preschool children

preschool children
Development and Relationships

Mollie S. Smart / Russell C. Smart
Department of Child Development and Family Relations
University of Rhode Island

MACMILLAN PUBLISHING CO., INC.
New York

COLLIER MACMILLAN PUBLISHERS
London

MINISTRY OF EDUCATION, ONTARIO
COMMUNICATION SERVICES BRANCH
13TH FLOOR, MOWAT BLOCK
TORONTO, ONTARIO M7A 1L3

Copyright © 1973, Macmillan Publishing Co., Inc.

Printed in the United States of America

All rights reserved. No part of this book may be reproduced or transmitted in any form or by any means, electronic or mechanical, including photocopying, recording, or any information storage and retrieval system, without permission in writing from the Publisher.

Reprinted with modifications from *Children: Development and Relationships,* Second Edition, by Mollie S. Smart and Russell C. Smart, copyright © 1967 and 1972 by Macmillan Publishing Co., Inc. and *Readings in Child Development and Relationships,* by Russell C. Smart and Mollie S. Smart, copyright © 1972 by Macmillan Publishing Co., Inc.

Macmillan Publishing Co., Inc.
866 Third Avenue, New York, New York 10022

Collier-Macmillan Canada, Ltd., Toronto, Ontario

Library of Congress catalog card number: 72-75855

Printing: 4 5 6 7 8   Year: 4 5 6 7 8 9

contents

Introduction   vii

1. Personality and Body   1

Readings 41

Erik H. Erikson   *Autonomy vs. Shame and Doubt, Initiative vs. Guilt*   41
Dorothy V. Whipple   *Human Growth Through the Ages*   46
Mary F. Waldrop and Charles F. Halverson, Jr.   *Minor Physical Anomalies: Their Incidence and Relation to Behavior in a Normal and a Deviant Sample*   63

2. Intellectual Development   73

Readings 116

Lawrence Kohlberg   *Psychometric and Piagetian Measures of Preschool Intellectual Growth*   116
Edward A. Chittenden   *What Is Learned and What Is Taught*   124
N. Dickon Reppucci   *Individual Differences in the Consideration of Information Among Two-Year-Old Children*   132
Carol Feldman and Michael Shen   *Some Language-Related Cognitive Advantages of Bilingual Five-Year-Olds*   140
Maebah Becenti   *Children Who Speak Navajo*   149

3. The Role of Play in Development   151

Readings 180

David Elkind   *The Case for the Academic Preschool: Fact or Fiction?*   180 vi Contents

Rosalind Charlesworth and Willard W. Hartup *Positive Social Reinforcement in the Nursery School Peer Group* 189
Susan W. Gray and Rupert A. Klaus *The Early Training Project: A Seventh Year Report* 198

4. Socialization: Interaction and Results 213

Readings 247

David Rosenhan *The Kindnesses of Children* 247
Henry B. Biller *Father Absence, Maternal Encouragement, and Sex Role Development in Kindergarten-Age Boys* 263
Norman L. Thompson, Jr., and Boyd R. McCandless IT *Score Variations by Instructional Style* 269
Russell DiBartolo and W. Edgar Vinacke *Relationship Between Adult Nurturance and Dependency and Performance of the Preschool Child* 279

5. An Overview of Human Life and Growth 287

Readings 315

William W. Ballard *The Rise and Fall of Humanity* 316
Lawrence K. Frank *Basic Processes in Organisms* 324
Erik H. Erikson *The Life Cycle: Epigenesis of Identity* 330
Jean Piaget *Equilibrium* 333
Myrtle B. McGraw *Major Challenges for Students of Infancy and Early Childhood* 337

Author Index 341
Subject Index 351

introduction

During the past decade, the preschool stage of life has received a great deal of public attention. Child development specialists have always been interested in preschool children for three main reasons: the preschool years are extremely important for the development of the human being; a great deal can be learned by studying the young child; young children are available for study. The current interest in the preschool years is probably due to growing recognition of this time of life as being crucial for life-long physical and mental development. It may be the latest period when it is possible to catch up from growth failure due to early deprivation. Although a large body of literature has been built up during the past 40 or 50 years, research on the preschool child continues with great enthusiasm. There is indeed much more to discover.

The final chapter is a general one about human life and growth. It deals with the various ways in which children interact with the physical and social surroundings, thereby changing, developing, and restructuring their bodies, minds, and personalities. Some principles of development are stated. Different ways of learning and maturing are discussed. The readings for the final chapter were chosen in order to show man as part of an ecosystem and to introduce the reader to the thoughts and styles of the great developmentalists.

The first four chapters of the book are about the child from 2 to 6 or 7. *Preschool* is an accurate term for this period of life in the sense that the child is not yet required to attend school. The term may be misleading if it suggests that preschool children are not educable. Indeed, the preschool years are vastly significant for learning and for all kinds of growth. Piaget places the end of one stage of intellectual growth at about 7 years. Erikson places the end of the main concern with the sense of initiative at about 7. Many educational systems throughout the world recognize 7 as a nodal age, a time when the child is appropriately occupied with learning the tools of his culture, whether they be reading, writing, and arithmetic, or work such as hunting, fishing, and child care. Therefore, in our consideration of the preschool child, we often include the 6-year-old, even though, strictly speaking, the American 6-year-old is a schoolchild, required by law to attend school.

Asserting his individuality, testing the limits of himself, his family, and his world, pushing out into that world, the preschool child is building his mental structures in complex and wondrous ways. With the problems of developing a sense of autonomy fairly well in hand by age 3½, he comes to grips with the development of a sense of initiative and imagination. His business is play, a widely varied activity through which he develops his body, personality, intelligence, and emotions. Although he thinks very concretely and cannot go beyond his own limited point of view in controlled thought, his imagination catapults him far and wide. Personality develops now through starting new activities, getting new ideas, and exploring everything—places, people, language, objects, art materials. New experiences give him not only starting points for flights of fancy, but the wherewithal for building his primitive, concrete concepts of the world. Repeated experiences are necessary, too, since only through repeated encounters with classes of objects can he pull abstractions from them, and only through repeatedly checking his interpretations with other people can his thinking become socialized. Nor does he have to figure out everything for himself, through experience. Other people give him words with which to label his experiences, and then those experiences take on wider meanings, meanings that are valid in his culture. Other people show him how to feel in this or that situation, how to heal a hurt, how to see the funny side. They tell him what is important in life and how to get it. Although such messages often come through straight, they do not always do so. And often the behavior of the child is a language that adults find difficult to understand. The study of child development helps adults to interpret the language of behavior and to respond to it in ways that are meaningful to the child.

Chapter 1

Merrill-Palmer Institute by Donna J. Harris

Personality and Body

No longer a baby, the preschool child interacts with an expanding world of people and things. Although physical growth is slower than it was during infancy, he is still growing faster than he will in the years which follow this period. Personality development is dramatic, as he moves from infantile concerns to the stage which gives color and focus to the preschool years.

Directions in Personality Growth

Two threads dominate the fabric of personality growth during the preschool years: the sense of autonomy and the sense of initiative. If all has gone well during infancy, a firm sense of trust is established by now. Further satisfactory experiences strengthen it, although shreds of mistrust are also present throughout life. Upon the foundation of a sense of trust, the child builds his sense of autonomy, and upon trust and autonomy, his sense of initiative. The success of his preschool interactions determines the adequacy of the sense of initiative and imagination which he builds.

Autonomy

The sense of autonomy blossoms as the child of 2 or thereabouts experiences the power of doing and deciding that comes with his wealth of budding abilities. Walking freely, although in a jerky trudging style, running a bit stiffly, climbing, bear-walking, knee-walking, galloping, riding a kiddy car, he has many independent modes of locomotion to exploit and choose from. The house and yard are for exploring. His hands easily do his bidding in reaching, grasping, letting go, throwing, turning, pulling, pushing. Toys to manipulate, tools that extend the powers of his hands, milk bottles with clothes pins, Daddy's old hat, Mummy's old purse, crayons and paper, sand and water, mud—all give him choices and successes. "Shall I play with it or not?... I'll do what I want with it.... What I do is all right."

Talking brings control over both the self and others and a corresponding strengthening of the sense of autonomy. The average increase in vocabulary from 18 months to 2½ years is from 22 to 446 words [66]. Four hundred and forty-six words represent a great many things, ideas, activities, and people brought into the child's orbit of influence. He has made the discovery that everything has a name and that when he can say the name, he can exert some control over the thing.

Even headier is the power to cooperate with people or not. If you ask a 2-year-old, "Do you want to go outdoors?" the chances are that he'll say *no*. Even though he really would like to go out, he gets tremendous momentary satisfaction out of deciding thus. If you say, "We're going out now," he'll most likely trot along happily, the decision having been kept out of his hands. Similarly with helping him finish a job that is too hard, like putting his rubbers on, it is better to do it than to ask, "Shall I help you?" There are many opportunities for choosing and deciding, even when adults limit them. The child decides whether to kiss, hug, and give other endearments, whether to finish his dinner and whether to urinate on the toilet or in his pants. The last decision mentioned, the question of toileting, is the one which, to the psychoanalysts, symbolizes the whole stage of developing autonomy. It is indeed an area where the sternest of parents has a hard time forcing the child and where the child can retain his autonomy under severe pressure. In the normal course of events in Western society, the child exercises autonomy as he brings his sphincters under control and takes on the toileting patterns approved by his family.

Autonomy in a group of nursery school children was measured by ratings of their behavior in separating themselves from their parents and becoming involved with peers and play in the nursery school [52]. Questionnaires answered by their parents showed the degree to which each parent expected autonomous behavior from the child. Significant relationships were found between the parents' expectations of autonomous behavior and the children's actual behavior. Autonomous behavior included practical independent performance which was helpful to the parent and also the child's insistence on doing for himself or acting on his own. For example, "Johnny is two years old. He refuses to eat at mealtime unless he can feed himself."

Autonomous behavior at 2½ predicts nonverbal intelligence and cognitive style at age 6 [55]. Nursery school teachers rated young children on behavior scales which measured their seeking of physical contact and attention, orality (licking, drooling, thumb-sucking, and mouthing), and sustained directed activity. The last includes contentment and absorption in play and following through in play. Performance IQ (solving nonverbal problems) correlated with autonomy at the earlier age as expressed in sustained directed activity and lack of contact-seeking and attention-seeking. It seems reasonable that 2-year-olds who pursue their own play interests independently and persistently would develop better problem-solving abilities than would children who seek contact and help instead of behaving autonomously.

The negative side of a healthy sense of autonomy is a sense of shame and worthlessness. These negative feelings creep in when the youngster cannot choose enough and act independently enough, when the results of his choices and actions are disastrous, and when adults use shaming as a method of control. Because the young child is vulnerable to shaming, adults may use it as a discipline technique, not realizing its dangers for personality development [20]. When a person is shamed, he does not want to be seen or noticed. The use of shaming as a technique of control does not promote good behavior but, rather, defiance and trying to get away with doing what one wants to do. Another unfortunate outcome of poor guidance of autonomy is compulsive repetition of certain acts, a stubborn exerting of power. This type of behavior is probably the source of conforming rigidly to rules as written, in contrast to flexible interpretation of meaning.

> Outer control at this age, therefore, must be firmly reassuring. The infant must come to feel that the basic faith in existence, which is the lasting treasure saved from the rages of the oral stage, will not be jeopardized by this about-face of his, this sudden violent wish to have a choice, to appropriate demandingly, and to eliminate stubbornly. Firmness must protect him against the potential anarchy of his yet untrained sense of discrimination, his inability to hold on and to let go with discretion. As his environment encouraged him to "stand on his own feet," it must protect him against meaningless and arbitrary experiences of shame and of early doubt [20, p. 252].

Initiative

Just as development of a sense of autonomy dominates the early part of the preschool period, the sense of initiative is the central theme of the latter part. Personality growth is never in a straight line. There is always some backing up and reworking of old problems. Even with a firm sense of trust, there are frights over Mother's being away too long or strangers threatening. Even with a strong sense of autonomy, a child occasionally asserts it in a temper tantrum, a refusal to eat, or a toilet "accident." Little threads of problems run through life as imperfections in trust and autonomy, demanding attention and solutions.

Now at 4 years or so, the sense of initiative claims the center of the stage. The preschool child is an explorer, curious and active. He seeks new experiences for their

4 Preschool Children

own sake, the sheer pleasure of sensing and knowing. He also seeks experience in order to fit it in with something he already knows and to make it more understandable. He pushes vigorously out into the world, seeking a wide range of information about it, about people and what they do, about what he himself can do. Grasping a piece of reality, like Mother's high heels and handbag, Daddy's briefcase, or a doctor's kit, he creates the experience he wants, trying on the role of a mother or father or doctor, contemplating what these adults do, imagining how it would be if he himself were doing it. Building a store with cartons, he becomes a storekeeper. He paints a picture. He creates a new world in a stream bed. It is at this stage that children put beans in their ears and stir eye shadow into cold cream. If the child's seeking is successful, then he finds a wide variety of things he can do, make, and create, with the approval of his family and other adults. If he succeeds, he continues as an older child and adult to look for new ideas, solutions, answers, reasons, creative experiences. Imagination will be discussed in greater detail in Chapter 3, where its development will be related to cognitive growth and where both these functions will be seen as integrated in play, which is the business of the preschool child.

Aggression, also, is a function of the sense of initiative, since aggression involves pushing out into the world and attacking. Since aggression is also involved with anger, its discussion will be postponed until Chapter 4, which deals with emotional development and control. Assertive behavior is similar to aggression in being a reaching out and pushing into the environment to explore and manipulate it. Assertion, unlike aggression, does not imply anger. Assertive behavior in 5-year-olds was studied by testing, observations, and teachers' ratings, focusing on the exploration-manipulation sort of behavior and upon destructiveness in the service of learning or exploring [17]. The test of instrumental destructiveness involved telling the child that he could get and keep an attractive top if he would first knock over a pile of plastic glasses that stood in front of the toy. Results showed that this test, as well as teachers' and observers' ratings, was correlated with intelligence as measured by the Stanford–Binet. The measures of assertion were reflections of the child's ability to interact with his environment and to master it. Since intelligence tests measure knowledge and mastery, the child who dealt assertively with his world would be more likely to score high on such tests.

Conscience begins to develop at this time, regulating initiative and imagination. The child takes the voice of his parents into himself, saying what he may do and what he may not do. When he does not obey it, he may feel guilty. Sometimes he even feels guilty for his thoughts and wishes which run counter to the commands of his conscience. His vigorous imagination can easily hit or kill people who oppose him or it can, more deviously, create a bear or a wolf to eat the annoying people. The bear may get out of control and threaten the child himself, especially in a dream. Conscience development will be considered further in the framework of parent–child relationships.

Exploration also involves noticing how other people solve problems and trying their solutions by imitating them. Not only are parents imitated, but peers, older children, and adults may also serve as models. Children select certain models to imitate and they also select certain behavior patterns from the models' repertory, rather than trying to imitate everything that certain models do. Styles of expressing curiosity were noted in a study in a Head Start setting [50]. Some children used mostly verbal methods, some visual, and others manipulative.

Thus do the forces of creativity and social control struggle in the person of a young child, producing dreams of beauty and fright, glimpses of new worlds of achievement, the constriction of guilt. The establishment of a healthy sense of initiative means that the child can interact vigorously under the control of a conscience that is strong enough but not too punishing.

Activity and Passivity. While the expression of initiative includes pushing out, exploring, and making beginnings, being active is also an aspect of initiative. Therefore, it is worthwhile to note what has been found about activity and passivity in the early years of life. Individual differences in activity have been observed in infancy, as well as during the preschool and school years [21, 51]. Differences were seen in motor activity and in sensitivity to the environment. Motor differences included those in total amount of activity and those in ways of using the body. For example, some babies were very active with their arms and legs, whereas others turned and rolled more. Some moved quickly, others slowly, some mildly, some forcefully. They varied in the distribution and length of periods of quiet and activity. Some children seemed to keep quiet in order to think [51, p. 5]. At each age, degree of activity and degree of perceptual sensitivity determine certain aspects of interactions with the environment, including people, and thus affect the course of personality development [21, pp. 21–29].

Another approach to the understanding of activity was through a longitudinal study which followed children from birth to maturity [37]. Passivity was defined as the tendency to acquiesce to or withdraw from frustrating situations, instead of dealing with them actively. The opposite of passivity, then, sounds very much like the sense of initiative. Passivity was found to be a highly stable personality characteristic during the first ten years of life. Another characteristic studied was dependence, defined as the child's tendency to seek affection, help, and company of female adults, usually his mother. The opposite of dependency also sounds like an aspect of initiative, since initiative includes independent action. Dependency was found to be a moderately stable personality characteristic during the first ten years of life [37, pp. 50–54].

Achievement and Competence. During the preschool years, when the development of the sense of initiative dominates life, it seems more important to get things started than to finish them. Planning, undertaking, exploring, pushing out, and attacking are all of the essence of this period. Achieving (finishing jobs, doing well) becomes much more important during the stage which follows, the period of the development of a sense of industry. Since preparations for each stage of personality development are made during preceding stages, some of the foundations for later achievement can be studied during the preschool years. The young child has experiences that affect his efforts, persistence, and expectations of himself in regard to excellence. As the youngster pushes forward to explore and to try new activities, his parents take certain attitudes toward what he is doing. Some parents hold high standards of excellence for their children; others hold lower standards. Some push children to do well; others let them do more as they will. Some give them a large measure of independence; others control them tightly. There are steps in between each of these pairs of extremes. Research shows that achievement motivation and behavior are affected by experience during the period of development of the sense of initiative and even more in the years which follow [14]. Observations at home and at school showed certain children to be consistently interested in achievement-oriented play. The mothers of these children tended to reward their achievement efforts and their seeking of approval and to ignore

6 Preschool Children

requests for help. These children, in contrast to those less interested in achievement, were less dependent upon adults for help and for emotional support [15].

Competence in preschool children is correlated with parental practices which are intellectually stimulating and somewhat tension producing, such as demands for mature behavior and firm discipline [4]. These conclusions came from factor-analytic studies of parent interviews and ratings of children's behavior. Parental techniques which fostered self-reliance, such as demanding self-control and encouraging independent decision making, promoted responsible, independent behavior. In another study [3], a group of preschool children were chosen for being highly socialized and independent, as shown by their self-reliance, exploring, self-assertion, self-control, and affiliation. The parents of these children, as contrasted with the parents of a control group, were consistent, loving, and demanding, respecting the child's decisions, using reason, and maintaining a firm stand when a stand was taken. These parents displayed high nurturance, high control, clear communication, and clear policies of regulation. Thus the parents encouraged initiative in children, but limited the area within which the child could operate. The children were therefore protected from disastrous failure while benefiting from appropriate freedom.

Parent–child interactions in the preschool years are related to achievement behavior at later ages. At age 8 to 10, boys with high achievement needs and high achievement ratings, as contrasted to low achievers, had mothers who had demanded more independence, maturity, and achievement of their sons and who also had rewarded them liberally for fulfilling the demands [80]. In other words, the mothers' demands and rewards during the preschool years were related to the children's achievement during the elementary school years. Figure 1–1 shows the number of demands for mastery and independence made between the ages of 1 and 10 on high-achieving and low-achieving boys. The development of achievement motivation becomes increasingly important during the early school-age period. An extensive body of research on achievement is reported in Smart and Smart, *School-Age Children,* Macmillan, 1973.

Sex Differences. Common observation indicates that boys explore the world more vigorously than do girls. Any teacher of young children will agree that, in general, boys are harder to control than girls. A study of dependency shown by children in the nursery school demonstrated greater dependency behavior in girls than in boys [31]. Boys have been found to be more curious than girls in their reactions to novelty in pictures and toys [46, 67].

Cultural influences in traditional Chinese and Japanese families encourage children to be dependent, obedient, and cautious, and discourage them from exploring, behaving impulsively, and deciding [39]. We have observed the same phenomena in India. Especially when children live in joint families, adults are ever present to supervise, restrain, and protect, preventing an active reaching out and intrusion by young children. Often we have seen young Indian children taken to parties or visiting by their parents. The little child sits beside the mother or close to her, simply looking and listening, or maybe daydreaming, or if given something to play with, quietly playing. An American child his age would most likely explore the room and objects in it, approach some of the people and intrude upon his mother's conversations. Such differences in Asian and American child behavior reflect different cultural values as well as child-rearing methods which support the values.

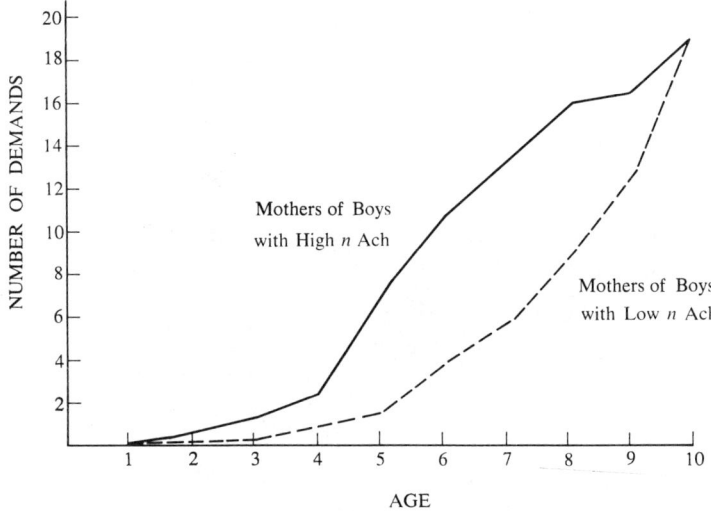

Figure 1–1. Demands for mastery and independence made by mothers of boys with high need for achievement and by mothers of boys with low need.

SOURCE: Reprinted by permission from M. R. Winterbottom, "The Relation of Need for Achievement to Learning Experiences in Independence and Mastery," in J. W. Atkinson [Ed.], *Motives in Fantasy, Action and Society*. Princeton, N.J.: Van Nostrand Co., 1958. Copyright © 1958, Van Nostrand Co.

Physical Characteristics, Experiences, and Their Implications

Although much more independent than infants, preschool children are able to operate independently only within circumscribed areas. The protective and nurturing roles of parents are understood best in the light of the young child's physical characteristics.

Growth Rates

Height and Weight. Growth in height is not so fast as it was during infancy. The growth rate decelerates slowly throughout the preschool period. At 2 years, a child has added 75 percent of his birth length to his height [10, p. 248]. At 4 years, he has added 100 percent to it. Thus the second 2-year period of life sees only one-third as much gain in height as do the first 2 years. A boy's height at 2 is about half of his adult height, a girl's is a little more than half. To estimate her adult height, double the height at 2 and subtract 10 or 12 centimeters [76]. Thus the first doubling of height takes place in 4 years while the doubling which results in the final height takes 16 years. Rate of weight gain follows a slow deceleration from 2 to 3 years and a gradual acceleration from 3 to 5. Birth weight is quadrupled by 2½, showing the rapid rate for weight gain in infancy. Between 2 and 5, the weight gain is less than the amount gained during the first year of life, showing the slower rate at which weight is gained in the preschool period as contrasted with infancy [10, p. 254]. Since the size of a child at any age bears some relation to his size at adulthood, it is possible to predict final height with fair accuracy. Several methods and

Table 1–1 Fels Multipliers for Stature Prediction of Boys and Girls of Average Parental Stature

Multiplier BOYS	Age	Multiplier GIRLS
2.46	1	2.30
2.06	2	2.01
1.86	3	1.76
1.73	4	1.62
1.62	5	1.51
1.54	6	1.43

SOURCE: Reprinted by permission from S. M. Garn, "Body Size and Its Implications," in L. W. Hoffman and M. L. Hoffman (Eds.), *Review of Child Development Research*, Vol. 2. New York: Russell Sage Foundation, 1966. Copyright © 1966 Russell Sage Foundation.

tables for prediction exist. An example is the Fels multipliers for stature prediction, given in Table 1–1.

Sex differences in height show up in these early years, girls progressing faster toward maturity than boys. The same is true of weight; girls are farther along toward their mature weights than are boys of the same age. However, during the preschool period, boys are slightly heavier and taller than girls, on the average, since their eventual heights and weights are greater.

Slow growth in height and weight has been reported for children in lower socioeconomic groups all over the world, including the United States. The bulk of children in underdeveloped countries are retarded in height and weight, the usual average being below the sixteenth percentile for well-nourished children in the United States and Western Europe. In these same countries, the growth of children in the favored socioeconomic groups has been found to be comparable with that of children in the United States and Western Europe [80]. Such studies strongly suggest that nutrition, rather than racial or genetic factors, plays the main role in the growth failure occurring in deprived parts of the world [81, 34].

Tissues and Proportions. Rates of growth change for various tissues, as well as for height and weight. The growth of fat and muscle is especially interesting, because of the consequent change from babylike to childlike appearance. Fat increases rapidly during the first 9 months of life, decreases rapidly in thickness from 9 months to 2½ years, and decreases slowly until 5½. At 5½, it is half as thick as at 9 months. Thus does the chubby baby grow into a slender child. Muscle tissue follows a different pattern, growing at a decelerating rate throughout infancy and childhood, lagging behind other types of tissue growth until the puberal growth spurt. (See Figure 1–2.)

Sex differences show up in tissue growth, too. Boys have more muscle and bone than girls; girls have more fat than boys. Of course, there are individual differences, too, in all aspects of growth. Individual differences in amount of fat are greater than sex differences [10, pp. 260–262].

Bodily proportions change due to differential growth rates of various parts of the body. The principle of developmental direction is illustrated here by the growth which takes place in a cephalo-caudal (head to tail) direction. Development is at first more rapid in the head end of the body, with the tail end reaching maturity

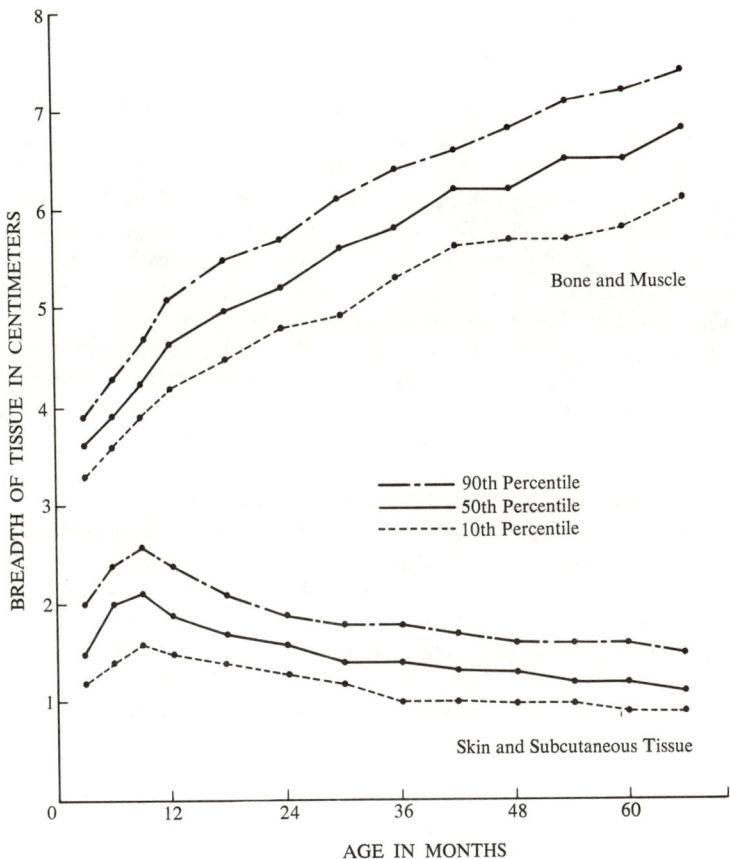

Figure 1–2. Rates of growth of bone and muscle tissue and of skin and fat.
Source: Reprinted by permission from M. E. Breckenridge and M. N. Murphy, *Growth and Development of the Young Child*, 8th edition. Copyright © 1969, W. B. Saunders Company.

later. At age 2, the head is still large in relation to the trunk and legs. The abdomen and chest measure about the same but after 2, the chest becomes larger in relation to the abdomen [76, p. 84]. The abdomen sticks out, since a relatively short trunk has to accommodate the internal organs, some of which are closer to adult size than is the trunk. Thus the toddler is top-heavy. The head itself grows according to the same principle, with the upper part closer to completion than the lower part. A large cranium and a small lower jaw give the characteristic baby look to a 2-year-old's face. These proportions, plus fat, result in the diminutive nature of immature creatures which adults find emotionally appealing. Americans call baby humans, puppies, kittens, and other animal infants cute. Germans add *chen* to their names and French *ette*. As the legs, trunk, and jaw grow in relation to the head, the baby loses his "cute" or diminutive look. This is what happens to the human baby between 2 and 5 years of age. By the time he starts to kindergarten or first grade, his proportions more nearly resemble those of the children in the rest of the grades than they resemble his preschool brothers and sisters at home.

10 Preschool Children

Bones of preschool children have their own qualitative characteristics as well as proportional. The younger the child the more cartilage there is in his skeletal system and the less the density of minerals in the bones. The joints are more flexible; the ligaments and muscles are attached more tenuously than in an older child. Thus it is easier to damage young bones, joints, and muscles by pressure and pulling and by infections. The skeletal system is very responsive to changes in environment that produce malnutrition, fatigue, and injury [10, p. 267]. Bone maturation, evaluated by the thickness, number, and shape of small bones showing in X rays of the hand and wrist, has been found to be retarded by two or three years in preschool children of poor, underdeveloped countries [61]. Head circumference was found to be smaller in malnourished preschool children as compared with well-nourished children of the same ethnic origin [61].

The brain is more nearly complete, as to total weight, than the rest of the body. By 3 years, the brain is about 75 percent of its adult weight and by 6 years almost 90 percent. At age 5 the total nervous system is one-twentieth the total weight, in contrast to the adult nervous system, which is one-fiftieth the total weight [76, p. 217].

The fact that there is relatively little increase in brain weight at this time does not mean that brain development is not proceeding rapidly. There is every reason to believe that during the preschool period, there is a continuous increase in the number, size, and complexity of connections between cells in the cortex and in connections between the different levels of the brain [70]. Evidence strongly suggests that Piaget's successive stages of cognitive growth occur as the cortex matures and becomes progressively organized.

The patterning of brain waves shown by electroencephalograms shows characteristic changes during the preschool period [75]. The very slow rhythms prominent in infancy decline, and a faster rhythm reaches its peak of frequency in the preschool period. It has been observed that the time of the rise in frequency of the preschool rhythm is associated with the time of the rise in frequency of temper outbursts. Specific incidents of temper outbursts were associated with immediate, specific increases in this type of brain wave. Another rhythm emerges at about age 5 [76, p. 220].

Of the special senses, *vision* and *taste* are noteworthy in the preschool years. The macula of the retina is not completely developed until about 6 years, and the eyeball does not reach adult size until 12 or 14 [76]. The young child is farsighted because of the shape of the eyeball. Estimates for visual acuity, taken from several studies [19] are: at 2 years, 20/100 to 20/40; at 3, 20/50 to 20/30; at 4, 20/40 to 20/20; at 5, 20/35 to 20/25; at 6, 20/27. Thus even at 6 years of age, the estimated acuity is not yet 20/20. Investigations of the ways in which children use their visual mechanism show that they function in immature ways during the preschool years [24]. Vision screening by trained nonprofessionals has been the means of finding preschool children who need the attention of professionals [29]. An analysis of 109 vision-screening projects shows that 6 percent of the children were referred for professional eye examinations and that 75 percent of those examined had abnormal eye conditions. One to 3 percent of preschool children require glasses [71].

Taste buds are more generously distributed in the young child than in the adult, being scattered on the insides of the cheeks and the throat as well as on the tongue. He probably is highly sensitive to taste. The ear too is significantly different in the young child because of the Eustachian tube which connects the middle ear with the throat. The tube is shorter, more horizontal, and wider in the infant and preschool child than in the older child and adult. Invading organisms find an easy entrance route from the young child's throat to his middle ear. Hence he is more susceptible to ear infections than is the older child.

The internal organs show various immaturities, with implications for child care. For example, the stomach, at 4 to 6 years, has less than half the capacity of the average adult stomach. Calorie requirements at that age, however, are more than half as great as that of an active adult. The shape of the stomach is straighter than in older children and more directly upright than an infant's or older child's. Thus it empties rather readily in either direction. The lining of the digestive tract is easily irritated by seasonings and roughage. The respiratory system matures sufficiently during the preschool years to establish the adult type of breathing, combining abdominal and chest movements. However, air passages are relatively small at this time and the lymphatic system prominent so that tonsils and adenoids are at their maximum size.

Methods of Assessing Growth

A child can be compared with other children his age or he can be evaluated in terms of his own past growth. His heredity can be taken into account by using a mid-parent height table when considering his height. Speed of growth can be calculated at two points in time. An individual's speed of growth can be compared with that of other children.

Comparisons with Peers. Height-weight-age tables represent the most common instrument used for making such assessments of growth. Tables 1–2, 1–3, 1–4, and 1–5 give for each age and sex the heights and weights which are at seven points on a percentile scale [76, pp. 89–92]. For example, 4-year-old David is 42¼ inches tall and weighs 34 pounds. Table 1–4 shows that he weighs less than 75 percent of children his age, whereas Table 1–2 indicates his height to be above that of 75 percent of children. These figures suggest that David is slim, but they tell nothing about his body build. Width is taken into account by another type of table [56], combining age, height, weight, and width. This rather complicated table has been little used for practical purposes.

Comparisons with Self. Another method of assessing growth is by means of a special record form on which repeated measurements are entered. The Wetzel

Table 1–2 Height Percentile Table for Boys from age 2½ through age 5½

Age	Length in Inches						
	3%	10%	25%	50%	75%	90%	97%
2½ yr.	34¼	34¾	35½	36¼	37	38	39¼
3 yr.	35¾	36¼	37	38	38¾	39½	40½
3½ yr.	37	37¾	38½	39¼	40¼	41	42
4 yr.	38½	39	39¾	40¾	42	42¾	43½
4½ yr.	39½	40¼	41	42	43¼	44¼	45
5 yr.	40¼	41¼	42¼	43¼	44½	45½	46½
5½ yr.	41½	42½	43¾	45	46¼	47¼	48

SOURCE: From *Growth and Development of Children*, 5th edition, by Ernest H. Watson and George H. Lowrey. Copyright © 1967, Year Book Medical Publishers, Inc., Chicago. Used by permission of Year Book Medical Publishers.

12 Preschool Children

Table 1-3 Height Percentile Table for Girls from Age 2½ through Age 5½

Age	Length in Inches						
	3%	10%	25%	50%	75%	90%	97%
2½ yr.	33¼	34	35¼	36	37	38	39
3 yr.	34¾	35½	36¾	37¾	38½	39¾	40¾
3½ yr.	36¼	37	38	39¼	40¼	41½	42½
4 yr.	37½	38½	39½	40½	41½	43	44¼
4½ yr.	38½	39¾	40¾	42	43	44¾	45¾
5 yr.	40	41	42	43	44¼	45½	46¾
5½ yr.	41¼	42½	43½	44½	45¾	46¾	48

SOURCE: From *Growth and Development of Children*, 5th edition, by Ernest H. Watson and George H. Lowrey, Copyright © 1967, Year Book Medical Publishers, Inc., Chicago. Used by permission of Year Book Medical Publishers.

Table 1-4 Weight Percentile Table for Boys Age 2½ through Age 5½

Age	Weight in Pounds						
	3%	10%	25%	50%	75%	90%	97%
2½ yr.	25¼	26½	28½	30	32¼	34½	37
3 yr.	27	28¾	30¼	32¼	34½	36¾	39¼
3½ yr.	28½	30½	32¼	34¼	36¾	39	41½
4 yr.	30	32	34	36½	39	41½	44¼
4½ yr.	31½	33¾	35¾	38½	41½	44	47½
5 yr.	34	36	38½	41½	45¼	48¼	51¾
5½ yr.	36¼	38¾	42	45½	49¼	53	56½

SOURCE: From *Growth and Development of Children*, 5th edition, by Ernest H. Watson and George H. Lowrey. Copyright © 1967, Year Book Medical Publishers, Inc., Chicago. Used by permission of Year Book Medical Publishers.

Table 1-5 Weight Percentile Table for Girls Age 2½ through Age 5½

Age	Weight in Pounds						
	3%	10%	25%	50%	75%	90%	97%
2½ yr.	23½	25½	27½	29½	32	35½	38¼
3 yr.	25½	27½	29½	31¾	34½	37½	41¾
3½ yr.	27½	29½	31½	34	37	40½	45¼
4 yr.	29¼	31¼	33½	36¼	39½	43½	48¼
4½ yr.	30¾	33	35¼	38½	42	46¾	51
5 yr.	33	35½	38	41	44½	48¾	52¼
5½ yr.	35	38	40¾	44	47¼	51¼	55½

SOURCE: From *Growth and Development of Children*, 5th edition, by Ernest H. Watson and George H. Lowrey. Copyright © 1967, Year Book Medical Publishers, Inc., Chicago. Used by permission of Year Book Medical Publishers.

Grid [77] is a well-known example of this method. The Grid can be used to indicate the child's body type as obese, stocky, good (average), borderline, fair, or poor and to compare a child with other children in height, width, body volume, and rate of growth. The child can be compared with himself at any time in the past. Growth can be seen as even or uneven. The Wetzel Grid is used by physicians for supervising health and growth.

Personality and Body 13

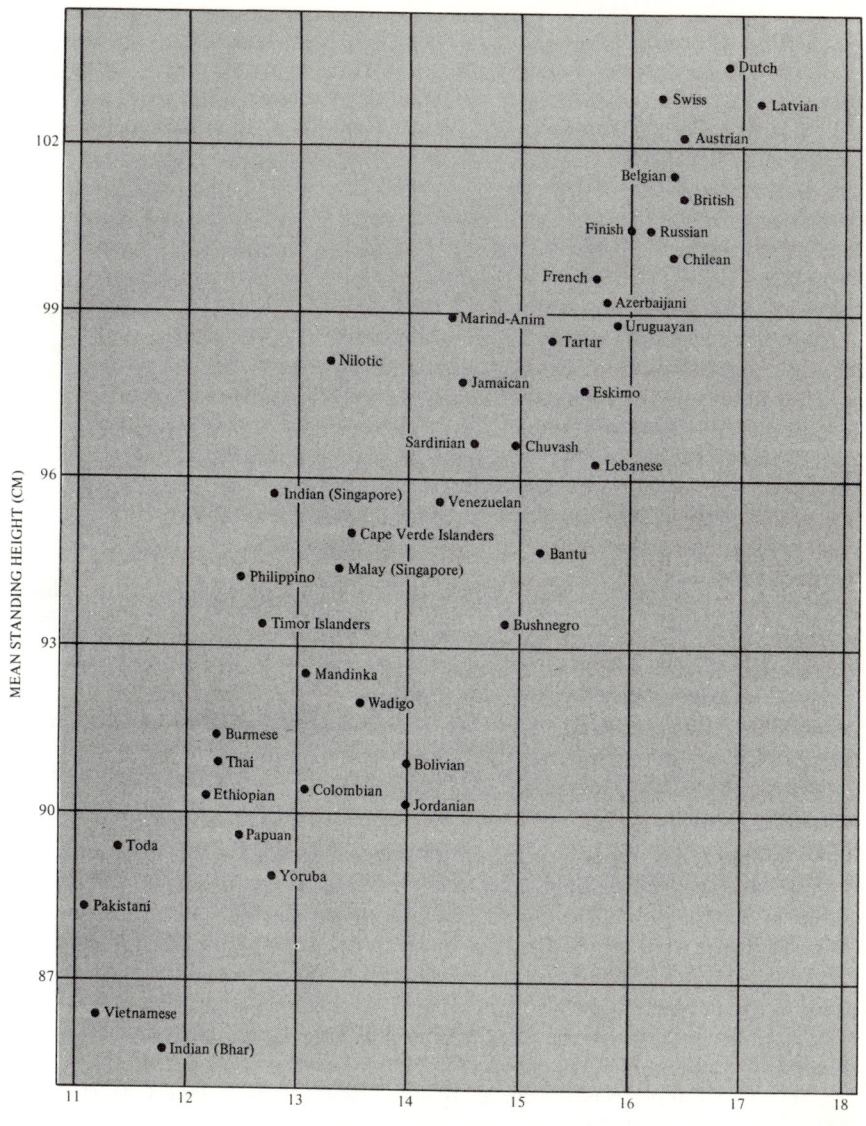

Figure 1–3. Mean heights and weights of preschool children in different parts of the world.

SOURCE: Reprinted by permission from H. V. Meredith, "Body Size of Contemporary Groups of Preschool Children Studied in Different Parts of the World," *Child Development*, **39**, Figure 1, p. 359. Copyright © 1968, by the Society for Research in Child Development, Inc.

Cross-Culture Comparisons. Body size varies in different parts of the world. Physical measurements on 160 samples of 4-year-old children represent Africa, Asia, Australia, Europe, the Americas, West Indies, and the Malay archipelago [47]. These samples differed as much as 7 inches in average height and 13 pounds in average weight.

14 Preschool Children

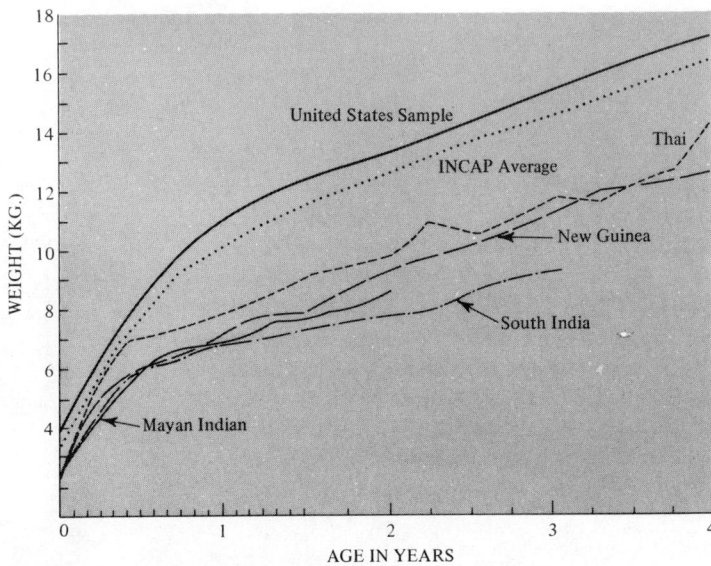

Figure 1–4. Average weight-for-age of children in four underdeveloped countries, shown in relation to average weight according to the standards of the Institute for Nutrition in Central America and Panama. The median of the Iowa curves is also indicated, showing that averages for normal Central American children are very close to those for a sample of North American children.

SOURCE: Data from M. Béhar, "Prevalence of Malnutrition Among Preschool Children of Developing Countries," in N. S. Scrimshaw and J. E. Gordon [Eds.], *Malnutrition, Learning and Behavior*. Cambridge: M.I.T. Press, 1968. Also from R. L. Jackson and H. G. Kelly, "Growth Charts for Use in Pediatric Practice," *Journal of Pediatrics*, 1945, **27**, 215–229.

The shortest group was from Bihar, an Indian state known for its famines. The sample of over 3000 children averaged 85.8 centimeters in height. The diet in Bihar is commonly deficient in calories, proteins, calcium, and vitamins. The Bihar children were fifth lightest, at an average weight of 11.8 kg. The lightest sample was from East Pakistan, another area prone to famine and found by a survey team to be deficient in total calories, protein, vitamin A, riboflavin, and iron. The Pakistani 4-year-olds were taller than only three other groups: the Indians, Kwango Negroes, and Vietnamese.

The tallest sample was Czech, at 103.8 centimeters. Next tallest were Dutch, 103.5, and next, United States whites, 102.9. The heaviest children were Lithuanians, at 17.3 kilograms, then Latvian, 17.2, and Czech, 17.1. Norwegian and Dutch were also heavier than United States white children, who averaged 16.7 kilograms.

In the middle of the height ranks were Polynesians, at 96.6 centimeters. Children in the West Indies and Jamaica were midway in weight, averaging 14.5 pounds. Figure 1–3 shows the relation between mean height and mean weight in some of the samples studied.

Growth in weight among preschool children from several underdeveloped countries is shown in Figure 1–4. The children are compared with INCAP standards (Institute of Nutrition of Central America and Panama). The children from Thailand and New Guinea followed an almost normal course of growth for the first 3 months, fell farther and farther below normal for the next year, and then maintained a low level of weight growth. The Guatemalan and Indian children showed a pattern similar to the other two groups in the first 3 months, but after that diverged farther from the INCAP standard. As far as these graphs show, the children do not seem to be dropping farther below the standard line.

Skeletal Age

Another way of assessing growth is to measure the maturity of the skeleton, by means of X rays. Early in prenatal life the precursors of most bones appear as cartilage. (The bones of the upper part of the skull develop from membranous tissue.) The cartilage is gradually replaced by bone beginning in the sixth week after fertilization. From this time until the individual is in his twenties bone is being laid down, starting from centers of ossification which appear in highly uniform places in each cartilage. Ossification takes place in the cells through a process of formation of organic salts of calcium and phosphorus. The centers of ossification appear in a fairly uniform order. Bones grow in width or diameter by the addition of bony material on the outer surface of the bone underneath the periosteum (a membrane which surrounds the bone). Long bones grow longer by the addition of ossified materials at their ends. During the growth period, therefore, any given bit of bone is overlaid by later ossified material, not replaced by it.

In long bones another ossification center appears at the end of the cartilage which forms the model of the growing bone. This separate piece of bone is called the epiphysis. The cartilage between the epiphysis and the shaft of the bone (the diaphysis) appears to become thinner and thinner as growth proceeds. Eventually, in normal human beings the epiphysis and diaphysis fuse into one piece of bone, and lengthwise growth in that bone ceases. Just as the timetable of the appearance of centers of ossification is fairly regular for the individual, so the fusion of epiphyses and diaphyses follows a time pattern [57]. As each piece of bone grows, its size and shape changes in a systematic fashion which varies relatively little from one person to another.

All of these changes in bony tissue can be followed in X rays of the bones. The cartilaginous material is transparent to X rays; the ossified material, opaque. Most of the studies of skeletal development have been done using X rays of the left hand and wrist. The developed film is compared with standard illustrations in order to match it as closely as possible to one of them. The skeletal status of a child is expressed in terms of skeletal age, which corresponds to the chronological age at which the children on whom the standards were based usually attained that same degree of skeletal development [26]. Mental age, which is to be discussed in the next chapter, is a similar derived measure of development and is defined in much the same way as skeletal age.

Bone Growth as a Record of Health. X rays of the hand yield information about the quality of a child's growth. Lightly mineralized bones may be due to insufficient intake of calcium, or insufficient metabolism of calcium, or both. An X ray film may therefore yield supplemental information concerning the nutritional status of a child. Some kinds of illnesses and other traumatic events in the child's life may result in bands of increased density of the bone at the growing end of the long

16 Preschool Children

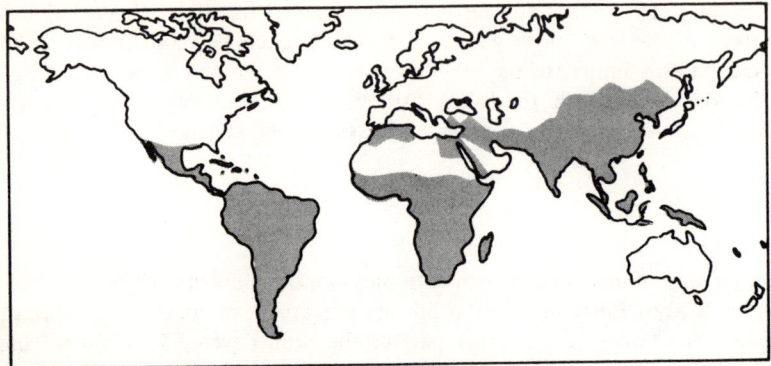

Figure 1–5. Geographic distribution of protein-calorie malnutrition.
SOURCE: Fig. 8, p. 40, adapted from M. Béhar, "Prevalence of Malnutrition Among Preschool Children of Developing Countries." In N. S. Scrimshaw and J. E. Gordon [Eds.], *Malnutrition, Learning and Behavior*. Cambridge: M.I.T. Press, 1968, pp. 30–42.

bones [26, p. 19]. If they occur, they become permanent records of disturbances in the body's metabolism during that period of the child's life.

The principle of critical periods is apparent in the disruption of the orderly sequence of appearance of ossification centers during illness [26, p. 18]. If there is a disturbance in the calcium metabolism, such as occurs during illnesses, at the time when an ossification center is due to appear, its appearance may be delayed until a later time, even until after the appearance of the next scheduled center. When this happens, an X ray film taken subsequently, even perhaps several years later, will show imbalances in the development of individual bones and centers of ossification. Since the age of the bones that are present can be judged from their appearance, it becomes possible to make a judgment as to the time of the crisis and about how severe was the impact on the skeleton (and presumably the total organism). Later X ray examinations can tell at what point the child has made complete recovery.

Feeding the Young Child

Over 60 percent of the world's preschool children are malnourished [5]. This figure represents 300 million of the 400 million preschool children who live in the underdeveloped areas of the world shown in the shaded portions of the map in Figure 1–5. The figure is conservative, since over 75 percent of these children are underweight. The 60 percent does not include malnourished children in the more prosperous parts of the world; and yet in our own country, a recent nutrition survey found large numbers of children suffering from stunted growth and deficient in many different nutrients [60].

An analysis of the food intake of 121 healthy, middle-class preschool children showed that recommendations for iron were not being met [16]. Although the average child received enough vitamin C, there were a substantial number who had intakes of less than 50 percent of the recommended allowance. While one child may not get enough of a certain nutrient because his mother does not offer it to him, another may refuse to eat any or enough of the food she does give him.

Nutrients. Since the majority of the world's children do not have an ample diet

Personality and Body 17

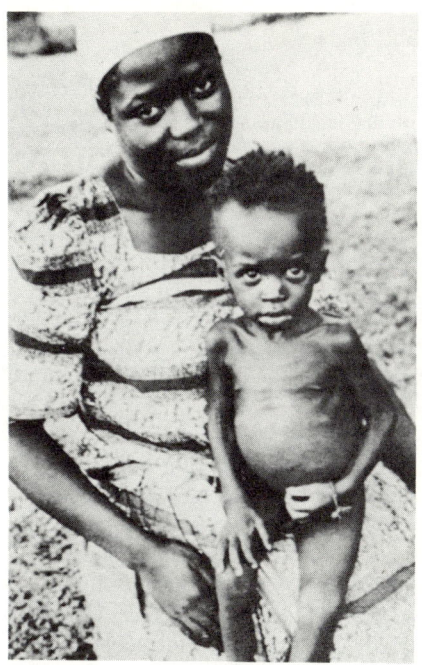 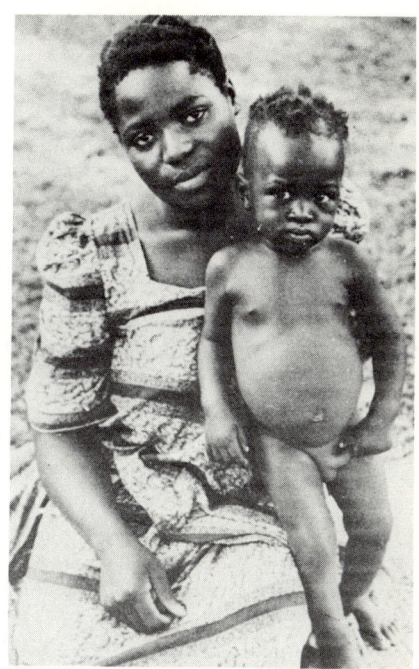

Figure 1–6. A two-year-old child with marasmus was photographed on admission to the Nutrition Rehabilitation Unit, Kampala, and again after six weeks on a high protein diet based on local foods.
SOURCE: D. B. Jelliffe, *Child Nutrition in Developing Countries.* Washington, D.C. Agency for International Development, 1969.

from which to select, the most pressing nutritional problem is to make enough good food available to all. The problem is political, economic, agricultural, educational, religious, and social. Even when a fairly good diet is available, young children often do not get full benefit of it. If they are simply expected to eat what they can of the family diet, they may have to contend with peppers and strong seasonings which may damage their gastric systems [11]. A nutritionist [79] who has observed African children for 40 years comments that poor preparation of food, methods of presenting it, and timing of meals are important factors in preschool malnutrition. The bad effects of emotional disturbances, and excessive bulk, roughage, and spices have not been acknowledged sufficiently. When the culture recognizes that young children need special diets, the food offered is usually high in starch and low in protein. Thus the 4-year-old, who needs 50 percent more protein per pound of body weight than his father, receives bananas, arrowroot, maize, and rice gruel while his father gets meat or beans. The inequity continues throughout the childhood period, being most serious when growth is most rapid. The Food and Nutrition Board of the National Research Council regularly publishes recommended allowances of food elements for people of all ages. The following guide (Agricultural Research Service) for feeding the preschool child translates the most recent table of recommended nutrients into

18 Preschool Children

foods for each day:

> 3 or more cups of milk and milk products
> 2 or more servings of meat, poultry, fish, and eggs
> 4 or more servings of vegetables and fruits, including a citrus fruit or other fruit or vegetable high in vitamin C, and a dark-green or deep-yellow vegetable for vitamin A at least every other day
> 4 or more servings of bread and cereal of whole grain, enriched or restored variety
> Plus other foods as needed to provide additional energy and other food values

Figures are not to be taken completely literally. Individuals vary in the amounts they need and in the amounts they eat from one day to another and from one meal to another. If the foods offered are chosen along the lines of this plan, most preschool children will take what they need from it.

Timing. Because a small child's capacity is limited while his needs for growth-promoting and protective foods are great, his nutritional program merits careful planning. Menus and timing are both important. Although feeding a new baby when he cries for food contributes to the early building of a sense of trust, the preschool child benefits from a structured program, including regular mealtimes that fit his stage of maturity. If the child comes to meals hungry but not famished and exercised but not exhausted, he is likely to take in adequate nutrients. For most American children, it works out well to have three meals a day, with a snack in the middle of the morning and another in the middle of the afternoon. The snacks can be planned as to time, quality, and quantity to make the youngster appropriately hungry at family mealtimes. If completely unplanned, snacks are all too prone to be long on carbohydrates and fats and short on proteins, minerals, and vitamins. With his limited capacity for intake and high need for growth-promoting foods, a preschool child cannot afford to eat many empty calories (foods devoid of proteins, minerals, and vitamins). With good planning, eating and sleeping can be tied together in rhythms which assure adequate sleep for the young child. Insufficient sleep leads to fatigue which depresses the appetite.

Sensory Aspects. Taste sensitivity varies from one individual to another, in preschool children as well as in older children and adults. An investigation [38] of preschool children's thresholds for the basic tastes—salt, sweet, bitter, and sour—showed degrees of sensitivity to all four tastes to be highly correlated. Preschool children tended to be at the extreme ends of the scale for tasting bitter. That is, they either tasted it or they did not, whereas for sweet, salt, and sour, they could be arranged into groups of high, medium, and low sensitivity. The number of subjects reporting that they were always hungry for meals increased as taste sensitivity decreased. Breakfast was the meal most enjoyed, in contrast to teen-age girls, who have been found to enjoy breakfast least.

Nutritionists recommend variety in the textures of foods which make up a meal. A combination of crisp, chewy, and soft foods is usually enjoyed. Common observation, as well as research [18], shows that preschool children often accept a raw vegetable in preference to the same vegetable cooked. Such a preference may be based on flavor as well as texture. None of the foods liked best by preschool children contained anything gritty or stringy [38].

Taste is not the only sense involved in eating. Sensations of touch come from fingers as well as mouth when young children eat. They often want to feel the slipperiness of gelatin and spaghetti, the crinkliness of lettuce, and the cloudlike softness of a soufflé. Bright colors and color contrasts are thought to be effective in making meals attractive to children as well as to adults. Young children prefer lukewarm food to hot food [10, p. 201]. The sense of smell doubtless plays an important part in enjoyment of eating.

Favorite foods, according to mothers' reports on what preschool children ate, were headed by meats [16]. Next in order came fruits, sweets, and cereals. While some vegetables such as beets and corn were liked and eaten by many children, vegetables were most often mentioned as disliked foods. The most disliked vegetable was lima beans, with spinach, squash, asparagus, and sweet potatoes also unpopular. Fourteen out of 121 children refused all vegetables. Twenty-two specific vegetables were refused by one or more children.

Emotional Aspects. Emotional surroundings can enhance or depress appetite. Conversely, hunger disposes the child toward anger outbursts. Excitement and upset conditions cause the stomach to stop its movements. To eat with the family may be too stimulating for a young child, or it may add to his happiness and feelings of belonging, depending on what goes on at the family table. Whatever the arrangements, the preschool child has the best chance of eating an adequate diet in an atmosphere that is calm and pleasant.

Avoiding Problems. The year between age 2 and 3 is a time when eating problems often begin. Because the rate of growth has slowed down appetite is likely to be smaller. Parents, remembering the joyous abandon with which their baby waded into his food, may worry when they see that the same child at 2½ toys with his food and fusses over what he will eat and what he will not eat. Urging and forcing at this point often prolong and complicate the problem. Eager to exercise his autonomy, the 2-year-old wants to choose and decide for himself. It is satisfying to decide to eat a small serving and then to ask for more or to refuse it; it can be very annoying to have too large an amount presented, especially if poked at you in spoonfuls. If the child can do it himself, his sense of autonomy is enhanced. He can make progress with a spoon and even more with his fingers if given foods that are easy to pick up. Custard and soup are easier to drink than to spoon up. The young child profits from all arrangements which facilitate self-help and from wide limits within which to do it himself. He does need limits, though, for healthy development of the sense of autonomy. The child suffers, as well as the family, when he is allowed to throw his applesauce on the floor or to grab the food from his neighbor's plate. It is important for him to feel that what he does is all right, and for him to have that feeling, his behavior has to be acceptable to the people around him.

Planning for Sleep and Rest

Sleep is a protective function which allows for repair and recovery of tissues after activity. Cognition is more adequate and emotional life more positive under conditions of enough sleep.

As children mature, they sleep less. They also change in the proportion of the two types of sleep, as Figure 1–7 shows [59]. Children and adults dream during the rapid eye movement (REM) phase of sleep, which seems to be essential to psychological well-being. REM sleep makes up about 25 percent of sleep at age 2, and nonrapid eye movement (NREM) about 75 percent. Between ages 3 and 5, REM

20 Preschool Children

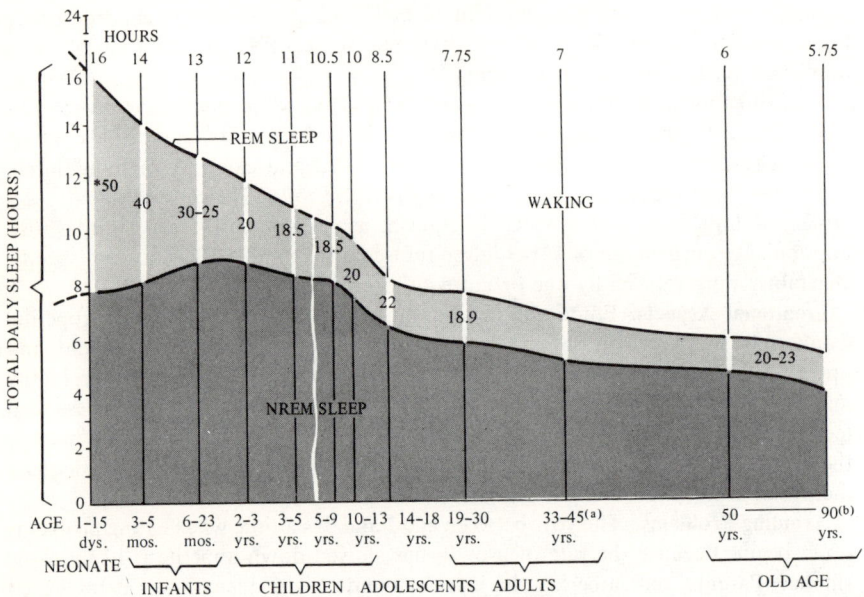

Figure 1-7. Ontogenetic development of the human sleep-dream cycle.
SOURCE: Reprinted by permission from H. P. Roffwarg, J. N. Muzio, and W. C. Dement, "Ontogenetic Development of the Human Sleep-Dream Cycle," *Science*, 152, 604–619, 29 April, 1966. Copyright 1966 by the American Association for the Advancement of Science. Revised since publication in *Science* by Dr. Roffwarg.

constitutes about 20 percent of sleep. The average total hours of sleep at age 2 to 3 is almost 12 and at age 3 to 5, about 11. During the second year a common pattern is two naps a day and an all-night sleep. One nap is more usual between age 2 and 5 and after that, no nap. In some cultures, an afternoon nap is normal for everybody, adults as well as children. Children who had recently given up napping, a group between 4½ and 7 years, were found to take a longer time than children who napped and also a longer time than older children to get into REM sleep [59]. The 4½ to 7 group had a long period of deep NREM sleep before starting REM, suggesting that they were especially fatigued.

Children vary widely, in hours of sleep, consistency of patterns, distribution of sleep between night and day, soundness of sleep, and effects of various influences on sleep. How much sleep is enough? This is a very difficult question to answer with scientific evidence or even to answer in a home situation. A practical way for adults to judge whether children are getting enough sleep is to use as criteria such signs as readiness to get up in the morning, good appetite, emotional relaxation, cheerfulness, warm skin with good color, bright eyes, good posture, activeness in play, curiosity, enthusiasm.

Pediatricians have commented that mothers often find it more difficult to let children establish their own sleep patterns than to let them regulate their own feeding [10, p. 263]. Only 7 percent of parents in an American study [62, p. 269] and 9 percent in an English study [53, p. 246] said that they had no particular bedtime and let the child go to bed when he liked. The majority of parents had a certain bed hour in mind, but they varied considerably as to how strictly they maintained it. Among the English parents variations in strictness were related to class, those in higher occupations reporting more insistence upon prompt bed-going.

While unspecified bed hours may be infrequent, many children manage to postpone bed-going and sleep, with the result that they sleep for shorter periods of time than children who go to bed promptly. Whether permissively reared children get enough sleep is a difficult question to answer because of the problem of defining *enough* sleep. In countries such as Italy and India, where babies and preschool children go out in the evening with their parents, falling asleep here and there on a friend's sofa or an extra chair at a concert, we have not noticed hyperactivity or signs of fatigue. Young children seemed to sit around more than Americans, but in a relaxed, not tense, way. Extra sitting around might be due to more relaxed adults, fewer toys, less stimulating conditions, and possibly lower available energy due to poor nutrition.

Avoiding Problems. Children generally benefit from parental supervision which makes regular sleep and rest a part of their lives. At developmental periods when certain influences disturb sleep, guidance is appropriate. For instance, toward the end of the first year, when strangers are recognized as strange and frightening, it is important for baby-sitters to be well acquainted with the baby, in order to prevent fright when he wakens from sleep. In the latter part of the second year and for some time after that, when motor activities are thrilling and the sense of autonomy is at a crucial stage of growth, a child may find it very hard to accept bed and sleep. Here is where a routine and careful guidance can prevent sleep problems from getting established. It is easiest to go to bed and to sleep after a period when stimulation has been cut down (that is, excitement minimized), and when a regular series of steps toward bed (such as washing, tooth brushing, story, putting teddy bear in bed), and an affectionately firm parent have indicated that sleep is imminent. Dreams are likely to be disturbing, because they are not clearly distinguished from reality. Reassurance after a fright or disturbance is conducive to sleep, as long as it is calm, confident, and given in the child's room. When parents make a big entertainment production out of the incident or take the youngster into their bed, reassurance may come to be a goal in itself.

Illness and Accidents

Prevention. Maintaining life and health in young children is no simple matter for parents, even in the favored environment of western civilization. (In some parts of the world, the odds are against an infant's surviving.) Preventive care means taking a young child regularly to a physician or to a well-baby clinic, where he is immunized against diseases, assessed as to growth and health, and his mother is given advice as to nutrition, physical care, and attention to defects. Dental care is necessary from the preschool period onward. It has been estimated that among American children under 5 years of age, 10 percent have more than eight cavities [7, p. 5]. In areas without fluoridated water, 70 to 80 percent of preschool children have decay requiring treatment, whereas in communities with fluoridation, only 30 to 40 percent suffer such decay [71].

Promotion of health and growth through routines of feeding, sleep, and activity has been discussed. Parents also have the jobs of promoting community health

Preschool Children

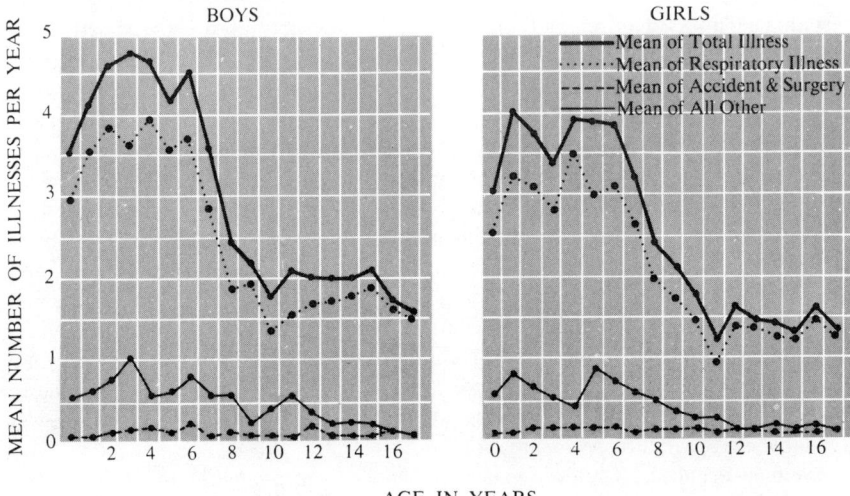

Figure 1-8. Incidence of illnesses and certain types of illnesses in boys and girls.

SOURCE: Reprinted by permission from I. Valadian, H. C. Stuart, and R. B. Reed, "Studies of Illnesses of Children Followed from Birth to Eighteen Years," *Monographs of The Society for Research in Child Development*, **26**:3, Figure 13. Copyright © 1961, The Society for Research in Child Development, Inc.

measures, supervising general hygiene in the home, nursing ill children, and keeping children from injury. Although most of the serious childhood diseases are preventable through immunization and many of the lesser illnesses are preventable through home hygiene, many respiratory disturbances and some gastrointestinal illnesses are common even in preschool children living under favorable circumstances. The immaturity of the systems involved makes them prone to infections and disturbances. As shown in Figure 1-8, the peak period for American children's illnesses, with respiratory ailments predominating, is the time from age 2 to 6.

Accidents. A young child is more likely to die from an accident than from any of the next five ranking causes of death [49]. Figure 1-9 illustrates this fact, showing that 37 percent of male deaths and 32 percent of female deaths between the ages of 1 and 4 were caused by accidents. These rates are over three and a half times the death rate from pneumonia, the second ranking cause, and nearly four and a half times that from cancer. The accident rates have increased during the past decade largely because of the increase in number of motor vehicle accidents. The other main types of accidents to young children are from traffic, fires, explosions, burns, drowning, poisoning, falls, and inhaling or ingesting food and other objects. Supervision of children outdoors is thus seen to be vital—not only telling them what not to do but watching them and keeping them out of the way of traffic, water, and other hazards. Making and keeping the home safe for young children require constant planning and vigilance. Over two fifths of accidents to young children occur in the home.

Another Metropolitan Life Insurance study [48] showed that about 25 percent of the annual deaths from accidental poisoning in the United States were deaths of children between 2 and 4 years of age. The agents of death were chiefly aspirin and other salicylates, petroleum products, lead, and household pesticides. The obvious implications are that safety of preschool children requires keeping them

Personality and Body 23

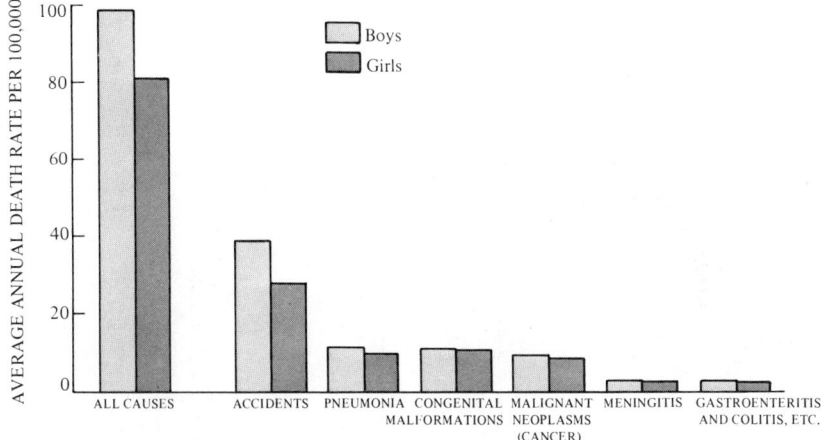

Source: Basic data from Reports of the Division of Vital Statistics, National Center for Health Statistics.

Figure 1–9. Accidents and other major causes of death among children between 1 and 4 years of age.

SOURCE: Reprinted by permission from *Statistical Bulletin*, Metropolitan Life Insurance Company, September 1969.

away from many substances of common use in the home. Saying *no* is not enough at this age. Since preschool children tend to be good climbers, the problem of where to keep poisons out of their grasp is an important one to solve.

Studies on children over 6 indicate that accident-proneness is associated with stereotyped patterns of impulsively discharging anxiety through motor activity [43]. Preschool children tend to be impulsive in motor acts, anyway. While the anxiety is the primary place to focus for prevention, it may also be worthwhile to try to help preschool children to act less impulsively.

International Differences in Threats to Children. International differences in mortality and illness rates are greatest at the 1-to-4-age-level. Countries with low death rates include the United States, Great Britain, Denmark, Netherlands, Norway, Sweden, and Australia. Death rates in some of the nations with high rates are as much as 40 times the rates in the countries with low rates [63, pp. 206–207]. Figure 1–10 shows the contrast in preschool mortality rates between the United States and three other American countries. Not only are the rates ever so much higher in Columbia, Mexico, and Guatemala, but the leading cause is different. Disturbances of the gastrointestinal tract rank last among principal causes of death in the United States and first in the other countries. Accidents (or violence), the first cause of death in the United States, does not appear as a principal cause in the other countries. The infectious diseases, whooping cough, and measles are still important in Colombia, Mexico, and Guatemala.

A new threat to child health knows no national boundaries. *Air pollution* most likely has adverse effects on health and development, according to a committee of the American Academy of Pediatrics [2]. A review of studies suggests that toxic substances in the air are now contributing to respiratory infections and that they may lead to permanent lung damage. Since pollutants emitted in England fall on Sweden, to cite only one example, the problem is truly international.

24 Preschool Children

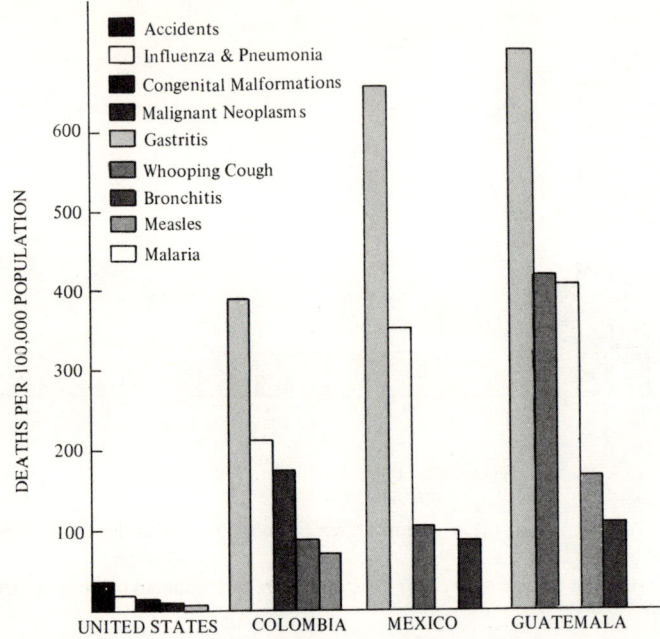

Figure 1-10. Five principal causes of death in children 1 to 4 years in United States and three other American countries.
SOURCE: From *Dynamics of Development: Euthenic Pediatrics* by Dorothy V. Whipple, M.D. Copyright © 1966 by McGraw-Hill, Inc. Used with permission of McGraw-Hill Book Company.

Psychological Care of Ill and Injured Children. It is frightening to be hurt or sick—frightening to anyone, but especially to a preschool child. Pain itself can be frightening as well as unpleasant. Reduced to a lower level of autonomy, he is disturbed at not being able to control himself and the environment as efficiently as normally. His thinking and his actions are less adequate for coping with the world.

Reassurance from parents makes the pain and fright possible to bear, just as Mother's presence in a disturbingly new situation gives a young child courage to explore. The most reassuring parent is one who combines sympathy with the calm expectation that balance and normalcy will be restored in due time. The ill or injured child is comforted and strengthened by having the limits of his activity redefined appropriately. For instance, "You are going to stay in your bed, but you can move around it all you like. I'll give you this box of toys to play with now. After your nap, you can choose a story for me to read to you." If toys and activities require less effort than his normal top speed, then he can still feel satisfied with what he achieves.

Hospital care for young children has been slowly undergoing a revolution, sparked by the research of Bowlby [8] and Spitz [68, 69] and pushed along by writers such as Robertson [58]. Gradually doctors, nurses, and parents are accepting the evidence that it is damaging for children between 6 months and 3 years to be separated from their mothers, and that even after 3 years of age, separation may be harmful. Some hospitals now permit and even encourage parents to stay with their young children so as to give them the emotional support which they

Courtesy John E. Ball

need every day but all the more when they are ill. Visiting rules have been liberalized in many places, too. Continuing research efforts confirm the earlier findings on young children's need for closeness to loved people while undergoing traumatic experiences. For example, when 197 British children under 6 years of age underwent surgery for tonsils and/or adenoids, half were admitted to the hospital with their mothers and half were alone. The young patients accompanied by their mothers suffered significantly fewer complications afterwards, both emotional and infective [9]. Interviews with parents of Swiss preschool children showed that emotional reactions after discharge were less frequent among children whose parents had visited them frequently in the hospital and who had had close contact. The differences between frequently visited, closely contacted children and infrequently visited children were very significant [12]. There is still a big educational job to be done in adapting hospitals to children's emotional needs.* Unfortunately many medical personnel still interpret a young child's stony silence as good adjustment, and the flood of tears released by his parents' arrival as evidence that parents are bad for him.

Parents as Sources of Physical Danger. Parents are the second most frequent cause of physical injuries to children, ranking second to motor vehicles [28]. The authors of this report strongly suspect that child-beating inflicts many more injuries on children than do even motor vehicles, but that most parental violence is not reported. They estimate that for every child brought to the hospital with positive evidence of parentally inflicted damage, 100 such cases remain undetected.

* An illuminating film: *A Two-Year-Old Goes to the Hospital* (British National Health Service and World Health Organization).

26 Preschool Children

Physical Structures and Behaviors

A child's appearance gives some hints as to how he will behave. Some impressions come from his body build and some from his features. Some research has been done on relationships between physical and behavioral measures.

Body Build. Three main types of physique have been described by Sheldon [64]; *endomorph*, round, soft, and plump with more fat and less muscular tissue than other types; *mesomorph*, strong, well-developed muscles and bones; *ectomorph*, tall, thin, delicate-looking. When preschool children were rated by their mothers and teachers and the rating related to physique types, some relationships were established [74]. The adults were likely to see the endomorphic girl as cooperative and cheerful, socially extraverted, and low in tension and anxiety. The mesomorphic girl was often described as energetic. The adults tended to rate the ectomorphic girl as uncooperative, not cheerful, anxious, and aloof. Among boys, relationships were not as clear, but the mesomorphic boy was seen as energetic, aggressive, assertive, cheerful, and social while the ectomorph was depicted as unsocial, shy, reserved, cooperative, and unaggressive, and the endomorph as amiable, and socially outgoing. It is impossible to tell how much the ratings were influenced by what adults expected to see in children of various body types rather than by what the children actually did. However, it does look as though there is some relationship between build and behavior.

Minor Physical Anomalies. In order to explore relationships between congenital factors and behavior, a longitudinal study has been done on a group of nursery school children who had been judged normal at birth [72, 73]. Each child was scored for anomalies of hair, eyes, ears, mouth, hands, and feet, such as very fine electric hair, eyelid fold, ears set low, curved fifth finger, third toe longer than second. These anomalies are so slight that they are ordinarily not noticed. Each child's total score was based upon the degree as well as the presence of such anomalies. Behavior measures were obtained at 2½ years by observers who measured time spent in various activities and counted incidences of specific actions, and by teachers' ratings. High scores for anomalies were associated with inability to delay gratification, nomadic play, frenetic play, spilling, throwing, opposing peers, and intractability.

Five years later, a replication of the study [72] showed stable anomaly scores and poor motor control associated with high scores. Such children shifted location more, were less able to delay response, and showed more frenetic behavior than children with low anomaly scores. High-scoring girls were more likely to be fearful and withdrawn, boys to be hyperactive.

The results of this study suggest that the slight physical anomalies and the somewhat disturbed behavior had a common source, rather than that one caused the other. One might reason that very noticeable physical abnormalities cause negative reactions toward children, who then behave poorly. The subjects of this study were normal physically, however, with deviations which could be noticed only through a careful examination. It is very unlikely that they experienced negative reactions due to their appearance. It is possible, however, that hyperactive behavior in infancy elicited hostility from parents which intensified the condition.

Motor Development

Watch a group of preschool children playing. The first impression is of constant motion. Closer inspection reveals some children sitting looking at books, others squatting in the sandbox, and one or two in dreamy silence beside the record player. The younger the child, the shorter the interval during which he is likely to stay put. Carrying out simple motor acts, he tends to finish quickly. In contrast, the older preschooler weaves simple acts together into more complicated units which take longer to perform. To crawl through a piece of culvert, for instance, takes only a minute and to crawl through several times takes only five, whereas to make that culvert into the Holland Tunnel and to use it as such may take half the morning.

Motor control includes inhibiting actions as well as initiating them and controlling their speed of execution. The ability to perform certain motor acts very slowly was found to be associated with high levels of intelligence in preschool children [42]. In a group ranging from average to very high IQs, the higher IQ children were more likely to do well in tests of drawing a line slowly, walking slowly between two lines, and making a truck move slowly by means of a winch. The experiment also showed that children of higher IQ were just as active in free play as those of average intelligence. It is not certain whether superior ability to inhibit motor acts is the result of superior intelligence or if a common cause, superior development of the nervous system, is responsible for the high scores on both types of tests.

The Development Sequence

The chart of motor behavior, Table 1-6, drawn from several sources, shows how development between age 2 and 5 results in a child who moves and manipulates more like an adult than he does like the toddler he used to be. Having worked through stages of using a spoon and fork, holding a glass, and pouring from a pitcher, he can feed himself neatly without having to try very hard. He can even carry on a conversation at meals. He can cut and fold paper. From imitating a circular stroke at 2, drawing a vertical line at 3, and copying a square with some accuracy at 5, he is poised on the brink of learning to write. The 2-year-old, to whom walking steadily, running, and climbing are thrilling achievements, advances through walking tiptoe, hopping, jumping, tricycling, agile climbing, and stunting to the graceful age of 5. Skipping, hopping skillfully, running fast, he looks into an exciting future of skating, swimming, and riding a two-wheeler. Balls, the toys beloved by babies, children, and adults, are used with increasing maturity [27, 36, 41].

Individual Differences. One child differs from another in the speed with which he progresses through a sequence of behavior patterns. Individual differences in rate of motor development were apparent in 152 children between 3 and 7 years, who were tested for skill in cutting and tracing a straight line [40]. Although these skills showed fairly high correlations with age (0.63 for cutting and 0.70 for tracing), 2 of the 50 youngest children ranked in the upper third in cutting and 2 in tracing. Four of the 49 oldest children ranked in the bottom third in cutting and 4 in tracing. We have seen 4-year-olds who could swim and ride bicycles and 6-year-olds who spilled their food consistently. Children differ also in speed, power, and accuracy of their muscular coordinations, as witness the "natural athletes" who throw and catch balls efficiently in the preschool years. They differ, too, in balance and grace. When reading a chart that shows average development for various ages, it is important to keep in mind that this is a summary of a group of children and that it does not picture any one child as he is.

Table 1-6 Some Landmarks in Motor Development During the Years from 2 to 6, from Basic Normative Studies. The Item is Placed at the Age Where 50 Percent or More of Children Perform the Act. (Initials in parentheses refer to sources. See footnotes.)*

	Age Two	Age Three	Age Four	Age Five
Eye-Hand	Builds tower of 6 or 7 blocks (GA) Turns book pages singly (GA) Spoon into mouth without turning (GA) Holds glass in one hand (GA) Imitates circular stroke (GA) Puts on simple garment (GA)	Builds tower of 9 blocks (GA) Makes bridge of 3 blocks (TM) Catches ball, arms straight (MW) Spills little from spoon (GA) Pours from pitcher (GA) Unbuttons, puts shoes on (GA) Copies circle (TM) Draws straight line (TM)	Cuts on line with scissors (GI) Makes designs and crude letters (GI) Catches small ball, elbows in front of body (MW) Dresses self (GI)	Folds paper into double triangle (TM) Copies square (TM) Catches small ball, elbows at sides (MW) Throws well (G) Fastens buttons he can see (GI) Copies designs, letters, numbers (GI)
Locomotion	Wide stance, runs well (GA) Walks up and down stairs alone (GA) Kicks large ball (GA) Descends large ladder, marking time (MW) Jumps 12" (MW)	Walks tiptoe (GA, B) Jumps from bottom stair (GA, B) Stands on one foot (GA, B) Hops, both feet (MW) Propels wagon, one foot (J) Rides tricycle (GA) Descends long steps, marking time, unsupported (MW) Jumps 18" (MW)	Gallops (G) Descends small ladder, alternating feet easily (MW) Stunts on tricycle (G) Descends short steps, alternating feet, unsupported (G)	Narrow stance (GI) Skips (G, MW) Hops on one foot, 10 or more steps (MW) Descends large ladder, alternating feet easily (MW) Walks straight line (GI)

* SOURCES:
B —Bayley, N. "Development of Motor Abilities During the First Three Years," *Mono. Soc. Res. Child Devel.*, 1935, **1**.
GA —Gesell, A. and Amatruda, C. A. *Developmental Diagnosis* (New York: Hoeber, 1951).
GI —Gesell, A. and Ilg, F. L. *Child Development* (New York: Harper, 1949).
G —Gutteridge, M. V. "A Study of Motor Achievements of Young Children." *Arch. Psychol.*, 1939, No. 244.
J —Jones, T. D. *Development of Certain Motor Skills and Play Activities in Young Children*, Child Development Monographs (New York: Teachers College, Columbia University, 1939), No. 26.
MW—McCaskill, C. L. and Wellman, B. L. "A Study of Common Motor Achievements at the Preschool Ages." *Child Devel.*, 1939, **9**, 141-150.
TM —Terman, L. M. and Merrill, M. A. *Stanford-Binet Intelligence Scale* (Boston: Houghton Mifflin, 1960).

Personality and Body   29

Sex Differences. At all ages, males tend to do better than females on tests of large muscles coordination, most likely because of their superior strength and muscular development [23]. Girls begin early to show superiority in manual dexterity. Between age 2 and 6, boys have been found to excel in going up and down ladders and steps, throwing, catching and bouncing balls, and jumping from boxes and ladders [41]. Girls performed better than boys in hopping, skipping, and galloping [27]. The latter can be confirmed by observing a kindergarten in the fall, where there are almost sure to be several little boys who merely run or gallop while the other children skip.

Throughout the preschool period, boys continue to show the exploratory, assertive, and vigorous play that has been noted as a sex difference in infancy. Their behavior is also shaped by sex-typing experiences which influence what they have to play with and what restrictions and directions are brought to bear on them. Different cultures have different ways of emphasizing sex-appropriate behavior, some stressing masculine, some feminine, some maximizing sex differences, and some minimizing them.

Posture

Posture is the way in which the whole body is balanced, not only in sitting and standing, but also in play and rest. Posture is neuromuscular behavior, just as surely as bouncing a ball and drawing a circle are. Parents and teachers rarely make great headway when they try to get children to stand up straight or otherwise consciously improve their posture according to standard ideas of what good posture is. The ways in which a child stands, sits, and moves are the results of a dynamic interplay of forces which cannot be controlled by holding his head up or throwing back his shoulders. This is not to say that good posture is unimportant in its influence on health, growth, and efficiency of movement. It is very important indeed, but it is achieved through good muscle tone and healthy skeletal development, as well as through general physical and mental health. Figure 1-11 illustrates good and poor posture in the preschool child.

Breckenridge and Murphy [10, p. 282] distinguish five important factors when considering body dynamics:

1. *Gravity*. The body is most efficient motorwise if it is arranged symmetrically about a line that passes through the center of gravity (see illustration). The center of gravity drops in the trunk as the child's proportions change, and the lower it is, of course, the easier it is for him to maintain his balance in the upright position. The transverse line in Figure 1-12 shows the location of the center of gravity in the body from birth to adulthood. During the years from two to five, the center of gravity drops from just above the umbilicus to just below it [54, p. 89].
2. *Muscles and bones*. Good tone is important in all muscles. If opposing pairs of muscles are unequal in pull, faulty balance between them results in poor posture.
3. *Stage of development*. We have already mentioned that the young child has flexible joints, due to looser attachment of ligaments and muscles. Also, his center of gravity shifts downward, causing him to adjust gradually to the change. Standing on a wide base at first, in order to maintain his balance, the young child toes out and takes much of his weight on the inner part of his feet.

30 Preschool Children

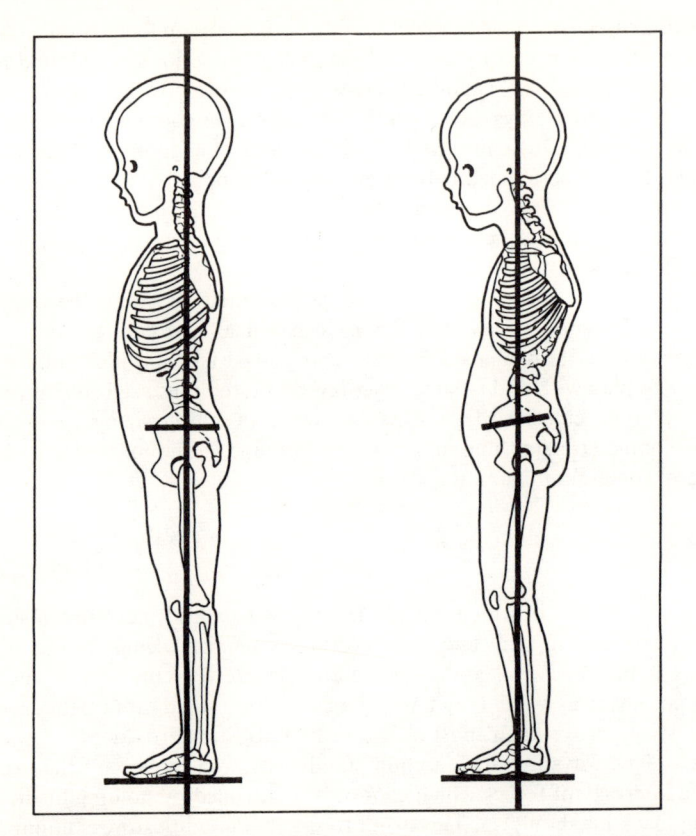

Figure 1–11. The child on the left shows good posture, the child on the right, poor posture. The first child's body is arranged symmetrically about a line that passes through his center of gravity. The head and chest are high, chin in, abdomen in, shoulder blades in, curves of back small and knees straight.

SOURCE: Figure 4.3 on page 90 of *Good Posture and the Little Child*, Children's Bureau Publication 219. Washington, D.C.: U.S. Government Printing Office, 1935.

The arch is protected with a fat pad at this point, and it makes him look as though he had flat feet. Knock-knees and lordosis (small of back curving in excessively) are so common in the preschool period as to be considered normal. These conditions usually improve with age.

4. *Individual differences.* There is no one best posture for all, since a child's body dynamics are individual. A stocky child must balance his body in one way, a thin child in another. Varieties of proportions will have their own dynamics.
5. *Environmental influences.* The child's whole regime affects his posture. Obviously, nutrition determines what materials build and maintain his body, and hence is one key to the efficiency with which the body can operate and balance itself. Rest and fatigue, with their intimate connection with nutrition, nerves, and muscles, play a big role in determining posture. Activity is essential, too, for developing coordination, maintaining muscle tissue and promoting its growth. A variety of equipment and opportunities for large-muscle play is hygienic. Shoes, clothing, and furniture all have roles to play in promoting or hampering the dynamic coordination which is ideal for a given child.

Personality and Body

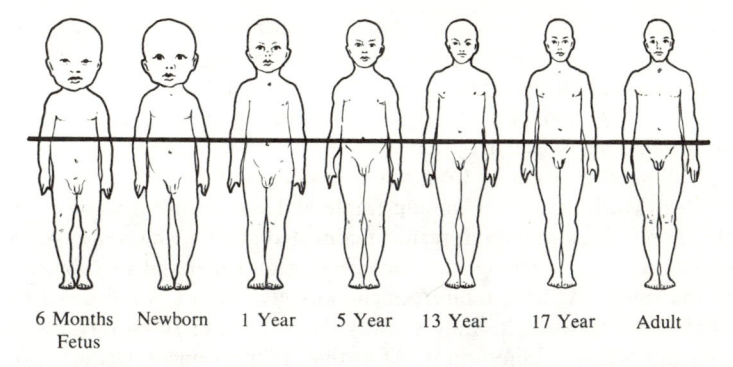

| 6 Months Fetus | Newborn | 1 Year | 5 Year | 13 Year | 17 Year | Adult |

Figure 1–12. The horizontal line shows the center of gravity which changes its location in the trunk as body proportions change.

SOURCE: Reprinted by permission from C. E. Palmer, "Studies of the Center of Gravity in the Human Body," *Child Development*, **15**, Figure 7. Copyright © 1944, The Society for Research in Child Development, Inc.

The child's own personality is expressed in his posture, both his general attitudes toward himself and the world and his specific ups and downs. Sometimes a sagging, slumping body is the first indication that something is wrong. A handicap, such as blindness or deafness, often leads to a characteristic posture. A beautifully balanced body is one indication of a healthy child.

The influences of culture on posture can be seen as early as the preschool years. Mead [44, p. 40] gives illuminating examples from three different cultures. In Bali, girls of 2 and 3 walk with a "pregnant" posture because there is much teasing about pregnancy. A girl is told that she is probably pregnant and older people will often hit her on the abdomen, asking, "Got a baby in there?" Among the Iatumul, it is almost impossible to tell boys and girls apart, even with moving pictures, because they are dressed like girls, and all move like girls. Among the Manus, Mead could not tell the little girls and boys apart because they were all dressed like boys and moved like boys.

Physical Fitness

The past decade has seen the arousal of interest on a nationwide basis in the topic of physical fitness of children. Programs to improve the health and fitness of preschool children have paid more attention to nutrition than to exercise, and rightly so. Many authorities on preschool children take the point of view that preschool children will take appropriate exercise in play if they are given a healthy general program which includes opportunities for using outdoor space and wide variety large-muscle play equipment. Tests of physical fitness on nursery school children have shown a wide range of results, however [65]. While some children scored the maximum on tests of muscular strength and flexibility, others could pass none, and most scored between the two extremes. Since these children had rich opportunities for motor play, other factors must have accounted for their differences. In fact, the study indicated relationships between healthiness of personality and muscular strength and flexibility. Further study has confirmed the relationship between body flexibility and personality, as expressed in a test that explores the child's concept of his body [25].

32 Preschool Children

Motor skills were developed in a sedentary nursery school child as a demonstration of the use of reinforcement principles [35]. Mark, age 3 years 8 months, spent most of the first half of the school year in much random wandering and avoidance of boards, ladders, and other kinds of climbing equipment. One such piece, a climbing frame, was selected by the experimenters as the focus of the behavior which Mark was to acquire. Continuous social reinforcement was given by a teacher when Mark used the climbing frame and was withheld when he was not using the frame. The social reinforcement consisted of watching Mark, speaking to him, smiling at him, touching him, or bringing him material to supplement his play on the frame. At first, reinforcement was given when Mark came near the frame and withheld when he moved away from it. After seven days he touched the frame and began to climb on it. After that, reinforcement was given only for climbing on it. By the second day he spent 25 percent of his outdoor time on the frame, and by the ninth day 67 percent. Later phases of the experiment included reinforcement for other vigorous motor activities and a gradual change to intermittent, rather than constant, reinforcement. Mark then used all the climbing equipment in the yard. When he returned to school the next fall, he spent 50 to 60 percent of his time in vigorous activity and used all the climbing equipment. While few children require as much help as Mark did in establishing patterns of motor play, the study has important implications for nursery school teaching. Probably many more young children would benefit from some reinforcement of vigorous motor activities.

Hand Preference

By age 2 most children show a preference for the right hand, a few for the left, and a few seem to have little preference. During the next three years, the hand preference becomes more firmly established, and established in more children. Thus hand preference is a developmental trait, a trait which increases with increasing maturity. While there are probably genetic foundations to laterality, social learning also influences hand preference. Figure 1–13, based on data from several investigators, shows how right-handedness increases with age. Note that the preschool years are the time when the greatest increase in established preferences occurs.

Studies on hand preference use an index of handedness derived from sampling a variety of activities. The formula for the index of dominance is $\frac{R - L}{R + L}$. (R is right hand, L is left hand.) Thus $+1$ would be complete right dominance and -1 left dominance. Figure 1–14 shows the distribution of such handedness indices for 44 nursery school children [32] who took part in experiments to determine hand preference and who were also observed eating and playing. For example, hand preference was noted while the child ate with a spoon, ate with his fingers, threw a ball, and drew with crayons. The lowest indices for hand preference were found while children ate with their fingers. Random observations for spontaneous acts also gave indices close to zero. About 11 percent of the children showed dominant left-handedness.

Sex differences are small but consistent. All studies concerned with such differences show a greater incidence of left-handedness and ambidexterity in boys. The

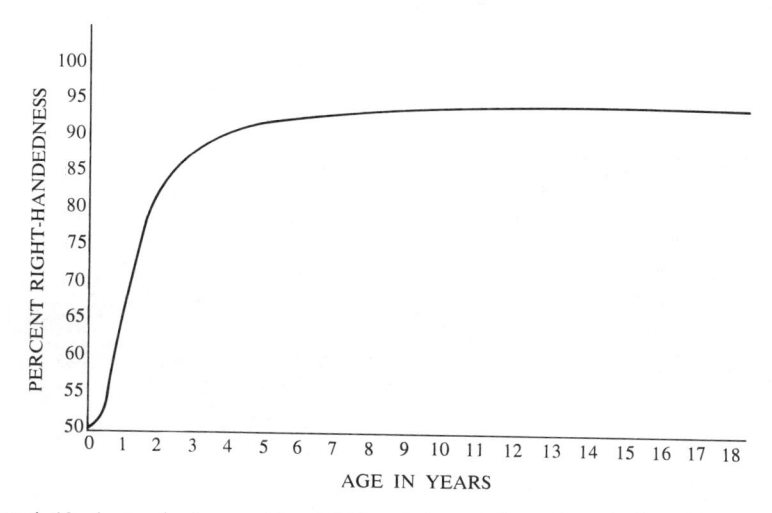

Figure 1-13. A steady increase in right-handedness takes place during the preschool years.
SOURCE: Reprinted by permission from G. Hildreth, "The Development and Training of Hand Dominance: II. Developmental Tendencies in Handedness," *Journal of Genetic Psychology*, **75**, 221–254. Copyright © 1949, The Journal Press.

difference may be due somewhat to social conditioning, since girls engage in more hand play than boys, and are more amenable to training.

Stuttering and handedness have long been thought to be associated. Low left dominance or partially converted dominance has been shown to occur in stutterers more than in the general population. Which is cause and which effect, or whether either is cause or effect, is not definitely established. Stuttering tends to occur first at 3 or 4 years, the age when hand preference is being established ordinarily. It has been found that when manual dominance is established, stuttering tends to disappear, at least at this age [32].

The left-handed person incurs many disadvantages in addition to possible speech disturbance. In a world designed for right-handed people, he has to adjust to scissors, golf clubs, classroom chairs, table settings, and countless other arrangements that are awkward for him. There are certain prejudices against left-handers,

Table 1-7 Incidence of Left-handedness in Schoolchildren over Three Decades

Author	Year	Percentage of Children Writing with Left Hand
Hildreth	1932	2.2
Hildreth	1937	4.1
Hildreth	1941	6.2
Carrothers	1945	8.2
Belmont & Birch*	1963	10.0

* In addition to writing as a criterion of handedness, this study also used ball throwing, turning a doorknob, and cutting with scissors.

SOURCE: Data from Belmont and Birch [6], Carrothers [13], and Hildreth [33].

34 Preschool Children

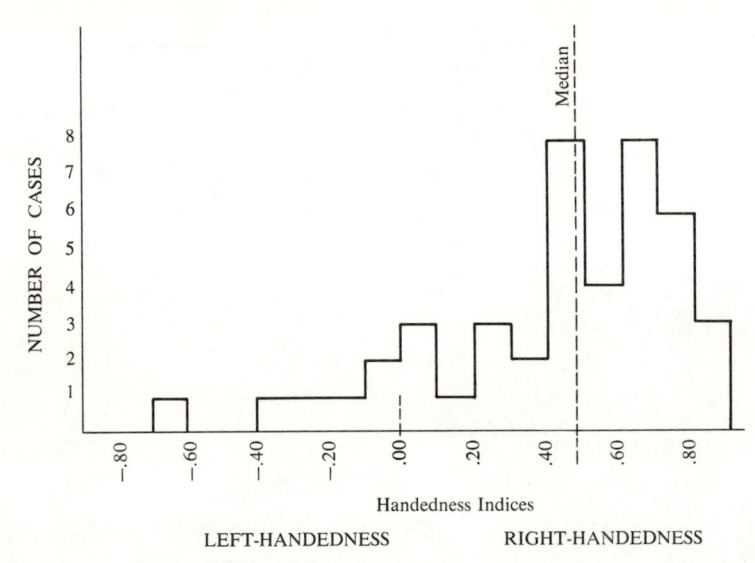

Figure 1-14. Distribution of handedness in nursery school children. Zero indicates no preference, +1 extreme right-dominance, −1 extreme left-dominance.

SOURCE: Reprinted by permission from G. Hildreth, "Manual Dominance in Nursery School Children," *Journal of Genetic Psychology*, 72, 29–45. Copyright © 1948, The Journal Press.

although feelings against them vary from time to time and from culture to culture. A small percentage of children develop a strong preference for the left hand, in spite of living among right-handed arrangements. It seems wise, for teachers and parents, to respect such a preference and to help the child by giving him left-handed equipment when possible and showing him how to adapt in places where he has to use right-handed tools and arrangements.

Since hand preference is definitely a behavior pattern that becomes established, not one that appears at birth, it is reasonable to expect that experience will influence it. If teaching and learning are important factors in establishing right-handedness, then permissiveness for choosing a preferred hand would increase the incidence of left-handedness. During the years from 1913 to the present, the incidence of left-handedness has indeed gone steadily up [33]. Table 1–7 shows results from studies in different decades.

Handedness and Eye Preference. There are preferences in the use of eyes and feet, just as there are for hands, and these preferences are not always consistent. The eye–hand preferences of a large number of black 4-year-old boys and girls were studied in relation to their performances on intelligence tests and perceptual-motor tests [22]. Hand dominance was judged by noting which hand was used in copying geometric forms (part of the perceptual-motor test). Eye dominance was determined by seeing which eye the child used in looking through a hole in a box to see an object at the other end. Eighty-five percent of the children were right-handed, but only 58 percent were right-eyed. Half of the children were right-handed and right-eyed, 31 percent right-handed and left-eyed, 4 percent left-handed and left-eyed, and 11 percent indeterminate. The left-handed, left-eyed group gave the poorest performance of all groups in both perceptual and intelligence tests. The investigators suggest that a neurological deficit underlies both the left dominance and the lower test scores of these children. This explanation fits with the findings of a study which showed disturbed hand dominance in 16- to 22-year-olds who had suffered oxygen deprivation at birth.

The question of laterality is a significant one during the elementary school years, when its reference to writing is obvious.

Summary

Two stages of personality development occur during the preschool period: the development of the sense of autonomy, during the early years, and the development of the sense of initiative, from about 3 years to 6 or 7 years. The sense of autonomy is promoted by clear, firm guidance which permits successful decision making within the limits it imposes. The opposite of sense of autonomy includes feelings of shame and doubt. Initiative and imagination grow as the child explores the world of people and things, as he imagines himself into a variety of roles and activities, and as he successfully seeks reasons, answers, solutions, and new ideas. Conscience develops, along with guilt, requiring a balancing with initiative for adequate personality development. Beginnings of initiative can be seen in infancy, when children differ in activity and passivity. During the preschool years, differences in achievement behavior represent differences in the sense of initiative. Parental encouragement of achievement behavior at this age is likely to have lasting effects. The sense of initiative results from the interaction of a variety of influences, including genetic, constitutional, cultural, and familial.

Physical growth is slower than it is in infancy. The rate of growth in height decelerates slowly during the preschool years. Although boys are slightly larger than girls, girls are closer to maturity than boys. Retarded growth occurs in children in the lower socioeconomic levels in the United States and in the majority of children in underdeveloped countries. Appearance and proportions change from the chubby, babylike configuration to the more slender, childish pattern, due to changes in amount and distribution of fat, as well as growth of muscle and skeletal tissues. Evidence of changes in the nervous system is more in terms of function than of size and structure. The structures of vision are immature. Taste buds are more numerous than in the older child. Characteristic shape, position, and structure make for significant differences, as compared with older children, in the preschool child's middle ear, digestive system, and respiratory system.

Assessment of growth is most often done in terms of a child's height and weight, which are compared with a standard derived from measurements of a large number of children. Or the present status may be evaluated according to a record of past growth. Growth can also be judged from skeletal development. X rays of the bones provide information on the health history of the child, as well as on his present status.

The majority of the world's children are malnourished. Their food is insufficient in quantity and quality. Since fatigue depresses appetite, health care includes careful guidance of rhythms of eating and sleeping. Eating problems are avoided by such guidance plus attention to the physiological, sensory, and emotional aspects of preschool children's eating and by recognition of his eagerness for autonomy. Sleep problems, also, are avoided by appropriate timing, nonstimulating bed-going routines, reassurance in frightening situations, and gentle firmness.

Many illnesses and accidents are preventable by planning, guidance, careful arrangement of the environment, hygiene, immunizations, and medical supervision. Preschool children are especially vulnerable to illness. International differences in preschool illness and death are enormous. Gastrointestinal disturbances rank first as cause of death in many poor countries; accidents rank first in the United States. Parental child abuse contributes heavily to the high "accident" rate. Easily frightened by illness or injury, the young child is reassured by the presence of a loved person, especially if that person is calmly sympathetic.

Physical structure and behavior are related. Body build shows some correlation with personality characteristics. Minor physical abnormalities are related to mild behavior disturbances.

Motor development proceeds through a fairly stable sequence of patterns. Individual children differ in speed of sequential development as well as in quality of performance, as shown in speed, power, and accuracy. In many, but not all, motor performances, boys excel girls. Posture, or body balance, expresses health and influences it. Young children vary in muscular strength and flexibility. Hand preference is established in most children during the first five years of life. Right-handedness increases with age. Left-handedness and ambidexterity occur more often in boys than in girls. Disturbances in lateral dominance are associated with poor perceptual-motor performances, implying an underlying neurological deficit.

References

1. Agricultural Research Service. *Food for fitness.* Washington, D.C.: United States Department of Agriculture, 1964.
2. Altman, L. K. Pollution danger to children seen. *Wall Street J.*, 1970, November 15.
3. Baumrind, D. Child care practices anteceding three patterns of preschool behavior. *Genet. Psychol. Mono.*, 1967, **75**, 43–88.
4. Baumrind, D., & Black, A. E. Socialization practices associated with dimensions of competence in preschool boys and girls. *Child Devel.*, 1967, **38**, 291–327.
5. Béhar, M. Prevalence of malnutrition among preschool children of developing countries. In N. S. Scrimshaw & J. E. Gordon (Eds.), *Malnutrition, learning and behavior.* Cambridge, Mass.: M.I.T. Press, 1968, pp. 30–41.
6. Belmont, L., & Birch, H. G. Lateral dominance and right-left awareness in normal children. *Child Devel.*, 1963, **34**, 257–270.
7. Berland, T., & Seyler, A. *Your children's teeth.* New York: Meredith, 1968.
8. Bowlby, J. *Child care and the growth of love.* London: Pelican, 1953.
9. Brain, D. J., & Maclay, I. Controlled study of mothers and children in hospital. *Brit. Med. J.*, 1968, **1**, 278–280.
10. Breckenridge, M. E., & Murphy, M. N. *Growth and development of the young child* (8th ed.). Philadelphia: Saunders, 1969.
11. Calder, R. Food supplementation for prevention of malnutrition in the preschool child. In National Research Council, *Preschool child malnutrition: Primary deterrent to human progress.* Washington D. C.: National Academy of Sciences, 1966, pp. 251–257.
12. Cardinaux-Hilfiker, V. Elternbesuche bei hospitalisierten vorschulpflichtigen Kindern. *Heilpädagogische Workblätter*, 1969, **38**, 6–15. (Abstract).

13. Carrothers, G. E. Left-handedness among preschool pupils. *Am. School Board J.*, 1947, **114**, 17–19.
14. Crandall, V. C. Achievement behavior in young children. *Young Children*, 1964, **20**, 77–90.
15. Crandall, V. J., Preston, A., & Rabson, A. Maternal reactions and the development of independence and achievement behavior in young children. *Child Devel.*, 1960, **31**, 243–251.
16. Dierks, E. C., & Morse, L. M. Food habits and nutrient intakes of preschool children. *J. Am. Dietetics Assoc.*, 1965, **47**, 292–296.
17. Dorman, L., & Rebelsky, F. Assertive behavior and cognitive performance in pre-school children. Paper presented at the meeting of the Society for Research in Child Development, Santa Monica, Calif., March 29, 1969.
18. Dudley, D. T. Effects of methods of vegetable preparation on choices and amounts eaten by nursery school children. Unpublished Master's Thesis. Iowa State University. Cited by Korslund [38].
19. Eichorn, D. H. Biological correlates of behavior. In H. W. Stevenson, J. Kagan, & C. Spiker, *Child psychology*. The Sixty-second Yearbook of the National Society for the Study of Education, Part I. Chicago: University of Chicago Press, 1963, pp. 4–61.
20. Erikson, E. H. *Childhood and society*. New York: Norton, 1963.
21. Escalona, S. K. *The roots of individuality*. Chicago: Aldine, 1968.
22. Flick, G. L. Sinistrality revisited: A perceptual-motor approach. *Child Devel.*, 1966, **37**, 613–622.
23. Garai, J. E., & Scheinfeld, A. Sex differences in mental and behavioral traits. *Genet. Psychol. Mono.*, 1968, **77**, 169–299.
24. Gesell, A., Ilg, F. L., & Bullis, G. E. *Vision*. New York: Hoeber, 1949.
25. Gollerkeri, S. B. Relationship between body image and muscular fitness of preschool children. Unpublished Master's thesis. University of Rhode Island, 1963.
26. Greulich, W. W., & Pyle, S. I. *Radiographic atlas of skeletal development of the hand and wrist* (2nd ed.). Stanford, Calif.: Stanford University Press, 1959.
27. Gutteridge, M. V. A study of motor achievements of young children. *Arch. Psychol.*, 1939, **244**.
28. Gwinn, J. L., Lewin, K. W., & Peterson, H. G., Jr. Roentgenographic manifestations of unsuspected trauma in infancy. *J. Am. Med. Assoc.*, 1961, **176**, 926–929.
29. Hatfield, E. M. Progress in preschool vision screening. *Sight-Saving Rev.*, 1967, **37**, 194–201.
30. Hicks, R. A., & Dockstader, S. Cultural deprivation and preschool children's preferences for complex and novel stimuli. *Percept. Motor Skills*, 1968, **27**, 1321–1322.
31. Hicks, S. E. Dependence of children on adults as observed in the nursery school. Unpublished Master's thesis. Pennsylvania State University, 1962.
32. Hildreth, G. Manual dominance in nursery school children. *J. Genet. Psychol.*, 1948, **72**, 29–45.
33. Hildreth, G. The development and training of hand dominance. II: Developmental tendencies in handedness. *J. Genet. Psychol.*, 1949, **75**, 221–254.
34. Jackson, R. L. Effect of malnutrition on growth of a pre-school child. In National Research Council, *Pre-school child malnutrition: Primary deterrent*

to human progress. Washington, D.C.: National Academy of Sciences, 1966, pp. 9–21.
35. Johnston, M. K., Kelly, C. S., Harris, F. R., & Wolf, M. M. An application of reinforcement principles to development of motor skills of a young child. *Child Devel.*, 1966, **37**, 379–387.
36. Jones, T. D. The development of certain motor skills and play activities in young children. *Child Devel. Mono.*, New York: Teachers College, Columbia University, 1939.
37. Kagan, J., & Moss. H. A. *Birth to maturity.* New York: Wiley, 1962.
38. Korslund, M. K. Taste sensitivity and eating behavior of nursery school children. Unpublished Master's thesis. Iowa State University, 1962.
39. Kurokawa, M. Acculturation and childhood accidents among Chinese and Japanese Americans. *Genet. Psychol. Mono.*, 1969, **79**, 89–159.
40. Lueck, E. Ability of young children to execute tracing and cutting tasks. Unpublished Master's thesis. Iowa State University, 1962.
41. McCaskill, C. L., & Wellman, B. L. A study of common motor achievements at the preschool ages. *Child Devel.*, 1938, **9**, 141–150.
42. Maccoby, E. E., Dowley, E. M., & Hagen, J. W. Activity level and intellectual functioning in normal preschool children. *Child Devel.*, 1965, **36**, 761–770.
43. Marcus, I. M., et al. An interdisciplinary approach to accident patterns in children. *Mono Soc. Res. Child Devel.*, 1960, **25**:2.
44. Mead, M. In J. M. Tanner & B. Inhelder (Eds.), *Discussions on child development.* Vol. 3. New York: International Universities Press, 1958.
45. Meichenbaum, D., & Goodman, J. Reflection-impulsivity and verbal control of motor behavior. *Child Devel.*, 1969, **40**, 785–797.
46. Mendel, G. Children's preferences for differing degrees of novelty. *Child Devel.*, 1965, **36**, 463–465.
47. Meredith, H. V. Body size of contemporary groups of preschool children studied in different parts of the world. *Child Devel.*, 1968, **39**, 335–377.
48. Metropolitan Life Insurance Company. The frequency of accidental poisoning. *Stat. Bull.*, 1960, **41**:3, 8–10.
49. Metropolitan Life Insurance Company. Accidental deaths high at the preschool ages. *Stat. Bull.*, 1969, **50**:6–8.
50. Minuchin, P. Correlates of curiosity and exploratory behavior. Paper presented at the meeting of the Society for Research in Child Development. Santa Monica, Calif., March 27, 1969.
51. Murphy, L. B. The widening world of childhood. New York: Basic Books, 1962.
52. Nakamura, C. Y., & Rogers, M. M. Parents' expectations of autonomous behavior and children's autonomy. *Devel. Psychol.*, 1969, **1**, 613–617.
53. Newson, J., & Newson, E. *Four years old in an urban community.* Chicago: Aldine, 1968.
54. Olson, W. C. *Child Development.* Boston: Heath, 1959.
55. Pederson, F. A., & Wender, P. H. Early social correlates of cognitive functioning in six-year-old boys. *Child Devel.*, 1968, **39**, 185–193.
56. Pryor, H. B. Width-weight tables (revised). *Am. J. Dis. Child.*, 1941, **61**, 300–304.
57. Pyle, S. I., Stuart, H. C., Cornoni, J., & Reed, R. Onsets, completions and spans of the osseous stage of development in representative bone growth centers of the extremities. *Mono. Soc. Res. Child Devel.*, 1961, **26**:1.

58. Robertson, J. *Young children in hospitals.* New York: Basic Books, 1958.
59. Roffwarg, H. P., Muzio, J. N., & Dement, W. C. Ontogenetic development of the human sleep-dream cycle. *Science,* 1966, **152,** 604–617.
60. Schaefer, A. E., & Johnson, O. C. Are we well fed? The search for an answer. *Nutrition Today,* 1969, **4**(1), 2–11.
61. Scrimshaw, N. S. Malnutrition, learning and behavior. *Am. J. Clinical Nutrition,* 1967, **20,** 493–502.
62. Sears, R. R., Maccoby, E. E., & Levin, H. *Patterns of child rearing.* Evanston, Ill.: Row, Peterson, 1957.
63. Shapiro, S., Schlesinger, E. R., & Nesbitt, E. L. *Infant, perinatal and childhood mortality in the United States.* Cambridge, Mass.: Harvard University, 1968.
64. Sheldon, W. H. *The varieties of human physique.* New York: Harper, 1940.
65. Smart, R. C., & Smart, M. S. Kraus-Weber scores and personality adjustment of nursery school children. *Res. Quart.,* 1963, **3,** 199–205.
66. Smith, M. E. An investigation of the development of the sentence and the extent of vocabulary in young children. *Univer. Iowa Stud. Child Welf.,* 1926, **3**:5.
67. Smock, C. D., & Holt, B. G. Children's reactions to novelty: An experimental study of curiosity motivation. *Child Devel.,* 1962, **33,** 631–642.
68. Spitz, R. A. Hospitalism: An inquiry into the genesis of psychiatric conditions in early childhood. *Psychoan. Stud. Child.,* 1945, **1,** 53–74.
69. Spitz, R. A. Hospitalism: A follow-up report. *Psychoan. Stud. Child.,* 1946, **2,** 113–117.
70. Tanner, J. M. *Education and physical growth.* London: University of London, 1961.
71. U.S. Public Health Service News Release. Quoted by A. F. North, Jr., in Research Issues in Child Health I: An Overview. In E. Grotberg (Ed.), *Critical issues in research related to disadvantaged children.* Princeton, N.J.: Educational Testing Service, 1969.
72. Waldrop, M. F., & Halverson, C. F., Jr. Minor physical abnormalities: Their incidence and their relation to behavior in a normal and deviant sample. Paper presented at the meeting of the Society for Research in Child Development, Santa Monica, Calif., March 29, 1969.
73. Waldrop, M. F., Pedersen, F. A., & Bell, R. Q. Minor physical anomalies and behavior in preschool children. *Child Devel.,* 1968, **39,** 391–400.
74. Walker, R. N. Body build and behavior in young children. *Child Devel.,* 1963, **34,** 1–23.
75. Walter, W. G. Electroencephalographic development of children. In J. M. Tanner & B. Inhelder, *Discussions on child development.* Vol. 1. New York: International Universities Press, 1953, pp. 132–160.
76. Watson, E. H., & Lowrey, G. H. *Growth and development of children* (5th ed.). Chicago: Year Book, 1967.
77. Wetzel, N. C. *Instruction manual in the use of the grid for evaluating physical fitness.* Cleveland: NEA Service, 1941.
78. White, B. L. An overview of the project. Paper presented at the meeting of the Society for Research in Child Development, Santa Monica, Calif., March 27, 1969.
79. Williams, C. D. Malnutrition and mortality in the preschool child. In National Research Council, *Pre-school child malnutrition: Primary deterrent to human progress.* Washington, D.C.: National Academy of Sciences, 1966, pp. 3–8.

80. Winterbottom, M. R. The relation of need for achievement to learning experiences in independence and mastery. In J. W. Atkinson (Ed.) *Motives in fantasy, action and society*. Princeton N.J.: Van Nostrand, 1958, pp. 453–494.
81. Woodruff, C. W. An analysis of the ICNND data on physical growth of the preschool child. In National Research Council, *Preschool child malnutrition: Primary deterrent to human progress*. Washington, D.C.: National Academy of Sciences, 1966, pp. 22–28.

Readings in
Personality and Body

The section on the preschool child begins with Erik H. Erikson's description of the two stages pertinent to this period. Although the critical period for development of the sense of autonomy begins in late infancy, it continues into the early preschool stage, the second and third years of life. The development of the sense of initiative then becomes crucial.

Because the student of child development needs a perspective on growth through childhood, the next selection is not confined to the preschool period. Pediatrician Dorothy V. Whipple writes on the nature of human growth and how it is measured, evaluated, and influenced. The term ages *in the title refers not only to stages of an individual's growth but also to historical ages. The measurement not only of height and weight, but of body build, the configuration of the human body, are dealt with here. We particularly wish to draw the reader's attention to Whipple's conclusions.*

One article relates physical development to behavior. The relationship between mildly deviant behavior and minor physical anomalies is explored in a study by Mary F. Waldrop and Charles F. Halverson, Jr.

Autonomy vs. Shame and Doubt
Initiative vs. Guilt

Erik H. Erikson
HARVARD UNIVERSITY

AUTONOMY VS. SHAME AND DOUBT

In describing the growth and the crises of the human person as a series of alternative basic attitudes such as trust vs. mistrust, we take recourse to the term a "sense of," although, like a "sense of health," or a "sense of being unwell," such "senses" pervade surface and depth, consciousness and the

Reprinted from *Childhood and Society*, pp. 251–258. Copyright © 1963 by W. W. Norton & Company, Inc. By permission.

unconscious. They are, then, at the same time, ways of *experiencing* accessible to introspection; ways of *behaving*, observable by others; and unconscious *inner states* determinable by test and analysis. It is important to keep these three dimensions in mind, as we proceed.

Muscular maturation sets the stage for experimentation with two simultaneous sets of social modalities: holding on and letting go. As is the case with all of these modalities, their basic conflicts can lead in the end to either hostile or benign expectations and attitudes. Thus, to hold can become a destructive and cruel retaining or restraining, and it can become a pattern of care: to have and to hold. To let go, too, can turn into an inimical letting loose of destructive forces, or it can become a relaxed "to let pass" and "to let be."

Outer control at this stage, therefore, must be firmly reassuring. The infant must come to feel that the basic faith in existence, which is the lasting treasure saved from the rages of the oral stage, will not be jeopardized by this about-face of his, this sudden violent wish to have a choice, to appropriate demandingly, and to eliminate stubbornly. Firmness must protect him against the potential anarchy of his as yet untrained sense of discrimination, his inability to hold on and to let go with discretion. As his environment encourages him to "stand on his own feet," it must protect him against meaningless and arbitrary experiences of shame and of early doubt.

The latter danger is the one best known to us. For if denied the gradual and well-guided experience of the autonomy of free choice (or if, indeed, weakened by an initial loss of trust) the child will turn against himself all his urge to discriminate and to manipulate. He will overmanipulate himself, he will develop a precocious conscience. Instead of taking possession of things in order to test them by purposeful repetition, he will become obsessed by his own repetitiveness. By such obsessiveness, of course, he then learns to repossess the environment and to gain power by stubborn and minute control, where he could not find large-scale mutual regulation. Such hollow victory is the infantile model for a compulsion neurosis. It is also the infantile source of later attempts in adult life to govern by the letter, rather than by the spirit.

Shame is an emotion insufficiently studied, because in our civilization it is so early and easily absorbed by guilt. Shame supposes that one is completely exposed and conscious of being looked at: in one word, self-conscious. One is visible and not ready to be visible; which is why we dream of shame as a situation in which we are stared at in a condition of incomplete dress, in night attire, "with one's pants down." Shame is early expressed in an impulse to bury one's face, or to sink, right then and there, into the ground. But this, I think, is essentially rage turned against the self. He who is ashamed would like to force the world not to look at him, not to notice his exposure. He would like to destroy the eyes of the world. Instead he must wish for his own invisibility. This potentiality is abundantly used in the educational method of "shaming" used so exclusively by some primitive peoples. Visual shame precedes auditory guilt, which is a sense of badness to be had all by oneself when nobody watches and when everything is quiet—except the voice of the superego. Such shaming exploits an increasing sense of being small, which can develop only as the child stands up and as his awareness permits him to note the relative measures of size and power.

Too much shaming does not lead to genuine propriety but to a secret determination to try to get away with things, unseen—if, indeed, it does not result in defiant shamelessness. There is an impressive American ballad in which a murderer to be hanged on the gallows before the eyes of the community, instead of feeling duly chastened, begins to berate the onlookers, ending every salvo of defiance with the words, "God damn your eyes." Many a small child, shamed beyond endurance, may be in a chronic mood (although not in possession of either the courage or the words) to express defiance in similar terms. What I mean by this sinister reference is that there is a limit to a child's and an adult's endurance in the face of demands to consider himself, his body, and his wishes as evil and dirty, and to his belief in the infallibility of those who pass such judgment. He may be apt to turn things around, and to consider as evil only the fact that they exist: his chance will come when they are gone, or when he will go from them.

Doubt is the brother of shame. Where shame is dependent on the consciousness of being upright and exposed, doubt, so clinical observation leads me to believe, has much to do with a consciousness of having a front and a back—and especially a "behind." For this reverse area of the body, with its aggressive and libidinal focus in the sphincters and in the buttocks, cannot be seen by the child, and yet it can be dominated by the will of others. The "behind" is the small being's dark continent, an area of the body which can be magically dominated and effectively invaded by those who would attack one's power of autonomy and who would designate as evil those products of the bowels which were felt to be all right when they were being passed. This basic sense of doubt in whatever one has left behind forms a substratum for later and more verbal forms of compulsive doubting; this finds its adult expression in paranoiac fears concerning hidden persecutors and secret persecutions threatening from behind (and from within the behind).

This stage, therefore, becomes decisive for the ratio of love and hate, cooperation and willfulness, freedom of self-expression and its suppression. From a sense of self-control without loss of self-esteem comes a lasting sense of good will and pride; from a sense of loss of self-control and of foreign overcontrol comes a lasting propensity for doubt and shame.

If, to some reader, the "negative" potentialities of our stages seem overstated throughout, we must remind him that this is not only the result of a preoccupation with clinical data. Adults, and seemingly mature and unneurotic ones, display a sensitivity concerning a possible shameful "loss of face" and fear of being attacked "from behind" which is not only highly irrational and in contrast to the knowledge available to them, but can be of fateful import if related sentiments influence, for example, interracial and international policies.

We have related basic trust to the institution of religion. The lasting need of the individual to have his will reaffirmed and delineated within an adult order of things which at the same time reaffirms and delineates the will of others has an institutional safeguard in the *principle of law and order*. In daily life as well as in the high courts of law—domestic and international—this principle apportions to each his privileges and his limitations, his obligations and his rights. A sense of rightful dignity and lawful independence on the part of adults around him gives to the child of good will the confident expectation that the kind of autonomy fostered in childhood will not lead to undue doubt or shame in later life. Thus the sense of autonomy fostered in the child and modified as life progresses, serves (and is served by) the preservation in economic and political life of a sense of justice.

INITIATIVE VS. GUILT

There is in every child at every stage a new miracle of vigorous unfolding, which constitutes a new hope and a new responsibility for all. Such is the sense and the pervading quality of initiative. The criteria for all these senses and qualities are the same: a crisis, more or less beset with fumbling and fear, is resolved, in that the child suddenly seems to "grow together" both in his person and in his body. He appears "more himself," more loving, relaxed and brighter in his judgment, more activated and activating. He is in free possession of a surplus of energy which permits him to forget failures quickly and to approach what seems desirable (even if it also seems uncertain and even dangerous) with undiminished and more accurate direction. Initiative adds to autonomy the quality of undertaking, planning and "attacking" a task for the sake of being active and on the move, where before self-will, more often than not, inspired acts of defiance or, at any rate, protested independence.

I know that the very word "initiative" to many, has an American, and industrial connotation. Yet, initiative is a necessary part of every act, and man needs a sense of initiative for whatever he learns and does, from fruit-gathering to a system of enterprise.

The ambulatory stage and that of infantile genitality add to the inventory of basic social modalities that of "making," first in the sense of "being on the make." There is no simpler, stronger word for it; it suggests pleasure in attack and conquest. In the boy, the emphasis remains on phallic-intrusive modes; in the girl it turns to modes of "catching" in more aggressive forms of snatching or in the milder form of making oneself attractive and endearing.

The danger of this stage is a sense of guilt over the goals contemplated and the acts initiated in one's exuberant enjoyment of new locomotor and mental power: acts of aggressive manipulation and coercion which soon go far beyond the executive capacity of organism and mind and therefore call for an energetic halt on one's contemplated initiative. While autonomy concentrates on keeping rivals out, and therefore can lead to jealous rage most often directed against encroachments by younger siblings, initiative brings with it anticipatory rivalry with those who have been there first and may, therefore, occupy with their superior equipment the field toward which one's initiative is directed. Infantile jealousy and rivalry, those often embittered and yet essentially futile attempts at demarcating a sphere of unquestioned privilege, now come to a climax in a final context for a favored position with the mother; the usual failure leads to resignation, guilt, and anxiety. The child indulges in fantasies of being a giant and a tiger, but in his dreams he runs in terror for dear life. This, then, is the stage of the "castration complex," the intensified fear of finding the (now energetically erotized) genitals harmed as a punishment for the fantasies attached to their excitement.

Infantile sexuality and incest taboo, castration complex and superego all unite here to bring about that specifically human crisis during which the child must turn from an exclusive, pregenital attachment to his parents to the slow process of becoming a parent, a carrier of tradition. Here the most fateful split and transformation in the emotional powerhouse occurs, a split between potential human glory and potential total destruction. For here the child becomes forever divided in himself. The instinct fragments which before had enhanced the growth of his infantile body and mind now become divided into an infantile set which perpetuates the exuberance of growth potentials, and a parental set which supports and increases self-observation, self-guidance, and self-punishment.

The problem, again, is one of mutual regulation. Where the child, now so ready to overmanipulate himself, can gradually develop a sense of moral responsibility, where he can gain some insight into the institutions, functions, and roles which will permit his responsible participation, he will find pleasurable accomplishment in wielding tools and weapons, in manipulating meaningful toys—and in caring for younger children.

Naturally, the parental set is at first infantile in nature: the fact that human conscience remains partially infantile throughout life is the core of human tragedy. For the superego of the child can be primitive, cruel, and uncompromising, as may be observed in instances where children overcontrol and overconstrict themselves to the point of self-obliteration; where they develop an over-obedience more literal than the one the parent has wished to exact; or where they develop deep regressions and lasting resentments because the parents themselves do not seem to live up to the new conscience. One of the deepest conflicts in life is the hate for a parent who served as the model and the executor of the superego, but who (in some form) was found trying to get away with the very transgressions which the child can no longer tolerate in himself. The suspiciousness and evasiveness which is thus mixed in with the all-or-nothing quality of the superego, this organ of moral tradition, makes moral (in the sense of moralistic) man a great potential danger to his own ego—and to that of his fellow men.

In adult pathology, the residual conflict over initiative is expressed either in hysterical denial, which causes the repression of the wish or the abrogation of its executive organ by paralysis, inhibition, or impotence; or in overcompensatory showing off, in which the scared individual, so eager to "duck," instead "sticks his neck out." Then also a plunge into psychosomatic disease is now common. It is as if the culture had made a man over-advertise himself and so identify with his own advertisement that only disease can offer him escape.

But here, again, we must not think only of individual psychopathology, but of the inner powerhouse of rage which must be submerged at this stage, as some of the fondest hopes and the wildest phantasies are repressed and inhibited. The resulting self-righteousness—often the principal reward for goodness—can later be most intolerantly turned against others in the form of persistent moralistic surveillance, so that the prohibition rather than the guidance of initiative becomes the dominant endeavor. On the other hand, even moral man's initiative is apt to burst the boundaries of self-restriction, permitting him to do to others, in his or in other lands, what he would neither do nor tolerate being done in his own home.

In view of the dangerous potentials of man's long childhood, it is well to look back at the blueprint of the life-stages and to the possibilities of guiding the young of the race while they are young. And here we note that according to the wisdom of the ground plan the child is at no time more ready to learn quickly and avidly, to become bigger in the sense of sharing obligation and performance than during this period of his development. He is eager and able to make things cooperatively, to combine with other children for the purpose of constructing and planning, and he is willing to profit from teachers and to emulate ideal prototypes. He remains, of course, identified with the parent of the same sex, but for the present he looks for opportunities where work-identification seems to promise a field of initiative without too much infantile conflict or oedipal guilt and a more realistic identification based on a spirit of equality experienced in doing things together. At any rate, the "oedipal" stage results not only in the oppressive establishment of a moral sense restricting the horizon of the permissible; it also sets the direction toward the possible and the tangible which permits the dreams of early childhood to be attached to the goals of an active adult life. Social institutions, therefore, offer children of this age an *economic ethos*, in the form of ideal adults recognizable by their uniforms and their functions, and fascinating enough to replace, the heroes of picture book and fairy tale.

Human Growth Through the Ages

Dorothy V. Whipple
GEORGETOWN UNIVERSITY SCHOOL OF MEDICINE

A human being starts being himself as a single cell. In 9 months he becomes a 6- or 7-lb baby; in less than 20 years he achieves 5 to 6 ft in height and 100 to 200 lb in weight. During this time there is a great temptation to evaluate how well he is doing by how big he has become. While in general there *is* a correlation between his size at any given time and his general well-being, the use of height/weight data as a measure of health is fraught with danger. However, although it is not possible to construct absolute standards of growth, enough is known to justify the cautious use of height/weight data.

THE NATURE OF GROWTH

Each animal species has a growth pattern characteristic of itself. Birds do not grow as do cows, but all birds follow a bird pattern. A hummingbird and an eagle follow similar patterns, even though the absolute values of their weights at any age are very different. In the same way a Jersey cow and a Holstein cow

From *Dynamics of Development: Euthenic Pediatrics* by Dorothy V. Whipple, M.D. Copyright © 1966 by McGraw-Hill, Inc. Used with permission of McGraw-Hill Book Company.

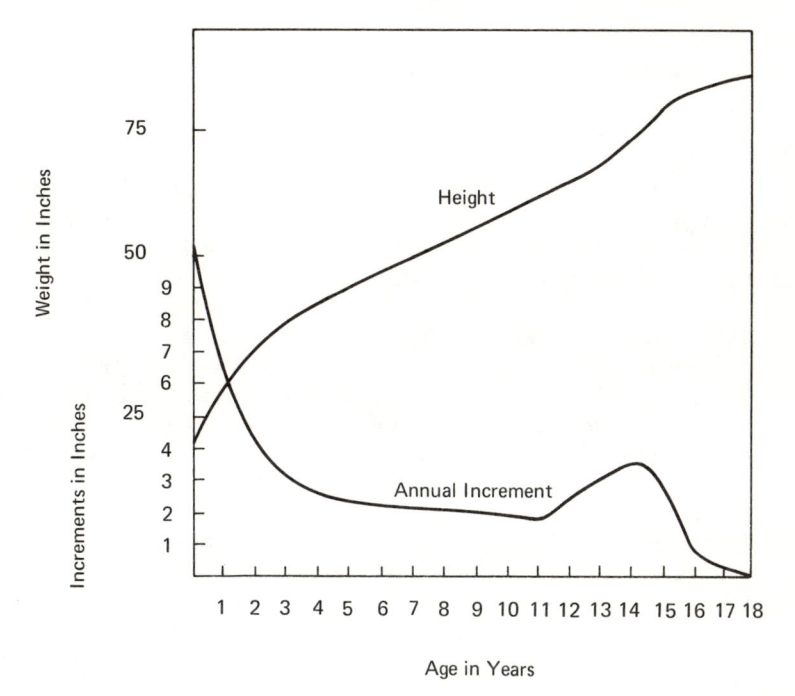

FIGURE 1. *Human growth pattern.*

have in common a cow pattern. This is as true of the human species as it is of the other animal species. A pigmy baby in Africa grows in the same way as a baby in Scandinavia or a baby in a Park Avenue apartment in New York (Figure 1).

Mammals below the human being (except the primate group to which human beings belong biologically) grow rapidly in early life and soon reach their mature size. They do not pass through the long, slow growing period of middle childhood, nor do they show a pubescent spurt in growth. In most mammals puberty comes soon after weaning and is not accompanied by an increase in the rate of somatic growth.

The long postponement of puberty in the human being is an evolutionary trait. The development of the brain is the distinguishing factor that separates man from lower species, and it takes time for this elaborate mechanism to complete its development. The hypothalamus controls the onset of puberty. When this part of the brain reaches maturity, it triggers an endocrine mechanism that initiates the maturation of reproductive function. The long childhood of the human being allows time not only for somatic growth but also for the development of the qualities of humanness. During the early years the child is prepared for adulthood in all areas of development; his body increases in size and develops increasingly intricate motor capacities, his personality emerges, he absorbs his culture. Under optimal conditions he becomes not only a full-sized adult competent in motor activities but an adult mature on the human level. The changes are so profound that it is not surprising that optimal development on all fronts is not always achieved. While development takes place in all areas simultaneously, the rate of development varies from area to area. Somatic growth and development will be considered in this section.

The greatest increments in human growth take place prior to birth; in children in the United States this is roughly 20 in. During the first year another 10 in. is added, and during the second year another 5 in. The human child achieves approximately half his ultimate height by the age of 2 years. During the third year the annual increment slows down to 3 to 4 in. and thereafter to 2 to 3 in. per year, until the growth spurt of puberty begins to makes its appearance.

During intrauterine life nourishment is absorbed and body substances that did not exist before are created. The increase in size of the fetus is due to creation of nervous tissue, of bone, of muscle, of connective tissue, and of all the multitudinous tissues which compose the animal organism. Later in life, new-cell creation slows down in most tissues, and most of the further increase in size is due to enlargement of the already created cells.

The early growth of the fetus and the infant appears to be primarily under control of the genes (Goldberg, 1955). Retardation of growth prior to the age of 2 years is usually attributed to primordial dwarfism (Kogut et al., 1963) or intrauterine growth retardation (Szalay, 1964). The anterior pituitary hormones, especially the growth hormone, are thought to be responsible for the steady growth through the years of middle childhood. Thyroxin initiates the development of centers of ossification in the long bones. In the period immediately preceding puberty, androgens from the adrenal cortex and the testes and estrogens from the ovary begin to make their appearance, stimulated probably by gonadotropins from the hypophysis.

In the girl, the estrogens stimulate both the growth of the long bones and finally maturational changes in the epiphyses followed by their closure; simultaneously the estrogens stimulate reproductive maturing. In the boy, androgens stimulate growth of the long bones more than estrogen does in the girl, both in duration of effect and in magnitude of increments. Ultimately androgens bring about closure of the epiphyses in the male, and growth in height comes to an end. It is the androgens which are responsible for maturation of the male reproductive system and the male secondary sexual characteristics.

The controlling factors of human growth inherent in the organism are thus seen to be the genes and the endocrines. Since it is, in the last analysis, the genes which control the endocrines, the growth potential of any individual human being can be thought of as lying within his genes. The actual growth of an individual, however, is determined both by his genetic potential and by the environmental stresses and strains to which he is subjected. The assumption that there is an optimal growth for each individual predetermined in his genes leads logically to a second assumption, namely, that deviants from this optimum reflect environmental hazards.

There are mountains of figures on human growth; nevertheless, what is optimum for any individual is still difficult to determine. It is possible, however, to cull from the available data some information that is useful in helping children attain their maximum well-being.

All growth studies fall into one of two categories: cross-sectional and longitudinal. Confusion between these categories is responsible for much of the prevalent misinformation about growth.

CROSS-SECTIONAL STUDIES

In a cross-sectional study all the children are measured once. Data are obtained, for example, from a school population of children varying in age from 6 to 18 years. The end result of such a study gives information on a group of 6-year-olds, a group of 7-year-olds, and so on for each age group. When all the data on the 6-year-olds are averaged, a figure of what the "average 6-year-old" has accomplished in 6 years is obtained. The meaning of this figure depends upon how homogeneous the group of 6-year-olds is. Size at age 6 varies with genetic background, with socioeconomic level, with physical and emotional health, and probably with other factors as well. If the population measured contains children who fall in many of these different categories, the average figure is not of much value as a standard against which to compare the accomplishments of any given child in 6 years. Average figures from a cross-sectional study are useful in comparing groups. The average size of 6-year-olds in a New York City public school can be compared with the average size of the 6-year-olds in a Japanese school or a French school or a Mississippi school or in an English school in 1850.

In a cross-sectional study the figures represent a static phenomenon. They are not a continuum, because no child moved from one group to the next. In many cross-sectional "growth" studies the data are used as though they were a continuum. The average figures of distance attained at the various ages are put together, and the resulting curve is called a "growth" curve (though nothing grew—all was static). In using cross-sectional data in this way the assumption is made that all children of age 6, when the study was made, will be of the same size 1 year hence as those age 7 at the time of measurement. This assumption is not valid; children do not progress at the same rate at different ages. Differences in the rate of progression exist at all ages, but during the spurt of growth at puberty the differences are very marked indeed. Each child grows rapidly for 1 or 2 years during his period of sexual maturation. However, there is about an 8-year span during which individual children pass through this growth spurt. Girls mature earlier than boys, but even within the same sex there is a range of several years during which maturation may take place.

A girl who has not started to mature may grow 1 in. in height between 11 and 12 years of age; another girl in early puberty at this age may grow 5 in. in this same chronological time. The difference obtained in a cross-sectional study of height between the average 11-year-old girl and the average 12-year-old girl gives a figure which distorts the amount of gain of the early- and late-maturing girls.

In Figure 2a the growth of girls maturing at different ages is plotted in individual increments. The dotted line represents the average figure, which bears little resemblance to the individual curves. In Figure 2b these data are replotted in such a way that peak growth in height of all the girls is placed at a single point. Again the dotted lines represent the average, which comes much

A—Plotted Against Age   B—Plotted Against Time of Maximum Growth
Solid lines are increments of individual girls • Dotted lines are averages of all four girls.

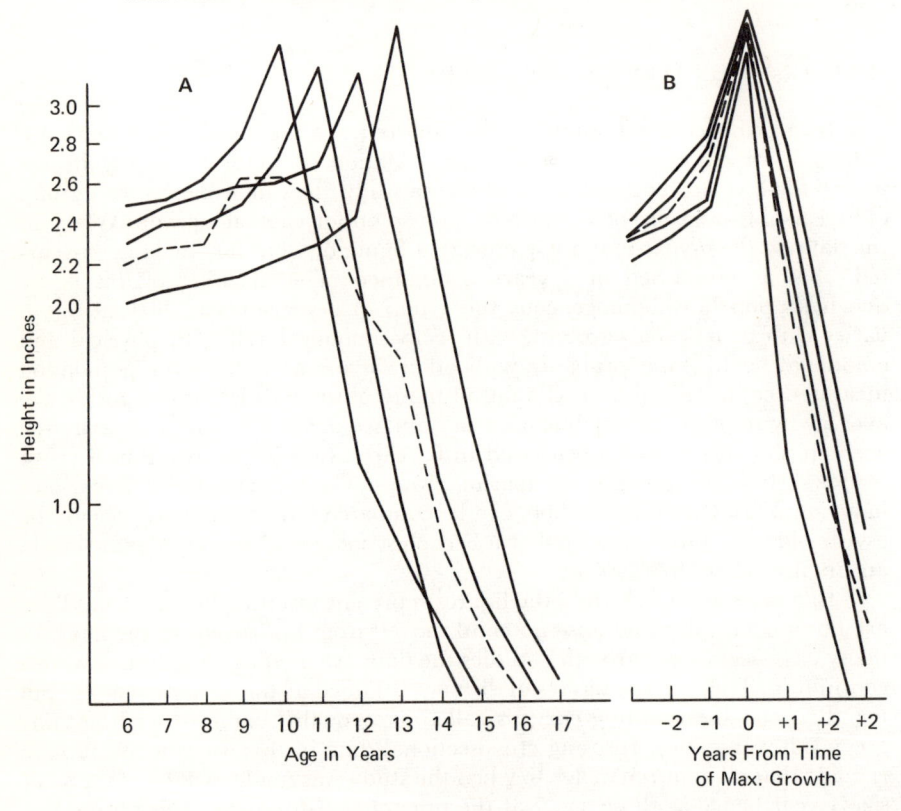

FIGURE 2.   *Height increments of girls maturing at different ages.*

closer to demonstrating the magnitude of the pubertal growth spurt than did the first average.

Valuable information can be obtained from cross-sectional studies, but such studies are of relatively little value in studying the velocity of growth—the increment per unit of time.

LONGITUDINAL STUDIES

In a longitudinal study a group of children is followed over a period of time. The same children are measured at successive periods. *Growing*, not merely growth accomplishment, is measured. Data from individual children can be combined and recombined in many ways. For example all the girls who reach the menarche at age 12 can be put in one group and their growth compared with girls who reach the menarche at age 13. It is soon seen that age of menarche has far more significance for growth than chronological age.

Longitudinal studies are more difficult to conduct than cross-sectional ones. It takes years to complete a study in which the investigator is waiting for his subjects to grow up; families move about, so it is difficult to maintain a group of children for a long span of years; longitudinal studies are expensive; and investigators as well as children grow older with the years!

At the present time in the United States there are a number of large-scale longitudinal studies, some under way, others completed. The Brush Foundation Study of Child Health and Development in Cleveland, the Fels Research Institute Study of Prenatal and Postnatal Environment at Antioch, Longitudinal Studies of Child Health and Development of the Harvard School of Public Health in Boston, Studies of the Institute of Human Development in Berkeley, California, are some of the most outstanding studies.

GENETIC INFLUENCES

There are many genes which influence growth. Since it is of course impossible to identify them individually, the problem is to relate observable and measurable qualities of a child with his growth potential. Growth in childhood is correlated with (1) size at birth, (2) sex, (3) speed of maturation, and (4) body build, and perhaps with other factors, too.

Of these four factors sex, with only rare exceptions, is readily observable at birth. It is certainly genetically determined, and there is no conceivable environmental factor which can change this basic fact about the individual.[1]

Birth weight is information easy enough to come by, but by itself it does not offer enough information to warrant prediction of growth.

Body build and rate of maturing are probably genetically determined. Rate of maturing, while not determinable at birth, shows itself during the early years. Combined with sex and birth weight, it offers the best information for predicting what a given child should accomplish under good conditions.

There is considerable evidence to suggest that although both body build and rate of maturing are genetically determined, they, unlike sex, may both be subject to change by environmental forces (see below).

SIZE AT BIRTH   The size at birth after full-term pregnancy is an index, although a rough one, of the ultimate size of the mature man. While dependent upon the genetic growth potential operating since conception, birth weight is influenced by many other factors. It is only a first step in estimating the growth potential of any given child.

First-born infants are usually smaller by some ounces than later-born infants (Meredith, 1950). Why this should be so is unknown, and there seems to be no correlation between this small difference and growth potential.

Infants born to small women and fathered by large men are often smaller at birth than would be expected as judged by their ultimate growth (Tanner, 1956). Apparently some dampening effect from the mother keeps an infant in utero from becoming too large to pass through her small birth canal.

Birth weight is related to duration of gestation. Lubchenco, Hansman, Dressler, and Boyd related birth weight to gestational age in a large series of

---

[1] Some of the new work on chromosomal patterns has cast doubt upon the absolute quality of sex. However, even for these infinitesimally few individuals with atypical chromosomal patterns, sex can still be considered a gene-determined absolute.

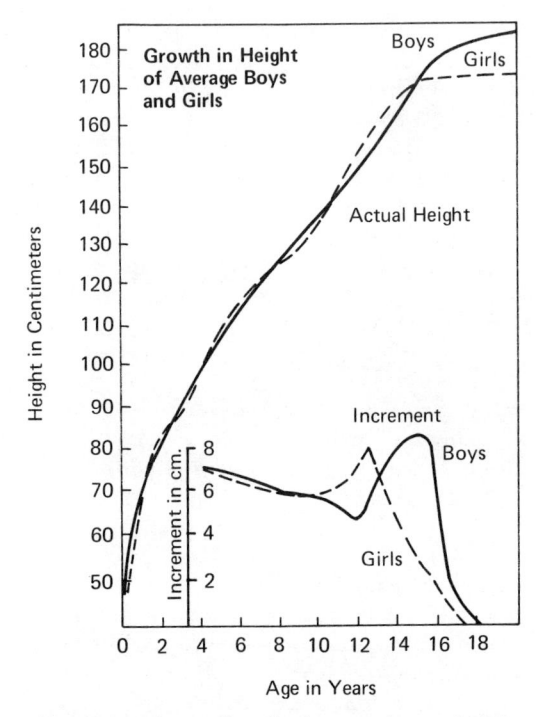

FIGURE 3. *Growth of average boys and girls.*

premature and full-term infants. Their data suggest that infants destined to be large are already large by the end of 24 weeks of gestational age.

SEX   Boys and girls have different growth patterns. At birth boys are slightly bigger (between 1 and 4 per cent) than girls in both height and weight. During the first year of life boys grow slightly faster than girls, but between the ages of 1 and 9 the growth rate differences between boys and girls are almost nonexistent.

At puberty the first significant differences in height and weight between the sexes become evident. It is at this time that the different endocrines exercise their effects—androgens in the male and estrogens in the female. Girls mature earlier than boys, so that for a few years the girls in any population group are larger than the boys in almost all dimensions. Then the boys begin their pubertal spurt; they catch up and pass the girls and end up roughly 10 per cent bigger (Figure 3).

SPEED OF MATURING   Some children progress along their predetermined growth pattern at a faster rate than others. The age at which a child matures sexually is a milestone that is convenient to use as a peg. Some girls accomplish sexual maturity in eleven years from birth; others take 16 or even 17 years to reach the same level of maturity. Boys are not so speedy as girls. The speediest can reach manhood in 12 years; the slow ones may take 18 years.

FIGURE 4.   *Classic body builds: Uncle Sam, John Bull, and Hercules.*

Early maturers are early in all their physiologic accomplishments (Reed and Stuart, 1959). In general, during childhood they are taller and heavier than later maturers. Their skeletons grow faster, they get their teeth earlier, they develop muscular capacity and coordination a little sooner than the late maturers. The speed of maturation is a gene-determined phenomenon. The early maturers become adults who have more weight for height than late maturers.

BODY BUILD   Adult human bodies vary in all their external dimensions. Almost all classifications consist of two extreme types and one intermediate one. At one extreme human beings are tall and thin, the typical Uncle Sam; at the other extreme they are short and fat, the John Bull. In between there is the strong muscular athlete, the Hercules (Figure 4).

Sheldon uses the terms *endomorph, mesomorph,* and *ectomorph* to describe the three types (Figure 5). The endomorph has a round head and large, fat abdomen predominating over this thorax. His arms and legs are short, with considerable fat in the upper arm and thigh but with slender wrists and ankles. He has a great deal of subcutaneous fat. His body is thick, his skeleton large. The endomorph is plump as a child and tends to put on weight as he gets older.

The mesomorph is the strong athlete. Bone and muscle predominate, but he has much less fat than the endomorph. He has broad shoulders and chest and heavily muscled arms and legs with the lower segment strong in relation to the upper.

The endomorph is the linear man; he has a thin, peaked face with a receding forehead, a thin, narrow chest and abdomen, spindly arms and legs.

A **B** **C**

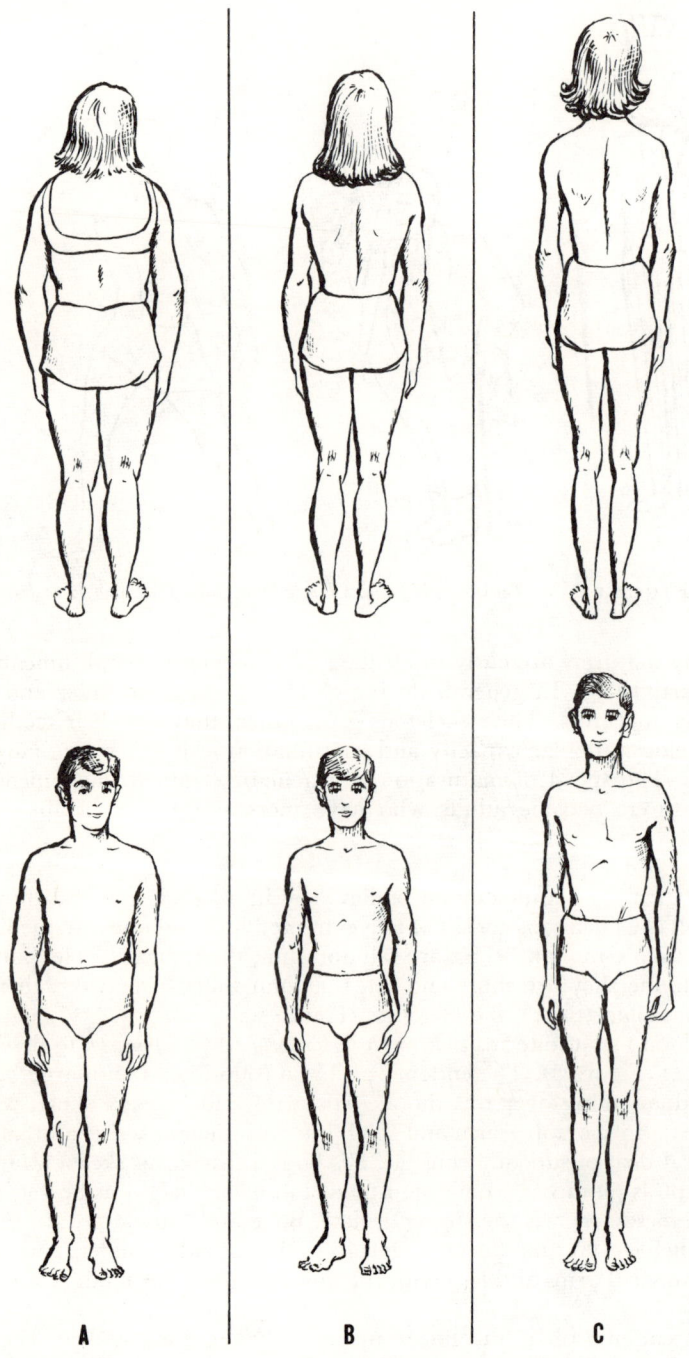

FIGURE 5. *Somatypes: (A) endomorph, (B) mesomorph, (C) ectomorph.*

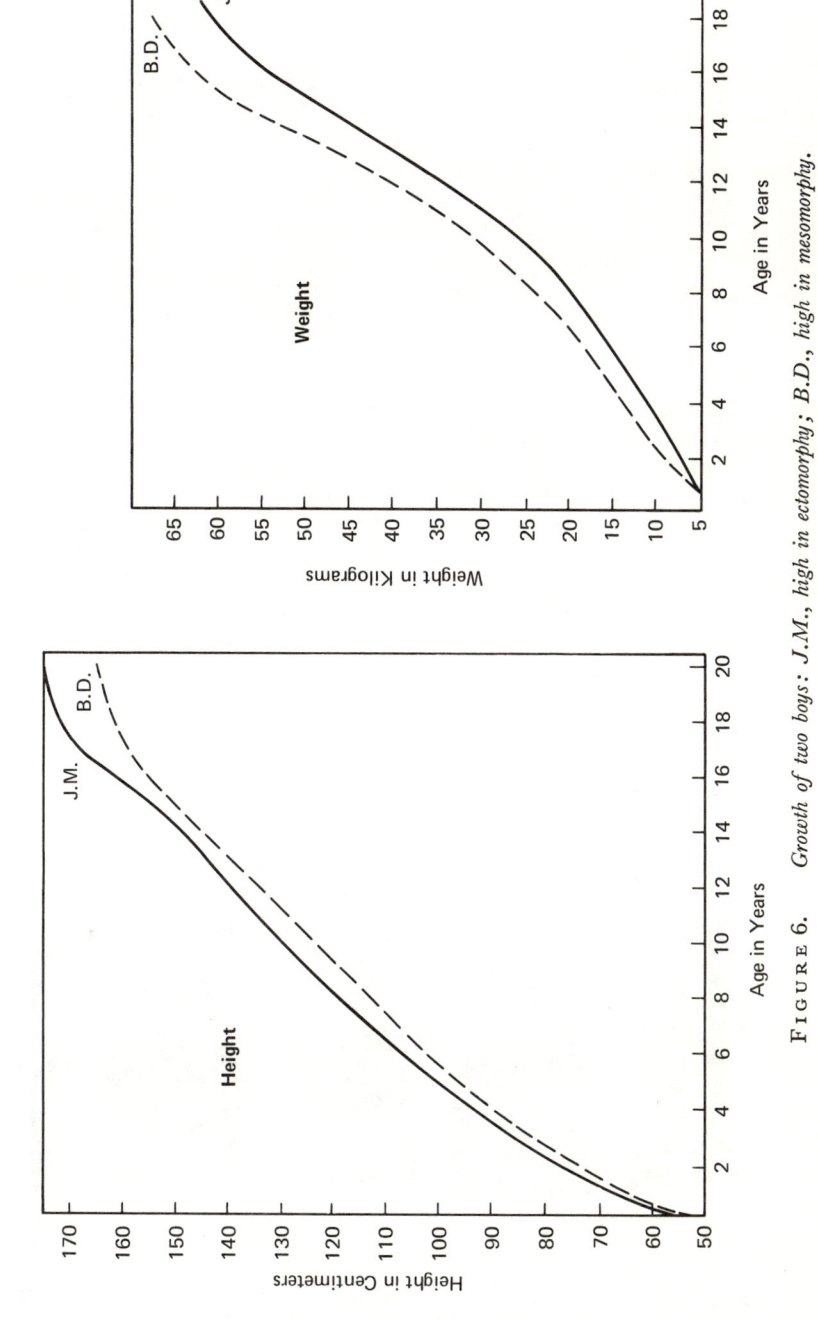

FIGURE 6. *Growth of two boys: J.M., high in ectomorphy; B.D., high in mesomorphy.*

His muscles are neither large nor strong. He has very little subcutaneous fat. He seldom becomes obese.

The majority of people have a moderate amount of each component in their somatotype. Virtually all somatotyping has been done on adults. In the Brush Foundation Growth Study a group that had been followed since childhood was somatotyped in early adult life. With the knowledge of their adult somatotypes their growth records were sorted out and recombined into groups of homogeneous somatotypes. The ectomorphs were taller than the mesomorphs at all ages from 4 onward, but the mesomorphs were heavier from age 2 onward. From the age of 2 the mesomorphs had more weight for height than the ectomorphs. (Figure 6 shows the growth of two boys, one high in ectomorphy, the other high in mesomorphy.)

Unfortunately somatotyping at the early ages has not at present been worked out. From longitudinal growth studies it was obvious, after the subjects reached adult size and could be somatotyped, that their growth in childhood varied according to the body build they finally achieved. This is important, but at present data are lacking with which to predict growth based on somatotype at birth (Dupertuis and Michael).

Bayley and Bayer (1946) have suggested another way of classifying body builds. They describe androgyny, the degree of masculinity in the female and femininity in the male. Androgyny emphasizes the fact that every individual has some characteristics of the opposite sex. Bayley and Bayer describe an undifferentiated pattern of body build characteristic of the neuter gender quality of early childhood. At puberty the pattern fans out either toward the hyperfeminine or the hypermasculine or remains intermediate (asexual). Some individuals travel all the way to the extreme of their sex; others stop part way, retaining elements of the undifferentiated pattern of childhood (Figure 7).

While the final measurement of androgyny cannot be made until maturity is reached, nevertheless, like the somatotypes of Sheldon, the androgyny type is, Bayley and Bayer believe, an innate trait uniquely characteristic of the individual and possessed by him all his life. By means of certain anthropometric

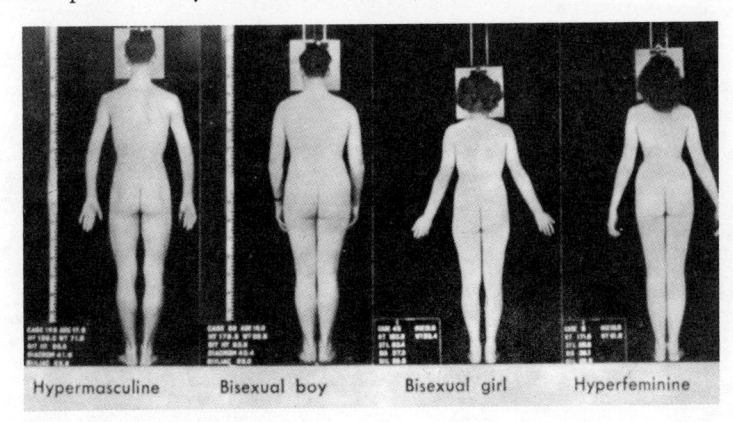

FIGURE 7. *Androgynic patterns.* (From Bayley and Bayer, Photos of Cases 5, 45, 66 and 168 in The Assessment of Somatic Androgyny, *Am. J. Phy. Anthrop.* 4:433, 1946. Courtesy of the Wistar Institute of Anatomy and Biology, Philadelphia.)

measurements during childhood these investigators have been able, at least roughly, to categorize children before puberty with respect to their androgyny scores.

In the androgyny score considerable emphasis is placed on the distribution of subcutaneous fat and muscles. Women on the whole deposit more fat than men, and men develop larger muscle mass than women. Amount of muscle and of fat are also factors in the somatotyping system of Sheldon.

These two different methods of describing body build overlap. The mesomorph of Sheldon is the muscular type and is closely related to the hypermasculine on the androgyny scale. As a male this type tends to mature early. The endomorph deposits an abundance of fat and is related to the hyperfeminine on the scale of Bayley and Bayer. As a female this type tends to mature early. The ectomorph of Sheldon, the linear person, is the asexual person of Bayley and Bayer; in both sexes they are late maturers. The muscular girl is high in mesomorphy on Sheldon's scale, high in masculinity on that of Bayley and Bayer. Unlike the muscular boy, she tends to be a later maturer. The fat boy is high in endomorphy and high in femininity. He does not follow the early-maturing pattern of the endomorphic girl, he tends to be a late maturer (Bayer, 1940).

Brozek raises the question of how stable the body type of an individual remains through the life span. He feels that while there are stable (genetic) aspects to body build, the variable (environmental) aspects have been confused in most of the attempts to categorize body build.

It is doubtless true that body build is not a simple, single, gene-directed characteristic. Body build is the result of the growth and development of the skeletal structure, the muscles, and the adipose tissue. Each of these parts of the organism is acted upon by many things, both intrinsic and extrinsic. Nevertheless there are measurable tendencies toward one or another of the recognized body types which are useful clinically.

ENVIRONMENTAL INFLUENCES

There is good reason to believe that nutrition is a factor not only in the rate of growth but also in the speed of growth and the ultimate stature achieved. Children known to be on poor diets can be stimulated to grow at a more rapid rate by improvements in their diets. Where the optimum is reached in relation to diet is not so clear. Can children on adequate diets (adequate to the best of our present-day knowledge) be stimulated to grow more by supplements of protein, minerals, vitamins, or anything else? Opinion is divided on this matter. There is also this question, by no means answerable at present: Is more necessarily better?

It is also obvious that physical health has an effect on growth. Children with serious organic disease such as congenital heart disease, nephritis, or some of the inborn errors of metabolism do not grow as do normal children. The decreased incidence of serious acute disease in children since the introduction of antibiotics and improved immunization procedures may play a role in the larger size of today's children. Emotional factors also affect growth. Infants deprived of maternal care fail to gain weight adequately even on excellent diets.

But here, as in so many places in human development, the resultant growth depends not only upon the amount and kind of emotional deprivation but also upon the inherent traits of the child reacting to the deprivation.

An interesting trend in growth over the last hundred years is thought probably to be related to nutrition. The data on heights and weights of school children indicate that the whole process of growth has been undergoing a speeding-up process. Children born in the 1930s are appreciably larger at age 5 (and probably before) than children born at the beginning of the century (Meredith, 1941). The amount of this secular change is quite considerable. . . .

American (Meredith, 1941), British (Clements, 1953) and Swedish (Broman et al., 1942) data all give similar trends. The average gain between 1880 and 1950 is about $1\frac{1}{2}$ cm and $\frac{1}{2}$ kg per decade at ages 5 to 7 and about 2 cm and $\frac{1}{2}$ kg per decade during puberty. The fully grown adult (Tanner, 1956) has increased in height about 1 cm per decade for the past century.

Hathaway compared the figures obtained by various American investigators from 1902 to 1952 (Figure 8). The data from Hathaway's compilations are averages based on cross-sectional studies. Data from Bayley's longitudinal study of California children showed a similar increase in size of the children over their parents. The range of heights and weights at all ages has been unaffected over the years. There have been, and still are, big children and adults and little ones But big and little alike are all a little bigger than they used to be.

How long has the secular trend been in operation? There is very little reliable data before 1880; however, Robert, in 1876 made a significant comment in discussing the physical requirements of factory children: "A factory child of the present day at the age of 7 years weighs as much as one of 8 did in 1833—each age has gained one year in 40 years" (Tanner, 1955); and Clements comments on the small size of the armor worn in the Middle Ages.

In this connection it should be pointed out that uniformly a high socioeconomic level is reflected in greater weight gains. Every study made the world over has shown that those children from the more privileged groups gain more and gain it sooner than the less privileged in any society. . . .

The effect of socioeconomic levels has been demonstrated in many studies (Meredith, 1941). Chinese girls of upper class in Hong Kong grow larger and mature earlier than girls of similar genetic background but of a less favored economic level (Lee, Chang, and Chan, 1963). That economic level makes a difference is a clearly established fact. Why it should be so is not so clear. Probably, like the secular trend, nutrition is a factor, but so too may be other factors, like regularity of sleep and meals, more outdoor exercise, better medical care—factors that go along with a higher level of education and greater ease of life in the more prosperous groups in any society.

Does climate have an effect on growth? Mills has made a case for the gradual change in the world temperature to be at least partly responsible for the secular trend. He suggests that difficulty in heat loss may retard human growth as it does in experimental animals. However, current studies on children in the tropics and in temperate and cold regions do not seem to bear out this hypothesis. Race and climate are difficult factors to disentangle from nutrition and socioeconomic level. West African children (Mackay, 1952) are a good deal retarded in relation to American children, but Whites and Negroes in New York

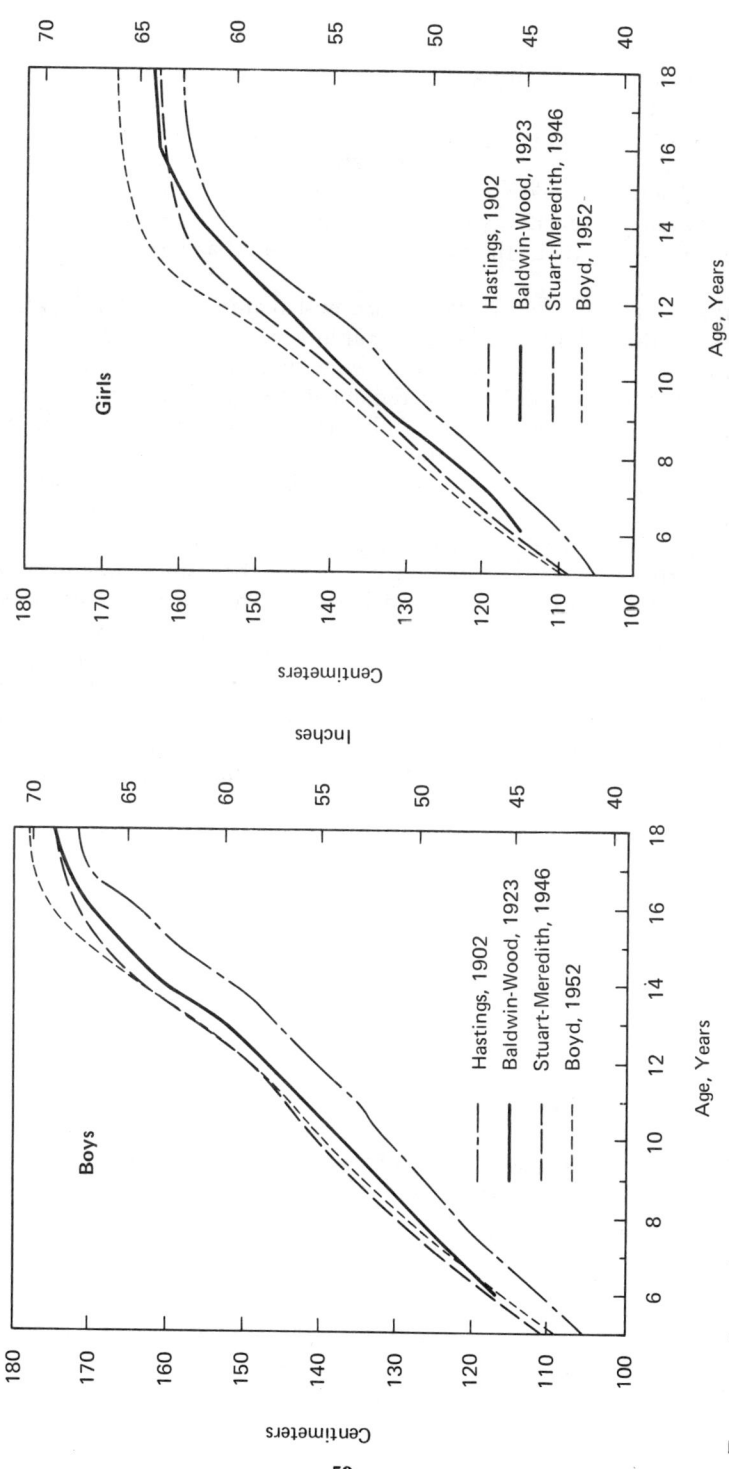

FIGURE 8. *Average heights of American children by various investigators.* (From Hathaway, *Height and Weights in Children and Youths in the U.S.*, U.S., Dept. Agric., 1957.)

City in similar economic circumstances showed no appreciable differences (Michelson, 1944), indicating that race was not a significant factor here. But how about climate? Using age of menarche (see below) as a criterion, Ellis gives 14.3 years as the mean age at menarche in Nigerian school girls of upper socioeconomic level and Levine 14.4 years as that of Eskimo girls. Wilson and Sutherland found the expected class difference in school girls in Colombo, Ceylon, to range from 12.8 years for the menarche in the upper group to 14.4 years in the lower, about the same class differential as found in the temperate zone.

Japanese children (Ito, 1942) born and reared in California were taller and heavier than children of similar parentage who remained in Japan. The California-reared Japanese children were also more advanced in skeletal development than the children who remained in Japan. This difference is usually attributed to better food and generally better living conditions, although the possible effect of climate cannot be ignored.

The effect of climate, if any, on growth is difficult to distinguish from the other variables affecting the children measured; however, it is clear that season has a definite influence on growth (Palmer, 1933; Reynolds and Sontag, 1944). In the Northern Hemisphere, October, November, and December are the months of greatest weight gain, and it may be five or six times as much as during the months of April, May, and June, when weight gain is at a minimum. ... About two-thirds of the annual gain in weight is made in the fall (the 6 months from September to February) and only one-third in the remaining 6 months of the year. Height gains are maximum in April, May, and June, and minimal in September, October, and November. The reason for the seasonal variation is quite unknown. It appears in well-nourished children as well as in poorly nourished ones. Suggestions have been made that hormone secretions are involved or that environmental temperatures or length of day are factors.

The age at which the changes of puberty take place is basically a genetically determined phenomenon; nevertheless, malnutrition can delay the events of puberty. In the secular trend the age of puberty is most pronounced. Maturation occurs earlier now than it did a century ago. Kiil found the average age of menarche of Norwegian girls in 1850 to be 17.0 years and in 1950 13.5 years. In the United States the average age of menarche has dropped from 14.2 years in 1900 to 12.9 years in 1950 (Mills, 1950). The effect of the economic depression as measured in Hagerstown, Maryland, was not sufficient to affect the growth of children measured. Nevertheless there was a demonstrable retardation of the age at which both boys and girls matured. Similar data were obtained both in France and in Belgium during World War II.

It would appear that the human body has to grow a certain amount before puberty can take place. If growth takes place rapidly, puberty comes early; if growth is slow, puberty must wait until the body has reached the requisite size, or more likely, maturity level.

The speed with which the human body *can* grow is doubtless genetically determined, but the actual speed is the resultant of the genetic potential and the opportunity afforded by the environment.

CONCLUSIONS

The following conclusions on the nature of human growth seem reasonably substantiated:

1. All children possess the potential for a pattern of growth characteristically human; every child (barring those with gross defects) passes through the same stages as every other child. These stages are related to most of the measurable aspects of growth, such as physical measurements, development of organs, and maturation of function and behavior.

2. The differences among normal children, within the range of the human pattern, are large. These differences are reflected not only in the magnitude of the measurements but in the tempo of growth itself.

3. Correlations exist between various aspects of growth. A child who deviates from the mean with respect to one type of growth is apt to deviate proportionately in other aspects. While correlations between the various aspects of growth are frequent, they are by no means universal; in some children progression is less uniform than in others.

4. Genetic and endocrine factors are responsible for the basic patterns of growth and maturation. These patterns tend to persist through the life span, contributing to the uniformity of individual growth.

5. Genetic patterns can be modified by environmental factors, such as disease, nutrition, emotions. The effect of quantitatively similar environmental factors varies, depending both on the time in the life cycle when specific deprivations occur and, probably, on the genetic makeup of the individual on whom they are acting.

References

BAYER, LEONA M.: Weight and Menses in Adolescent Girls with Special Reference to Build, *J. Pediat.*, *17*:345, 1940.

BAYLEY, NANCY, and LEONA M. BAYER: The Assessment of Somatic Androgyny, *Am. J. Phys. Anthropol.*, N.S. *4*:433, 1946.

BROZEK, JOSEPH: *Body Measurement and Human Nutrition*, Wayne State University Press, Detroit, Mich., 1956.

CLEMENTS, E. M. B.: Changes in the Mean Stature and Weight of British Children over the Past 70 Years, *Brit. M. J.*, *2*:897, 1953.

DUPERTUIS, C. W., and N. B. MICHAEL: Comparison of Growth in Height and Weight Between Ectomorphic and Mesomorphic Boys, *Child Development*, *24*:203, 1953.

ELLIS, R. W. B.: Age of Puberty in the Tropics, *Brit. M. J.*, *1*:85, 1950.

GOLDBERG, MINNIE B.: What Makes Us Grow As We Do, *J. Am. M. Women's A.*, *10*:110, 1955.

HATHAWAY, MILLICENT L.: Heights and Weights of Children and Youths in the U.S., Home Economics Research Report 2, U.S. Department of Agriculture, 1957.

ITO, P. K. Comparative Biometrical Study of Physique of Japanese Women Born and Reared Under Different Environments, *Human Biol.*, *14*:279, 1942.

KIIL, V.: (Quoted by J. M. Tanner) in *Growth at Adolescence*, Charles C Thomas, Publisher, Springfield, Ill., 1955.

KOGUT, MAURICE D., S. A. KAPLAN, and S. N. S. SHIMIZU: Growth Retardation, Use of Sulfation Factor as Bioassay for Growth Hormone, *Pediatrics*, *31*:538, 1963.

LEE, MARJORIE M. C., K. S. F. CHANG, and MARY M. C. CHAN: Sexual Maturation of Chinese Girls in Hong Kong, *Pediatrics, 32*:389, 1963.

LEVINE, V. E.: Studies in Physiological Anthropology: III. The Age of Onset of Menstruation of the Alaska Eskimos, *Am. J. Phys. Anthropol.*, N.S. *2*:252, 1953.

LUBCHENCO, LULA O., CHARLOTTE HANSMAN, MARIAN DRESSLER, and EDITH BOYD: Intrauterine Growth as Estimated from Liveborn Birth Weight Data at 24–42 Weeks of Gestation, *Pediatrics, 32*:793, 1963.

MACKAY, D. H.: Skeletal Maturation of the Hand: A Study of Development in East African Children, *Tr. Roy. Soc. Trop. Med. & Hyg., 46*:135, 1952.

MATTHEWS, C. A., and M. H. FOHRMAN: *Beltsville Standards for Growth of Jersey and Holstein Cattle*, U.S. Department of Agriculture Technical Bulletin, Nos. 1098 and 1099, 1954.

MEREDITH, H. V.: Stature and Weight of Children of the U.S. with Reference to Influence of Racial, Regional, Socio-Economic and Secular Trends, *Am. J. Dis. Child., 62*:909, 1941.

———: Stature and Weights of Private School Children in Two Successive Decades, *Am. J. Phys. Anthropol., 28*:1, 1941.

———: Birth Order and Body Size, *Am. J. Phys. Anthropol., 8*:195, 1950.

MICHELSON, N.: Studies in Physical Development of Negroes: IV. Onset of Puberty, *Am. J. Phys. Anthropol.*, N.S. *2*:151, 1944.

MILLS, C. A.: Temperature Influence on Human Growth and Development, *Human Biol., 22*:71, 1950.

PALMER, C. E.: Seasonal Variations of Average Growth in Weight and Height of Elementary School Children, *Pub. Health Rep., 48*:211, 1933.

REED, R. B., and H. C. STUART: Patterns of Growth in Height and Weight from Birth to 18 Years of Age, *Pediatrics*, 24 (supp.):904, 1959.

REYNOLDS, E. L., and L. W. SONTAG: Seasonal Variations in Weight, Height, and Appearance of Ossification Centers, *J. Pediat., 24*:524, 1944.

SHELDON, W. H.: *The Varieties of Human Physique*, Harper & Row, Publishers, Incorporated, New York, 1940.

SZALAY, GLENN C.: Intrauterine Growth Retardation versus Silver's Syndrome, *J. Pediat., 64*:234, 1964.

TANNER, J. M.: *Growth at Adolescence*, Charles C Thomas, Publisher, Springfield, Ill., 1955.

———: Adult Body Measurements, *Arch. Dis. Childhood, 31*:372, 1956.

WILSON, D. C., and I. SUTHERLAND: The Age of Menarche in the Tropics, *Brit. M. J., 2*:607, 1953.

Minor Physical Anomalies:
Their Incidence and Relation to Behavior
in a Normal and a Deviant Sample*

Mary F. Waldrop and Charles F. Halverson, Jr.
NATIONAL INSTITUTE OF MENTAL HEALTH

The cumulative incidence of certain minor physical anomalies was related to impulsive, fast-moving behavior in samples of normal preschool children (Waldrop, Pedersen, & Bell, 1968). These anomalies, which are typically associated with Down's Syndrome and other congenital defects have been thought to result from chromosomal irregularities or noxious agents which affect fetal development during the first weeks of pregnancy (Achs, Harper, & Siegel, 1966; Gustavson, K., 1964). Each anomaly does occur, however, in the normal population (Benda, 1960; Smith & Bostian, 1964).

The relation of the occurrence of these physical characteristics to behavior was interpreted as evidence for congenital contributors to poorly controlled, hyperactive behavior. The same factors which probably operated sometime during the first trimester of pregnancy could have influenced *both* the occurrence of the slight morphological aberrations and the hyperactive behavior so that where one was found the other tended to be present.

To extend and amplify the meaning of the findings from the original study (Waldrop et al., 1968) we will report here three additional studies involving the incidence of minor anatomical anomalies and their relation to hyperactive, uncontrolled behavior. First, we replicated the original study, again using normal two-and-a-half-year-old boys and girls who attended our research nursery school. Second, we extended the original study by evaluating the stability of the findings over five years for 84 per cent of the children in the original study. Third, we observed children with congenital defects in hearing and in speech production to provide further evidence on probable etiologies of these anomalies.

In all three of these studies, just as in the original study, each child was examined for the presence of the 18 minor physical anomalies and was given two scores—one was the total count of anomalies, the other was a sum of the weighted scores.[1] The original list (Waldrop et al., 1968) was revised as follows: (a) "Index finger longer than middle finger" was eliminated from the list

Reprinted from paper presented at meetings of The Society for Research in Child Development, Inc., Santa Monica, Calif., March, 1969. By permission.

* We wish to thank Mrs. Gerda Schoenfeld (teacher), Miss Beverly Whitlock (Director), and others at the Easter Seal Treatment Center, Rockville, Maryland, for their interest, expert assistance, and cooperation in part of this study.
[1] Weights of one or two, depending on severity, were given to the nine anomalies which Goldfarb and Botstein (unpublished manuscript) found were significantly more frequent among their sample of schizophrenic children than among their sample of normal children. Weights of one were given to the six anomalies which they found were more frequent, though not significantly so, among their deviant sample. No weights were given to the three anomalies which they found either to be nonexistant in their samples or more frequent—not significant—among their sample of normal children.

because of lack of incidence, (b) "Head circumference outside normal range" was added to the list, with a circumference deviating more than 1.5 standard deviations from the reported mean for that age and sex being weighted 2, and one deviating between 1.0 and 1.5 such standard deviations being weighted 1 (Vickers & Stuart, 1943) and, (c) other anomalies were defined more precisely.

TABLE 1

List of Anomalies and Scoring Weights

Anomaly	Weight
Head	
Fine electric hair:	
Very fine hair that will not comb down	2
Fine hair that is soon awry after combing	1
Two or more hair whorls	0
Head circumference outside normal range:	
$> 1.5\ \sigma$	2
$> 1.0 \leqslant 1.5\ \sigma$	1
Eyes	
Epicanthus:	
Where upper and lower lids join the nose, point of union is:	
Deeply covered	2
Partly covered	1
Hypertelorism:	
Approximate distance between tear ducts:	
$> 1.5\ \sigma$	2
$> 1.0 \leqslant 1.5\ \sigma$	1
Ears	
Low-seated ears:	
Point where ear joins the head not in line with corner of eye and nose bridge:	
Lower by > 0.5 cm	2
Lower by $\leqslant 0.5$ cm	1
Adherent ear lobes:	
Lower edge of ears extend:	
Upward and back toward crown of head	2
Straight back toward rear of neck	1
Malformed ears	1
Asymmetrical ears	1
Soft and pliable ears	0
Mouth	
High-steepled palate:	
Roof of mouth:	
Definitely steepled	2
Flat and narrow at the top	1
Furrowed tongue (one with deep ridges)	1
Tongue with smooth-rough spots	0

(continued)

TABLE 1 (*Continued*)

	ANOMALY	WEIGHT
Hands		
	Curved fifth finger:	
	Markedly curved inward toward other fingers	2
	Slightly curved inward toward other fingers	1
	Single transverse palmar crease	1
Feet		
	Third toe longer than second:	
	Definitely longer than second toe	2
	Appears equal in length to second toe	1
	Partial syndactylia of two middle toes	1
	Big gap between first and second toes	1

Table 1 is the revised list of the 18 minor physical anomalies along with the epitomical descriptions and scoring weights.

Because individual anomalies occurred with low frequency, only a cumulative score showed sufficient range for correlational analyses. Because the total score and the weighted score correlated greater than .85 in every sample, only the results using the weighted scores will be reported here. Inter-rater reliabilities for judging the anomalies was satisfactory for all samples (mean $r = .83$).

REPLICATION STUDY

The two-and-a-half-year-olds in the Replication Study were like the subjects in the original study except that they were not selected as newborns having hospital records free from complications of pregnancy and delivery. Twenty-six of the children who participated in the Replication Study were selected because their parents, when newlyweds, had participated in another phase of the longitudinal research program at the Child Research Branch, National Institute of Mental Health. The other 32 children lived in neighborhoods near our research nursery school. The procedures and measures, however, that were used to evaluate the 33 boys and 25 girls as they attended our research nursery school in groups of five for five weeks were the same as those used in the original study. In the original study all preschool behavior measures relating significantly to the anomaly score were factor-analyzed for both males and females, with the result that measures reflecting fast-acting, impulsive, uncontrolled behavior were loaded heavily on the first factor for males and the first factor for females. These two first factors, one for males and one for females, were labeled hyperactivity. The second factor for males represented a tractability factor, but the second factor for females represented intractability and inhibition. The measures included some ratings done independently by two teachers and some observations based on behavioral counts or times.

The mean anomaly score for the replication sample of 33 males was 4.09, standard deviation was 2.08, and the range was from 1 to 9. Since the correlates of the anomaly score in the replication sample of males were very similar to the correlates in the original sample, we obtained for each of the boys in the replication sample a factor score based on the weights from the previous hyperactivity factor. (For this replication sample of males, the reliabilities for the ratings and observations ranged from .72 to .92.) This hyperactivity factor score for the males in the replication sample was found to be significantly correlated with the anomaly score ($r = .49, p < .01$). That is, the boys in the Replication Study who had high anomaly scores tended to be high on the hyperactivity factor. Further substantiation of this relation was obtained by correlating the anomaly score with an objective count of times the child was restrained by the teachers during "resting" time ($r = .46, p < .01$). Frenetic, impulsive, poorly controlled behavior was again found to characterize preschool boys who had more than an average number of minor anomalies.

The mean anomaly score for the replication sample of 25 females was 3.56, standard deviation was 2.20, and the range was from 0 to 7. Relations to the cluster of variables making up the hyperactivity factor in the original sample of females were not found again in the replication sample of females. Instead, variables making up the intractability-inhibition factor seemed to characterize the replication sample of females with the high anomaly scores. A score for each girl based on the weighted measures from this previously obtained second factor was significantly related to the anomaly score ($r = .42, p < .05$). That is, girls with the greater number of minor anomalies moved about less, opposed peers more, and were more perseverative than girls with fewer anomalies. For this replication sample of females the inter-rater and split-half reliabilities for the ratings and observations ranged from .53 to .92. Also, during the five weeks of nursery school, the girls with high anomaly scores were rated by the teachers as showing more fearfulness ($r = .48, p < .01$) and more vacant staring ($r = .63, p < .001$), and as staying closer to an adult ($r = .44, p < .01$), than those with low anomaly scores. These three measures (Fearfulness, Vacant staring, Closeness to an adult base) were based on 11-point rating scales which had inter-rater reliabilities greater than .80. A child high on "Fearfulness" was described as characteristically appearing to be guarded, wary, defensive, apprehensive, frightened, or panicky. A child high on "Closeness to an adult base" was described as spending an unusually large amount of time clinging tightly to teacher, hiding her eyes, not exploring the situation either visually or otherwise. A child high on "Vacant staring" was described as being immobile and staring without apparent focus much more than other children did. Since these three measures were significantly interrelated, a composite was formed by summing her standard scores on the three ratings. This composite was significantly related to the anomaly score ($r = .59, p < .01$). Thus, girls with high anomaly scores in this sample were overcontrolled, inhibited, stubborn, and perseverative rather than hyperactive.

The higher incidence of these minor physical anomalies in the Replication Study when compared to the original study is due to having more precise norms making it possible to set a smaller deviation from the normal as a criterion for an anomaly. Also, we included in the Replication Study the anomaly "Head circumference outside normal range" that was not reported in the original study.

STABILITY STUDY

Other investigators have reported on the stability of hyperactivity between the preschool years and early adolescence. For example, Kagan and Moss (1962), using the term *hyperkinesis* to mean the inability to inhibit impulses to action, found that hyperkinetic behavior showed a high degree of stability over the years three to fourteen for both sexes. MacFarlane, Allen, and Honzik (1962) reported almost the same percentage of cases that showed "overactivity" at three showed "overactivity" at seven. They also reported an inter-age correlation of .42 between age five and ten years.

In the present investigation, the interest was in seeing if this stability of hyperactive behavior held true for the original sample over a period of five years, as well as in seeing if the anomaly scores were stable. In addition, it was expected that (a) hyperactivity at seven and a half would relate to the anomaly score at seven and a half and to the anomaly score at two and a half, and (b) hyperactivity at two and a half would relate to the anomaly score at seven and a half.

The stability data for the anomalies and hyperactive behavior were obtained from a follow-up study at age seven and a half of 35 males and 27 females who had been among the two-and-a-half-year-olds studied in the original sample. A person who had not known the children at age two and a half, and had no knowledge of their previous anomaly score or their nursery school behavior, assessed each child for the presence of the minor physical anomalies.

Impulsive, fast-moving behavior at age seven and a half was evaluated by one objective measure and two reliable ratings made of the child in free play and testing situations. Two ratings, "Frenetic behavior" and "Inability to delay," were made with no previous knowledge of the child. A child rated high on "Frenetic behavior" was one who much more than the others showed impulsive, fast-moving, ineffective, incomplete, and hyperactive play. A child rated high on "Inability to delay" was one who when required to wait to take part in any activity seemed unusually unable to wait for gratification. The objective measure of hyperactive free play was the distance (in 9 × 9 in. square floor units) traversed during free play divided by time, for each shift in location during 20 minutes of free play. The setting was a nursery school playroom very similar to the one used when the children were age two and a half. Data were obtained from a continuous narrative spoken by an observer into a tape recorder and subsequently scored for a number of shifts in location and rate of each shift.

In addition to evaluating minor physical anomalies and impulsive, fast-moving behavior, we tested each child for IQ and motor coordination. The IQ measure (WISC) was part of a larger assessment package concerned with longitudinal correlates of cognitive behavior. We plan to report this aspect of the study elsewhere. Our thinking regarding individual differences in motor coordination was that "clumsiness" might be correlated with the anomaly score since poor gross and fine motor coordination has often been found associated with an aggregate of symptoms defining hyperactivity. Both "hyperactivity," or "acting out," and motoric involvements such as athetoid movements and lack of balance have been considered "soft signs" of some minimal cerebral dysfunction. In order to measure individual differences in both fine and gross motor coordination we constructed a scale which combined adaptations of the Lincoln Oseretsky test of motor development (Sloan, 1955) and a neurological examination developed by Ozer (1968; unpublished manuscript). From the Oseretsky test we deleted a number of items that were either too easy or too difficult for our age range, and then added some of the tasks from the Ozer neurological examination.

The final version of the scale consisted of 34 items, most of which were scored on a simple pass-fail criterion. Typical tasks the child was asked to perform were balancing on each leg for at least ten seconds, touching each finger tip with the thumb in rapid succession, and sorting matchsticks into boxes as rapidly as possible. Inter-coder agreement for the motor scale was quite high ($r = .97$).

TABLE 2

Correlates of the Anomaly Score at Age 7½
(Stability Study)

VARIABLES	MALES N = 35 $\bar{X} = 4.91$, $\sigma = 2.66$, RANGE: 1–11	FEMALES N = 27 $\bar{X} = 3.74$, $\sigma = 2.33$, RANGE: 0–10
Anomaly score at 2½	.71**	.70**
Rate of shifts during free play at 7½	.30†	.36†
Inability to delay at 7½	.39‡	.63**
Frenetic behavior at 7½	.34†	.52‡
Motor coordination at 7½	−.41‡	−.48‡
Full scale IQ at 7½*	−.34†	−.46‡
Verbal IQ at 7½	−.35†	−.33†
Hyperactivity factor at 2½	.47‡	.69**
Inability to delay at 2½	.49‡	.41†
Frenetic behavior at 2½	.45‡	.43†

* Correlates with IQ measures based on total anomaly scores and other correlates based on weighted anomaly scores.
† $p < .05$
‡ $p < .01$
** $p < .001$

The results of the Stability Study are summarized in Table 2. This table shows the correlation of the anomaly score at age seven and a half with the following: (a) the anomaly score at age two and a half, (b) the three measures of impulsive, fast-moving behavior, (c) the motor coordination scale, (d) IQ measures, (e) a factor score based on the weighted measures included in the hyperactivity factor for males and hyperactivity factor for females and the original study, and (f) ratings of "Frenetic play" and "Inability to delay" when the children were two and a half. Of interest, too, is the fact that "Frenetic play" at seven and a half correlated significantly with the same rating done independently at two and a half: males, .34 ($p < .05$) and females,

.64 ($p < .001$). For "Inability to delay" the across-age correlates were: males, .50 ($p < .01$) and females, .40 ($p < .05$).

These data demonstrate that: (a) the weighted anomaly score tended to be stable over the five years, (b) children with high anomaly scores still tended to be more frenetic and have less behavioral control than children with few anomalies, (c) children at age seven and a half with high anomaly scores tended to be clumsy, (d) children at age seven and a half with more than an average number of minor physical anomalies tended to have lower than average IQ scores, (e) frenetic, fast-moving behavior showed continuity over five years, and (f) the children at age seven and a half with high anomaly scores tended to have been hyperactive as two-and-a-half-year-olds. In other words, generally speaking both the anomaly score and the associated hyperactive behavior were stable over the five-year period. Also, children at age seven and a half with high anomaly scores were likely to be poorly coordinated and to have lower than average verbal ability.

STUDY OF CHILDREN DEFICIENT IN SPEECH AND/OR HEARING

If minor anomalies do result from variations in embryological development, it is reasonable to expect that there would be a higher incidence of the anomalies in a sample of children selected for congenital deficiencies than there would be in a sample of normal children. To test this hypothesis we examined 31 boys and 10 girls who had been referred by physicians to an Easter Seal Treatment Center Nursery School because of deficiencies in speech and/or hearing. Mothers of 4 of the 31 boys and 7 of the 10 girls were thought to have had rubella while they were pregnant with these children.

The mean anomaly score for the Easter Seal samples was compared with the mean anomaly score for the replication samples of boys and girls. See Table 3. The replication samples were chosen for this analysis because we had used exactly the same method of scoring anomalies in these samples as in the Easter Seal samples.

TABLE 3

Comparison of Anomalies in Easter Seal and Replication Samples

	\multicolumn{4}{c}{MALES}	\multicolumn{4}{c}{FEMALES}
SAMPLE	N	$\bar{X}$	σ	RANGE	N	$\bar{X}$	σ	RANGE
Replication Study	33	4.1	2.1	1–9	25	3.6	2.2	0–7
Easter Seal	31	7.6	2.3	3–12	10	8.3	2.3	4–11
Rubella Subsample	4	7.2	2.3	5–11	7	9.0	1.8	6–11

A t value of 6.35 ($p < .001$) was obtained when the means of the anomaly scores for males in the Easter Seal sample were compared with the means for males in the Replication Study. For females this t value was 5.39 ($p < .001$).

In the small subsample of four boys and seven girls from the Easter Seal samples where there was direct evidence of a teratogenic agent (rubella) present during early prenatal development, the mean anomaly scores were also significantly higher than the mean anomaly scores in the replication samples. For males the t was 2.32 ($p < .05$), for females the t was 6.48 ($p < .001$), and for the combined sample the t was 5.96 ($p < .001$).

From Table 4 we can make interesting comparisons across two male samples (replication and Easter Seal) of the percentage of children having each of the observed anomalies. Indeed, it was surprising to find that close to three-fourths of the boys in the Easter Seal Center sample had curved fifth fingers, high-steepled palates, partial syndactylia of the second and third toes, and epicanthus.

TABLE 4

Incidence of Anomalies

Anomalies	Easter Seal Males (%)	Replication Study Males (%)
Curved 5th finger	88	21
High steepled palate	72	48
Partial syndactylia	68	30
Epicanthus	68	42
Asymmetrical ears	64	27
Abnormal head circumference	56	30
Hyperteliorism	56	15
Soft pliable ears	48	21
Big gap between 1st and 2nd toes	48	9
Two or more hair whorls	44	27
Third toe longer than 2nd	32	39
Low seated ears	28	21
Electric hair	16	12
Malformed ears	16	6
Adherent ear lobes	12	27
Single palmar crease	4	12

No behavior measures were collected on the Easter Seal children. Their teachers, however, characterized at least 32 of the 41 children as hyperactive, and used phrases such as "destructive," "overactive," "management problem," "unable to wait," "constantly demanding attention," "jumpy," "very aggressive," "a behavior problem," "swings from the rafters" to describe them.

The results from the Easter Seal samples are evidence that there is a higher incidence of these *minor* physical anomalies among children with *major* congenital problems. This finding, plus the well-known fact that an even higher incidence of these minor anomalies is found among children with gross chromosomal defects (Down's Syndrome), argues for the congenital etiology of the anomalies. Thus it would seem that the higher the incidence of multiple minor physical anomalies the greater the severity of the congenital problem.

DISCUSSION

These analyses have not been directed to the location of cut-off points where the presence of a certain number of minor physical anomalies might indicate impulse-control problems; but some suggestions based on clinical observations can be offered. Consistently across samples, boys with some of these anomalies (4–8) seemed to have trouble with inner controls—they were active, frenetic, unable to wait, intractable, and had poor motor control. Girls with the same number of anomalies (4–8) were variable across samples. In one sample they were very similar to the boys, that is, they were fast-moving, frenetic, and intractable; in another sample they were still intractable, but instead of being fast-moving and having poor motor control they tended to be immobile, to stare vacantly, and to have excessive motor control. Both boys and girls seemed to have difficulties with control, whether too much or too little. The children who had a major deficiency typically considered congenital (i.e., impaired speech and/or hearing) had on the average four more of these anomalies than the "normal." It is well known that those children with a great many anomalies tend to have major, specifically congenital defects, such as Down's Syndrome. Thus it seems that the higher the incidence of multiple minor physical anomalies the greater the severity of a congenital problem or vice versa.

It is plausible to think in terms of the neurological substrate for control of impulsive behavior as developing at the same time as these minor anomalies develop. The same insult (about which we can only speculate at this time) most likely results in *both* the occurrence of the anomalies and the relatively poor control over behavior which was seen in children with high anomaly scores.

The causes for the anomalies and the predisposition to fast-moving behavior in boys and to either fast-moving or immobile behavior in girls could be genetic, such as some chromosomal irregularity; or the cause could be the result of a noxious agent affecting embryological development, such as the rubella virus; or the cause could be subtle variations in early embryological development. At this time we can only speculate about which of these alternatives may be true.

References

Achs, R., Harper, R., & Siegel, M. Unusual dermatoglyphic findings associated with rubella embryopathy. *New England Journal of Medicine*, 1966, 274, 148–150.
Benda, C. E. *The child with mongolism.* New York: Grune & Stratton, 1960.
Goldfarb, W., & Botstein, A. Physical stigmata in schizophrenic children. Unpublished manuscript, Henry Ittleson Center for Child Research, Brooklyn, N.Y.
Gustavson, K. *Down's syndrome: a clinical and cytogenetical investigation.* Uppsala: Institute for Medical Genetics of the University of Uppsala, 1964.
Kagan, J., & Moss, H. A. *Birth to maturity.* New York: Wiley, 1962.
MacFarlane, J. W., Allen, L., & Honzik, M. A developmental study of the behavior

problems of normal children between 21 months and 14 years. Berkeley & Los Angeles: University of California Press, 1962.

OZER, M. N. The neurological evaluation of school-age children. *Journal of Learning Disabilities*, 1968, *1*, 84–87.

——, & MILGRAM, N. A. The effects of neurological and environmental factors on the language development of Head Start Children: an evaluation of the Head Start Program. Unpublished manuscript.

SLOAN, W. The Lincoln-Oseretsky motor development scale. *Genetic Psychology Monograph*, 1955, *51*, 183–252.

SMITH, E. W., & BOSTIAN, K. E. Congenital anomalies associated with idiopathic mental retardation. *Journal of Pediatrics*, 1964, *65*, 189–196.

VICKERS, V. S., & STUART, H. C. Anthropometry in the pediatrician's office. Norms for selected body measurements based on studies of children of North European stock. *Journal of Pediatrics*, 1943, *22*, 155–170.

WALDROP, M. F., PEDERSEN, F. A., & BELL, R. Q. Minor physical anomalies and behavior in preschool children. *Child Development*, 1968, *39*, 391–400.

Chapter 2

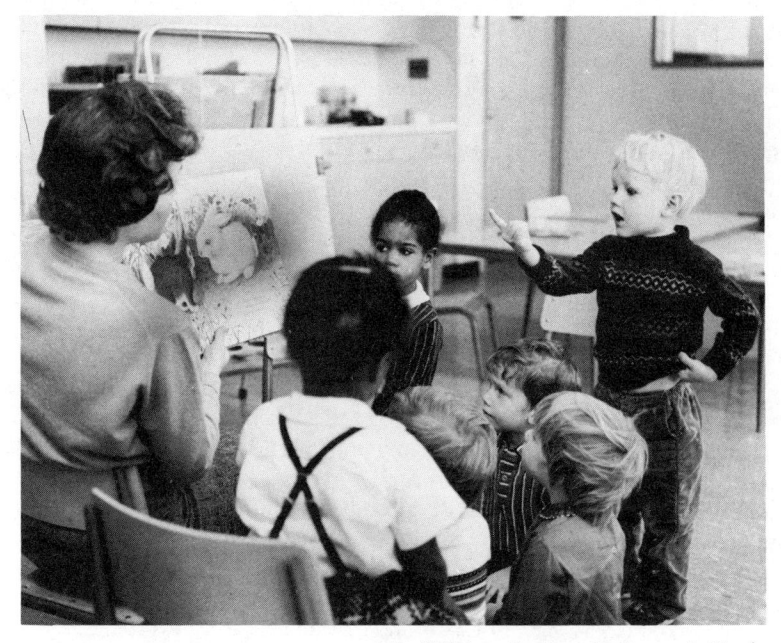

Merrill-Palmer Institute by Donna J. Harris

Intellectual Development

This chapter and the next concern the preschool child's intellectual development, and the measurement and stimulation of that development. Thinking, concept formation, intelligence, and language make up the subject matter of this chapter. Imagination and stimulation of development are the focus of the next. Thought, language, and imagination interweave and overlap as cognitive growth proceeds. Language provides symbols for thinking, and also socializes thought, through interaction with other people. Children talk to others and talk to themselves. Young children talk out loud to themselves. Imagination or fantasy, an unfettered kind of thought or inner life, expresses emotion and complements controlled thought. Fantasy is both inner language and, on occasion, outer language. It is dreams and artistic expressions. Sometimes fantasy is equated with egocentric thought, because both are the means of pleasure seeking rather than truth seeking. Although fantasy is not limited by reality and does not purposefully deal with reality, it sometimes achieves solutions to problems which controlled thought cannot solve. An adult may "sleep on" a problem and awaken with the solution. A child may work through his problems in dramatic play or with dolls. The role of controlled thought is widely appreciated in children's education and development, but fantasy is little understood. Adults tend to dismiss it as a whimsical activity which will pass with time. Some schoolteachers deplore it as a waste of time; others see it as one of the keys to understanding children's thoughts and emotions. [43].

Other keys are available for unlocking the mysteries of children's minds. Tests and experiments are used to investigate cognitive processes and factors which influence them. Observations are made under controlled conditions and the results analyzed. Children are rated by adults who have certain bases for agreeing or disagreeing with statements about their behavior. Results of tests, experiments, observations, and ratings are treated statistically so as to extract generalizations from them and then those generalizations are tested for significance. Knowledge gained from research is then applied, in the case of cognition, by educators. The last part of the following chapter is concerned with some recent developments in preschool education which stem from new knowledge of cognitive development.

Thought Processes and Conceptual Development

The intellectual landmark of the end of infancy is the completion of the period of sensorimotor intelligence, a phase of cognitive development discussed in Chapter 3 of Smart and Smart, *Infants* (Macmillan, 1973). At this point, the child has achieved two major feats, the control of his movements in space and the notion of object constancy. He realizes that an object continues to exist even when he does not perceive it and that it can move in space which also is there when the child is not dealing with it.

Sensorimotor intelligence links successive perceptions and movements, with brief anticipations and memories. It does not take a large, sweeping view: "Sensorimotor intelligence acts like a slow-motion film, in which all pictures are seen in succession but without fusion, and so without the continuous vision necessary for understanding the whole" [63, pp. 120–121].

Representational thought is what makes the period of preoperational thought distinctly different from the sensorimotor period [65]. Instead of confining his interactions to the here and now, the child can think about objects, people, and actions that are not present. He shows that he does this by imitative and imaginative play. Representational thought can be applied to the past, when the youngster acts upon an event that has happened, and to the future in the form of planning which also appears as play. Both actions and objects are used in symbolic ways to serve representational thought. The child begins to use language at about the same time that he starts to use objects and actions in representational thought. Language quickly becomes a powerful tool of thought. Even so, imaginative and symbolic acts continue to be useful throughout life.

The period of *preoperational thought* ordinarily lasts from 18 months or 2 years to 7 or 8. During this time, the child is building mental structures which will eventually result in logical thinking or operations. This he does through his interactions with objects and people. The interaction takes the form of the two complementary processes, assimilation and accommodation [68, pp. 1–6]. The child assimilates by acting on the environment and fitting it into existing schemas. For instance, when first given a wagon or a kiddy car, the young child manipulates the wheels, using an examining schema which is already established. Further examination shows this toy to be different from his other toys and he adapts old schemas and develops new schemas for playing with it, thus accommodating to the wagon as he loads it, pulls and pushes it and unloads it, or as he propels the kiddy car. Through assimilation and accommodation, he learns the properties of toys and other objects, materials such as water, clay, and paint. He also learns ways of manipulating objects through "logico-mathematical experiences" [67]. By arranging, grouping, and counting his blocks, sticks, cars, or anything else, he is *operating* on them. Through repeated actions of this type, he internalizes these experiences into concrete logical operations. While he is working his way through the period of preoperational thinking, his thought has certain characteristics that distinguish it from concrete logical operations, the period that is to follow.

Characteristics of Preschool Thinking

1. The young child cannot think from any point of view except his own and he does not realize that he is limited in this fashion. His thought is centered on one perspective, his own. An example of centered thinking in an adult makes this limitation more clear, because it is obviously inappropriate for adults.

> Mrs. A : My, what a charming accent you have, Mrs. B. I think it is so quaint the way you say "two-dooah Foahd cah" for "two-door Ford car." I'd just love to have an accent like yours.
> Mrs. B : Your own accent is interesting, Mrs. A. I've never heard anyone say "caow" for "cow," as you do.
> Mrs. A : Why, *I* don't have an accent. I was born right here in Ohio.

Mrs. A could not consider her own speech from Mrs. B's point of view, nor could she hear Mrs. B's speech from her point of view or from that of anyone but herself. In addition, she could not comprehend that there existed other points of view. She centered in her own and could not move off or decenter.

The preschool child characteristically has but a dim awareness of his psychological self in relation to the rest of reality even though he knows that his body is a separate and distinct object among other objects. He does not know that his thoughts and actions make up part of the situation in which he is. He has little objectivity, or relativism, which means looking from another person's point of view, from another angle in space or time, or imagining how it would be if you were somewhere else. This is not to say that the preschool child cannot step into the role of someone else. He can do it very well indeed, but when he does it, he loses himself. He cannot stand off and view himself from the angle of somebody else, but he can become the other person. He can do through fantasy, in taking the role of another, what he cannot do through controlled thought. Through neither fantasy nor controlled thought, however, can he see both points of view at once and weigh them.

2. Perceptions dominate the young child's thinking. He is greatly influenced by what he sees, hears, or otherwise experiences at a given moment. Literally, seeing is believing. The static picture is what he believes. He does not pay attention to transformations or changes from one state to another. What he perceives at any one time is, however, only part of what a more mature person would perceive. Carolyn, the 2-year-old who remarked, "Choo-choo going fwimming," was beholding on the river a large object, followed by several similar, rectangular objects,

76 Preschool Children

which did in fact resemble a train. The pointed prow of the tug, the decks, the small size, the absence of wheels—all these features did not indicate to her that this object was not an engine, although they would have done so to an older child. If Carolyn saw these aspects of the tug, she ignored past experiences which would have been brought to bear on the situation by a more sophisticated observer. Nobody has seen a train moving itself on anything but a track. Carolyn's thinking was not flexible enough to watch the tug and barges, think of trains and how they run, compare this event with past observations of trains, and then come to a conclusion based on both present and past. Another illustration of the dominance of perception is the ease with which young children can be fooled by a magician. Although the older members of the audience reject the evidences of their senses because they reason on the basis of past experience, the preschool children really believe that the magician found his rabbit in the little boy's coat pocket and that the card flew out of the air into the magician's hand.

One of Piaget's famous experiments is done by pouring beads from one glass container to another glass, taller and thinner than the first. When asked whether there are more or fewer beads in the second glass, the child answers either that there are more, because the level has risen, or that there are fewer, because the glass is narrower. The child centers on *either* height or width, in fact, more often on height, which is more salient [70]. In contrast, a child who had reached the next stage of thought, the period of concrete operations, would reason with respect to both relations and would deduce conservation. His perceptions would be placed in relation instead of giving rise to immediate reactions [63, pp. 130–131].

Perception becomes more flexible, "decentered," with increasing maturity [23]. Children between 4 and 12 were tested with cards containing at least three ambiguous figures apiece. The first cards showed a butterfly with a face in either wing. The score was for number of spontaneous perceptions. The number of perceptions increased with both age and IQ. Four-year-olds typically saw a butterfly but no faces, whereas children 9 and up ordinarily saw the butterfly and both faces. A few of the preschool children with high IQ's gave responses much like those of sixth graders. Thus, with intellectual growth, children became less rigid perceptually, less tied to the first perceptual response made in the given situation.

3. Reasoning at this age is from the particular to the particular rather than from general to particular. Piaget [64, p. 231] tells how Jacqueline, age 34 months, ill with fever, wanted oranges to eat. Her parents explained to her that the oranges were not ripe yet, they had not their yellow color and were not yet good to eat. She accepted the explanation until given some camomile tea, which was yellow. Then she said, "Camomile tea isn't green, its yellow already.... Give me some oranges!"

Thus she reasoned that if camomile tea was yellow, the oranges must have become so. She went from one concrete instance to another, influenced by the way she wanted things to be.

4. Preschool thinking is relatively unsocialized. The young child feels no need to justify his conclusions and if he did, he would not be able to reconstruct his thought processes so as to show another person how he arrived at his conclusions. He takes little notice of how other people think, sometimes even ignoring what they say when he is talking. He begins to adjust his thinking to that of other people only as he becomes aware of himself as a thinker and as he grows in power to hold in mind several aspects of a situation at a time. Through years of interaction with

other people, discussing, disagreeing, coming to agreements, the child gradually adopts the ground rules necessary for logical thinking.

Growth in Conceptualizing

Most 2-year-olds can name pictures or drawings of familiar items, showing that they have inner representations of those objects. The child need not have seen a previous picture of the object in order to recognize what it depicts, thus showing that he has some sort of generalized representation, which might be considered a primitive concept. The Stanford–Binet test shows that the preschool child's typical response to pictures is the naming of figures in them, while the child of 6 or 7 and 11 or 12 tells about actions as well and the child over 12 gives a theme. Thus the conceptualizing of pictures develops from simple and concrete to abstract and complex.

The young child is hard at work organizing his experiences into concepts of classes, time, space, number, and causality. The fact that he does not quite make it until around 4 years is reflected in Piaget's term, *preconceptual thought*, which refers to the first half of the period of preoperational thought. The second half of this period, the stage of *intuitive thought* is characterized by judgments being made on the basis of perceptions rather than on reason. He classifies more and uses more complex representations of thought than he does in the period of preconceptual thought.

Class Concepts. Even before the stage of preconceptual thought, children perceive certain similar or identical aspects in objects or in repeated events. One-year-olds will show a primitive kind of grouping behavior when presented with two sets of dissimilar objects, as did the infants who touched several clay balls in succession or several yellow cubes in succession [72]. Preconceptual children will group objects readily on a perceptual basis rather than according to any inclusive and exclusive categories. *Chaining* is a kind of grouping often employed by young children. Given blocks in various shapes, colors, and sizes, a child might put a red triangle next to a red cube, then add a blue cube, a long blue rod, a short blue rod, and a small green rectangle. Each object is related to the one beside it, but there is no overall relationship tying the collection together.

Four-year-old children will group words together in categories when they try to recall them, instead of recalling them more in the order given [74]. For example, a child would be more likely to recall *hat* with *coat* or *dress*, than with *mouth* or *queen*, the words given before and after *hat*. In this grouping we see a conceptualizing of verbal stimuli.

Preoperational children cannot conceive of a given object as belonging simultaneously to two classes, such as a block going with the red things and the wooden things. Nor can they understand a class including a subclass.

The first concepts are concrete, tied to definite objects of events. Through repeated experiences, especially those verbalized by other people in certain ways, the child develops abstract concepts. The concepts he builds will always be affected by the people around him, through the give and take of social living. For example, most children acquire the abstract concepts *red* and *black*. Figure 2–1 shows how a group of American preschool children increased in their successes on tests of matching and naming colors. Living in a culture that uses abstract color names, these children were in the process of acquiring abstract concepts of color, as shown

78 Preschool Children

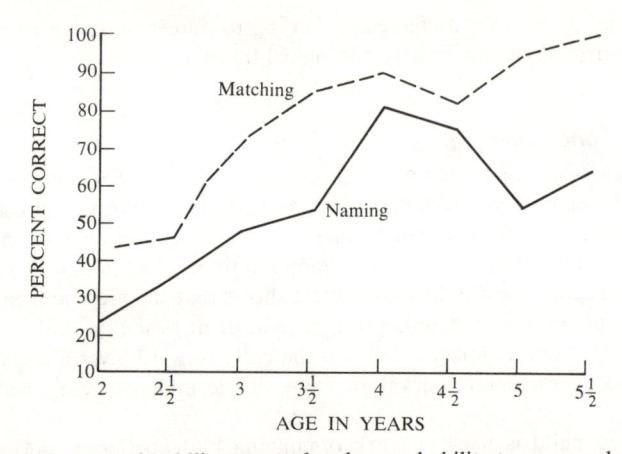

Figure 2-1. Age increases in ability to match colors and ability to name colors.
SOURCE: Reprinted by permission from W. M. Cook, "Ability of Children in Color Discrimination," *Child Development*, **2**, Figure 3. Copyright © 1931, The Society for Research in Child Development, Inc.

by naming. How much more difficult, or even impossible, it is for a child to develop an abstract concept of red when *gab*, the word for red, is also the word for blood. Thus *red* and *blood* are forever tied together, as are *black* and *crow* in the word *kott-kott*. Even more concretely tied to perception is the Brazilian Indian word *tu ku eng*, which is used for any and all of these colors: emerald green, cinnabar red, and ultramarine blue. *Tu ku eng* is also a parrot which bears all three colors. Thus green, red, and blue are not only bound up with the parrot but also with each other [100, pp. 234–241].

Sensory, motor, and emotional experiences all enter into the early building of concepts. Young children often group together things that they have experienced together, as did the child who used *quack* to mean duck, water, and all other liquids and the child who used *afta* to mean drinking glass, pane of glass, window, and what was drunk out of the glass [100, p. 226]. The experience of the family group is often used in ordering objects which have no claim to family membership other than belonging in a category. For example, 2-year-old Dickie called two half dollars *daddy* and *mummy*, a quarter *Dickie*, and a dime *Baby*. Children frequently take into account physical qualities such as heaviness, clumsiness, pliability, or prickliness, when naming objects. The name itself is thought to be part of the object, and language can express such qualities. Two children who made up a language used the word *bal* for *place*. The longer the vowel was held, the larger the place. *Bal* therefore meant village, *baal*, town and *baaal*, city. The word *dudu* meant go. The speed with which it was spoken indicated how fast the going was [100, p. 261].

Several experiments have been devised to find out how children will classify (group) objects spontaneously when not given labels to aid in abstraction. The role of perception in concept formation can thus be seen more clearly. In the first experiment [44], children between 3 and 5 years were asked to choose from a group of red triangles and green circles the figures which were the same as another figure. The other figure was either a green triangle or a red circle. (See Figure 2-2.) The younger children chose quickly, without hesitation, usually on the basis of color

Intellectual Development   79

Figure 2-2. An ambiguous situation. Matching can be done by either form or color.

Source: Reprinted by permission from H. Werner, *Comparative Psychology of Mental Development*. New York: International Universities Press, Inc., 1957. Copyright © 1957, International Universities Press, Inc.

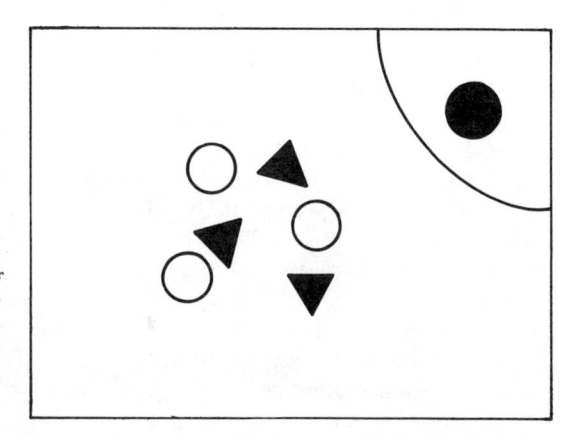

rather than form. With increasing age, form more often became the basis of choice. Another experimenter [20], using what was essentially the same situation, found that when faced with the choice between form and color as a way of grouping, the older children often showed concern over the ambiguity of the choice. A number of experiments [16, 17, 18, 86] have confirmed the finding that the younger preschool children are likely to classify on the basis of color and older ones on form. It is suggested that contrast effects from color stimuli are dominant and that the young child has a built-in tendency to attend to such contrast. There is evidence to show that there is a hierarchy of stimuli in terms of attention and that the hierarchy changes as the child matures [50]. The salience of the type of stimuli in the child's life is probably a determining factor. These experiments show how the perceptual processes in young children are almost automatic in grouping certain elements. When a grouping is formed, it predominates over other possible groupings, because of the child's inflexibility and lack of control of thought.

Further research dealing with the use of categories shows that the salience of various concepts is related to age during the preschool years [48]. Children between $3\frac{1}{2}$ and $6\frac{1}{2}$ years of age were given systematic choices in how to group a collection of toys. It was possible to classify the toys in terms of color, size, number, form, analytic characteristics (such as having four wheels or two arms), or sex type (for girls or for boys to play with). In general, the children found it easier to use color, number, form, and size for classifying toys than to use analytic concepts or sex type. There were age differences in the use of color, size, and form, the younger children using color and size more easily than form, the older ones using form more easily than color and size. It was suggested that although 6-year-olds are capable of classifying by color and size, form has greater significance for them, because they are learning to read and write, tasks in which form is very important.

When once a preschool child has sorted objects in terms of one particular classification, he finds it difficult or impossible to abandon that classification and sort them into another [46]. The following experiment [34] demonstrates the gradual elaboration of classifying which takes place with growth. Children were given forms of several shapes and colors and told to put them into groups. The first step in ordering is to put the objects into groups of either form or color. The young child (78 percent of 3-year-olds and 33 percent of 4-year-olds) was unable to arrange the objects further even after the examiner set an example. In step 2, most 6-year-olds made subgroups by form after having grouped all the objects by color.

In step 3, still another subgrouping was made. That is, after arranging the objects into colors, and into forms within the color groups, the child then ordered them according to size. Step 4, characteristic of the adult, involves taking more than one category into account at a time. In order to do this, the person has to abstract the categories completely. He has to be able to consider form, color, and size entirely apart from the objects in which he perceived them. This process is a freeing of thought from sensory perception. No child under 8 achieved it unaided. Thus preschool children are ordinarily dominated by their perceptions and unable to deliberately select or reject a category as a way of ordering.

A concept of *all* is built during the preschool years. In the early part of this period, the child does not know whether a succession of objects which look alike are one and the same object or a series of objects. Jacqueline, age 2½, walking in the woods with her father, was looking for slugs (snails). Catching sight of one she commented, "There it is." Seeing another, several yards away, she cried, "There's the slug again." Piaget took her back to see the first one again and asked if the second was the same or another. She answered "yes" to both questions. Jacqueline had no concept of a class of slugs [64, p. 225]. A 2-year-old ordinarily has the concept of "another" when it is a case of wanting a cookie for each hand, or asking for more. The difference between cookies in the hands and slugs on Jacqueline's walk is that the two cookies are present at the same time, whereas the slugs were seen in succession.

A step beyond Jacqueline's dealing with a concept of slugs was shown by Ellen, at 3½. Looking up at the blue Michigan sky surrounding her, she asked, "Is our sky at camp joined onto our sky at home?"

Thus Ellen showed that she realized that the sky in New York State and the sky in Michigan were either the same thing or of the same order of things. By asking, she was trying to develop the appropriate concept.

Adults often wonder why young children accept a succession of streetcorner Santa Clauses as Santa Claus. The reason is seen above, in the child's uncertainty as to whether similar objects constitute an individual or a class. Through experience and discussion, the child builds concepts of *one*, *some*, and *all*. At first, *all* means that he perceives in a given situation. The toddler, listening to his bedtime story about Sleepyboy taking off his clothing, gets up at the mention of Sleepyboy's shoes and points out the shoes of everyone in the family. This early form of generalization is a *plural concept*. It is less mature than the concept of *all shoes*, which begins at around 5. This stage was demonstrated in an experiment where each child was shown two series of trays. The trays in the first series contained a dog and a bird, a dog and a pig, a dog and a cow, a dog and a sheep. Although every child could recognize that this tray had a dog, and that tray, and the other tray, few children under 5 could express the fact that all the trays contained dogs [34].

Time Concepts. The earliest experiences of time are most likely those of bodily rhythms, states which recur in regular patterns, such as hunger, eating, fullness. Interactions with the environment impose some patterns on bodily rhythms, calling them by such names as breakfast, nap time, and bath time. Other early experiences which form the basis of time perception include dealing with a succession of objects, such as filling a basket with blocks; taking part in an action which continues and then stops, such as pushing or pulling a wheeled toy; hearing sounds of varying lengths. These experiences, each a seriation of events, are one type of operation which is basic to the notion of time, according to Piaget [69, p. 198],

Intellectual Development

Events such as these constitute the order of temporal succession. A second type of experience basic to time concepts comes from temporal metrics, the repetitions of stimuli in patterns, such as music and dance, or even rhythms of patting which a parent might do to a child in arms. A third notion, that of duration, is necessary for mature time concepts. Duration involves appreciation of the intervals between events. In early childhood, time is not "an ever-rolling stream" but simply concrete events, embedded in activity. Time and space are not differentiated from each other. Having no overall, objective structure, time is largely the way that the preschool feels it or wants it. To put it in Piaget's terms, the young child judges duration in terms of content, forgetting speed. Adults can appreciate this quality when they consider how long 10 seconds can be under the dentist's drill and how brief a hit Broadway show can be. Or, looking back at events such as your first formal dance or first trip alone, the vivid scene is as yesterday. Accepting the objective nature of time, the dental patient "knows" that the drilling was really only 10 seconds, the audience admits that the show lasted for $2\frac{1}{2}$ hours and the adult realizes that his solitary trip to Grandpa's was 10 years ago.

Time is structured differently by different cultures, groups, and individuals. A Balinese child must learn to orient himself within several simultaneously running calendars. An Eskimo gets a concept of night and day as varying dramatically from season to season, whereas to an Indonesian, night and day are very stable. Minute-conscious Americans are scheduled throughout the days, weeks, and years, equipped with abundant watches, clocks, timers, and calendars. The ages at which American children replace egocentric time concepts with objective ones are not necessarily those of other children in the world. In fact, in primitive time systems, nobody detaches time concepts from the concrete activities in which they are embedded, such as milking time, apple blossom time, or the year that a certain field was planted with yams. Emotional experiences may divide time into lucky and unlucky periods. While Western civilizations have attained considerable objectification of time, there are still many time structures based on personal, emotional, and spiritual experiences—spring, holy days, vacation, mourning period, anniversaries. A child's concepts will be molded by the time concepts he encounters in other people—his family, friends, and teachers. As he checks his notions with theirs, he gradually changes his private, egocentric (self-referred) ones to generally held concepts.

Time concepts of children between 18 and 48 months were studied by both observation and questioning for two consecutive years in a nursery school [1]. All the children in the school were used both years, and all spontaneous verbalizations involving or implying time were recorded. The results show the trend of development in time concepts throughout the preschool period, although since the subjects ranged from high average to very superior intelligence, the age levels at which concepts occurred must be considered as applying to children of above average intelligence. Note, they do show the trend of development in time concepts from egocentric to objective:

> *18 months:* Some sense of timing, but no words for time.
> *21 months:* Uses *now*. Waits in response to *just a minute*. Sense of timing improved. May rock with another child, or sit and wait at the table.
> *2 years:* Uses *going to* and *in a minute, now, today*. Waits in response to several words. Understands *have clay after juice*. Begins to use past tense of verbs.

> *30 months :* Free use of several words implying past, present and future, such as *morning, afternoon, some day, one day, tomorrow, last night.* More future words than past words.
> *3 years :* Talks nearly as much about past and future as about the present. Duration : *all the time, all day, for two weeks.* Pretends to tell time. Much use of the word *time : what time? it's time, lunchtime.* Tells how old he is, what he will do tomorrow, what he will do at Christmas.
> *42 months :* Past and future tenses used accurately. Complicated expressions of duration : *for a long time, for years, a whole week, in the meantime, two things at once.* Refinements in the use of time words : *it's almost time, a nice long time, on Fridays.* Some confusion in expressing time of events : "I'm not going to take a nap yesterday."
> *4 years :* Broader concepts expressed by use of *month, next summer, last summer.* Seems to have clear understanding of sequence of daily events.*

Another study [82] traces the development of time concepts from egocentric to objective by showing how children learn to use a clock. When asked what time events in their day took place, a quarter of 4-year-olds, a tenth of 5-year-olds, and no 6-year-olds either recited their schedules or used words like *morning* and *early*. Numbers, either unreasonable, approximate or correct, were used by the rest of the children.

Space Concepts

The young child's concepts of space, like his concepts of time, are derived from bodily experience. He gets sensations from within his body and from his interactions with the rest of the world. During the sensorimotor period, he looks, touches, mouths, and moves to build concepts of his body and other objects. During the period of preoperational thought, space is still egocentric, related to the child's body, his movements, and perceptions. Four-year-old Laura named a certain tree "the resting tree" because she often sat under its cool branches for a few minutes on her way home from kindergarten. The land where the "resting tree" was located was the "resting place," and the family who lived there was "the resting tree people."

Space concepts were studied in nursery school children in the same way in which the time study, reported above, was conducted [2]. The order of appearance of verbalized concepts of space is thus shown. As in the time study, the ages given are for children who measured above average on intelligence tests.

> *1 year :* Gestures for *up* and *down.*
> *18 months :* Uses *up, down, off, come, go.*
> *2 years : Big, all gone, here.* Interest in going and coming.
> *30 months :* Many space words are rigid, exact ones : *right, right here, right there, right up there.* Words were combined for emphasis and exactness ; *way up, up in, in here, in there, far away.* Space words used most : *in, up in, on, at.*
> *36 months :* Words express increased refinements of space perception : *back, corner, over, from, by, up on top, on top of.* A new interest in detail and direction : tells where his daddy's office is and where his own bed is, uses names of cities.
> *42 months :* Next to, under, between. Interest in appropriate places : *go there, find.* Interest in comparative size : *littlest, bigger, largest.* Expanding interest in location : *way down, way off, far away.* Can put the ball *on, in, under* and *in back of* the chair.

* Reprinted by permission from L. B. Ames, "The Development of the Sense of Time in the Young Child," *J. Genet. Psychol.,* 1946, **68**, 97–125.

Intellectual Development 83

48 months : More expansive words : *on top of, far away, out in, down to, way up, way up there, way far out, way off.* The word *behind.* Can tell his street and city. Can put a ball in front of a chair. Space words used most : *in, on, up in, at, down.**

Primitive languages contain many space words which refer to the body or its motion and location in space. So does everyday (nonscientific) English in such words and expressions as groundwork, sky-high, eye-level, handy, backside; neck and neck. When asking directions from the man in the street, how often does one get an answer such as, "Follow Elm Street for half a mile and then turn right onto Route 4?" Not very often. It is much more likely to be, "You know where the Mobil gas station is down past the cemetery? No? Well then, go to the second stop light and turn kitty-corner to the Catholic Church. You can't miss it." *You can't miss it* is almost inevitable at the end of a set of directions so firmly rooted in concrete experience. The person giving such directions is doing it so much from an egocentric standpoint that he cannot imagine anyone finding the route less clear than it is in his own mind.

The child's progress toward objective space concepts depends not only upon his bodily experiences, moving through space and perceiving objects, but also upon the concepts which adults offer him. Although it is necessary to have experience and to internalize it, the child also checks his interpretations with those of other people.

* Reprinted by permission from L. B. Ames and J. Learned, "The Development of Verbalized Space in the Young Child," *J. Genet. Psychol.*, 1948, **72**, 63–84.

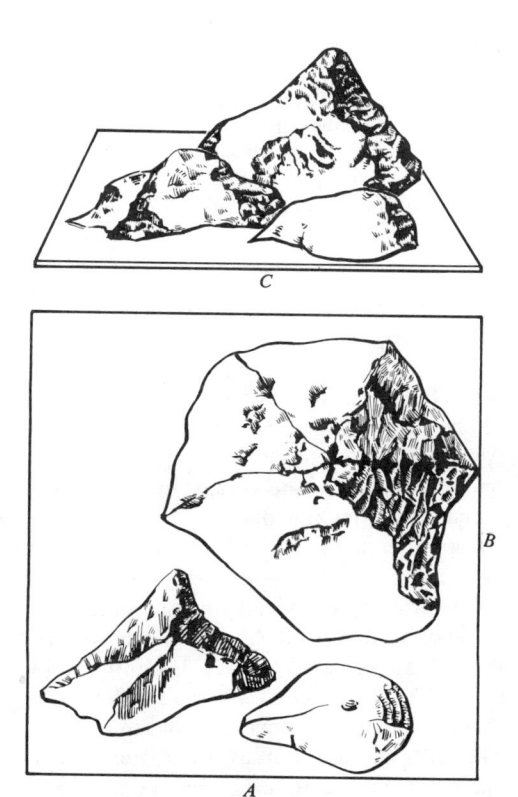

Figure 2–3. Model of mountains, as seen from different viewpoints, used in testing children for egocentric concepts.

SOURCE: Adapted from J. Piaget and B. Inhelder, *The Child's Conception of Space.* London: Routledge & Kegan Paul Ltd., 1948. Copyright © 1948, Routledge & Kegan Paul Ltd. Reprinted by permission of the publishers.

84 Preschool Children

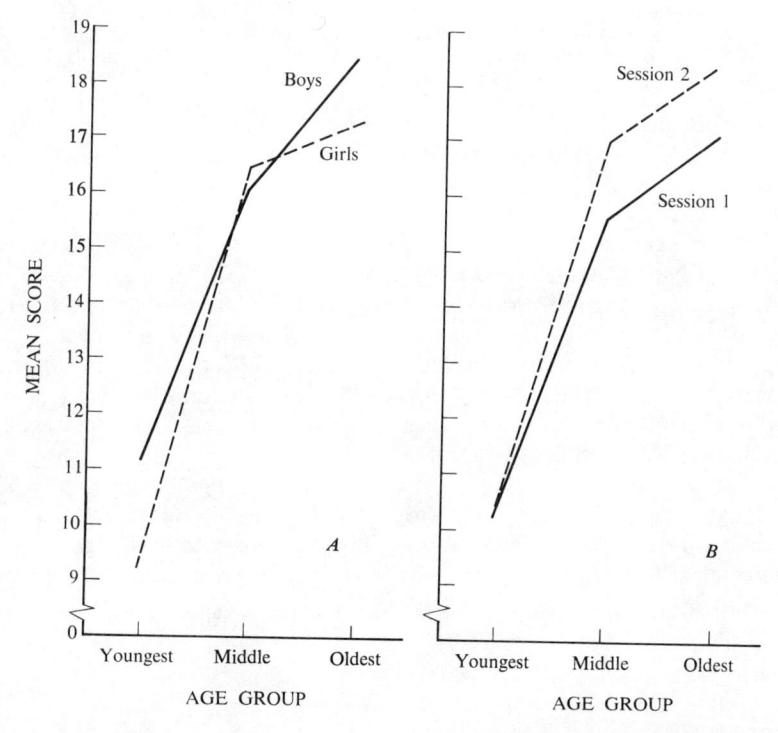

Figure 2-4. Scores of children between ages 3 and 6 on a test of ordering in space. The figure on the left shows mean scores of boys and girls on two testing sessions, indicating significant increases with age for ability to order space. The figure on the right shows scores on two tests, two weeks apart, indicating significant increases over a 2-week period.

SOURCE: Reprinted by permission from J. Gottschalk, M. P. Bryden, and M. S. Rabinovitch, "Spatial Organization of Children's Responses to a Pictorial Display," *Child Development*, **35**, Figure 1, p. 813. Copyright © 1964, The Society for Research in Child Development, Inc.

Thus he comes eventually to have an idea of space existing independently of his perception of it.

Piaget [68, p. 211] demonstrates egocentric space concepts by his mountains test. Three mountains are placed on a table, as in Figure 2-3. A doll is placed first at one side of the table, then at another and another. The child is asked to choose from pictures or cutouts what the doll would see in the various positions. A child under 7 or 8 shows no understanding of the problem. He cannot conceive of the mountains as looking different from the way in which he is viewing them, because his space concepts are still tied to his own perceptions. All he can do with the problem is to attribute his own view to the doll.

The ordering of space by preschool children has been studied in terms of their methods of dealing with columns and rows of pictures [30]. Children between 3 years 3 months and 6 years 3 months were tested in two sessions two weeks apart. The child was given a card with rows of pictures of 20 familiar objects and asked to name all the pictures and to report "I don't know" for unfamiliar ones. The order and direction used were noted. Responses were scored for organization, one point being given each time the picture named was adjacent to the one named previously. As Figure 2–4 shows, scores increased very significantly with age and also increased with the same groups over a 2-week period. Therefore, as children grew older, they applied more order to the way in which they dealt with objects in space, as though they realized increasingly that they could be more efficient if they organized their behavior.

The ability to copy the order of the set of objects is first observable between 4 and 5 years of age. It is easier for a child to pile blocks in a certain order than it is for him to make a row which corresponds to a model [40]. In the pile, there is only one way to go, up. In making a row, one can add to the left or to the right. Even when frames were supplied in order that adding to the rows could be done in one direction only, the row constructed was still more difficult. The difference in ease of ordering may be connected with the space orientation of the body itself, up and down being an unchanging dimension, while left and right aspects of the environment change constantly.

Quantity Concepts. While a hungry 4-year-old could readily choose the plate with more cookies on it rather than the plate with less, he probably would not be able to understand the words *more* and *less* with complete accuracy. When tested for comprehension of these two words, children between $3\frac{1}{2}$ and 4 reacted about the same to either word [21]. *More* and *less* were undifferentiated from each other, and both were usually taken to mean *more*. This experiment illustrates why a child's use of a certain word cannot be taken as proof that he understands it in its full and accurate meaning. Quantity concepts develop gradually, as do concepts of time, space, and causality.

Like concepts of time and space, number concepts are rooted in early concrete experience. The toddler does not have to count at all in order to choose the plate containing four cookies rather than the plate with two cookies. A configuration of objects, up to 5 or 6, can be grasped perceptually without true number concepts being employed. A larger group may be seen as complete or not because every object is known as an individual. For instance, a 2-year-old (like the others) in a family of eight realizes that eldest brother is absent, not because he has counted and found only seven members present, but because he does not see a certain individual who is often part of the family configuration. The development of perceptual discrimination of numbers of objects was demonstrated in a study of children between 3 and 7 years [51]. The children were asked to discriminate 10 marbles from smaller groups of marbles, to match a group of marbles varying in number from 2 to 10, and to select larger and smaller groups of marbles as compared with a group of 4. Figure 2–5 shows the results of the tests. Perceptual discrimination of number improved steadily, with number discrimination developing first, then number matching, and then group matching. A score of 10 would indicate exact matching, which would involve true counting and comparison. Note that the average scores reached in this period were approximately 8, 7, and 6, suggesting that the discrimination was indeed done on a perceptual, not conceptual, basis. The process by which children learn to match numbers was analyzed from the behavior of children between 3 and 5 years of age [87]. The child was asked to build a row of M & M candies equal in number to one built by the examiner. The youngest children usually aligned the start of the row with the standard and then added candies without regard to density until the rows were approximately equal. The next oldest group placed a candy opposite each end of the model row and then filled in with more candies than the standard contained. The

86 Preschool Children

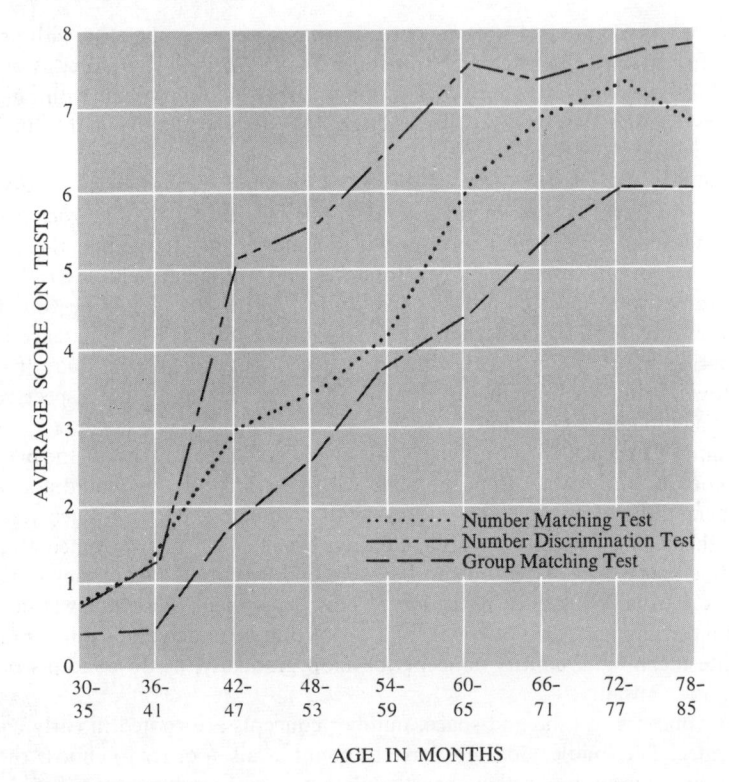

Figure 2–5. Improvement between ages 3 and 7 on tests of matching numbers, discriminating numbers, and matching groups.

SOURCE: Adapted from L. Long and L. Welch, "The Development of the Ability to Discriminate and Match Numbers," *Journal of Genetic Psychology*, **59**, 377–387.

oldest group matched the model row in both length and number. Thus the performances of the three age levels demonstrated the development of one-to-one mapping. Even the youngest children showed some notion of a relation between length of line and numerosity.

When a child counts objects and tells accurately that there are 7 apples or 7 blocks, he has a concrete number concept, a more exact way of dealing with numbers of objects than does the child who discriminates on a perceptual basis. An abstract concept, in contrast to a concrete one, is not involved with apples or blocks but with 7. Many experiences with 7 of this and 7 of that occur before 7 becomes free from objects and stands alone. As has been shown with concepts of classes, time, and space, the preconceptual period is a time when thought is quite concretely and specifically tied to personal experience. During this period, however, thought becomes progressively freer.

Certain primitive number concepts illustrate the stage of preconceptual thought. Werner [100, pp. 289–290] tells of cultures where a different type of number name is used for each of seven classes of objects: indefinite and amorphous; long, round, or flat; human being; boats; and measures. He tells of a language where 10 baskets are *bola* and 10 coconuts *koro*. Partially fused, 10 changes as the objects do. A step toward abstraction is shown in the language where *lima*, the word for *hand*, is also the word for *five*. The use of the body as a natural number schema is found in primitive cultures and in children, and alas, in an occasional college student. Number systems based on five or ten obviously have their roots in the human hand. Werner [100, p. 291] says, "At the beginning, no schema is an abstract form purely mathematical in significance; it is a material vessel in which the concrete fullness of objects is poured, as it were, to be measured."

A relationship has been shown, at least in retarded children, between the ability to articulate the fingers and the development of number concepts. Each child was asked to point, with eyes closed, to the finger touched by the examiner. A group showing high ability in number concepts made almost no errors, whereas a group with mathematical disability showed many errors [100, p. 296].

Children who grow up in cultures using abstract number systems must go through the primitive stages of enumeration, but they are offered the abstract concepts to grasp when they are able to do so [11]. (Or, unhappily, they may have the abstract concepts pushed at them before they have built the conceptual bases which underlie them.) Three developmental stages in number conception were described for 72 children between 4 and 7 years: (1) Preconceptual. Number is responded to in purely perceptual terms. When the arrangement of objects changes the perception of number may change. (2) Individual numbers are responded to in conceptual terms. The verbal terms are very helpful here in achieving concepts. (3) Relationship among the individual numbers is understood [101].

Perceptual dominance can be demonstrated in young children's quantification by some of Piaget's tests [61, pp. 49–50]. For example, the child is given a number of flowers and the same number of vases and asked to place a flower in each vase. Then the examiner takes out the flowers and puts them in a bunch. He spreads out the vases and asks, "Are there more flowers or more vases?" The child under 7 or 8 usually says that there are more vases. If the vases are bunched up and flowers spread out, he is likely to say that there are more flowers. He bases his answer on the perception of the amount. The flowers, in a bunch, cover less area than the vases spread out. Therefore he concludes that there are more vases. Instead of recalling his experience of matching flowers to vases, and reasoning that the quantities must be equal, he is so dominated by what he sees that he is not free to use concepts.

Being able to count is no guarantee of being able to cope with a situation similar to the flowers test. Children between 5 and 9, all of whom could count beyond six, were asked to place a rubber doll in each of six little bathtubs, which were placed side by side [41]. Upon questioning, the child agreed that there were the same number of dolls and tubs. Then the experimenter asked him to remove the dolls and place them in a heap. Answers to the questions as to whether there were more dolls or more bathtubs usually brought the answer that there were more bathtubs.

An objective number concept involves knowing that the number of objects is the same, no matter how they are arranged. ...... = ::: = :..: The difference between 5- to 6-year-olds and 7- to 7½-year-olds in regard to this kind of understanding is demonstrated by this experiment [52]. Children were given two groups of four beans to represent eight sweets. Four sweets were to be eaten in midmorning and four more at teatime. Then two more sets of four were presented, and the children were told that these represented sweets to be eaten the following day, when only one was to be eaten in the morning and the remaining three would be eaten with the four teatime sweets. While the children watched, three sweets were taken from the group and added to the other group of four. Thus the children had in

88 Preschool Children

front of them two sets, one being 4 + 4 and the other 1 + 7. The experimenter then asked each child if he would eat the same number of sweets on each day. The younger children said "no" that 1 + 7 was either larger or smaller then 4 + 4. The older children gave the correct answer promptly. Questioning showed that they understood the equivalence of the sets and the compensation occurring in the change. The children under 7 demonstrated inability to weigh more than one factor at a time and their centering on what they first perceived. They compared either 1 or 7 with the 4's. The older children, having considerable freedom from perceptual dominance, could consider the several aspects of the situation in relation to one another.

Cardinal number concepts are built from putting objects into groups or classes and then abstracting out the number. Ordinal number concepts come from putting objects in series and then abstracting out the order. Classifying and seriation are therefore both essential activities in building number concepts. Piaget [66, p. 156] maintains that classification and seriation are necessarily learned simultaneously, since the processes are complementary. Below about 5 years a child cannot make a series of objects, as of dolls of increasing size, but between 5 and 6 he does so. At this point, he has great difficulty in finding the correct place for an object which has been omitted from the series, but at around 7 he can do this task easily. At 7 he is sufficiently freed from the perception of the dolls to conceive at the same time of the first doll being smaller than the second and the second smaller than the third.

Causality Concepts. The idea of universal laws is absent in primitive and childish thinking. What explanations are given tend to be in concrete and personal terms. Egocentrism in regard to causality occurs at the same time and for the same reasons as egocentrism in concepts of space, time, and number.

The events of the outer world are closely linked with the child's inner world and his needs. During the preschool and school years, causality becomes less subjective. It can be followed through three stages of subjectivity. At first events are explained in terms of the child's own feelings and actions or in terms of people close to him or perhaps in terms of God. Although he does not consider all events to be caused by his own action, as he did in the sensorimotor period, he understands causes as forces resembling personal activity. "The peaches are growing on our tree, getting ready for us to eat." "The moon comes up because we need some light in the night." The next step toward maturity is to see natural events as caused by forces contained in themselves or by vague agents called *they*. "The radish seed knows it is supposed to make a radish." Increasing sophistication of thought decreases egocentrism, and the child begins to see causes as impersonal. For instance, heavy things sink and light things float. Progress in understanding cause is from concrete toward abstract. At first, explanations are merely descriptions of events. QUESTION: "What makes a sailboat move?" PETER: "My daddy takes me out in our sailboat. Mummy goes and Terry goes. Daddy starts the motor and we go chug, chug, chug down the pond."

The idea of universal, impersonal causes is beyond even the stage of childhood thinking and is not achieved by naive adults. The concept of chance is related to the concept of necessity. Both require some logical or formal thought. Young children's explanations tend to be diffuse and inconsistent. Several events are explained by several different causes instead of by a unifying cause. Piaget [61, p. 137] gives these accounts of conversations of an adult with two 5-year-old children, Col and Hei, dealing with the concept of floating:

Col: Rowing boats stay on the water because they move.—**Adult:** And the big boats? —They stay on the water because they are heavy.
Adult: Why does the boat (a toy) remain on the water?—**Hei:** It stays on top because it's heavy.... The rowing boats stay on top because they're big.—Fifteen days later Hei says, on the contrary, that boats stay "because they're not heavy." But comparing a pebble with a plank, Hei again says: "This pebble will go to the bottom because it isn't big enough, it's too thin." Finally Hei says that a stone goes to the bottom because "it's stronger" (than the wood).—And the boats, why do they stay on top? Because the water is strong.

These children give different, and what look like conflicting, explanations of events which an adult would unify under universal laws of floating. The children are showing their inability to consider several factors at one time and their consequent inability to come to general conclusions.

Achievements in Thinking During the Preoperational Period

In all areas of thinking, the preschool child increases in speed and flexibility. Strongly dominated by perception and by his wishes in the early years, he moves toward greater control of his thinking. His earliest concepts of classes, space, numbers, time, and causes are rooted in concrete, personal experience, gradually becoming more objective and abstract as he has more experience, especially interactions with other people, who check his thoughts and conclusions.

Intellectual Development as Revealed by Standardized Tests

Many tests of intelligence have been invented, each according to the concept of intelligence defined by its creator. Binet, who with Simon, developed the first standardized intelligence tests, considered three different capacities as constituting intelligence—the ability to understand directions, to maintain a mental set, and to correct one's own errors [57, p. 349]. Terman [88], whose revisions of Binet's tests have had the greatest influence on modern intelligence testing, thought of intelligence as the ability to think abstractly and use abstract symbols in solving problems. Thorndike [90], who accepted a concept of intelligence as comprising problem solving through use of abstract symbols, defined three dimensions of intelligence: altitude, breadth, and speed. Altitude referred to difficulty of problem, the more intelligent person being able to solve the more difficult problem; breadth meant the number of tasks a person could do; speed, of course, referred to how fast problems were solved. Thorndike considered altitude the most important of the three attributes of intelligence. Guilford [32, 33] thinks of intelligence as consisting of many different abilities, possibly 120, about 80 of which are already known. He stresses creativity as a component of intelligence.

Measurement of Intelligence

Many tests have been designed to measure preschool intelligence, the best known of which is the Stanford–Binet [89], a derivative of Binet and Simon's original tests. The Stanford–Binet yields a single mental age score, from which an intelligence quotient, the IQ, is computed. Although the Stanford–Binet can be given to most 2-year-olds, it is often easier to interest them in tests which have more manipulative materials and which involve more sensory stimulation, such as the Merrill–Palmer Test [85] or the Gesell Test [27]. Advantages of the latter type include the adaptability of the scoring to the child's refusing some items and the fact that more than one score can be obtained from each of these tests. The Merrill–Palmer can be scored for verbal and nonverbal items and the Gesell for four areas of development, called motor, adaptive, language, and personal social. Merrill–Palmer scores can be expressed as percentiles, standard deviations, or IQs. Gesell scores are expressed as developmental quotients. The Wechsler Intelligence Scale for Children [97] is favored over the Stanford–Binet by the same examiners for elementary school age children. The Wechsler can also be used for preschool children. Like the Merrill–Palmer, the Wechsler yields verbal and nonverbal scores. The Peabody Picture Vocabulary Test [22] is primarily a screening test which can be given without requiring the child to speak. It has been used widely in Head Start groups. The Peabody test materials consist of 150 plates, each with four pictures. The examiner says a word and the child is asked to point to the picture which best illustrates the word. Quick and easily administered, this test correlates well with other tests of intelligence.

Mental age (MA) is a construct conceived by Binet. A child's MA is found by comparing his test performance with the average performance of a large number of children. Binet gave a large number of tests to a large number of children, found the ages at which most children passed each test, and arranged the tests in order of difficulty. This procedure is essentially the one which has been followed in constructing intelligence tests since then. To show how the MA is found, take, for example, a child who passes the items passed by the average 8-year-old. The child's MA is 8. If his chronological age (CA) is also 8, then he is like the average child of his age. If, however, his CA is 6 he has done more than the average. If his CA is 10, he has done less.

Intelligence quotient (IQ) is a construct originated by Stern, a German psychologist. IQ is a ratio of CA to MA, which has been found to be fairly constant. IQ is found by dividing MA by CA and multiplying by 100. 100MA/CA = IQ.

IQ as an Expression of Rate of Growth

The intelligence quotient is a measuring of rate of growth in mental age, although the convention of multiplying by 100 obscures this fact. Tom, age 70 months, earns a score of 77 months of mental age. His average rate of mental growth throughout the whole of his 70 months is 1.1. For each month of CA he has achieved 1.1 month of MA. His IQ (MA divided by CA × 100) is 110. Margery, also age 70 months, earns a score of 63 months of mental age. Her mental growth has averaged .9 months for each month of CA. Her IQ is 90. If Tom and Margery continue to grow at their present rates, Tom's IQ will continue to be 110 and Margery's 90. Suppose, however, each grows at the rate of 1 month of MA per month of CA for the coming year. Each will gain 12 months of MA. Tom's MA will be 89, his IQ, 108; Margery's MA will be 75, her IQ 91. The MA changes are large, but the IQ changes are small. At each test the resulting IQ expresses the average mental growth since birth.

IQ as a Measure of Brightness

The common concept of IQ is as a measure of quality or strength of intelligence. The higher the IQ, the brighter the child and the more capable he is of doing good work at school. Tom, who has been growing at the rate of 1.1 months of mental age for each month of chronological age for 70 months, is brighter than Margery,

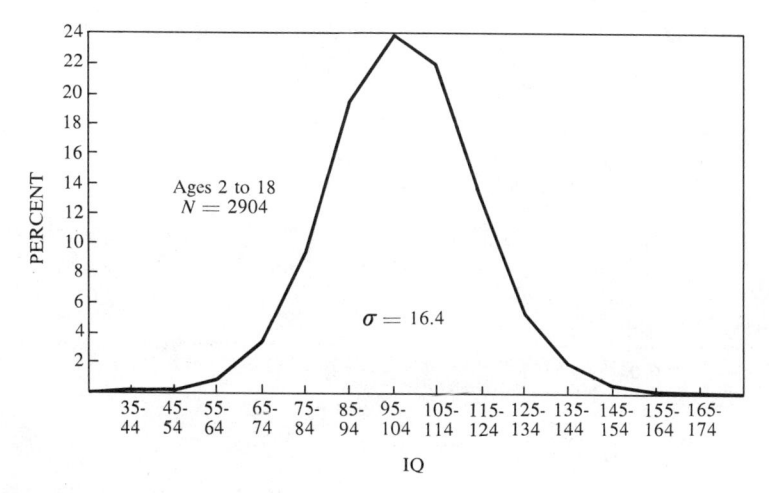

Figure 2–6. Distribution of Stanford–Binet IQs in the population on which the test was standardized.

SOURCE: Reprinted by permission from L. M. Terman and M. A. Merrill, *Measuring Intelligence*. Boston: Houghton Mifflin Company, 1937. Copyright © 1937, Houghton Mifflin Company.

who has been growing at an average rate of 0.9 MA months per chronological month. Jean, age 50 months, has been growing at the 1.1 rate and therefore has an IQ of 110. She is just as far above the average 50-month-old child as Tom is above the average child of 70 months. By the time Jean is 70 months old, if her mental growth continues at the same rate, her mental age will be 77 and her IQ will still be 110.

Distribution of IQs

Figure 2–6 and Table 2–1 show how IQs were distributed in the 1937 Stanford–Binet [89]. *Average* includes 79.1 percent of the population. *Defective*, with 8.23 percent, is a little smaller than *superior*, with 12.63 percent, although the most inferior categories match the most superior in size.

Another way of showing how IQs are distributed is to tell how often a given IQ occurs in 100 cases, or in the case of extreme IQs, how often in 1000 or 10,000. Table 2–2 expresses IQs thus.

Table 2–1 Distribution of IQs in Children Tested in the Standardization of the Stanford–Binet Test

Category	IQ range	Percent in category
Very superior	140–169	1.33
Superior	120–139	11.3
High average	110–119	18.1
Normal or average	90–109	46.5
Low average	80–89	14.5
Borderline defective	70–79	5.6
Mentally defective	30–69	2.63

SOURCE: L. M. Terman and M. A. Merrill, Stanford–Binet Intelligence Scale. Boston: Houghton Mifflin, 1960.

Table 2-2 Frequency of Occurrence of Common and Uncommon IQ Levels

The Child Whose IQ Is	Is Equalled or Excelled by	Child of IQ:	Equals or Exceeds (%)	Child of IQ:	Equals or Exceeds (%)
160	1 out of 10,000	136	99	94	36
156	3 out of 10,000	130	97	89	25
152	8 out of 10,000	120	89	85	18
148	2 out of 1,000	113	79	80	11
144	4 out of 1,000	105	62	70	3
140	7 out of 1,000	100	50	64	1

SOURCE: R. Pintner, A. Dragositz and R. Kushner. *Supplementary guide for the revised Stanford-Binet Scale*, Form L. Stanford: Stanford University Press, 1944

Errors of Measurement

Errors are likely to affect any test through less-than-perfect presentation and scoring, through the subject's not performing at top capacity, and through poor conditions of testing, such as noise or discomforts. The standard error of measurement has been calculated for various ages and IQ ranges [89]. For practical purposes, *five* is the standard error. In interpreting any IQ, then, ±5 should be added to the figure. If Mary's measured IQ is 107, there are 68 chances in 100 that her "real" IQ lies between 102 and 112. There are 95 chances in 100 that Mary's IQ lies between 97 and 117.

The standard error must be used when comparing the IQs of two children and also when comparing two tests on one child. In the first case, the difference between IQs must be at least 10 before a real difference can be said to exist. When tests on the same child are compared, the difference between the two tests must be 10 or more before a real change in growth rate is indicated.

Predicting Intelligence

Preschool intelligence tests correlate positively with intelligence tests given later. The longer the interval between tests, however, the lower the correlation. At 3 years, intelligence tests have some predictive value, and by age 6, considerable value. The stability and predictive value of intelligence test scores have been explored in a study in which 252 children were tested repeatedly at specified ages between 21 months and 18 years [39]. Figure 2-7 shows how tests given during the preschool years correlated with tests given during the middle school years and during adolescence. A look at what actually does happen to individual IQs is helpful in understanding why statistical prediction has to be done within large ranges. In another study [81] of repeated tests, the greatest gain in an individual case was 58 points, the greatest loss, 32. Figure 2-8 shows records of individual children which illustrate different patterns of changes in IQ. About 25 percent of the cases showed irregular patterns, typified by Case 105. About 20 percent were steady, as shown by Case 112. Other patterns of rising and falling can be seen in the other cases.

In predicting later IQ from preschool IQ, socioeconomic status and initial IQ level are significant. A survey of research on IQ change showed that when children

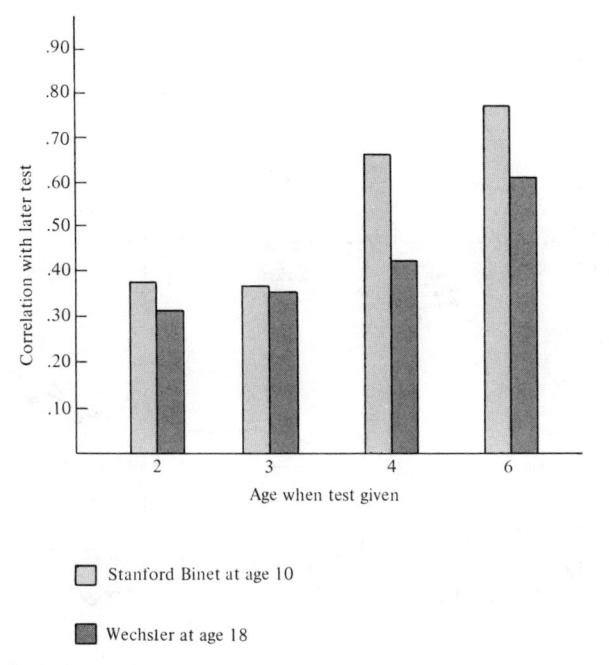

Figure 2-7. Coefficients of correlation between scores of mental tests given to children at ages 2 years through 6 and tests given to the same children at ages 10 and 18. The Stanford-Binet was used at age 10, the Wechsler-Bellevue at 18.

SOURCE: Adapted from M. P. Honzik, J. W. Macfarlane, and L. Allen, "The Stability of Mental Test Performance Between Two and Eighteen Years of Age," *Journal of Experimental Education,* **17,** 309-324.

scored below the median at age 6, changes in IQ were related to socioeconomic status [71]. Children of high SES continued to rise in IQ, while those of low SES continued to drop. This finding is consistent with the results of a study on infants showing that babies with low developmental status were likely to improve if they belonged in families of high socioeconomic level but not if they were in families of low socioeconomic level. A low IQ, then, is sensitive to the socioeconomic environment, whether it be favorable or unfavorable, while an above-average IQ is less likely to be affected by SES. While the child was young, socioeconomic status was more strongly related to IQ than when the child was older [71].

Radical changes in the environment are likely to produce radical changes in IQ, especially if the environmental change comes early in the child's life. Compensatory education programs are based on this knowledge. (Such programs will be discussed in the following chapter). The first compensatory education experiments, done at the University of Iowa in the 1930s, illustrate the enormous IQ changes which can result from environmental change [77]. Thirteen mentally retarded children, between 7 and 36 months of age, were transferred from a crowded, unstimulating orphanage to a home for the retarded where each child had a loving substitute mother, attentive aunties, toys, and individualized interaction. At entrance, the retarded children ranged from 35 to 89 IQ with an average of 64. Length of stay

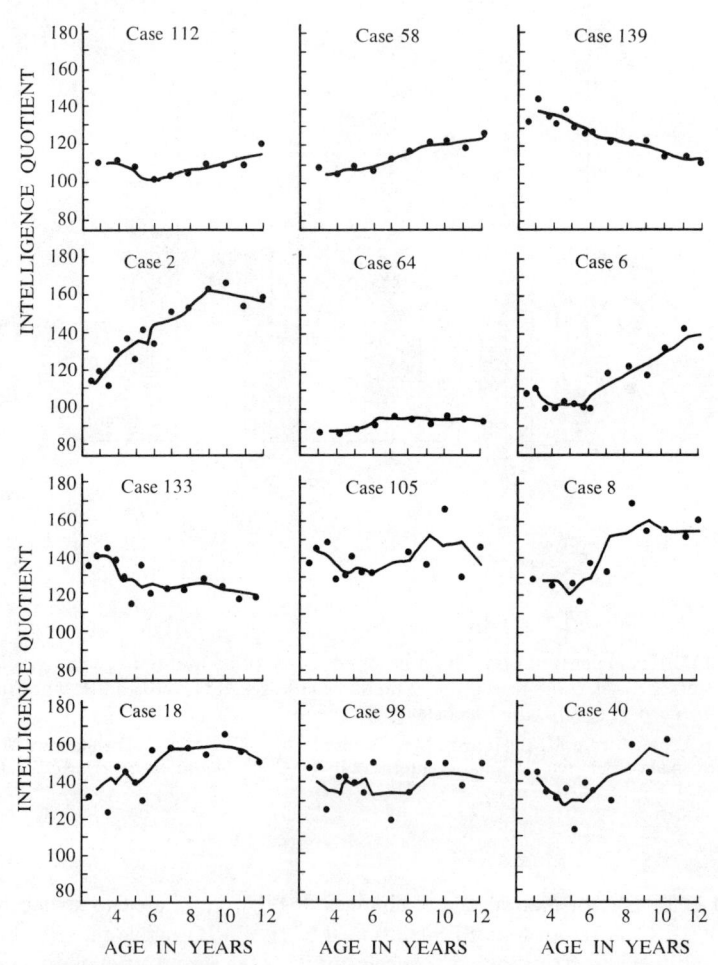

Figure 2–8. Examples of individual records of IQs from 2 to 12 years of age, illustrating variation in mental growth patterns.

SOURCE: Reprinted by permission from L. W. Sontag, C. T. Baker, and V. L. Nelson, "Mental Growth and Personality Development: A Longitudinal Study," *Monographs of The Society for Research in Child Development*, **23**, Figure 1. Copyright © 1958, The Society for Research in Child Development, Inc.

was from 6 to 52 months. Every child gained in IQ, all but two more than 15 points. Three gained over 45 points. The highest gain was 58. Over a 2-year period, the experimental group made an average gain of 28 IQ points, while a control group (of the same original average IQ) lost 26 points.

A child's IQ gives a good indication of how well he can do in school now and in the near future. It shows what he is likely to achieve in school in the more distant future. What the IQ tells is in terms of chances and probabilities. It is only a measurement of a limited sample of the child's behavior, telling something about him, but not everything. An IQ should never be thought of as fixed, definite, or final. It should never be used to place a child in a slot from which he cannot move.

Organization of Measured Intelligence

The abilities which constitute adult intelligence have been studied and delineated by several investigators, using factor analysis. Thurstone [91] identified these factors in intelligence: *space*, the ability to visualize objects; *number*, facility with simple arithmetic; *verbal comprehension*, dealing with verbal concepts and reasoning; *word fluency*, ability to produce appropriate words; *memory*, storing and retrieval of experiences and concepts; *induction*, finding principles; *deduction*, use of principles in problem solving; *flexibility and speed* of thought. Thurstone [92] has devised tests for measuring "primary mental abilities" in children as young as 5, the tests being grouped into motor, verbal, spatial, perceptual, and quantitative categories. Bayley [4] sees intelligence as "a complex of separately timed developing functions ... with the more advanced ... functions in the hierarchy depending on the maturing of earlier, simpler ones."

Structure of intellect was compared across race and class for 4-year-olds from black and white, middle- and lower-class groups [76]. Seven factors were found. The largest difference between groups was found in the factor representing verbal comprehension. Here the white middle class was highest, the lower white and middle black equal, and the lower black lowest. There were no group differences for ideational fluency, the free and expansive use of language. The verbal differences between classes and races, then, had to do with functions that use standard English and not with unrestricted production of ideas and language. Nonsignificant differences on the other factors generally showed the middle class exceeding the lower. On black–white comparisons, blacks were superior on some factors and whites on others.

Class and Ethnic Differences in Response to Tests

Preschool children have recently been studied by many researchers concerned with differences in cognitive structure and function and in reasons for those differences. The widespread interest in preschool education as a way to preventing school problems has led to the search for basic facts on which to build compensatory and preventive programs [37].

Until about the third year of life, social class differences in measured intelligence are not usually found. The time of emergence of these differences is not clear. By kindergarten age or before, disadvantaged children are likely to score lower than other children in general intelligence, language, fine motor coordination, and most cognitive variables on which they are tested [35, 75]. For white children between 2½ and 5, the difference between means of the highest and lowest of seven socioeconomic groups was 22 points [89]. When advantaged and disadvantaged children between 4 and 6 were compared on the Stanford–Binet Test, the difference was 30 points [56]. A longitudinal study of black children showed no difference in intelligence at 18 and 24 months, but at 3 years the difference between the means of the highest and lowest of three socioeconomic levels was 19 points [29]. Of these three groups, the middle-class children obtained the highest IQs, the children from the poor stable families the next, and those from fatherless welfare families, the lowest. Another longitudinal study of black boys showed almost no socioeconomic differences at age 3 years 8 months [58]. Lower- and middle-class boys were compared on the Stanford–Binet IQ, Peabody Picture Vocabulary, Concept Familiarity Index, and a number of perceptual and motor tests. (The lower-class boys were from poor but stable families, not from the lowest class.) Only the picture vocabulary test showed any significant difference. The author suggests that previous studies showing class differences did not include enough precautions for making the lower-class children comfortable in the testing situation. Middle-class children adapt more easily to testing, while lower-class children need extra time and reassurance from the examiner. Since occupation and education are not as highly correlated among blacks as among whites, socioeconomic differences are not likely to follow the same patterns.

Class and race differences were the focus of a comparison of children's cognitive functioning [84], as part of a series of studies which would yield knowledge about the influence of maternal behavior, its effect on children's cognition and implications for desired changes. Disadvantaged mothers and children 4 and 5 years old, both black and white, were tested before the beginning of a Head Start program. There was a lower-class control group which was not going to Head Start and a middle-class group, all white. Tests were selected for measuring skills that might be important in achieving academic success. Many significant social class differences were seen but only a few racial differences. Middle-class children scored higher than lower-class in impulse control, persistence, modeling (imitating an adult in verbal, nonverbal, and prosocial behavior), pointing to colors, and developing strategies of solving pegboard problems. Class differences in maternal behavior were impressive [4]. The middle-class mother most often let her child set his own pace, offered many suggestions on how to find solutions, told her child what he was doing right, and encouraged learning strategies that could generalize to future problems. The lower-class mother often made very specific suggestions, intruded physically into the child's problem solving, and told him what *not* to do. The greater success of the middle-class children in problem solving, self-control, persistence, and imitation seems logical in view of the type of teaching used by their mothers. Only two race differences occurred among the children. The black children had trouble solving the pegboard problems. On level of aspiration, black children pitched their goals higher than either white group, thus aspiring to levels they were very unlikely to reach. The white children, in choosing more feasible goals, were more likely to feel satisfied with the efforts.

The behavioral style of the culture is demonstrated in the family and shown in the child's way of coping with problems. Middle-class American children and working-class children of Puerto Rican origin were compared in responses to the Stanford–Binet test, as part of comprehensive longitudinal research [35]. The Puerto Rican children were tested by a bilingual Puerto Rican psychologist, who chose the language most appropriate for the child. The expected class difference in IQ was found, the average of the middle-class children being 122 and the other group 96.

Each child was observed in his way of responding to the examiner's request for work, whether he started trying right away or delayed his efforts, refused, looked for more, what he said about it. A comparison of the two total groups showed the middle-class children making significantly more work responses. However, the middle-class children made the same proportion (82 and 86 percent) of work responses to verbal and nonverbal items, whereas the Puerto Ricans made only 66 percent responses to verbal items and 85 percent to nonverbal. The groups were the same, then, in responses to nonverbal work demands but significantly different in responses to verbal work demands.

Another difference was in the way a child acted when he did not respond by working. The Puerto Ricans were more likely to be passively unresponsive. When the Puerto Rican child did make a nonwork response, it was likely to be an irrelevant substitution, such as "I want to go to mommy . . . I want a drink." The middle-class children were likely to say *no* and to add some comment explaining that they were not able to do the test. When a comparison was made between the two groups using only children between 90 and 110 IQ, thus equating them for IQ, the same differences in response style appeared. The Puerto Ricans still responded more to nonverbal work demands, while the middle-class children responded equally to verbal and nonverbal tasks. The nonwork responses noted for the total groups also held in the comparison of groups equated for IQ. Therefore the differences between the groups seem to reflect a difference in ethnic style rather than a difference in intellectual competence.

Clinical observations of the examining psychologists amplify the comparisons between the groups. The middle-class children were friendly, interested in the tests, ready to follow instructions, pleased to show what they could do, steady, persistent, likely to tell what they were thinking, and often able to tell whether or not they knew the answer. Although curious about the examiner and the surroundings, their interest did not interfere with their attention to the tasks set for them. The Puerto Rican children were friendly and responsive to the examiner as a person and the situation as social. They were insufficiently task-oriented, as indicated by insisting on playing with toys, being easily distracted, making irrelevant responses or passively failing to respond. The investigators point out the difficulties inherent in the American elementary school for these children whose work style fits better with performance demands than it does with verbal demands.

Recognition, recall and conceptualizing of visual and verbal materials were studied in disadvantaged children between 5 and 7½ years [73]. The main results were consistent with the previously described class differences between middle-class Americans and lower-class children of Puerto Rican origin. That is, the children did better with visually presented materials than with those given auditorily. However, ability to deal with the auditory stimuli increased with age, suggesting, then, that in disadvantaged children processes concerned with visual material develop earlier. When the disadvantaged child enters school, he may be quite adequate in looking at his environment and organizing it visually but quite inadequate in attaching verbal labels, organizing them, and storing them so as to be able to retrieve them easily. He catches up somewhat during the first three years of school and brings his auditory system closer to the level of efficiency of the visual system. In contrast, the middle-class child is likely to start school able to process both kinds of stimuli satisfactorily.

Language Development

Language supplements the tactile link between the young child and other people and supplants that link in many of the child's relationships with others. Language is a vital tie between past, present, and future, both for the individual and for groups of people. The rapid acquisition of language by the preschool child, shown by increase in vocabulary and development of grammatical structures, is intimately related to the development of autonomy and initiative, to the growth from

98 Preschool Children

egocentric thought to objectivity, and to social relationships. And it is also closely related to general intelligence, vocabulary being one of the best single measures. American middle-class culture emphasizes verbal modes, sometimes neglecting other avenues of expression and experience.

Fusion of Thought and Language

The linking of thought and speech marks the beginning of the period of preoperational thought. During the sensorimotor period, children think and reason, but they do it slowly and concretely, in terms of the experience of the moment. Higher animals do the same kind of thinking and reasoning that infants do. They also make sounds which have meaning. Baboons use 18 different sounds meaningfully. Some animals can recognize a few words which stand for people, objects, and actions.

Intellectual development receives a big impetus when thinking and speech come together in the discovery that everything has a name. The average timing of the discovery is between 18 months and 2 years, when the vocabulary increases from around 20 words to almost 300 words. Over 600 words are added annually for the next two years, and then the rate of vocabulary increase drops somewhat [80].

After discovering that everything has a name and that names are very handy in thought and deed, the toddler concentrates on learning as many names as possible. He also invents names, as did a boy of 16 months, who called *yoyo* all portable things with handles and *gogo* all yoyos with lids [96. pp. 34–35]. In a similar vein, a little girl called all drinkable liquid *gaggle-gaggle*. A pair of twins, before using any regular words, said *ee-ee* to each other to call attention to an interesting change in the environment and *aw-aw* when they wanted an exchange of toys. Similarly, a more involved invention of names was noted [34, p. 249] in two boys, 4 and 6, playing with blocks. One did the building while the other handed to him, and together they invented the following names for the blocks: Big thin Window, Little Big Thin Window, Big Stone, Little Stone, Big Knups, Little Knups, Big Peppermint, Little Peppermint.

At about the time when children discover that everything has a name, they think that a name is an intrinsic part of the object. Preschool children say that the names come from the objects or that they were made with the things themselves. When Piaget [62, p. 536] asked a young child how people knew that the sun was called the sun, he got this answer, "They saw it was called the sun because they could see it was round and hot."

This notion is strong throughout the period of preconceptual thought and in the thinking of primitive people. To know the name, then, is to have some control over the object. The idea persists beyond the preschool period. The power of names is implied in the cancellation games which schoolchildren play. For instance, Dorothy Levin, contemplating Harry Rogers, wonders if he would make a good husband for her. She puts their names down, one above the other, and cancels the letters. With the remaining letters she recites a stage of courtship for each: like, love, courtship, marriage, like . . . Aha! The magic contained in their names together could get Dot and Harry to the "like" stage only. No marriage! Many if not most adults show some lingering belief in the power of words when they react emotionally to a curse.

Uses of Language

Verbal Mediation. One of the important differences between the infant and preschool child is the latter's verbal control of learning. When the child can attach labels to objects and processes, then he can generalize more readily. It is easier to discover principles and act according to them. For example, here is a situation which distinguishes between children in the stage of preverbal learning and those who use verbal mediation in learning [42]. The experimenter hid candy under the smaller of two boxes, presenting the boxes in random arrangement until the child learned to pick up the smaller box. Then a new set of boxes was used in the same way, with the candy under the smaller one. In the second set, the larger box was about the same size as the smaller box in the first pair. The child who had learned to choose according to a specific-sized box would choose the larger from the second set, but the child who had used verbal mediation (saying to himself or aloud something such as "The candy is under the smaller box") would choose the correct one promptly. The third phase of the experiment used two equal-sized boxes, one bearing the picture of a mouse, the other an elephant. The child who had learned the task by verbal mediation immediately knew that the candy was under the mouse, since he had a concept of smallness as indicating location of candy.

Short-term memory, as well as problem solving, is greatly aided by verbal labels. When given labels in connection with remembering colors, preschool children did almost as well as adults [7].

Reversal-shift problems are tasks that require a person to respond in the opposite way to that to which he has been successfully responding. For example, a child who has been rewarded for choosing triangles rather than squares is now rewarded for choosing squares rather than triangles. The choice remains in the same dimension, shape. If he had to change from triangles to red or small, that is, from the dimensions of shape to the dimension of color or size, the task would be a nonreversal shift. Reversal shifts are more difficult than nonreversal shifts for most children below 5 years of age. Between 5 and 7, few children make reversal shifts readily, while above 7, the majority do [45]. Verbal mediation is thought to make the difference, the problems being easy if one can say to himself, "Color is what counts. Now the red is right instead of the black." The age-related rise in ability to solve reversal shift problems most likely reflects a rise in ability to use verbal mediation.

There is evidence to show that a preschool child can communicate with himself silently, but that if he verbalizes his message aloud, it will help him to remember the mediator and hence make it more useful [19]. Three-to-five-year-olds were given tasks of matching, naming, and recognizing colors. First the child found a chip "just like this one" from the array of 14 colors. Then the array was covered, one chip shown and the child was asked, "What do you call this color?" Lastly, with the array covered, the child was told that he would be shown a color which would then be hidden while he found one just like it. Most of the children used color names consistently, applying them to a set of colors adjacent in the color circle. In the majority of cases, errors in matching represented choices of colors which the child named with the same term as the stimulus. All children showed this tendency on the matching task, suggesting the use of some sort of covert naming. On the recognition task, however, those who named the stimulus aloud did better. Apparently being able to rehearse internally develops with age, and during the preschool period, saying the mediator aloud helps the child to pay attention to it and to remember it.

The more a child learns through verbal mediation, the more resources he has available to tackle new problems and learn new material. The more words he learns the more readily he stores his experiences as memories. The more memories he stores, the more available is past experience for use in thinking and problem solving. Hence the acquisition of language is an integral part of cognitive growth. The child who does not acquire adequate verbal symbols and who does not use them in thinking is likely to be at a disadvantage in our culture. Problems can, however, be solved without language. Older deaf children [102] and older monkeys [93] can solve reversal shift problems more easily than nonreversal. There are doubtless mediators other than verbal ones.

Private Speech. Speech is not always for the purpose of communicating with another person. Sometimes it is for oneself. Some of the speech of preschool children expresses their wishes, needs, intentions, and experiences without regard for any effect that the comments might make on the listeners. The other person's thoughts, feelings, needs, wants, and comments are not taken into account [69, pp. 120–122] Piaget calls this type of speech *egocentric*. By this term, he refers to the fact that the young child is limited to and centered on his own point of view, not that he is selfish. His thought processes are not sufficiently flexible to permit him to consider what the other person is experiencing. Egocentric speech is like a monologue, even when it is broken by remarks from other people. When two people carry on egocentric speech at the same time, it gives a very disjointed result. Stone and Church [83, p. 282] gives this intriguing example of a collective monologue by two 4-year-olds in the Vassar nursery school:

Jenny: They wiggle sideways when they kiss.
Chris: (*vaguely*) What?
Jenny: My bunny slippers. They are brown and red and sort of yellow and white. And they have eyes and ears and these noses that wiggle sideways when they kiss.
Chris: I have a piece of sugar in red pieces of paper. I'm gonna eat it and maybe it's for a horse.
Jenny: We bought them. My mommy did. We couldn't find the old ones. They were in the trunk.
Chris: Can't eat the piece of sugar, not unless you take the paper off.
Jenny: And we found Mother Lamb. Oh, she was in Poughkeepsie in the trunk in the house in the woods where Mrs. Tiddywinkle lives.
Chris: Do you like sugar? I do, and so do horses.
Jenny: I play with my bunnies. They are real. We play in the woods. They have eyes. We *all* go in the woods. My teddy bears and the bunnies and the duck, to visit Mrs. Tiddywinkle. We play and play.
Chris: I guess I'll eat my sugar at lunch time. I can get more for the horses. Besides, I don't have no horses now.

Socialized speech, in contrast to egocentric, involves an exchange with others, through asking and answering questions, commenting on what the other person has said, giving him information which has some pertinence. Piaget noted that egocentric speech decreased and socialized speech increased with age, showing a real change in proportion at the end of the period of preoperational thought. At age 4, bright and average children used the same proportion (about 30 percent) of egocentric speech but at age 6, bright children used egocentric speech in only 5 percent of their utterances while average children did so in 18 percent [47].

Vygotsky [95, pp. 16–24], disagreeing with Piaget's contention that egocentric speech simply dropped out with increasing maturity, devised experiments to reveal its function. He put children in what appeared to be quite free situations. Just as the child was getting ready to draw, for instance, he would discover that he had no paper or that his pencil was not the color he needed. In such frustrating situations, the proportion of egocentric speech doubled, in comparison with Piaget's figure for children the same age and also in comparison with Vygotsky's findings for children under nonfrustrating circumstances. (His own figure for egocentric speech in normal circumstances was slightly lower than Piaget's.) The child would say such things as: "Where's the pencil? I need a blue pencil. Never mind, I'll draw with the red one and wet it with water; it will become very dark and look like blue." Vygotsky maintains that egocentric speech is not a mere accompaniment of activity but a means of expression, a release of tension, and a true instrument of thought, in finding the solution to a problem. He showed developmental changes in the use of egocentric speech. In the younger child, it marked the end of an activity, or a turning point. Gradually, it shifted to the middle and then to the beginning of an activity, taking on a planning and directing function. He likens this process to the developmental sequence in naming drawings. First, a little child names what he has drawn; a few months later, he names his drawing when half done; later, he announces what he is going to draw before he does it.

Vygotsky suggests that egocentric speech is a transitional stage between vocal and inner speech, which is a kind of thought. Egocentric speech, he says, "goes underground."

Vygotsky's findings are supported by subsequent studies which show that spontaneous verbal self-expression and self-communication are important means of problem solving for young children [28]. Different levels of cognitive development involve different uses of private speech [47]. A hierarchy of five levels is outlined, as follows:

1. *Presocial self-stimulating language:* words and phrases are repeated for their own sake. The child seems to be playing with words, such as "Pillow pum pum pum, pill, pum."
2. *Outward-directed private speech:* the child speaks to nonhuman objects, such as "Come here, stick." He describes what he is doing but does not add any information to what the other person can easily see for himself, such as "Going up" when he is climbing the stairs.
3. *Inward directed or self-guided private speech:* he asks himself questions and answers them; he guides his own activities by speaking aloud. On this level, comments are goal-directed, whereas in the previous level, they are merely descriptive.
4. *External manifestations of inner speech:* he speaks in such a low voice that nobody can hear what he says.
5. Silent inner speech or thought.

Private and Communicative Speech: An Example. The perceptive observations of a linguistically trained mother showed a young child distinguishing between communicative and noncommunicative speech [12]. Richard, at 21 months, when intending to communicate, spoke in a loud voice, made eye contact or bodily contact, and repeated his comments over and over until he got a response from the person addressed. Styles of noncommunicative speech were varied. One was a staccato rhythm; another, beginning by 27 months, a joking tone that was low in pitch, forced, and accompanied by a half smile. Yet another, occurring when he knew he would be forbidden to do what he was asking, included a low, soft voice, fuzzy enunciation, head twisting, and some agrammatical deviation. Between 21

Figure 2-9. Number of spoken words added to vocabulary each year from ages 1 to 6. SOURCE: Data from M. E. Smith [80].

and 27 months, about 20 percent of Richard's utterances were communicative in a normal play situation, but while looking at the book with his mother, the percentage was much higher.

Culture and Language

What could be more obvious than the fact that children speak the language into which they were born, the *mother* tongue? The earliest observable effect of the mother tongue is on the tones produced by the baby. Two Chinese babies, at $6\frac{1}{2}$ months, made sounds very different from those made by Russian and American infants [99]. The Chinese babies made mostly monosyllabic sounds with much tonal variation over individual vowels; the Russian and American infants showed little tonal variation over single vowels but made intonation patterns over several syllables. Other students of infant speech have noticed response to intonation by the fifth month.

The mother tongue also shapes the child's thinking. In Piaget's words, "... language conveys to the individual an already prepared system of ideas, classification, relations—in short, an inexhaustible stock of concepts which are reconstructed in each individual after the age-old pattern which previously molded earlier generations" [63, p. 159]. Commenting on Indians who speak English as well as Hindi, a famous Indian author wrote, "English has given them minds which are deeper, wider and more complex in all the mental facilities ... those who know English well in India constitute a psychological species which is different from those who do not know the language" [14].

Growth Trends in Acquisition of Language

Figure 2-9 illustrates the spectacular increase in vocabulary during the preschool years. These data are from a classic study of language, in which pictures and

Intellectual Development   103

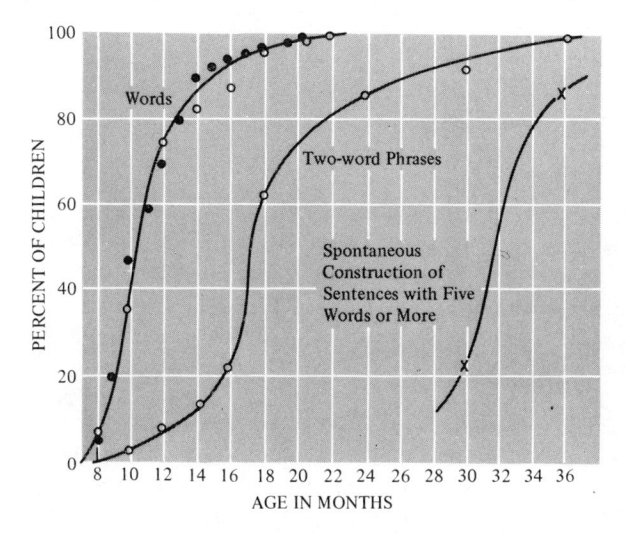

Figure 2–10. Emergence of three levels of language development, words, two-word phrases, and sentences.

SOURCE: Reprinted by permission from E. H. Lenneberg. *Biological Foundations of Language.* New York: John Wiley & Sons, Figure 4.1, p. 133. Copyright © 1967, John Wiley & Sons, Inc.

questions were used to elicit words from children. The number of children represented at each age varied considerably, from 52 at 1 year to 9 at 6 years. The increase from 3 to 272 words during the second year represents a change from nonspeaker to speaker. From 272 words to 896 in the third year also indicates a big change in control of language.

While there are individual differences in the emergence of language, there is also great regularity in this process. Of 486 normal children (free of nervous and mental disease), raised in an adequate environment, less than 7 percent were below the following norms of language development [49, pp. 133–135]. By 39 months, the child names most of the objects in his home, speaks quite intelligibly, understands spoken instructions, makes complex sentences, and communicates spontaneously. Figure 2–10 shows ages at which three major language developmental levels are attained.

Sentences. The first type of sentence produced is active, next negative, then question, and last passive [26]. The order for understanding is different from the order for producing. Active comes first, then question, passive, and negative.

One-word sentences of course come first. The second stage, the early sentence, typical of age 2, lasts for a period of four to seven months. The early sentence includes a preponderance of nouns. Lacking articles, it has few auxiliary and copulative verbs and few prepositions and conjunctions. The third stage of sentence formation produces sentences of about four words. Only 1 or 2 sentences out of the 50 are compound or complex. The following story told by a 2-year-old includes second-stage and third-stage sentences:

> Me tell story about angleworm. One time go angleworm. Little girl pick up angleworm. Know dat? Angleworm cry. Angleworm lie down

pillows. Angleworm go sleep pillow. Two pillows. Two angleworms. Angleworm wake up.

The fourth stage of sentence formation, appearing at about age 4, yields sentences of six to eight words in length and more complex structure. This story illustrates the fourth stage:

The first Christmas was Jesus' birthday and Santie Claus did come. And I was afraid of him. And after that I was happy that I played with my toys.

An analysis [98] of the presleep utterences of Anthony, a 2½-year-old boy, provides, among other interesting data, information about the number of words in the sentences he used. Anthony used two-word sentences most and three-word sentences almost as often. Figure 2–11 shows percentages of various sentence lengths in his talking.

Mean Length of Utterance. The mean length of utterance is a measure which is useful in language studies. The units counted are morphemes, the smallest meaningful units in a language. For example: *cat, eat, ed* (as in *chased*), *ing* (as in *reading*). Table 2–3 shows the mean number of morphemes in each utterance of 13 young children [9]. Mean length of utterance varies from one individual to another. Notice Grace, at 27 months, with an MLU of 3.5, and Betty, at 31½ months, with MLU 2.1. The table also shows whether each child has acquired the use of *be* in the progressive tense (I *am* going rather than I going) and whether he uses *will* or *can*.

Grammar. Children can imitate the speech of others before they understand it and they understand more than they can produce independently. The imitation-comprehension-production sequence has been demonstrated for normal children between 2 and 6 years of age and for retarded 6- and 7-year-olds [15, 53]. However, imitation is not the chief mode of language acquisition. If it were so, children would

Table 2–3 Estimates of Lengths of Utterance and Some of the Grammatical Forms Used by 13 Young Children

Name of Child	Age in Months	Mean Number Morphemes*	*Be* in Progressive	Modal Auxiliaries *will* or *can*
Andy	26	2.0	no	no
Betty	31½	2.1	no	no
Charlie	22	2.2	no	no
Adam	28½	2.5	no	no
Eve	25½	2.6	no	no
Fanny	31½	3.2	yes	no
Grace	27	3.5	yes	yes
Helen	30	3.6	yes	yes
Ian	31½	3.8	yes	yes
June	35½	4.5	yes	yes
Kathy	30½	4.8	yes	yes
Larry	35½	4.8	yes	yes
Jimmy	32	4.9	yes	yes

* Mean count from 100 consecutive utterances.

SOURCE: Reprinted from R. Brown and C. Fraser, in U. Bellugi and R. Brown (eds.), "The Acquisition of Language," *Monographs of The Society for Research in Child Development,* **29**:1, Table 13. Copyright © 1964, The Society for Research in Child Development, Inc.

Intellectual Development 105

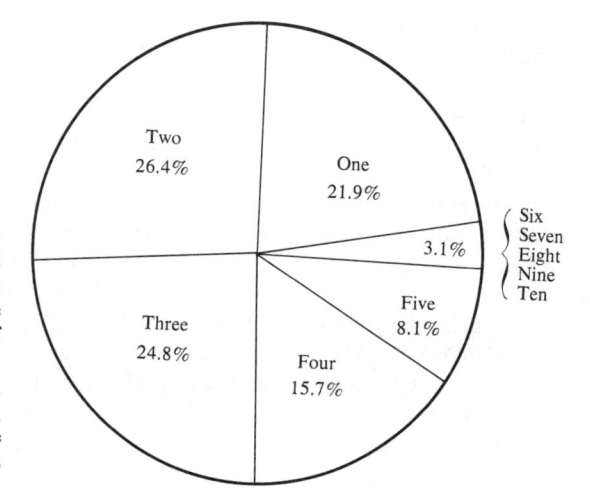

Figure 2-11. Presleep utterances of Anthony divided as to number of words in showing relative frequence of use of sentences of various lengths.

SOURCE: Reprinted by permission from R. H. Weir, *Language in the Crib*. The Hague: Mouton & Co. N.V., 1962.

Pie chart values:
- One 21.9%
- Two 26.4%
- Three 24.8%
- Four 15.7%
- Five 8.1%
- Six, Seven, Eight, Nine, Ten: 3.1%

say what they heard others say, instead of generating new statements. After trying to speak a foreign language by using the phrases in the tourist book, the adult knows how impossible it is to communicate with imitated phrases. One has to make the comment to fit the occasion, and this is what children do from the beginning. From their very first attempts to put words together, they do so according to rules. They discover the rules of the mother tongue systematically and apply them as they gain control of them. Research suggests that a child stores fragments of speech which are tagged for meaning and with bits of information concerning context [13]. He gradually analyzes the stored information to produce the rules that govern his speech. The first rules are simple ones. The rules are different from those governing adult speech, approximating them more as the child analyzes the language on more complex levels and as he has new experiences that require revision of the rules he has.

Syntax, the ordering of words, is important from the beginning. Perhaps the first rule is "the subject comes before the verb." Of course we know that the young child does not formulate it like this, but we wonder how he does do it. The first sentences are called *telegraphic speech*, because they include only words carrying essential meaning. In comments such as "See doggie," "Mommy come home," and "Go car," only words carrying necessary information are used. However, these sentences can be understood, because the order of the words is correct. Even though the child reduces sentences to the barest essentials, he usually preserves the word order, an extremely important dimension of English grammar. When passive sentences are first encountered, they are often understood in terms of the order of an active sentence. For instance, 3-year-olds, when asked to show the picture indicating "the cat is chased by the dog," would point to the picture of the cat chasing the dog [5]. This finding indicates that syntax (order) is more important than form to the young child. This finding is not unexpected for speakers of English, a language in which syntax is very important. It is surprising, however, to find that Russian children also order their first two-word sentences strictly, even though Russian is a heavily inflected language, and word order is not so important as it is in English [78]. In fact, it seems to be universal that the subject precedes the object in the dominant actor-action form of a language [31].

Another example of the ways in which children simplify adult grammar is the childish tendency to produce regular inflections. Children and adults were shown a picture of a man swinging something above his head and told: "This is a man who knows how to gling. He glings every day. Today he glings. Yesterday he—?" Adults hesitated and offered *gling, glang, glung* and even *glought;* children confidently replied, "Glinged." [6] There is considerable evidence that the various aspects of grammar are learned in a consistent order [5]. For example, plurals were made by adding *s* before irregular forms were used. Every one of 18 children said *mans* before he used the word *men* [55]. There is also consistency across measures of language acquisition. Turning again to Table 2-3, it can be seen that children whose mean length of utterance was below 3.2 said "I going" and not "I am going." When the MLU was below 3.5, the children omitted *will* or *can* from statements such as "I will go out," saying instead, "I go out." Cross-culture consistencies in language development are also seen. For example, with both Russian and American children, the first negative sentence is a three-word sentence beginning with *no* (*nyet*), in spite of the adult Russian form which usually includes two negative words, *nyet* and *ni* [78].

Learning Language. Language research indicates that a great deal goes on inside children which is difficult to detect and amazing in its complexity. Sometimes, however, children verbalize revelations of how they learn, and if a knowledgeable person is listening then we can learn from people such as Richard and Anthony.

The young child plays with words in two main ways, sometimes combining these two approaches in the same utterance. He plays with sounds and with the words themselves; he learns to use the language for expressing ideas and communicating. The former function, sometimes called the poetic function, is illustrated by the following quotation from Anthony: "Look at those pineapple . . . in a pretty box . . . and cakes . . . what a sticks for cakes . . . for the click." Learning to use language correctly, Anthony practices and drills himself in sounds, words, and syntax. The records of his bedtime talks show systematic manipulations of language which often resemble the grammars written for the study of a foreign language [98]. The following excerpt is an exercise in noun substitution: what color—what color blanket—what color mop—what color glass. Noun modifiers are explored in this sequence: there's a hat—there's another—there's hat—there's another hat—that's a hat. A verb substitution pattern occurred thus: go get coffee—go buy some coffee. Negatives are practiced: like it—don't like it—like it daddy. He holds a question-and-answer dialogue with himself: There is the light—where is the light—here is the light. Some of Anthony's verbalizations have a large amount of sound play in them, such as: train—Anthony can see the plane—plane—plane—see bubble—bubble's here—bubbles—flowers—bed flowers. Sometimes he comments on his achievements: one two three four—one two—one two three four—one two three—Anthony counting—good boy you—one two three.

One of the important revelations of Anthony's bedtime talks is the self-motivated nature of his language learning. Nobody was responding to him with praise or criticism. Nobody was answering his expressed needs. Nobody was even listening, as far as he knew. Anthony's exploratory combining of words and his persistent drilling must have been for the reward of increased competence. Motives for other aspects of his language activity were probably sensory and expressive pleasure in the sound play and a seeking for understanding of experience.

Since the book on Anthony was published, his two younger brothers have also made their contributions to the study of language development [99]. The private speech of Michael and David showed the same self-motivated aspects seen in Anthony's, the same persistent drilling and creative play, but also individual features.

Teaching Language. As long as the normal child is exposed to language, he begins to talk. No special teaching is necessary for the emergence of language [49, pp. 135–137]. However, the way in which language develops is very much influenced by environment. And while a deprived environment leads to poor development, subsequent enrichment instigates improvement. In other words, language potentiality seems not to be injured by environmental deprivation. Research shows that middle-class children usually have larger vocabularies and make more effective use of language than do disadvantaged children. The obvious conclusion is that different experiences at home account for a large part of the difference. But what, exactly, are those experiences?

It was formerly thought that children were helped in learning grammar if the parents expanded their toddler's telegraphic speech. For instance, if Becky said, "Mommy cake," her mother would reply, "Mommy is making a cake," thus showing Becky how to expand her telegraphic statement grammatically. A longitudinal study of children and their mothers does indeed show different language development in Sarah, whose mother made few expansions, and in Eve, whose mother made many [13]. The difference, surprisingly, is in the richness and meaning of what the children said. When compared at the same point in mean length of utterance, although Sarah was older than Eve in months, Sarah's speech had more grammatical words and parts, and Eve's more content words. Sarah said what she said more grammatically, but Eve said more. The implications in this comparison were confirmed by an analysis of 2800 parent utterances in response to child utterances. Sarah's telegraphic comments were followed less frequently by maternal expansions than were Eve's. Apparently, Eve's mother's elaboration of the child's utterances led to more complexity in what the child was trying to express. These findings suggest that richness of ideas and content of speech are more affected by parental teaching than is the acquisition of grammatical forms. There is no indication from research that parental responses of expansion or approval-disapproval have any effect on the child's learning of grammar [8]. It looks as though children learn grammar if exposed to it, but need meaningful interaction in order to elaborate ideas.

The effect of the mother's language and teaching style was examined at the University of Chicago [36]. Black mothers and their preschool children were drawn from four socioeconomic levels, interviewed at home, and then brought to the laboratory for testing and observation. The mothers' patterns of language are of special interest here. The middle-class mothers talked a great deal *more* to their children, in answering questions and instructing them on the tasks set up by the experimenters. The upper-middle-class mothers' verbal output was almost twice as great as that of mothers in the two lowest groups. Quality was different, as well as quantity. Mothers in the highest group were more likely to use abstract words, complex syntactic structures, unusual phrases, and, in general, an elaborate code. Thus these mothers led their children to manipulate the environment symbolically, to recognize subtle differences in language, and to use language in thinking. Through use of language, they encourage children to anticipate what would happen as a result of this or that action, and to delay action while deciding. Contrasting teaching styles can be seen in the following examples of mothers teaching their children to sort toys:

Mother I: All right, Susan, this board is the place where we put the little toys; first of all you're supposed to learn how to place them according to color. Can you do that? The things that are all the same color, you put in the same section; in the second section, put another group of colors, and in the third section, you put the last group of colors. Can you do that? Or would you like to see me do it first?
Child I: I want to do it.
Mother II: Now, I'll take them all off the board; now you put them all back on the board. What are these?
Child II: A truck.
Mother II: All right, just put them right here; put the other one right here; all right, put the other one there.
Mother III: I've got some chairs and cars, do you want to play the game? (No response) O.K. What's this?
Child III: A wagon?
Mother III: Hm?
Child III: A wagon?
Mother III: This is not a wagon. What's this?

The middle-class children performed much better than the working-class children on the sorting tests and also verbalized the bases on which they were sorted. They also reflected more before answering. Planning was much more evident in the middle-class mothers and children, whereas in both verbal and motor behavior, the working-class mothers and children tended to act out of context, without meaning, without anticipation. For instance, a mother would silently watch her child make an error and then punish him. The other mother would anticipate the error, warn the child to be careful, to avoid the mistake, and to consider the important cues before making a decision.

Social class differences in language and teaching style have been confirmed by other studies, showing middle-class mothers using more complex, elaborated speech patterns, more instruction, less physical intrusion, and less negative feedback [4]. Middle-class mothers were more likely to react sensitively to each child as a unique individual.

A class difference in the use of language has been found in a British study of three-year-olds from middle-class and working-class families [94]. The children were matched for IQ and verbal output, but their styles of language use were quite different. The middle-class children talked more about qualitative features of the environment and about cause-and-effect relations and other relations between these features. That is, the children did more analysis and synthesis in their speech than did the children from less educated families. The less favored children were more concrete and personalized in their speech. From a review of studies of children's use of language, Bruner concludes that more highly educated children, as well as adults, use language more analytically, synthetically and without dependence on context, shared percepts and actions [10]. Less educated people speak with more affect and metaphors, more narrative, more ties to places and people, more concreteness ("I said ... and he said ...").

These experiments emphasize the interrelatedness of language, thought, and behavior style. Through their use of language, mothers influence their children's development in all these areas.

Intellectual Development 109

Bilingualism in Young Children

When his family speaks more than one language, a baby begins speaking by using forms from both or all languages [24]. By around age 3, he separates one from another. He may have accents in both languages at first.

As international communication grows more and more important, it becomes more and more desirable for children to speak more than one language. In an earlier era, it was thought to be disadvantageous for a preschool child to learn a second language. Current research suggests the very opposite, that the best time to learn is early and the best way to learn is from a person who speaks that language as his mother tongue, that is, a native speaker. Advantages are in terms of ease of learning sounds, flexibility of brain function, and related cognitive development.

Learning the Sound Typical of a Language. Experience during infancy seems to shape the tones produced in babbling, as shown by studies of Chinese, American, and Dutch babies [79, pp. 155–169]. The Chinese baby sounded different to Americans. American listeners could pick out the babbling of an American baby from non-Americans and Dutch listeners a Dutch baby from non-Dutch. However, it seems to be possible throughout the childhood period to produce the sounds of another language quite easily, whereas a person who learns a second language in adolescence rarely sounds like a native speaker and almost always has an "accent."

The learning and production of grammatical and nongrammatical sounds and sequences were investigated in normal, monolingual children between 4 and 9 years of age [54]. For example, *strut*, *drin*, and *stais* are grammatical phonological sequences in English; *Tsut*, *dlin*, and *srais* are not grammatical in English, although they appear in other languages. The children were required to learn, remember, and produce sets of grammatical and nongrammatical sequences of sounds. The youngest children did equally well with learning and remembering both types of material. The oldest could learn and remember the grammatical material more easily than the nongrammatical. All age levels found it easier to reproduce grammatical material rather than nongrammatical. Older children did better than younger in learning, remembering, and producing. While older children learned more efficiently, then, the younger children had less relative difficulty with what was similar to learning a second language.

Flexibility of Brain Functions. A brain surgeon [60] reports that the speech area of the cortex can be relocated on the opposite side of the brain if the original area is damaged before about 12 years of age. After that time, the functions of the cortex are quite firmly fixed and the brain cannot build a new speech center. (Age 12 is also the time when the brain reaches maximum weight.) If a second language is learned before age 12, the brain develops a switch mechanism, whereby the child can easily change from one of his languages to another, without confusion, without translating, and without an accent. This switch mechanism works for additional languages, also. The brain specialist recommends beginning a second language in the preschool age, if possible, and says that confusion will not occur if the second language is spoken either by a different adult or by the same adult in a different place. Most important is that both or all languages be learned in childhood, at first from a native speaker, behaving as a mother does with a young child.

Cognitive Advantages of Bilingualism. When 4- to 6-year-old Head Start children were tested for their understanding of object constancy, naming objects and using names in sentences, bilingual children were superior on all measures. An analysis of their performances makes clear the advantage that the bilingual child has. Bilinguals did much better in switching labels assigned to objects, such as calling a cup a plate. The subject was asked which object was really a cup and which was called a cup. Bilinguals did better also in using regular labels in sentences and using nonsense labels in sentences. These results suggest greater flexibility in the bilingual and, more specifically, suggest that the bilingual child may be more aware that there are different ways of saying the same thing and that the name is assigned rather than an intrinsic part of the object [25].

Summary

Thinking, language, and imagination are intimately associated with one another in such a way that each is necessary to mental life. The preschool (or preoperational) stage of thought begins when infant thinking ends, with grasping the idea of the permanence and constancy of objects and also when the child has achieved control of his own movements in space. From this time until about 7 years of age, thinking is dominated by the perceptual experiences of the moment. Thought is centered, since the preschool child finds it extremely difficult to consider how any situation looks to another person. He feels no need to justify his thinking to anyone else. As he moves through the preschool years, his thinking becomes increasingly flexible, less centered, and less dominated by perception. Concepts are at first embedded in concrete experience, becoming more and more abstract as the child has more experiences in grouping objects, dealing with time, space, and numbers, experimenting with processes. The process of abstraction is aided by the abstractions offered by language. Both language and concepts are learned through interactions with people, where the child checks and rechecks his accuracy, eventually achieving socialized thought.

Tests measure certain aspects of intelligence, each test being designed to measure intelligence as defined in a certain theory. Mental age is a score found by matching a child's test performance with that of the average child and noting the age at which the average child succeeded. Intelligence quotient (IQ) is the ratio of mental age to chronological age, a ratio which has some constancy through the years. IQ can be used to express rate of mental development and brightness of quality. Measured intelligence has been analyzed statistically into factors which wax and wane at various ages.

Language develops rapidly in the second year of life, speeding up thought and also making it more precise and flexible. The use of verbal symbols makes problem solving much more efficient. Since the preschool child is centered on his own point of view, his speech reflects this fact. As he gradually increases, through social interaction, in his ability to take into account the viewpoints of other people, he continues to talk to himself as an aid to problem solving and planning and directing his activities. Through social interaction, he also comes to possess and use the concepts with which his culture organizes experience. He also progresses toward the use of adult structure in language, increasing the number of words, refining his use of grammar, and speaking in longer, more complex sentences. The emergence of language behavior is strongly influenced by maturation. The language community determines which sounds shall be retained and which particular language acquired. Parental teaching strongly influences the thinking in which language is involved and which language facilitates.

Intellectual Development

References

1. Ames, L. B. The development of the sense of time in the young child. *J. Genet. Psychol.*, 1946, **68**, 97–125.
2. Ames, L. B., & Learned, J. The development of verbalized space in the young child. *J. Genet. Psychol.*, 1948, **72**, 63–84.
3. Bayley, N. On the growth of intelligence. *Am. Psychol.*, 1955, **10**, 805–818.
4. Bee, H. L., et al. Social class differences in maternal teaching strategies and speech patterns. *Devel. Psychol.* 1969, **1**, 726–734.
5. Bellugi-Klima, U. Language acquisition. Paper presented at the symposium on "Cognitive studies and artificial intelligence research," Sponsored by the Wenner-Gren Foundation for Anthropological Research. Chicago: University of Chicago, March 2–8, 1969.
6. Berko, J. The child's learning of English morphology. *Word*, 1958, **14**, 150–177.
7. Bernbach, H. A. The effect of labels on short-term memory for colors with nursery school children. *Psychon. Sci.*, 1967, **7**, 149–150.
8. Brown, R., Cazden, C., & Bellugi-Klima, U. The child's grammar from I to III. In J. P. Hill (Ed.), *Minnesota Symposia on Child Psychology.* Vol. 2. Minneapolis: University of Minnesota Press, 1969, pp. 28–73.
9. Brown R., & Fraser, C. The acquisition of syntax. In U. Bellugi & R. Brown (Eds.), The acquisition of language. *Mono. Soc. Res. Child Devel.*, 1964, **29**:1, pp. 43–98.
10. Bruner, J. S. *Poverty and Childhood.* Detroit: Merrill-Palmer Institute, 1970.
11. Burn, M. H. Children learning mathematics. *Arithmetic Teacher*, 1963, **10**, 179–182.
12. Carlson, P., & Anisfeld, M. Some observations on the linguistic competence of a two-year-old child. *Child Devel.*, 1969, **40**, 569–575.
13. Cazden, C. B. The acquisition of noun and verb inflections. *Child Devel.*, 1968 **39**, 433–448.
14. Chaudhuri, N. C. The Hindi-English conflict. New Delhi: *Times of India*, October 2, 1967.
15. Cohen M. B. Active and passive language development of grammar. *Conn. College Psychol. J.*, 1967, **4**, 20–24.
16. Corah, N. L., & Gospondinoff, E. J. Color-form and whole-part perception in children. *Child Devel.*, 1966, **37**, 837–842.
17. Corah, N. L., & Gross, J. B. Hue, brightness, and saturation variables in color-form matching. *Child Devel.*, 1967, **38**, 137–142.
18. Cramer, P. The Stroop effect in preschool aged children: A preliminary study. *J. Genet. Psychol.*, **111**, 1967, 9–12.
19. Dale, P. S. Color naming, matching and recognition by preschoolers. *Child Devel.*, 1969, **40**, 1135–1144.
20. Descoeudres, A. Le développement de l'enfant de deux à sept ans. 1921. Cited in Werner [100].
21. Donaldson, M., & Balfour, G. Less is more: A study of language comprehension in children. *Brit. J. Psychol.*, 1968, **59**, 461–471.
22. Dunn, L. M. *Peabody Picture Vocabulary Test.* Minneapolis: American Guidance Service, 1959.
23. Elkind, D., & Scott, L. Studies in Perceptual development. I: The decentering of perception. *Child Devel.*, 1962, **33**, 619–630.

24. Ervin-Tripp, S. Language development. In L. W. Hoffman & M. L. Hoffman (Eds.), *Review of Child Development Research*. Vol. 2. New York: Russell Sage Foundation, 1966, pp. 55–105.
25. Feldman, C., & Shen, M. Some language-related cognitive advantages of bilingual five-year-olds. (Mimeo.) University of Chicago, Chicago Early Education Research Center, 1969.
26. Gaer, E. P. Children's understanding and production of sentences. *J. Verbal Learning & Verbal Behavior*, 1969, **8**, 289–294.
27. Gesell, A., & Amatruda, C. S. *Developmental diagnosis*. New York: Hoeber, 1951.
28. Gever, B. E., & Weisberg, R. W. Spontaneous verbalization of children during problem solving: Effects of task difficulty, age and social class. *Proceedings, 78th Annual Convention, Am. Psychol. Assoc.*, 1970, 297–298.
29. Golden, M., Birns, B., Bridger, W., & Moss, A. Social class differentiation in cognitive development among black preschool children. *Child Devel.*, 1971, **42**, 37–45.
30. Gottschalk, J., Bryden, M. P., & Rabinovitch, M. S. Spatial organization of children's responses to a pictorial display. *Child Devel.*, 1964, **35**, 811–815.
31. Greenberg, J. H. *Universals of language*, 2nd ed. Cambridge, Mass.: M.I.T. Press, 1966.
32. Guilford, J. P. The structure of intellect. *Psychol. Bull.*, 1956, **53**, 267–293.
33. Guilford, J. P. Intelligence: 1965 model. *Am. Psychol.*, 1966, **21**, 20–26.
34. Hazlitt, V. Children's thinking. *Brit. J. Psychol.*, 1929, **30**, 20. Cited in Werner [100].
35. Hertzig, M. E., Birch, H. G., Thomas, A., & Mendez, O. A. Class and ethnic differences in the responsiveness of preschool children to cognitive demands. *Mono. Soc. Res. Child Devel.*, 1968, **33**:1.
36. Hess, R. D., & Shipman, V. C. Early experiences and the socialization of cognitive modes in children. *Child Devel.*, 1965, **36**, 869–886.
37. Hodges, W. L., & Spicker, H. H. Effects of preschool experience on culturally deprived children. In W. W. Hartup & N. L. Smothergill (Eds.), *The young child: Reviews of research*, Washington, D.C.: Nat. Assoc. Educ. Young Children, 1967, pp. 262–289.
38. Holtzman, W. H., Diaz-Guerrero, R., Swartz, J. D., & Tapie, L. L. Cross-cultural longitudinal research on child development: Studies of American and Mexican schoolchildren. In J. P. Hill (Ed.), *Minnesota Symposia on Child Psychology*. Vol. 2. Minneapolis: University of Minnesota Press, 1969, pp. 125–158.
39. Honzik, M. P., Macfarlane, J. W., & Allen, L. The stability of mental test performance between two and eighteen years. *J. Exper. Educ.*, 1948, **17**, 309–324.
40. Huttenlocher, J. Children's ability to order and orient objects. *Child Devel.*, 1967, **38**, 1169–1176.
41. Hyde, D. M. An investigation of Piaget's theories of the development of the number concept. Unpublished doctoral dissertation, University of London. Cited in Lovell [52].
42. Jensen, A. R., Learning in the preschool years. In W. W. Hartup & N. L. Smothergill (Eds.), *The young child: Reviews of research*. Washington, D.C.: Nat. Assoc. Educ. Young Children, 1967, pp. 125–135.

43. Jones, R. *Fantasy and feeling in education*. New York: New York University Press, 1968.
44. Katz, D., & Katz, R. *Gespräche mit kindern*. 1928. Cited in Werner [100].
45. Kendler, T. S. Development of mediating responses in children. In J. C. Wright & J. Kagan (Eds.), Basic cognitive processes in children. *Mono. Soc. Res. Child Devel.*, 1963, 33–52.
46. Kofsky, E., & Osler, S. F. Free classification in children. *Child Devel.*, 1967, **38**, 927–937.
47. Kohlberg, L., Yeager, J., & Hjertholm E. Private Speech: Four studies and a review of theories. *Child Devel.*, 1968, **39**, 691–736
48. Lee, L. C. Concept utilization in preschool children. *Child Devel.*, 1965, **36**, 221–227.
49. Lenneberg, E. H. *Biological foundations of language*. New York: Wiley, 1967.
50. Lewis, M., & Harwitz, M. The meaning of an orienting response: A study in the hierarchical order of attending. Princeton, N.J.: Educational Testing Service, 1969.
51. Long, L., & Welch, L. The development of the ability to discriminate and match numbers. *J. Genet. Psychol.*, 1941, **59**, 377–387.
52. Lovell, K. *The growth of basic mathematical and scientific concepts in children*. New York: Philosophical Library, 1961.
53. Lovell, K. Some recent studies in cognitive and language development. *Merrill-Palmer Quart.*, 1968, **14**, 123–138.
54. Menyuk, P. Children's learning and reproduction of grammatical and non-grammatical phonological sequences. *Child Devel.*, 1968, **39**, 849–859.
55. Miller, W., & Ervin, S. The development of grammar in child language. In U. Bellugi & R. Brown (Eds.), The acquisition of language. *Mono. Soc. Res. Child Devel.*, 1960, **31**, 9–34.
56. Mumbauer, C. C., & Miller, J. O. Socioeconomic background and cognitive functioning in preschool children. *Child Devel.*, 1970, **41**, 471–480.
57. Murphy, G. *An historical introduction to modern psychology*. New York: Harcourt, Brace, 1930.
58. Palmer, F. H. Socioeconomic status and intellective performance among Negro preschool boys. *Devel. Psychol.*, 1970, **3**, 1–9.
59. Pedersen, F. A., & Wender, P. H. Early social correlates of cognitive functioning in six-year-old boys. *Child Devel.*, 1968, **39**, 185–193.
60. Penfield, W. The uncommitted cortex, the child's changing brain. *Atlantic*, 1964. **214**, **1**:77–81.
61. Piaget, J. *The child's conception of physical causality*. London: Routledge and Kegan Paul, 1930.
62. Piaget, J. Children's philosophies. In C. Murchison, *A handbook of child psychology*. Worcester, Mass.: Clark University, 1933.
63. Piaget, J. *The psychology of intelligence*. London: Routledge and Kegan Paul, 1950.
64. Piaget, J. *Play, dreams and imitation in childhood*. London: Heinemann, 1951.
65. Piaget, J. The attainment of invariants and reversible operations in the development of thinking. *Soc. Res.*, 1963, **30**, 283–299.
66. Piaget, J. *The child's conception of number*. New York: Norton, 1965.
67. Piaget, J. Introduction to M. Almy et al. *Young children's thinking*. New York: Teachers College Press, 1966.

68. Piaget, J., & Inhelder, B. *The child's concept of space.* London: Routledge and Kegan Paul, 1958.
69. Piaget, J., & Inhelder, B. The psychology of the child. New York: Basic Books, 1969.
70. Poteat, B. W., & Hulsebus, R. C. The vertical dimension: A significant cue in the preschool child's concept of "bigger." *Psychon. Sci.,* 1968, **12,** 369–370.
71. Rees, A. H., & Palmer, F. H. Factors related to change in mental test performance. *Devel. Psychol. Mono.,* 1970, 3:2, Part 2.
72. Ricciuti, H. N. Objects grouping and selective ordering behavior in infants 12 to 24 months old. *Merrill-Palmer Quart.,* 1965, **11,** 129–148.
73. Rifkin, S. H. A developmental study of the effect of auditory and visual language input on the conceptual ability and memory efficiency of culturally disadvantaged children. Paper presented at the Southwestern Psychological Association. February 27, 1969.
74. Rossi, S. I., & Wittrock, M. C. Clustering versus serial ordering in recall by four-year-old children. *Child Devel.,* 1967, **38,** 1139–1142.
75. Ryckman, D. B. A comparison of information processing abilities of middle and lower class Negro kindergarten boys. *Except. Child.,* 1967, **33,** 545–552.
76. Sitkei, E. G., & Meyers, C. B. Comparative structures of intellect in middle- and lower-class four-year-olds of two ethnic groups. *Devel. Psychol.,* 1969, **1,** 592–604.
77. Skeels, H. M. Adult status of children with contrasting early life experiences. *Mono. Soc. Res. Child Devel.,* 1966, **31,** 3.
78. Slobin, D. L. The acquisition of Russian as a native language. In F. Smith & G. A. Miller (Eds.), *The genesis of language.* Cambridge, Mass.: M.I.T. Press, 1966, pp. 129–148.
79. Smith, F., & Miller, G. A. *The genesis of language.* Cambridge, Mass.: M.I.T. Press, 1966.
80. Smith, M. E. An investigation of the development of the sentence and the extent of vocabulary in young children. *Univer. Iowa Stud. Child Welf.,* 1926, **3:**5.
81. Sontag, L. W., Baker, C. T., & Nelson, V. L. Mental growth and personality development: A longitudinal study. *Mono. Soc. Res. Child Devel.,* 1958, **23:**2.
82. Springer, D., Development in young children of an understanding of time and the clock. *J. Genet. Psychol.,* 1952, **80,** 83–96.
83. Stone, L. J., & Church, J. *Childhood and adolescence.* New York: Random House, (2nd ed.) 1968.
84. Streissguth, A. P. Social class and racial differences in preschool children's cognitive functioning. Paper presented at the meeting of the Society for Research in Child Development, Santa Monica, Calif., March 28, 1969.
85. Stutsman, R. *Scale of mental tests for preschool children.* New York: World, 1930.
86. Suchman, R. G., & Trabasso, T. Color and form preference in young children. *J. Exper. Child Psychol.,* 1966, **3,** 177–187.
87. Syrdal, A. K., Pufall, P. B., & Shaw, R. E. Development of number in very young children. Paper presented at the meeting of the Society for Research in Child Development. Santa Monica, Calif., March 28, 1969.
88. Terman, L. M. *The measurement of intelligence.* Boston: Houghton Mifflin, 1916.

89. Terman, L. M., & Merrill, M. A. *Measuring Intelligence.* Boston: Houghton Mifflin, 1939.
90. Thorndike, E. L. *The measurement of intelligence.* New York: Teachers College, Columbia University, 1926.
91. Thurstone, L. L. Theories of intelligence. *Sci. Month.*, 1946. **62**, 175–197.
92. Thurstone, L. L., & Thurstone, T. G. *SRA primary abilities for ages 5–7.* Chicago: Science Research Associates, 1950.
93. Tighe, T. J. Reversal and nonreversal shifts in monkeys. *J. Compar. Physiol. Psychol.*, 1964 **58**, 324–326.
94. Tough, J. An interim report of a longitudinal study. Institute of Education, Language and Environment. University of Leeds, 1970. Cited in Bruner [11].
95. Vygotsky, L. S. *Thought and language.* Cambridge, Mass.: M.I.T. Press, 1962.
96. Watts, A. F. *The language and mental development of children.* London: Harrap, 1944.
97. Wechsler, D. *Wechsler intelligence scale for children.* New York: Psychological Corporation, 1949.
98. Weir, R. H. *Language in the crib.* The Hague: Mouton & Company, 1962.
99. Weir, R. H. Some questions on the childs' learning of phonology. In F. Smith & G. A. Miller (Eds.), *The genesis of language.* Cambridge, Mass.: M.I.T. Press, 1966, pp. 153–168.
100. Werner, H. *Comparative psychology of mental development.* New York: International Universities Press, 1957.
101. Wohlwill, J. F. A study of the development of the number concept, by scalogram analysis. *J. Genet. Psychol.*, 1960, **97**, 345–377.
102. Youniss, J. Concept transfer as a function of shifts, age and deafness. *Child Devel.*, 1964, **35**, 659–700.

Readings in
Intellectual Development

The first two authors, psychologists Lawrence Kohlberg and Edward Chittenden, discuss the process of cognitive development according to Piaget. Kohlberg describes what traditional intelligence tests measure and compares them with what Piagetian tests measure, giving some insights into what aspects of intelligence are inherited, what are modifiable by training and what can be depressed by a very impoverished environment. Chittenden illustrates Piaget's theory with practical examples, stressing the major role of the child's own activity and the minor but supporting role of the teacher.

Children differ in their patterns of inhibiting action while planning and considering information. Such differences in reflectivity were found in two-year-olds by N. Dickon Repucci, who related these measures to sustaining of involvement in play. Results suggest a biological component in reflectivity which is modified by experience as the child matures.

Bilingualism is the topic of the last two articles. Carol Feldman and Michael Shen show that there are advantages to speaking two languages. Bilingual Head Start children did better than monolinguals in tests of appreciation of object constancy, naming and using labels in sentences. Knowing that the same thing is called by two different names is probably helpful to the young child in coming to realize that names are arbitrary, rather than attributes of objects. The short article by kindergarten-training-instructor Maebah Becenti is a poignant description of what the non-English-speaking child encounters when he enters a school where only English is spoken. The author knows from firsthand experience as a Navajo child.

Psychometric and Piagetian Measures of Preschool Intellectual Growth

Lawrence Kohlberg
HARVARD UNIVERSITY

I. PSYCHOMETRIC GENERAL INTELLIGENCE IN THE PRESCHOOL PERIOD

The claim that early stimulus deprivation leads to irreversible cognitive deficit must be viewed with great caution. As increasingly careful work has been done in the effects of early deprivation in infants, the impressionistic conclusions of

Reprinted from "Early Education: A Cognitive-Developmental View," *Child Development*, 39, 1048–1055. Copyright © 1968 by The Society for Research in Child Development, Inc. By permission.

Spitz and Bowlby as to massive irreversible cognitive and developmental retardation due to maternal and stimulus deprivation in infancy have come increasingly under question (Robinson, 1968; Yarrow, 1964). A number of studies (Dennis & Najarian, 1957; Rheingold & Bayley, 1965) indicate that some observed retardation due to infant institutional deprivation, and some observed compensation by infant enrichment programs, wash out in later development.

The major factual considerations leading to the notion of a preschool critical period in cognition derive from neither animal nor institutionalization studies. The real basis for stressing preschool cognitive programs comes from the belated recognition by educators that differences in the child's educational achievement are primarily due to the characteristics of the child and of his home environment rather than to the child's elementary schooling as such. This point has been ably documented by Bloom (1964). According to Bloom, longitudinal studies indicate that about 50 per cent of the child's final intelligence and about 33 per cent of his performance on school achievement tests is predictable from measures of his intelligence before he enters school. While the fact that later achievement is quite predictable from intelligence test functioning at school entrance is unquestionable, the implication that the preschool era is a "critical period" for the environmental stimulation of intellectual development and that raising the IQ in this period is a practical and feasible goal for preschool programs is questionable.

The critical-period interpretation of test stabilization data starts from the finding that tests administered in the first year of life do not predict adult intelligence scores, that tests administered at school entrance sizably do predict these scores, and that there is only a small increase in predictability found if tests are administered later than school entrance. The critical-period interpretation of this large increase in predictability from age 1 to age 6 is due to the fact that environmental stimulation has "fixed" intellectual growth and functioning during this period. This interpretation, as elaborated by Bloom (1964), is based on two assumptions. The first is that the degree of predictability from a childhood test to an adult ability test is a function of the proportion of the pool of adult knowledge and skills tested which has developed at the childhood age. The second assumption is that the filling in of the ability pool between the two time points is largely a function of differential environment. Neither assumption seems tenable in light of other known findings concerning intelligence. The stability of intelligence tests after age 6 is not necessarily due to the completion of development at age 6 of half the elements composing adult ability but may be due to the continuing stable influence of both heredity and environment after this age. With regard to stabilization due to the environment, it should be recognized that the stimulation potential of home and neighborhood are more or less constant throughout childhood. The fact that low IQ of 6-year-olds from culturally deprived homes predicts to low IQ in adolescence does not necessarily indicate that the effect of environment on adult intelligence occurred primarily in the preschool years. The deprivation of the environment is fairly constant and continues to operate throughout the childhood years and accordingly contributes to the predictability of the preschool IQ to later intelligence.

With regard to stabilization due to heredity, there is also no reason to assume that this factor is completely manifest in early infancy or in the preschool years. With regard to the hereditary, no new evidence has accumulated in the last 25 years to modify earlier conclusions as to massive genetic components of general intellectual ability. It is not meaningful to specify definite quantitative estimates of hereditary and environmental contributions to intelligence, because such estimates depend upon the range of variation of heredity and of environments considered. If all the children considered grow up in middle-class suburban homes and schools, then most of the variation in their intelligence will be due to hereditary variability. If environments vary tremendously, so that some children are raised in orphanages without stimulation and some in a rich environment, then environment will account for much more of the variability in intelligence. In spite of these qualifications, it is safe to say that the twin studies suggest that at least 50 per cent of the reliable variation in general intelligence test scores (if reliably or repeatedly measured) at the school-age level among a "normally" reared, medically normal group of American children is contributed by hereditary factors. A very large portion of the predictability of later intelligence and achievement scores from scores on intelligence tests given at entrance to school, then, is the product of hereditary factors.

The major reason the hereditary contribution to stability of intelligence scores has been questioned recently is that infant tests do not predict to adult status, and it has been assumed that a hereditary factor should be manifested at birth. In fact, however, baby tests simply do not measure the same dispositions as do later intelligence tests, whether these dispositions be viewed as due to hereditary or to environment. Baby tests were not constructed to measure cognition (i.e., eduction of relations and categories) but to record the age of appearance of sensory and motor responses.[1] Factor analytic studies indicate very little overlap between the content of baby tests and the content of intelligence tests, whereas they indicate something like a general cognitive factor in intelligence tests given after age 4.

Accordingly, the hereditary components of adult intelligence are not manifested in baby tests, which represent hereditary (and environmental) factors quite different than those influencing school-age or adult intelligence test functioning. Because of this, much of the difference between the adult predictive power of infant tests and of school entrance tests is due to the fact that only the latter tap the hereditary contribution to adult intellectual status. This is demonstrated by the studies of Skodak, Skeels, and Honzik, reviewed by Jones (1954), which indicate a regular rise up until age 5 in the correlations between the IQ of children in foster homes and the education of their real mothers; this almost exactly parallels the rise in infant-mother correlations found for home-reared children. These correlations, then, cannot be attributed to stimulation by the real parents themselves. Rather, they indicate that the cognitive abilities of the adults (reflected in educational status or test per-

---

[1] This assumption is not clearly implausible, however, for the cognitive baby tests patterned after Piaget's baby observations, developed by Uzgiris and Hunt (1964) and by this writer (Kohlberg, 1961).

formance) represent hereditary factors, which influence later cognitive performance of their children and are quite different from the hereditary factors influencing baby test performance.

The increase of predictability between infant tests and tests at school entrance is, then, largely the result of the fact that infant tests do not reflect the hereditary contribution to adult intelligence and is only in part the result of the filling in of intellectual skills by environment in these years. The weakness of the alternative "critical period" interpretation may be indicated by imagining findings in which baby tests at 1 month did not predict to adult intelligence, but baby tests at 7 months predicted 40 per cent of the variance of adult intelligence. The critical-period interpretive model would then require one to say: first, that 40 per cent of adult intellectual abilities were acquired in the first 6 months and, second, that their acquisition was primarily due to environment. In fact, the only plausible interpretation of the finding would be that the 1-month test was invalid as an intelligence test and that the 7-month test was a good indicator of the hereditary components of adult intellectual functioning.

We have claimed that neither cognitive-developmental theory nor empirical findings support the notion that the preschool period is a specially open period for stimulating general intelligence or general cognitive development. These conclusions are strengthened by the rather disappointing findings concerning the actual effects of preschool cognitive stimulation upon performance on psychometric tests of general intelligence. Morrisett (1966) summarizes reviews of the literature (Fowler, 1968; Robinson, 1968) as well as unpublished work suggesting "that there is no compelling evidence for the long-term effectiveness of short-term educational intervention at the preschool level. Many preschool programs for disadvantaged children have shown that they make relatively large gains in intelligence test performance during the first year of the program; but this characteristic acceleration in intellectual growth is not always maintained during a second preschool year or when the children enter first grade." As one of many examples of such findings, we may cite a study of our own (Kohlberg, 1968). An integrated Montessori program for Head Start children aged 3 and 4 led to a mean 14-point increase in Stanford-Binet IQ in the first 6 months. No significant further increase in IQ was found during the remaining 1½ years in which the children were in the program. The initial IQ increases could not be considered actual increases in general cognitive-structural development, since they were not paralleled by any significant increases in performance upon Piaget cognitive-structural tasks. The primary cause of the IQ increase was an improvement in attention and rapport with adults. Increases in rated attention in the classroom (as well as in the test situation) were marked during the first 6 months, and individual improvement in rated attention correlated .63 with improvement in Stanford-Binet IQ's during this period. In addition to attention, verbalization showed a sharp initial spurt related to improvement on IQ performance. In summary, then, it appears that the IQ changes were more a result of changes in cognitive motivation than a change in cognitive capacity. These changes in turn had a ceiling rather than moving continuously upward, and the motivational changes themselves did not lead to a later increase in cognitive capacity because of increased general learning.

II. PIAGET CONCEPTS AND MEASURES OF PRESCHOOL INTELLECTUAL GROWTH

In the preceding section, we concluded that studies using psychometric tests indicate a heavy hereditary determination of intelligence and suggests that the effects of programs of preschool stimulation upon intelligence are rather minor and transient. We must now consider Hunt's (1961) suggestion that these conclusions may be specific to the concepts and methods employed by psychometric tests and might be revised by work with the newer concepts of methods of studying intelligence developed by Piaget.

It is not surprising to find that psychometric tests include a core of performance due to general cognitive ability of a partially hereditary nature, when this core constituted the rationale for their construction. The rationale of the general intelligence test of Binet, Spearman, and Wechsler (Spearman, 1930) is that of measuring a fixed biological capacity, as is implied in the division of performance into "g" (general ability) and "s" (specific experience) factors. Experience factors are largely consigned to "specificity" rather than to general intelligence. This rationale led to the construction of tests designed to wash out experience effects, partly by providing novel tasks and partly by providing a random and heterogeneous sample of tasks. Such tests lead to a sum score in which individual differences in experience with specific tasks might be expected to balance out. Stated differently, the Binet-Spearman approach has avoided defining basic cognitive achievements except in highly general terms ("eduction of relations and correlates") applicable to any task. Any item or achievement is a good intelligence test item if it elicits individual differences relating to other ability items. The more the item fails to correlate generally with all other items the worse or the more "specific experience loaded" the item is assumed to be.

There can be no question that this approach has yielded longitudinally stable and situationally general measures, which predict to all sorts of good outcomes in personality adjustment and in general problem solving as well as in scholastic achievement. However, the Spearman-Binet-Wechsler approach is not the only approach to yielding longitudinally stable and situationally general measures of cognitive development. In contrast to the psychometric approach to intelligence, the Piaget approach attempts to specify the basic concepts or operations characterizing each developmental era. It does not range over a wide variety of developmental items in order to wash out specific experience effects and leave a general rate of learning or development factor. Instead, it attempts to theoretically define some general cognitive operations and restricts items to those which may elicit such operations.

In a sense, then, Piaget's definition of intelligence or intellectual development is an a priori theoretical one, and it is irrelevant to him whether or not it leads to measures of situationally general and longitudinally stable individual differences. However, it is obvious that cognitive age-development as defined by Piaget's conceptions and cognitive age-development as defined by the Binet sampling approach must have some relation to one another. In fact the correlations between summed scores on Piaget tests and Binet scores are in the .70's for children of a given age (Kohlberg, 1966; DeVries, in preparation). These findings seem to accord with Piaget's view that psychometric tests of intelligence get at the same thing as his tests, but in less pure and conceptually understandable form (1947, p. 154):

> It is indisputable that these tests of mental age have on the whole lived up to what was expected of them: a rapid and convenient estimation of an individual's general level. But it is no less obvious that they simply measure a "yield," without reaching constructive operations themselves. As Pieron rightly pointed out, intelligence conceived in these terms is essentially a value-judgment applied to complex behavior. Inhelder was able to distinguish moronism from imbecility by the presence of concrete groupings and slight backwardness by an inability to reason formally. This is one of the first applications of a method which could be developed further for determining level of intelligence in general.

In this spirit, Pinard and Laurendeau (1964) have been developing a standardized method of assessing general intelligence or mental age with the Piaget procedures.

The writer's own view on this problem is somewhat different than that expressed by Piaget. My interpretation is that there is a hereditary general ability component of psychometric tests, a general "eduction of relations and correlates" or "rate of information-processing" factor, which contributes, along with other factors, to general cognitive-structural development as defined by Piaget. As I stressed earlier, the insistence of Piaget that *universal cognitive structures* are the result of interaction and are not pre-formed or maturational does not constitute a denial of the quantitative influence of heredity upon *individual differences in rate* of formation of these structures. It might be found that the rate at which experience was assimilated to create new cognitive structures was largely a function of genetic factors, and yet these structures would still be said to depend upon experiences as long as it was found that every child who developed the structures had had certain universal physical or social experiences.

While hereditary factors may enter into Piaget level, Piaget's theory also provides a definite rationale for the existence of item-general and longitudinally predictive differences in cognitive level based on differential amounts of general experience. The Piaget approach allows experiential effects to define general rather than specific differences in performance. General effects of experience are revealed in manner of handling a familiar object, specific effects in familiarity with the object itself. As an example, the dream experience is familiar to all children at every age, and the dream scale attempts to assess the qualitative mode of thought-response to the dream, not familiarity with it. It assumes that the structural level of the concept involves the general effects of experience and is not much affected by highly specific experience with the object in question. This focus is supported by the assessment of presence or absence of a level of thought or an intellectual operation, not assessment of speed and facility in its use. Piaget procedures treat the high school boy and Einstein as alike in possession of formal operations, though they differ greatly in their use. The generality of intellectual level in the Piaget view results from the fact that cognitive stages are structured wholes rather than from an innate rate factor. Intellectual performance is general because it rests on general operations which develop as total structures, not because it represents a general biological factor intersecting with specific experience or learnings (Smedslund, 1964).

In similar fashion, Piaget's theory may be used to account for the stability of intelligence without postulating an innate rate of growth factor. Longitudinal stability of cognitive level is implied by the existence of invariant sequences in cognitive development which has been found for many Piaget-type tasks (Sigel, 1964; Sigel & Hooper, 1968). Attainment of a given level of development implies successive attainment of all the preceding levels of development. Accordingly, relative cognitive maturity at a later age should be predictable from maturity at an earlier age without the assumption of an innate rate factor. If all children must go through an invariant sequence in cognitive development, children at a lower level at an earlier time point must go through more intervening stages and therefore will be relatively low at a later time point.

The writer and his colleagues (DeVries, in preparation; Kohlberg, 1963; Kohn, in preparation) have been engaged in research comparing psychometric and Piaget intellectual measures at ages 4 to 7 with regard to the following hypotheses derived from the framework just stated:

1. There should be a "general factor" among Piaget tests greater than that found among general psychometric items, but largely accounting for the general factor in the psychometric items.
2. Relative level on the Piaget tasks should be more longitudinally stable in the years 4 to 7 than would be expected from the stability of psychometric intelligence in this period.
3. Piaget items should depend more on general experience, and hence chronological age, than psychometric items. Accordingly older average children should be more advanced on Piaget tasks than younger bright children matched for psychometric mental age.
4. Mere chronological aging should not, however, lead to greater development on Piaget items if the environment is very deprived. Culturally disadvantaged children, then, should show more retardation on nonverbal Piaget tasks than control children matched for psychometric mental age.

While much of the data from this research program has not yet been processed, some preliminary findings are available. While correlating with the Binet, Piaget tasks also hang together after Binet and other psychometric intellectual factors are removed. Presumably the intertask consistency of Piaget level represents a "general factor" independent of any innate rate factors entering into the Binet. The fact that chronological age correlates with the Piaget factor, with Binet mental age controlled, but that this correlation does not hold under conditions of cultural deprivation, gives additional support to the notion that the Piaget "factor" represents a general and longitudinally predictive residue of effects of experience upon cognitive development.

The logic and preliminary findings just mentioned suggest a number of reasons why Piaget measures might reflect general increments in cognitive development due to natural or educational experience better than do psychometric measures. In principle they resolve the paradox of the Binet, which almost forces us to view any educational increments as specific contents or as motivational sets not truly reflecting cognitive-structural development.[2] Insofar as Piaget measures of intelligence define general and sequential (longitudinally predictive) structural effects of general experience, they should be valuable in assessing the effects of various types of general cognitive-stimulation programs, whether or not these programs define accelerating Piagetian intellectual development as explicit objectives.

The possibility that Piagetian measures will detect some general and stable effects of preschool cognitive-stimulation programs more clearly than do psychometric measures does not, however, change the fundamental caution about preschool stimulation of general intelligence or cognitive development reflected in the previous section. The findings on acceleration of Piaget concrete operations indicate that such acceleration is neither easy nor does it typically generalize, either to other Piaget tasks or to Binet mental age tasks. With regard to the critical-period issue, it also does not appear that a wave of longitudinal, twin, and experimental studies using Piagetian measures would lead to radically different conclusions than those of the psychometric studies as to the role of heredity and of preschool experience upon long-range intellectual development. The fact that Piagetian and psychometric measures correlate as well as they do seems to preclude this possibility.

References

BLOOM, B. *Stability and change in human characteristics.* New York: Wiley, 1964.
DENNIS, W. and NAJARIAN, P. Infant development under environmental handicap. *Physchological Monographs*, 1957, 71 (7, Whole No. 436).
DEVRIES, R. Performance of bright, average, and retarded children on Piagetian concrete operation tasks. Unpublished monograph, University of Chicago, Early Educational Research Center, in preparation.
FOWLER, W. The early stimulation of cognitive development. In R. Hess and R. Bear (Eds.), *Preschool education: Theory, research and action.* Chicago: Aldine, 1968.
HUNT, J. McV. *Intelligence and experience.* New York: Ronald, 1961.
JONES, H. Environmental influences in the development of intelligence. In L. Carmichael (Ed.), *Manual of child psychology.* New York: Wiley, 1954.
KOHLBERG, L. A schedule for assessing Piaget's stages of sensorimotor development in infancy. Unpublished schedule, Yale University, 1961, mimeographed.
———. Stages in children's conceptions of physical and social objects in the years 4 to 8—a study of developmental theory. Unpublished monograph, 1963, multigraphed (in preparation for publication).
———. The Montessori approach to cultural deprivation. A cognitive-development

---

[2] This was our interpretation of Binet increments in the Montessori program. We claimed they were due to attentional and verbalization factors rather than to general or cognitive-structural development, since the changes were not reflected in increments in Piaget performance. The study also suggested that this was not due to any failure of the Piaget tasks to assess general cognitive level. It was found that Piaget tests were more stable than the Binet tests, i.e., they yielded test-retest reliabilities between a 2- to 4-month period in the 90's. It was also found that when a child was initially high on the Piaget tests and low on the Binet tests, he would increase markedly on the Binet test at the later period. In other words, the Piaget tests were more situation-free measures of cognitive capacity. Using nonverbal techniques (choice of lengths of gum, glasses of Coca Cola) to indicate possession of the conservation concept, the Piaget tasks elicited evidence of cognitive maturity masked by distractibility or shyness in the Binet situation. The Piaget tests, then, seemed to eliminate some "noncognitive" situational and verbal factors due to experience.

interpretation and some research findings. In R. Hess and R. Bear (Eds.), *Preschool education, theory, research and action.* Chicago: Aldine, 1968.

———. Cognitive stages and preschool education. *Human Development*, 1966, *9*, 5–19.

———, and LESSER, G. *What preschools can do: theories and programs.* Chicago: Scott, Foresman, in press.

KOHN, N. The development of culturally disadvantaged and middle class Negro children on Piagetian tests of concrete operational thought. Doctoral dissertation, University of Chicago, in preparation.

MORRISETT, L. Report of a conference on preschool education in *Items of the Social Science Research Council*, June, 1966.

PIAGET, J. *The psychology of intelligence.* London: Routledge, Kegan, 1947.

PINARD, A. and LAURENDEAU, M. *Causal thinking in children.* New York: International University Press, 1964.

RHEINGOLD, H., and BAYLEY, N. The later effects of an experimental modification of mothering. In C. B. Stendler (Ed.), *Readings in child behavior and development.* New York: Harcourt, Brace & World. 1965.

ROBINSON, H. The problem of timing in preschool education. In R. Hess and R. Bear (Eds.), *Preschool education: theory, research and action.* Chicago: Aldine, 1968.

SIGEL, I. The attainment of concepts. In M. Hoffman and L. Hoffman (Eds.), *Review of child development research.* Vol. 1. New York: Russell Sage, 1964.

———, and HOOPER F. (Eds.), *Logical thinking in children: research based on Piaget's theory.* New York: Holt, Rinehart and Winston, 1968.

SMEDSLUND, J. Concrete reasoning: a study of intellectual development. *Monographs of the Society for Research in Child Development*, 1964, *29* (2, Serial No. 93), 3–39.

SPEARMAN, C. The psychology of "g." In C. Murchison (Ed.), *Psychologies of 1930.* Worcester, Mass.: Clark University Press, 1930.

UZGIRIS, I., and HUNT, J. McV. A scale of infant psychological development. Unpublished manuscript, University of Illinois, 1964.

YARROW, L. Separation from parents during early childhood. In M. L. Hoffman (Ed.), *Review of child development research.* Vol. 1. New York: Russell Sage, 1964.

What Is Learned and What Is Taught

Edward A. Chittenden
EDUCATIONAL TESTING SERVICE

Much of the knowledge children absorb is best acquired by exploration in the real world where they may freely, actively construct their vision of reality, rather than be passively instructed about it. Such is the view of Piaget and other advocates of a "natural" approach to child development.

What is the place of planned instruction in programs for young children, and in what ways does such instruction contribute to the child's cognitive development? When is a highly structured approach in teaching young children

Reprinted with permission from *Young Children*, Vol. XXV, No. 1, October, 1969. Copyright © 1969, National Association for the Education of Young Children, 1834 Connecticut Ave., Washington, D.C. 20009.

appropriate, and when does a more supportive, less directive role seem called for? These questions have been discussed and debated by teachers for many years; they are important questions which raise complex issues and defy simple answers.

In this article, some of these issues are looked at in the light of two quite different, but complementary, sources of evidence. One source stems mainly from the investigations of Piaget and his colleagues on the development of intellectual processes. The other source stems from the many educational studies which have failed, in one way or another, to obtain clear evidence of differential effects of instruction.

Research workers in education have long been aware of the uncomfortable fact that a great many educational "experiments" fail to produce any objective, quantifiable evidence indicating that one approach in instruction is any better (or worse) than the next in terms of the child's intellectual growth. Whether the outcomes in these experiments are measured by IQ change, reading readiness tests or by teacher ratings, children seem to be remarkably impervious to most experimental efforts of the educator. The reasons offered for such findings of "no-effects" are complex and varied, and they range from problems of statistical inference to the question of appropriate criterion measures. In a recent review of this "no-effect" question, Stephens (1967) argues that the number of studies, at all levels of education, reporting negative findings of this sort is now so substantial that educators should stop trying to explain the result away, and should instead examine the result for what it may really represent.

A current study directed by Dr. Millie Almy of Teachers College provides the opportunity to look at the question of instruction and its effects (or lack of effects) on cognitive development, from the point of view of developmental psychology. In carrying out her earlier research (Almy, Chittenden & Miller, 1966), Dr. Almy had become interested in the apparent relationship between the developmental theory of Piaget and the new curricula for teaching science and math. New math, for example, with its emphasis on ways of thinking was much closer to Piaget's studies than was the older, traditional arithmetic. The new science curricula were quite compatible with Piaget's emphasis on abilities to order, to classify, etc. Moreover, it seemed that the new curricula which stressed discovery and exploration on the part of the learner, expressed an orientation toward teaching which resembled instructional implications of Piaget's theory.

The curricula involved in Dr. Almy's current research are: Karplus's Science Curriculum Improvement Study (SCIS), the AAAS Science programs, and the Greater Cleveland Mathematics Program. Schools on the east and west coasts were identified in which the Math and one of the science programs, or Math only, had been introduced in the kindergarten and first grades. Children in these schools, and a control group of children with no special programs, were followed longitudinally from kindergarten to second grade. In all, over 600 children were studied.

The cognitive measures used by Dr. Almy were directly adapted from Piaget's work. The measures included: conservation tasks, class inclusion problems, serial ordering items, tests of the understanding of transitive relations ($A > B$, $B > C$, $A ? C$), and matrices. The tasks were selected for the purpose of distinguishing between responses which Piaget would classify as "logical operations" and responses which would be classified as "pre-operational." In addition to examining the effects of instruction upon cognition, Dr. Almy also undertook a content analysis of the programs and an investigation of teachers' reactions to curricular innovation.

An analysis of her results shows that there is little evidence that the new programs had any acceleratory effect on the development of logical operations. The children with no special instructional programs performed as well on the Piagetian tasks as did children who had had these programs for two years. This result appears to hold regardless of verbal abilities.

In some ways, these could be considered surprising results. The tests appear to be appropriate measures of the kinds of abilities supposedly fostered by the new instructional programs, yet no major difference between the groups of children is evident. On the other hand, such no-effects findings might well be anticipated on the basis of previous instructional studies, and also on the basis of Piaget's research on intellectual development.

PIAGET: A DEVELOPMENTAL PERSPECTIVE OF LEARNING

During the past 10 years, the work of Jean Piaget and his colleagues has moved from a status of relative obscurity in this country, to a status of relative fame. Perhaps the most widely cited aspect of his work relates to his accounts of the major stages in the development of human intelligence. In particular, much of the research in this country, including the many studies of conservation, has centered on the characteristics of the preoperational stage (ages two to seven) and the stage of concrete logical operations (ages seven to eleven).

While Piaget's analysis of stages is becoming well known, his ideas regarding the factors which bring about cognitive change are less widely discussed. What stimulates cognitive growth during the course of a stage of development? What factors contribute to the change from one level of thought to another?

ASSIMILATION/ACCOMMODATION

The central assumption in Piaget's (1967) analysis of cognitive change is his belief that development depends upon a continuous interaction between organism and environment—an interaction which involves, on the one hand, environmental forces (objects, people, events) acting upon the child and, on the other hand, the child acting selectively upon the environment. The two-way exchange is given form by the two complementary processes of "assimilation" and "accommodation." Simply stated, assimilation represents the organism acting upon the environment, and accommodation represents the influence of environmental constraints upon the organism.

The process of assimilation is perhaps most clearly illustrated with reference to observations of infant behavior. At a certain age, give a baby something new and what does he do with it? He probably puts it into his mouth. He may then take it out of his mouth and go through a little shaking routine, with movements resembling those used on his rattles. If he's about one year of age, his repertoire may include throwing it on the floor, banging it on the table, and looking or listening with interest at the result. Each of these means for exploring an object may be thought of as representing assimilatory actions for they are the baby's way of acting on his environment. They are his means of trying to assimilate objects or events of his world. Very young infants may exhibit only staring or sucking "schemas" while older ones exhibit more variety and complexity in assimilatory schemas. Children in nursery school have even richer and more elaborate ways of exploring and investigating their world.

In the very attempt to assimilate and to act upon the environment, the environment brings about changes in the assimilatory structures. The baby encounters objects that don't fit into his mouth, or objects that don't make a banging noise, and gradually he begins to differentiate between objects to suck, ones to bang, ones to squeeze, etc. The nursery school child may have the idea (the assimilatory expectation) that all big things are heavy—too heavy for him to lift—a generally accurate expectation that is built upon considerable experience. Now he is given a large block of styrofoam and finds he can lift it! His expectations are not met, and he encounters an exception which along with other exceptions will eventually lead to differentiation between the physical properties of size and weight.

These changes in concepts of size and weight, and changes in the baby's reactions to objects, are the kinds of changes which reflect the process of accommodation. Through accommodation, the realities of the environment act upon the organism and force changes in the assimilatory patterns, and thus gradually contribute to the formation of new and more elaborate ways of exploring the world.

It is important to emphasize the fact that attempts at assimilation and cognitive exploration on the part of the baby, the child, or the adult, will occur only when the object in question is perceived as familiar to some extent, and hence can activate assimilatory action. As an everyday illustration, perhaps you have noted an episode resembling the following. At the zoo, a father, mother and older child will be staring in awe at a giraffe or some other exotic creature. The three-year-old, however, is tugging at his mother's hand, not intrigued with the giraffe but wanting her to come with him while he feeds the pigeons—common, ordinary park pigeons. Pigeons are familiar to him, and their tameness in the situation intrigues him much more than the bizarre animals behind bars. For the adults, pigeons are too familiar to be interesting. For the baby in the stroller, pigeons are too distant and he spends most of his time batting at a plastic disc which hangs on the stroller and shines in an interesting way in the sun.

These common observations simply illustrate the point that curiosity and assimilatory action are aroused by the new or the novel in the context of the familiar. It is an obvious point, but a valuable one for educators to remember. In classrooms, in order to stimulate interest we sometimes devote too much effort to stressing what is new or novel and neglect the importance of familiarity.

Through assimilation and accommodation, the constraints of the environment force change in the cognitive system and thus lead to the development of new and more comprehensive assimilatory patterns. This spiral of action and reaction, described as an "equilibration" process, is central to Piaget's analysis of cognitive change.

From the teacher's point of view, Piaget's theoretical analysis of the assimilation/accommodation processes suggests several other important characteristics of learning and cognitive change.

Action   First, there is a stress on the role of action on the part of the learner. Children do not learn new ways of thinking through passive absorption of events, and Piaget's model does not depict them as sponges, soaking up wisdom. Instead, Piaget stresses the central role of active exploration. The baby is active in his carriage as he scratches the sides, stares at objects, studies his hands. The toddler lifts things, carries them about, and arranges them. Nursery school and kindergarten children are continually on the go. Of course, some of this activity can be rather aimless or frivolous, but most of it in normal settings is activity with purpose. Piaget states: "Knowledge is not a copy of reality. To know an object, to know an event, is not simply to look at it and make a mental copy, or image, of it. To know an object is to act on it" (1964, p. 8).

Repetition   Not only is action an important part of the Piagetian model, but it appears to be an action of a somewhat repetitious sort. The observant parent or teacher can give many illustrations of what appear to be repetitious behaviors associated with cognitive development. A three-year-old for several days in a row may elect to complete one puzzle. Each day he appears to go through the same sequence, but probably if we had complete movie records we would find evidence of slight, purposeful variations. The toddler laboriously piles his blocks in one chair, then transports them to another—one by one—then when finished, starts all over again. A five-year-old may spend several successive days in pouring water into various containers, mixing in color, etc.

Assimilation and accommodation are gradual processes and the child's actions upon the environment are repeated again and again with slight modifications each time. The young child who begins to differentiate the properties of size and weight has learned to do so on the basis of many liftings and pushings of objects, and only several years later will the distinction between the two be formally recognized. Concepts of weight (as an attribute separable from size) are not suddenly or quickly learned. Rather, Piaget's work implies that these and other concepts are the product of a long history of actions upon the world. It seems that Piaget differs on this point from Bruner in that Piaget depicts the child as somewhat slower and methodical, somewhat more systematic in acquisition of new ideas, while Bruner tends to depict moments of discovery and cognitive leaps.

Variation   Size and weight concepts come not only from experiences with styrofoam blocks, but they stem from experiences in all kinds of situations with all kinds of objects. Basic abilities to handle quantity and number come not just from manipulating counting cubes, but from a variety of interactions which range from block construction to handing out cookies, one to a customer. The modification of assimilatory schemas requires a variety of experiences as well as repetition and time.

Objects   Finally, we should note in Piaget's model the emphasis which is placed on the role of the object world, or the physical environment, in contrast to the adult and social world. The role of the physical world appears to be especially critical in relation to the development of logic, science and math concepts.

Piaget has described two distinct kinds of experiences with objects. First, there is physical experience which "consists of acting upon objects in order to find out something from the objects themselves" (1966, p. v.). Experiences of weighing, mixing things in water and modeling clay, would be of this type.

Secondly, there are "logicomathematical" experiences. Here, the child is also manipulating objects, but attention is not directed to the *properties* of the objects but rather to the *actions* of manipulating them. If a child counts 10 stones, if he arranges them in some way, the weight or other physical properties of the stones are in this case quite unimportant. Instead, what is important are the actions of counting, whether stones, beads or blocks are counted. Objects are essential here, but the child is learning from the actions he performs on them (the act of counting; the act of grouping, etc.) and not from the properties of the objects. Around the ages of seven or eight, these actions of ordering, enumerating and grouping, become "internalized" as concrete logical operations.

In summary, the following educational implications can be drawn from Piaget's theory.

- The theory points up the importance of exploration and activity.
- The theory stresses the important function of real events and concrete objects in children's learning. For areas of science and math, it implies that what is learned from the physical environment, through actions upon that environment, may be more important than what is learned from people, books, or TV.
- Finally, equilibration and the process of assimilation/accommodation stress the significance of self-directed and self-regulated learning. On this third point, Piaget has been rather clear: "In the area of logico-mathematical structures, children have real understanding only of that which they invent themselves, and each time that we try to teach them something too quickly, we keep them from reinventing it themselves" (1966, p. vi).

These ideas are not new to educational thought. What is new is that they are stated in the context of a comprehensive theory of intellectual development —a theory based on a half century of research.

The actions and operations of comparing objects constituted the basis for one of the tasks which Dr. Almy used to assess the cognitive development of her subjects. The task, which is intended to appraise the child's understanding of transitive relations, is posed in the following way: using three wooden rods, A is demonstrated to be longer than B, and B demonstrated to be longer than C; the subject is then asked about A and C. Since the problem, in its several variations, is set up in a way which prevents the subject from making an easy perceptual comparison of A and C, correct responses indicate the use of concrete logic. On such a task, older children will readily respond that A is longer than C, and when asked "Why?" they may assert "This (A) was bigger than that (B) and that (B) was bigger than that (C); so the first one *has* to be longer!" Their explanations and their tone of voice denote a conviction about the accuracy of their logical answer. In Piaget's terms, this would be considered an "operational" response, since the actions of comparing (A greater than B, etc.) have become internalized and are coordinated into a group of logical operations.

Younger children of five or six behave differently on such a task. They may say that C is longer, because "I can tell!", "I can see it." Or, they may say that they do not know which is longer, and will ask to compare A and C directly by placing them close together. This is a preoperational response, characterized by a dependence on intuition and perception, rather than by a reliance on logic.

Piaget has argued that the kind of ability required in the transitivity problem is an ability which is not readily taught. Most children learn eventually to handle this problem, but the ability to do so rests upon an extensive developmental history of action on objects, over time, in a variety of settings. It is not directly taught by parents or teachers. Piaget believes that similar complex histories underlie the related operational abilities tested on such other tasks as serial ordering, class inclusion, conservation. In a recent review, Kohlberg (1968) suggests that we might distinguish between the basic concepts and abilities of Piaget's studies ("natural" or "spontaneous" concepts) and the concepts or abilities that are products of specific learning situations. Most Piagetian tasks would measure abilities at the "natural" end of this spectrum while the traditional achievement tests, for example, might primarily measure the outcomes of specific instruction.

The curricula studied by Dr. Almy undoubtedly led to learning of specific concepts, but contrary to what might be anticipated from the manuals for these curricular programs, there was little evidence that they appreciably affected the development of more basic or "natural" thought processes. The growth of concrete logical operations was not markedly influenced by these programs.

Such a finding, while disappointing to some, can nevertheless be interpreted as supporting Piaget's theory. If we accept Piaget's model, we would assume that the abilities tested in Dr. Almy's posttest require a developmental background so broad and varied that it would extend well beyond the boundaries of any instructional program. We would also assume that the condition of self-regulated equilibration, through assimilation and accommodation, could not be met in the confines of an instructional program, even a loosely structured program which permits considerable individual exploration.

Her results and the theory of Piaget would also support a proposal set forth by Stephens in his intriguing book, *Process of Schooling* (1967). Stephens proposes that to understand the effectiveness or apparent lack of effectiveness of schools and instruction, we should adopt the model of agriculture rather than the model of the factory. The factory educator, he says, looks at schooling as an assembly line and expects that for every innovation on the instructional assembly line of the classroom you should get some measurable effects on the product— on the pupils coming out. The agricultural model, on the other hand, views schooling differently.

> In agriculture we do not start from scratch, and we do not direct our efforts to inert and passive materials. We start, on the contrary, with a complex and ancient process, and we organize our efforts around what seeds, plants, and

insects are likely to do anyway ... we do not supplant or ignore these older organic forces. We always work through them [1967, p. 11].

In this way, Stephens reminds us to look at all the forces at work in education, at developmental and cultural factors as well as at the instructional variables.

By adopting this view, we do not fall into the trap that has snared a number of researchers, particularly those in educational technology who tend toward the factory model and expect a revolutionary product as a result of their revolutionary hardware. ("Revolution" is a favorite word.) If Stephens is correct, they are headed for some major disappointments in this regard. The agriculture model, while less neat and precise, appears to be a more realistic one and does not mislead teachers, or pupils, or parents of pupils into expecting revolutionary results from important, but humanly limited, innovations in education.

In conclusion, Piaget's work and the kind of evidence reported by Almy and by Stephens gives us a clearer picture of the course of cognitive growth and the function of instruction. For Piaget, the distinguishing quality of human intelligence is the fact that man creatively acts upon his environment and *constructs* a reality; ideas of conservation, understanding of transitive relations, are but examples of such constructions. If the early years of childhood are given over to the business of *constructing*, then it is not surprising that *in*struction, in the more formal sense of the word, would sometimes seem out of place. From the teacher's point of view, then, the young child embodies two puzzling qualities—while he readily learns a great deal, he is, paradoxically, rather difficult to teach.

While such evidence may moderate our expectations regarding the effects of instruction on cognitive development, it should also give us a better understanding of the positive contributions of instruction. Piaget's work and the related studies suggest at least two important functions of instruction, or "directive" teaching. First, instruction in the classroom can serve the function of setting into motion the processes of assimilation and accommodation for a particular area of exploration. The teacher can arouse curiosity by introducing the novel in the context of the familiar, and through planned discussions and activities can encourage the child's subsequent investigations. Secondly, instruction can serve an equally important function of helping the child consolidate what he has been learning. The child can be taught what he already "knows." Some of the best (although unnoticed) teaching at any level of education is probably of this consolidating type.

Teachers of young children are often observed to proceed in precisely these ways. When a good teacher is observed to instruct, in a directive sense, she is either involved in getting a child or children "launched" or in helping a child consolidate or "digest" what he has lately been learning. But for the central period of self-directed exploration between the "start" and the "finish" these teachers often adopt a much less directive, but supporting role.

In our programs for young children, whether in fields of math and science or in art, we should ask whether we focus too much on the "middle," prolonged period of learning and equilibration, where instruction may be of least value, to the neglect of the initial and the consolidation phases where the teacher's efforts might be of very great value.

References

ALMY, M., CHITTENDEN, E. & MILLER, P. *Young Children's Thinking.* New York: Teachers College Press, 1966.
KOHLBERG, L. Early education: a cognitive-developmental view. *Child Develpm.*, 1968, 39, 1013–1062.
PIAGET, J. In R. E. Ripple & V. N. Rockcastle, (Eds.). *Piaget rediscovered: a report of the Conference on Cognitive Studies and Curriculum Development.* School of Education, Cornell University, March, 1964.
———. Introduction to Almy, M., *et al. Young Children's Thinking.* New York: Teachers College Press, 1966.
———. *Six Psychological Studies.* New York: Random House, 1967.
STEPHENS, J. M. *The Process of Schooling: A Psychological Examination.* New York: Holt, Rinehart & Winston, 1967.

Individual Differences in the Consideration of Information Among Two-Year-Old Children*

N. Dickon Reppucci
YALE UNIVERSITY

One central aspect of children's behavior in play and in situations of response uncertainty may involve the degree to which the child considers available information and forms a plan to guide behavior. Twenty-five boys and 25 girls, aged 27 months, were observed in a 30-minute free-play session in which mobility and time spent in sustained involvement with toys were coded. In addition, the response times on an embedded figures task and on a two-choice discrimination task which induced conflict were obtained. Sustained involvement with toys was positively related to response times in conflict situations, and negatively related to motor activity.

Reflection-impulsivity refers to individual differences among school-age children in their decision time in a problem situation containing a number of simultaneously available solutions (Kagan, 1964, 1965b). Reflection is the tendency to respond slowly and consider the alternatives; while impulsivity is the tendency to respond quickly without evaluating adequately the alternative

Reprinted from *Developmental Psychology*, 1970, 2, 240–246, by permission of The American Psychological Association.

* This article is based on a dissertation submitted to the faculty of the Graduate School of Harvard University in partial fulfillment of the requirements for the PhD degree. The author wishes to thank Jerome Kagan, Michael Novey, and all those members of Jerome Kagan's staff who contributed to this project. This research was supported in part by a Predoctoral Research Fellowship MH-15, 206 OIAI from the National Institute of Mental Health and from research Grant MH-8792, from the National Institute of Mental Health, United States Public Health Service, to Jerome Kagan.

hypotheses. Match-to-sample tests, for example, the Matching Familiar Figures (MFF) and the Haptic Visual Matching test (HVM), typically have been used to assess reflection-impulsivity (Kagan, 1965a, 1965b, 1965c). In these tests, the child is asked to select from an array of similar stimuli the one which is identical to a standard stimulus. Decision time is the operational measure of reflection-impulsivity. This dimension has been shown to be stable across varied tasks (Kagan, 1965b), reliable over time (Kagan, 1966), and modifiable (Kagan, Pearson, & Welch, 1966).

Recently, Pedersen and Wender (1968) reported a relation between a style of play behavior at $2\frac{1}{2}$ years of age and test performance at 6 years that may be related to reflection-impulsivity. The behavior of thirty $2\frac{1}{2}$-year-old boys was rated over 4 weeks in a nursery school situation. Four years later, each subject was administered the Sigel Sorting Test and a shortened form of the Wechsler Intelligence Scale for Children (WISC). Verbal ability at 6 years was independent of the earlier behavior ratings but children who frequently sought physical contact and attention from adults and spent little time in sustained directed activity (SDA) with toys did poorly on the performance scales of the WISC and used a relational strategy of classification on the Sigel Sorting Test. These subjects behaved as if they were impulsive (Kagan, Rosman, Day, Albert, & Phillips, 1964). In comparison, subjects who had long periods of sustained play did well on the performance scales and used categorical sorts which is more typical of reflective children. A negative correlation between attention-seeking behavior and sustained directed activity affirmed the independence of these two groups of children. Thus, it appears that $2\frac{1}{2}$-year-old children who display long periods of sustained involvement with toys are more likely to be reflective than those who have short epochs of play.

One central aspect of children's behavior in play and in situations of response uncertainty seems to involve the degree to which the child considers available information and forms a plan. The tendency to form a plan to guide behavior may increase sustained involvement in play and prolong response time in ambiguous situations. For example, one child in a room with toys immediately begins playing with blocks and does so for a few seconds before going to another toy; another child in the same situation looks over the toys and then plays with the blocks for 60 seconds or more. Correspondingly, in a situation of choice between alternatives, the child who played with blocks for a few seconds makes a decision almost immediately; in comparison, the long-playing child makes a choice after considering the alternatives. In both situations, the fast responding child seems to act on impulse with no plan to guide his behavior; whereas the slow-responding child appears to reflect on the available alternatives in a more thoughtful fashion before acting. This example is not meant to imply that one child has more information than another but rather that the second child considered the available information in both situations more deliberately than the first child and then made use of it.

In a study related to information processing in a conflict situation, Maher, Weisstein, and Sylva (1964) found a wide range of oscillation responses among young children when confronted with a choice between different goal objectives; some never oscillated and others did so with great frequency. The stability of the response was demonstrated in a correlation of .94 between children's oscillations on a risk of no reward condition and those on a certainty of some reward condition. The children who oscillated the least seemed to consider the alternatives and then responded, whereas children who oscillated the most did not seem to form a plan before responding. The former may have a more reflective attitude and the latter a more impulsive one.

In another study, Scarr (1966) devised a task directly analogous to those used to assess reflection-impulsivity. Each of 61 pairs of monozygotic and dizygotic twin girls, aged 6–10 years, had to choose between a hidden toy which she had not seen and a second toy which she had seen and which was placed in a box identical to the one containing the hidden toy. On the variable of decision time, the identical twins demonstrated greater within-pair similarity than the fraternal twins. This finding may constitute evidence for a hereditary component in the reflection–impulsivity dimension.

Finally, there is evidence to indicate that motorically active children are more impulsive and less likely to consider information for any sustained time period. Heider (1966) found that highly active infants were often characterized by minimum delay in response as preschool children. Kagan (1965a) found that preschool children who engaged in vigorous activities were impulsive in their responses to MFF and HVM tests administered between the ages of 7 and 13 years. Shaefer and Bayley (1963) found that very active 10-month old boys were rated as low on attentiveness during the period 27–96 months of age.

The purpose of the present investigation is to demonstrate a correlation between indexes of reflection–impulsivity in tasks of uncertainty and indexes of sustained involvement in play among 2-year-old children. It is expected that these two dimensions share variance because they are both influenced by the tendency to consider available information and to form a plan to guide behavior. Moreover, a measure of motor activity is expected to be negatively related to both sustained involvement with toys and longer decision times because motorically active children are less likely to sustain involvement and consider information.

METHOD

SUBJECTS

The subjects for this study were 50 white children, 25 boys and 25 girls, aged 27 months who were originally recruited by advertisements in one of the local newspapers as part of an extensive longitudinal study being conducted by Jerome Kagan.[1] The children were seen as close to 27 months from their date of birth as possible within 14 days. With the exception of 1 child who was accompanied by her older sister (the child's chief caretaker because of the mother's paralytic condition), all children came to the laboratory with their mothers. Social class was indexed by parents' educational level[2] and children from varied educational levels were represented in the sample.

---

[1] J. Kagan, R. McCall, N. D. Reppucci, J. Jordan, and C. Minton, unpublished study entitled "Change and Continuity in the First Two Years: An Inquiry into Early Cognitive Development," 1969.
[2] Social class was indexed by parent's educational level using the following metric: 6 = postcollege, 5 = college degree, 4 = part college, 3 = high school diploma, 2 = ninth grade completed, and 1 = ninth grade not completed.

Procedure

Free Play The experimenter escorted the mother and child into a large (21 × 15 feet) furnished playroom. Brown masking tape on the floor divided the room into 35 equal squares, 3 × 3 feet. The experimenter offered the mother a seat on the end of the couch, but gave her no explicit instructions. The mother and child were left in the room alone for a 5-minute adaptation period in order to alleviate any fears which the child might have regarding this new environment. At the end of this adaptation period, the experimenter returned and arranged 10 toys (bell-boys, mallet, playdough, pixie doll, wagon, colored wooden blocks, large clear plastic box, flutterball, riding train, and toy rule) in a standard pattern on the rug. The experimenter gave the mother two magazines and asked her not to initiate any interaction with the child, not to encourage him to act in any particular way, and not to prohibit any activity unless she considered his safety at stake; but, within the context of these restrictions, to be as natural as possible. The experimenter then left the room and the child was allowed to play with the toys for 30 minutes.

During the 30-minute free-play session, the major variable coded was length of involvement in SDA with toys. The SDA was defined as a single uninterrupted behavioral involvement with toys that might include one or more act changes, for example, ringing the bell on the train, sitting on the train, loading blocks into the train, riding the train around the room, ringing the bell, and then loading blocks into the train again; this behavior would be scored as one SDA, even though there were six act changes and four different acts. Two assistants independently coded SDA on an Esterline Angus event recorder for all 50 children. The mean of these two recordings was used unless the difference between the coders was more than 5 seconds. In such cases, SDAs were corrected by listening to a tape-recorded description of the session. If any questions of accuracy remained, a permanent television tape of the session was used. The initial reliability coefficients for uncorrected SDA for 20 children ranged .72–1.00, with a mean reliability coefficient of .97. Since these figures seemed inflated by a very high agreement between the coders on SDAs 100 seconds in length or longer, reliability coefficients were obtained for uncorrected SDAs less than 100 seconds in length. The range was .64–1.00 and the mean reliability coefficient was .88.

A record of the child's locomotor movement (the number of squares traversed) was also obtained. The mean reliability coefficient for five children was .97.

Embedded Figures Task (EFT) The experimenter presented the child with a figure of a girl and taught him to touch the figure. Next, while keeping this model within the child's view, she presented him with a series of backgrounds with the figure embedded in them. The child's task was to find and touch the figure. Following the initial learning, the experimenter showed the child six sets of embedded figures, each consisting of a model and three embeddings of the model. The first three sets were relatively easy discrimination tasks consisting of a dog, horse, and bird in backgrounds containing a number of colored figures that looked progressively more like the model as the difficulty increased. The final three sets were schematic drawings of a cat, car, and flower, embedded in black and white line backgrounds. If possible, at least one response to each embedding was obtained. Only two children refused to play at all, and only two others failed to complete at least the first four sets. Length of fixation time to the stimulus before making a response was recorded. The mean reliability coefficient for three children was .99.

136 Preschool Children

Conflict Situation Task (CST) The experimenter told the child they were going to play a game with candy (M&Ms). The conflict apparatus had two cups in the front below two white plastic encasements. Each encasement contained both a red and yellow light which were invisible unless turned on. The experimenter controlled the lighting and could turn on any single light or any combination of one light on each side. Each time the child touched the yellow light first, he was rewarded with an M&M which was delivered in the cup below the correct light. Once the experimenter felt confident that the child had learned the discrimination she used a fixed schedule for alternative stimuli, in which the most probable chance score would be 50% correct (Gellermann, 1933). After the child had five *consecutively* correct trials in this schedule, two red lights were presented, producing a negative conflict situation in which there was no correct answer (negative). After receiving two more red and yellow light discrimination trials, the child was presented with two yellow lights, a positive conflict situation in which both choices were correct (positive). Seventy percent of the children learned the task and were presented with the conflict situation. Length of fixation time before making a choice was recorded and mean reliability coefficient for three children was .99.

RESULTS

The hypothesis that a conflict had been induced in the child had to be demonstrated. Berlyne (1960) stated that "situations in which uncertainty is of importance are situations of conflict [p. 29]" and showed that increased reaction time in a two-choice discrimination situation is a measurable index of conflict (Berlyne, 1957, 1960, 1965). Therefore, if conflict had been successfully induced,

TABLE 1
t Test for Matched Decision Times of the Conflict Situation Task

Variable	Difference Between Means	df	t
Girls			
Neg-Pre tr	2.12	16	2.88†
Pos-Pre tr	0.69	15	2.06
Neg-Cri	2.46	16	3.91‡
Pos-Cri	0.58	15	1.95
Boys			
Neg-Pre tr	3.15	17	4.60‡
Pos-Pre tr	1.04	15	2.41*
Neg-Cri	3.24	17	4.58‡
Pos-Cri	1.04	16	3.29†

NOTE.—Neg-Pre tr = decision time to the negative conflict trial minus decision time to the immediately preceding trial; Pos-Pre tr = decision time to the positive conflict trial minus decision time to the immediately preceding trial; Neg-Cri = decision time to the negative conflict trial minus the mean decision time to the five criterion trials; Pos-Cri = decision time to the positive conflict trial minus the mean decision time to the five criterion trials.

* $p < .05$, two-tailed test.
† $p < .01$, two-tailed test.
‡ $p < .001$, two-tailed test.

the response time to the conflict trials should have increased over the response times to the mean of the five criterion trials and to the trials immediately preceding each conflict trial, regardless of individual differences among the children. The t tests were performed and the p values are presented in Table 1. The results clearly indicate that conflict was induced.

Seven variables from the three tasks—free play, EFT, and CST—were investigated. The measures of sustained involvement in the free play were the length of the median and 75th percentile SDAs. The measures of reflection-impulsivity were the mean first response times (length of fixation time before

TABLE 2
Product-Moment Correlations Between All Variables

Variable	Median SDA	75th Percentile SDA	Response Time to DHB	Response Time to CCF	Decision Time to Negative Conflict	Decision Time to Negative Conflict	Mobility
Girls							
Social class	−.13	.06	−.06	.09	.34	.35	.18
Median SDA		.68†	−.01	.33	.51†	.52†	−.39†
75th percentile SDA			.09	.21	.17	.29	−.42†
Response time to DHB[a]				.33	.02	.29	−.23
Response time to CCF[b]					.32	.23	−.44†
Decision time to negative conflict						.73‡	−.17
Decision time to positive conflict							−.06
Boys							
Social class	.34	.50†	.23	.31	−.13	−.06	−.02
Median SDA		.78‡	.08	.31	.35	.38	−.36*
75th percentile SDA			.09	.25	.44*	.71‡	−.42†
Response time to DHB				.67‡	.08	.20	−.24
Response time to CCF					.05	.34	−.38†
Decision time to negative conflict						.75‡	−.29
Decision time to positive conflict							−.48†

NOTE.—SDA = sustained directly activity; DHB = dog, horse, bird; CCF = cat, car, flower.
[a] Mean first fixation time before response to the dog, horse, bird series of the embedded figures task (EFT).
[b] Mean first fixation time before response to the cat, car, flower series of the EFT.

* $p < .10$, two-tailed test.
† $p < .05$, two-tailed test.
‡ $p < .01$, two-tailed test.

making a response) to the dog, horse, bird (DHB) series and to the cat, car, flower (CCF) series of EFT, and the decision times (length of fixation time before making a response) to the negative and positive conflicts of CST. The measure of mobility was the number of squares traversed during the free play. The correlation matrix for these variables plus social class is presented in Table 2.

The indexes of sustained involvement were correlated with a tendency toward longer decision times in the conflict situations. The relations between the decision times in the conflict situations and the length of sustained directed activity were striking. The correlations between response times to EFT, especially the CCF series, and sustained directed activity were generally in the expected direction but were not statistically significant. Social class was positively related to the 75th percentile SDA for boys but was not related to any of the other variables for either sex. Moreover, as predicted, mobility was negatively related to the other measures.

DISCUSSION

The establishment of a relation between long epochs of sustained involvement in play and long response times in situations of conflict among 2-year-old children provides support for the hypothesis that a dimension involving the tendency to consider available information and to form a plan to guide behavior is operative during the third year of life. This finding, in conjunction with that of Pedersen and Wender (1968), strengthens the belief that a dimension influencing reflection–impulsivity in grade-school children might be detected during the preschool years. The lack of relation between response times to either of the EFT series and the other variables suggests that in relatively easy situations of response uncertainty the influence of the reflection–impulsivity dimension is less than in more difficult ones. The pattern of increasing correlation between response time to the CCF series and the other variables adds credence to this argument, since the CCF series were more difficult than the DHB series (the mean first response time to the DHB series for all children was 3.0 seconds; for the CCF series, it was 5.2 seconds).

It is expected that the 2-year-old children who had long decision times and long involvements with toys are reflective on tests like MFF and HVM at 5 and 6 years of age. Observation of six of the children at 3 years of age revealed remarkable stability over the 9-month period from 27 to 36 months. In a 20-minute free-play session in which there were three toys in the play-room, three children, who spent long periods of time involved with toys at 27 months, had very long SDAs (75th percentile SDAs were 408, 565, and 1,194 seconds) at 36 months; whereas three children, who had short periods of involvement at 27 months had short SDAs (75th percentile SDAs were 62, 71, and 92 seconds) 9 months later. In addition, on a revised and more difficult version of the EFT, the three children with long SDAs had longer response times (mean of 15 trials = 12.9 seconds) and fewer errors (mean of 15 trials = .20) than the three children with short SDAs who had shorter response times (M = 6.2 seconds) and increased errors (M = .53). The children with long SDAs performed in a manner similar to reflective grade-school children while children with short SDAs resembled impulsive older children.

The moderate relation between social class and sustained involvement in play among boys indicates that level of cognitive development may influence the dimension, but the lack of relation between educational level and any of the other measures for either sex argues against this as the major explanation of the results. The inverse relation between mobility and both sustained involvement and decision time suggests a possible biological influence. The explanation which is favored is that a child's tendency to consider information and to form a plan to guide behavior is a basic variable which is modified by the environment as the child matures. This notion implies that the tendency to consider information is not dependent on existing cognitive structures—all children have the tools to consider information before responding but this is not the preferred mode of functioning for many of them. With age, of course, consideration of information increases for all children (Kagan, Rosman, Day, Albert, & Phillips, 1964). Flavell, Beach, and Chinsky (1966) have shown that while the 5-year-old child has learned words for familiar objects, he may not have learned to use these words in a problem context. That is, a child may "have" a language but not "use" it. Impulsive children *have* information but do not use it as extensively as reflective children do.

If the assumption that part of the variance in the reflection–impulsivity dimension is the result of a biological predisposition, then one should be able to find antecedents of this dimension during the first year of life. In conjunction with Jerome Kagan and others, the author is currently in the process of analyzing data collected as early as age 4 months with this goal in mind.

References

Berlyne, D. E. Conflict and choice time. *British Journal of Psychology*, 1957, **48**, 196–118.

———. *Conflict, arousal and curiosity*. New York: McGraw-Hill, 1960.

———. Uncertainty and conflict: A point of contact between information-theory and behavior-theory concepts. In R. J. C. Hayser, C. C. Anderson, C. M. Christensen, & S. M. Hanka (Eds.), *The cognitive processes readings*. Englewood Cliffs, N. J.: Prentice-Hall, 1965.

Flavell, J. H., Beach, D. R., & Chinsky, J. M. Spontaneous verbal rehearsal in a memory task as a function of age. *Child Development*, 1966 **37**, 283–299.

Gellermann, L. W. Change orders of alternating stimuli in visual discrimination experiments. *Journal of Genetic Psychology*, 1933, **42**, 206–208.

Heider, G. M. Vulnerability in infants and young children: A pilot study. *Genetic Psychology Monographs*, 1966, **73**, 1–216.

Kagan, J. Developmental studies in reflection and analysis. In A. H. Kidd & J. L. Riviori (Eds.), *Perceptual and conceptual development in the child*. New York: International Universities Press, 1964.

———. Impulsive and reflective children: Significance of conceptual tempo. In J. Krumboltz (Ed.), *Learning and the educational process*. Chicago: Rand McNally, 1965. (a).

———. Individual differences in the resolution of response uncertainty. *Journal of Personality and Social Psychology*, 1965, **2**, 154–160. (b).

KAGAN, J. Reflection-impulsivity and reading ability in primary grade children. *Child Development*, 1965, **36**, 609–628. (c).

———. Reflection-impulsivity: The generality and dynamics of conceptual tempo. *Journal of Abnormal Psychology*, 1966, **71**, 12–24.

———, PEARSON, L., & WELCH. L. The modifiability of an impulsive tempo. *Journal of Educational Psychology*, 1966, **57**, 359–365.

———, ROSMAN, B., DAY, D., ALBERT, J., & PHILLIPS, W. Information processing in the child: Significance of analytic and reflective attitudes. *Psychological Monographs*, 1964, **78** (1, Whole No. 578).

MAHER, B. A., WEISSTEIN, N., & SYLVIA, K. The determinants of oscillation points in a temporal decision conflict. *Psychonomic Science*, 1964, **1**, 13–14.

PEDERSEN, F. A., & WENDER, P. H. Early social correlates of cognitive functioning in six-year-old boys. *Child Development*, 1968, **39**, 185–194.

SCARR, S. Genetic factors in activity motivation. *Child Development*, 1966, **37**, 663–673.

SCHAEFER, E. S., & BAYLEY, N. Maternal behavior, child behavior and their intercorrelations from infancy through adolescence. *Monographs of the Society for Research in Child Development*, 1963, **28**(87, Serial No. 3).

Some Language-Related Cognitive Advantages of Bilingual Five-Year-Olds*†

Carol Feldman
UNIVERSITY OF CHICAGO

Michael Shen
UNIVERSITY OF PENNSYLVANIA

It was an accepted notion for many years that bilingual children had serious deficits in contrast with their monolingual peers (3). But recent research has shown that some bilingual children do *not* do worse than monolinguals on

   Reprinted from a paper presented at meetings of The Society for Research in Child Development, Inc., Santa Monica, California, March, 1969. By permission.

* The research or work reported herein was performed pursuant to a contract with the Office of Education, U.S. Department of Health, Education, and Welfare through the Chicago Early Education Research Center, a component of the National Laboratory on Early Childhood Education. Contractors undertaking such work under Government sponsorship are encouraged to express freely their professional judgment in the conduct of the work. Points of view or opinions stated do not, therefore, necessarily represent official Office of Education position or policy.
† The claims made in this paper are limited by the following considerations:
  (1) The bilingual subjects must speak enough English to understand the test questions.
  (2) The results only apply to lower-class subjects, since middle-class monolinguals may do much better.
  (3) The advantages as discerned here are temporary, applying only to five-year-old subjects. By six or seven years, most subjects get close to 100% of the test items correct.

general measures of intellectual development (5). Fishman (4) argues that disadvantages commonly associated with bilingualism would not appear in bilinguals whose languages were situation specific. In fact one might expect that in some cognitive areas, the bilinguals' knowledge of two languages might be advantageous. In particular one might expect that functions related to labelling would be advanced by having two languages, for the child would thus be facilitated in his acquisition of a mature notion of the nature of labels.

Piaget (6) argues that object constancy must be established before the child can learn to use verbal labels as names for objects. And the ability to use labels alone as names for objects ought to be a precursor to more elaborate cognitive skills involving the use of labels in sentences. Object constancy, naming, and the use of names in sentences ought to emerge in that order in development and the order ought to be apparent in the five-year-old child for whom object constancy is almost an accomplished fact and for whom the use of sentences is just beginning to emerge. One might expect that all three of these skills would be better in bilingual than monolingual children.

Inasmuch as I expect this advantage to be apparent simply because the bilinguals have two languages, one might expect that the advantages of the middle class child [who, according to Bernstein (2), has two language codes] over the lower class child could be looked at in the same way. The middle class child is said to have both an elaborated and a restricted language code while the lower class child is said to have only a restricted code. Bernstein has attributed the middle class child's advantage to special properties of the elaborated code. The more elaborate syntax of this code is said to be suited to a facilitation of the encoding of abstract and complex ideas. However at the age of five none of these subtle syntactic aspects of the elaborated code would be apparent as syntactic development is not sufficiently advanced. I suggest that at five years the middle class child may have an advantage nonetheless, because he has two codes rather than one. For either the bilingual or the middle class child having two codes may facilitate his awareness that there are different ways to say the same thing. This is turn may facilitate a decline in seeing names as a part of the things which they name, a characteristic of thought which Piaget (7) attributes to childhood egocentrism.

The notion that the two codes of a middle class child are similar to the two languages of a bilingual lower class child is supported by Fishman (4) who argues that bilingualism which is situation specific (bilingualism with diglossia) may appear in "speech communities whose linguistic diversity is realized through varieties not yet recognized as constituting separate languages." This is much like arguing that Bernstein's middle class children were actually bilinguals with diglossia and suggests that there might be comparable advantages from the two sorts of codes found in the lower class bilingual and in the middle class monolingual child.

The present study attempts to show that in bilingual five year olds there are advantages that would be expected from their having two languages: in object constancy, in naming, and in the use of names in sentences. Secondarily, it is suggested that object constancy should be in advance of naming, as Piaget suggests, and that naming should be in advance of using names in sentences.

METHOD

SUBJECTS   The subjects were fifteen bilingual and fifteen monolingual Head Start children. The bilinguals were primarily of Mexican origin. Approximately half of the monolinguals were Negro and half of them of Mexican origin. The children lived in the same neighborhood and were enrolled in the same classes.

The bilinguals were selected by asking classroom teachers and a special language teacher to identify bilinguals. To be classified as bilingual children had to demonstrate understanding of several simple Spanish questions and to speak Spanish at home. These criteria meant that several children whom the teachers classified as bilingual on the basis of Spanish surnames were here considered to be monolingual.

The children were four, five and six years of age with a mean age of five years. There were the same number of male and female children at each age in each group.

PROCEDURE   The children were taken to a room removed from the classroom and were told that they were going to play a "candy game." They were given candy non-contingently at the beginning of the session, during breaks between the main sections, and at the end of the experiment. The experimenter was seated in front of a table on which he variously placed the toys that were being named.

1. *Object Constancy*   In the first part of the procedure each of several objects (cup, plate, sponge, etc.) was physically transformed. The transformations were that a cup was crushed, a paper plate was spray painted, a sponge was dirtied, a match was burned, and a suction cup soap holder was adhered to a wall so that the child saw it sideways and straight on. The transformations were done in view of the child and then the transformed object was placed with a second object identical to the pre-transformed object. The child was asked, "Which was the one that I showed you before?" and was required to pick one object from the pair.

2. *Naming*   In the second part of the procedure the child was told that he was going to play the "name game." The experimenter pointed out that objects, just like people, have names. The purpose of this section was to test the child's ability to use verbal labels to name familiar objects which were present. Three kinds of labelling ability were tested: The ability to use common names (i.e., call a cup "cup"), the ability to learn nonsense names (i.e., call a cup "wug"). and the ability to switch common names (i.e., call a cup "plate"). For each of these the subject was required in some cases to demonstrate his knowledge by speaking (production) and in other cases by pointing (comprehension).

The subject was presented with pairs of familiar toy objects (car, airplane; frog, lamb; monkey, squirrel). The experimenter switched the names of the objects in the pair (e.g., by holding up the car and saying "The name of this is 'airplane'"). The subject was asked both which object was called an "airplane," and which one was really an airplane. A similar procedure was followed in relabelling objects with nonsense syllables [e.g., "wug," "niss," (1)] and asking which one was called a "wug" and what it really was.

3. *Sentences*   In the third part of the experiment the child was required to demonstrate his ability to use the three sorts of labels described in part two (common, switched common, and nonsense labels) in simple relational sentences like "The cup is on the plate," by placing objects in a relationship stated by E and in other cases by describing the relationship in which E placed them. The labels used in the sentences were "cup," "plate," "can," "car," and "airplane" and the objects that were named were presented.

The rationale for using simple relational sentences was that referential word meaning, which can account for most of the meaning in these sentences, is the simplest sort of meaning and earliest to emerge. The notion is that such words as "table," "cup" get their meaning by standing for or referring to a thing. Simple relational sentences are syntactically simple and semantically simple since most of the meaning of the sentence can be conceived of as lying in the referential meaning of the component words. Words like "cup," "plate," and even the verb part of the predicate "on" can all be thought of as referring to things or states of the world.

RESULTS

The results were analyzed in terms of the number of correct responses. The results were first analyzed by looking at performance of the two groups of subjects in the three sections of the experiment (Table 1). The range of performance on the three tasks (bilingual: 94–54 per cent, monolingual: 84–35 per cent) suggests the appropriateness of the tasks for the age tested. The three tasks: object constancy, naming, using labels in sentences were increasingly difficult in the order expected. That is, both bilinguals and monolinguals found object constancy easier than naming, and naming easier than the use of names in a sentence.

Bilinguals did significantly better than monolinguals at all three tasks. The apparently uniform advantage that appears in this analysis will be seen in later analyses not to actually exist, but it would otherwise raise serious questions about the legitimacy of comparing the two groups.

As a post-hoc analysis the results in Table 1 were split for both subject groups within each task into verbal or production and pointing or comprehension responses (Table 2). I call the pointing responses comprehension measures because the subject had to understand what E asked him to point to. I chose this terminology because it implies that the underlying knowledge is the same in the two procedures and only the nature of the performance is different. There were only comprehension measures in the object constancy task, which was intended to be as purely cognitive as possible. Performance in equivalent tasks was broken down into comprehension and production for parts two and three of the experiment. In every case bilinguals did better than monolinguals on the comprehension measures. However in parts two and three where there were also production measures bilinguals did better one time (part three) but not the other (part two). It appears that the bilinguals' advantage in these tasks is most evident in comprehension measures.

In general, comprehension scores were superior to production scores for both groups (bilinguals: 80 per cent vs. 63.7 per cent; monolinguals: 65 per cent vs. 54 per cent; Table 3). This is interesting because it corroborates a notion common in the psycholinguistic literature; namely, that comprehension tends to be in advance of production in language development. Comprehension may be more reliable for looking at these processes largely because the subjects are so young.

Table 1 shows that we found the tasks appropriate for five year olds, tasks one through three increasingly difficult for both groups, and bilinguals better than monolinguals at all three tasks. In Table 2 we found that the bilinguals' advantage over the monolinguals was more apparent in compre-

TABLE 1
*The Percent of Correct Responses on Three Tasks:
Object Constancy, Naming and Use of Names in Sentences
in the Monolingual vs. Bilingual Subjects*

	BILINGUALS % CORRECT	MONOLINGUALS % CORRECT	t	p
1. Object constancy	94.7	84.0	1.71	<.05
2. Object relabelling	80.7	69.1	1.93	<.05
t	1.81	1.74		
p	<.05	<.056		
2. Object relabelling	80.7	69.1	1.93	<.05
3. Relations	54.1	35.6	2.42	<.025
t	6.59	6.46		
p	<.001	.001		

TABLE 2
*The Mean Number of Correct Comprehension and Production Responses for Each of the Three
Tasks and the Two Groups in Table 3*

	BILINGUALS $\bar{X}$	MONOLINGUALS $\bar{X}$	t	p
1. Object constancy				
A. Comprehension	4.73	4.20	1.71	<.05
B. Production	–	–	–	–
2. Object relabelling				
A. Comprehension	12.20	10.07	2.39	<.025
B. Production	3.13	3.07	–	N.S.
3. Relations				
A. Comprehension	2.27	1.33	1.81	<.05
B. Production	2.60	1.87	2.21	<.025

TABLE 3
Percentage of Correct Responses of Monolinguals vs. Bilinguals on Questions Requiring Verbal and Non-verbal Responses

	BILINGUAL (%)	MONOLINGUAL (%)
Comprehension	80.0	65.0
Production	63.7	54.8

hension than production measures, and that comprehension was generally better than production (Table 3).

It is not until well past the age of five that children understand sentence meaning, but there may well be precursors to their understanding sentence meaning. These might logically emerge around five years. I suggest that the precursor state to the adult concept of sentence meaning would be the child's understanding that meaning is a function of use. A child could clearly demonstrate this understanding by his use of words in a sentence. He could also demonstrate it by his ability to switch names. While he might be able to learn common labels, and still think that names are parts of things, his willingness to rename things implies that he knows that the meaning of a word is just what a person uses it to mean.

In parts two and three there were three kinds of labelling tasks which we will now separate (Table 4): (1) switched common labels; (2) common, correct labels; and (3) nonsense labels, which were used in two sorts of situations: (A) alone as a label, and (B) in a sentence. As would be expected from

TABLE 4
Percentages of Correct Responses with Three Kinds of Labels (1, 2, and 3) Used Alone (A) and in Sentences (B) in Bilingual and Monolingual Subjects

		BILINGUAL (%)	MONOLINGUAL (%)	t	p
1. Switched common label					
A. Used alone		68.8	31.1	3.37	<.005
B. In a sentence		6.7	13.3	–	N.S.
	t	7.29	1.89		
	p	<.001	<.05		
2. Regular common label					
A. Used alone		85.9	85.2	–	N.S.
B. In a sentence		73.3	52.0	2.18	<.025
	t	3.42	4.23		
	p	<.005	<.001		
3. Nonsense label					
A. Used alone		91.1	93.3	–	N.S.
B. In a sentence		53.3	16.7	3.22	<.005
	t	3.45	10.69		
	p	<.005	<.001		

Table 1, the ability to use names as labels (A) is in advance of the ability to use the names in relational statements (B) in both bilinguals and monolinguals. Further it is found that task 1 is harder than 2 and 1 is harder than 3. That is, in general switching names is harder than either using ordinary names or learning new nonsense names (Table 5). This is true for both the monolingual and bilingual subjects and for both task types A and B with a single exception: monolinguals do so poorly at using both switched names (13 per cent) and nonsense names (16 per cent) in sentences that there is no difference between the two measures.

TABLE 5
Percentage of Correct Responses of Bilingual and Monolingual Subjects Comparing Three Kinds of Labels: (1, 2, and 3) Used in Two Kinds of Tasks: Alone (A) and in Sentences (B)

		A		B	
		BILINGUAL (%)	MONOLINGUAL (%)	BILINGUAL (%)	MONOLINGUAL (%)
1. Switched common label		68.8	31.1	6.7	13.3
2. Regular common label		85.9	85.2	73.3	52.0
	t	2.36	6.35	9.85	5.06
	p	<.025	<.001	<.001	<.001
1. Switched common label		68.8	31.1	6.7	13.3
3. Nonsense label		91.1	93.3	53.3	16.7
	t	3.88	4.77	5.11	.23
	p	<.001	<.001	<.001	N.S.

The most interesting findings lie in the contrast between the bilingual and monolingual groups (Table 4). Here it is clear that the bilinguals are not just generally superior to the monolinguals. In tasks 2A, the use of common names alone, and 3A, the use of nonsense names alone, the subject groups are equally competent. However, the bilinguals are better than the monolinguals in the use of these same names in relational statements (2B and 3B). Task 1, switching names, was found to be generally more difficult for both groups than tasks 2 or 3. The use of switched names as labels was superior in the bilinguals but the use of these names in a sentence was so poor in both groups there was no difference between them.

DISCUSSION

First, why should the ability for both monolinguals and bilinguals to use names as labels be in advance of the ability to use them in statements? It seems intuitively reasonable that one has to learn how to use the labels as such before one can use them in a more complex structure like a statement. Although this is consistent with Piaget's notion, there is a twist obtained here. It appears that the ability to use names as labels has to reach some threshold level before the child is able to use them correctly in relations any significant percentage of time. Hence, in task 1 where labelling is correct only about 60 per cent (bilinguals) and 30 per cent (monolinguals) of the time, the use of labels in relations is correct close to 0 per cent of the time. Whereas in tasks 2 and 3 where labelling is correct around and above 85 per cent of the time, in three out of four cases (except in 3B) labels are used correctly in relations a significant percentage of time (around 50 per cent). It appears tentatively that labelling has to consolidate before use in sentences of those labels can occur and not simply that labelling is a precursor function.

It may not be the case that labelling is important because it is a basic and paradigmatic function but because until it occurs and consolidates, other language functions, which are different in kind from labelling, cannot occur at all. The fact that there is an apparent ceiling effect rather than co-variation supports the notion that labelling may be necessary for later language functions but different in kind from them.

The second set of findings involves the difference for both groups obtained between task 1 and tasks 2 and 3. Changing a label is harder than knowing a correct one, or learning a new one. One can argue that around this age children are rapidly acquiring new words and hence are receptive to learning nonsense words which may be perceived as new labels by the child. However, five-year-old children are rigid in being unwilling to give up what they have already learned as it is such a recent and tenuous acquisition. On another level one may suggest the unwillingness to switch names represents an inability to see language meaning as a function of the speaker's use of the word, an inability to see that the name of a thing is just what a speech community chooses to call it.

Bilinguals then are superior in their ability to switch names used alone and also in the use of common names and nonsense names in relational statements. The ability to use names in statements clearly involves some ability to see language as usable by people in linguistic contexts. Similarly an ability to switch names may be said to require a notion of meaning as use; whereas, the ability to know names and to learn new ones is possible for a child who thinks names are a part of things and has no notion of use.

Naming is subject to two possible interpretations. The first is that names get their meaning by standing for or referring to objects. The second is that they are like all other language functions in depending for their meaning on use.

Hence I am proposing that naming is important because it is the first place that the child learns that language meaning is related to use. Until he has naming mastered at a fairly high level he cannot switch from the first gear of name meaning as reference to a second gear of name meaning as a function of use. Naming is nonetheless important because it appears that a certain threshold level of success at naming is required before the child can develop his first true language function, a notion of meaning as use.

The advantage of the bilingual child in switching names and using labels in sentences can be taken as evidence for a notion of meaning as a function of use. This advantage is not identical to an ability to use names as labels for in their acquisition of common names and their ability to learn new nonsense names, the bilinguals and monolinguals are equal. The threshold effect observed further suggests a difference in kind between naming ability and a notion of meaning as use. I am suggesting then that the mere presence of two language codes as in the case of a lower class bilingual, or perhaps a middle class monolingual, facilitates the shift from a notion of meaning as word reference into seeing meaning as a function of use which I believe to be the precursor to an adult meaning system.

SUMMARY

Monolingual and bilingual five-year-old Head Start children were compared in their ability at tasks involving object constancy, naming, and the use of names in sentences. The three tasks constitute a natural sequence of language skills. They were all found easier for bilinguals than monolinguals, and this was clearest on non-verbal measures. In a further analysis it was found that switching names and using names in sentences was better in bilinguals but the knowledge of names and facility for acquiring new names was equivalent in the two groups. It was suggested that young children might first perceive names as attributes of things they name. With such a notion they might nonetheless easily learn new words. However they later learn that names refer to the things they name because someone so uses them. Having a notion of meaning as a function of use might facilitate acquisition of the ability to use labels in sentences.

References

1. BERKO, J. The child's learning of English morphology. *Word*, 1958, 14, 150–177.
2. BERNSTEIN, B. Social class and linguistic development: A theory of social learning. In A. Halsey, J. Floyd, & A. Anderson (Eds.), *Society, Economy, and Education*. Glencoe: Free Press, 1961.
3. DARCY, N. A review of the literature on the effects of bilingualism upon the measurement of intelligence. *J. Genet. Psych.*, 1953, 82, 21–58.
4. FISHMAN, J. A. Bilingualism with and without diglossia; diglossia with and without bilingualism. *J. Soc. Issues*, 1967, 23, 29–38.
5. PEAL, E. & Lambert, W. E. The relation of bilingualism to intelligence. *Psychol. Monogr.*, 1962, 76(27), 1–23.
6. PIAGET, J. *The Construction of Reality in the Child*. New York: Basic Books, 1954.
7. ———. *The Child's Conception of the World*. Totowa, New Jersey: Littlefield, Adams, and Co., 1967.
8. ———. *Six Psychological Studies*. New York: Random House, 1967.

Children Who Speak Navajo

Maebah Becenti
TOADLENA BOARDING SCHOOL, NEW MEXICO

Navajo families do not speak English among themselves. Thus, when a Navajo child begins school, he has difficulty learning English, much as the English-speaking child encounters when learning Spanish, French, or any other foreign language.

Have you ever tried to correct a foot fault in tennis, to stop biting your fingernails or to stop smoking? It wasn't easy, was it? Modifying your speech habits can be just as difficult. I have chosen to write on the problems of the child who speaks Navajo to make teachers of Navajo children aware of the problems of the bilingual child, and to attempt to answer some of the questions commonly raised by those interested in Navajo education. I believe that similar difficulties are faced by any child who must be educated in a second language.

Experiences and skills that are taken for granted by the teachers of first-grade white children cannot be expected of the Navajo children. Many Navajo children come to school the first day lacking a familiarity with the English language or much of the background experience which is common to the lives and environment of most white children. The teachers are confronted with students who have been speaking and thinking only in their native tongue.

One of the difficulties encountered by the child is his inability to make correctly all of the sounds in the new language. In most cases he is unaware that his speech differs from that of the teacher. His ear has not been trained to note the distinction. It seems more appropriate to correct a child when he is young, less sensitive, and more easily changed than to wait until he is older and less receptive.

Sounds that cause trouble are the ones not found in the child's own language. For example, the Navajo children substitute "d" for "th" because the Navajo language has no "th" sound. They substitute "b" for "v" for the same reason. The Navajos have trouble pronouncing endings on words such as ing, k, s and t. Glottal stops are the most common consonantal sound in Navajo. An example of this is "ha' a' aah," which means the word *east*. The features of the Navajo vowels are nasality, tone and length.

Some of our parents do not speak English. Therefore, whenever we go home we cannot help but speak the native language to make communication possible. I believe this is one of the bad influences on those of us who are trying to improve our English.

Even though a child learns to speak by imitation, he is handicapped for some time because he does not think in the second language. When an English-speaking person first learns to say "adios," for example, he thinks "goodbye." The translation process slows up the pace for the bilingual child because he

Reprinted with permission from *Young Children*, Vol. XXV, No. 3, January, 1970. Copyright © 1970, National Association for the Education of Young Children, 1834 Connecticut Ave., N. W., Washington, D.C. 20009.

is trying to think how he can best translate a certain word or sentence. Sometimes, the word needed does not exist. For instance, we do not have a word for "sorry" and therefore have to describe a situation similar to the word.

A Navajo child is often confused with negative questions, such as, "You are not hurt, are you?" Instead of answering "No" he will answer "Yes," the way he would answer that question in his native language. It requires drilling and practice to correct this problem.

Teachers of Navajo children frequently ask why Navajos are shy and reluctant to speak. As a Navajo, I know that this problem exists and wonder how we can solve it. One solution might be simply to make it possible for the Navajos to mingle with the English-speaking children more. By this method, we may be able to overcome the inferiority and inadequacy that the Navajo children feel. But as far as I know, shyness is not a custom of the Navajo people or anything of the like. One of the reasons Navajo children are reluctant to respond orally may be fear. A certain child may know the answer to a specific question, and he wants to answer that question. But he is afraid and embarrassed that he will be ridiculed by his fellow classmates. The Navajo students tend to ridicule students who recite in class a great deal. This reason may also explain low voice volume in class. Sometimes, a child is not sure whether he will say the right thing(s).

Some Navajo students write English better than they speak it. This may come about because the bilingual child has more time to think while writing than while speaking.

As teachers of these bilingual students, let us make every effort and use every opportunity for the Navajo children to become proficient in communication skills. It is my sincere hope that someday we will speak as fluently as the English-speaking people.

Chapter 3

Merrill-Palmer Institute by Donna J. Harris

The Role of Play in Development

Reporting to the parents of a 3-year-old, the teacher said: "Laura works a great deal with water. She and Cindy have been working in the doll corner most of the time during the past week."

To the uninitiated, the word *work* would seem farfetched in describing anything that Laura, or any 3-year-old, did in the nursery school or at home. Understanding the meaning of play in the child's life, the teacher equated it with work. Play is what the preschool child does when he is not sleeping, eating or complying with

152 Preschool Children

other such routines or requests. Although to an adult, play may be just a time filler, to a child play is serious business. Engaging in this serious business, he develops his mind and body, integrating social and emotional functions and the intellectual functions of thinking, reasoning, problem solving, talking, and imagining [1, 52]. Physical environment and guidance are vital influences on the child's development through play. As the last section of this chapter will show, the preschool years are important ones for intellectual growth, even though many people erroneously consider them a time of waiting for education to begin. A more modern mistake is sometimes made by adults who know that enormous cognitive development occurs during the preschool years. They unfortunately jump to the conclusion that preschool children should work on intellectual lessons to the exclusion of growth through play and imagination.

Play

There are many theories as to the origin, purpose, and function of play. They can be grouped into *psychogenic* and *sociogenic* theories [53]. The former stress the fact that in play, the child uses former experiences and reworks them or assimilates them. The latter focus on the role of novel responses as preparation for future adaptation. Play actually performs both functions and others as well. While promoting and enhancing many kinds of development and relationships, play is its own reward.

Differentiation and Integration

The developmental principle of differentiation and integration is illustrated by many sequences observable in play. Just as the newborn baby starts with his reflexive patterns to build a new pattern of grasping an object and bringing it to his mouth, so the 2-year-old refines some of his crude coordinations into smaller units which he improves and then combines into complex units. Thus he develops new patterns of thinking and acting which are different from the older, simpler ones and yet include them.

Having only recently progressed from walking to running, the 2-year-old runs just for the fun of it. Stepping high and alternating his feet faster than when he walks, he may add little speed. He climbs for the fun of it, too, on stairs, furniture, jungle gym or inclined boards, going up and down, backward, frontward, on his stomach, on his seat, trying out all possibilities, enjoying the feel of all. Even after walking, running, and climbing have become integrated into more complex motor patterns, they are still used sometimes by themselves and apparently enjoyed for their own sakes. Similarly, tricycle riding, ball throwing and catching, jumping, and cutting with scissors—these are all activities which are used sometimes for themselves and at other times for other ends. As running and climbing become easy and automatic, they are used for other ends, integrated with other actions. The child runs and waves his arms, being a bird; he runs to reach the doll carriage before his sister gets it; he climbs the stairs to get Mommy's knitting for her; he scrambles onto the kitchen counter to find crackers and peanut butter. He modifies walking and running motions to ride a kiddy car and later a tricycle.

By the end of the preschool period, many complex patterns of play have been developed from simple forms of motor play, imagination, manipulation, and perception, but growth is merely off to a good start. Mental development goes on, building more and more involved structures through the interaction between child and environment. The coordinations of ball throwing, catching, running, counting, and others, can be integrated into playing basketball, baseball, and tennis. Counting may be used eventually in playing bridge. Dramatic play can be integrated into acting and writing.

Sensorimotor Play

Infant play is predominately sensorimotor, since intellectual growth has not progressed beyond the sensorimotor level. Although with increasing maturity play becomes more differentiated and parts of it more complex, the child continues to engage in sensorimotor play. So do the adolescent and the adult. Age is no selector of who lingers beside a tidal pool to bathe his senses in sparkles, clarity, colors, undulating form, chill, salt, and prickles. Anyone can enjoy making a snowball and throwing it. Preschool play has a large sensorimotor component, as anyone who observes young children will notice. Exploration is one facet of the developing sense of initiative. The young child touches objects eagerly, grasps them, runs his fingers lightly over them, even scratches them with his fingernails. Although he has learned, to a large extent, to keep objects out of his mouth, such inhibitions are not complete and he often finishes an examination with his lips and tongue. Color is important, often featured in his comments and greatly enjoyed in toys, art, clothing, and nature. He experiments with sounds, using his voice, musical instruments, and any casual sound makers which come into his grasp.

Social Play

Infants show interest and pleasure in the company of other infants. During the preschool years, children seek one another and give evidence of enjoying play together. Parents usually recognize some of the benefits of social play. Very often they say, as the reason for sending a child to nursery school: "He needs playmates. We want him to learn to play with other children."

Working with a friend or companion can make a difficult task more acceptable. When 5-year-olds were given a target game, children assigned to work in pairs were more willing to try than those working alone [54]. Those who were least willing to do the task were the ones who were asked to do it alone in front of the class.

The ordinary course of group play as seen in nursery schools or neighborhood is a progression from simple to complex. Two-year-olds watch others, cooperate momentarily, often engage in the same activity as someone else (parallel play), such as shoveling or sliding, but they play in an essentially solitary style. However, even though they may not appear to be interacting, there seems to be a satisfaction in just being near each other. For instance, a rocking boat is a popular plaything in which a group of young children can be together. They tend to be rough with each other, hitting, pushing, poking, grabbing, often seeming to explore each other as *things* rather than as people. Of course, they recognize each other as people, but they are in a process of finding out the basic characteristics of people, especially of children similar to themselves. Will this person fall over when I push him?

What happens when I pull that shiny long hair? How does it feel to hug him? What kind of noise does she make? Egocentric, he seeks information which will eventually help him to grow beyond egocentrism.

At the 2-year level pushing or hitting with the apparent intent to hurt is infrequent. The pushing and hitting that does go on is most often for the purpose of getting a toy that someone else has. Sometimes a child hurts others unintentionally because he does not even recognize them as being there, walking into their play, pushing them aside. Such actions are egocentric, since the child has a limited awareness of himself in relation to the rest of the world and is unable to comprehend the situation as it is to someone else.

Gradually interchange grows more frequent, longer, with more cooperation and more conflict. A nursery school study has shown positive, friendly behavior to be more frequent than negative behavior in social interaction [8]. The former increased with age. With the development of language, more communication takes place. Two children play together, talking about what they are making in the sand, putting dolls to bed, dressing up, pretending a scene that requires two cooperating characters, such as a mother and a baby. Groups of three children playing together are common between 3 and 6 years. While three seems to be the preferred number, groups do increase up to five or six members, especially at the older ages.

In the early stages of group play, children tend to move in and out of the group without changing the content of the play (shifting group play). For instance, Tom, Hal, and Barbie were digging and making dribble castles near the water's edge. Barbie took her periwinkles to visit the hermit crab that Tom and Hal were tending in the pool between their castles. Just as Barbie took off to find another hermit crab, Dulcy settled down beside Barbie's castle to keep the pool from filling in. Later Barbie returned, all four played for a few minutes and then Tom and Hal departed, leaving Barbie and Dulcy with all three castles, pools, and wild life. Play groups are more stable in the older preschool years, as activities become more structured and complex. Conflicts over toys decrease as children learn how to take turns and as their behavior becomes more flexible, with more possibilities for action.

Friendly Behavior. Young children have definite preferences in playmates. They can tell which children they like best and least. Observations in nursery schools reveal children playing consistently with liked peers. Degree of popularity can be assessed by sociometric methods adapted to young children. Instead of asking the child the names of his best friends, a useful technique is to show him a board mounted with photographs of all the children in his play group. He can then name or point to the one he likes to play with, the one he doesn't like to play with, one he would like to take home after school, and so on. Popularity scores can be derived from numbers of choices, and characteristics of low, high, and medium scorers can be studied.

High scorers on a picture-board sociometric test were found to be more likely than other children to use positive social reinforcement and to use it with a large number of children [25]. Positive social reinforcers were attention, approval, affection, acceptance, submission, and tokens. Low scorers (rejected children) were likely to give negative social reinforcement, which included noncompliance (refusing to submit or cooperate, ignoring overtures of others), interferences, such as taking property or disrupting activity, ridiculing, blaming, tattling, attacks, threats, and demands. Giving and receiving positive reinforcement were found to be reciprocal activities. That is, those who gave the most got the most. Four-year-olds gave more than 3-year-olds and also spread their reinforcements over a large number of recipients [8]. Boys gave more to boys and girls to girls.

Popular children sometimes use negative reinforcement with their peers. Other children seem to take into consideration the type of aggression used and the situation in which it occurs [39]. Peers are likely to tolerate provoked aggression directed toward an appropriate object, thus considering the intensity of the act and the degree of threat to the recipient.

When 3-year-olds were strongly dependent on their mothers for contact comfort, they were likely to be victims of aggression by other children in the nursery school [35]. That is, children who were immature in their dependent behavior at home elicited aggression at school. More mature dependent behavior, the seeking of help or affection, did not seem to detract from popularity unless it interfered with play [39]. If a young child insists upon sitting on the teacher's lap and monopolizing her attention, then the other children are likely to disapprove. If, however, a child seeks the teacher's help in ways that enhance group play, or if he elicits help and affectionate response from a friend, then he probably gains support and friendship. Some of the conditions which enhance basic sympathetic responses between playmates go back to experiences in the family [27]. Preschool children's consideration for others develops most readily when parents include with their disciplining of children the pointing out the consequences of children's behavior toward other people. (Parent–child relationships are discussed in the following chapter.)

Compliant behavior was studied in 3- to 5-year-olds in a nursery school [10] using time sample observations. *Compliance* was defined as the "frequency and alacrity with which the children acceded to the commands and suggestions of other persons." Degree of compliance with peers was not found to be related to intelligence, nor was there a sex difference. The most compliant children sought more help and more emotional support from other children than did the less compliant children. The most compliant tended to be less aggressive and dominating with their peers than did the least compliant children. The following differences in social behavior between peer-compliant and peer-noncompliant children were found to be statistically significant: opinions are more readily influenced by others; has higher energy level; is more spontaneous and uninhibited; is more distractible; is more suggestible; more often seeks praise and attention from others; is warmer, friendlier; shows more empathic sensitivity to others' feelings; appears more relaxed and easygoing; is less rigid, less inflexible; is less of a perfectionist; exhibits less self-pity; finds it less difficult to make mistakes. In the nursery school, complying with peers seemed to occur in a give-and-take situation rather than in one of dominance and submission. The child who makes many suggestions for play is likely to be a child who frequently agrees with the suggestions of others. It is noteworthy that the children who showed the greatest degree of compliance with peers were also high in the characteristics of mental health.

Sources of friendly behavior are not confined to the child himself. The situation also contributes to how a youngster feels and behaves in relation to another. Experimental proof of the importance of the situation was provided by pairing preschool children in cooperative tasks under three conditions [5]. The picture-board technique was used to find sociometric scores. Children of similar moderate degrees of popularity were paired. The task involved pressing buttons cooperatively.

Reinforcement, in the form of small tokens for cooperative button pressing, was given to experimental groups and not to a control group. Posttesting with the picture board showed an increase in friendship (sociometric) status of the children who had received reinforcement. Therefore, children's social attitudes can be influenced by the conditions under which they interact with each other. The personality characteristics of the participants do not tell the whole story.

Nursery school teachers make use of the knowledge that children's social attitudes and behavior can be changed by the situation in which they interact. Important influences include the planned settings of the nursery school and the teacher's own actions. For example, a 4-year-old boy's antisocial behavior improved greatly when a special teacher consistently reinforced socially acceptable acts and carefully avoided reinforcing antisocial acts [46]. For example, the teacher would say, "Yes, that's right," or smile, nod, and show interest when the little boy helped, showed concern for others, shared ideas or toys, conversed, or otherwise showed friendliness. When he threatened, assaulted, derogated, or disrupted other children, the teacher took action to protect the other children and turned her attention away from the little boy.

Social play becomes more complex as children learn not only more subtle ways of approaching and interacting with each other but also as they develop in motor coordination, language, concepts, and imagination. Play is the arena in which all of these behavior patterns are developed, often simultaneously. The various patterns are analyzed and discussed separately only because the whole picture is too complicated to deal with at once.

Imagination

Preschool thinking is "cute" in much the same way that infant proportions are "cute"; preschool imagination is beautiful. Imaginative behavior gives the preschool child a special place in the adult's heart. Adults look wistfully at young children's original interpretations of commonplace events, their fresh, bright paintings, poetry, and free-wheeling dramatics. Almost every adult has at least a fleeting memory of being that kind of person himself. "Every child an artist." "The magic years." "The golden years of childhood." What happens to imagination?

Imagination as Part of the Sense of Initiative

Having developed a firm sense of autonomy and a consequent concept of himself as a person, the child wants to find out what he can *do*. To this end, he explores the world through his senses, through thinking and reasoning, and through imagination. In most situations, of course, these three instruments of exploration are combined. The essential part played by imagination, however, is probably least understood and appreciated. Through imagination, the young child tries on the roles of the important people in his world, the people who do things which he might some day do. Most vital of all are the roles of his parents, and these are the parts he plays first and most often, especially the part of the parent of the same sex. The child imagines being and/or replacing the parent of the same sex. In doing so, he imitates some of the parent's behavior and thinking, including his standards and goals. His own conscience develops through this activity, modeled upon the parent's, encouraged by his desire to be the parent. Gradually, through interaction with both parents, the youngster faces the facts that he can neither be nor replace his parent and that he himself can one day be a parent through growing up and behaving in grown-up ways. He is continually fascinated by the exploration of adult roles, which he does first and foremost through dramatic play, but also through literature and fantasy and even through dancing, painting, and other creative media.

Guilt is a necessary product of the developing sense of initiative, as the child changes from a simple pleasure-seeker to a complex self-regulator. Erikson [17, p. 256] expresses it thus:

> Here the most fateful split and transformation in the emotional powerhouse occurs, a split between potential human glory and potential total destruction. For here the child becomes forever divided in himself. The instinct fragments which before had enhanced the growth of his infantile body and mind now become divided into an infantile set which perpetuates the exuberance of growth potentials, and a parental set which supports and increases self-observation, self-guidance and self-punishment.

Through imagination, the child appeases and allays some of the conflicts which arise between these two parts of himself, the part which desires and the part which controls (the conscience). When his conscience punishes him too severely with guilt, he can ease the load through imagination. Not only does expression through some creative medium make him feel better; it is a way of solving problems. Imagination is also a powerful means of pushing aggressively out into the world and incorporating some of it into himself.

If life's problems are solved satisfactorily during the years when imagination predominates, then a residue of imaginative activity and a resource of initiative remain, to enliven, sparkle, inspire, and push throughout the rest of life. Such a person will get fresh ideas and will not be afraid to experiment with them. Even though he has attained objectivity, his thinking and feeling will be so flexible that he will be able to take off on flights of imagination. Both creativity and true recreation have their roots in imaginative play.

Imagination as a Part of Intellectual Development

In its simplest form, imagining consists of representing some part of outer reality by an inner image. Without the ability to use images as representations, man would forever stay in the sensorimotor stage of intellectual development. The first indications of imitative and imaginative play occur in babies during the final period of the sensorimotor stage, when the child imitates his own past actions in very simple, concrete ways. Thus he shows that he has mental images of these actions. For instance, he pretends to go to sleep, curling up in the doll bed or on a pillow, shutting his eyes momentarily. He pretends to eat, perhaps taking a real lick of sand or other make-believe food. He imitates the actions of others, especially his mother. He hugs and loves dolls and soft animals, feeds them, washes them, and puts them to bed. He uses objects imaginatively in order to extend the meaning of newly acquired words, as did 22-months-old Richard [7]. After being told that nodding the head means *yes*, he nodded his own head, saying "Yes, yes, boy." Next he waved his cup up and down, saying, "Yes, yes, cup." Then he did the same with his bowl and fork.

Piaget [43] shows how symbolic games contribute to development during the preconceptual period. The transition from the sensorimotor period to preconceptual is marked by using symbolic patterns with new objects. Jacqueline, having pretended to sleep and pretended to cry, made her toys sleep and cry. Later she pretended to play with a cousin (who was not there) and then to be the cousin. Symbolic play represents experiences the child has had and the meaning that they have for him. It also can be what the child wants life to be. Egocentric, the child becomes submerged in action, loses awareness of himself as separate from the play, and lives in the role that he is dramatizing. The very act of living in that other role, however, leads him away from egocentrism, because it lets him see and feel how it is to be that other person or dog or airplane. As mental growth continues through the preconceptual stage, through symbolic play as well as other experiences, egocentrism gives way to objectivity. Piaget calls imaginative play "the purest form of egocentric and symbolic thought" [42, p. 127]. Symbols, he says, are needed as long as egocentric action prevails, since ready-made language is inadequate for the child's purposes. Language, being the product of society, cannot express all the experience and needs of the individual child, nor can the child master the language enough to serve him very flexibly.

Types of Imaginative Play

The major forms of imaginative expression in early childhood are discussed in this section. Anyone who works with young children needs to know a great deal about the development and guidance of imagination. The following comments are intended only as an introduction to the topic.

Fantasy. Everyone does some thinking which is undirected, free, somewhat symbolic, and difficult or impossible to put into words. Fantasy serves pleasure rather than being directed toward reality or practical issues. Even so, it often produces solutions to problems. Sometimes it is called daydreaming. Fantasy, imaginative thinking, and symbolic thinking all refer essentially to this kind of behavior. Since people engaging in fantasy are not paying attention to the lesson that may be in progress, teachers have traditionally looked upon daydreaming with disfavor. Research in children's thinking shows, however, that fantasy has an essential role to play. Through her studies on imagination in Australian and English children, Griffiths [23] came to see fantasy and symbolic thinking as useful and adaptive ways of coping with life's problems. Instead of being a waste of time, a blank, or a pursuit of pleasure, imagination is a way of dealing with reality which is particularly appropriate for the young child. He can, of course, direct his thoughts to a limited extent, but this free-reining, personal, inner method of symbolic play is his natural medium of action. He makes objective contact with reality and then employs fantasy [23, p. 174].

> Like those simple animalculae that stretch out long pseudopodia into surrounding water in search of food, retiring afterward into a state of apparent passivity while digestion takes place, so does the child seek experience, and, having come into contact with reality in some form, retires within himself to understand and consolidate what he has acquired. He cannot tackle a problem all at once, immediately, even such problems as seem insignificant to us. This is surely the meaning of childhood; time is needed for adaptation.

Griffiths conducted a series of 20 interviews with each of 50 5-year-olds in situations where the child played freely with drawing materials and was encouraged to say anything he wished. Ink blots and an imagery test were used in addition to the recording of what the child said. For the first few days, comments were controlled and reality-adapted. After three or four days, nearly all children revealed evidence of fantasy. At first, items appeared scattered and chaotic in arrangement, but gradually the elements were linked, themes emerged, and the whole content became complex and closely knit. The whole was not static, but constantly developing in relation to the child's problems and experiences [23, pp. 14–31]. Through fantasy, the child moved from a personal, subjective and egocentric point of view to a more socialized and objective attitude. In order to illustrate this process, there follows a rather long, repetitive account from Griffiths [23, pp. 175–177] of stories told by Dick, reflecting on the subject of possessions and the best ways of coming to own the things that he wants. The repetitive nature of this account demonstrates the ways in which fantasy operates, working over and over ideas, varying them, returning to a theme, adapting it, and moving on to a solution of the problem.

First phase: Theft
1. (Third day of the work.) "There was an old man and he had some greengages. And there was a great big giant, and he came and pinched all these greengages, and went away to his house. And this man he went to his house too."
2. (Also on third day.) "And once upon a time there was a lady and she had some eggs. And she was eating these eggs, and an old man came along, and he saw her eating them, so he went up to her and pinched 'em all."
3. (Fifth day.) "Once upon a time there was a burglar and he stole something. And so the copper saw him and this copper took him to prison. He stole a watch and the man was hitting him."

The three stories just given represent what may be called the first phase. At first there is the idea of theft successfully carried out. In the third story two days later he is doubtful already of the advisability of the method, for in spite of extenuating circumstances a thief is punished. He hastens to the next phase.

Second phase: Goods purchased
4. (Also on fifth day.) "Once there was a lady and she had some eggs, and a man came down the street, and *he* wanted some. So he went to the stall where the lady bought hers, and he got some and he ate 'em all up."
5. "Some old man had some greengages, and he ate 'em all up, and he said, 'They're good. I think I'll go and buy some more.'"
6. (Sixth day.) "Once upon a time there was a lady running down the street with some apples, and a man wanted some too. And so he asked the lady where she bought 'em. And so *he* went and bought some."
7. (Eighth day.) "Once upon a time there was a lady and a man. So this man he had some apples, and so this lady wanted some. And she asked him where he got his apples so he said out of his garden, and but he didn't. And then the lady found out, and she went to the stall where he bought 'em, and she found out that he was telling lies."

This is the end of the second phase in which the desired article is purchased. In the last story it is interesting to note the emergence of the "garden" idea, anticipating the next phase.

Third phase: Fruit is grown from seeds
8. (Ninth day.) "Once upon a time there was a lady, and she was running down the street, and she had some apples and a man saw them, and so he wanted some. So he planted some apple seeds, and some apples grew."

Creative Language. Stories and poems are imaginative in both the giving and receiving. Symbolism and beauty can be noted in the form as well as the content. Teachers of young children, and sometimes parents, regard their telling of poems and stories as creative activity. Although there is no definite proof that listening and perhaps writing down the story encourage the child to further expression, adults who work with preschool children generally believe that this is so. Rhythm and imagery are apparent in this moon song, chanted and enjoyed by Ellen at 2½.

> Crescent, crescent, crescent, crescent,
> Crescent goes to sleep, crescent wakes up.
> Ballie, ballie, ballie, ballie,
> Ballie goes to sleep, ballie wakes up.

Sometimes one story will reveal progress in solution of emotional problems. Four-year-old Susan used the following tale with which to struggle symbolically with confusion, fear, good and bad:

> Once Susan was in a theater seeing a grown-up movie. The lady who was giving the movie said, "Our magic fairy who is asleep will have to come out." And so the magic fairy woke up and came out. She chased everybody down the stairs and made everybody dance down the stairs. She chased me down the stairs. When we went out, she spoke to each person as they went out the door and I do not know what she said to the other people, but she said this to me, "You did dance down the stairs but you did not like it." She said that she'd go back in the building and for me to stay there.
> She chased me in front of the first car parked outside the theater. Then I started to run up across the bridge as quietly as I could. Then I just had time to sneak into a house and hide. When the good fairy came up, pat-a-pat, pat-a-pat, making a funny pat-a-pat, pat-a-pat, pat-a-pat noise. So I just had time to sneak up into my own house on Giles St. and lock the door when the good fairy came up and went ding-dong, ding-dong on my door bell. I would not open it or Mummy or Daddy or my sister, so the fairy could not get in.
> Then the fairy went up and down, flying on top of my roof, for she thought that my house would burn down if she did. But it did not. There was a good fairy inside my house. And she, the good fairy, would not let my house burn down, for she took away the bad fairy's wand, and would not return it. So the bad fairy died, because fairies die when their wands are taken away. And so that was the end of the bad fairy and we all lived happily ever after.

Often the expression of fears and problems helps to minimize them. Adults know how much it helps to talk to a friend about a bad experience, past or anticipated. Young children often do not know exactly what is bothering them, or if they do, they cannot express it straightforwardly. To express it in a story or poem or in another artistic medium can relieve tension, clarify the trouble, and help the youngster to find solutions.

Sometimes hostility shows through the symbols, even when the comment is understood by all to be imaginary and not a real threat. This 5-year-old shows a certain flair for creative imagery, violent as his product is:

I'll push you out the window and you'll make a mess on the pavement and my Daddy will scrape you up with a knife and spread you on bread and eat you. Then he'll vomit you up.

A large number of stories, collected from preschool children, contributed to a study of fantasy [19]. Age trends showed increasing length, complexity, and expansion, along with increasing use of fantasy. A 2-year-old boy's story was: "Tractor fall down boom. Fall right down and bust his head off. And he run, run, run" [19, p. 31]. A typical story by 5-year-olds took from half a page to a page.

Sex differences were revealed. Boys seemed to be more intrusive and active and to use more themes of aggression, greater variety of characters, more objects of transportation, objects of nature, and other objects. Girls' stories were more intensive, detailed, involved with feeling, people, the domestic, the here and now. Compare the story of the 2-year-old boy (above) with the following one from a 2-year-old girl: "Once upon a time there was a little girl and she hurt herself. And her mommy came here and she kissed her and made her better" [19, p. 39].

Symbolism. The child's fears and problems are often symbolized by the toys he chooses and by the content of his imaginative games. Discovering an analogy between two objects and situations, he invests one as a symbol for the other. The story of 5-year-old Joyce illustrates this process [23, pp. 141–148]. Joyce and Dorothy were sisters whose father had died two years earlier. More recently, two neighbor children had died, one of them being their playmate, Dorothy L. Joyce sometimes went on errands for Dorothy L.'s mother, who called Joyce "my little girl" and sometimes acted as though Joyce had taken Dorothy's L.'s place. Joyce was rivalrous with her sister Dorothy, a delicate child who received fussing and petting from their parents. Joyce had a china doll which was to her a little girl, and, after Dorothy L.'s death, a dead little girl. When telling the thoughts that came into her mind during a series of play interviews, Joyce disclosed that Dorothy L.'s mother had allowed her to see the dead child in her coffin, where "she was like a china doll." Shortly after this time, sister Dorothy became ill and had to go to the hospital. At this point, her daddy and Dorothy L. disappeared from Joyce's dreams and conversation. She became afraid of her china doll. Instead of taking it to bed with her, she put it on a chair. Waking in the night, she wanted to take the doll into bed, but was afraid that a mouse might get her. "They might get my dolly and get her eyes out with their claws."

Thus Joyce pushed away the reality of her father's death and her sister's frightening disappearance, centering her fears upon an object, the doll, which she used to symbolize all these disturbing occurrences. The doll had formerly been a comforting object. She was still dealing with that object in the daytime, although not at night, when fears were most oppressive. Perhaps she was hanging onto the possibility of getting control of the whole terrifying situation through the doll, which served as such a powerful symbol.

Summarizing the functions of symbolic thinking or fantasy in the life of the child, Griffiths [23, p. 187] makes several points: Fantasy is the normal means of problem solving. Problems are attacked indirectly, often symbolically. The child is only vaguely aware of what he is trying to do. The problem is solved piecemeal, through a series of solutions. The process results in both acquisition of information and a change of attitude. The change of attitude is from personal and egocentric toward socialized and objective.

162 Preschool Children

Dramatic Play

Dramatic play, or pretending, is a kind of symbolism. A child can pretend by himself, on a very simple level, as does the toddler who pretends to eat and sleep. Or a child can carry on dramatic play with other children. The make-believe play of children under age 3 is largely personification, such as talking to dolls and other objects, imitative use of objects such as drinking cups, and taking part in such situations as washing clothes. Between 3 and 5, children become more active with materials and engage in more frequent, longer, and more complex imaginative games.

Sociodramatic Play. The Israeli effort to educate disadvantaged children has led to research on play. Sara Smilansky's analysis of play clarifies its role in normal development [48]. Sociodramatic play is, as its name implies, both social and dramatic. It serves to promote and integrate young children's social, emotional, and intellectual growth. Smilansky [48, p. 9] gives six essential elements of sociodramatic play:

1. Imitative role play. The child expresses a make-believe role in imitative acts and/or words.
2. Make-believe with objects. Actions or words are substituted for objects.
3. Make-believe in substituting words for acts and situations.
4. Persistence in the episode for at least ten minutes.
5. Interaction of at least two participants.
6. Verbal communication about the play.

The first four elements occur in dramatic play. The addition of the last two are essential for sociodramatic play.

Smilansky has observed that until about 3, a child imitates small pieces of his parents' (and other significant adults') behavior, expressing his identification with them through dramatic play. Thus he irons as Mommy does or drives a tractor like Daddy. After 3, he begins to see that the thoughts, feelings, and actions he has been imitating are not merely single episodes but that they are also reactions to other people. Sociodramatic play is born of the understanding that people react to each other and interact with each other. He needs other children, for now he wants to imitate both actions and reactions. He wants to reproduce the world as he understands it [48, p. 71].

Sociodramatic play was the setting for 65 percent of the positive social reinforcement given by nursery school children to their peers, in the previously mentioned study [8]. Thus they interacted more in dramatic play than they did during involvement with art, music, table games, and such. In response to other children, children gave attention, approval, and submission. They were likely to initiate an exchange by offering affection, personal acceptance, and tokens. Dramatic play also facilitates the use of language, playful expression of anger and hostility, and the trying on of various roles.

By 4½ or 5 years, children who have had rich play experience can make use of a wide range of topics for sociodramatic play. Going beyond home and family, even beyond store and post office, they may explore the moon in an episode that lasts for several days. Astronauts build with large blocks, packing cases, and planks. They store food and drink. They launch, fly, and land. The following half-hour incident illustrates sociodramatic play with a strong adventure theme:

Bill and Grant were digging with shovels in the dirt in a far corner of the yard. They piled the dirt in a mound against the fence. Both looked excited. Grant said, "We'll have a pile way up to the sky." Bill asked, "How long will it take to get down to the bottom?" Grant replied, "All night and all day and all night."

Bill accepted the answer without comment. Another boy came over to watch the digging. Bill exclaimed in a high voice, "We smell a *bad* bear and a *good* bear here. So it's very *dangerous*. We're going to find the bears in China. I sleep with the bears at night. I lock them in a cage tight. Then I turn out the light."

Bill and Grant went into the building and came out with a small bottle of water. They poured it on the roots which had been exposed by the digging. "Put the poison on my roots, too" Bill told Grant. "Kill them all."

The teacher told the boys it was time for milk. Sitting on the bench in the coat room, Bill leaned towards Kit and told him earnestly, "The *good* bears and the *bad* bears both know me, but only the good bears know you, cause I've known 'em longer than you have. And do you know what happened one night? A *bad* bear visited me [51]."

An incident is rarely a pure example of one kind of play or another. In this bit of play, Bill and Grant practice the coordinations of digging, try on the roles of explorers going to China, and explore the nature of bears and feelings toward bears. Bill seems to be getting the upper hand of a fear of bears, or perhaps of a less specific fear which he has chosen bears to symbolize. The power of imagination makes water into poison, and the little boys can use that poison to kill roots. Probably the roots symbolized a fear or a threat.

Imaginary Playmates

Imaginary companions of preschool children have long intrigued students of behavior. A frequent production of children in the stage of developing imagination and initiative, imaginary playmates can be human or animal, fleeting or long-enduring, single or multiple, ideals or scapegoats. Studies report a fourth to a third of children as having imaginary companions. The children who create these playmates come in as great a variety as the imaginary creatures themselves, strongly suggesting that the creations serve the needs of the children. Bright children are somewhat more likely to have imaginary companions (or to tell about them) than are children of below average intelligence. Girls are more prone than boys to create their own playmates [28, pp. 394–397]. A study of college students who had had imaginary companions in childhood showed them to have tendencies toward higher than average grades and toward cooperation, friendships, and the experiencing of strong feelings and emotions [16]. Among creative adolescents, producers in literary fields reported more imaginary companions in childhood [45].

Humor

Humor is an intellectual process which reduces anxiety. Developmentally, the first joke is the game of peek a boo, which dramatizes the baby's anxiety over his mother's disappearance, then presumably reduces his tension. Joking makes psychological pain bearable, expresses fears and wishes which cannot be faced directly, and gratifies forbidden desires. One of man's most creative achievements, humor partakes of both language and gesture, with emphasis on gesture during the preschool period. Humor depends on flexibility of thought, which the preschool child possesses to a very limited extent. The punch line, so important to adult jokes, is beyond his cognitive powers. Therefore, his amusements and his attempts to be funny are not amusing but seem silly to an adult. He may actually be funny in the simplicity of his jokes. Although incongruity and surprise are of the essence of grown-up jokes, a certain subtlety is usually necessary for adults. Furthermore, preschool humor is too far removed from adult problems to be tension-reducing to adults. Incongruity takes precedence over surprise in preschool humor, although surprise can add to the fun.

Falling down is often hilarious, since it includes both aspects of the joke. The person suddenly gets into the wrong position, in the wrong relationship to the floor. A fillip is added by the involvement of the whole body in the situation. Language jokes tend to be in the form of calling objects or events by inappropriate names, especially forbidden words, such as bathroom terms. Long, rambling (pointless to adults) stories may be offered and accepted as jokes, since the surprise element is not essential. These lengthy tales often concern creatures falling down, falling apart and growing together again, getting lost and found, hurt and well, having toilet accidents or performing deliberate excretions. Underlying young children's jokes are their envy of adult size, power, and privileges, worries over the wholeness and safety of their bodies, resentment of adult control in the face of their own autonomy strivings, aggressive impulses which frighten them.

Music and Dance

Creativity exists both in performance and in enjoying the music and dancing of others. In these areas, as in other parts of the preschool child's experience, exploration is vital. A rich environment offers opportunities to experiment with sound and gesture and with putting them together. Infants enjoy and respond to songs. By age 2, the child who has had some experience with singing will listen to others and will sing spontaneously as he plays. He likes action songs, in which he responds to words with gestures. He joins in with a few words as others sing. His first efforts to sing with a group will probably not be well coordinated, but they soon lead to his being able to follow along with others' singing. Soon he recognizes and asks for certain songs and recognizes various pieces of music [33, pp. 361–365]. Creative expression flows when the few necessary facilities are present—a chance to listen; a chance to sing; the simplest of instruments to play (some can be made from scrap materials [40, p. 13]); a group with whom to play, sing, and dance; experience to play, sing, and dance about. In a simpler society, a child can grow into the music and dance of his parents, watching, imitating, being taken through the motions, and joining in adult dances and music groups when he is sufficiently grown up. In complex western culture, it often takes an adult with special skill and understanding to appreciate and facilitate the young child's creations in music and dance. Such a teacher develops the cognitive processes basic to the child's understanding and appreciation, as well as the feeling aspects [2, pp. 20–27]. As one student of the dance has said, "A child cheerfully undertakes a multiple career as singer, instrumentalist, actor, and dancer. In what we call 'play', he dramatizes poetry and makes it blood-brother to song" [37, p. 5].

In the machine age many children see little of rhythmic muscular activity which seems to them worth imitating. In contrast, primitive children experience the rhythms of weaving, grinding, and chopping. In a preschool day camp dancing grew out of the small happenings of every day: a Moon Time Dance when the children noticed the moon in the daytime sky, The Sunflower Dance, created by a 4-year-old and 2-year-old who found sunflowers, The Chocolate Sellers, dances of

Mollie Smart

fears, of wonder of God, of cooking [15]. The teacher found that the higher the emotional content in the thought expressed, the more the child seemed to need rhythmic action to express it. With young children, there was rarely dancing without singing or rhythmic language.

With music, as well as dance, young children have potentiality for expression and enjoyment, perhaps even more than that of the average adult. It has been shown that music produces an emotional response in people and a more pronounced response in children than in adults, as measured by the galvanic skin response [57].

Creative Materials

The same statement could be made of young children's expression through *paint*, *clay*, *blocks*, and other materials. These media offer the same types of benefits that the child gets from fantasy, dramatic play, and creative language—increased understanding of the world and his relation to it, expression and understanding of his questions and problems, release of emotional tension, satisfaction from creating beauty and order. In fact, some of the most creative programs for children encourage the use of all forms of artistic expression and enjoyment in relation with one another [50]. Emotionally disturbed children indicate in their artistic expression some of their malaise. Psychology students and professors, with no previous training in understanding children's art, were able to do significantly better than chance in matching paintings to personality descriptions [49]. The judges also separated the paintings of disturbed children from those of normal children. Since the judges could not tell how they did it, the investigators suggest an unidentified intuitive process at work.

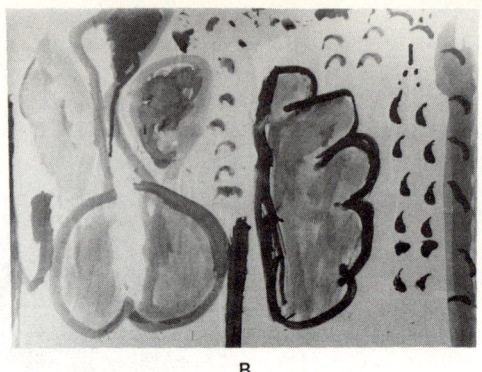

Figure 3–1. Development of graphic representation.
A. Scribble
B. Design
C. Pictorial, using circles and rectangles
D. Pictorial

Figure 3–2 (opposite page). Development of representation of human form between the ages of three and seven years.

Series by Ellen S. Smart

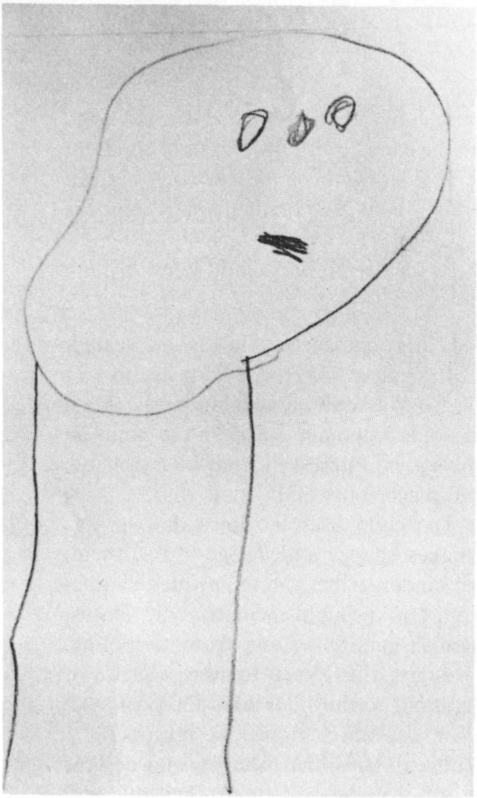

A

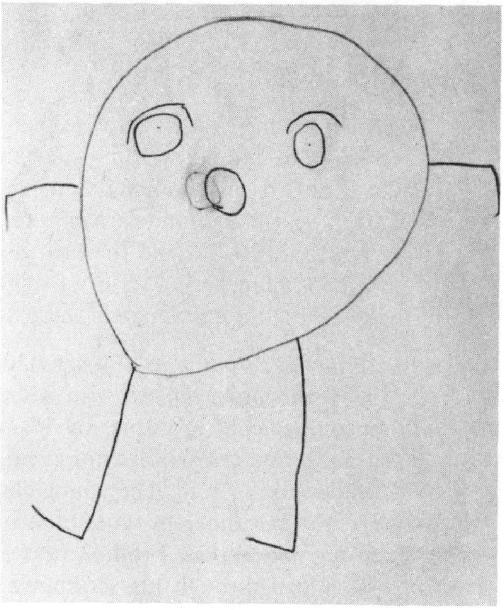

B

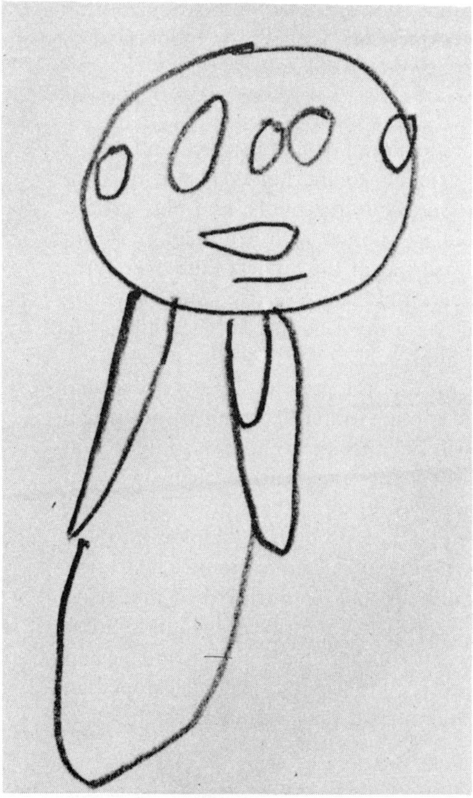

C

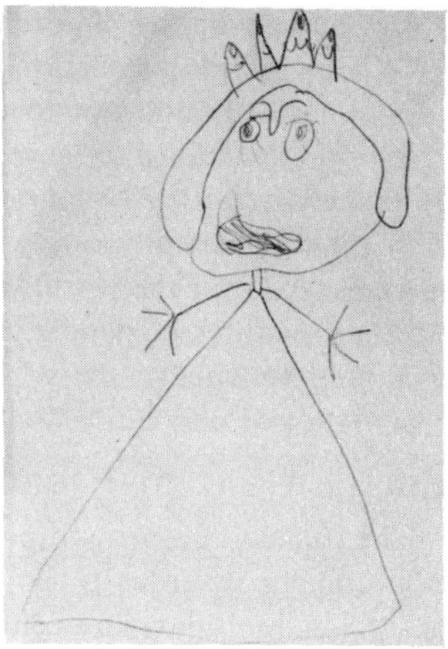

D

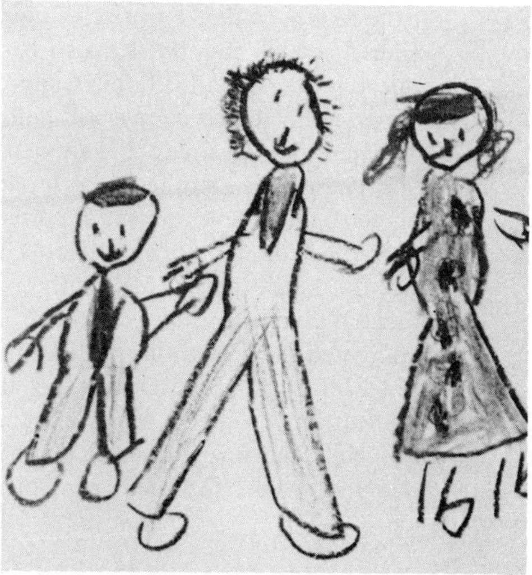

E

When a child first encounters paint, clay, or any other new material, he has to explore it, to find out what it is like and what he can do with it. (Not only children. Watch an African graduate student in the first snowfall of the North American winter!) Set-up and limits are important here—"paint goes on the paper," "blocks are not to throw," "hold the saw this way."

In the graphic arts, a series of stages can be identified. Each child goes through these stages at approximately these ages:

1. *Scribbling, from 1 to 3 years.* During the first quarter of the second year, a baby will make marks with a crayon on a paper, after a demonstration or encouragement to do so. By 18 months, he will scribble spontaneously. Even if paper and crayons are not given, 2-year-olds will make marks in the sand, on a sidewalk, or wall. The young child shows great interest in what he has made. He tries out different types of strokes and placements [32].
2. *Shape and design.* From 2 to 5 years. The child uses the lines that he has developed through his scribbling and makes shapes and designs from them. Even though he cannot write, the average kindergartner can tell printed characters from scribbling [18]. In a kindergarten of high socioeconomic status, 75 percent of the children could distinguish cursive writing from scribbling. When children are making shapes and designs, they do so for the pleasure of making them and not to represent something. A child develops his own style and preferences while discovering how to make more complex designs.
3. *Pictorial, from age 4 onward.* Now the child uses his lines, shapes, and designs to represent reality. Drawings of people are usually the first recognizable pictures. All over the world, children make their early drawings in the same ways. Their pictures of people, houses, trees, suns, boats, trains, and cars give little hint as to whether the young artists were American, Scottish, or Indonesian.

Enrichment of Preschool Life

The tremendous growth potential of young children demands a rich and varied environment in order to be realized. Supplements to the home, in the form of nursery school, day-care centers, kindergartens, church schools, and play groups provide places where children can reach out to interact with a nurturant world. Although the kibbutzim of Israel and the yasli-sad of the Soviets take over some of the functions that American families reserve for themselves, schools for young children in this country are also based on the idea of adding to the child's life opportunities which his family cannot give him.

Even today, many people still hold the view that the preschool years are a time when the child "just plays," waiting to be old enough to start learning lessons which really count. Even mothers who spontaneously enhance their children's intellectual and personality development are often surprised when they learn of their own vital influence. Although nursery schools have been operating in the United States ever since 1921, the public has neither understood nor promoted their educational potential. Suddenly, however, the problems of poverty and educational deprivation highlighted the growth possibilities that exist in all children during their first years of life. Infancy and preschool years are seen as the time to prevent mental retardation, learning problems, school failure, poor self concept, inadequate language and antisocial tendencies. Special compensatory programs have been developed in attempts to meet the needs of deprived children and their families. First, let us take a look at the traditional nursery school and then at some of the outstanding approaches to compensatory preschool education.

Traditional Nursery Education

The preschool child is treated as a whole person who grows through differentiation and integration of body, personality, and intellect. Provisions for play, health, and growth are carefully planned and maintained. Social growth is promoted by arrangements which facilitate cooperative play, and guidance which gives insight into motivations and feelings of oneself and others. Equipment and program are attuned to the stages of personality growth which dominate the preschool years.

Building the Sense of Autonomy. The miniature world, which strikes the casual visitor as so cute, is child-sized in order that the child can *do the utmost for himself*. He hangs his snowsuit on the hook that is just the right height; his feet touch the floor when he sits on the toilet. The child-sized world is arranged in such a way that its occupants can *make many decisions for themselves*, decisions which turn out to be right. A child selects a puzzle from the puzzle rack and puts it back before he takes another. An easel with fresh paper, paints, and brushes invites him to paint, standing on a floor protector which keeps a spill from being a disaster. The housekeeping corner is full of equipment which children can manage—doll clothes with wide armholes and big buttons, a low bed in which children can snuggle with dolls, a sturdy, stable ironing board with small iron, unbreakable dishes and a place to wash them, grown-up purses, shoes, and hats, for easy dressing up.

The teachers appreciate what it means to young children to be independent successfully, to make decisions that turn out well and to feel worthwhile in what they do. In addition to encouraging and facilitating such behavior, teachers also know what not to do, never to use shaming as a way of controlling behavior, never at any age, but especially at this time of life, since doubt and shame undermine the growth of autonomy. Neither is competition used as an incentive, since it too would threaten the child's growing sense of autonomy.

Discipline in the nursery school is not quite the same as the discipline that many students and parents have known in their lives. It is easier to understand in terms of the sense of autonomy. The teacher sets limits on what the child may decide for himself and what he may do. She makes the limits clear and sticks to them firmly, giving him freedom within them. She does not say, "Wouldn't you like to come indoors now?" She says, "Now it's time to go indoors." She does not say, "Nice little boys don't grab toys from little girls." She says, "Jilly is using the doll carriage now, Tommy. You may have it when she is finished. Could you use the rocking bed now?" Thus a choice really is a choice and a direction is definite. The teacher understands that the children will often test the limits she sets, as part of their growing up. Because the child knows she respects and accepts him as a person, because he trusts her, he can usually accept the limits she sets for him. Because he likes her and wants to be like her, he often wants to do what he perceives she wants. Thus discipline in the nursery school is carefully planned and carried out in such ways that children can grow in autonomy through successful deciding and doing [44, pp. 222–247].

Building Initiative and Imagination. Motivational and intellectual aspects of growth are involved here, as this chapter and Chapter 1 have shown. The nursery school's stress on creative activities is one of its most vital ways of contributing to preschool growth. Not only is creativity valuable in itself now and in the future, but imagination is more than a supplement to controlled thought during the preschool years. The young child solves through imaginative processes many problems which he cannot handle by controlled thinking.

Setting him free within comfortable limits, the nursery school invites the child to reach out into his world, to explore it vigorously and curiously, to imagine himself in a multitude of roles, to create a variety of beauty. All of this magic is implicit in the combination of children, raw materials, space, some carefully chosen equipment, and teachers who love children and know a great deal about them. Dramatic play requires only a few simple props, but it needs a push at the right moment and hands off at other moments. The skillful teacher will suggest straightening the corner block before the whole post office tumbles down. She is quick to produce paper that will do for letters for the postman to carry. She suggests that Ronnie could be a customer at the stamp window after he has hung on the fringes unable to get into the game.

Managing paints, clay, paste, and such is so simple that first-time observers often see the teacher doing nothing. It takes real understanding of initiative and imagination, however, to let children create freely, often by keeping quiet and doing nothing. Teachers never "fix up" children's products. They accept them. They never draw models to be copied. They never tell children what to make with materials. They don't say, "What is it?" They listen to what the child spontaneously says about his creations. They show that they realize it meant something to him to do what he did.

Initiative and imagination are stimulated by books, stories, music, trips, pets, plants, and visitors with special messages for children. Such experiences provide ideas which are worked over in dramatic play and creative work with materials.

Perhaps it is in the area of initiative and imagination where the nursery school supplements the home most generously. What home can provide such a constant flow of fingerpaint and play dough? What mother can arrange for a group of peers for daily playmates or be on hand constantly to supervise dramatic play constructively? Or to play the piano for a group of elephants who turn into butterflies? Or to take children to see a hive of bees working behind glass? Or to arrange for her child to find out how a pipe organ works? Or to have his teeth cleaned with a group of his friends, attending the dental hygiene clinic after a child-oriented introduction?

Facilitating Intellectual Development. The tremendously rich environment of the nursery school offers never-ending opportunities for building mental structures. The child constantly perceives, integrates his perceptions, and integrates sensory experience with verbal. Toys and materials are readily available for handling in addition to looking, a condition which stimulates richness in thinking about objects [20]. Since most preschool children think preconceptually and intuitively, a nursery school curriculum is designed to give them problems which they are capable of solving. Through building with blocks they learn that two of these equal one of those and that a square can be divided into two triangles. Counting may result from figuring out how many blocks to bring from this shelf and how many from that, when blocks are kept sorted according to size and shape. Counting happens in many situations which have real meaning—two cookies for each child at snack time, time before lunch for singing three songs. How many children go home with

Peggy's mother? The workbench is a place for dealing with linear measure, roughly, of course, in terms of *longer* or *shorter than* or *about the same size as*. The sink is for learning about volume, if you are allowed to pour water back and forth instead of just washing your hands. Useful equipment includes containers graduated as to size and another series of similar size but different shapes. Clay, sand, and mud offer chances to experiment (loosely speaking, not scientifically) with size, shape, and volume. So do many other materials found in nursery schools offer opportunities for development of the schemas of cognition—pegs and pegboards, puzzles, shoes to lace, matching games, color sorting games, musical instruments, records, books.

Language is a vital part of the curriculum. The teacher is a model of clear, pleasantly toned, noncolloquial speech. Skilled in understanding baby talk, she replies in speech which the child comes to imitate. She encourages children to talk, to tell her and other children about their experiences and feelings. New words and concepts come from books, stories, songs, and the many planned new experiences of nursery school. The beautiful books and satisfying storytimes make children look forward eagerly to learning to read to themselves. Here is preparation for reading—good speech, something to talk about, a love of books. Here also is intellectual development taking place through language, when children communicate with others and acquire verbal symbols with which to think.

Concepts of *time* are part of preschool endeavors, even though young children do not handle chronology very objectively. Many of their comments and questions and much of their play shows efforts to straighten out their ideas of time and to understand how life changes. While children make barely a beginning in comprehending the historic past by 8 years of age preschool children are deeply concerned with the sweeping changes in life which have occurred with the passage of time. Before they are interested in or able to tell minutes by the clock, they hear about dinosaurs, horse and buggies, steam locomotives. Through play, conversation, and thought, children arrange these past events and phenomena into a very rough historical concept. In India we found that relatively uneducated people would often tell us, "It happened in ancient times," meaning that it happened before Independence. It could have occurred any time between 3000 B.C. and 1947. "Ancient times" is probably the way children think of the past before they have had the rigors of history lessons brought to bear upon them. The history lessons will be richer in meaning if they come after the past has content for the children, even though it is content without much chronology.

A review of research on teaching in the nursery school [47] yields considerable evidence that nursery school attendance promotes social, language, and intellectual growth. The quality of the nursery school seems to make a difference in whether such growth can be demonstrated. Gains are greatest in the children who start with the greatest room for improvement. Those from homes providing meager stimulation are likely to make the greatest intellectual gains.

Educational Deprivation

The culture of poverty includes restrictions which affect every member of the family in every aspect of life and development. By about 2 years of age, the child is missing more and more experiences basic to the type of intellectual growth required for participation in the mainstream of culture. Living in a crowded,

172 Preschool Children

noisy home, he learns to ignore sounds, since few of them have any relevance for him. When people speak to him, they speak in single words or in short sentences, often in commands. He may not discover that everything has a name. Lacking this powerful piece of knowledge, he does not seek out names, does not add to his vocabulary, and hence drops farther and farther behind the average child in thinking as well as in talking and understanding language. Nobody corrects his pronunciation, since the adults and older children articulate poorly. Inaccurate phonetically and grammatically, his speech is not easy for the teacher to understand when he goes to school. The child then has trouble understanding the teacher, because she talks in longer, more complicated sentences than he has heard, she sounds her words differently, she uses words he does not know, and she talks about things, places, and events which he has never experienced [29].

Slum homes, in contrast to middle-class homes, offer young children few toys and play materials. Deprived children may never have the visual and tactile stimulation which comes from play with color cones, blocks, nests of cubes, puzzles, paints, clay, crayons, and paper. They lack the emotional satisfactions of cuddly toys and the imaginative and social possibilities of dolls, housekeeping equipment, costumes, and transportation toys. Their motor development is not encouraged, as it would be through the use of climbing apparatus, tricycles, and large building materials. Nature is not seen as orderly, beautiful, and wondrous, since nature is hardly seen at all. Preschool children in slum areas rarely go more than a few blocks from home. A woman who grew up in a slum recalls that as a child, the only beauty she saw was in the sky.

Upon entering first grade, educationally deprived children are at a severe disadvantage in many ways, but most seriously in the main job of the beginner in school, learning to read. In contrast to children from more educated families, they are more personal and concrete, more dependent on action and context, and lacking in the skills of linguistic analysis and synthesis [6]. Disadvantaged children differ from middle-class children in what the teacher's words mean to them, in what they know about themselves. First grade is baffling to those who lack meaningful experiences with language and ideas, toys and places, people and other living things. Unable to cope with reading and other school activities, the educationally deprived child falls farther behind in second grade and still farther as he grows older [12, 13]. His IQ declines. Somewhere around third or fourth grade, he feels hopeless and defeated. Intellectually and educationally retarded, he is a serious problem to the school and to himself.

Many children live under conditions which deprive them of opportunities for normal intellectual development. The culture of poverty, according to various estimates, envelops 15 to 20 percent of the population [26]. While sharing a lack of education and inability to earn an adequate living, these people differ in ethnic subculture. It is estimated that the severely disadvantaged include about 20 million English-speaking Caucasians, 8 million Negroes, 2 million Spanish-Americans, 700,000 Puerto Ricans, and 500,000 American Indians. About 10.7 million children are poor. They are 15 percent of all children under 18 [9].

Compensatory Programs for Disadvantaged Children

In the early 1960s, Americans began to develop programs designed to promote normal intellectual growth in children of the very poor. Already the Israelis were tackling such problems with considerable success. The Oriental Jews who had migrated to Israel had a disproportionate number of children with low IQs, as compared with children of European Jews. When reared in the kibbutzim, the Oriental children's IQs equaled those of the Europeans. Americans also had the example of Maria Montessori, who created and directed a highly successful school for poor children in Rome, in 1907. After the United States government created Head Start, in 1965, programs multiplied and the public became interested. Many people's hopes were raised too high and they were disappointed when children were not transformed magically, promptly, permanently, and cheaply. Results to date show that good programs can improve the functioning of children and families, that intellectual factors are closely related with physical, social, sociological, and economic factors, and that brief, inexpensive programs are likely to make only temporary changes.

Basically, the nursery schools for deprived children are like the good nursery school described above, dedicated to providing opportunities for full development. Since the disadvantaged child must catch up with what he has missed, in addition to growing in the regular way, his preschool is necessarily adapted to his special needs. Therefore such schools lay particular stress on teaching verbal and perceptual skills, promoting the child's self concept and self-confidence, stimulating curiosity and building a need for achievement. These nursery schools, in contrast to those for normally advantaged children, usually structure their programs more, providing for a great deal of adult–child interaction. Some schools stress the learning of perceptual, conceptual, and verbal skills, paying little or no attention to social and emotional development. The Bereiter and Engelman [3] approach is probably the most famous of such programs. Using tangible rewards and punishments, with verbal drills, learning of rules and application of rules, Bereiter–Engelman programs have produced substantial IQ gains, such as an average gain of 14 points in the first year [30]. Gains tend to continue when the program is continued into the early grades, and academic success is usual. A language tutoring program for 3- and 4-year-olds produced substantial (14.5 in one group, 7 in another) average IQ rises plus enthusiasm for learning and excitement over mastery [4].

Contrasting with programs built on drills, rewards, and punishments is Smilansky's approach to treating deprivation through sociodramatic play [48]. Advantaged Israeli children were found to differ greatly from disadvantaged in terms of their use of play, analyzed by the six criteria presented on page 162. After diagnosing the play level of the children, they were given meaningful experiences which could serve as themes for play; a clinic, a grocery store, and a story. Visits, conversations, observations, toys, and materials were appropriately supplied. Teachers first tried to stimulate sociodramatic play without entering in and then took active part in the play. Children's play improved greatly under these conditions. Meaningful experiences and materials without teacher intervention were not enough, but teacher intervention alone was of some help. Achievement in sociodramatic play was not related to IQ, although minimal normal intelligence seems to be required. Girls made more progress in play than did boys. Although the disadvantaged children remained below the verbal level of the advantaged control group, there was improvement in verbal patterns during the experiment.

Several studies have compared results from two or more types of programs [14, 41, 56]. *Concept training* and *discovery* were used with 2-year-old black boys, half of them lower class and half middle class [41]. In each of the experimental conditions, the child was alone with an instructor for two one-hour periods a week, over eight months. In the concept-training condition, the teacher demonstrated and labeled a concept, such as *on top of, under, rough, smooth, wet, dry*. Then the child performed an act related to the concept and the teacher labeled it, the child demonstrated an instance of the concept and the child used the label correctly. In the discovery condition, the child freely used the same materials that were presented to the concept-training group, and the instructor played with him as though they were in a regular nursery school, letting the child take the initiative. After the eight-month period, both experimental groups were superior to controls on tests. A year later the experimental groups were still superior to controls. Differences between the two experimental groups favored the concept-training group after the eight months' experimental period, but favored the discovery group a year later. Apparently both methods were beneficial, with discovery having more lasting effects. The investigators suggest that the main reasons for success were an early beginning and a systematic, uninterrupted relationship between teacher and child over a period of time.

The more comprehensive programs such as the Early Training Project at Peabody College [22] and the Perry Preschool Project [55] in Ypsilanti have also produced dramatic gains in IQ. There is evidence that any good preschool program produces some rise in IQ. In fact, IQs tend to go up during the first year after school entrance [22]. The important question is whether IQ gains can be *maintained*, and if so, under what circumstances. The Early Training Project report shows that the experimental groups have maintained their superiority over the control groups for three years after the end of the intervention program. Although all groups showed some decline in Stanford–Binet IQ between first and fourth grade, the groups paralleled each other. Therefore, while the school, or perhaps the general culture of poverty, exerted a depressing effect, the gains made by the children in the project were not lost. Tests of school achievement also showed the experimental group to be superior, but the differences between experimental and control groups decreased as the children moved up through the grades. By fourth grade there was a small but nonsignificant difference.

The other results of the Early Training Project are also important, since raising IQs and inducing academic achievement are only fragments of the massive help needed by the very poor. The intervention began as a summer preschool, followed by a year-round program of weekly home visits by a teacher who worked with the child and the mother. The children in this group had three summers of nursery school, and three winters of teacher visits. Another group had two years of summer school and teacher visits for the remainder of the time. By having one control group in the same community and another in a town 60 miles away, the investigators were able to measure the diffusion of the intervention program to relatives and friends of the families in the program. They found solid evidence of diffusion to relatives and friends and also to children in the same family, especially to younger siblings close to the ages of the children in the program. Younger siblings of experimental children tested significantly higher over a two-year period than did younger siblings of control children. It seems reasonable that changes made in the mother benefited the younger siblings as well as the children to whom the program was directed. It is also reasonable that one way of maintaining IQ gains is to involve mothers in the educational process. When mothers learn how to teach their children and when they experience the rewards from it, then they are likely to exert steady and lasting influence on their children's intellectual development. In fact, when children had no nursery school, educated, involved mothers had a greater stimulating effect than similar mothers did on children who were attending preschools [21].

Another important finding from several preschool programs is that greater gains were shown in the programs that started at younger preschool ages. For example, in the Perry Preschool Project study which showed very large gains, the 3-year-olds gained an average of 27.5 to 30.2 IQ points, while the 4-year-olds gained 17.6 to 24.4 [56]. Initial ability is another condition related to gain. The greatest gains tend to be made by children with moderate or slight retardation, whose IQs are in the high 70s and low 80s [21]. The Perry Preschool children were in this IQ range.

Benefits from intervention programs do not always show up immediately. The first group in the Perry Preschool project did not test significantly higher than their control group at the end of kindergarten, but at the end of first grade, they were superior on reading tests and other achievement tests [55]. Likewise, in the Early Training Project, achievement scores of experimental children were more superior to those of controls at the end of the second grade than they were at the end of the first grade.

It is unfortunate that the results of intervention programs are measured so often in terms of IQ points and achievement test scores and so seldom in relation to other important benefits, such as the delight a child shows in mastery of problems, the social adjustment which has been characteristic of the Perry children who gained in IQ, the vision screening, medical and dental examinations and resulting treatments given to 90 percent of Head Start children [36], and the changes in life style among families in the Early Training Project "from the status of environmental victims to people who are beginning to develop environmental mastery." [38].

When it became apparent that an early start and parent participation were important in helping disadvantaged children, before-and-after programs were initiated and attempts were made to find new ways of working with children and parents. Parent and Child Centers [31] were started in order to reach children under 3. Follow Through was begun in order to maintain gains made by preschool programs. A television program, "Sesame Street," was designed for disadvantaged preschool children, offering them daily, repeated opportunities to learn language and concepts in a setting of kindness, human dignity, and fun [34]. The potential audience of "Sesame Street" was 12 million children between 3 and 5 years. During the first two weeks of the program, it was estimated that 6 million children watched it. Later, a study of one area found 90 percent of children between 3 and 5, not in day-care centers, watched the program [11]. Viewers have shown substantial gains in learning letters, numbers, sorting, and problem solving. At the beginning of the second year of "Sesame Street," studies showed that children who had watched the program had made greater gains in learning than those who had not watched [24]. The more time they had spent watching the show, the more they had gained. Effects were noted among urban and rural, rich and poor, English-speaking and non English-speaking. Unfortunately, however, many children in poor neighborhoods were not seeing "Sesame Street." Opportunities for viewing "Sesame Street" are to be extended in the United States and offered in at least 50 other countries.

Although the recent increase in day-care centers is motivated by commercial interests as well as by interest in benefiting children, well-run programs can be very valuable to children and families. A good program includes the educational opportunities of a nursery school plus physical care, nutrition, and parent involvement.

Summary

Play, the main occupation of the young child, is his mode of learning new patterns of thought, feeling and action and of integrating them. While sensorimotor play persists throughout life, social and imaginative play become increasingly influential upon the preschool child's develoment. Play is its own reward. It enhances all of life.

Early social play involves exploration of other children as objects and as persons. Parallel play, typical of 2-year-olds, means engaging in the same activity with little interaction other than watching and imitating. Interactions between young children are temporary and fleeting, increasing as children mature. The earliest group play is loosely structured, permitting children to shift in and out of the activity easily. Sympathetic and cooperative behavior occur in young children. Leadership involves opening possibilities for activities to others and integrating their play. Children vary considerably in the degree to which they can and will fit in with the play of others. Quarrels are common when conflicts occur, but most quarrels are settled rather simply, with little aftermath. As children grow older, they tend to quarrel less frequently but more aggressively. Positive, friendly behavior increases with age, occurring very often in well-liked children. Reinforcement of positive social behavior is effective. Immature children are likely to elicit aggression from children the same age who are more mature.

Imagination, the key to preschool personality development, complements controlled thinking. Through mental images, the child represents experiences and objects to himself. He invents symbols to stand for the images and uses those symbols in his thinking. As he acquires language, he is able to think more and more with the words which his culture gives him as representatives of experiences and objects. In imagination, however, he continues to use some of his own private symbols, and to invent more for his own purposes, in fantasy, symbolic thinking, and dreams. Other forms of imaginative expression include dramatic play, in which human relationships and roles are explored, creative language, which produces stories and poems and humor, which reduces anxiety. Sex differences are apparent in the stories children tell. Young children perform and enjoy in all fields of art, music, dance, painting and sculpture. With all art media, such as paint, clay, and blocks, children develop through an orderly sequence of stages. Children use all forms of imagination in solving problems and in expressing their thoughts and feelings.

Schools for young children supplement homes by providing constructive play opportunities. An excellent nursery school (preschool) offers an environment in which the sense of autonomy and the sense of initiative are nurtured. Guidance and discipline provide limits within which the child can make successful decisions and free choices. Intellectual development is promoted through a rich variety of sensory experiences, available in contexts which lead to conceptualization. The learning of language is encouraged. Preschools have a special contribution to make to culturally disadvantaged children, who are going to school in increasing numbers. Enrichment programs have been successful in raising IQ, improving language, concepts, self concepts, self-confidence, and curiosity, and in preventing progressive retardation in the elementary school. The preschool must work with the family, as well as the child, if the child is to gain maximum benefit from his school.

Federal projects in preschool education, day care, health and family welfare are based on the conviction that the preschool years offer the most promising opportunities for breaking the cycle of poverty. These projects emphasize the promotion of normal, healthy growth before drastic remedial measures become necessary.

References

1. Almy, M. Spontaneous play: An avenue for intellectual development. *Young Children*, 1967, **22**, 265–277.
2. Aronoff, F. W. *Music and young children.* New York: Holt, Rinehart and Winston, 1969.
3. Bereiter, C., & Engelmann, S. *Teaching disadvantaged children in the preschool.* Englewood Cliffs, N.J.: Prentice-Hall, 1966.
4. Blank, M., & Solomon, F. A tutorial language program to develop abstract thinking in socially disadvantaged preschool children. *Child Devel.*, 1968, **39**, 379–389.
5. Blau, B., & Rafferty, J. Changes in friendship status as a function of reinforcement. *Child Devel.*, 1970, **41**, 113–121.
6. Bruner, J. S. *Poverty and childhood.* Detroit: Merrill-Palmer Institute, 1970.
7. Carlson, P., & Anisfeld, M. Some observations on the linguistic competence of a two-year-old child. *Child Devel.*, 1969, **40**, 569–575.
8. Charlesworth, R., & Hartup, W. W. Positive social reinforcement in the nursery school peer group. *Child Devel.*, 1967, **38**, 993–1002.
9. Committee for Economic Development. Profile of the poor. *Sat. Rev.*, May 23, 1970, p. 23.
10. Crandall, V. J., Orleans, S., Preston, A., & Rabson, A. The development of social compliance in young children. *Child Devel.*, 1958, **29**, 430–443.
11. Culhane, J. Report on Sesame Street. New York Times Magazine, May 24, 1970, pp. 34 ff.
12. Deutsch, M. Facilitating development in the preschool child: Social and psychological perspectives. *Merrill-Palmer Quart.*, 1964, **10**, 249–263.
13. Deutsch, M. The influence of early social environment on school adaptation. In D. Schreiber (Ed.), *The school dropout.* Washington, D.C.: National Education Association, 1964, pp. 89–100.
14. Dickie, J. P. Effectiveness of structured and unstructured (traditional) methods of language training. *Mono. Soc. Res. Child Devel.*, 1968, **33**:8, 62–79.
15. Dixon, C. M. *High, wide and deep.* New York: John Day, 1938.
16. Duckworth, L. H. The relationship of childhood imaginary playmates to some factors of creativity among college freshmen. Unpublished Master's thesis, University of Alabama, 1962.
17. Erikson, E. H. *Childhood and society.* New York: Norton, 1963.
18. Gibson, E. J. The ontogeny of reading. *Am. Psychol.*, 1970, **25**, 136–143.

19. Goodenough, E. G., & Prelinger, E. *Children tell stories.* New York: International Universities Press, 1963.
20. Goodnow, J. J. Effects of active handling, illustrated by uses for objects. *Child Devel.*, 1969, **40**, 202–212.
21. Gray, S. W. *Selected longitudinal studies of compensatory education—A look from the inside.* Nashville, Tenn.: Demonstration and Research Center in Early Education, George Peabody College for Teachers, 1969.
22. Gray, S. W. & Klaus, R. A. The early training project: A seventh-year report. *Child Devel.*, 1970, **41**, 909–924.
23. Griffiths, R. *A study of imagination in early childhood.* London: Routledge & Kegan Paul, 1935.
24. Groseclose, E. Teachers find ABCs are too elementary. *Wall St. J.*, November 15, 1970.
25. Hartup, W. W., Glazer, J. A., & Charlesworth, R. Peer reinforcement and sociometric status. *Child Devel.*, 1967, **38**, 1017–1024.
26. Havighurst, R. J. Minority subcultures and the law of effect. *Am. Psychol.*, 1970, **25**, 313–322.
27. Hoffman, M. L. Parent discipline and the child's consideration for others. *Child Devel.*, 1963, **34**, 573–588.
28. Jersild, A. T. *Child psychology* (6th ed.). Englewood Cliffs, N.J.: Prentice-Hall, 1968.
29. John V. P., & Goldstein, L. S. The social context of language acquisition. *Merrill-Palmer Quart.*, 1964, **10**, 265–275.
30. Karnes, M. B. *Research and development program on disadvantaged children.* Final Report, Vol. 1, May, 1969, University of Illinois, Contract No. OE–6–10–325, U.S. Office of Education.
31. Keliher, A. V. Parent and child centers. *Children*, 1969, **16**, 63–66.
32. Kellogg, R., & O'Dell, S. *The psychology of children's art.* New York: CRM–Random House, 1967.
33. Leeper, S. H., Dales, R. J., Skipper, D. S., & Witherspoon, R. L. *Good schools for young children*, 2nd ed. New York: Macmillan, 1968.
34. Lesser, G. S. Television and the language development of children. Paper presented at the meeting of the New England Psychological Association, Boston, November 8, 1969.
35. Maccoby, E. E. Stability and change in attachment behavior during the third year of life. Paper presented at the meeting of the Western Psychological Association, Vancouver, 1969.
36. McDavid, J. W., et al. Project Head Start: Evaluation and research, 1965–67. A Summary. (Mimeo.) Washington, D.C.: Division of Research and Evaluation, Project Head Start.
37. Maynard, O. *Children and dance and music.* New York: Scribner's, 1968.
38. Miller, J. O. Diffusion effects in disadvantaged families. Urbana, Ill.: *ERIC Clearinghouse on Early Childhood Education*, University of Illinois, 1968.
39. Moore, S. B. Correlates of peer acceptance in nursery school children. *Young Children*, 1967, **22**, 281–297.
40. Office of Economic Opportunity. *Project Head Start Equipment and Supplies.* Washington, D.C.: U.S. Govt. Printing Office, 1965.
41. Palmer, F. H., & Rees, A. H. Concept training in two-year-olds: Procedures

and results. Paper presented at the meeting of the Society for Research in Child Development, Santa Monica, Calif., March 27, 1969.
42. Piaget, J. *The psychology of intelligence.* London: Routledge & Kegan Paul, 1950.
43. Piaget, J. *Play, dreams and imitation in childhood.* London: Heinemann, 1951.
44. Read, K. H. *The nursery school* (4th ed.). Philadelphia: Saunders, 1966.
45. Schaefer, C. E. Imaginary companions and creative adolescents. *Devel. Psychol.*, 1969, **1**, 747–749.
46. Scott, P. M., Burton, R. V., & Yarrow, M. R. Social reinforcement under natural conditions. *Child Devel.*, 1967, **38**, 53–63.
47. Sears, P. S., & Dowley, E. M. Research on teaching in the nursery school. In N. L. Gage (Ed.), *Handbook of research on teaching.* New York: Rand McNally, 1963, pp. 814–864.
48. Smilansky, S. The effects of sociodramatic play on disadvantaged preschool children. New York: Wiley, 1968.
49. Smith, H. P., & Applefeld, S. W. Children's paintings and the projective expression of personality: An experimental investigation. *J. Genet. Psychol.*, 1965, **107**, 289–293.
50. Snow, A. C. *Growing with children through art.* New York: Reinhold, 1968.
51. Student observation. Merrill-Palmer Institute (unpublished).
52. Sutton-Smith, B. The role of play in cognitive development. *Young Children*, 1967, **22**, 361–370.
53. Sutton-Smith, B. Novel responses to toys. *Merrill-Palmer Quart.*, 1968, **14**, 151–158.
54. Torrance, E. P. Peer influences on preschool children's willingness to try difficult tasks. *J. Psychol.*, 1969, **72**, 189–194.
55. Weikart, D. P. (Ed.) *Preschool intervention: Preliminary report of the Perry Preschool Project.* Ann Arbor, Mich.: Campus Publishers, 1967.
56. Weikart, D. P. Comparative study of three preschool curricula. Paper presented at the meeting of the Society for Research in Child Development, Santa Monica, Calif., March 28, 1969.
57. Zimny, G. H., & Weidenfeller, E. W. Effects of music upon GSR of children. *Child Devel.*, 1962, **33**, 891–896.

Readings in
The Role of Play in Development

Play is the young child's chief mode of interaction and development. Although there seems to be a growing appreciation of the fact that children learn through play, there are also increases in efforts to program and control young children's learning. In the traditional nursery school, play is respected and facilitated. Compensatory education for young children is a new field in which many approaches to children's learning are being tried by professionals from a variety of disciplines. Some of these programs include play as a mode of learning, others do not.

The value of play is emphasized by David Elkind in his analysis of the contribution that the traditional nursery school makes to middle-class children and to education in general. Elkind is convinced that a structured nursery school can be worthwhile for deprived children and can help them catch up with the development that the middle-class child achieves at home, in interaction with his family. He is very convincing in arguing that the remedial program for the deprived child should not be inflicted on the well-developed child. Social play in the nursery school is the setting of a study by Rosalind Charlesworth and Willard Hartup. This study is part of a series dealing with the reinforcements that children give each other during play.

Of the many reports of research on compensatory education, only one is reprinted here. Susan W. Gray and Rupert A. Klaus report on The Early Training Project, seven years after its beginning. In addition to its age and the careful controls used, the project is noteworthy for its parent program and research methods which permit accurate estimates of its results.

The Case for the Academic Preschool: Fact or Fiction?

David Elkind
UNIVERSITY OF ROCHESTER

The advantages an academic preschool offers to an underprivileged child are considerable. The school can provide kinds of stimuli he would probably not otherwise receive and help him acquire the skills and knowledge needed to cope effectively with later learning. But

Reprinted with permission from *Young Children*, Vol. XXV, No. 3, January, 1970. Copyright © 1970, National Association for the Education of Young Children, 1834 Connecticut Ave., N.W., Washington, D.C. 20009.

what about the privileged middle-class child? What has the academic preschool to offer him?

Over the past few years there has been a remarkable growth of professional interest in young children and in the preschool education they receive. In part, this new interest in young children derives from research (some of which is reviewed by Scott, 1968, and by Stevenson, Hess & Rheingold, 1967), which suggests that the preschool years are of great importance not only for social and emotional but also for intellectual growth. While the research findings came as no surprise to nursery school teachers, they seem to have come as something of a revelation to many educators and psychologists (e.g., Bruner, 1960; Fowler, 1962; Hunt, 1961).

This "new" recognition of the importance of the preschool years for mental growth has had two major consequences. One of these is a movement (that has succeeded or will soon succeed in states such as California, Massachusetts and New York) to provide preschool education for all children whose parents desire it. The second major consequence of this new focus upon the preschool child is a growing sentiment towards changing the character of preschool education. While the advocates of change in preschool education (e.g., Berlyne, 1965; Fowler, 1962; Hunt, 1961; Sava, 1968) are somewhat vague in their specifications, it seems fair to say that they appear to advocate more formal, academic types of instruction. In the present essay, I want to deal primarily with this second consequence and to examine some of the arguments for the formalization of preschool education.

Those who advocate more structured nursery school instruction (e.g., Sava, 1968) seem to base their position on four types of arguments: (a) The earlier we start a child in the formal academic path, the earlier he will finish and the cheaper the total educational cost; (b) learning comes easy to the young child and we should take advantage of the preschooler's learning facility and eagerness to learn; (c) intellectual growth is rapid in the preschool years and instruction will help to maximize that growth while failure to provide appropriate intellectual stimulation may curtail the child's ultimate level of achievement and (d) traditional preschool experience is too soft, too directed towards emotional well-being and too little concerned with cognitive stimulation. Let us take up each of these arguments in turn.

IS THE ACADEMIC PRESCHOOL ECONOMICAL?

There is certainly a sense in which preschool instruction may be more economical than later educational interventions. In the case of disadvantaged children who do not profit from what Strodtbeck (1964) called "the hidden curriculum of the middle-class home," there is a real need for more structured learning experiences such as those provided by Bereiter and Englemann (1966); Kami and Radin (1967) and Blank and Solomon (1968). To the child who comes from the often chaotic stimuli of the ghetto, the structure of a formal instructional program is a needed counterpoise to his experience at home. The structured preschool experience offered to the disadvantaged child helps compensate for the cognitive and linguistic preparation that the middle-class child receives in the home. In the case of disadvantaged children, then, preparation is certainly cheaper in the long run than reparation or remedial education later.

The advocates of preschool instruction have not, however, limited their sights to the disadvantaged child only, but aim their arguments at the middle-class child as well. There is so much to learn these days, it is argued, that we need to start children earlier if they are to complete their education while still young. Besides it is more economical to educate at the preschool than at the college level. While these arguments seem to have merit, they do not really hold up under careful scrutiny.

It is true of course that we are living in an era of explosive increases in knowledge and that our highly technical civilization will require ever more highly trained individuals. Our task is thus to speed up the educational process. Such a speedup, however, can be accomplished in several ways just as it can be done in industry. If a manufacturer wishes to speed up his production, he can either get his workers to work longer hours or make his production facilities operate more rapidly and efficiently. In most cases, the latter solution results in a more economical manufacture and a better product. The same probably holds true in education.

Our educational system today is really not geared to the needs of young people growing up in today's world. Too much of it is geared to the acquisition and storing of information and too little to teaching young people how to retrieve information. By the time we are adults most of us have forgotten about four-fifths of what we learned in school. That, after all, is a pretty poor yield. Our educational system, thus, has a lot of dead wood and could be streamlined so there would be no need to start children at the preschool level in order to complete their education in a reasonable time. Children in Western Europe often do not begin school until age six or seven but are better educated than our young people when they complete high school. In any case, if we taught children to read and write at the preschool level there would still have to be a total change and reorganization at all educational levels. It might be more profitable in the long run to streamline our existing instructional institutions before creating new ones.

Formal instruction of the middle-class child does not appear, then, to have any economic advantages. Nor does it have the necessary preparatory quality it has for the disadvantaged child. The typical middle-class home provides a good deal of structure and instruction. Middle-class parents are constantly conversing with their children, labeling things for them, answering their questions, providing them with "educational" toys and instilling them with the idea that they, the parents, look favorably upon academic achievement. In the context of this structured tutelage in the home, additional instruction in the preschool would merely gild the lily. We shall, at a later point, return to the role of the preschool for middle-class children. At this point, it is only necessary to say that formal instruction of the middle-class preschool child is probably a less effective procedure than streamlining the educational system as a whole.

IS THE ACADEMIC PRESCHOOL EFFICIENT?

Those who advocate preschool instruction for the middle-class child argue that the preschool youngster is an eager and facile learner. While both of these contentions are true, they do not necessarily imply the efficacy of preschool instruction in the formal sense. Let us look first at the young child's eagerness to learn. This eagerness is present in his constant questions, his curiosity and exploratory behavior. Actually, this eagerness is present at the kindergarten and first grade levels as well. But by the time children reach the fifth and sixth grade, more than 50 percent of the children once eager to learn dislike school, the prime agency of instruction. *It is at least possible that the dislike of school and of learning is a direct result of our lock step instructional processes which kill spontaneous interest.* The introduction of formal instruction at the preschool level could thus well have the effect of bringing children's eagerness to learn to an earlier grave than heretofore.

If we look now at the young child's facility in learning, it too offers no direct invitation for formal instruction. The young child learns quickly but what he learns, he learns by rote—not by reason and thought. Read a story to him several times and he will know it by heart. But in problem solving and in other types of learning situations, he has great difficulty and uses trial and error. In all but rote situations he is a terribly inefficient learner. This observation has now been substantiated by evidence from many different kinds of studies (White, 1965), which strongly suggest that something happens between the ages of four and seven which transforms the young child who learns merely on the basis of association to an older one who learns with the aid of language mediation and with deductive reasoning.

These data are important because as the writer has argued elsewhere (Elkind, 1969a), most of the tool skills required of the young child, such as reading and arithmetic, require the logical and linguistic structures that usually do not emerge until age six or seven. Accordingly, if we try to teach children to "read" and "do math" while still at the preschool level, they may learn by different means than they will at a later time. Such training could actually produce difficulties later and interfere with the successful mastery of these tasks at the cognitive level. Moreover, since such skills cannot be easily learned by rote means, children will have to invest much more time in the preschool learning to read than they would have to invest had they waited until they were older before learning this tool skill.

This is not to say—I want to emphasize—that the preschool period is not a very important one in preparing children for formal instruction in tool subjects. Listening to stories, learning the alphabet and familiarity with numbers and quantitative relations are all important preparatory education for formal instruction. Preparing children for reading and mathematics is, however, different from teaching them reading and arithmetic, which should be delayed until the child gives evidence of having attained mediational learning—the ability to learn with the aid of rational and linguistic formulae. Of course, no blocks should be placed in the path of the exceptional child who learns to read and do math through his own efforts and interest. Accordingly, while it is true that the young child is an eager and facile learner, this does not imply that he be given formal instruction in tool subjects. Such instruction could well stifle his spontaneous interest in learning because the skills themselves call for learning abilities the young child does not yet possess. His facility in rote learning is of little help in learning skills such as math and reading that require rational learning processes. In view of these considerations, it makes more sense for preschool education to focus upon preparation for formal instruction than upon formal instruction itself.

DOES THE ACADEMIC PRESCHOOL MAXIMIZE MENTAL GROWTH?

Those who argue for an academic preschool suggest that early childhood is a "critical period" in mental growth. The idea of critical periods in human development derives from analogies with animal studies. Such studies show that during certain periods in their development, animals are particularly susceptible to environmental influence. Young chicks, to illustrate, become attached to the prominent object about them approximately 17 hours after birth. Thereafter, the chick responds to this object as if it were his "mother," whether it is a box, balloon or graduate student (Scott, 1968). In humans, the period of primary socialization appears at the last quarter of the first year, when the infant gives evidence of fear of strangers and anxiety over the mother's departure (Schaffer & Callender, 1959).

While there is thus some evidence for a critical period for human socialization, there is no unequivocal evidence for such periods in *mental* development. The evidence adduced by those who favor the critical period hypothesis is of three sorts: (a) mental growth curves, (b) case histories and (c) data from academic preschools. Let us examine the evidence.

The argument for critical periods based on mental growth curves derives from the writings of psychometricians such as Bloom (1964). Bloom suggests that half the child's intellectual capacity is attained by age four and another 30 percent by age eight. There is, therefore, evidence that early childhood is a period of very rapid intellectual growth. This evidence, however, does not necessarily imply that the period is critical in the sense that if stimulation is not received during this epoch, later stimulation will not be able to accomplish the same result. Let us look at the mental growth curves in more detail since they appear to be the primary basis for the critical period notion with respect to mental growth.

Unlike growth curves for height and weight, which involve merely recording the successive measurements on the same individuals across time, mental growth curves involve the correlations between test scores at successive age levels. What mental growth curves really tell us is not how much of a child's total mental capacity he has at any given time, but only how much of his total intellectual ability we can predict at any age. To illustrate, from a child's IQ score at age four, we can predict with 50 percent accuracy what his IQ will be at age 17. That is the *only* straightforward interpretation of the mental growth curves report by Bloom (1964).

Suppose, however, that we accept the interpretation that ability to predict is related to total ability, and that a child does attain half his total mental ability by age four and 80 percent by age eight. Does this imply we ought to start academic instruction early to capitalize on this rapid growth period? Not at all! In the first place, the rate of mental growth appears to decline as the rate of formal instruction increases. That is, almost 75 percent of a child's mental growth takes place before he receives formal schooling and the rate of mental growth declines as the amount of formal schooling increases—only 20 percent growth between eight and 17. There is, in effect, *a negative correlation between mental growth and formal instruction!* Looked at in this way, one could legitimately argue that formal schooling ought to be *delayed* rather than introduced early to maximize mental growth.

Another argument for the criticalness of early childhood for mental growth comes from the writings of Fowler (1968), who states:

"The unvarying coincidence of extensive early stimulation with cognitive precocity and subsequent superior competence in adulthood suggest that stimulation is a necessary if not sufficient condition for the development of his abilities" (p. 17). What Fowler forgets, however, is that correlation is *not* causation. It is true that many great scientists and artists received early instruction, but it is also true that they had gifted parents and were genetically well endowed. Furthermore, and more importantly, what of all those children whose parents stimulated and instructed them almost from the day of their birth and who did not achieve later eminence? In science, it is necessary to acknowledge negative as well as positive instances, and my guess is that the negative instances far exceed the positive. I have seen one such product of early stimulation, an autistic (schizophrenic) boy who believed he was a tape recorder. When he was an infant, his mother bathed him in a sea of tape-recorded sound to stimulate his musical talents. In arguing about the benefits of early instruction, it is only fair to report the possible costs of intense instructional pressure at home and at school.

Finally, a third argument for the criticalness of the preschool period comes from those who cite the effects of preschool instructional programs, such as those of Head Start, Bereiter and Englemann (1966), and so on. To the extent that these programs are directed at disadvantaged children, the gains may be very real indeed but are probably of smaller magnitude than they appear (Jensen, 1969). This is because when the children take the initial pretest before the training, they are strange to the situation and examiners, whereas afterwards they feel at home and their test performance reflects that fact (Zigler & Butterfield, 1968). As I indicated earlier, however, there may be real benefits for disadvantaged children in an academically oriented preschool.

The question I wish to raise is whether such instructional programs would equally benefit middle-class children. Recently, Gottesman (1968) reviewed some of the animal and human research relevant to this issue. In general, the studies show that enriched environments benefit disadvantaged or deprived subjects to a much greater extent than they do advantaged or non-deprived subjects. As Jensen (1969) suggests, there seems to be a minimum level of stimulation necessary for children to realize their abilities. If the actual level is below that minimum, they do not realize their full potential. If, however, the environment is richer than necessary, it does not further implement their growth. If this view is correct, mental growth would have to be regarded as analogous to physical growth. Poor diet can stunt a child's height, but an abundantly rich one will not increase his ultimate height beyond a certain limit. If this analogy holds true, the level of stimulation children need to maximize their intellectual growth may be far less than we imagine and excessive enrichment wasteful.

Indeed, most middle-class preschool children are probably over- rather than understimulated. Such overstimulation occurs because we frequently overestimate the young child's ability to assimilate new experience. Most parents have had the experience of taking their preschoolers to the circus, carnival or zoo. Children are usually more interested in the food than other attractions. Usually it is not until weeks later that the youngster will begin to talk about or draw the events which transpired at the event. Children cannot assimilate new experiences in as large a dose or as rapidly as adults, and protect themselves by tuning out the stimulation they cannot process.

In summary, we have reviewed three arguments for the criticalness of early childhood intellectual stimulation and have not found any one of them entirely satisfactory. I do not wish, however, to deny the importance of the early childhood period for intellectual growth. The preschool period is important, even critical, but not because growth is most rapid at the time, or because great men received early stimulation, or because there is evidence to show the lastingness of early instruction. No, the preschool period is important for a simple reason, namely, mental growth is cumulative and depends upon what has gone before.

Whether we are talking about Piagetian stages, the acquisition of a skill such as playing the piano or knowledge in a particular area, there is a cumulative learning aspect. What the child learns in the preschool period must adequately prepare him for what he is to learn later. It is in this sense, and this sense only, that early childhood is a critical period in intellectual development. In the next section, we will deal in more detail with the preparatory role of the preschool.

IS THE ACADEMIC PRESCHOOL SUPERIOR TO THE TRADITIONAL PRESCHOOL?

The advocates of an academic preschool see little of intellectual value in traditional preschool education perpetuated by, as Sava (1968) derogatorily put it, the "child lovers." Such attitudes seem to reflect a boundless ignorance of what is accomplished in the traditional preschool and of the skill required to run such a school effectively. What the supporters of the academic preschool fail to realize is that the preschool child is a very different psychosocial being than the school-age child, and that the traditional preschool is well suited to his intellectual and emotional needs.

In the first place, emotions and intellect are not as separate at ages three and four as they will be later and an emotionally distraught preschooler is cognitively disorganized as well. The preschool teacher's concern with and response to the young child's feelings have cognitive as well as emotional benefits. Then too, preschool represents the child's first separation from home, his first experience with a peer group and a substitute mother figure. The preschool child still has a lot of social learning to do, and the traditional preschool provides the opportunity, security and structure for such learning.

Secondly, and more importantly, the traditional preschool does provide for cognitive stimulation and instruction in the most general and significant sense of that term. Play is, after all, the child's work and much of his motor play is preparatory to later cognitive developments. In stacking and building with blocks, the child learns about spatial relations, balance, weight and gravity. Likewise in large motor play such as climbing, swinging, running, he learns the motor and perceptual coordinations that are essential to later fine motor coordinations involved in reading and writing. Those who deride play in the preschool ignore the fact that all play has a cognitive component and role in all creative endeavor, whether it be intellectual or artistic.

Finally, the traditional preschool program has incorporated for many years some of the most innovative ideas in educational practice today. The traditional nursery school has, to illustrate, always sought to *individualize instruction* and allow each child, in today's lexicon, to do "his thing" whether it be carpentry, doll play, painting or block building. Also, *discovery learning* is built into many preschool activities, such as dramatic play. When a child play-acts roles with other children, he is learning about adult roles and reciprocal rules of behavior. He is, moreover, engaging in the social interchanges with peers that Piaget (1948) regards as so important to the overcoming of egocentrism. Finally, in providing a range of materials and allowing the child to engage in those which send him at the moment, the traditional preschool capitalizes upon *intrinsic motivation* to learn in the best sense of that term (Elkind, 1969b).

The traditional preschool, thus, does much more than the advocates of the academic preschool credit. Indeed, the traditional preschool already embodies ideas that are only now beginning to appear at higher education levels, such as individualized instruction, discovery learning, peer group stimulation and use of intrinsic motivation. This is not to say, of course, that the traditional preschool is perfect and that there is no room for improvement. For one thing, the value of the preschool will vary with the quality of the teacher. Teacher variability at the preschool level is as great as at every other level of education and can always stand improvement. For another thing, traditional preschools may have too little material for spontaneous practice in logical and mathematical thinking and teachers might benefit from our new knowledge about the thinking capacities of preschool children (Inhelder & Piaget, 1969).

In short, with respect to middle-class children, the traditional preschool still appears to be consonant with the maximum benefit to intellectual and emotional growth of the preschool child. While the traditional preschool can probably increase considerably its effectiveness in preparing children for academic instruction, there is no strong evidence for exposing young, middle-class children to academic instruction itself. Indeed, it would be ironic if, in the name of progress, preschools were forced to adopt the lock step curricula already being given up at higher levels of education.

SUMMARY AND CONCLUSIONS

In this essay I have discussed four of the arguments for introducing an academic curriculum into preschool education. These arguments are that academic instruction is: (a) more economical; (b) more efficient; (c) more necessary and (d) more cognitively stimulating than the traditional preschool. I have tried to show that each of these arguments is weak at best and that there are stronger arguments for not having an academic preschool, at least for the middle-class child. There is no preponderance of evidence that formal instruction is more efficient, more economical, more necessary or more cognitively stimulating than the traditional preschool program. Indeed, while there is room for improvement in the traditional preschool, it already embodies some of the most innovative educational practices extant today. It would, in fact, be foolish to pattern the vastly expanded preschool programs planned for the future upon an instructional format that is rapidly being given up at higher educational levels. Indeed, it is becoming more and more apparent that formal instructional programs are as inappropriate at the primary and secondary levels of education as they are at the preschool level.

References

BEREITER, C. & ENGLEMANN, S. *Teaching Disadvantaged Children in the Preschool.* Engelwood Cliffs, N.J.: Prentice Hall, 1966.

BERLYNE, D. E. Curiosity and education. In J. D. Krumboltz (Ed.), *Learning and the Educational Process.* Chicago: Rand McNally, 1965, 67–89.

BLANK, MARION & SOLOMON, FRANCES. A tutorial language program to develop abstract thinking in socially disadvantaged preschool children. *Child Develpm.,* 1968, 39, 379–390.

BLOOM, B. S. *Stability and Change in Human Characteristics.* New York: Wiley, 1964.

BRUNER, J. S. *The Process of Education.* Cambridge, Mass.: Harvard Univ. Press, 1960.

ELKIND, D. Developmental studies of figurative perception. In L. P. Lipsitt & H. W. Reese (Eds.), *Advances in Child Development and Behavior.* New York: Academic Press, 1969, 1–28a.

———. Piagetian and psychometric approaches to intelligence. *Harvard educ. Rev.,* 1969, 39, 319–337b.

FOWLER, W. Cognitive learning in infancy and early childhood. *Psycholog. Bull.,* 1962, 59, 116–152.

GOTTESMAN, I. I. Biogenetics of race and class. In M. Deutsch, I. Katz & A. Jensen (Eds.), *Social Class, Race, and Psychological Development.* New York: Holt, Rinehart & Winston, 1968, 11–51.

HUNT, J. McV. *Intelligence and Experience.* New York: Ronald Press, 1961.

JENSEN, A. R. How much can we boost IQ and scholastic achievement? *Harvard educ. Rev.,* 1969, 39, 1–123.

KAMI, C. & RADIN, N. A framework for a preschool curriculum based on some Piagetian concepts. *J. creative Behav.,* 1967, 1, 314–324.

PIAGET, J. *The Moral Judgment of the Child.* Glencoe, Ill.: The Free Press, 1948.

———. *The Early Growth of Logic in the Child.* New York: Norton, 1969.

SAVA, SAMUEL G. When learning comes easy. *Saturday Rev.,* Nov. 16, 1968, 102–119.

SCHAFFER, H. R. & CALLENDER, W. M. Psychologic effects of hospitalization in infancy. *Pediatrics,* 1959, 24, 528–539.

SCOTT, J. P. *Early Experience and the Organization of Behavior.* Belmont Calif.: Wadsworth, 1968.

STEVENSON, H. W., HESS, E. H. & RHEINGOLD, HARRIET L. (Eds.). *Early Behavior.* New York: Wiley, 1967.

STRODTBECK, F. L. The hidden curriculum of the middle-class home. In C. W. Hunnicutt (Ed.), *Urban Education and Cultural Deprivation.* Syracuse: Syracuse Univ. Press, 1964, 15–31.

WHITE, S. H. Evidence for a hierarchical arrangement of learning processes. In L. P. Lipsitt & C. C. Spiker (Eds.), *Advances in Child Development and Behavior,* Vol. 2. New York: Academic Press, 1965, 187–220.

ZIGLER, E. & BUTTERFIELD, E. C. Motivational aspects of changes in IQ test performance of culturally deprived school children. *Child Develpm.,* 1968, 39, 1–14.

Positive Social Reinforcement in the Nursery School Peer Group*

Rosalind Charlesworth
ANN ARBOR PUBLIC SCHOOLS

Willard W. Hartup
UNIVERSITY OF MINNESOTA

An observational method was devised for obtaining normative information on the amount and kinds of positive social reinforcement dispensed by preschool-age children to each other in nursery school. Data were collected in 4 preschool classes. It was found that children in the older groups reinforced their peers at a significantly higher rate than those in the younger groups and that the amount of reinforcement given was positively related to the amount received. Reinforcement was dispensed in a higher proportion when a child was engaged in dramatic play activity than when he was engaged in other pursuits (such as art, music, or table games). About half the reinforcements were given in response to overtures from the recipients and half spontaneously. The consequence of reinforcement was, in largest proportion, the continuation of the recipient's activity at the time of reinforcement.

Numerous attempts are currently being made to study patterns of young children's social behavior within the conceptual framework of reinforcement theory. Only a few studies (Floyd, 1964; Hartup, 1964; Patterson, Bricker, & Greene, 1964), however, have dealt particularly with preschool-age peers as agents of reinforcement. The results of the Patterson et al. (1964) study strongly support the utility of applying reinforcement theory to the observational study of aggressive behavior as it occurs in the nursery school. The present study investigated patterns of positive social behavior in the nursery school peer group considered in terms of this theory. Previous studies of positive social behavior have used more molecular descriptive concepts (Swift, 1964), such as "cooperation," "leadership," "sympathy," and "social participation."

Skinner's rubric "generalized reinforcer" was chosen as the basis for defining positive social reinforcement. Skinner (1953) postulates that reinforcement from people gives rise to several important forms of generalized social reinforcers: attention (attending to another), approval (praise or acceptance), affection (physical gestures or verbal statements), submissiveness (following a request or suggestion), and tokens (giving tangible physical objects). Gewirtz (1961) has elaborated further the processes by which these stimuli acquire reinforcing properties in early infancy and become the prime

Reprinted from *Child Development*, 38, 993–1002. Copyright © 1967, by The Society for Research in Child Development, Inc. By permission.

* The authors wish to acknowledge the assistance of Elizabeth Konen, Nancy Mann, and Marilyn Rausch in carrying out this study. They also extend thanks to the staff of the University of Minnesota Laboratory Preschool for their cooperation, and to Sandra Cohen and James Bryan for their helpful reviews of an earlier manuscript. This project was carried out while the first author was supported by NICHD grant No. T1-HD-105-01.

maintainers of social life. For the present study, Skinner's conceptualization was used as a guide for defining categories of social behavior, and an observational method was then designed for obtaining information concerning reinforcement frequencies occurring in the nursery school peer group.

METHOD

SUBJECTS   The children observed were enrolled in a laboratory preschool. They were, for the most part, children of university faculty members and other professional people. The subjects for the principal investigation consisted of two groups of children between the ages of 4-1 and 4-9 and two groups between 3-4 and 4-0. The total sample included 35 boys and 35 girls, divided into preschool classes of 16, 17, 18, and 19 children each. The major portion of the children in the two older groups had had previous nursery school experience. One group of 3-year-olds consisted of children with no previous experience, while the other group was about equally divided between new children and nursery school veterans. One of the older and one of the younger groups met five mornings per week, while the other two groups met three afternoons per week.

THE OBSERVATIONAL TECHNIQUE   *Procedure*[1]   The observer arrived in the room before the children. Prior to collecting any data, the observer spent time sitting in the room practicing the observational technique, learning the children's names, and allowing the children to become accustomed to her presence. The observations began during the fourth week of the school year and continued for 5 weeks. Each day the observer began as soon as half the children had arrived and continued until cleanup was announced. The children were observed in random order for 3-minute periods. A child was never observed more than twice on the same day. Twelve 3-minute time segments were recorded for each child in each of the older groups, ten segments for one of the younger groups, and eight for the other. For purposes of statistical analysis, the scores for the younger groups were extrapolated to 12 observation periods. Tally was made of the location of the observers during each observation period.

The following information was recorded: the child's name and the names of the other children and adults engaged in the same activity or in parallel activity; the activity in which the child was engaged; a detailed running account of the child's behavior and the behavior of any child with whom he interacted.

There were two observers. Two of the groups (one 3-year-old and one 4-year old) were observed exclusively by O_1 and one (4-year-old) by O_2. In the fourth group (3-year-old), half of the observations were carried out by the O_1 alone and half by both observers simultaneously. A comparison of the

[1] An observation and Coding Manual containing a description of the conditions for observation, instructions for recording observations, the coding procedure, and sample protocols has been deposited as Document No. 9617 with the ADI Auxiliary Publications Project, Photoduplication Service, Library of Congress, Washington, D.C. 20540. A copy may be secured by citing the Document No. and by remitting $2.50 for photoprints or $1.75 for 35 mm. microfilm. Advance payment is required. Make checks or money orders payable to: Chief, Photoduplication Service, Library of Congress.

number of codeable incidents recorded by each observer showed that O_1 recorded 16 per cent more codeable incidents than did O_2.

The observation protocols were coded using the following group of categories:

>   I. *Giving positive attention and approval:* attending, offering praise and approval, offering instrumental help, smiling and laughing, verbal help, informing another of a third person's needs, general conversation.
>   II. *Giving affection and personal acceptance:* physical and verbal.
>   III. *Submission:* passive acceptance, imitation, sharing, accepting another's idea or help, allowing another child to play, compromise, following an order or request with pleasure and cooperation.
>   IV. *Token giving:* giving tangible physical objects, such as toys or food, spontaneously.

These categories coincide with those listed by Skinner (1953) as possessing widely shared reinforcing value in humans, It is not argued that the ratings covered all classes of social stimuli having reinforcing value. Crying, for example, can be positively reinforcing in peer interaction but was not tabulated in this study. Judgments concerning the frequency of social reinforcers were made using the following considerations: (a) the occurrence of a reinforcement was defined in terms of the kind of action involved, rather than in the effects the action had upon the child perceiving it; and (b) the record needed to contain evidence that the recipient perceived the potentially reinforcing activity of his peer. The reinforcements were also coded as to whether they were accepted, rejected, or ignored. In the data analysis, the frequencies of reinforcements *given* are those positive social reinforcements which were followed by positive behavior on the part of the recipient. Also tabulated were instances for each child in which he received reinforcement from other children as recorded in the other children's protocols.

The observations were coded by one of the observers and a naïve coder in order to obtain information on the reliability of the coding procedure. Two ratios were computed. The first, .77, is a ratio of agreement/agreement + disagreement in which agreement concerns the presence of positive social reinforcement (even though there might be disagreement as to the category of the reinforcement). A second ratio, in which agreement concerned the presence of a particular category of reinforcement, was .64, These reliability checks were based on 20 per cent (161) of the 3-minute protocols. A third coder tallied information on location, presence or absence of an overture, and consequences of reinforcement.

RESULTS AND DISCUSSION

GIVING POSITIVE SOCIAL REINFORCEMENT   *Findings*   Age and sex differences in frequency of giving positive social reinforcement were revealed by means of a series of two-way analyses of variance for unequal cell frequencies (Table 1). For total frequencies (the sum of all reinforcements regardless of category), there was a significant age difference, with the 4-year-olds giving more reinforcement than 3-year-olds ($F = 9.30$, $p < .01$). Most of this difference is accounted for by Category I: Giving Attention and Approval ($F = 15.03$, $p < .01$). For Category II, a significant age by sex interaction was found ($F = 5.68$, $p < .025$). When the means are examined (Table 2), it can be seen that younger and older boys gave affection and personal acceptance in almost

TABLE 1
Summary of Analyses of Variance for Positive Social Reinforcement Scores for Two Age Groups

REINFORCEMENT SCORE

Source	df	Total Frequency (F)	Category I (F)	Category II (F)	Category III (F)	Total N Different Peers (F)
Age	1	9.30†	15.03†	3.29	1.51	21.25†
Sex	1	3.31	1.03	1.30	6.03*	2.73
A × S	1	1.35	<1.00	5.68*	<1.00	3.53
Within	66	–	–	–	–	–

* $p < .02$.
† $p < .01$.

TABLE 2
Means and Ranges of Positive Social Reinforcement Scores for Four Sex and Age Groups

REINFORCEMENT SCORE

			Total Frequency		Category I		Category II		Category III		Total N Different Peers	
Sex	Age	N	$\bar{X}$	R	$\bar{X}$	R	$\bar{X}$	R	$\bar{X}$	R	$\bar{X}$	R
M	4	17	22.82	6–49	10.29	2–24	3.18	0–10	8.47	0–23	5.76	2–11
F	4	16	21.06	2–54	9.56	1–24	4.06	0–14	6.19	0–18	5.88	2–9
M	3	18	17.77	4–35	6.09	1–15	3.58	0–16	7.74	3–25	4.44	2–8
F	3	19	9.79	0–33	4.36	0–14	1.07	0–5	3.82	0–15	2.74	0–7

equal amounts, while younger girls gave much less frequent affection than older girls or either group of boys. Boys were found to give submissive types of reinforcements (Category III) significantly more frequently than girls ($F = 6.03$, $p < .025$).[2] It was also found that older children reinforced a significantly greater number of other children than did the younger children ($F = 21.25$, $p < .01$).

Another set of analyses was conducted in order to test classroom and sex

[2] No separate analysis of Category IV was completed due to the small frequencies obtained.

TABLE 3
Summary of Analyses of Variance of Positive Social Reinforcement Scores for Two 4-Year-Old Classes

REINFORCEMENT SCORE

SOURCE	DF	TOTAL FREQUENCY (F)	CATEGORY I (F)	CATEGORY II (F)	CATEGORY III (F)	TOTAL N DIFFERENT PEERS (F)
Class	1	5.91†	8.01‡	4.50*	2.25	10.14‡
Sex	1	<1.00	<1.00	<1.00	1.54	<1.00
C × S	1	<1.00	<1.00	<1.00	<1.00	<1.00
Within	29	–	–	–	–	–

* $p < .05$.
† $p < .02$.
‡ $p < .01$.

TABLE 4
Summary of Analyses of Variance of Positive Social Reinforcement Scores for Two 3-Year-Old Classes

REINFORCEMENT SCORE

SOURCE	DF	TOTAL FREQUENCY (F)	CATEGORY I (F)	CATEGORY II (F)	CATEGORY III (F)	TOTAL N DIFFERENT PEERS (F)
Class	1	<1.00	<1.00	<1.00	<1.00	5.52†
Sex	1	6.74†	1.69	7.79‡	5.12*	10.16‡
C × S	1	<1.00	<1.00	<1.00	<1.00	1.01
Within	33	–	–	–	–	–

* $p < .05$.
† $p < .02$.
‡ $p < .01$.

differences in giving reinforcements within the two age groups separately (Table 3 and Table 4). For the 4-year-olds, there were significant classroom differences on four of the five variables tested; only the frequency of submissive reinforcers did not differ significantly between the two classes for 4-year-olds. For the younger children, there were significant sex differences in favor of the boys in four of the five categories, with only attention and approval not reaching a significant level. There was also one significant classroom difference for the younger children. Subjects in one classroom reinforced a larger number of children than those in the other ($F = 5.52, p < .025$).

Differences in the mean number of positive reinforcements given were also analyzed according to the sex of the recipient. Boys gave significantly more reinforcements to other boys than they gave to girls ($t = 4.43, p < .002$), and girls gave more reinforcements to other girls than to boys ($t = 2.18, p < .05$).

The proportions of each type of reinforcement given were tabulated. Most frequently given by the 4-year-olds was attention and approval (46 per cent), followed by submission (35 per cent), affection and personal acceptance (16.8 per cent), and token giving (2.27 per cent). The proportions of two categories of reinforcers show a slight age shift: the 3-year-olds used a larger proportion of attention and approval (37 per cent) than the 4's. The 3-year-olds give almost exactly the same proportion (16.5 per cent) of affection and personal acceptance and more (5.5 per cent) tokens.

Discussion The findings presented above show that considerably more positive social reinforcement was given by 4-year-olds than by 3-year-olds. Also, the older children distributed their reinforcements to a larger number of other children than did the younger children. These findings parallel the classic findings of Parten (1932) and others concerning the association between chronological age and social participation. The present findings, however, document the fact that the preschool years encompass a period of marked increases in the child's use of generalized social reinforcers in his interactions with peers.

The findings also reveal early differences between boys and girls with respect to certain aspects of peer interaction and utilization of social reinforcers. Boys participated in more give-and-take play in the nursery school than did girls; that is, they gave more submissive reinforcements generally, and they gave more reinforcements during dramatic play. The finding that younger girls gave considerably less affection and personal acceptance than boys and that 82 per cent of this type of reinforcement was given spontaneously indicates that when girls are placed in a group setting at age 3 they are less socially active than boys. Further, the younger girls gave less total reinforcement than younger boys. Thus, sex differences in use of social reinforcers, particularly by younger nursery school children, are clearly revealed by the data. On the other hand, measures of what might be called "social activity level" or "general social participation" were not procured. Therefore, it cannot be argued, without further study, that the sex differences (or the age differences discussed in the preceding paragraph) are independent of differences in general activity or participation.

The differences between the older classes in the number of reinforcements given may be related to two factors. The teacher of the group in which the most reinforcements were given felt that this was an unusually socially active group. In contrast to the other older group, these children not only gave more reinforcements but also had a lower frequency of rejected reinforcements (these were not included in the totals given). There was also a significant difference in the number of different individual children reinforced in each of these two groups. The group in which more reinforcements were given was the 3-day-per-week group.

Evidence for the early formation of a sex schism is apparent in the data on object choice. Boys tended to reinforce boys and girls to reinforce girls. These data indicate that the relative deprivation of reinforcing stimuli from persons of the opposite sex cited by Stevenson (1965) extends from early in the preschool years in the interaction of the child with his peers.

GIVING AND RECEIVING OF REINFORCEMENT *Findings* The relationship between giving and receiving of positive social reinforcement was tested by the use of the within-groups correlation coefficient (Walker & Lev, 1958). The correlation between the total numbers of reinforcements given and the total number received was large ($r = .79$) and highly significant ($p < .01$). Each separate category of giving reinforcement was significantly related to each category of receiving it, with correlations ranging from $r = .38$ ($p < .01$) to $r = .64$ ($p < .01$) (Table 5). Also highly related were the number of individual

TABLE 5
Within-Groups Correlations Between Frequencies of Giving and Receiving Positive Social Reinforcement for Four Classrooms

RECEIVING POSITIVE SOCIAL REINFORCEMENT	GIVING POSITIVE SOCIAL REINFORCEMENT		
	CATEGORY I (r)	CATEGORY II (r)	CATEGORY III (r)
Category I	.39	.45	.64
Category II	.51	.38	.65
Category III	.69	.54	.58

Note. All correlations are significant beyond .01 ($N = 70$).

children reinforced by a child and the number of individuals he received reinforcements from ($r = .46$, $p < .01$). The total frequency of reinforcements given and the number of people to whom they were distributed were correlated $r = .62$ ($p < .01$), and the total number of reinforcements received and the number of people they were received from were correlated .70 ($p < .01$).

Discussion The results on the giving and the receiving of reinforcement indicate that these are reciprocal activities. Those who give the most get the most, and vice versa. Since precaution was taken to base the measures of giving and receiving on different events, this finding is of substantial interest. For one thing, it suggests that reinforcement giving is an operant which comes under the control of generalized social reinforcers of other children at very early ages. This finding also is reminiscent of the commonality between dependency behavior and nurturance giving found by Hartup and Keller (1960) and Eininger (1965).

LOCATION, OVERTURES, AND CONSEQUENCES *Findings* Each reinforcing incident was categorized as to the type of play occurring at the time the child was reinforcing the "other." The type of play (or location of the child) was categorized: (a) dramatic play—housekeeping area, blocks, trucks, puppet play, and so forth; (b) table activities—puzzles or other manipulative table toys, art activities, stories or flannel board, and so forth; (c) wandering—going from place to place without engaging in the available activities or standing on the sidelines observing. Overall, 65 per cent of the reinforcement was given during dramatic play activities. The following proportions of specific kinds of reinforcement occurred during dramatic play: Category I, 59 per cent; Category II, 70 per cent; Category III, 67 per cent; and Category IV, 77 per cent. Boys gave a larger proportion of their reinforcements (74 per cent) during dramatic play than did girls (51 per cent).

A tally was made of the types of activity in which children were engaged when no reinforcements were given during the 3-minute observation period. During these observation periods, children were usually engaged in table activities (60 per cent) or wandering about the room (19 per cent), while only 21 per cent of these observations found the child in a play area where dramatic play was in progress or was a possibility.

Each reinforcement was also coded as to whether an overture had been made by the recipient, that is, whether an indication was given that reinforcement was desired. Overtures, overall, were present almost half (47 per cent) of the time but the proportions differed for each category of reinforcement. For attention and approval, the proportion was 49 per cent; for submission, 67 per cent; for affection and personal acceptance, 18 per cent; and for tokens, 4 per cent. There were no age or sex differences in proportion of overture present for total frequencies.

The coder found it somewhat difficult to code the consequences of reinforcement, and thus, the following results are tentative. For the most part (58 per cent), reinforcement was followed by the recipient continuing the activity in which he was engaged at the time of reinforcement. Sixteen per cent of the reinforcements were followed by a change in behavior, 6 per cent were rejected, 8 per cent were ignored, and 12 per cent could not be rated.

Discussion   The data on location of reinforcement show that opportunities for dramatic play activities are particularly conducive to the child's acquisition of positive social skills with peers. It is clear from the results of this study that, as would be expected, activities which involve attending to a project or to an adult do not elicit as large quantities of social reinforcement from peers as do dramatic play activities. It is also interesting that boys, who are usually characterized as being more active than girls in the nursery school play group, do indeed engage in a larger proportion of social reinforcing peer interaction during dramatic play than girls, who divide their reinforcements almost equally between dramatic play and more sedentary activities.

The data on overture present or absent suggest that different stimuli elicit the giving of different kinds of social reinforcers. Attention, approval, and submission seem to require a prior social response from another child. On the other hand, affection, personal acceptance, and tokens appear to function as instrumental actions used to initiate an interaction sequence. The data concerning the consequences of peer reinforcement are particularly important, although in need of replication. It appears that reinforcement (as defined by the actions observed in the present study) usually sustains ongoing behavior and that very few reinforcements are rejected.

CONCLUSIONS

The observational method used, although time consuming and comparatively subjective, yielded promising results concerning the positive social reinforcement behavior of preschool children. The results indicated that children of this age manifest a wide variety of positive behaviors, and developmental changes are apparent. The ultimate value of the present observational method will depend on the predictive value of the information obtained. As is reported elsewhere (Hartup & Coates, 1967; Hartup, Glazer, & Charlesworth, 1967), the present measures of classroom behavior have been found to be predictive of behavior in two other situations. Consequently, further work utilizing this approach to the study of peer reinforcement seems warranted.

References

EININGER, MARY ANN. Dependency behavior as related to two kinds of nurturance in young children. Unpublished M.A. thesis, University of Minnesota, 1965.

FLOYD, JOANNE. Effects of the amount of reward and friendship status of the other on the frequency of sharing in children. Unpublished doctoral dissertation, University of Minnesota, 1964.

GEWIRTZ, J. L. A learning analysis of the effects of normal stimulation, privation and deprivation on the acquisition of social motivation and attachment. In B. Foss (Ed.), *Determinants of infant behavior.* New York: Wiley, 1961.

HARTUP, W. W. Friendship status and the effectiveness of peers as reinforcing agents. *Journal of experimental child Psychology*, 1964, **1**, 154–162.

———, & COATES, B. Imitation of a peer as a function of reinforcement from the peer group and rewardingness of the model. *Child Development*, 1967, **38**, 1003–1016.

———, GLAZER, JANE, & CHARLESWORTH, ROSALIND. Peer reinforcement and sociometric status. *Child Development*, 1967, 38, 1017–1024.

———, & KELLER, E. D. Nurturance in preschool children and its relation to dependency *Child Development*, 1960, **31**, 681–689.

PARTEN, MILDRED B. Social participation among preschool children. *Journal of abnormal and social Psychology*, 1932, **27**, 243–269.

PATTERSON, G. E., BRICKER, W., & GREEN, M. Peer group reactions as a determinant of aggressive behavior in nursery school children. Paper presented at the meetings of the American Psychological Association, 1964.

SKINNER, B. F. *Science and human behavior.* New York: Macmillan, 1953.

STEVENSON, H. W. Social reinforcement of children's behavior. In L. P. Lipsitt and C. C. Spiker (Eds.), *Advances in child development and behavior.* Vol. 2. New York: Academic Press, 1965. Pp. 97–126.

SWIFT, JOAN. Effects of early group experience: the nursery school and day nursery. In M. Hoffman and L. Hoffman (Eds.), *Review of child development research.* Vol. 1. New York: Russell Sage Found., 1964. Pp. 249–288.

WALKER, HELEN, & LEV, J. *Elementary statistical methods.* New York: Holt, 1958.

The Early Training Project: A Seventh Year Report*

Susan W. Gray and Rupert A. Klaus
GEORGE PEABODY COLLEGE FOR TEACHERS

This is a report at the end of fourth grade of a preschool intervention project for children from low income homes. Its purpose was to investigate whether one could offset progressive retardation in elementary school. Special experiences provided for the 44 experimental children were based upon variables associated with attitudes and aptitudes conducive to school achievement. Intensive work was done for three summers; in the remaining months there were weekly home visits. Over the years the experimental children remained significantly superior to control children on intelligence tests. On measures of language and achievement trends still remained, but differences were no longer significant by the end of fourth grade. There is a slight but parallel decline across groups. Evidence is presented on younger siblings.

The Early Training Project has been a field research study concerned with the development and testing over time of procedures for improving the educability of young children from low income homes. The rationale, the general design and methodology, and findings through the second year of schooling have been reported in some detail in *The early training project for disadvantaged children, a report after five years*, by Klaus and Gray (1968). A briefer report, up to school entrance, is given in Gray and Klaus (1965). The purpose of this report is to present the findings at the end of the fourth grade, three years after all experimental intervention had ceased.

The major concern of the Early Training Project was to study whether it was possible to offset the progressive retardation observed in the public schooling careers of children living in deprived circumstances. In addition, the writers undertook to study the spillover effect upon other children in the community and upon other family members.

The general research strategy was one of attempting to design a research "package" consisting of variables which—on the basis of research upon social class, cognitive development, and motivation—might be assumed to be relevant to the school retardation which is observed in deprived groups and which at the same time might be subject to the effects of manipulation. Because this was a problem with major social implications, we also tried to design a general treatment approach which it would be feasible to repeat on a large scale, in the event that the procedures proved successful.

Subjects were 88 children born in 1958. Sixty-one of these lived in a city of 25,000 in the upper South. The remaining 27, who served as a distal control

Reprinted from *Child Development*, 41, 909–924. Copyright © 1970, by The Society for Research in Child Development. Inc., By permission.

* Major financial support for this study was received from the National Institute of Mental Health, under Mental Health Project Grant 5-R11-MH-765. Additional support for research staff during the later phases of the study was made possible through Grant HD-00973 from the National Institute of Child Health and Human Development, from the Office of Education, Contract OEC 3-7-070706-3118, and Grant 9174 from the Office of Economic Opportunity.

group, resided in a similar city 65 miles away. The children were all Negro. When we initiated the study the schools of the city were still segregated; we chose to work with Negro children because in this particular setting we had reason to believe that our chances of success were greater with this group.

The children were selected on the basis of parent's occupation, parent's education, income, and housing conditions. At the beginning of the study incomes were considerably below the approximate $3,000 used as the poverty line for a family of four. Occupations were either unskilled or semi-skilled; the educational level was eighth grade or below; housing conditions were poor. The median number of children per family at the beginning of the study was five; in about one-third of the homes there was no father present.

From the 61 children in the first city three groups were constituted by random assignment. The first group (T1) attended, over a period of three summers, a ten-week preschool designed to offset the deficits usually observed in the performance of children from disadvantaged homes. In addition, this

TABLE 1
Layout of General Research Design

TREATMENTS	T1 THREE SUMMER SCHOOLS	T2 TWO SUMMER SCHOOLS	T3 LOCAL CONTROLS	T4 DISTAL CONTROLS
First winter 1961–62	(Criterion development, curriculum planning, general tooling up)			
First summer 1962	Pre-test Summer school Post-test	Pre-test Post-test	Pre-test Post-test	Pre-test Post-test
Second winter 1962–63	Home visitor contacts			
Second summer 1963	Pre-test Summer school Post-test	Pre-test Summer school Post-test	Pre-test Post-test	Pre-test Post-test
Third winter 1963–64	Home visitor contacts	Home visitor contacts		
Third summer 1964	Pre-test Summer school Post-test	Pre-test Summer school Post-test	Pre-test Post-test	Pre-test Post-test
Fourth winter 1964–65	Home visitor contacts	Home visitor contacts		
Fourth summer 1965	Follow-up tests	Follow-up tests	Follow-up tests	Follow-up tests
Fifth summer 1966	Follow-up tests	Follow-up tests	Follow-up tests	Follow-up tests
Seventh summer 1968	Follow-up tests	Follow-up tests	Follow-up tests	Follow-up tests

group had three years of weekly meetings with a specially trained home visitor during those months in which the preschool was not in session. The second group (T2) had a similar treatment, except that it began a year later; the children received two summers of the special preschool and two years of home visits. The third group (T3) became the local control group, which received all tests but no intervention treatment. The fourth group (T4), the distal control group, was added to the design because of the somewhat ghetto-type concentration of Negroes in the first city. The local and distal control groups also made possible the study of spillover effects upon children and parents living in proximity to the experimental children. The general layout of the experimental design is given in Table 1.

By reading down the columns, one may see the particular treatment and testing sequence followed for each of the four groups. Periodic testing is continuing for the children through elementary school.

THE INTERVENTION PROGRAM

The overall rationale for the intervention program grew out of the literature on child-rearing patterns in different social classes, plus the writers' own observations in low income homes. On the basis of this study, the intervention program for children was organized around two broad classes of variables: attitudes relating to achievement, and aptitudes relating to achievement. Under attitudes we were particularly interested in achievement motivation, especially as it concerns school-type activities, in persistence, in ability to delay gratification; and in general interest in typical school materials, such as books, crayons, puzzles, and the like. We were also concerned with the parent's attitude toward achievement, particularly in their aspirations for their children, especially as they related to schooling.

In the broad class of aptitude variables relating to achievement we were particularly interested in perceptual and cognitive development and in language. Children from low income homes have been shown to have deficits in these areas, all of which appear closely related to school success in the primary grades.

In the summer months, for 10 weeks the children met in assembled groups. Each of the two experimental groups had a head teacher, who was an experienced Negro first grade teacher. There were in addition three or four teaching assistants. These assistants were divided about equally as to race and sex.

The work with the parents in the project was carried on largely through a home visitor program in which a specially trained preschool teacher made weekly visits to each mother and child. Both the home program and the school program are described in considerable detail in *Before first grade* (Gray, Klaus, Miller, and Forrester, 1966) and in Klaus and Gray (1968).

Prior to and after each summer session children in all four groups were tested on several instruments. From the first summer certain standardized tests of intelligence and language were used, along with a number of less formal instruments. At the end of first grade, achievement tests were added. This testing schedule is shown in Table 1. In general the .05 level of significance was used.

RESULTS

The detailed results of the testing program through May, 1966, the end of the second grade for the children, are given in Klaus and Gray (1968). This paper gives the results as they relate to the spring and summer testings of 1968 with some additional information on performance of younger siblings. The same kinds of analyses were used for the 1968 data as were used in the earlier paper.

In 1968 the following tests were administered to all children still residing in middle Tennessee: the Binet, the Peabody Picture Vocabulary Test, and the Metropolitan Achievement Test. The analyses here reported are based only upon those children available for testing with the exception of one child in the distal control group.

TABLE 2
Mean Stanford-Binet MA and IQ Scores for the Four Treatment Groups at Each Administration

Date of Administration	T1($N = 19$) MA (mo.)	IQ	T2($N = 19$) MA (mo.)	IQ	T3($N = 18$) MA (mo.)	IQ	T4($N = 23$) MA (mo.)	IQ
May 1962	40.7	87.6	43.8	92.5	40.3	85.4	40.3	86.7
Aug. 1962	50.7	102.0	46.9	92.3	44.3	88.2	43.4	87.4
May 1963	55.6	96.4	56.0	94.8	53.2	89.6	50.4	86.7
Aug. 1963	59.3	97.1	60.6	97.5	55.0	87.6	52.3	84.7
Aug. 1964	68.0	95.8	71.6	96.6	62.3	82.9	59.4	80.2
Aug. 1965	83.8	98.1	86.3	99.7	79.4	91.4	77.0	89.0
June 1966	88.7	91.2	93.4	96.0	86.8	87.9	82.9	84.6
July 1968	106.0	86.7	111.4	90.2	104.7	84.9	96.2	77.7

The Stanford-Binet scores are given in Table 2, and are portrayed graphically in Figure 1. A Lindquist (1953) Type 1 analysis of the results of 1962–1968, in terms of IQ, gave a significant F of 4.45 for the four groups, and F of 16.81 for repeated measures, and F for interaction of groups over time of 3.51. All of these were significant at the .01 level or beyond. Next an analysis was made by the use of orthogonal comparisons. These are given in Table 3. Here it may be seen that the two experimental groups remained significantly superior to the two control groups.

The comparison of the first and the second experimental groups for 1968 showed an F of less than 1.00. The comparison of the two control groups, however, yielded an F that, although not conventionally significant, was still large enough (3.52 where $F_{.95} = 3.96$) to be suggestive of a sharper decline in the distal than in the local control group. As was true of earlier analyses the larger part of the variance appeared to be carried by the second experimental group and the distal control group.

The scores across the ten administrations of the Peabody Picture Vocabulary Test are given in Table 4 in MA and IQ form. A Lindquist (1953) Type 1 analysis of variance was performed for the MA scores.

TABLE 3
Orthogonal Comparisons of Treatment Group Sums for Binet IQ Scores for the Eight Administrations

Date of Administration	HO: T1 = T2 + T3 + T4 F Ratio	Conclusion	HO: T2 = T3 + T4 F Ratio	Conclusion	HO: T3 = T4 F Ratio	Conclusion
Aug. 1962	12.67*	T1 > T2 − T3 + T4	1.44	T2 = T3 + T4	<1.00	T3 = T4
May 1963	2.91	T1 = T2 + T3 + T4	3.36	T2 = T3 + T4	<1.00	T3 = T4
	HO: T1 + T2 = T3 + T4		HO: T1 = T2		HO: T3 = T4	
May 1962	2.07	T1 + T2 = T3 + T4	1.53	T1 = T2	<1.00	T3 = T4
Aug. 1963	18.53*	T1 + T2 > T3 + T4	<1.00	T1 = T2	<1.00	T3 = T4
Aug. 1964	29.94*	T1 + T2 > T3 + T4	<1.00	T1 = T2	<1.00	T3 = T4
Aug. 1965	11.12*	T1 + T2 > T3 + T4	<1.00	T1 = T2	<1.00	T3 = T4
June 1966	5.99*	T1 + T2 > T3 + T4	1.18	T1 = T2	<1.00	T3 = T4
July 1968	7.50*	T1 + T2 > T3 + T4	<1.00	T1 = T2	3.53	T3 = T4

* $p < .05$; $F_{.95} = 3.97$.

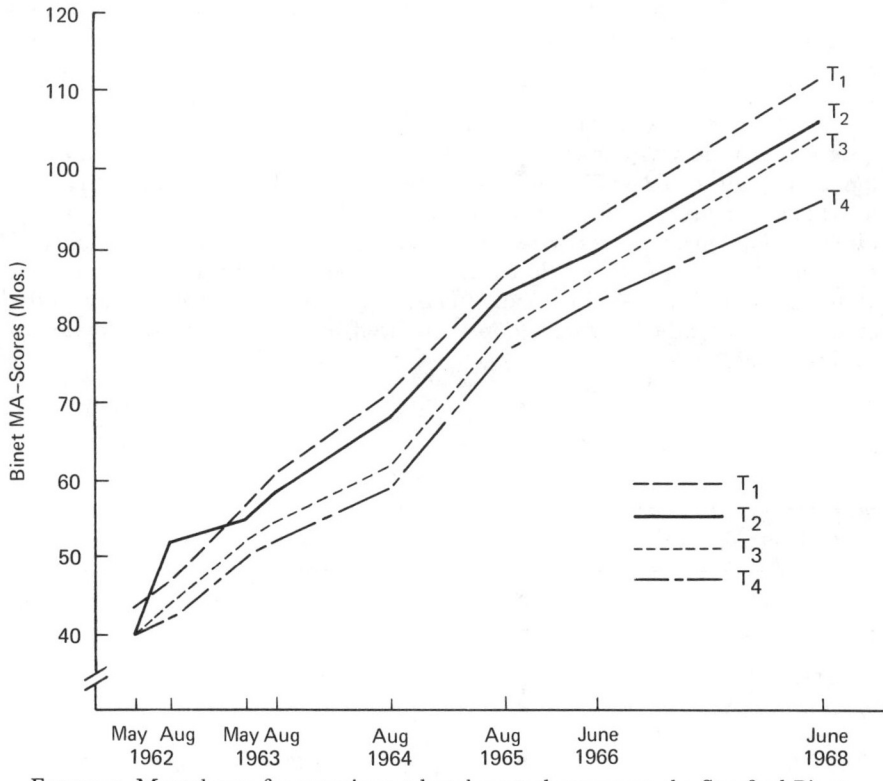

FIGURE 1. Mental ages for experimental and control groups on the Stanford-Binet.

TABLE 4
Mean PPVT Mental Age Scores and IQ Equivalents for the Four Treatment Groups for the Ten Administrations

DATE OF ADMINIS-TRATION	TEST FORM	T1($N = 19$) MA (MO.)	IQ	T2($N = 19$) MA (MO.)	IQ	T3($N = 18$) MA (MO.)	IQ	T4($N = 23$) MA (MO.)	IQ
May 1962	A	30.0	69.5	30.6	70.1	29.4	66.4	32.2	74.0
Aug. 1962	B	36.8	75.3	33.1	63.9	32.7	65.8	30.7	62.8
May 1963	A	44.8	79.0	40.7	69.6	39.1	69.3	39.5	69.8
Aug. 1963	B	45.0	78.4	50.7	83.6	38.4	64.0	37.6	63.8
May 1964	B	55.6	81.2	60.1	85.5	45.8	65.4	48.7	70.9
Aug. 1964	A	59.1	83.0	62.0	87.0	50.6	72.4	48.7	69.6
June 1965	B	74.2	89.0	76.2	90.3	67.6	83.0	67.3	84.0
Aug. 1965	A	70.6	86.2	76.5	91.8	65.4	80.2	66.3	83.4
June 1966	A	78.1	86.7	81.9	89.3	75.4	83.9	71.2	80.7
July 1968	A	96.4	84.5	100.3	86.7	91.7	81.8	89.3	78.7

F for groups was 5.16, indicating a significant effect of the experimental treatment upon the children's performance. F for repeated testings was 376.73, an effect that would be clearly expected when MA scores were used. These were selected in preference to IQ scores on this particular test since the IQ scores appear to lack discrimination at certain levels. The interaction between groups and time was non-significant. Orthogonals were next used. Here was found that T1 + T2 was significantly greater than T3 + T4 up until 1968, in which year differences were not significant. As may be seen from Table 4, differences in mean scores were still apparent. Heterogeneity had increased over time, however, so that differences were no longer significant. In no analysis at any point of time was either experimental group significantly superior to the other. Nor did either control group show itself to be significantly superior to the other one.

TABLE 5
Metropolitan Achievement Test Grade Equivalent Mean Scores for the Various Subtests for the Three Administrations

SUBTEST AND YEAR	T1	T2	T3	T4
Word knowledge:				
1965	1.69	1.73	1.79	1.37
1966	2.32	2.47	2.29	1.98
1968	3.58	3.90	3.54	3.27
Word discrimination:				
1965	1.68	1.81	1.82	1.37
1966	2.64	2.73	2.65	2.20
1968	3.73	3.95	3.76	3.47
Reading:				
1965	1.72	1.82	1.84	1.46
1966	2.52	2.75	2.56	2.11
1968	3.52	3.89	3.72	3.10
Arithmetic computation:				
1965	1.52	1.62	1.54	1.43
1966	2.41	2.55	2.49	2.05
1968	3.92	4.07	4.06	3.79
Spelling:				
1966	2.42	2.85	2.60	1.99
1968	4.26	4.69	4.24	3.67
Language:				
1968	3.52	4.00	3.63	3.17
Arithmetic problem-solving and concepts:				
1968	3.31	3.54	3.75	3.26

The results for the Metropolitan Achievement Test are given in Table 5. A Lindquist (1953) Type 1 analysis was performed on each subtest, and orthogonal comparisons made. In the interest of brevity a table of orthogonal comparisons is not given. In 1965, at the end of first grade, the experimental children were significantly superior on three of the four tests used at that time: word knowledge, word discrimination, and reading. For arithmetic computation scores, F was less than 1.00. The local controls were also somewhat superior to the distal controls on these tests, an indication possibly of horizontal diffusion or, either in interaction or independently, a somewhat better instructional program. In 1966 five subtests were given. This time only two were significant, word knowledge and reading. On the other three tests, however, the F's ranged from 2.69 to 2.84, suggesting probabilities at about the .10 level. In neither year was T1 significantly superior to T2. The highest F was 1.16, where $F_{.95}$ is 3.97. In the comparisons of T3 and T4, T3 was superior to T4 on reading and arithmetic computation. On word knowledge, word discrimination, and spelling the F's ranged from 3.19 to 3.85, suggesting probabilities beyond the .10 level ($F_{.90} = 2.77$). At the end of the fourth year no significant effects were found with the single exception of reading, on which T3 was superior to T4. There is some suggestion of residual effect since in six of the seven possible comparisons of experimental and controls, the experimentals were superior. Also on all seven possible comparisons the local control group was superior to the distal control group.

The Binet was administered in all four groups to those younger siblings who were of testable age. This was first done in 1964 and again in 1966. Since

TABLE 6
Initial Binet Scores of Treatment Group Children and Younger Siblings in Two Testings

Testing	Groups	Mean Scores (First Testing, 1962) for Treatment Group Children with Younger Siblings			Mean Scores for Younger Siblings		
		N	CA	IQ	N	CA	IQ
1964 testing of younger siblings born in 1959 and 1960	T1	12	47	82	13	54	82
	T2	16	46	89	21	53	83
	T3	7	50	84	9	54	71
	T4	12	48	88	14	62	74
1966 retesting of younger siblings initially tested in 1964	T1	12	47	82	13	78	85
	T2	14	46	92	19	76	85
	T3	5	46	82	7	76	78
	T4	11	48	86	13	77	75
1966 testing of younger siblings born in 1961 and 1962	T1	10	44	87	11	58	84
	T2	9	47	91	10	52	87
	T3	7	48	83	9	56	76
	T4	12	47	88	15	55	84
1966 testing of all younger siblings	T1	15	50	84	24	69	84
	T2	17	46	91	29	68	86
	T3	8	47	84	16	65	77
	T4	15	47	86	28	63	80

TABLE 7
Orthogonal Comparisons of Binet Scores of Younger Siblings

	HO: T1 + T2 = T3 + T4		HO: T1 = T2		HO: T3 = T4	
	F Ratio	Conclusion	F Ratio	Conclusion	F Ratio	Conclusion
All younger siblings 1966	3.48	T1 + T2 = T3 + T4	.75	T1 = Y2	.00	T3 = T4
Younger siblings first tested in 1966	.77	T1 + T2 = T3 + T4	.04	T1 = T2	.80	T3 = T4
Younger siblings retested in 1966						
1964 results	8.13*	T1 + T2 > T3 + T4	.74	T1 = T2	.01	T3 = T4
1966 results	4.72*	T1 + T2 > T3 + T4	5.11*	T1 > T2	2.07	T3 = T4

* $p < .05$; $F_{.95} = 3.97$.

the 1966 findings have not been previously reported they are presented here in Table 6. In 1964, 57 children were tested. Fifty of these same children were tested again in 1966, along with 43 additional siblings who were too young to test in 1964.

An analysis of co-variance was performed on these scores, with the IQ's at first testing of the target-age children used as the covariable. Also, where there were two younger siblings in the same family, one was dropped, so that the analysis was based on 87 children. Separate analyses were also performed for the 1964 and the 1966 results of all children who were retested. In addition, an analysis was performed on the 1966 results for those children who were being tested for the first time.

On all younger siblings tested in 1966 the F between groups was not significant at the .05 level ($F = 3.97$). It was significant beyond the .10 level, and therefore we made further analyses. Orthogonal comparisons were used, with the hypotheses shown in Table 7. This is the same general approach as used with the target children. All orthogonal comparisons showed significant differences for the testing of all younger siblings in 1966: the combined experimental group siblings were superior to the combined control group siblings; the T1 siblings were superior to the T2 siblings; and the T3 siblings were superior to the T4 siblings. When the children who were tested for the first time are separated out, it is clear, both in the 1966 and the 1964 data, that most of the variance was being carried by younger siblings closer in age to the target age children. There are some interesting implications of these general results on younger siblings which will be examined in more detail in the discussion section.

DISCUSSION

The results on the one test of intelligence which was used consistently from the initiation of the program in 1962 until the testing at the end of the fourth grade, in 1968, are very much in line with what might be expected, for this was an intervention program that used a broad gauge approach and which was relatively successful in terms of improving the educability of young children from low income homes. Intervention caused a rise in intelligence which was fairly sharp at first, then leveled off, and finally began to show decline once intervention ceased. The control groups on the other hand tended to show a slight but consistent decline with the single exception of a jump between entrance into public school and the end of first grade. Differences between experimentals and controls on Binet IQ were still significant at the end of the third year after intervention ceased. All four groups have shown a decline in IQ after the first grade but the decline, as shown in Figure 1, tended to be relatively parallel. Perhaps the remarkable thing is, with the relatively small amount of impact over time that differences should still be significant. After all, the child experienced only five mornings of school a week for ten weeks for two or three summers, plus weekly home visits during the other nine months for two or three years. This suggests that the impact was not lost. It was not sufficient however, to offset the massive effects of a low income home in which the child had lived since birth onward.

The results on the PPVT showed a pattern that is not dissimilar. There was a rise during intervention, including the first grade, then a leveling-off and a slight decline. Here, however, differences between groups, although consistent were no longer significant.

The importance of the school situation for the maintenance or loss of a gain should be weighed. The children for the most part remained in schools in which the entire population was Negro. Eight of the local children at the end of first grade did enroll in schools that had previously been all white. Four more changed during the next two years. None of the distal children attended schools with white children. Since in this area, as in many places, race tends to be confounded with social class, the children in the study did not in general have the advantage of classmates with relatively high expectancies. There is some evidence that in both of the all-Negro schools the general teaching-learning situation, although fair, was less adequate than in the schools that have formerly been all white. This, plus the continuing effect of the home situation and the immediate community, took its toll. There are some data on achievement test scores to be presented later which suggest the impact of the two all-Negro schools which most of the children attended.

On the one achievement battery administered from first to fourth grade, the Metropolitan Achievement Test (Table 5), significant differences did not appear in 1968 on any of the subtests with sole exception of the reading score, in which the local control group was superior to the distant control group. The experimentals had been superior to the controls on three tests in 1965 and on two tests in 1966. One might interpret this as showing that the intervention program did have measurable effects upon test performance at the end of first grade, but that by the end of fourth grade, the school program had failed to sustain at any substantial level the initial superiority. Although disappointing, this is perhaps not surprising in a test battery so dependent upon specific school instruction.

An interesting sidelight is thrown on this matter by looking at the performance on the Metropolitan Achievement Test of the eight children from the local school who at the end of first grade enrolled in previously all-white schools.

TABLE 8

Mean Gains on the MAT over a 3-Year Period for 8 ETP Children in Integrated Schools and Matches in Negro Schools

	WORD KNOWL.	WORD DISC.	READ.	ARITH.
ETP *S*s in integrated schools beginning fall 1965	3.1	2.8	2.7	2.9
ETP *S*s in negro schools matched to the first group on spring 1965 *MAT* and on verbal rating by home visitor	1.7	2.0	1.6	1.7
Difference	1.4	.8	1.1	1.2

(Mean Gains 1965–68)

An attempt was made, on the basis of first grade achievement tests and home ratings of educational aspirations, to match these eight children with eight who remained in the Negro school. Admittedly, this is a chancy business, and one which should not be taken too seriously. Table 8 presents the gains in grade equivalents on the Metropolitan Achievement Tests from the end of first grade to the end of fourth grade.

On the four subtests common to both grade levels the picture is a clear one of more gain in the children who changed schools, varying from .8 to 1.4 years' greater gain. These data did not seem appropriate for subjection to statistical analysis. They do suggest however, the fairly obvious: that performance on achievement tests is directly related to school experience. The children who changed schools have made approximately "normal" gains for their three years; the children who did not change have gained two years or less during the three years from first through fourth grade.

The results on the younger siblings are to the writers among the most interesting findings of the study. We have termed the process by which such results are achieved and the product of that process as vertical diffusion, to suggest that this is a spread of effect down the family from the mother and possibly the target-age child to a younger child. In this study the effects of the older sibling and the mother upon the younger child were confounded. Some research currently being carried on under the direction of one of the writers has made possible the separation of the influence of mother and older siblings. Results so far indicate that most of the effect is coming from the mother. It is plausible to assume that the role of the mother was the more influential since considerable effort was expended by the home visitor over a period of three years with the first experimental group and over two years with the second experimental group. The emphasis of the home intervention was on making the mother a more effective teacher, or more generally, an effective educational change agent for her target-age child. Also worthy of note is the finding that vertical diffusion appeared more clearly in the younger siblings born in 1959 and 1960, who were within one to two and a half years in age of the older siblings. The siblings born in 1961 and 1962, when pulled out for separate analysis, did not show an effect which approached statistical significance. Vertical diffusion also appeared more operative in the first than in the second experimental group. A plausible explanation is that intervention lasted a year longer with the first group and began a year earlier. There is also in the data some suggestion of a process we have examined in more detail elsewhere (Klaus and Gray, 1968), one that may be termed horizontal diffusion, the spread of effect from one family to another. This we have in general analyzed by comparing the local and distal control groups. Here we found that the younger siblings in the local control group showed themselves to be superior to the distal control group.

To the extent that the findings on vertical diffusion have generality, they seem to point to the efficacy of a powerful process in the homes, presumably mediated by the parent, which may serve to improve the educability of young children. Before a second conclusion is reached by the reader, however, to the effect that "parent education" is the answer, we would like to point out that our procedure was clearly parent education with a difference. It was conducted in the home; it was done by skilled preschool teachers with some experience in working in the homes; it was highly concrete and specific to a given mother's life situation; it was continuous over a long period of time. Indeed, parent education probably is the answer, but in low income homes a very different kind of parent education from that usually provided may be needed.

Seven years after the Early Training Project began, in 1969, intervention programs for young children from low income homes are nationwide. These programs differ tremendously in the length and timing of the intervention, in the objectives and consistency with which they are followed, in the degree of specificity of the program, and in the length and extent of follow-up study of the sample.

It is hardly surprising, with the wild heterogeneity of such programs, that nationwide assessment of programs, such as the Westinghouse Survey of Project Head Start (1969), would find relatively small evidence of positive effects upon the child's achievement and personal adequacy. Leaving aside all the problems of measuring personal adequacy and even achievement in young children, such lack of results is only to be expected in situations where the bad or inappropriate so cancels out the good that little positive effect can be found, especially if the evaluation is somewhat premature.

At this point in time it seems appropriate to look more closely at those programs which have clearly followed an adequate research design, specified and carefully monitored their treatments, and conducted adequate follow-up study of the sample. Such programs are relatively few in number, for their history is short.

In the Early Training Project we have been more fortunate than most. The study was initiated nearly four years before the tidal wave of interests in such early intervention that came about through such nationwide programs as Project Head Start and Title I and III of the Elementary and Secondary Education Act. We have worked in a setting in which we have been free from administrative pressures either to change our procedures or to make premature conclusions from our data. The two communities in which families live have had little outward mobility; even at the end of seven years attrition is only a minor problem. For these reasons we believe the data collected over seven years with our four groups of children do shed some light upon the problem of progressive retardation and the possibility that it can be offset.

Our answer as to whether such retardation can be offset is one of cautious optimism. The effects of our intervention program are clearly evidenced through the second year of public schooling, one year after intervention ceased. There is still an effect, most apparent in the Binet, after two more years of non-intervention. Our data on horizontal and vertical diffusion, especially the latter, gives us some hope that intervention programs can have a lasting effect that goes beyond the children that were the target of that intervention program.

Still, it is clear from our data, with a parallel decline across the four groups in the second through fourth grades, that an intervention program before school entrance, such as ours, cannot carry the entire burden of offsetting progressive retardation. By some standards the Early Training Project might be seen as one of relatively massive intervention. And yet a colleague of ours (Miller, 1969) has estimated that in the years prior to school entrance the maximum amount of time that the children in the project could have spent with the Early Training Project staff was approximately 600 hours, less than two percent of their waking hours from birth to six years. Perhaps the remarkable thing is that the effect lasted as well and as long as it did. In a similar vein, we have estimated the amount of these contacts which was in the home as a maximum of 110 hours, are about 0.3 percent of the waking hours of the child from birth to six years. Surely it would be foolish not to realize that, without massive changes in the life situation of the child, home circumstances will continue to have their adverse effect upon the child's performance.

In 1968 the authors wrote:

> The most effective intervention programs for preschool children that could possibly be conceived cannot be considered a form of inoculation whereby the child forever after is immune to the effects of a low income home and of a school inappropriate to his needs. Certainly, the evidence on human performance is overwhelming in indicating that such performance results from the continual interaction of the organism with its environment. Intervention programs, well conceived and executed, may be expected to make some relatively lasting changes. Such programs, however, cannot be expected to carry the whole burden of providing adequate schooling for children from deprived circumstances; they can provide only a basis for future progress in schools and homes that can build upon that early intervention.

In 1969 we see no reason to alter this statement. Our seventh year results only serve to underscore its truth.

References

GRAY, S. W., & KLAUS, R. A. An experimental preschool program for culturally deprived children. *Child Development*, 1965, **36**, 887–898.

———, KLAUS, R. A., MILLER, J. O., & FORRESTER, N. J. *Before first grade*. New York: Teachers College Press, Columbia University, 1966.

KLAUS, R. A., & GRAY, S. W. The early training project for disadvantaged children: A report after five years. *Monograph of the Society for Research in Child Development*, 1968, *33* (4, Serial No. 120).

LINDQUIST, E. R. *The design and analysis of experiments in psychology and education*. Boston: Houghton Mifflin, 1953.

MILLER, J. O. Cultural deprivation and its modification; effects of intervention. In Haywood, C. H. (Ed.) *Social-cultural aspects of mental retardation*. New York: Appleton-Century-Crofts, Inc., 1970.

Westinghouse Learning Corporation. *The impact of Head Start: An evaluation of the Head Start experience on children's cognitive and affective development*. Westinghouse Learning Corporation, Ohio University, 1969.

Chapter 4

Merrill-Palmer Institute by Donna J. Harris

Socialization: Interaction and Results

An increasing complexity of feelings and emotions accompany the child's growing variety of interactions with people and objects. At the same time, he learns to understand and control his emotions, although not completely, of course. He makes a beginning in the long process of learning to behave and to feel in ways that are acceptable to himself and to society. At the beginning of the preschool period, he has some concept of himself as a physical object in space; by the end of this time, he can think of himself as a person-among-persons. He is affected by the religious–philosophical orientation of his family and his culture.

Emotional Development

Evidence for emotional differentiation during the preschool years is supplied by a study on awareness of affect concepts in 4-, 5-, and 6-year-olds [34]. With increasing age, children tended to differentiate more between affect concepts, as shown in tests such as sorting pictures with different facial expressions, knowing affect words (happy, sad, mad, angry), inferring subjective state from stick figures, and acknowledging experiences ("a scary dream") and feelings ("Do you sometimes feel lonely?"). Children high in affect awareness were likely to be also empathic in relations with peers and imaginative in art and in play.

Love

The discussion of love in infancy pointed out that love, at all ages, involves delight in being with, desire to be with, and desire for contact and response from another person. Early in the course of development, certainly by the time the baby becomes a toddler, love includes another dimension, the desire to give to the other person, expressed in attempts to promote his happiness and well-being. The first dimension, the desire to be with the love object, was explored as *attachment behavior*. Preschool love has been studied in terms of the attitudes of adults in the family, especially *nurturant behavior*, and also in terms of *dependent behavior* in children. The child has a variety of love relationships with those who occupy different family positions. He also has love relationships with peers. This topic was discussed in the previous chapter, in the context of play [20, pp. 204–207].

General emotional atmosphere in the family is ordinarily thought to affect the well-being of the young child. A demonstration of this relationship is offered by a study of parental tensions in relation to child adjustment [11]. Seventy-six preschool children were observed and rated on quality of emotional adjustment. Their parents were interviewed about their relationships to each other. Healthy child adjustment was shown to be related to positive husband–wife adjustment in the areas of sex, consideration for one another, ability to talk over difficulties, and expression of affection. The data gave some indication that girls were more adversely affected by parental tension than were boys. Corroboration of the importance of general emotional atmosphere comes from a study [51] of two groups of preschool children, one from intact families and one from homes broken by divorce. Matched for IQ and age, the children were drawn from community-supported day nurseries. On a projective test of anxiety, the children from broken homes showed more disturbance than did the controls.

Nurturance. Probably the most studied component of love, nurturance is a willingness or even eagerness to promote the well-being and development of the loved one. Parents ordinarily have a large feeling of nurturance for their children. Many, perhaps most, adults feel nurturant toward all children. Erikson [30, p. 138] speaks of the sense of generativity, an essential of the mature personality. "Generativity is primarily the concern for establishing and guiding the next generation...." A high degree of nurturance is involved in generativity.

There is a mutuality to nurturance, the other side of the coin being an acceptance of it. The love that a child feels for a parent has a large measure of this acceptance in it. He counts on the parent's nurturance, expecting it and accepting it as a continuing part of life. The development of the baby's sense of trust was due in large part to the nurturance he received or, in Erikson's terms, to the strengths of his parents' sense of generativity. Having learned to trust his family in this way, the child accepts love as the foundation of his world. Even when parental nurture is not very dependable, some of it is much better than none at all. Bowlby has written about the nurturing function of mothers in these words [19, p. 68]:

> In no other human relationship do human beings place themselves so unreservedly and so continuously at the disposal of others. This holds true even of bad parents . . . Except in the worst cases, she is giving him food, shelter, comforting him in his distress, teaching him simple skills and above all providing him with that continuity of human care on which his sense of security rests.

The child's sense of security also requires continuity of the first aspect of love, that his parents will continue to find pleasure in his company. When he acts affectionate, cute, sweet, amusing, and otherwise endearing, part of his motivation is doubtless that of making his parents enjoy him. Although a preschool child's sense of generativity is only in the beginning stages, he does show kindness and generosity to peers and family [76, 77]. Nursery school children have been found willing to share candy, cookies, and money with other children. Generosity, kindness, sympathy, and helping are called *prosocial* behavior. Moral behavior is often understood as including prosocial behavior. This aspect of development is discussed in greater detail in Smart and Smart, *School-Age Children* and *Adolescents* (both Macmillan, 1973). Jimmy proudly helps Mother to carry the groceries in from the car. Donald tenderly pats Daddy's head on hearing that he has a headache. Polly carries a mug of coffee to Mommy in bed on Sunday morning. All three children promote their parents' comfort in ways that are simple and temporary yet realistic. And while a pat on the head is rather minute when compared to what Daddy did that day for Donald, it is an act of love, recognized and accepted as such by parent and child.

Nurturance in parents is vitally related to the socialization of children. Children are more likely to imitate nurturant models and to identify with them. Parental nurturance is correlated with children's moral development and prosocial behavior. It seems to be literally true that love begets love. Problem solving is also affected by nurturance. Preschool children, when faced with a complex puzzle task, did better under conditions of nurturance from an adult [27]. Highly dependent children were more affected by adult nurturance than were less dependent children.

Attachment. Attachment is an ongoing, durable affectional tie of one person to another [1]. It is something inside the person, formed by him through experience with the attachment object. Attachment is what most people understand as love. In Chapter 4 of Smart and Smart, *Infants* (Macmillan, 1973), we described the development of ties between the infant and mother and between the infant and other people. Attachment behavior includes clinging, following, smiling, watching, calling, listening, and any other attempts to make and maintain contact, plus crying and protesting at separation. Such behavior continues throughout the second year and most of the third year, in the normal course of development [20, pp. 204–207]. At age 2, the child is likely to cling or climb into his mother's lap when a stranger enters, but at 3, he is more likely to simply stand close to her [58]. At an average age of 2 years and 9 months, attachment behavior changes in such a way that children are much more willing to be separated temporarily from their mothers, more able to feel secure in a strange place and with subordinate attachment-figures [20]. Between 3 and 4, the need for frequent and intense contact decreases, and continues to decrease after 4. However, at 5 and 6 and even older, children like to cuddle occasionally, to hold hands when walking, and to have immediate contact when frightened.

As clinging and proximity-seeking decline, the child increases in making contacts from a distance [58]. He smiles, calls to his mother, talks to her, and shows her things. Another developmental change from 2 to 3 is seen in manipulative play. When left alone and then with a stranger, exploration is more depressed in 1- and 2-year-olds than in 3-year-olds.

Dependency. The constructs *dependency* and *attachment* overlap but they are not identical. An attachment is a durable affectional tie to another person. Attachment behavior is oriented to a particular person. Dependency involves seeking help, attention, approval, recognition, contact, and proximity. What is sought is significant, not the person giving it [1]. The same piece of behavior, say, a 3-three-year-old trying to get attention by showing his painting, might be attachment behavior if done in relation to his mother or dependent behavior if done in relation to his baby-sitter. The same piece of behavior also takes on different meanings at different ages and under different circumstances. Normal attachment behavior during the second year includes clinging to the mother when a stranger approaches. The average 4-year-old does not cling to his mother when a stranger approaches. If he does, *dependency* describes it better than *attachment*.

While dependency carries some implication of helplessness and immaturity, there are competent and mature ways of seeking help, contact, and recognition. Dependent behavior is necessary and normal for human beings. Some modes of dependent behavior are immature. The Harvard Preschool Project is concerned with competent behavior of children 3 to 6 years old. Social behavior characteristic of well-developed children was found to include getting and keeping the attention of adults, using adults as sources of information and help, and expressing affection under appropriate circumstances [70]. Less competent children were more likely to seek adults' attention through misbehavior.

As children grow, they change in their ways of seeking help, contact, proximity, attention, and recognition. They are expected to use more mature ways as they get older, ways appropriate to age, stage, and sex. For example, crying is socially acceptable in young children, as long as they do not cry as often as babies do. For school-age children, it is occasionally appropriate for girls, rarely for boys. Adolescent girls and women may properly cry in emotional crises, but adolescent boys and men are not supposed to resort to tears in any but the most extreme situations. Dependent behavior can therefore be classified as to appropriateness of maturity level, as well as according to degree.

Another age change in dependency behavior is in its relation to mutuality. As the person matures he gives more nurturance. Still dependent on others for company and nurturance, he can give as he accepts. The objects of dependency relationships also change. Dependent in the beginning on his mother, the child comes to depend upon other family members, then peers, teachers, other adults, eventually a husband or wife, and, perhaps, finally children.

There are wide cultural differences in parental attitudes toward independence. For example, an observer of another culture commented:

> it appeared that the child in Brazil is fondled, cuddled, hugged more often and to a later age than is general in the United States. There is a strong tendency for parents to be overprotective and indulgent as well,

behavior which is reflected in the cultural conception of the child as "the protected one"—a fragile creature ("his bones are soft") who needs constant warmth, care and protection [75].

North American parents tend to be concerned about dependency in children [29, p. 29]. Often one of their main goals in sending a child to nursery school is to encourage independence.

Many studies have dealt with the effects of mothers' behavior on dependency in children [36]. The availability of the mother has a bearing on the young child's seeking of contact. Two- and 3-year-old boys sought more affectionate contact with their female nursery school teachers when they (the children) came from large families where children were spaced close together [90]. There is some agreement that frustration and punishment in infancy and preschool years are associated with dependency in the preschool period. Evidence comes from studies which correlated mothers' feeding practices and discipline practices with later behavior in their children. The preschool child's dependency tended to be greater if his mother used withdrawal of love to discipline him, showed signs of rejection, punished parent-directed aggression, and was demonstrative with affection [80]. There is agreement in the literature that maternal rejection is associated with dependency in children. Cross-culture research [93] suggests that frustration and punishment in early childhood may affect adult dependency behavior. In cultures where children are punished severely for dependency behavior, adults show greater dependency than adults do in cultures where children's dependency behavior is indulged.

Fathers as well as mothers were included in an extensive study of relations between behavior of children and behavior of parents [13]. Children were observed in a nursery school and in a puzzle task where each child experienced easy success, probable success, and failure. Parent behavior was studied in two 3-hour home visits and in structured interviews with the mother and father. A group of children were identified as highly self-reliant, self-controlled, explorative, and content. Their parents tended to be warm, rational, and receptive to the child's communication, controlling, and demanding. Children who were the least self-reliant, incompetent, and aimless were likely to have permissive-indulgent parents. These parents were warm, encouraged autonomy, and made an effort toward cognitive enrichment. They were low on control, discouraging infantile dependency and rejecting. That is, they accepted dependent behavior and gave little firm direction.

In another study of parents and children, competence and dependent behavior were assessed by observation and interviews [25]. In general, children tended to be most competent and nondependent when parents treated them on their own level of maturity, rather than behaving as though the children were either adults or infants. In this dimension, fathers' behavior had more effect on girls, and mothers' on boys. A study of development from birth to maturity indicated that personality in childhood and adulthood was related to mothers' protective behavior when children were under 3 [46]. The definition of protection was not what many people would think of as an aspect of love or nurturance but was really overprotection. Rather than being a warm, helpful, cherishing pattern, it was rated on "(a) unsolicited and unnecessary nurturance of the child, (b) consistent rewarding of the child's requests for help and assistance, (c) encouraging the child to become dependent on her, (d) overconcern when the child was ill or in danger." A large measure of this kind of "protection" during the first 3 years in girls' lives was

Courtesy Frank Porter Graham, Child Development Center of the University of North Carolina.

associated with a tendency to withdraw from anxiety-arousing situations in adulthood. In boys' lives, "protection" during the first 3 years was associated with passivity at the 6- to 10-year age.

A certain amount of protection, control, and nurturance are essential for a child's existence and healthy development. Parents are faced with many decisions as to how to give their children enough response, help, contact, proximity, attention, and recognition without forcing or dominating and yet encouraging the child toward independent effort.

Sibling Love. Sibling love has a large measure of pleasure in being with the other person, and a less important component of nurturance and dependency. Koch has explored the attitudes existing between 5- and 6-year-olds and their siblings. Since these children are summing up their experiences of the preschool years, and since their younger brothers and sisters are preschoolers, some of the findings are pertinent here. The reasons children gave for wanting to play with their sibs and for not wanting them to leave the family were companionship, protection, general liking for the other child, and appreciation of his services. Older children spoke more of personal qualities such as "cuteness" or "niceness," while second-borns mentioned more the sib's services and protection. Girls reported playing more with younger sibs than did boys. Sibs close in age played together more than those with a greater age difference. Second-borns more often stated a preference for play with the sib and at the same time tended to believe that they played little with the sib. Thus the preschool children did not get all the companionship they sought from their older brothers and sisters.

Grandparent Love. Grandparent love relationships between children and grandparents have qualities different from parent–child and sib–sib love. Anthropological studies show that friendly equality between grandparents and children is a product of a certain kind of social structure [86]. Formality between grandparents and children is related to association of grandparents with family authority, through grandparents' either exercising authority or being the parents of the parent who definitely exercises authority over the children. Indulgent, close, and warm relationships are more likely to be built when grandparents have little authority in the family. The age and maturity of the child also influence the relationship [47].

When grandparents (70 grandfathers and 70 grandmothers) were questioned, it became apparent that the role of grandparent is played in a variety of ways [66]. Grandparenthood was comfortable and pleasant to 59 percent of the grandmothers and 61 percent of the grandfathers but difficult and uncomfortable to 36 percent and 29 percent, respectively. According to the style in which roles were played, there emerged three main types of grandparents and a fourth type, the parent surrogate, which applied to grandmothers only. The *fun-seeking* grandparent (29 percent of grandmothers, 24 percent of grandfathers) is probably the type referred to in the study mentioned above. These grandparents are informal and playful, joining the child for the purpose of having fun and mutual satisfaction. Authority lines are unimportant. The dimension of love featured in this relationship, therefore, is the one of delight in the company of the beloved and desire for response from him. The *formal* grandparent (31 percent of grandmothers, 33 percent of grandfathers) probably represents a more old-fashioned type of relationship. The formal grandparent takes an interest in the child, gives treats and indulgences, and occasionally helps the parents, but sees his (or her) role in strict terms. This grandparent does not offer advice and leaves parenting strictly to the parents. Nurturance and pleasure in the child's company are both aspects of the formal grandparent's relationship, with perhaps more emphasis on nurturance, and neither aspect being very strong. The *distant figure* (19 percent of grandmothers, 29 percent of grandfathers) feels remote from the child and acknowledges little effect of the child upon his life. Although this grandparent maintains a benevolent attitude, gives gifts on ritual occasions, and goes through certain motions, there is little feeling or response.

The love which a child experiences with his grandparent will, then, depend on the role his grandparent plays in relationship to him. He will most likely establish a mutually joyous relationship with the fun-seeker, where child and grandparent respond to each other, savoring the pleasures of each other's company. From the formal grandparent, the child will derive a certain satisfaction, knowing that nurturance and some response are forthcoming. The distant figure will probably be the object of indifference to the child, just as the child is to him, although the child will perhaps have some pleasant expectations of material benefits on Christmas and birthdays. The surrogate mother, the role played by some grandmothers, takes on many of the emotional characteristics of the mother–child relationship, although if the mother is also in the picture, the three-way relationship is more complex.

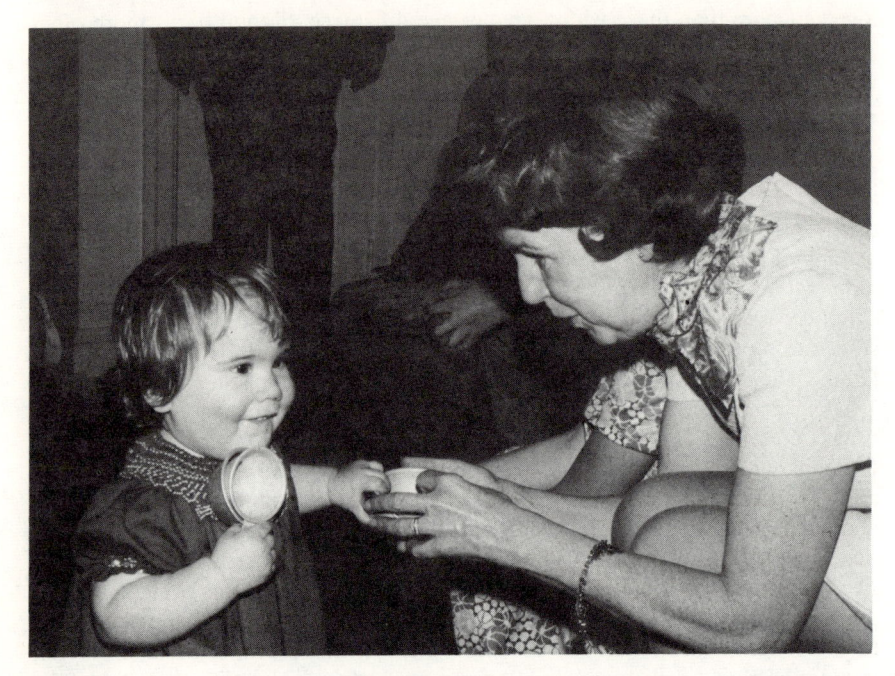

Ellen S. Smart

When grandparents were studied in relation to family structure, differences emerged between paternal and maternal grandparents [48]. Maternal grandmothers were much more positive in their perceptions and reactions than were paternal grandmothers. A majority of the former approved of the parents' child rearing, felt affectionate toward the child, and saw similarities between the child and themselves. Paternal grandparents were different in that it was the grandfather who had very positive responses, much more so than the maternal grandfather, who was quite uninvolved with the grandchild.

Matriarchal families are very common among lower-class black people [74]. Child care is often turned over to the grandmother while the mother earns money. Overburdened by poverty and responsibilities, with no male support, both the mother and grandmother are severe, inconsistent, and inattentive in relation to the child.

Anger and Aggression

Anger is the distress that accompanies being restrained or blocked in progress toward some sort of fulfillment. Diffuse and unproductive expressions of anger, such as crying, kicking, and throwing, are frequent in late infancy and the early part of the preschool period, when the child's desire for autonomy is strong and when he experiences many frustrations. Aggression is sometimes conceived as a controlled and productive attack on problems, resulting in increased knowledge, power, and/or status for the aggressor. In the latter context, the anger which accompanies aggression is a stirred-up, energized feeling which aids in problem solving and contributes to the development of the sense of initiative. Competition between people can involve either hostile aggression or controlled and productive aggression. Many practical dilemmas arise from the dual nature of anger and aggression. While a hostile attack is dangerous and destructive, there is great advantage in being able to fend off an attack and in taking the initiative. Some children use aggression very often in order to cope with frustration; others display little aggression but use dependent behavior in the face of frustration. Aggression can also occur when frustration is not involved.

Experiments by Bandura, Walters, and their associates have shown that children readily imitate aggressive behavior shown to them by live models and by models in films, both human and cartoon [5]. Children reproduced in detail the attacks of an adult model on a large inflated doll. When one group of children saw a model rewarded for aggression and another saw the same model punished, the first group imitated the model and the second did not. Both groups expressed disapproval of the model's behavior, however, calling him mean, wicked, harsh, and bossy. Thus, even though the children considered aggressive behavior undesirable, they imitated what paid off. They made some attempts to justify their choice by calling the victim dumb and selfish. The children who had observed the punished model were then offered rewards for aggressive behavior. They promptly imitated what they had seen the model do, thus showing that they had learned the aggressive behavior, even though they had not performed it when they observed it.

When adults are permissive of aggressive behavior, children tend to act aggressively. Parents vary in how much aggression they permit, against whom they permit it, and how it may be expressed. A group of highly educated parents ranked aggression as high in a list of undesirable behavior. Only avoidance (being aloof, timid, and withdrawn) was less desirable [29]. Middle-class parents usually try to substitute verbal forms of aggression for physical, although they tend to feel that boys should be able to defend themselves by fighting "if necessary." Lower-class parents are more permissive of fighting and may actually encourage it in boys. Most parents discourage aggression against themselves but permitted and encouraged it against other people [8]. In punishing the child physically, parents are effectively demonstrating to the child how to act aggressively. Since they do not permit it toward themselves but encourage it toward others, the child learns how, when, and to whom to behave aggressively.

Applications of Research on Anger. Many of the studies mentioned indicate that the results of parental behavior are often unintentional. When one considers that what parents do in the first 3 years of life is likely to be reflected in children's behavior patterns, he is impressed with the complexity of parent–child relationships [74]. Parental action springs from a wide variety of sources other than pure reason and self-control. Even so, there are some steps a parent can take consciously in order to make it easy for a preschool child to do the acceptable thing. Including here the information derived from Goodenough's study of anger the following list indicates conditions which discourage physical aggression and encourage the development of self-control:

1. The child is cared for on a flexible routine which provides food, rest, and activity before the child is acutely and painfully in need of these things.
2. Parents and other caretakers answer his calls for help promptly.
3. He is offered many opportunities to achieve and decide in approved ways.
4. Parents disapprove of hostile aggression and stop this behavior firmly.

222 Preschool Children

5. Parents clearly express what behavior is permitted and what is not.
6. Physical punishment is avoided.
7. Avoidance of television programs, films, and books showing aggression and violence.
8. An atmosphere of emotional warmth prevails in the home.

Jealousy and Rivalry

Jealousy is the angry feeling that results when a person is frustrated in his desire to be loved best; rivalry is the angry feeling that results when a person is frustrated in his desire to do best, to win or to place first. Very often an individual feels jealous and rivalrous toward the same person, although sometimes these emotions can be separated. A child is likely to feel jealous of the baby who displaces him as youngest in the family and to feel rivalrous with the older child, who is stronger and abler than he. Parents and children also feel jealousy and rivalry toward one another. The themes of jealousy and rivalry within the family flame in the most ancient literature. Cain and Oedipus symbolize some of the most disturbing situations which exist in family life.

Jealousy of parents and the resolution of that jealousy make up the psychoanalytic story of the preschool period. The play age, the stage when the sense of initiative is developing, is the phallic stage in *psychoanalytic* terms. Almost every little boy says at least once, "Mummy, I'm going to marry you when I grow up," and every little girl has the equivalent plan for the future with her father. Wanting to be first in the affections of the opposite-sexed parent has as its corollary jealousy of the like-sexed parent. The like-sexed parent represents a powerful, full-blown picture of what the little child hopes to become, even the person who attracts and holds the other parent. As recognition of reality (that he cannot win over the powerful, wonderful parent) helps the boy to give up his attempts to be first with mother, he continues to try to grow more like his father. He identifies with him, feeling less jealous and more affectionate and sympathetic with him. He gains strength by joining with the father. A similar mechanism is thought to work through the girl's attempt to be first with her father.

Jealousy of siblings is usual in western culture, in the typical small family, consisting of parents and children. "Let's send the baby back to the hospital" is the classic suggestion of the preschool child who has just lost his place as youngest in the family.

Two or three decades ago, authorities who advised parents placed great emphasis on the value of preparing the child for a new baby. The hope was that jealousy would be eliminated if the young child understood the reproductive process and the characteristics of neonates and if he realized that such a baby was about to enter the family. He was to "help" get clothes and equipment ready and to learn how to share in the baby's care. Attractive books with such titles as "Your New Baby" were read to the young child as preparation.

Modern experience has not shown any of these actions to be wrong or even useless. On the contrary, the most accepted authorities today still recommend them. While we are not aware of studies definitively proving the worth of "preparing for the new baby," common sense and common experience show that the young child feels more loving and less jealous toward the baby who is introduced thus into his family. The difference today is that some jealousy and rivalry are regarded as inevitable in American culture—in fact, in most cultures. The reason for it is the same reason which the Book of Genesis puts forth in the story of Cain and Abel. Every child wants to be the best loved by his parents. The first child wants it most deeply, since he once was the only child and knew what it was like to have all the attention, company, endearments, and gifts. Interviews with 202 families revealed that the first child was regarded as more selfish and more jealous in families of every size, both white and black [26, pp. 119–131]. In studying two-child families, they found that the second was happier and more generous than the first and that on the average the first child was still reported by mothers as being the more jealous and selfish no matter what type of training he had received, no matter whether he was treated more indulgently than the second child. The authors concluded that no type of training whatever, whether severe, moderate, or indulgent, is likely to eliminate the first child's sense of having been replaced by the second and of having lost some of his parents' love.

The child's interpretation of the new-baby situation is based on reality, as shown by a study of 46 children and their mothers [4]. The behavior of the mother toward the child was rated before, during, and after pregnancy. Substantial and continuing decreases were found in child-centeredness, approval, acceptance, affectionateness, and rapport. Declines occurred in duration of contact, intensity of contact, effectiveness of policy, and babying (an aspect of indulgence). Increases occurred in restrictiveness of policy and severity of penalties. It is possible that some of these changes would have occurred with increasing age of the child, but since they did occur along with the mother's pregnancy and the birth of a baby, it is easy to understand how the young child would hold the new baby responsible for the unhappy turn of events. In addition, he sees the baby enjoying privileges he would like to have or which he is trying to give up, such as sucking a bottle, wetting his diapers, being carried and fondled, crying. One 5-year-old said: "Yes, I would like to change places with my baby brother. Then I could yell my head off and mamma would take care of nobody but me." Another commented, "Sometimes I wish I could tear magazines myself" [50].

Jealous actions include suggestions for getting rid of the baby and attacks on the baby (the most direct) and more devious attacks such as accidents and rough play, acting out aggression with toys, attacking the mother, whining, withdrawing, protesting extreme love and concern for the baby. Later on, jealousy takes such forms as bickering, fighting, teasing, taking toys away. Reasons why parents behave in jealousy-inducing ways are to be found in the culture. In the small American family, there is not enough time and energy to go around after a new baby comes. In contrast, the joint family system provides for several adult women and adolescent girls too who are responsive to all the young children. When a young child's mother is pregnant or busy with a new baby, the child still has the support and attention of women to whom he is attached. The young child's affection and desires for approval are focused less intensively on one person. Therefore one person cannot let him down so severely and even if his mother does disappoint him, aunties and grandmothers are ever ready to care for him and comfort him.

The materialistic and relativistic standards of American society have some bearing on the forms which jealousy and rivalry take. Parents' approval and resulting rewards often depend on how the child compares with his siblings, as well as with children outside the family. To look good and thereby be most approved and loved, he has to be better than someone else, often his brother or sister. If he were loved for himself and if his achievements were measured against some absolute standards, he would have less reason to be jealous of his siblings.

Jealous as siblings are, they normally love each other, too. They often feel ambivalent, pulled in two directions, "Sometimes I love you, sometimes I hate you" is a key to understanding many incidents in behavior of siblings (indeed, of most people) toward each other. When questioned about their relationships, 28 percent of 360 5- and 6-year-olds said that they quarreled constantly with their sibs, 36 percent reported a moderate amount of quarreling, and 36 percent stated that they quarreled rarely [50]. When these children were asked if they would be happier without the sister or brother, about a third of them reported that they would. When the sib was an infant, especially of the same sex, there was less desire to be rid of him than when he was beyond infancy. Apparently infants disrupt their siblings' lives less than do older children. Second-born children, more than first-borns, wanted to be rid of the other children. The wider the age difference between sibs, the more the second-borns wanted to be rid of the first-borns. The second-borns' reasons were largely in terms of the behavior of the sibs themselves, such as, "He always socks me," "She likes to boss me too much," "Sometimes she wishes I were gone." When first-born children wanted younger ones out of the way, their reasons were often in terms of parents' attitudes, especially favoritism toward the other child.

Children often express jealousy and rivalry in play and creative media. The following story by a 4-year-old illustrates imaginative expression of these emotions:

> You see, there was a little pussy and do you know, that the little pussy had to go to the bathroom so badly. He couldn't find a place to go. Finally he found a little girl and she said she'd take him into her house and he could go to the bathroom. The kitty said he'd like to be her pet. Where do you think he went to the toilet? In a pot. That little girl had him for a pet and was so nice to him. One day when the little girl's father came home, he brought a dog for a pet. But that dog was mean to the little kitty and hurt him *so* much. So the little girl didn't like the dog and she just had the kitty for a pet.

This little girl had a sturdy, aggressive toddler brother who knocked down her block buildings and spoiled her doll play. Still in diapers, he was a reminder of her rather recent achievements in toileting and other self-care. It seemed to us that the little girl, represented by the kitty, planned to ignore her little brother, represented by the doggie, as a way of coping with her jealousy and anger at him for intruding in her otherwise satisfactory life.

Applications of What Is Known About Jealousy and Rivalry. Jealousy and rivalry are so common in the American family as to be almost inevitable. These feelings can probably be minimized, if not eliminated, by some of the following procedures:

1. Preparing the young child for the birth of a sibling by telling him that the baby is coming, teaching him what babies are like, helping him to understand his own infancy, and assuring him of the parents' continued affection for him.
2. Understanding and accepting imaginative expression of jealousy and rivalry, while firmly limiting direct expression.
3. Acceptance and appreciation of each child as an individual.
4. Avoidance of comparisons between children.
5. Avoidance of the use of competition to motivate siblings.

Fear

In infancy, fear has an innate basis in terms of stimuli which induce withdrawal. As the child interacts with his environment, he also learns to be afraid in certain situations. The hereditary basis of fears continues to contribute to emotional development [59, pp. 13–35].

As a child grows up, he goes through age-related stages in regard to what frightens him and how he needs and uses his mother in coping with fears [23]. In early infancy, his mother soothes his fears by relieving distress. After the baby has become attached to his mother, fear of visual novelty occurs, as can be seen in reactions to strangers. Clinging and otherwise contacting the mother alleviates this type of fear and helps him to approach and explore strange objects. Pain and sudden intense stimuli continue to be frightening, as they were in infancy, and to be relieved through the mother or other familiar and nurturant people.

A close friend can have a reassuring and comforting effect on a child who is in a stressful situation, as shown in a study of 4- and 5-year-olds [79]. Beginning in the preschool period and increasingly throughout the rest of childhood, increasing competence enables the child to cope with new situations without help from his mother or other adults.

Sources of Fear. Like infants preschool children can acquire fears through *conditioning*. Sometimes one painful experience is sufficient to establish a fear, as when a toddler comes to fear dogs by being pushed over, barked at, or bitten. Or a fear can be acquired from another person in as few occasions as one. For example, a young child can become afraid of thunderstorms through an experience of being in a storm with a person who displays fear of the situation. The fears of parents and children show a correspondence as to both kind and number [35]. In Britain, during World War II, children's reactions to air raids were greatly influenced by whether their parents showed calm attitudes or fearful ones [44].

Television has been found to contribute to fears in 4- and 5-year-old children [71]. Through measures of palmar sweating and through follow-up interviews, children were found to be frightened by violent cartoons and by violent human characters shown on TV. A week later, the children remembered more details from the human violence film than from the cartoon violence or from the two nonviolent shows.

An overly demanding social situation puts the child into a position where he has no appropriate response at his command, and hence withdrawal is what he attempts. Johnny comes into the living room suddenly to find several strange adults there. Mother tells him to speak nicely to the ladies, but he is shy and silent. He could have spoken to old friends, or he could have spoken to the new ladies too had he been prepared ahead of time to expect strangers and to say something to them.

Imagination, *initiative*, and *conscience* contribute to fears at this time of life. Eager to explore and to try out new activities, the child tends to push beyond limits set by his parents. When his budding conscience tells him he is doing wrong, or that he wants to do wrong, he may create imaginative satisfactions, only to have those creations frighten him. He is especially likely to imagine animals which have powers he would like to have and to use, such as great strength for attacking other creatures, biting, kicking, or eating them. He may disguise his aggressive wishes quite elaborately, dreaming about such animals instead of telling stories about them or using them in dramatic play. The dream animals sometimes attack their creator, who feels guilty about his destructive wishes and thus suffers punishment.

226 Preschool Children

Table 4–1 Fears Shown by Children Age 2 to 6, in Several Experimental Situations

	Percentage of Children Showing Fear			
Situation	24–35 MONTHS	36–47 MONTHS	48–59 MONTHS	60–71 MONTHS
1. Being left alone	12.1	15.6	7.0	0
2. Falling boards	24.2	8.9	0	0
3. Dark room	46.9	51.1	35.7	0
4. Strange person	31.3	22.2	7.1	0
5. High boards	35.5	35.6	7.1	0
6. Loud sound	22.6	20.0	14.3	0
7. Snake	34.8	55.6	42.9	30.8
8. Large dog	61.9	42.9	42.9	
Total	32.0	30.2	18.1	4.5

* SOURCE: Reprinted by permission from Arthur T. Jersild and Frances B. Holmes, "Children's Fears," Child Development Monographs, No. 20 (New York: Bureau of Publications, Teachers College, Columbia University, 1935), Table 14, page 237.

Dreams containing animals have been found to make up 61 percent of the dreams of 4-year-olds, whereas at 5 and 6 the figure is only 39 percent 89]. The proportion of animal dreams drops steadily with age, reaching a low of 7.5 percent in adulthood. Fear of the dark may accompany the young child's fears of imaginary animals and bad dreams. When parents were questioned about the fears expressed by their children between birth and 6 years, results showed a progressive decrease in fears which were responses to such tangible stimuli as objects, noises, falling, and strange people and an increase in fears of intangibles, such as imaginary creatures, darkness, being alone or abandoned, threat or danger of injury and harm [42].

The answers of 130 children to the question "What are things to be afraid of?" give information on the fears of children 5 years old and over [61]. Animals were mentioned most often, but less frequently as age increased. Eighty percent of children were afraid of animals at age 5 and 6, 73 percent at 7 and 8. Snakes were mentioned more often than any other animals. Then came lion, tiger, and bear. A third of children under 7 admitted to fear of the dark. Children rarely reported fear of the type which parents try to teach, such as fear of traffic, germs, and kidnapers.

An experimental study of children's fears confirmed the finding that expressed fear of tangible situations decreases with age throughout the preschool period [42, pp. 167–296]. Children were carefully observed when left alone, while walking across inclined boards which fell a distance of 2 inches, entering a dark room, meeting a peculiarly dressed stranger, walking across high boards, hearing a sudden loud sound, picking a toy out of a box containing a live snake, and being asked to pat a dog brought in on a leash. Their actions were judged as indicating fear or not. The percentage of children showing fear at four different age levels between 2 and 6 are shown in Table 4–1.

Fear can be widespread and generalized, in contrast to being focused on a particular object or situation. When fear is widespread, generalized, and unfocused, it is called *anxiety*. The preschool child is likely to experience anxiety when separated for a long time from his mother, father, or main object of attachment. Considerable research has been concerned with what it means to a young child to be separated from his mother and some research has dealt with the question of separation from the father. Maternal deprivation has been extensively studied and it was shown that deprivation can be either sensory or emotional or both and that the breaking of established bonds between baby and mother has quite a different result from that of separation when attachment is not involved. The effects of partial and complete separation of toddlers from their mothers were explored with children between 16 and 27 months of age [37]. Two groups, carefully equated as to age and sex, were selected, one from each of two nurseries. All subjects were from intact families, without history of separation and with no indications that the children had been rejected. No subject had a sibling in the same nursery. The two nurseries were run identically, with one exception. In the first, the children stayed all day but went home at night; in the second, the children lived 24 hours a day in the nursery. The two groups did not differ in behavior for the first two days, but after that, the residential children showed more intense symptoms of anxiety. They sought relations with adults more intensely, sought affection more, cried more, did more thumb and finger sucking, lost sphincter control more often, and had more colds. The most striking difference was that the residential children showed more and greater hostility. This study indicates that although partial separation from parents is not necessarily destructive, *complete* separation is likely to be so.

Maternal employment is a tempting situation to fasten upon when searching for conditions causing anxiety in young children. Public opinion is often expressed against young mothers who hold jobs outside the home. A thorough review of research on this topic concludes that maternal employment is too global a condition to use as a variable in investigating causes of children's behavior [84]. For example, 26 kindergarten children of fully employed mothers were matched in family factors, age, and sex with 26 kindergarten children whose mothers had never been employed during the lives of these children. No differences were found between the two groups on the nine personality characteristics investigated [82]. Rather than studying such a general condition as employment of the mother, separation might be understood more clearly in terms of the mother's acceptance of her role, the quality of substitute care provided, the age and sex of the child, the relation of the mother's employment to family functioning and its meaning to husband–wife relations [84].

It is sometimes held that when a parent leaves the family through divorce, death, or any other separation, a preschool child is likely to interpret the disruption as due to his own unworthiness. Hence he would suffer a separation anxiety. Since fathers leave households more often than mothers, they are more likely than mothers to cause this kind of fear in preschool children.

Applications of Research on Fear and Anxiety. Although some fears are inevitable and even desirable (caution has survival value), children can learn to deal with frightening situations, and adults can help them to do so. Adults can also arrange and plan so as to prevent the development of extreme fears and anxiety. The following procedures are often valuable:

1. When the child is to be separated from the people to whom he is attached, make the transition gradual.
2. At times of crisis, such as illness, keep the child with a person to whom he is attached.
3. Teach the child techniques for coping with situations in which he is inadequate.

228 Preschool Children

4. Prepare the child for dealing constructively with situations which are about to come up. Talking, stories, and dramatic play are useful for this purpose.
5. Use the child's spontaneous expressions of fears, in fantasy, dreams, dramatic play, and artistic productions, to gain insight into what he fears and why he does so, in order to help him deal with the fears.
6. Never force a child into a situation he fears. Rather, minimizing the threat, such as by caging the animal which frightens him, encourage him to approach it in such a way that no harm occurs to him.
7. When a child is frightened by bad dreams, comfort him immediately, make sure that he wakens and agrees that the experience was a dream, not real, and put him back in his own bed, with a light if he wishes.

Character Development

Both common sense and research show that the American child develops his morality largely through family living. His parents teach him what is right and what is wrong. They push him toward what they consider good behavior and pull him away from the bad. They hold up their ideals for him to see, their inspirations to light the way for him, too. In addition to all this conscious, direct teaching, parents and others exert influences of which they are not aware and which they can turn neither off nor on.

Definition of Character

"Character is the habitual mode of bringing into harmony the tasks presented by internal demands and by the external world" [72, pp. 1–2]. One function of the personality is to find these modes and to carry through the organizing and integrating required. Another function is to determine what demands from the external world shall be heard. Other demands come from the individual's body and some from unconscious parts of his being. For instance, the child, feeling hungry, searches around to get food in a way he feels to be acceptable, such as asking Mother for a cookie and a glass of milk rather than climbing onto the counter or opening the refrigerator.

Sequence of Development

The schemas of character, like all the other behavior patterns of the child, undergo changes with experience and age. Although the preschool child is very different from the infant in his moral behavior, he still has a long way to go on the path toward character maturity. The 2-year-old is in the "into-everything" stage. Able to run, climb, manipulate, explore, feed himself, and talk, he can get many gratifications for himself.

Responsive to rewards and punishment, he modifies some of his behavior without thinking or evaluating [3]. For example, in experiments where children are punished for choosing certain toys, they avoid those toys even after the experimenter has left the room. That is, the suppression behavior is internalized in response to punishment.

A parental *no* may function as punishment, especially if said harshly or coldly Or it may be said in conjunction with some action that prevents behavior, as when the adult removes the pointed scissors from the young child's hand. While the physical world presents some limits to the child, social demands come largely through Mother's voice and hands, supplemented by Father's and other adults. The toddler will pause in what he is doing when someone tells him to stop, or he will do so most of the time. Unless a toy is substituted for the cigarette lighter or the honey pot placed out of reach on the table, the next moment is likely to find the young child once more trying to make fire or to lick and stick.

The next easily observed step in character development occurs when the child obeys rules while watched. Ellen, just under 3, was fascinated by Lucy, a doll that belonged to Susan, age 5. Susan, knowing Ellen's passion for poking Lucy's blue glass eyes fringed with long black lashes, made a strict rule that Ellen was never to touch Lucy. One day Ellen came home from nursery school to behold Lucy sitting on the sofa. She fell on the doll with cries of joy, began to poke Lucy's eyes, and paused when her mother chided her, "Ellen, you know Susie doesn't want you to touch Lucy."

"But Mummy," Ellen said in hurt surprise, "Susie isn't here!"

The voice which commanded Ellen to inhibit impulses toward Lucy was entirely external. When the voice was away at kindergarten, it simply wasn't there, and Ellen felt no restraint.

During the years between 3 and 6, some of the voice of society, via the family, is taken into the child, internalized, made his own, integrated with the rest of his personality. Research shows that internalization takes place most readily when parents are warmly affectionate, firm, and consistent [41, 65, 72]. When the love of the parents has become important to the child, then the winning of their approval is also important. Indeed, the child often takes the role of the parents in talking to himself, either aloud or silently, as did the 2-year-old who wet her pants and then said to her uncle, who was taking care of her: "Naughty girl! You must come and tell Mommy" [57]. The child was playing the mother role, making comments appropriate to the disciplinary function of the mother. This incident, implied many times in many settings, suggests how the child comes to withdraw approval from himself when he does "wrong" and approves himself when he does "right." Warmly affectionate (nurturant) parents who have thus been rewarding to the child will be imitated more and their roles learned better and internalized more into the child. Hoffman [41] shows that children whose internalized moral standards are adaptive and realistic tend to have parents who show disappointment when the child does not live up to their standards. Instead of threatening to withdraw their love or belittling the child, such parents show that they believe the child can live up to the ideal if he would. Thus although the child feels hurt at the time, he too believes that he can do what the parents expect.

Hoffman says, "... we may tentatively conclude that an internalized moral orientation is fostered by an affectionate relationship between the parent and child, in combination with the use of discipline, techniques which utilize this relationship by appealing to the child's personal and social motives."

The mechanisms by which a loving, nurturant parent figure becomes the most effective punisher are analyzed by Unger [88], who argues that strong internal controls cannot grow in a child without an adult who combines the nurturing and punishing functions.* Throughout infancy, the parent's presence is associated with

---

* Some critics challenge this theory by citing what happens to children brought up in communal nurseries. In both Russia and Israel, the children who live in nurseries receive little or no punishment from their parents but from the resident nurses and caretakers. Parents and children have

comfort, pleasant stimulation, relief of hurts and tensions. Absence or unavailability means the opposite, especially during the time when fear of strangers is dominant. The child learns that certain acts on his part result in withdrawal of the parent and consequent anxiety for him. The parent makes it easier for the child to identify these acts and their results by verbalizing it. "That was naughty. You make Mommy angry when you hit the baby." Sending the child to his room or otherwise isolating him has the same effect. Facial cues and tones of voice associated with these situations become sufficient to induce anxiety over the possibility of parental withdrawal. Thus a parent who has never given a spanking or other harsh punishment may be able to control a child by a mere frown or look. This is the foundation of love-oriented discipline. The child regulates his behavior so as not to lose the nurturing presence or approval of a loving adult. The indication that loss of approval is imminent comes first from the parent, either verbally or in gesture, and secondly from the child's own language, aloud in the beginning and silent inner language eventually.

Guilt, according to Unger, is a two-stage process. The first stage is verbal. The child says to himself, "I shouldn't have done that," and the second stage is an autonomic-visceral reaction of fear or anxiety, triggered by the first stage. The second stage is the same reaction which earlier was set off by the withdrawal or threatened withdrawal of the nurturing parent but now is activated by the child's own words to himself. The words to himself are, of course, derived from previous situations where the loving and beloved adult expressed disapproval. Now, in order to end the unpleasant autonomic-visceral reaction of fear or anxiety, he must undo the situation which caused his words to himself. If his past experience with the loving adult taught him that a confession or apology would undo or make up for what he did wrong, then he will confess or apologize and will feel better. If he learned that he must pay for wrongdoing by enduring a spanking or giving up a privilege, then he will attempt to find a punishment that represents these punishments. Or he may have learned that wrongdoing cannot be undone and that he must bear a burden of guilt indefinitely. In the meantime as he continues to grow up, he is having more experiences with parental love and punishment, with doing wrong, and with reinterpretation of moral behavior.

Knowing all this, can parents control their own behavior so as to produce ideal character in children? Some can more than others, but nobody can behave perfectly with his children or elsewhere. Some acts can be direct and intentional while others cannot. Love or rejection, firmness or vacillation, rigidity, or flexibility, emanate from parental personalities with spontaneity. Although much parental behavior springs from unconscious sources and from parts of the personality which cannot be changed at will, there are still parts of parental roles which can be learned and can be consciously controlled. Parents "teach" some of the behavior patterns which constitute character by making their demands clear, consistent,

---

companionship and enjoyment for the brief time that they are together. The nursery caretakers do the punishing. However, the caretakers surely also reward the children with affectionate approval as well as tangible rewards. It is hard to believe that these women would be coldly mechanical disciplinarians, since they choose their jobs and are chosen for them on the basis of having some ability with children and desire to be with children. Why, then, would they not have many of the affectional characteristics of foster parents? It may be that the peer group takes a large part of what Americans think of as the parental role, both the rewarding and punishing aspects. Observations in both Russia [22] and Israel [55] indicate that this may be so.

firm, and suited to the child's abilities, by showing their pleasure in the child's "good" behavior, by giving understandable reasons but not substituting them for firmness, and by avoiding physical punishment.

Factors in Moral Development

Moral behavior results when a person knows and does what is right and good.

Cognition. To know what is right or good involves making a moral judgment. Various cultures give concrete expression to the idea that a certain stage of mental maturity is necessary before the child can exercise either judgment or volition necessary for moral behavior. The Roman Catholic first communion, at age 7, is an example. So is the widespread assumption among tribal people that a child reaches the age of reason and responsibility at about 7. Six or 7 is the common age for starting school in earnest. The transition from preconceptual thought to the stage of concrete operations occurs at about the same time when changes occur in character. What precedes these changes?

The earliest judgments about what is good and bad come from what the parents impose in the way of rules and requirements. As a child comes to know the rules, *good*, to him, means following the rules and *bad* means not following them. Moral realism, according to Piaget [73, p. 106], has these features: (1) Any act which shows obedience to a rule or to an adult is good; a rule is not something thought of by a person, but rather something ready-made, which has been revealed to the adult and is now being imposed by him. (2) The letter rather than the spirit of the law shall be observed. (3) Acts are evaluated according to how well they keep to the rules rather than according to the motives which prompted them. Results, rather than intentions, are what count.

Moral realism is illustrated by 2-year-old Jacqueline Piaget, who had been told what would be the results of a laxative which her mother gave to her [73, pp. 177–191]. She nevertheless came close to tears and looked very distressed when she lost control of her sphincters. To Jacqueline, it was bad not to follow the rule about going to the toilet, even though her mother had explained that she was not responsible for the lapse. Another time, Jacqueline broke a fragile shell which Piaget had given her to play with. She was very upset over the breakage, even though her father tried to persuade her that it was not her fault.

By age 3 or 4, Piaget says, a child shows that he sees a difference between his own intentional breaking of rules and his unintentional breaches. He will plead "Not on purpose" to excuse himself. With the misdeeds of others, however, his attitude differs. Because of his egocentrism, his inability to see anything from someone else's point of view, he does not understand that another person's breaking of rules could be "not on purpose." He judges the other person's acts by the results, since the results are all that he can perceive.

The next stage of moral judgment, that of evaluating an act in terms of right and wrong intentions, is achieved as the child becomes freed from egocentrism. Piaget believes that this comes about not merely through the passage of time but through certain kinds of interactions with the environment, largely interactions with the parents. A child is helped to grow beyond egocentrism as adults cooperate with him by discussing things on an equal footing, encouraging him to find facts and to analyze them. He is hindered when adults behave authoritatively, especially when they give verbal instructions instead of letting children experiment and figure things out. Speaking of the child whose parents take pleasure in wielding authority, Piaget says, "Even when grown up, he will be unable, except in very rare cases, to break loose from the affective schemas acquired in this way, and will be as stupid with his own children as his parents were with him" [73, p. 19].

The question of the timing of Piagetian processes has been of special interest to Americans. For example, some American preschool children have developed faster than Piaget's Swiss subjects in being able to distinguish verbally between intentions and consequences of acts [18]. Maturity of moral judgment was tested in 51 preschool children from two socioeconomic levels: middle class and working class. More than a third of the children were able to judge intentions in one of the stories, although none of Piaget's had done so. Mental age and cultural background seemed to have some influence on the age of attaining the more mature kind of judgment, with a larger proportion of the more mature children in the middle-class and in the Jewish groups. The results of this study are in harmony with Piaget's comments on the role played by parents in helping their children to achieve moral maturity. It is consistent with other studies which indicate that the middle-class families would exceed working-class families in democratic discussion [3, pp. 326–328; 39; 59] and that the Jewish families would similarly exceed the non-Jewish [56]. The changes which Piaget urged in parental use of authority seem actually to have taken place in the trend toward democratic parent practices noted in America [63]. Perhaps the acceleration of a sample of American children in regard to moral judgment can be attributed to such changes in parental practice.

Volition. Moral action depends upon willing to do the right and good thing. Moral judgment of itself does not imply action. Everyone has had the experience of judging that an act was wrong and then doing it anyway, or judging that an act was good and failing to do it. Experiments on children's aggression (page 221) showed that children sometimes perform the very acts that they condemn verbally.

The idea of an age or stage of reason and responsibility comes into the topic of moral action, as well as moral judgment. Nobody expects a newborn baby to choose to do right or wrong, but almost everyone considers a 7-year-old to have some freedom of choice. The development of a sense of self gives conviction of freedom of choice. So do the experiences of temptation and guilt. The rightness and wrongness of the child's choices are strongly related to his experiences with parents and other socializing agents. Language is an important tool of volition.

Language. The language development which takes place during the preschool period is fundamental to voluntary behavior and hence to moral action. On the basis of his work with Russian children, Luria [54] traced four stages through which speech comes to exercise a regulating influence on behavior. A replication of Luria's study showed the same sequential development in Australian children [45].

1. At 18 months to 2 years, the *initiating function* can be seen. The toddler will clap his hands on command. Instructions will not change an activity that is under way, however. If you tell a child to take off his socks while he is putting them on, or to put rings on a bar while he is taking them off, he cannot change his actions. He only intensifies the efforts he is making.
2. At 3 to 4 years, the child can follow both initiating and inhibiting instructions. He can *wait* for a signal, after being told to do so. However, the initiating part of the instruction is stronger and often the child can inhibit only briefly. If he gets continuous verbal instruction, however, he can inhibit more easily.

3. At about 4 years, when the child's own speech is well developed, he can use it to *start and stop* his own actions. He can follow instructions as to using his own speech for voluntary acts.
4. External regulatory speech becomes internal. The child no longer says it out loud but to himself when he regulates his behavior.

In regard to moral behavior, language has another important function in addition to that of starting and stopping actions. Language is the means by which the child evaluates his actions. "I shouldn't have done that" is the first part of the process of guilt as described by Unger. (See page 230.) There is widespread agreement that signs of guilt in children can be seen first at 4 or 5 years of age, the very time when children reach Luria's third stage in the use of speech to regulate behavior. "I shouldn't do that" is avoidance-mediating, anticipating an anxiety reaction. Talking to oneself is thus involved in feeling guilt and in avoiding guilt by means of controlling one's behavior. Since a certain stage of language development has to be reached before speech can regulate behavior, it follows that intellectual growth plays an essential role in moral behavior. Parents and other family members influence the child enormously in helping him to use language in organizing his mental processes and his behavior. Table 4-2 summarizes moral development in childhood.

The Self

An adult knows himself as both subject and object. He feels, he knows, he is; he can stand off and look at himself, his feelings, his actions, his relationships. As far as anyone knows, man is the only creature who can look at himself as an object. It is a viewpoint which begins as the infant distinguishes between his body and the rest of reality and which develops gradually, during the preschool period, as the child moves from preconceptual thought toward objectivity. Further elaboration of the self takes place throughout the whole period of development, perhaps throughout all of life.

The development of a sense of autonomy means that the child gets a clearer and clearer concept of himself as a person separate from other objects and other people, distinct in body and distinct in actions. With the growth of the sense of initiative, the child enlarges his concept of self by relating it to the world. Having made

Table 4-2 Summary of Developmental Changes Basic to Character

Age	Moral Behavior	Cognitive and Volitional Behavior
1	Obeys commands sometimes	Cooperative with adult who cooperates with him
2	Obeys more commands	Initiating function of speech.
	Good means following the rule or instruction.	Verbalizes role of parent.
3	Obeys when watched.	Inhibiting function of speech.
4	Begins to internalize demands of parents	Judges other people by acts, not intentions. but sees difference between his own intentions and unintentional breaking of rules.
	Some feelings of guilt.	Uses his own speech to initiate.
6	Conscience fairly internalized.	Uses language to evaluate his actions.
	Definitely feels guilt.	

himself separate and distinct, he integrates his self concept by trying on different roles (playing fireman, nurse, teacher), exploring, and expressing himself in various media.

Investigations of the development of the self concept have taken two main forms, observing overt actions that have to do with the self and examining evidence from the unconscious. Ames [2] has traced verbalized concepts of self by noting comments made by children of different ages. The 2-year-old's typical remarks are about *me* and *mine*. The 3-year-old says *me too, we, our, let's, I like you, do you like me?* A typical 4-year-old's comment is "I'm bigger than you are." These verbalizations show first a concern with the self, then some thinking of the self along with others, and finally, a comparing of the self with others.

Problems in Developing Self Concepts

Deprived Children. One of the outstanding characteristics of severely deprived children is a negative self concept or even lack of self concept. A child may not even realize that he is a person or that he has a name which distinguishes him from others. The conditions associated with positive self concept or high self-esteem are often found lacking in the families of disadvantaged children [43]. Conditions leading to high self-esteem are acceptance of the child, well-defined limits and values, and respect for the child's decision making within those limits. In very poor families, parents tend to be indecisive, disorganized, apathetic, and rejecting. Low in self-esteem themselves, they do not believe that they can control their own lives, let alone their children's. While they may sometimes be warm and nurturant, they are more likely to try to give children immediate pleasure, through candy, money, toys, and clothes rather than to guide them to develop competency.

In comprehensive compensatory programs, parents are offered help in developing their own competence and self-esteem, as well as effective behavior in relation to their children [38]. Teachers try to show the child that he is a distinct individual, important because he is a person. The child is helped to establish self-confidence and self-esteem as he forms a clear and definite idea of himself. Teachers use many methods for promoting self concepts. They provide mirrors, full length if possible, in places where children can easily look at themselves. They take pictures of the children, show them and discuss them. They may draw pictures or silhouettes of the children. Songs and games are made up to include the children's names. Feelings of autonomy and worthiness are stimulated by opportunities for successful decisions, achievement, and recognition. The teacher's respect for the individual child and her warm response to him are very basic in the development of his self concept.

Black Children. Children of any minority group are likely to have some problems with self concepts, but black children in predominantly white societies are especially vulnerable. Studies on racial awareness in preschool children have shown consistently that 3-year-olds can discriminate black–white differences and that negative attitudes are often shown by 5 years [83]. Black children were less likely than white children to choose children of their own race as playmates and guests, and more likely to name their own race as aggressors and less likely to offer aid to a hurt child. Thus black preschool children reflect stereotypes of their own race. Knowing that he is a black child and seeing blacks negatively, a young child develops low self-esteem.

Rising black pride is reflected in the results of a study which compares children's self-identification and preference with findings of an identical study done 11 years ago [28]. More than twice as many in the present-day black preschool group identified the black doll as looking like themselves. While there was an increase in choosing the black doll over the white as a preferred playmate, the difference between eras was not significant, and about half of the black children chose white playmates in preference to black. The white children also showed an increase in those identifying their color correctly and a significant increase in those preferring to play with children the same color.

Some encouraging findings are available. Studies of modification of racial attitudes have shown that white preschool children respond to a reading program that presents black people favorably [87] and to reinforcement procedures designed to encourage positive evaluation of black stimuli by white children [94]. Such programs have good chances of success with young children, since they have had less time than older children for learning unfavorable racial attitudes [49].

Body Image

An interesting approach to the study of the self is through the study of body image as conducted by Fisher and Cleveland [33]. The common idea of body image is probably the mental picture of one's body. To these authors, however, body image includes the images, attitudes toward and feelings about the body, many of them unconscious, which represent the self and summarize the effects of the child's interaction with the world. The relationships a child has with important people, especially the baby with his mother, are internalized as part of the body image. (This idea is similar to the widespread view that the child sees himself as others see him, that his concept of self grows from the roles he takes with other people and his interpretation of their roles.)

Fisher and Cleveland measured the clarity of body image in terms of the definiteness with which the person perceives the boundary between his body and the rest of the world.* They have found interesting relationships between methods of child rearing and personality characteristics. Comparing nine cultural groups, they concluded that high boundary scores (definite, clear body image) were associated with permissive acceptance of impulse release in young children. The Bhils, an Indian tribe, who made the highest average score, nurse their children until about 3, feed them when they cry, toilet-train them in relaxed style, and express feelings freely. The authors theorize that the more a parent inhibits a child, the more antagonistic their relationship becomes, the harder it is to work out close communication between them, the less easily will the child take the parent as a model, and the less definite will the child's body image be.

Evidence obtained from psychiatric patients suggests that low scorers (indefinite body image) tend to have spent their early years in a family atmosphere of restrictiveness, narrow range of permissible behavior, blocked outlets for relieving tension; they tend to see their parents as threatening, destructive, and disrupting. High scorers tend to come from families where expectations of children are clear and firm, modes of controlling them are open and defined, and the parents represent devotion to a limited number of primary values and lines of living.

* Using data from Rorschach tests to give two scores relating to body image.

Whether one starts with the concept of *character* or *self* or *body* or *body image*, the research results converge on the topic of teaching and learning within the family during the early years of life. There is agreement about the importance of clarity, firmness, affection, and commitment to values on the part of parents. However, it is an open question as to how much parents can purposely and voluntarily influence children's personality growth.

Sex Typing

Sex typing is a process through which a child comes to feel, think, and act in ways considered by his culture to be masculine or feminine. By age 3, a child knows very well whether he is a boy or a girl and has considerable knowledge of and preference for sex-appropriate behavior [32, 78]. Attitudes toward sex role, as shown by tests and observations of dependency, attachment, and imitation, change as the child matures. An investigation of bright and average children showed that sex role attitudes were related to mental age [52]. The same changes occurred in all, but at earlier ages in the brighter children. Thus the child's perception of sex roles and his attitudes toward them are related to the maturity of his cognitive structure.

Definition of Male and Female Roles

Every culture defines the meaning of male and female, basing it somewhat but not consistently on biological characteristics. The variety of definitions is amazing. In Mead's [62] words:

> Now it is boys who are thought of as infinitely vulnerable and in need of special, cherishing care, now it is girls. In some societies it is girls for whom parents must collect a dowry or make husband-catching magic, in others the parental worry is over the difficulty of marrying off the boys. Some peoples think of women as too weak to work out of doors, others regard women as the appropriate bearers of heavy burdens, "because their heads are stronger than men's".... In some countries the women are regarded as sieves through whom the best-guarded secrets will sift; in others it is the men who are the gossips.

Even though there is wide variety in sex typing, there is a strong tendency for masculinity to be defined in terms of independent, competitive, instrumental coping, and femininity in terms of being loving, attractive, sensitive, and supportive to others. A study of 110 cultures [10] showed widespread trends in sex role teaching. A majority of societies stressed achievement and self-reliance in boys and nurturance and responsibility in girls. In societies where obedience was required, it tended to be of girls more than of boys. Thus, while certain kinds of work or functions can be assigned to either sex, there is considerable consistency in the personality traits which human beings attempt to encourage in one sex or the other. The following list of characteristics was judged by college students and fifth graders to be typical [68]:

Masculine	Feminine
Never afraid of anything.	Always does what teacher says.
Likes to show off.	Likes to act grown up.
Likes noisy fun.	Is always polite.
Sticks up for own rights.	Likes to do for others.
Is bossy.	Is easily embarrassed.
Likes to tease others.	Careful not to hurt others' feelings.

The defining of masculine and feminine behavior is not identical with requiring it. While simple, stable societies tend to have clear definitions and requirements which jibe with them, a complex, fast-changing society tends to vary in requirements, from one ethnic group to another, between social classes, and from family to family.

Differential Treatment of Boys and Girls

Once we gave a pink sweater before a baby was born. When the baby turned out to be a boy, the mother expressed regrets that she would have to save the sweater until she had a girl. That little boy's color scheme was to leave no doubt in him or in anybody else as to what sex he was! He soon received a wealth of trucks, cars, and erector sets but no dolls. His father played boisterously with him, stimulating vigorous motor play, acting casual about bumps, discouraging tears. And what happened when someone came along to occupy our pink sweater? She received dolls and homemaking toys. She was held tenderly. Her father stroked her curls, tickled her chin, and taught her to bat her long eyelashes at him. Big Brother stroked her curls, tickled her chin, and elicited eye-batting too. The mother applauded when Brother was aggressive, active, and courageous and when Sister was nurturant, beguiling, and sensitive. Often the parents' techniques of influence were subtle—a pat, a shove, a smile, a frown, a tight voice, a song. At other times they were direct—"Don't do that, Brother. Be a big man, like Daddy" or "I was so proud of my girl, acting like a regular little lady."

Reinforcement of sex role behavior by teachers has been observed in nursery schools [31]. After listing all types of play behavior and the proportion of time spent by each sex in each kind of behavior, the investigators concluded that there was a clear sex difference in play preferences. On 27 items, one sex was significantly different from the other. Boys definitely did more of the following: building blocks, playing with transportation toys, riding tricycles, and playing in the sandbox. Girls did more: art activities, playing in kitchen and doll house, doll play, and listening to stories. Girls spent less time in opposite-sex-preferred behavior than did boys. Of the sex-preferred behaviors that were reinforced, 83 percent were feminine. (Reinforcement was recorded when the teacher commented favorably, initiated, or joined in.) That is, teachers who were feminine themselves reinforced both sexes for feminine behavior. Even so, the boys did not become more feminine in their behavior preferences. As mentioned in the previous chapter, boys reinforce boys more, and girls, girls. An analysis of peer reinforcements showed that boys reinforced behavior preferred by boys, and girls reinforced behavior preferred by girls. One boy who had a very high number of feminine choices received ordinary treatment by teachers but much criticism and isolation by peers. These findings suggest that people (both children and adults) reinforce child behavior which is in their own repertoires. While same-sex reinforcement agents are therefore crucial in a child's acquisition and maintenance of sex-appropriate behavior, a variety of agents can serve the purpose. In the children studied here, peer reinforcement, plus interaction at home, were sufficient to assure sex-appropriate play in almost all of the children. An indication that siblings influence sex typing comes from a study of 3- and 4-year-olds making sex-typed discriminations on the *It* test. Children with an opposite-sex sibling scored high in sex-appropriate choices [78]. A child tends to reinforce the characteristics of his own sex in his sibling, no matter which the sex of the sibling. When the sibling doing the reinforcing is also older and consequently has power over the younger one, the reinforcement is likely to be more effective than when the dispenser is younger [85].

Teaching Biological Sex Differences

The little boy learns that he is a boy before he realizes that the possession of a penis makes a child a boy. Similarly for the girl. The differential treatment of boys and girls makes it clear to them that they belong to one sex or the other. In a clothed society, especially one which prescribes highly distinctive dress for the sexes, children first express the difference between boys and girls in terms of their outfits and hairdos. Parents often avoid labeling the sexual parts of the body, sex feeling, and activities [80, p. 412]. However, when a person knows the name of something, he can discuss it better and reason about it, since labeling is an important aid to learning. Advice to parents from authorities has consistently stated the desirability of telling children the names of their sex organs and of answering their questions directly. Questions during the preschool year are usually first about the names of the sex organs, then about sex differences, such as whether a girl has lost her penis and if not why not. Answers that clarify and reassure are, "A boy has a penis and testicles." "A girl has a vulva and vagina." "Boys grow up to be fathers; girls grow up to be mothers."

Questions about where babies come from are to be expected. "The baby grew inside its mother" is simple and true. The next question, "How did it get out!" is almost inevitable in a preschool child whose questions have been answered in a trust-promoting way. "The vagina stretches to let the baby out. The mother works to push him through." This type of answer is reassuring if it implies that both mothers and babies can cope with the process of birth and if it leaves the way open for more questions. Questions about fertilization and mating rarely come during the preschool period, and if they do, they are simple questions about physiology, not love.

In actual practice, the teaching of sex differences and reproduction rarely takes the simple, straightforward course described above. Because adults have strong feelings about sexual matters, they convey some of them in what they say and leave unsaid and in how they talk and remain silent. The sex education of 4-year-olds in an English city is reported in detail, showing typical behavior of mothers in five social classes [67]. For example, with the question of whether the child knew that babies grow inside their mothers, 20 percent had already told their children, 34 percent said that they would tell if asked, and 46 percent would either evade the question or tell falsehoods [67, p. 377]. The higher the social status of the mother, the more likely she was to tell her child by age 4 and to answer his questions honestly.

Israeli children between 4 and 5½ were questioned about their concepts of sex differences and reproduction [53]. These young subjects proved very willing to discuss the matter and revealed some interesting conceptions and misconceptions which were classified as to the family's ethnic origin (Oriental or Western). About 90 percent of the children knew that there was a relation between the mother's enlarged abdomen and the subsequent birth of the baby. When asked how it is that the baby is inside the mother, the most frequent answer was that he was formed from the food the mother ate. The next most popular explanation was that the baby had always been in his mother's belly and then came the answer that the mother had first swallowed the baby. The notion of the baby entering through the sexual organ was held by only 5 percent of Western boys and 2 percent of Western girls. No Oriental children had this idea. The function of the father was thought of mainly in terms of helping the mother. When asked how the baby came out of the mother, the commonest answer was that the belly was cut open. As for having some notion of birth through the birth canal, 33 percent of Western girls did so, no Oriental girls, 8-percent of Western boys, and 4 percent of Oriental boys.

Sex Role Preference

Certain objects and actions are generally considered typical of masculine or feminine involvement. For instance, a lipstick is feminine, a football masculine. Preference for a masculine or feminine role is measured by having the subject choose between objects or activities connoting culturally defined masculine and feminine behavior. Toy preference tests are used to investigate children's sex role preferences. The child is asked to choose the toy he would most like to play with from masculine–feminine pairs, such as a dump truck and a set of doll dishes. Between 3 and 5, children show sex-appropriate preferences [92], boys showing them more consistently than girls [14, 24].

Sex Role Identification

The process of learning to feel and behave like a member of one sex or the other is known as sex role identification. As mentioned above, parents define sex roles for their children, reward them for playing the appropriate roles, and punish, or at least withhold rewards, when the children play the wrong sex roles.

Children learn sex-appropriate behavior through *modeling* as well as by reinforcement [9]. That is, the child takes on the motivations and the overt behavior of the model. Children are most likely to imitate a *nurturant* model and will often reproduce even incidental details of behavior [6]. Kindergarten boys who scored high in masculinity were likely to portray their fathers as warm and nurturant and also as giving punishment [64]. The mothers of the high-masculine boys confirmed the warm, nurturant relation between fathers and sons but not the punitive one.

Another salient characteristic of models for children is *power* or *status*. A child is likely to imitate a model whom he sees as controlling resources. The person controlling resources has been shown by experiments to be an even more attractive model than the person giving out rewards [7]. Thus the young child will model both his father and mother, practicing their roles in fantasy and play. Most likely, the mother seems to the toddler to control the most important resources, since she can give or withhold most of what he needs. As the father increases in salience, he becomes a more powerful model. The kindergarten boys who portrayed their fathers as punishing must have perceived the fathers as powerful. In addition to being influenced by the father's warmth, such a boy may take on the feelings and behavior of the father because he also wants the status and power that he sees his father as having.

The importance of father–son interaction for masculinity in the son is shown in studies of boys whose fathers were absent from the home [17]. Five-year-old father-absent boys gave less masculine responses on tests than did father-present boys [15]. When father absence occurred before the fifth year, masculine responses were significantly less than when the father left during the fifth year, suggesting that the young child is more vulnerable to father absence or that the length of time of absence is important, or both.

Perceptions of Roles of Family Members

Since parent-child interactions occur in the context of the family, sex typing is related to the family organization, not only to the parents as individuals. For example, the power relationship between husband and wife is pertinent. Sex role preference similarity and imitation in preschool and school-age children was found to be related to dominance in parents [40]. Boys from mother-dominated families were less likely to have masculine preferences than were boys from father-dominated families. With girls differences were not significant. The feminine role preference and orientation of girls was shown, by another study, to be related to the daughter's perceptions of the mother as salient in the family [16]. Salience was not the same as dominance in relation to the father, but depended upon how the girl saw her mother in terms of nurturance, limit setting, and competence, as well as decision making. Girls were likely to be feminine in orientation and preference when they saw their mothers as salient controllers of resources, but they also were likely to regard their fathers positively and as important.

Concepts of sex role are derived to a large extent from concepts of what fathers, mothers, and other family members do. The way in which the child sees the child-father relationship now will also contribute to how he sees it when he plays the father role with his own child. Likewise, his childish observations of the husband-wife roles have implications for his adult life. Tests and anecdotal records of 319 children between 3 and 6 give some indication of preschool children's concepts of fathers and mothers [91]. Since several socioeconomic levels were sampled, the results can be considered representative of a large part of the population. Some of the questions asked were these: What are daddies for? What are mothers for? What are families for? Results showed that concepts of fathers were much more limited than concepts of mothers; mothers were seen as busier than fathers, with many of the mothers' activities focused on children, and fathers being more impersonal; mothers were seen as more supporting and more punishing than fathers; fathers' affections were considered to include mothers and children, with mothers occupying a prominent place, but little indication was given that children realized that they shared the mothers' affection with the fathers.

Religion

Religion contributes to understanding of self by placing the self in relation to the rest of reality, past, present, and future. While the preschool child is extremely concrete in his concepts of relationships, he does have experiences determined by the religious setting into which he is born.

Parents determine the religious orientation of their child both by uniting him with their religious community, as through circumcision or baptism; by their interpretation of man's relationships to God or gods, to man, to present, past, and future; by the expressed thoughts and feelings about beauty, love and truth, animate and inanimate nature. More indirectly, parents' behavior in general is influenced by their religion.

The religious community may have little or no direct bearing on the young child, depending on how it defines him and how it contacts him. Church nurseries and Sunday school groups can be very important in the child's life. He may enter into them eagerly and actively as his only experience with a peer group. A desirable church school takes account of the child's physical and psychological needs just as a nursery school does, although it stresses religious experiences, such as sacred stories and music, enjoyment of creativity, appreciation of beauty and of nature, worship, and giving. Symbolic and ritualistic performances appeal to children in the stage of developing initiative and also give them concrete experience of their religion.

The sense of trust developed in the beginning of life is the basis for faith in God or gods or the state or whatever one trusts. Since the mother first and then the father and the rest of the family are key figures in the development of the sense of trust, the family is the primary religious agent. They also play the most important roles, with the young child, in the creation of his sense of autonomy, the development of his self, his character, the standards of right and wrong which he makes his own.

The child begins early to muse upon the religious mysteries of which he becomes aware. "What does God look like?" "Why do the angels just come at Christmas time?" "What does *dead* mean?" "When do the seeds start to grow under the earth and how do they know it's time?" "You won't die before I'm grown up, will you?" "Do you think the astronauts will find heaven?" "Why doesn't God give me the toys I've been praying for?" "Don't you hate the people who killed Jesus?"

Answers to questions such as these depend upon the parents' own religion. What they say or do not say affects their child in a religious way, either helping him to build, restricting him to primitive thinking, or leaving him with gaps. Religious practices in the home can have deeply emotional as well as intellectual effects. Grace before meals, family Christmas dramatics, the seder—each of these events is a scene of family unity in which a little child feels a sense of belonging to his group and to something bigger. A memorable religious occasion often touches many of the senses and thus becomes an all-over experience for the child. Consider the variety of experiences during the Hindu celebration of the festival of Ganesh or Gumpati, the god of luck who is a favorite with children. The family brings home a clay model of Gumpati, a fat little boy with an elephant's head and trunk. Placing him on a stand or table in a bare room, they heap flowers, fruit, sweets, and incense at his feet. The child has large muscle experience in the walk home. He sees and touches Gumpati. He smells the flowers and incense. He eats some of the treats. He hears the story of Gumpati's birth and early childhood. After a week or so, there is a parade with music to make and hear. Gumpati in all his glory is transported to the river or lake, where an older boy lets him sink under the waters. The child sees the dramatization of the fact that his Gumpati was only a clay figure and not the real spirit which it represented. He does not *understand* the full meaning of the drama, but he has the picture of it which can later give shape and fullness to the idea.

Summary

Emotions increase in differentiation during the preschool period, as the child takes part in more interactions and more complex interactions with his parents, siblings, grandparents, and other people. Nurturance offered by adults to children is an expression of their own personality, indicating degrees of development of the sense of generativity. Children's responses to adults include a small measure of nurturance and a large measure of dependence, which varies with the attitudes and behavior of the adults. Siblings are ordinarily ambivalent to each other, showing nurturance, dependence, jealousy, and rivalry, according to the types of experiences they have with one another and to the attitudes and guidance techniques used by adults. Anger, an emotional response to frustration, can be hostile or constructive. Hostile aggression, an angry attack, is often but not always disapproved by parents. The developing imagination of the preschool child contributes to intangible fears, which increase greatly at this time. Concrete fears decrease. As with the infant, the presence of a loved person (attachment object) reassures the frightened child. Research suggests methods of controlling and minimizing anger, jealousy, rivalry, and fear in young children.

Character is the characteristic way in which a person harmonizes his own needs and desires with the demands of the outside world. Considerable development of character takes place during the preschool years, when the child increases in knowledge of rules, in his ability to judge right from wrong, and in his will to do right. Beginning as a person who requires outer control, he grows toward self-control, internalizing the demands of himself. Parental practices and attitudes are extremely significant in determining the type of character built by the child. The child's intellectual growth is part and parcel of his moral growth.

The young child gradually becomes more and more aware of himself as a distinct body and person, separate from other objects and persons. His increasingly complex interactions contribute to his growing concept of self. Through language and dramatic play, he explores, integrates, and expands this concept. His increasing intellectual powers permit greater flexibility of thought, which he eventually uses to view himself as others see him. The establishment and acceptance of his sex role contributes to the concept of self. Male and female roles are outlined by the culture and defined in detail by the family. The family teaches by direct instruction and prohibition, by sex-typing the environment, and by differential treatment of boys and girls. Children respond by identifying with one role or another, by their preference for either role, and by the concepts of family members which they build. Religion contributes broadly to the self concept, by placing the person in a broad orientation to all of existence.

References

1. Ainsworth, M. D. S. Object relations, dependency and attachment: A theoretical review of the infant-mother relationship. *Child Devel.*, 1969, **40**, 969–1025.
2. Ames, L. B. The sense of self of nursery school children as manifested by their verbal behavior. *J. Genet. Psychol.*, 1952, **81**, 193–232.
3. Aronfreed, J. *Conduct and conscience.* New York: Academic, 1968.
4. Baldwin, A. L. Changes in parent behavior during pregnancy. *Child Devel.*, 1947, **18**, 29–39.
5. Bandura, A. The role of modeling processes in personality development. In W. W. Hartup & N. L. Smothergill (Eds.), *The young child: Reviews of research.* Washington, D. C. National Association for the Education of Young Children, 1967, pp. 42–58.

6. Bandura, A., & Huston, A. C. Identification as a process of incidental learning. *J. Abn. Soc. Psychol.*, 1961, **63**, 311–318.
7. Bandura, A., Ross, D., & Ross, S. A. A comparative test of the status envy, social power and secondary reinforcement theories of identificatory learning. *J. Abn. Soc. Psychol.*, 1963, **67**, 527–534.
8. Bandura, A., & Walters, R. Aggression. In H. W. Stevenson (Ed.), *Child Psychology*. The sixty-second Yearbook of the National Society for the Study of Education. Chicago: University of Chicago Press, 1963, pp. 364–415.
9. Bandura, A., & Walters, R. H. *Social learning and personality development.* New York: Holt, Rinehart and Winston, 1963.
10. Barry, H., Bacon, M. K., & Child, I. L. A cross-cultural survey of some sex differences in socialization. *J. Abn. Soc. Psychol.*, 1957, **55**, 327–332.
11. Baruch, D. W., & Wilcox, J. A. A study of sex differences in preschool children's adjustment coexistent with interparental tensions. *J. Genet. Psychol.*, 1944, **64**, 281–303.
12. Baumrind, D. Child care practices anteceding three patterns of preschool behavior. *Genet. Psychol. Mono.*, 1967, **75**, 43–88.
13. Baumrind, D. Current patterns of parental authority. *Devel. Psychol. Mono.*, 1971, **4**:1, Part 2.
14. Biller, H. B., & Borstelman, L. J. Masculine development: An integrative review. *Merrill-Palmer Quart.*, 1967, **13**, 253–294.
15. Biller, H. B. Father dominance and sex role development in kindergarten-age boys. *Devel. Psychol.*, 1969, **1**, 87–94.
16. Biller, H. B. Maternal salience and feminine development in young girls. *Proc. 77th Annual Convention, Am. Psychol. Assoc.*, Washington, D.C., 1969, **4**, 259–260.
17. Biller, H. B. Father absence and the personality development of the male child. *Devel. Psychol.*, 1970, **2**, 181–201.
18. Boehm, L. The development of conscience of preschool children: A cultural and subcultural comparison. *J. Soc. Psychol.*, 1963, **39**, 355–360.
19. Bowlby, J. *Maternal care and mental health.* Geneva: World Health Organization, 1951.
20. Bowlby, J. *Attachment and loss.* Vol. I: *Attachment.* London: Hogarth, 1969.
21. Breznitz, S., & Kugelmass, S. Intentionality in moral judgment: Developmental stages. *Child Devel.*, 1967, **38**, 469–479.
22. Bronfenbrenner, U. Soviet methods of character education: Some implications for research. *Am. Psychol.*, 1962, **17**, 550–564.
23. Bronson, G. W. The development of fear in man and other animals. *Child Devel.*, 1968, **39**, 409–431.
24. Brown, D. G. Sex-role development in a changing culture. *Psychol. Bull.*, 1958, **55**, 232–242.
25. Clapp, W. F. *Competence and dependence in children: Parental treatment of four-year-old girls.* Washington, D.C.: U.S. Department of Health, Education, and Welfare, 1968.
26. Davis, W. A., & Havighurst, R. J. *Father of the man.* Boston: Houghton Mifflin, 1947.
27. DiBartolo, R., & Vinacke, W. E. Adult nurturance and the preschool child. *Devel. Psychol.*, 1969, **1**, 247–251.

28. Durrett, M. E., & Davy, A. J. Racial awareness in young Mexican-American and Anglo children. *Young Child.*, 1970, **26**, 16–24.
29. Emmerich, W. The parental role: A functional-cognitive approach. *Mono. Soc. Res. Child Devel.*, 1969, **34**:8.
30. Erikson, E. H., *Youth and crisis.* New York: Norton, 1968.
31. Fagot, B. I., & Patterson, G. R. An in vivo analysis of reinforcing contingencies for sex-role behaviors in the preschool child. *Devel. Psychol.*, 1969, **1**, 563–568.
32. Ferguson, L. R. *Personality development.* Belmont, Calif.: Wadsworth, 1970.
33. Fisher, S., & Cleveland, S. E. *Body image and personality.* New York: Van Nostrand, 1958.
34. Gilbert, D. C. The young child's awareness of affect. *Child Devel.*, 1969, **40**, 629–640.
35. Hagman, R. R. A study of the fears of children of preschool age. *J. Exper. Educ.*, 1932, **1**, 110–130.
36. Hartup, W. W. Dependence and independence. In H. W. Stevenson [Ed.], *Child psychology.* The Sixty-second Yearbook of the National Society for the Study of Education. Chicago: University of Chicago, 1963, pp. 333–363.
37. Heinicke, C. M. Some effects of separating two-year-old children from their mothers. *Hum. Relat.*, 1956, **9**, 102–176.
38. Hess, R. D., Gordon, I., & Scheinfeld, D. Intervention in family life. In E. Grotberg (Ed.), *Critical issues in research related to disadvantaged children.* Princeton, N.J.: Educational Testing Service, 1969.
39. Hess, R. D., & Shipman, V. C. Early experience and the socialization of cognitive modes in children. *Child Devel.*, 1965, **36**, 869–886.
40. Hetherington, E. M. A developmental study of the effects of sex of the dominant parent on sex role preference, identification and imitation in children. *J. Pers. Soc. Psychol.*, 1965, **2**, 188–194.
41. Hoffman, M. L. Childrearing practices and moral development: Generalizations from empirical research. *Child Devel.*, 1963, **34**, 295–318.
42. Jersild, A. T., & Holmes, F. B. Children's fears. *Child Devel. Mono.*, No. 20. New York: Teachers College, Columbia University, 1935.
43. Jessor, R., & Richardson, S. Psychosocial deprivation and personality development. In *Perspectives on human deprivation: Biological, psychological and sociological.* Washington, D.C.: U.S. Department of Health, Education, and Welfare, 1968, pp. 1–87.
44. John, E. A study of the effects of evacuation and air raids on children of preschool age. *Brit. J. Educ. Psychol.*, 1941, **11**, 173–182.
45. Joynt, D., & Cambroune, B. Psycholinguistic development and the control of behavior. *Brit. J. Educ. Psychol.*, 1968, **38**, 249–260.
46. Kagan, J., & Moss, H. A. *Birth to maturity.* New York: Wiley, 1962.
47. Kahana, B., & Kahana, E. Grandparenthood from the perspective of the developing child. *Devel. Psychol.*, 1970, **3**, 98–105.
48. Kahana, E., & Rosenblatt, I. E. Grandparenting as a function of family structure. Paper presented at the meeting of the Society for Research in Child Development, Santa Monica, Calif., March 29, 1969.
49. Katz, I. Factors influencing Negro performance in the desegregated school. In M. Deutsch, I. Katz & A. R. Jensen (Eds.) *Social class, race and psychological development.* New York: Holt, Rinehart & Winston, 1968, pp. 254–289.
50. Koch, H. L. The relation of certain formal attributes of siblings to attitudes

held toward each other and toward their parents. *Mono. Soc. Res. Child Devel.*, 1960, **25**:4.
51. Koch, M. B. Anxiety in preschool children from broken homes. *Merrill-Palmer Quart.*, 1961, **7**, 225–232.
52. Kohlberg, L., & Zigler, E. The impact of cognitive maturity on the development of sex-role attitudes in the years 4 to 8. *Genet. Psychol. Mono.*, 1967, **75**, 89–161.
53. Kreitler, H., & Kreitler, S. Children's concepts of sexuality and birth. *Child Devel.*, 1966, **37**, 363–378.
54. Luria, A. R. *The role of speech in the regulation of normal and abnormal behavior.* New York: Pergamon, 1961.
55. Luria, Z., Goldwasser, M., & Goldwasser, A. Response to transgression in stories by Israeli children. *Child Devel.*, 1963, **34**, 271–280.
56. Luria, Z., & Rebelsky, F. Ethnicity: A variable in sex differences in moral behavior. Paper presented at the meeting of the Society for Research in Child Development, Berkeley, April 1963.
57. Maccoby, E. E. Role-taking in childhood and its consequences for social learning. *Child Devel.*, 1959, **30**, 239–252.
58. Maccoby, E. E. Stability and change in attachment behavior during the third year of life. Paper presented at the meeting of the Western Psychological Association, Vancouver, June, 1969.
59. Marks, I. M. *Fears and phobias.* New York: Academic, 1969.
60. Marshall, H. Relations between home experiences and children's use of language in play interactions with peers. *Psychol. Mono.*, 1961, **75**:5.
61. Maurer, A. What children fear. *J. Genet. Psychol.*, 1965, **106**, 265–277.
62. Mead, M. *Male and female.* New York: Morrow, 1949.
63. Miller, D. R., & Swanson, G. E. *The changing American parent.* New York: Wiley, 1958.
64. Mussen, P., & Distler, L. Childrearing antecedents of masculine identification in kindergarten boys. *Child Devel.*, 1960, **31**, 89–100.
65. Mussen, P. H., & Parker, A. L. Mother nurturance and girls' incidental imitative learning. *J. Pers. Soc. Psychol.*, 1965, **2**, 94–97.
66. Neugarten, B. L., & Weinstein, K. K. The changing American grandparent. *J. Marr. Fam.*, 1964, **26**, 199–204.
67. Newson, J., & Newson, E. *Four years old in an urban community.* Chicago: Aldine, 1968.
68. Oetzel, R. M. Sex typing and sex role adoption in relation to differential abilities. Unpublished M.A. thesis, Stanford University, 1962. Cited in Ferguson [32].
69. Office of Economic Opportunity. *Project Head Start Daily Program I.* Washington, D.C.: U.S. Govt. Printing Office, 1965.
70. Ogilvie, D. M. Distinguishing social behaviors of competent and incompetent three- to six-year-old children. Paper presented at the meeting of the Society for Research in Child Development, Santa Monica, Calif., March 27, 1969.
71. Osborn, D. K., & Endsley, R. C. Emotional reactions of young children to TV violence. *Child Devel.*, 1971, **42**, 321–331.
72. Peck, R. F., & Havighurst, R. J. *The psychology of character development.* New York: Wiley, 1960.
73. Piaget, J. *The moral judgment of the child.* Glencoe, Ill.: Free Press, 1960.

74. Proshansky, H., & Newton, P. The nature and meaning of Negro self-identity. In M. Deutsch, I. Katz, & A. R. Jensen (Eds.), *Social class, race and psychological development*. New York: Holt, Rinehart and Winston, 1968, pp. 178–218.
75. Rosen, B. C. Socialization and achievement motivation in Brazil. *Am. Soc. Rev.*, 1962, **27**, 612–624.
76. Rosenhan, D. The kindnesses of children. *Young Children*, 1969, **25**, 30–44.
77. Rutherford, E., & Mussen, P. Generosity in nursery school boys. *Child Devel.*, 1968, **39**, 755–765.
78. Schell, R. E., & Silber, J. W. Sex-role discrimination among young children. *Percept. Motor Skills*, 1968, **27**, 379–389.
79. Schwarz, J. C. Presence of an attached peer and security. Paper presented at the meeting of the Society for Research in Child Development, Santa Monica, Calif., March 27, 1969.
80. Sears, R. R., Maccoby, E. E., & Levin, H. *Patterns of child rearing*. Evanston, Ill.: Row, Peterson, 1957.
81. Seltzer, A., & Beller, E. K. Moral and cognitive development in lower class Negro children. Paper presented at the meeting of the Eastern Psychological Association, Washington, D.C., April 1968.
82. Siegel, A. E., Stolz, L. M., Hitchcock, E. A., & Adamson, J. M. Dependence and independence in the children of working mothers. *Child Devel.*, 1959, **30**, 533–546.
83. Stevenson, H. W. Studies of racial awareness in young children. In W. W. Hartup & N. L. Smothergill (Eds.) *The young child: Reviews of research*. Washington, D.C.: National Association for the Education of Young Children, 1967.
84. Stolz, L. M. Effects of maternal employment on children: Evidence from research. *Child Devel.*, 1960, **31**, 749–782.
85. Sutton-Smith, B., & Rosenberg, B. G. Age changes in the effects of ordinal position on sex-role identification. *J. Genet. Psychol.*, 1965, **107**, 61–73.
86. Sweetser, D. A. The social structure of grandparenthood. In R. F. Winch, R. McGinnis, & H. R. Barringer, *Selected studies in marriage and the family*. New York: Holt, 1962, pp. 388–396.
87. Thompson, K. S., Friedlander, B., & Oskamp, S. Change in racial attitudes of preschool children through an experimental reading program. Paper presented at the meeting of the Western Psychological Association, Vancouver, June 18, 1969.
88. Unger, S. M. A behavior theory approach to the emergence of guilt reactivity in the child. *J. Psychol.*, 1964, **5**, 85–101.
89. Van de Castle, R. L. His, hers and the children's. *Psychol. Today*, 4(1), 37–39.
90. Waldrop, M. F., & Bell, R. Q. Relation of preschool dependency behavior to family size and density. *Child Devel.*, 1964, **35**, 1187–1195.
91. Wann, K. D., Dorn, M. S., & Liddle, E. A. *Fostering intellectual development in young children*. New York: Teachers College, Columbia University, 1962.
92. Ward, W. D. Process of sex-role development. *Devel. Psychol.*, 1969, **1**, 163–168.
93. Whiting, J. W. M., & Child, I. *Child training and personality*. New Haven, Conn.: Yale University Press, 1953.
94. Williams, J. E., & Edwards, C. D. An exploratory study of the modification of color and racial concept attitudes in preschool children. *Child Devel.*, 1969, **40**, 737–750.

Readings in
Socialization: Interaction and Results

Through his interactions with people, most of all parents, but also peers, other family members, and perhaps teachers, the young child develops patterns of social behavior and attitudes toward himself. Feelings as well as actions constitute his behavior in relation to himself and others. An abundance of research in this field reflects the great interest that it provokes. In light of the problem delineated by William Ballard in the last section of this book, it is heartening to notice a new emphasis in the area of socialization. Until quite recently, very little had been published on prosocial behavior and positive emotions. At present many psychologists are studying attachment, affection, generosity, kindness, and so on. We begin with a scholarly but tender and warming review, "The Kindnesses of Children," by David Rosenhan, in which he explores links between children's kindly behavior and other aspects of their development.

Henry B. Biller's study of sex role development in boys was based on boys' behavior and mothers' responses to questionnaires. Biller found differences between boys with fathers living in the family and boys whose fathers were absent. The masculinity of father-absent boys was affected by the mothers' behavior. Sex role preference in white and black children shows some significant race and sex differences in a study by Norman L. Thompson, Jr. and Boyd R. McCandless. Highly dependent and nondependent preschool children were compared as to performance on a puzzle task, given under two different conditions. Russell DiBartolo and W. Edgar Vinacke were the experimenters in this exploration of the effect of nurturance on performance of children who varied as to dependency.

The Kindnesses of Children*

David Rosenhan
SWARTHMORE COLLEGE

That we are occasionally deeply moved by the kindnesses of children needs no documentation here. One child's generosity to another, his spontaneous helpfulness to a needy adult, his willingness to forego his own pleasure without

Reprinted with permission from *Young Children*, Vol. XXV, No. 1, October, 1969. Copyright © 1969, National Association for the Education of Young Children, 1834 Connecticut Avenue, N.W., Washington, D.C. 20009.

* Some of the research reported here was conducted at the Center for Psychological Studies, Educational Testing Service, and was supported by Grant 1 PO 1 HD-01762 from the National Institute of Child Health and Human Development. Other research, and the writing of this report, was supported by MH-HD 13862 and MH-16462, both from the National Institute of Mental Health.

urging so that another may enjoy—these are the kinds of behaviors that make us feel that all is well in the world, however much our senses tell us otherwise. We are concerned in this paper with the origins of such behaviors, not only for their own sake but also because they appear to be progenitors of such behaviors in adults. And in adults they are not only moving but critically important, least of all, perhaps, for adult well-being, but mainly for society. Consider: the capacity of people to give much more than they apparently receive (and this is how we define altruistic or generous behavior)—as parents do for children, teachers for students, lovers for each other—forms one of the likely bases of socialization, education, patriotism, love, social order and cooperative cohesion. These capacities and social structures do not arise *de novo* in the adult, but rather spring from childhood antecedents.

Although rumor (buttressed by naive psychological theory) has it that man is selfish and concerned only with himself and his own gratifications, that is hardly the case. Indeed evidence for altruistic behavior can be found throughout the animal kingdom, and in large measure, too. After summarizing some of that evidence, Hebb and Thompson observe:

> The evidence indicates ... that a disinterested concern for others can be found in mammalian development. Although it reaches its greatest potential only in man, it is not foreign to any higher animal, and is not something that is imposed only by reward and punishment on the growing child. It can, of course, be stultified or fostered during growth, but by his intellectual and emotional characteristics man has a greater *aptitude* for altruistic attitudes than any other animal, and it is of great importance to gain a more precise knowledge of the conditions of its development [Hebb & Thompson, 1968, p. 746].

My concern here is to describe some of what is known about altruism in children. In a developmental context, I want to explore the roles of (1) affect, (2) observational learning and (3) moral preachings. I shall also want to speculate on the interrelations between these variables and others from the cognitive and social domains.

THE ROLE OF AFFECT

Common sense tells us that affect is involved in some forms of altruistic behavior. When the Actor assists the Recipient, presumably the latter experiences pleasure and the former empathizes that pleasure. This is likely to be particularly true for the initial acquisition of prosocial behaviors, and somewhat less so for their later maintenance. For lack of a better term I call this *acquisition affect*, to denote the close proximity of special affective states to the learning of prosocial behaviors.

There is a second kind of role for affect, one that predisposes a child to be kind to others. *Predisposing affects*, like acquisition affects, tend mainly (though, as we shall see, not always) to be positive. Anger, for example, does not predispose to kindness, but joy may. We shall consider these two roles for affect in turn.

ACQUISITION AFFECT   In 1963 and 1964 we interviewed intensively a group of people who had been active in the Civil Rights movement through

1961, with a view to determining whether they shared common psychological characteristics (Rosenhan, in press). We located two groups. Members of the first had been active participants in Civil Rights actions for a year or longer at the time of interview. We called this group the Fully Committed, mainly because they had given up their homes, occupations and educations to participate in these activities. The second group consisted of people who had been occasional activists, and whom we called the Partially Committed. They had limited their participation to one or two Freedom Rides, without relinquishing their other pursuits.

There were no population differences between the Fully and Partially Committed, except for income where, as one might expect, the Fully Committed were poorer. Nor were there differences in attitudes towards Civil Rights. Indeed, if one were to judge by their verbal behavior, the Partially Committed were greater believers in the equality of blacks and whites than were the Fully Committed. Only two really striking differences emerged between these groups, and both of these differences referred to events that took place in childhood. First, the Fully Committed had parents who were themselves active altruists. Second, our respondents had maintained a positive relationship with their parents during their childhood and through the time of interview.

Let us examine the first finding, for which data are presented in Table 1. The parents themselves were prosocial activists in the events of an earlier era, in such matters as the Spanish Civil War, the Second World War or religious education. So it was possible that our respondents learned by doing, or at least learned by seeing their parents do. One respondent observed that "my father carried me on his shoulders during the Sacco-Vanzetti parades" while another remarked that his mother "felt close to Jesus and was warmed by His teachings. She devoted her entire life to Christian education."

TABLE 1
Evidence for Discrepancy Between Teaching and Practice by the Socializers of Fully Committed and Partially Committed Civil Rights Workers

Discrepancy	Fully Committed	Partially Committed
Present	2	13
Absent	11	3
Evidence unclear or absent	2	5

$\chi^2 = 13.29$; df $= 2$; $p < .01$.

By contrast, the Partially Committed had parents who were at best mere verbal supporters of prosocial moralities, and at worst, hypocritical about those moralities. It was common for our Partially Committed to report that their parents preached one thing and practiced another. Moreover, our Partially Committed were so angered by the discrepancy between parental posture and action that we had reason to believe that our respondents had undergone nothing less than a "crisis of hypocrisy" during their childhood which resulted in their inability to make enduring commitments to prosocial (as to other) matters later on.

These data are amenable to a variety of interpretations, and I shall return to them later when I consider the role of observational learning in the development of altruism. For the present, however, it is useful to examine them in light of current theories of emotion. Schachter and Singer (1962) have observed that emotion results from the joint action of physiological arousal and cognitions appropriate to that arousal. In order to obtain arousal in the laboratory, Schachter and Singer injected their subjects with adrenaline (though they did not tell their subjects that). Aroused subjects subsequently observed a model go through a series of either joyful or angry antics. On a variety of measures, the subjects themselves subsequently manifested either joy or anger.

We speculate that our Fully Committed respondents were also aroused, not by injection, but by being family participants in what must have been very exciting events. Having been thus aroused, and having observed their parents participate in prosocial behavior (which is to say, serve as models) they, too, experienced emotion. Which emotion? Perhaps sympathy for the oppressed. Perhaps empathy. Perhaps affection for their parents. At this level our data are vague—they merely suggest that emotions of a prosocial kind play a significant role in the acquisition of altruistic behavior.

Data bearing more specifically on the role of affect in altruism were obtained in an experiment by Aronfreed and Paskal (1965). Six- to eight-year-old girls played a game involving two levers. If the child pressed one lever, she would often (60 percent of the time) get a piece of candy. If she pressed the other lever, a red light would go on with similar frequency. During the training phase of the experiment, a female experimenter sat close to the child and behaved in one of three ways each time the light went on. Either she exclaimed "there's the light," smiled at the child and gave her a warm hug; or she hugged the child without saying anything; or she said "there's the light" but did not hug the child. During the test phase of the experiment, the light on the front of the child's game was disconnected and the experimenter moved across from the child, facing the rear of the apparatus where there was an operative red light which she could see but the child could not. For this phase, each time the child pressed the lever that produced the light (for the experimenter), the experimenter exclaimed "there's the light."

It is clear that the red light, and the lever that activated it, are innocent or neutral stimuli: they have no special meaning. Paired with the experimenter's behavior, however, it should acquire meaning by classical conditioning, that is, it should come to mean "pleasure for the experimenter." The question is: Which of the three training experiences will most powerfully connect the red light to the experimenter's pleasure, such that the child will be most willing to press that lever and, at the same time deprive himself of candy?

The data from this experiment indicated that the *combination* of expressive cues ("there's the light") with affection (smiles and hugs) was so powerful that children in this condition pressed the red light lever more often than the candy lever! Children from the remaining two groups chose the candy-producing lever more often. Thus the combined effects of verbal expression and affection were more successful than either alone in conditioning pleasant affect to a neutral stimulus.

Midlarsky and Bryan (1967) repeated and elaborated this study in several significant ways. For half of their subjects, the experimenter remained impassive during the final testing. Even these children pressed the red-light lever more often than did children who had not witnessed expressive cues or experienced affection.

Midlarsky and Bryan (1967) also added an experimental condition which allowed them to assess the impact of the three treatment conditions upon charitability under conditions of anonymity. After they completed the task, the children were given some additional candies so that all children had an equal supply. They were then asked to donate candy to "needy children, whose parents can't afford to buy them any candy." Each child was told that the amount of the donation was her decision and that she need not donate at all if she did not choose to do so. In order to underscore the apparent privacy of her actions, the experimenter led her to the donation box and then waited outside of the room while she made (or failed to make) her contribution. Here, too, the combined effects of expressive cues ("there's the light") and affection (a smile and a hug) were greater than either alone in eliciting charitability.

PREDISPOSING AFFECTS   In the interview study of Civil Rights workers mentioned earlier, Fully Committed altruists appeared to have maintained a positive, cordial, warm and respecting relationship with their parent(s). That relationship extended far into childhood and continued through the time of the interview. True, there had been disagreements. True also, these disagreements sometimes extended to matters of considerable importance to both the respondent and his parent, including the matter of whether the respondent should be active in Civil Rights. Despite these differences, one sensed easily considerable fondness between parent and child.

The Partially Committed described their parents in negative or ambivalent terms. A substantial proportion described their relations with the socializing parent as downright hostile during the formative years and cool and avoidant at the time they were interviewed. One sensed discomfort, often anxiety and hostility, flowing from child to parent and perhaps vice-versa. These data are summarized in Table 2.

TABLE 2
Affective Reactions to the Primary Socializer by Fully Committed and Partially Committed Civil Rights Workers

VALENCE	FULLY COMMITTED	PARTIALLY COMMITTED
Positive	12	3
Negative or distinctly ambivalent	3	18

$\chi^2 = 15.55$; df = 1; $p < .001$.

Similar findings, this time in connection with student activists have been reported by Smith, Block and Haan.[1] Activists who participated in both protest and constructive volunteer activity contrasted clearly with "dissenters" who engaged only in protest. The former tended to report good relations with parents who were seen as humanistic but firm toward their children; the latter reported rather bad or ambivalent relations with parents, who were seen as inconsistent, lax and permissive.

The view that a positive affective relationship with a socializing agent facilitates altruism is supported not only by our naturalistic data but also by findings obtained by Rutherford and Mussen (1968). In their experiment, nursery school boys were given 18 identical pieces of candy which they could either keep for themselves or divide among themselves and two children in the class whom they liked best. Generous children (i.e., those who donated 15 or more candies to others) tended to see their fathers (though not their mothers) as nurturant in a doll play situation. Since the perception of parental nurturance is highly correlated with actual parental behavior in an interview situation (Mussen & Distler, 1960; Mussen & Rutherford, 1963), and since generous boys differentiated their parents in the imputation of nurturance, Rutherford and Mussen found it more plausible to view paternal nurturance as an antecedent rather than a consequence, of generosity.

It should be noted, however, that experimental attempts to manipulate directly the child's relationship to an altruistic socializer have *not* yet been successful. For example, children who had had a pleasant prior relationship with a charitable model were not subsequently more charitable than those who had a negative one (Rosenhan & White, 1967). Similar findings were obtained by Grusec and Skubiski (1969). Moreover, attempts by this writer to deepen the prior relationship by extending the period of exposure to the model have also been unsuccessful.

Success and Failure   Not only do long-term positive relationships predispose one to altruistic behavior, but brief bursts of positive affect seem to have similar effects. A series of experiments by Isen (1968) and Berkowitz and Connor (1966) have shown that the experience of success on a task generates significantly greater generosity in adults than does failure. Isen has interpreted her findings in terms of a "warm glow of success," suggesting that when people succeed, they experience positive affect which in turn expresses itself in increased willingness to be kind to others.

In an extension of these findings, Isen and Rosenhan (1969) gave fourth-grade children 25 cents for helping them test and give their opinions about newly manufactured toys. These children played a bowling game on which they either obtained many high scores (success) or many low ones (failure). Control children played a similar game which, however, lacked a score indicator. The experimenter (E_1) absented herself during these games on a pretext of having work to do. When the game was completed, E_1 returned and, shortly thereafter, a second experimenter (E_2), ostensibly a stranger, knocked on the door and was admitted. Speaking directly to E_1, she said that she was collecting money for children who had no toys, and asked permission to leave her charity

[1] Personal communication from M. B. Smith, May 1969.

box in the laboratory. After ascertaining that "anyone can give—even the children who help us here," E_1 led E_2 to a second room in the laboratory ostensibly to take her name and address, closing the door of the room firmly behind her. During the 60 seconds that E_1 and E_2 conferred together, the child was alone in the laboratory, supposedly unobserved with regard to whether or not he contributed.

Children who had experienced positive affect through the success induction contributed far more than children in either the failure or control conditions. Moreover, the number of children who had contributed was greater in the success than in the other conditions.

It was important that the procedures of this experiment be described in detail in order to communicate its salient feature: that a third party, ostensibly unassociated with the toy company, was requesting a donation. Under that condition, children who had experienced positive affect contributed more than those who had experienced negative affect, or none at all. A second experiment was conducted which differed from the first experiment in an apparently trivial respect. Instead of having someone bring in the charity box, the children's attention was now directed to a box that was already in the laboratory. They were simply told that *we* had been asked to collect for the Toy Fund, that we ourselves were going to contribute and they could contribute too, if they so desired. A 60-second period, during which children were alone, was allowed to permit them to contribute.

Under these conditions, no significant differences were obtained between failure and success. Both contributed more than controls. Boys, however, contributed significantly more after they had *failed* than after they had succeeded.

We have then, an instance where negative affect has an impact on generosity that is even greater than that of positive affect. And it is not the only one. Staub (1968) exposed fourth- and fifth-grade children to success, failure and intermediate scores on a bowling game. After they had finished playing, and by way of thanking the children for their efforts, the experimenter brought out a bowl of candy and gave it to the children. She then remarked that "actually we don't have enough candy and you should share some with another child. Why don't you take out your own candy and put it in this bag; whatever you want to leave for this other child you may leave in this bag." Under these conditions, fourth-grade children who experienced failure "shared" significantly *more* than children in the success condition.

How shall we reconcile these differences? Our present view, which remains to be tested, is that the crucial differences between these experiments lie in whether, in the subject's mind, generosity was directed to the primary experimenter (through whom he had either succeeded or failed) or to vaguely identified needy others. The "warm glow of success" hypothesis predicts that the positive affect generated by success will express itself in a desire to be helpful. Failure will not. Failure, however, does generate a desire to improve one's image in the eyes of another (Schneider, 1966). Thus, children who have failed will be generous if they feel that the experimenter might find out about it, but not otherwise. In Staub's (1968) experiment, as in the second experiment by Isen and myself, there were numerous cues which pointed to the possibility that we would know that the subject had contributed and would therefore think more highly of him. We shall return to the issues of "who knows whether I have been generous" in our discussion of the role of observational learning.

In summary, the evidence points strongly to the fact that positive affect is implicated in the acquisition of generous impulses and in the predisposition to behave generously. Similar observations have been made in regard to the acquisition of sympathy and empathy among children (Aronfreed, 1968; Lenrow, 1965). Negative affect becomes a factor in generous behavior only when the child is concerned with rectifying his negative self-image.

THE ROLE OF OBSERVATIONAL LEARNING

In a recent paper (Rosenhan, in press) we distinguished between two kinds of altruism: *normative altruism* and *autonomous altruism*. The first engenders a concern for others and is elicited and supported by a vast social network of relatively immediate rewards and punishments. Often characterized by low personal risk and cost to the actor, its central feature is the actor's concern for himself: whether *he* will be rewarded for engaging in an altruistic act, or *he* will be punished for failing to do so. In contrast, autonomous altruism is not legitimated by a visible system of reward and punishment but rather appears to derive its impetus from internalized cognitions and behavioral examples. Indeed, autonomous altruists quite often appear to disregard the external system of reward and punishment by sacrificing personal rewards to needy others for no visible immediate or future gain. In short, normative altruism seems characterized by the cluster of variables we associate with *social conformity*, while autonomous altruism reflects what we often call *commitment*.

Some evidence for this view was obtained in our study of Civil Rights activists. Fully Committed activists, you will recall, had parents who were themselves activists, who were exemplars of altruistic behavior. They had learned the altruistic norm by example as well as precept. Partially Committed activists were socialized by parents whose altruism was limited to preaching, and whose preaching was often violated in practice. Lacking a directly learned basis for altruism, the Partially Committed relied on more immediate (and, it might be added, transient) stimuli, such as group esprit and camaraderie and short-term personal rewards.

On the basis of the interview study, then, we concluded that the behavioral example provided by other altruists was a critical component of full altruistic commitment. We next sought to confirm this observation under controlled laboratory conditions. In an experiment conducted by Professor Glenn White and myself, children in the fourth and fifth grades alternated turns on a bowling game with an adult model. Each time the model obtained a winning score of 20, he took two 5 cent gift certificates from a large pile on a nearby table. These gift certificates served as money surrogates and were redeemable at a nearby candy store known to all the children. The model then deposited one of the gift certificates into a container labelled "Trenton Orphan's Fund." While the subject played, the model looked away, ostensibly waiting for his turn. This was done in order to minimize the possibility that the attention of the adult model might influence whether the child gave.

Model and child each had 10 turns, during which the model won and contributed twice. At the end of the game, the model pretended to have work to do elsewhere. After ascertaining that the child would like to play again by himself, the model departed, telling the child to return to his class when he was finished. The child then played 20 trials and obtained winning scores on four of them.

We had three concerns in this experiment. First, would children who were not exposed to a charitable model also contribute? After all, these children were 10 and 11 years old, old enough to understand who orphans were and what their needs might be. Moreover, they were likely to be aware that charitability was important and "good." For all of this, however, not a single child in this control condition contributed to the Orphans' Fund.

Our second question was concerned with whether the child would contribute in the presence of the charitable model. That a child contributes in the presence of an adult model would not really be surprising; since however much the model attempted to ignore the child's behavior, the model was still present in the room and the child knew it. Children are socialized to please adults, and certainly not to offend them. So we had little doubt that many children would contribute in the model's presence, and we were not surprised: 63 percent of the children contributed when the model was in the room.

Our final concern was the critical one: How would they behave in the model's absence? In a very broad sense, many of us are not concerned with the way a child behaves in our presence; it is his behavior when he is out of sight that concerns us. In this instance, the child had nothing to gain by contributing, and gift certificates to lose. Ostensibly no one would know if he had contributed (and we have considerable evidence to indicate that the children did not know they were being observed). Nevertheless, nearly 50 percent of the subjects contributed.

Clearly then, observation of a charitable model facilitates charitability (cf. Bandura, 1969), not only of the *normative* kind—as indexed by behavior in the presence of the model—but also of the autonomous sort that occurs in the absence of the model. Moreover, as Table 3 makes clear, autonomous and normative altruism are not unrelated, at least among children. Those who

TABLE 3
Relationship Between Giving in the Presence of the Model and Giving in His Absence
(Adapted from Rosenhan & White, 1967)

Gave in the Model's Absence (Autonomous Altruism)	Gave in the Model's Presence (Normative Altruism)		
	Yes	No	Total
Yes	51	6	57
No	25	38	63
Total	76	34	120

$\chi^2 = 29.84$; df = 1; $p < .001$.

contributed in the model's presence were far more likely than those who did not to contribute in his absence. And conversely, those who did not contribute in the model's presence, failed to contribute in his absence. Apparently, observation of an altruistic model *and* rehearsal in his presence greatly increase the likelihood that the model's charitability will be internalized by the child (Rosenhan & White, 1967).

The effects of models on altruistic behavior have been found in several other studies (Bryan & Walbek, 1969; Grusec & Skubiski, 1969; Harris, 1968; Rosenhan, 1969b; White, 1967). An experiment that is especially illuminating in this regard was conducted by Hartup and Coates (1967). Nursery school children individually observed a peer model who, on each of 10 trials, allocated only one of his earned trinkets to himself and five of these trinkets to "Alec" or "Kathy" (other nursery school children). The subjects were either relatively "popular" or "unpopular" as determined by the amount of positive reinforcement they had been observed to receive during sampled observations that were taken over a five-week period. Moreover, the model had either been quite rewarding to the child (i.e., had given him considerable positive reinforcement) or had not rewarded him at all. Subsequently, the experimenter and model went to an adjoining room while the subject played the game and earned trinkets.

As Table 4 indicates, there is no question that the observation of a peer model facilitates charitability. But what is of considerable interest is the manner in which the popularity of the child interacts with the rewardingness of the

TABLE 4
Mean "Giving to Other" Scores as a Function of Popularity of Child and Rewardingness of Model
(Adapted from Hartup and Coates, 1967)

Group	First Five Trials	Second Five Trials
Relatively popular children:		
Rewarding models	21.00	19.25
Nonrewarding models	13.42	13.83
Relatively unpopular children:		
Rewarding models	17.50	17.08
Nonrewarding models	22.83	18.58
No model	5.63	3.75

model, particularly during the first five trials. Popular children were more influenced by models who had been kind to them (i.e., been rewarding) than those who had not. Unpopular children, on the other hand, tended to imitate those who have not been kind to them more than those who have. Clearly, the socialization history of the child and his relation to the model are critical here as they were in the naturalistic study cited earlier (Rosenhan, in press).

THE ROLE OF MORAL PREACHINGS

There is no question but that, in our socialization of children, we spend much of our time telling them what is right and what is wrong, what is moral and what is immoral. Such preachments are heard from parents and teachers and, indeed, from children to each other. Surprisingly, very little is known about the impact of these teachings on behavior, nor is much known about the comparative effects of preaching versus behavioral example. Clearly, preaching has its effects at the verbal level: Children are able, with increasing age, to *tell* you what is right and wrong, and even why (cf. Kohlberg, 1963). But what are the effects on behavior?

In a recent study, White (1967) compared the effects of telling children that they should contribute to a particular charity, with observing a charitable model and with observing and rehearsing with such a model. Not surprisingly, many more of the children who had been told to give, subsequently gave anonymously (and gave more) than those who had been in the two modeling conditions. In fact, nearly all of the verbally instructed children contributed. This, however, occurred only when the groups were tested immediately after they had been trained. Wisely, White tested three groups again after a one-week delay, and found that the impact of preaching had deteriorated to the point where there was no difference between children who had been verbally instructed and those who had observed charitable models. Indeed, the stability of behavior—whether children were consistent contributors or noncontributors across the two testings—was markedly lower for the children who had been instructed than for those who had learned by observation. Thus, it is possible to argue that relative to observing a model, prosocial instruction has powerful short-run effects producing nearly uniform obedience, but considerably weaker delayed effects. Long-term effects, as indexed by test behavior which is separated from training by, say, a month, remain to be explored but would likely show even further weakness for prosocial preaching.

PREACHING AND PRACTICING   In children's experience, moral preachings are as likely to be paired with practices as not. And moral practices may be consistent with the preachings or inconsistent with them. It has already been shown that the consistency of preaching and practice among altruistic parents seems to be a critical determinant of altruistic commitment in the child, now himself become a man. Fully Committed Civil Rights activists reported parents who were themselves activists, whose preachings were consistent with their behaviors. Partially Committed activists appeared to have been socialized by inconsistent or hypocritical parents who preached a morality which they violated in practice. As indicated earlier, these data were obtained through retrospective interviews. We turn now to experiments that have sought to examine the effects of consistency and inconsistency between preachings and practices.

There are really two kinds of inconsistencies that can occur between preaching and practice. In one, the model sets a *higher* standard for himself than for the child. We call this a *child-indulgent* pattern and, in a study concerned with the internalization of norms for self-reward (Rosenhan, Frederick & Burrowes, 1968), we found that this pattern yielded a high degree of norm internalization (and little norm violation). There is, however, a second kind of discrepancy which occurs when the model sets a *lower* standard for himself than for the child. It is to this kind of discrepancy that notions of hypocrisy are addressed. Studies by Mischel and Liebert (1966) and Rosenhan, *et al.* (1968) indicate that experience with *self-indulgent* models produces considerably more norm violation than consistent or child-indulgent conditions. The central message of these studies is that where the verbal and behavioral modes are in competition, children will be mainly guided by behavioral example and only secondarily by verbal preachments.

These studies, however, have concentrated on internalization of norms for self-reward. What of rewarding others? What, in particular, is the impact of consistency and discrepancy in preaching and practice on the charitable behavior of children? Bryan and his colleagues have examined these issues in detail (Bryan, 1968, in press; Bryan & Walbeck, 1968, 1969). Their basic procedure utilizes a model who, in the presence of the child, behaves charitably or greedily, while preaching either charity or greed. The model's preachings consist of general exhortations on the value of charity ("It is good to give to poor children"); these statements simulate the elements of moral training as given by parents or teachers. Occasionally, the procedure includes an attempt to alert the subject to the potentially rewarding consequences of charitability, such as reminding him that charitable children are liked by others. Regardless of the variation employed, these experiments have produced one consistent outcome: moral preachings have no effect on behavior.

If the model behaves charitably, so will the child—even if the model has preached greed. And conversely, if the model preaches charity, but practices greed (Bryan and his colleagues call this the Young Republican condition!), the child will follow the model's precept and will not contribute to the charity. Behavior in the prosocial area is influenced by behavior, not by words.

If this is the case, why is it that we place so much tacit and explicit emphasis on moral adjuration and moral precept? Several of these studies suggest a possible reason. In addition to being given an opportunity to contribute to the charity, children were asked to rate the attractiveness of the model. Here the model's verbalizations were found to have profound impact. Models who preached charity were much more attractive to children than those who preached greed, regardless of what the model practiced. Indeed, much as the model's preaching had little impact on the child's behavior, so his practice had minimal impact on the child's *evaluation* of him. Thus, it is conceivable that since children tend to value more highly people who say the right things, such people are thereby encouraged to go right on saying them!

DEVELOPMENTAL AND OTHER VARIABLES ASSOCIATED WITH PROSOCIAL BEHAVIOR IN CHILDREN

Prosocial behavior, in both children and adults, has been a relatively new topic for researchers. Except for some early, classic work by Hartshorne, May and Maller (1929) and Beatrice Wright (1942), most of the work in this area has been undertaken in the past decade. It may therefore be somewhat premature to generalize about the relationship of prosocial behavior to other aspects of the child's functioning. Yet, some of the existing evidence is of considerable interest, and it is useful to speculate on the meaning of this material.

DEVELOPMENT OF PROSOCIAL BEHAVIOR

The evidence is now strong indeed that the acquisition and elicitation of generous behavior increases with age (Handlon & Gross, 1959; Midlarsky & Bryan, 1967; Wright, 1942; Ugerul-Semin, 1952; Rosenhan, 1969a). Just when generous behavior begins to be displayed is not clear. Our own studies (Rosenhan, 1969a) had led us to believe that generosity is rare indeed in the six-year-old, but the work of Hartup and Coates (1967) made it quite evident that generosity could be elicited in nursery school children. Clearly, variations in findings are to be expected, depending on the manner in which the charitable situation is structured; others may reflect differences in the underlying psychological makeup of the child. What might some of these variables be?

Cognitive Development Our experiments have required that the children contribute to the Trenton Orphans' Fund, a fund that we established for these experiments. While we ascertained that our subjects knew what orphans are, we cannot be certain that all of them possessed the cognitive maturity to understand the needs of orphans. Younger children in particular would likely have difficulty putting themselves in the role of a needy other (Piaget, 1926; Flavell, 1968), however much they might know that orphans have no parents. Moreover, the concept of abstract charity might well elude them. "Giving to Alec," as used in the Hartup and Coates (1967) experiment, is considerably more concrete and does not tax a young child's empathic abilities.

Our own experiments and those of other workers have been predicated on the view that observational learning greatly facilitates the elicitation, if not the initial acquisition, of generosity in children. But capacities for observational learning are not themselves unrelated to cognitive development. Complex capacities for imitation and symbolic play do not really emerge until a child is two (Piaget, 1962), and consequently there is no reason to believe that the observational learning of this capacity can occur before then. Evidence that cognitive development is related to observational learning has recently been offered by Coates and Hartup (1969).

Autonomous vs. *Normative Altruism: The Potential Role of Prosocial Moral Development* Earlier, I distinguished two kinds of altruism, autonomous and normative. The latter appears to be controlled by the forces of social reward and punishment, the former (about which we know less) by internalized norms that direct a person to be helpful, with less regard to consequences. It would appear that normative altruism emerges earlier, that autonomous altruism develops later, and possibly from it. In all of our experiments we have been able to elicit considerably more normative altruism (i.e., generosity in the presence of the model) than autonomous altruism (i.e., generosity in his absence), at whatever age. It is possible to believe that the generosity obtained with very young children by Hartup and Coates (1967) was of the normative sort, since their subjects were separated from the experimenter and the model by an open door, which may have encouraged them to believe they were being observed.

The distinction between normative and autonomous altruism brings to mind Kohlberg's (1963) developmental stages of morality. Kohlberg's first level of morality is dominated by obedience and fear of punishment, while his highest levels reflect the operation of moral principles. It may be that generous impulses can be similarly characterized and undergo similar processes of development from lower to higher stages.

Social Comfort   It is an error to assume that all children are comfortable in experimental situations. Quite likely, the younger they are the less at home they feel, and the more frightened they are by the novelty of the experimental context and the strangeness of the experimenter. On the other hand, the older they are, the more sensitive children become to nuances of social rules, and these may restrict or inappropriately cue their behavior.

The sensitivity of older children to social rules, and their fear of engaging in behaviors lest they make a social error is illustrated in studies by Staub and his colleagues (Staub & Feagens, 1969). Kindergarten through sixth-grade children heard sounds of another child's severe distress from another room. Attempts to help the child, or to get an adult to help, increased markedly from kindergarten to second grade, but then dropped in the fourth and sixth grades. Staub speculated that the older children may simply have feared adult disapproval for leaving the room and therefore were unwilling to take action. In a subsequent experiment, Staub (1969) tacitly communicated to some of his older children that it was permissible to go into the adjoining room, and found that those children aided the "distressed" child significantly more than those who did not have this information.

CORRELATES OF KINDNESS   Beyond Hartshorne, May and Maller's (1929) observation that "service" behaviors correlate with few other variables, there has been relatively little work done on correlates of kindness. What does exist, however, is illuminating. Rutherford and Mussen (1968) found that generosity in nursery school boys was negatively correlated with competitiveness in a laboratory game, and negatively correlated with teachers' ratings of gregariousness. Staub and Sherk (1968) found need for social approval *negatively* correlated with sharing in fourth-grade children. In a similar (and surprising) vein, both normative and autonomous altruism were positively related to teachers' ratings of obedience among eight-year-olds. Among 10-year-olds, however, the situation was drastically changed. Normative altruism was *negatively* correlated with obedience, and autonomous altruism not at all correlated with it (Rosenhan, 1969a). These data again suggest that at younger ages, kindness may be a matter of social conformity, but among older children it clearly is not.

SUMMARY

Evidence is accumulating that kindness is pervasive in the behavior of young children; it can easily be elicited in a variety of experimental or naturalistic settings. While we have learned a good deal about the development of altruistic propensities and how such propensities can be amplified, we have yet to learn just how they originate.

Positive affect and observational learning have both been shown to facilitate the occurrence of kindness, and both are likely to be implicated in its acquisition. One senses, too, that cognitive development, particularly the capacity to take the role of others and to engage in symbolic play, are very much implicated in kindness just as these same factors are involved in moral development.

Preaching about prosocial behavior, as opposed to providing examples of such behavior, appears to have little impact on the behavior of children. Nevertheless, the type of preaching affects the manner in which children evaluate the preacher.

Developmental studies, with rare exceptions, indicate that the incidence of generosity increases with age, and that the patterns of correlation between generosity and other variables undergo dramatic and meaningful changes with age.

References

ARONFREED, J. *Conduct and Conscience: The Socialization of Internalized Control over Behavior.* New York: Academic Press, 1968.

—— & PASKAL, V. Altruism, empathy and the conditioning of positive affect, Unpubl. mss., Univ. of Pennsylvania, 1965.

BANDURA, A. Social-learning theory of identificatory processes. In D. A. Goslin (Ed.). *Handbook of Socialization Theory and Research.* Chicago: Rand McNally, 1969.

BERKOWITZ, L. & CONNOR, W. H. Success, failure and social responsibility. *J. Pers. soc. Psychol.*, 1966, 4, 664–669.

BRYAN, J H. Actions speak louder than words: Model inconsistency and its effect on self-sacrifice. Res. Bull. 68-16, Princeton: Educational Testing Service, 1968.

——. Children's reactions to helpers. In J. R. Macaulay & L. Berkowitz (Eds.), *Altruism and Helping.* New York: Academic Press, in press.

—— & WALBEK, N. Preaching and practicing self-sacrifice: Children's actions and reactions. Unpubl. mss., Northwestern Univ., 1968.

——. Determinants of conformity: The impact of words, deeds and power upon children's altruistic behavior. Unpubl. mss., Northwestern Univ., 1969.

COATES, B. & HARTUP, W. W. Age and verbalization in observational learning. *Develpml. Psychol.*, in press.

FLAVELL, J. H. *The Development of Communication and Role-Taking Skills in Children.* New York: John Wiley, 1968.

GRUSEC, J. & SKUBISKI, S. L. Model nurturance, demand characteristics of the modeling experiment, and altruism. Unpubl. mss., Univ. of Toronto, 1969.

HANDLON, B. J. & GROSS, P. The development of sharing behavior. *J. abnorm. soc. Psychol.*, 1959, 59, 425–428.

HARRIS, M. Some determinants of sharing behavior. Unpubl. doctoral dissertation, Stanford Univ., 1968.

HARTSHORNE, H., MAY, M. A. & MALLER, J. B. *Studies in Service and Self Control.* New York: Macmillan, 1929.

HARTUP, W. W. & COATES, B. Imitation of a peer as a function of reinforcement from the peer group and rewardingness of the model. *Child Develpm.*, 1967, 38, 1003–1016.

HEBB, D. O. & THOMPSON, W. R. The social significance of animal studies. In G.

Lindzey & E. Aronson (Eds.), *The Handbook of Social Psychology* Reading, Mass.: Addison-Wesley, 1968, 729–774.

ISEN, A. M. Success, failure, attention and reaction to others: The warm glow of success. Unpubl. doctoral dissertation, Stanford Univ., 1968.

────── & ROSENHAN, D. L. Success, failure and altruistic behavior. Unpubl. mss., Swarthmore College, 1969.

KOHLBERG, L. Moral development and identification. In H. Stevenson (Ed.), *Child Psychology: The 62nd Yearbook of the National Society for the Study of Education.* Chicago: Univ. of Chicago Press, 1963.

LENROW, P. B. Studies in sympathy. In S. S. Tomkins & C. E. Izard (Eds.), *Affect, Cognition and Personality.* New York: Springer, 1965.

MIDLARSKY, E. & BRYAN, J. H. Training charity in children. *J. Pers. soc. Psychol.*, 1967, 5, 408–415.

MISCHEL, W. & LIEBERT, R. M. Effects of discrepancies between observed and imposed reward criteria on their acquisition and transmission. *J. Pers. soc. Psychol.*, 1966, 3, 45–53.

MUSSEN, P. & DISTLER, L. Child-rearing antecedents of masculine identification in kindergarten boys. *Child Develpm.*, 1960, 31, 89–100.

────── & RUTHERFORD, E. Parent-child relations and parental personality in relation to young children's sex-role preferences. *Child Develpm.*, 1963, 34, 589–607.

PIAGET, J. *The Language and Thought of the Child.* New York: Harcourt Brace, 1926.

──────. *Play, Dreams and Imitation in Childhood.* New York: Norton, 1962.

ROSENHAN, D. L. Studies in altruistic behavior: Developmental and naturalistic variables associated with charitability. Paper presented at meeting of Soc. Res. Child Develpm., 1969 (a).

──────. Some origins of concern for others. In P. Mussen, M. Covington & J. Langer (Eds.), *Trends and Issues in Developmental Psychology.* New York: Holt, Rinehart & Winston, 1969, 134–153 (b).

──────. The natural socialization of altruistic autonomy. In J. Macaulay & L. Berkowitz (Eds.), *Altruism and Helping.* New York: Academic Press, in press.

──────, FREDERICK, F. & BURROWES, A. Preaching and practicing: Effects of channel discrepancy on norm internalization. *Child Develpm.*, 1968, 39, 291–302.

────── & WHITE, G. M. Observation and rehearsal as determinants of prosocial behavior. *J. Pers. soc. Psychol.*, 1967, 5, 424–431.

RUTHERFORD, E. & MUSSEN, P. Generosity in nursery school boys. *Child Develpm.*, 1968, 39, 755–765.

SCHACHTER, S. & SINGER, J. E. Cognitive, social, and psychological determinants of emotional state. *Psycholgl. Rev.*, 1962, 69, 379–399.

SCHNEIDER, D. J. Self-presentation as a function of prior success or failure and expectation of feedback of created impression. Unpubl. doctoral dissertation, Stanford Univ., 1966.

STAUB, E. The effects of success and failure on children's sharing behavior. Paper presented at meeting of Eastern Psycholgl. Assn., 1968.

──────. The effects of variation in permissibility of movement on children helping another child in distress. Paper presented at meeting of Amer. Psycholgl. Assn., 1969.

────── & FEAGANS, L. A child in distress: The influence of age and number of witnesses on children's attempts to help. Paper presented at meeting of Eastern Psycholgl. Assn., 1969.

────── & SHERK, L. Need for approval, children's sharing behavior and reciprocity in sharing. Unpubl. mss., Harvard Univ., 1968.

UGUREL-SEMIN, R. Moral behavior and moral judgment of children. *J. Abnorm. soc. Psychol.*, 1952, 47, 463–474.

WHITE, G. M. The elicitation and durability of altruistic behavior in children. Res. Bull. 67-27, Princeton: Educational Testing Service, 1967.
WRIGHT, B. Altruism in children and perceived conduct of others. *J. abnorm. soc. Psychol.*, 1942, 37, 218–233.

Father Absence, Maternal Encouragement, and Sex Role Development in Kindergarten-Age Boys*

Henry B. Biller
UNIVERSITY OF RHODE ISLAND

In order to ascertain the effects of father absence and degree of maternal encouragement of masculine behavior on boys' sex role development, matched father-absent and father-present kindergarten-age boys were studied. Compared to father-absent boys, father-present boys were found to be much more masculine in projective sex role orientation and slightly more masculine in game preference but were not significantly different in terms of a rating scale measure of overt masculinity. For father-absent boys, but not for father-present boys, degree of maternal encouragement of masculine behavior was related to masculinity of game reference and the rating scale measure of overt masculinity.

A review of studies dealing with father absence and sex role development suggests that the possible effects of differences in maternal encouragement of masculine behavior among father-absent boys has been overlooked (Biller & Borstelmann, 1967). Because most fathers are very critical of having their sons overprotected and because fathers generally serve as models for masculine-independent behavior, when the father is absent the probability of maternal overprotection seems increased. There is some evidence that father absence during the preschool years is associated with overdependency of the child on the mother (Stolz et al., 1954), but the results of a recent study (Pederson, 1966) seem to suggest that the mother-son relationship can have either a positive or a negative effect on the father-absent boy's personality development. It would seem that a mother might be able to facilitate at least some aspects of her father-absent son's masculine development.

It is also quite possible that father absence and maternal encouragement of masculine behavior have different effects on the various aspects of sex role.

Reprinted from *Child Development*. 40, 539–546. Copyright © 1969 by The Society for Research in Child Development, Inc. By permission.

* This study was supported by Public Health Service Predoctoral Research Fellowship 1-F1-MH-32, 808-01, from the National Institute of Mental Health. Appreciation is expressed to the kindergarten directors, teachers, children, and parents who cooperated in this study, and to Drs. Lloyd J. Borstelmann and Darwyn E. Linder, of Duke University, and David L. Singer, of Teachers' College, Columbia University, who gave valuable suggestions. A less-detailed version of this paper was presented at the meeting of the Eastern Psychological Association, Philadelpia, April, 1969.

Biller and Borstelmann (1967) consider three aspects of sex role: sex role orientation (the perception and evaluation of the maleness or femaleness of the self), sex role preference (the individual's preferential set toward symbols and representations of sex role that are socially defined), and sex role adoption (how masculine or feminine the individual's behavior seems to others). Because of deprivation effects, father-absent boys often seem to have strong motivation toward a father figure and, similarly, a desire to act masculine. A father-absent boy may become aware of the higher valuation of the male role in our society, especially if his mother encourages him to do so; and he may develop a masculine preference. Although motivation to be with a father figure and to be masculine may be very strong, such motivation may not be sufficient to promote a masculine orientation or adoption in the absence of a masculine model.

METHOD

SUBJECTS   There are many potential differences (e.g., IQ and SES) between father-absent and father-present children that might contribute extraneously to differences in sex role development. For this reason it was decided to match father-absent and father-present Ss as closely as possible. The Ss in this study were 34 5-year-old Caucasian boys attending kindergarten classes in the Durham, North Carolina, area and their mothers; 17 of the boys were father absent and 17 father present. (There was a total of 159 father-present boys from among whom the matched father-present group was selected. In terms of matching criteria, no match was available for one of the father-absent boys; and there was incomplete information on two other father-absent and seven father-present boys.) Matched Ss did not differ more than 4 months in age, one SES level in terms of a five-level scale of parent occupation, and 10 IQ points on the Peabody Picture Vocabulary Test (PPVT) (Dunn, 1965); and they were identical in terms of sibling distribution (number and sex of siblings and whether older or younger than the Ss). The father-present and father-absent groups were essentially identical in age, IQ, and SES; the Ss had a mean age of 65 months, were mostly from working-class and lower-middle class backgrounds, and had a mean PPVT IQ of 105. Father-absent boys had not had fathers or father surrogates living in their homes for at least a year. Father absence was due to divorce or separation. Eleven of the boys had been father absent for more than 2 years, and the mean length of absence was 3 years, 2 months. In contrast, father-present fathers were reported to be home on a regular basis, usually 2 or more hours per weekday (when the boy was home and awake) and most of the weekend. (Part of the maternal questionnaire included items concerning how much time the boy spent with various members of his family, the boy's and the parents' schedules, and details of any parental absence from the home).

GENERAL PROCEDURE   The investigation was initially described to kindergarten directors, teachers, and parents as a study of different types of boys' play. Information concerning age, SES, and sibling distribution was ascertained from school files. Children were seen individually for sex role orientation, sex role preference, and IQ assessments; and teachers' ratings were used to estimate sex role adoption. Mothers were sent questionnaires assessing father availability and maternal encouragement of masculine behavior. The questionnaires were sent along with letters signed by the investigator and the appropriate kindergarten director. Another letter and questionnaire (after 1 month) and then a telephone call (after 2 months) followed if the questionnaires were not returned. Based on data in school files, 18 of 20 mothers of father-absent boys and 159 of 166 mothers of father-present boys returned completed questionnaires.

MEASUREMENT OF MATERNAL ENCOURAGEMENT   An earlier pilot study involved the interviewing of a dozen mothers of kindergarten-age boys to determine what kinds of questions might reveal their reactions when their sons exhibited masculine or unmasculine behavior. From the interview data multiple-choice questions were constructed to assess degree of maternal encouragement for masculine behavior. Excluding the buffer items, there were seven questions to elicit the mother's reactions to her son's behavior. Questions pertained to such situations as the boy picking up a heavy chair, wrestling with another boy, playing in the mud, climbing a tree, falling off his tricycle, painting boxes, and responding to being pushed by a boy of his own size. For each question, choice of the alternative indicating strong encouragement of assertive, aggressive, or independent behavior was scored 3 points; the alternative indicating acceptance of such behavior, 2 points; the alternative indicating interference, but not the stopping of the behavior, 1 point; and the alternative indicating strong discouragement of the behavior, 0 points. Split-half reliability computed by the Spearman-Brown formula was .84.

MEASUREMENT OF MASCULINITY   An extensively modified version of Brown's IT Scale was used to measure sex role orientation. In order to make the IT figure more sexually neutral in appearance, following a suggestion by Hall (Brown, 1962), only the face was presented. The IT figure was described to the S as "a child playing a make-believe game," a game in which "the child can be anybody or do anything in the whole world." The S was then asked to designate who IT was being and what IT was wearing and doing from among various pairs of pictures including people (Indian Chief or Indian Princess; man or woman), wearing apparel (men's clothes or women's clothes; men's shoes or women's shoes), and tasks (working with building tools or cooking utensils; fixing broken objects or washing and ironing). Each masculine designation was given 1 point, and 2 additional points (1 each) were given if the boy, when questioned, gave the child a boy's name and said the child would become a father. (The possible range of IT scores was from 0 to 11.) Split-half reliability computed by the Spearman-Brown formula was .83.

A game-preference task was used to assess sex role preference. Pictures of the same two boys playing four masculine games (archery, baseball, basketball, and football) and four feminine games (hopscotch, jacks, dancing, and jump rope) were drawn on 3 × 5-inch cards. These games had been found to be highly sex-typed by Rosenberg and Sutton-Smith (1964). The S was shown two games at a time and asked to select which game he would like to play the most. There were 16 comparisons: every masculine game was paired with every feminine game, and 1 point was given for every masculine choice. Split-half reliability computed by the Spearman-Brown formula was .79.

A rating scale of sex role adoption was used to estimate relative assertiveness aggressiveness, competitiveness, independence, and activity directed toward physical prowess and mastery of the environment. Items relating to lack of masculinity in terms of the boy's relative passivity, dependency, and timidity were also included. There were 16 items in all, 9 assumed to be representative of high masculinity, 7 of low masculinity. Concrete definitions were given of each behavior to be rated (e.g., "is active and energetic, on the move, plays hard"; "leads other children, organizes play activities, assigns tasks to others"; "is timid around others, is fearful when introduced to new adults and children, fears physical contact"). Each S was rated on each item in terms of a 5-point scale; very frequently, frequently, sometimes, seldom, and never. Each item was scored either 0, 1, 2, 3, or 4. For example, for the nine items assumed to relate to high masculinity, 4 points were scored when the behavior was checked as very frequent, 0 points when it was checked as never occurring. Two teachers' ratings were available for 31 of the 34 Ss, and the correlation between total scores derived from the two teachers' ratings was .82.

RESULTS

One-tailed tests of significance are reported because specific predictions (e.g., father absence negatively related to masculinity and degree of maternal encouragement positively related to masculinity) were decided upon before data collection. Comparisons made by use of t tests for matched pairs (Bruning & Kintz, 1968) revealed that the father-present boys had much more masculine IT scores ($t = 4.33$, df = 16, $p < .01$) and slightly more masculine game-preference scores ($t = 1.92$, df = 16, $p < .05$) but did not differ significantly from the father-absent boys in their rating scale scores ($t = 1.21$, df = 16, N.S.). In terms of t tests for uncorrelated means, the boys who had been father absent 2 or more years ($N = 11$) had significantly lower mean IT scores ($t = 2.82$, df = 15, $p < .01$) than the boys who had been father absent for 1 to 2 years, but there was no significant difference between the game-preference scores of the two father-absent groups ($t = .76$, df = 15, N.S.).

TABLE 1
Means of Masculinity Scores for Father-Availability Groups

Group	N	IT	Game	Rating Scale
Father-present (FP)*	17	8.89	11.61	39.22
Father-absent (FA)	17	5.71	9.06	37.94
Father-absent (FA1)† (1 to 2 years)	6	6.78	9.46	38.15
Father-absent (FA2) (more than 2 years)	11	4.39	9.15	37.60

* FP's had significantly higher IT scores ($p < .01$) and game scores ($p < .05$) than FA's.
† FA1's had significantly higher IT scores ($p < .01$) than FA2's.

The mean scores of the father-present and father-absent boys can be described in relation to the possible range in scores of the different sex role measures: IT scores, 0 to 11; game-preference scores, 0 to 16; rating scale scores, 0 to 64. The mean IT score (see Table 1) seemed relatively masculine for boys who were father present, relatively neutral for boys father absent 1 to 2 years, and somewhat feminine for boys father absent more than 2 years. The mean game-preference score was relatively masculine for father-present boys and relatively neutral for father-absent boys. In terms of mean rating scale scores, the boys as a group appeared relatively masculine. The mean sex role scores of the father-present boys were similar to those obtained from a larger sample of 5-year-old boys (Biller, 1968a).

With respect to a t test for matched pairs, the mothers of the father-present boys appeared to be slightly more encouraging of masculine behavior than did the mothers of the father-absent boys ($t = 1.89$, df $= 16$, $p < .05$). An examination of group means suggests that the mothers of father-present boys were generally accepting of masculine behavior in their sons (mean score $= 11.52$), while the mothers of father-absent boys appeared more ambivalent concerning masculine behavior in their sons (mean score $= 9.31$). For father-absent boys, degree of maternal encouragement of masculine behavior was positively related to game-preference scores ($r = .49$, df $= 16$, $p < .05$) and to rating scale scores ($r = .42$, df $= 16$, $p < .05$) but not to IT scores ($r = .12$, df $= 16$, N.S.). There were no significant relationships for father-present boys concerning maternal encouragement and masculine behavior (IT scores: $r = .08$, df $= 16$, N.S.; game-preference scores: $r = .21$, df $= 16$, N.S.; rating scale scores: $r = .11$, df $= 16$, N.S.).

Age, sibling distribution, SES, maternal employment, IQ, and reason for father absence were not significantly related to any of the sex role measures or to maternal encouragement for masculine behavior. (It should be noted that there was a restricted range of S variability in all these variables). For both the father-absent and father-present boys the different measures of masculinity showed positive but nonsignificant relationships to each other; for the total group of Ss the interrelationships reached low levels of significance (IT and game preference: $r = .25$, df $= 33$, $p < .10$; IT and rating scale: $r = .23$, df $= 33$, $p < .10$; game preference and rating scale: $r = .31$, df $= 33$, p $< .05$).

DISCUSSION

The seemingly greater effect of father absence on boys' sex role orientation than on more manifest aspects of their sex role development was consistent with previous investigations (Barclay & Cusumano, 1967; Biller, 1968b), as was the suggestion that father absence beginning before age 4 has more of a retarding effect on the development of a masculine sex role orientation than does father absence beginning after age 4 (Hetherington, 1966). It is possible that the effects of father absence on sex role preference and sex role adoption may also be quite dependent on the length and timing of father absence. For instance, the impact of father absence on sex role adoption may be more noticeable in 3- and 4-year-old boys than in 5- and 6-year-old boys, who may have more opportunity to interact with same-sex peers, especially if they are in kindergarten.

Mothers of father-absent boys seem to be, as a group, slightly less encouraging of masculine behavior in their sons than are mothers of father-present boys. However, degree of maternal encouragement for masculine behavior appears more important for father-absent boys than it does for father-present boys, at least with respect to sex role preference and sex role adoption development. It seems that a mother of a father-absent boy can influence her son's cognitive awareness of the incentive value of the masculine role and her son's motivation to imitate other males and act masculine. The sex role development of the father-present boys seems very much influenced by the father-son relationship (Biller & Borstelmann, 1967), but the mother-son relationship may assume critical importance in the sex role development of the father-absent boy. The presence of an interested and masculine father may mitigate the influence of an overprotective mother in the father-present home, or, on the other hand, an encouraging mother may find it difficult to facilitate her son's sex role development if he has a passive-dependent father who is frequently present as an example of masculine behavior. The mother of the father-absent boy may have more potential for either encouraging or discouraging her son's masculine development.

This study supports the value of distinguishing among different aspects of sex role. Father absence, particularly if it occurs early, appears to affect sex role orientation most. In father-absent boys maternal encouragement of masculine behavior appears to affect more manifest aspects of sex role, such as sex role preference and sex role adoption. These results are consistent with a developmental conception in which orientation development precedes preference and adoption development and, possibly is more resistant to change.

References

BARCLAY, A., & CUSUMANO, D. R. Father absence, cross-sex identity, and field-dependent behavior in male adolescents. *Child Development*, 1967, 38, 243–250.

BILLER, H. B. A multiaspect investigation of masculine development in kindergarten age boys. *Genetic Psychology Monographs*, 1968, 78, 89–138, (a)

———. A note on father-absence, socio-cultural backgrounds, and sex role development in young lower-class Negro and White boys. *Child Development*, 1968, 39, 1003–1006. (b)

———, & BORSTELMANN, L. J. Masculine development: an integrative review. *Merrill-Palmer Quarterly*, 1967, 13, 253–294.

BROWN, D. G. Sex role preference in children: methodological problems. *Psychological Reports*, 1962, 11, 477–478.

BRUNING, J. L., & KINTZ, B. L. *Computational handbook of statistics*. Glenview, Ill.: Scott, Foresman, 1968.

DUNN, L. M. *Expanded manual for the Peabody Picture Vocabulary Test*. Minneapolis: American Guidance Service, 1965.

HETHERINGTON, E. M. Effects of paternal absence on sex-typed behaviors in Negro and White preadolescent males. *Journal of Personality and Social Psychology*, 1966, 4, 87–91.

PEDERSON, F. A. Relationships between father-absence and emotional disturbance in male military dependents. *Merrill-Palmer Quarterly*, 1966, 12, 321–331.

Rosenberg, B. G., & Sutton-Smith, B. The measurement of masculinity and femininity in children: an extension and revalidation. *Journal of Genetic Psychology*, 1964, 104, 259–264.

Stolz, L. M., et al. *Father relations of war born children*. Stanford, Calif.: Stanford University Press, 1954.

IT Score Variations by Instructional Style*

Norman L. Thompson, Jr. and Boyd R. McCandless
EMORY UNIVERSITY

Brown's It Scale for Children (ITSC) is an instrument widely used with young children for measuring sex-role preference. Evidence exists that many children may respond to masculine cues in It rather than projecting their own choices. In this study, the effects of three different instructions on the performance of Negro and white children were examined. These instructions were (a) projective, (b) semiprojective, and (c) objective. Each instruction was given to 72 lower-class prekindergarten children, 18 Negro boys, 18 white boys, 18 Negro girls, and 18 white girls. Race was an important variable in the responses to the test, many white girls apparently respond to masculine cues in the It figure; however, this was not true among Negro girls. This may be due to differences in sex-role prestige in these two subcultures. Lower-class Negro boys show greater preference for the feminine role as measured under the semiprojective and objective instructions. The relation of the ITSC scores and teacher ratings of the children's behavior supports the hypothesis that the development of sex-role preference precedes the development of sex-role adoption, suggesting that the rate of development may be faster among white boys.

The concept of sex-role identification occupies an important position in the attempt to understand personality development. A major research problem in the area concerns measurement. Thus, the authors of the present study have focused on Brown's (1956) It Scale for Children (ITSC), a widely used instrument for assessing sex-role development in children. This technique purports to measure sex-role preference, defined by Brown (1956) as "behavior associated with one sex or the other that the individual would like to adopt, or that he perceives as the preferred or more desirable behavior" (p. 3).

In the standard procedure, the child is presented with a modified stick figure, "It," which is assumed to be sexless. The task for the child is to choose

Reprinted from *Child Development*, 1970, *41*, 425–436, Copyright © 1970 by The Society for Research in Child Development, Inc. By permission.

* This research was supported in part by a U.S. Office of Education Small Grant to the Emory Division of Educational Studies, and by the Atlanta Education Improvement Program, Ford Foundation. Miss Elizabeth Perry of the Atlanta Education Improvement Program assisted centrally in data collection. This paper was presented March 1, 1969, at the meeting of the Southeastern Psychological Association, New Orleans.

what "It" likes in a series of pictures of various sex-typed items. The assumption behind the test is that the child considers himself as "It" and that the activities he chooses for "It" are actually those he would choose for himself (McCandless, 1967).

The major criticism leveled against the instrument is that "It" actually looks like a boy, rather than a neuter figure. Therefore, many children make choices for a boy figure rather than projecting their own choices onto "It" (Brown, 1962). There is considerable evidence to support such a criticism. Sher and Lansky (1968) found that girls as well as boys tended to see "It" as a male when asked the sex of the figure. They also found that boys tended to say "boy" and girls tended to say "girl" when asked the sex of the "It" figure while it was concealed in an envelope. When these children were then shown "It," more girls changed their attributions to "boy" than boys changed their attributions to "girl." Additional support for the hypothesis that "It" possesses masculine cues comes from the results of a study by Hartup and Zook (1960).

Lansky and McKay (1963) eliminated the possible masculine stimulus effect of "It" by testing kindergarten children with the figure concealed in an envelope. They found that boys were more variable than girls in this situation. Endsley (1967) obtained different results in a study in which he tested half the 3- to 5-year-old children with the standard instructions and half with "It" concealed in an envelope. He found that boys were less variable than girls under both conditions. There were no differences in the mean scores between the two conditions for the boys or girls. He thus found no support for the contention that "It" possesses a masculine bias.

Sher and Lansky (1968) tested kindergarten children randomly assigned to one of three different sequences. The first sequence began with the standard instructions. The second sequence began with "It" concealed in an envelope. In the third sequence, the children were first asked to attribute a sex to the picture of "It." The task for these latter children was to respond to the choices for an "It" of the sex they attributed to the figure. The results indicated that there were no differences among the three conditions for boys. However, the girls were more feminine on the concealed condition than on the other two conditions. As girls and boys also tended to see "It" as a boy when asked the figure's sex, Sher and Lansky concluded that it it is likely the "It" figure contains predominantly masculine cues. ITSC scores may reflect the child's attempt to match a sex-typed figure with its appropriate objects. Thus it appears the test may measure sex-role knowledge rather than sex-role preferences.

The present study was designed to explore further the effects of the instructions used with the ITSC. Three different sets of instructions were employed in the study. These instructions were designed to produce variations in the test situation ranging from projective to semiprojective to objective.

A second purpose was to explore the effects of the examiner's sex on the children's performance. It is possible that the examiner's sex has a systematic effect on the children's performance. However, this had not been previously tested.

The third purpose of this study was to add normative data for the ITSC for lower-class Negro and white children. Hartup and Zook (1960) found no social class differences among their preschool-aged *S*s. In a study of older children, Hall and Keith (1964) found socioeconomic class differences, largely among the boys. Thomas (1966) tested deprived and non-deprived Negro and nondeprived white children. The results indicated that sex-role preferences mature more slowly among deprived Negro children than among nondeprived Negro and white youngsters. The feminine role had greater prestige among the deprived Negroes, while the masculine role had greater prestige among the nondeprived whites. The relative prestige of the two roles among the nondeprived Negroes was in transition but closer to that found among the whites. The present study is an extension of such work.

The final purpose was to explore the relationship between sex-role preference as measured by the ITSC and sex-role adoption as measured by teacher ratings.

Six hypotheses can be formally tested in connection with the four main objectives of the study:

1. When boys are compared with girls in ITSC (a) the boys' mean scores for all three instructions will be significantly higher (more masculine) than the girls'; (b) the boys' variances for the three instructions will be significantly smaller than the girls', except for condition C. This double hypothesis comes directly from Brown's results (1956, 1957).

2. Data do not permit a directional hypothesis about the effect of the sex of the examiner on Ss' performance. However, information is needed.

3. This set of hypotheses concerns the performance of the girls on the ITSC. (a) There will be a significant difference between the mean scores of instructions A (standard instructions) and B ("It" is concealed). The A score will be higher (more masculine). (b) There will be a significant difference between the mean scores of instructions A and C ("It-is-you"). The A score will be higher. (c) There will be a significant difference between the mean scores of instructions B and C. The B mean score will be higher.

Hypothesis 3b is based on Hartup and Zook's (1960) results; hypotheses 3a and 3c, on those of Sher and Lansky (1968).

4. The fourth set of hypotheses relates to the performance of the boys on the ITSC. (a) There will be no significant difference between the mean scores of instructions A (standard) and B (concealed). (b) There will be no significant difference between the mean scores of instructions A and C ("It-is you"). (c) There will be no significant difference between the mean scores of instructions B and C.

Hypothesis 4b comes from Hartup and Zook (1960), while hypotheses 4a and 4c are based on Sher and Lansky's (1968) findings.

5. This set of hypotheses pertains to racial differences in performance on the ITSC. (a) Negro boys will score significantly more feminine than white boys on instructions A and B. (b) Negro girls will score significantly more feminine than white girls on instructions A and B. (c) Negro boys will be significantly more variable than white boys.

This set of hypotheses is based on Thomas's (1966) results.

6. There will not be a significant relation between sex-role preference as measured by the ITSC and sex-role adoption as measured by teacher ratings. This hypothesis is based on Ward's (1969) results. He found that sex-role preference develops before the age of five, while sex-role adoption comes later.

METHOD

SUBJECTS The Ss were 72 kindergarten children, 36 boys and 36 girls, ranging from 51 to 66 months with a mean age of 57.50 months. The mean ages in months and standard deviations, respectively, for the four racial and sex groups were as follows: Negro boys, 55.94 and 2.68; Negro girls, 56.56 and 3.75; white boys, 58.33 and 3.61; and white girls, 59.17 and 3.09. Although the children were born at approximately the same time, the testing schedule necessitated testing each school at different times during the late winter and spring of the year. Fifty-eight of the Ss were enrolled in a special prekindergarten program for deprived children in three schools of the Atlanta, Georgia, public school system. Two of the schools were entirely Negro, while the third was predominantly white. The remaining 14 Ss were enrolled in Project Head Start classes in the same neighborhoods as the Ss in the special prekindergarten program. These classes were racially mixed. All Ss were deprived, lower-class children (McCandless, 1968).

Subjects from each school were assigned to each of the treatment groups. Assignment was random except that the groups were matched for race and sex. Only one S refused to be tested, and she was replaced by a classmate. Two Ss refused to be tested by a male examiner and were consequently tested by a female examiner.

PROCEDURE The ITSC was administered individually in private rooms of the schools. Half of the Ss were tested by a male examiner and half by a female examiner. Each S was given the ITSC three times in one day according to his assigned sequence. Due to the sporadic attendance of many of the Ss, it was not feasible to lengthen the time between testings. One-third of the Ss were randomly assigned to the *ABC* sequence, one-third to the *BCA* sequence, and one third to the *CAB* sequence. The instructions were:

A (standard instructions).—These instructions were the same as Brown's (1956). The figure was called "It" and was visible to the child throughout this portion of the test.

B (concealed instructions).—This technique was developed by Lansky and McKay (1963). The figure remained in the envelope, and the child was told, "There is a child named 'It' in the envelope."

C ("It-is-you" instructions).—These instructions were developed by Hartup and Zook (1960). The figure was identified as the same sex as the child throughout this portion of the test.

The sections of the ITSC were administered according to Brown's manual (1956). However, the 16 pictured toys were presented in two groups of eight rather than one group of 16 pictures. Each group contained four boys' toys and four girls' toys arranged in the numbered order of the cards. Each S was instructed to choose four from each of the two groups.

The weighted scoring method developed by Brown (1956) was employed. Each masculine choice receives a positive score, and a feminine choice receives a 0. The possible scores range from 0 (most feminine) to 84 (most masculine).

TEACHER RATINGS   Sex-role adoption was measured by ratings of the Ss' behavior by the head and assistant teachers. The ratings were based on the teacher's observations of the Ss' behavior throughout the school year, or the entire summer Head Start program. The masculine rating scale was developed by Biller (1969). The feminine scale was constructed by McCandless and Thompson for this study and was based on Biller's masculine scale.

Each scale contains 16 items describing various behaviors. The masculine scale has nine items characteristic of masculine behavior in young children and seven items characteristic of feminine behavior. The feminine scale contains 10 items characteristic of feminine behavior in young children and six items characteristic of masculine behavior. The teacher is asked to rate the child on a scale ranging from *very frequently* to *never* for each item of behavior. The masculine scale is scored so that a high score indicates masculine behavior and a low score indicates nonmasculine behavior. The feminine scale is scored in such a manner that a low score indicates feminine and a high score indicates nonfeminine behavior. This scoring procedure was employed so that the scoring direction on these scales corresponded to the scoring direction of the ITSC.

The percentages of agreement between the two teachers was computed by comparing the teachers' responses on each item. A disagreement of one step gave a score of 75 percent agreement on that item, a disagreement of two steps gave a score of 50 percent agreement, etc. The overall percentages of agreement between the pairs of teachers ranged from 72.5 to 89.3 for the masculine scale and from 76.6 to 86.7 for the feminine scale.

RESULTS

The age differences among the various racial and sex groups were examined. The difference between boys and girls for both Negro and white was not significant (black, $t = .554$, df $= 34$; white, $t = .730$, df $= 34$). The difference between Negro and white girls was significant at the .05 level of confidence ($t = 2.212$, df $= 34$). The difference between Negro and white boys was also significant at the .05 level of confidence ($t = 2.176$, df $= 34$). Although these mean differences are significant, the differences of 2.66 months between the two groups of girls and 2.39 months between the boys are small for the overall age of the children. Correlations between age and the various instructions of the ITSC are given in Table 1. The only significant correlations work *against* the hypothesis regarding racial differences between boys, and *for* the hypothesis concerning girls.

An analysis of variance was performed on the order effect of the various instructional conditions for boys and girls. A nonsignificant F of .580 (df $= 2$) was obtained among the orders for boys, and a nonsignificant F of .348 (df $= 2$) was obtained for the girls. The order in which the children received the ITSC does not affect the scores significantly.

A separate analysis of variance that involved four factors—sex of child, sex of examiner, race, and instructions revealed that the effects of the child's sex were significant (F for 1 df $= 70.85$). This result, bearing on the validity of the ITSC, supports hypothesis 1a: Boys will score higher than girls. As shown in Table 2, the boys' mean scores were consistently higher than the

TABLE 1
Correlations Between Age and Instructional Conditions of the ITSC

Group	A (Standard)	B (Concealed)	C ("It-Is-You")
Negro boys	−.68†	.32	−.13
White boys	.16	.13	.03
Negro girls	−.51*	.16	.09
White girls	.06	.00	.07

* $p < .05$.
† $p < .01$.

girls' for all instructional conditions. The various combinations of variances were examined by F tests for each subgroup. Hypothesis 1b (boys less variable than girls) was not supported, nor were there between-race differences in variance.

TABLE 2
Means and Standard Deviations of Subjects on the ITSC

	A		B		C	
Group	Mean	SD	Mean	SD	Mean	SD
Males	54.22	17.60	56.67	16.13	61.50	15.28
Negro	46.78	14.73	53.33	13.03	56.56	14.76
White	61.67	17.08	60.00	18.12	66.44	14.15
Females	40.58	18.19	36.11	13.25	27.81	15.98
Negro	35.56	14.84	37.61	13.08	26.72	14.46
White	45.61	19.76	34.61	13.25	28.89	17.30

No hypothesis was made concerning the effect of the examiner's sex on the performance of the Ss. The results of the analysis of variance indicate that it produced no effect ($F = .188$).

The sex of child by instruction interaction was significant at less than the .01 level (F was 9.891 for 2 df). The effects of instructions were examined by means of t tests for correlated means. The results of these tests for boys and girls, separated by race, are shown in Table 3. Hypothesis 3a, which states that the girls' mean scores under A (standard instructions) will be higher (more masculine) than those under B (concealed instructions) is not supported for the total group. Hypothesis 3b, that the girls will score higher on A than on C ("It-is-you"), was supported for the total group and for white girls. Hypothesis 3c, which states that the girls will score higher on B and C, was supported for the total group and for black girls. The hypothesis was not supported for white girls. The hypothesis about effects of instructions on boys' performance, 4a ($A = B$), 4b ($A = C$), and 4c ($B = C$), were all supported for the total group and for the

TABLE 3
t Tests between the Instructional Conditions for Negro and White Subjects

Group	A–B	A–C	B–C
Males	.935	.826	1.404
Negro	2.408*	2.843*	.944
White	.390	1.000	1.322
Females	1.149	3.803‡	2.726*
Negro	.522	1.898	2.201
White	2.080	3.611‡	1.677

* $p < .05$.
† $p < .01$.
‡ $p < .002$.

white boys. However, the Negro boys were more masculine on both B and C than on A.

The analysis of variance indicated that race is a significant factor in ITSC scores. The data, which are summarized in Table 4, show that the Negro

TABLE 4
t Tests between Negro and White Subjects

Group	A	B	C	Total
Males	2.722†	1.233	1.992*	2.673†
Females	1.678*	.664	.397	.858

* $p < .10$.
† $p < .02$.

boys were more feminine than white boys on the three instructional conditions combined.[1] On the individual instructions the Negro boys were significantly more feminine than white boys on A, with condition C ("It-is-you") reaching borderline significance. It is doubtful that the age difference between Negro and white boys produced these results. There were no significant correlations for boys between age and ITSC score except −.68 on A for the Negro boys (see Table 1). This indicates that the older the Negro boy, the more feminine he is likely to score under the standard instructions. If there had been no age

---

[1] This difference cannot be accounted for by different father-absent ratios for the ethnic groups. For Negro boys, 14 fathers were living at home and four were absent, while the white boys had 12 present and six absent. The Negro girls had 10 fathers present with eight absent, and the white girls had 14 present with four absent. In addition, one father-absent Negro girl had a grandfather living at home. An analysis was done to see if there were any differences in ITSC performances between father-absent and father-present children. Due to the small N's for children separated by sex and race, the data were collapsed over race. There were no significant differences between father-absent and father-present children for any instructional condition. The full data may be obtained from the authors.

difference between the two groups of boys, the difference on A might have been larger. There was no difference between the Negro and white girls on the combined instructional conditions. On the individual instructions, only A (standard) approaches significance. The differences on B and C are not significant. Therefore, hypothesis 5a was partially supported, while 5b was not supported. Nor was hypothesis 5c supported; it states that the Negro boys will be significantly more variable than white boys.

Hypothesis 6 states that there will be no significant relationship between sex-role preference as measured by the ITSC and sex-role adoption as measured by the teacher ratings. The results (Table 5) support the hypothesis, except for

TABLE 5
Correlation for Teachers' Ratings with ITSC

Group	A	B	C
Males:			
Negro	−.029	−.216	.004
White	.512*	.301	.479*
Females:			
Negro	.134	−.489*	.355
White	−.017	.247	.001

* $p < .05$.

the white boys. It may be that sex-role preference and sex-role adoption are coming into congruence by the approximate age of 5 years for lower-class white boys but not for the other groups.

The correlations among the treatments are reported in table 6. These indicate that the Negro boys were consistent across instructions, with the correlation between B and C reaching borderline significance ($p < .10$). The white boys were only consistent between conditions A and B. There was no consistency among the Negro girls across instructions; the white girls were consistent between B and C, with the correlation between A and C reaching borderline significance ($p < .10$).

TABLE 6
Correlations among Treatments

Group	A–B	A–C	B–C
Negro boys	.662‡	.510*	.458
White boys	.475*	.170	−.198
Negro girls	.286	.093	−.163
White girls	.121	.440	.576†

* $p < .05$.
† $p < .02$.
‡ $p < .01$.

DISCUSSION

The data from this study clearly suggest that race is an important variable in the responding to the ITSC. The type of instructions used did not affect the performance of the white boys, but the Negro boys were significantly more feminine on the standard instructions than on the concealed or "It-is-you" conditions. It is possible that the white boys' attitudes concerning their own sex role have developed consistently with their knowledge of the masculine sex role. The Negro boys made more feminine choices when the "It" figure was shown but not identified as being one sex or the other. Perhaps they see "It" as feminine. Such a conclusion is reasonable if, as has been suggested, the feminine role is preferred in lower-class black culture (Rainwater, 1966).

There is some support for the hypothesis that white girls respond to masculine cues in the "It" figure when, as in standard instructions, the figure is not identified by sex. This was not true for Negro girls. This difference could be due to the relative prestige of the sex roles in the two subcultures. For lower-class white girls, a neutral figure may be seen as masculine because the masculine role is more favored. Lower-class Negro girls may be similar to white boys, in that their sex-role attitudes have developed consistently with their knowledge of cultural advantage for their sex. However, the patterning of the Negro girls' scores suggests an additional possibility. The mothers of these girls may be more assertive and engage in more "masculine" activities than mothers in many other groups in the United States. These daughters are probably reinforced for imitating these activities. Although on the one hand the Negro girls may be learning what is typically the feminine role in our society, on the other they are learning the attitudes associated with the assertive role lower-class black women are forced to play.

The evidence from this study, in conjunction with previous studies (Hartup & Zook, 1960; Lansky & McKay, 1963; Sher & Lansky, 1968), supports the conclusion that standard "It" instructions measure variables in addition to sex-role preference, at least for white girls and Negro boys. Use of these instructions to measure which sex role a child prefers may thus be suspect.

The Negro boys in this study scored more feminine than white boys on the ITSC, while the Negro girls were more feminine than white girls only under standard instructions. Only the Negro boys and white girls were consistent across instructions. (The only exception to this was the correlation between standard and concealed instructions for the white girls.)

These results fall into a reasonable pattern if we look at the possible meaning of each instructional condition. The standard instructions are semi-projective in the sense that they reflect an interaction between the "projective" or "true" self and social expectations. These expectations vary according to whether the child sees "It" as a boy or girl. "It" under concealed instructions is most likely a projective test. The "It-is-you" instructions induce clear social expectations which are overridden only for high-autonomy children with inappropriate sex preference.

Regardless of the stimulus conditions, the Negro boys in the sample did not vary their response pattern. This may be because they have few adequate male models in their coculture. This, plus possible reinforcement for feminine "good behavior" activities, may account for their rather feminine scores. The white girls may be exposed to similar social dynamics. They live in a coculture which provides unattractive feminine models, and where males are clearly dominant and more highly valued. The nonsignificant AB correlation for these girls may be due to the small N and random variation; it may be due to mixed perceptions of "It" by the Ss, some seeing "It" as male and responding according to social expectations, while others respond projectively.

The relationship between ITSC performance and teachers' ratings of behavior supports hypotheses about the deleterious affects of a predominantly feminine-dominated subculture on the Negro boys and a masculine-dominated subculture on the white girls. For neither group is there a translation into behavior, as seen by teachers, of either their "true" preference or their social expectations. It is possible that they do not perceive the social expectations, or that they perceive these expectations but do not have adequate models. In contrast, it appears that white boys perceive appropriate sex-role behavior and exhibit it.

The Negro girls seem to see that femininity for "true" selves (as measured by the projective condition) calls for a strong male social posture. This fits with the model of a matriarchal society in which a true woman has to be strong. There is no relationship between the behavior of these girls and the standard instructions, since the scores represent an interaction between responses shaped projectively, by expectations, or both. The correlation obtained between behavior and condition C (knowledge of social expectations) suggests that they may perceive the social expectations of the general society and translate them into action that is perceived as appropriately feminine by the teachers.

This study indicates the importance of racial socially mediated factors in the development of sex-role attitudes and behaviors in lower class children. Gewirtz and Stinel (1968) believe that their generalized imitation paradigm can account for the attitudes and behaviors that are usually subsumed under identification. This suggests that research is needed in the lower-class Negro and white communities to determine the types of models available to the children, and especially the types of behaviors reinforced by adults in these groups.

References

BILLER, H. B. Father dominance and sex-role development in kindergarten age boys. *Developmental Psychology*, 1969, **1**, 87–94.

BROWN, D. G. Sex-role preference in young children. *Psychological Monographs*, 1956, **70** (14, Whole No. 421).

———. Masculinity-femininity development in children. *Journal of Consulting Psychology*, 1957, **21**, 197–202.

———. Sex-role preference in children: methodological problems. *Psychological Reports*, 1962, **11**, 477–478.

ENDSLEY, R. C. Effects of concealing "It" on sex-role preferences of preschool children. *Perceptual and Motor Skills*, 1967, **24**, 998.

GEWIRTZ, J. J., & STINGLE, K. G. Learning of generalized imitations as the basis for identification. *Psychological Review*, 1968, **75**, 374–397.

HALL, M., & KEITH, R. A. Sex-role preference among children of upper and lower social class. *Journal of Social Psychology*, 1964, 62, 101–110.

HARTUP, W. W., & ZOOK, E. A. Sex-role preferences in three- and four-year-old children. *Journal of Consulting Psychology*, 1960, **24**, 420–426.

LANSKY, L. M., & McKAY, G. Sex-role preferences of kindergarten boys and girls: some contradictory results. *Psychological Reports*, 1963, **13**, 415–421.

McCANDLESS, B. R. Children: behavior and development. (2d. ed) New York: Holt, Rinehart & Winston, 1967.

———. Predictor variable of school success of slum children. Paper presented at the meeting of the American Psychological Association, San Francisco, August, 1968.

RAINWATER, L. Crucible of identity: the Negro lower class family. *Daedalus*, 1966, **95**, 172–217. (Republished in T. Parsons and K. B. Clark (Eds.), *The Negro American*, Boston: Beacon, 1967. Pp. 166–204).

SHER, M. A., & LANSKY, L. M. The It scale for children: effects of variations in the sex-specificity of the It figure. *Merrill-Palmer Quarterly*, 1968, **14**, 323–330.

THOMAS, P. J. Sub-cultural differences in sex-role preference patterns. *Dissertation Abstracts*, 1966, **26**, 6894–6895.

WARD, W. D. The process of sex-role development. *Developmental Psychology*, 1969, **1**, 163–168.

Relationship Between Adult Nurturance and Dependency and Performance of the Preschool Child*

Russell DiBartolo and W. Edgar Vinacke†
STATE UNIVERSITY OF NEW YORK AT BUFFALO

This study determined the relationships between adult nurturance and child dependency and performance in a complex task. Sex differences were also investigated. Hypothesis 1 was that performance of preschool children on a complex task is more efficient under nurturant conditions than under nurturance-deprivation conditions. Hypothesis 2 stated that under nurturance deprivation children high in dependency will perform less efficiently than children low in dependency. Sex differences were expected in performance and dependency behavior as a function of level of nurturance and nurturant versus nurturant-deprivation conditions. The subjects were twenty-four 4-year-old children, 12 of each sex, in a federally supported preschool program. They were divided into high- and low-dependency groups, and assigned randomly within each group to either a nurturant or nurturance-deprivation condition. A puzzle task was administered to assess performance. Both Hypotheses 1 and 2 received significant support. No sex differences were found.

Reprinted from *Developmental Psychology*, 1969, *1*, 247–251. Copyright © 1969 by the American Psychological Association. By permission.

* This investigation was supported by Public Health Service Training Grant No. CA 5016 from the National Institutes of Health.
† The authors are indebted to Joyce DiBartolo for her services as experimenter. The assistance of Robert Barcikowski, State University of New York at Buffalo, in the statistical portion of this investigation is gratefully acknowledged.

This study is concerned with relationships among adult nurturance, child dependency, and performance of 4-year-old children in a prekindergarten school situation. It is also intended to ascertain whether sex differences appear in these relationships.

Investigators (Beller, 1955, 1959; Heathers, 1955; Moustakos, Sigel, & Schalock, 1956; Sears, 1963) who have examined conditions antecedent to dependency have presented arguments that describe dependency as either an acquired motive or as operant activity beginning in the infant's striving for physical gratification from the adult.

After dependency motivation has developed, it may be argued that the nurturant behavior of an adult acts as a secondary reinforcer associated with satisfaction of needs for security or reassurance. Subsequently, either the loss or a threat of the loss of gratifying adult behavior signals that satisfactions of these kinds cannot be obtained, thus activating fear or anxiety. As development continues, this anxiety becomes less and less overt. As a result, deprivation of nurturance instigates internal dependency responses which lead to a heightened level of dependency responses. In this framework, a situation in which dependency gratification is withheld by an adult may be considered as stressful, especially for the highly dependent child who will be more sensitive to this deprivation than will a low-dependent child. Thus, it is reasonable to expect that highly dependent children, with their heightened perception of nurturance deprivation, should become even more dependent and at a faster rate than children low in dependency (Beller, 1959).

Although the development of dependency may be much the same process for boys and girls, it is possible that parent-daughter and parent-son relationships may produce latent differences which may be reflected under controlled experimental conditions. Here, the manipulation of nurturance behavior and the observation of its effect on dependency may systematically be introduced free from interference from extraneous variables which may be found in the usual home or school situation.

Hartup (1958) concluded that nurturance withdrawal has the effect of enhancing the learning of simple tasks eliciting adult approval. This is interpreted as an attempt by the child to restore the relationship previously available in the nurturant situation because of anxiety-produced dependency behaviors. It is possible, however, that heightened dependency may be manifested in decreased efficiency on a more complex task. Following Hartup's general line of approach, this study uses a complex task to determine the effect of change in dependency in a nurturant situation as compared to a condition of deprivation of nurturance.

In pursuing this problem, the following hypotheses may be stated:

1. Performance of preschool children on a complex task is more efficient under nurturant conditions than under conditions of deprivation of nurturance.
2. Under deprivation of nurturance, children high in dependency will perform less efficiently than children low in dependency.

It was also hypothesized that sex differences would be evident.

METHOD

Nurturance was defined in accordance with Murray's (1938) formulation, as the need to aid the helpless. More fully, it signifies,

to give sympathy and gratify needs of a helpless object: an infant or any object that is weak, disabled, tired, inexperienced, etc.; to assist an object in danger; to feed, help, support, console, protect, comfort, nurse, heal, etc.

Nurturant Situation To establish the required conditions, the experimenter carried out the following behavior: (a) permissiveness—each subject was told that he could walk around the experimental room if he wished, get a drink of water, and partake in the task only if he wished to; (b) praise—before the subject began the task, the experimenter (female) told him that he was a very nice boy (or girl), a good helper; during the task, the experimenter told the subject that he was doing a very good job—this behavior was carried out at 10-second intervals or whenever the subject looked up. No instrumental help or clues[1] were offered by the experimenter; (c) affection—the experimenter told the child that she liked him very much, smiling as she explained the task in a soft tone of voice; (d) verbal reward—the experimenter verbally praised the child after completion of each task on the basis of speed, dexterity, attention to the task, and helpfulness of the child; (e) nearness—during the task, the experimenter sat immediately next to the subject (within 1 foot); (f) attention—the experimenter kept her undivided attention on the subject and his work on the task.

Nurturant-Deprivation Situation In contrast, the experimenter acted in a manner intended to remove the components of nurturance. Each of the dimensions of the nurturant situation was absent. At the start of the second task, the experimenter went to the rear of the experimental room out of sight of the subject, saying that she had to look at some books or arrange some cards.

Dependency This variable was defined according to Beller's (1957) dimensions of seeking help, physical contact, proximity, attention, and recognition. To measure these responses, Beller's 7-point behavior rating scale based on the frequency and persistence of these behaviors in the classroom situation was used. The composite score has been shown to be an indicator of a general dependency motive in young children (Beller, 1957).

Dependency Rating For 1 month prior to the experimental sessions, two classroom teachers independently rated the children for dependency by use of Beller's scale as described above. Each teacher selected two 10-minute periods each day in which to make the observations. Each child was observed at least three times weekly. The usual total observation time for each child was 12–16 minutes by each teacher for the 4-week period.

The mean score for girls was 18.7 ($SD = 3.78$) and for boys, 19.7 ($SD = 3.86$) The mean difference was not significant.

Rank order interjudge correlations were .43 for the girls' ratings and .70 for the boys' ratings. The overall interjudge coefficient was .54.

Task The experimental setting was puzzle solving. One of four jig-saw puzzles, each with 12 pieces, was used to assess the effects of the variables on performance.[2]

---
[1] No help was given on the test puzzle under any condition.
[2] These puzzles are produced by the Judy Company, Minneapolis, Minnesota.

Subjects   Twelve males and 12 females in a federally supported, prekindergarten school situation (Early Push Program) were used as subjects. Ages ranged 4 years–4 years, 11 months with mean ages of 4 years, 5 months for the males and 4 years, 4 months for the females. All the subjects were from low-income urban families and all were within the normal range of intelligence. Each had been in the same class with the same teachers from the beginning of the school year in late September to the time of the study in late April. The ethnic breakdown of the subjects was as follows: nine of Italian descent, including five males and four females; six of Irish descent, three males and three females; eight of Puerto Rican descent, three males and five females; and one Afro-American male.

Procedure: Familiarization Period   In order to counteract differential puzzle-solving abilities and practice effects during the experimental situation, a 2-week period of familiarization with puzzles was held prior to the study. This consisted of ten 20-minute periods, under both directed and free-play classroom conditions, using four puzzles, each with 12 pieces. The puzzle used in the performance task was chosen at random from these four puzzles just prior to the beginning of the experiment. During the familiarization period, the experimenter was present in the classroom.

Division into Groups   The behavior ratings were pooled for each child with the mean score adopted as the indication of dependency level. Based on these scores, within each sex, the subjects were divided into high- and low-dependency groups. Further subdivision into groups receiving experimental nurturance and nurturance deprivation was made at random from within the dependency levels. This assignment yielded 12 boys and 12 girls, 3 of each sex in each combination of high- and low-dependency under nurturance or nurturance-deprivation conditions.

Performance Task   Since the situation is an important variable in the induction of dependent behavior (Beller, 1959), the most relevant setting for the present study was considered to be one readily identified as usual and meaningful for the child. For this reason, the experimental sessions took place in an 8 × 12 foot room adjacent to the classroom and employed objects familiar to the children. A female experimenter, similar in age, physical stature, and temperament to the classroom teachers was used. During the course of the experiment, this person was unaware of the dependency level of each child and was told only which treatments to administer.

Each subject was brought individually to the experimental room and allowed to look around for 1 minute. After that, the subject was seated at a table on which the puzzle was placed. The experimenter then asked the subject to solve the puzzle, adopting the nurturant pattern of behavior. Time spent in puzzle solving during this period ranged 35–330 seconds. After a 3-minute rest period which consisted of talking with the experimenter about things other than the puzzle, the subjects solved the puzzle again, either under the condition of nurturance deprivation or under conditions of continued nurturance. Second-session performance times ranged 65–380 seconds.

RESULTS

The hypotheses were tested by a three-way analysis of covariance of second situation performance times with first task performance times taken as the covariate. The Scheffé method of post hoc comparisons was used for further analysis (Guenther, 1964). The dependency scores were considered independent of the performance scores. Tables 1 and 2 show the results of this analysis.

TABLE 1
Analysis of Covariance of the Effects of Nurturance, Dependency, Sex, and Their Interactions on Performance Times on the Test Puzzle

Source of Variation	DF	MS	F
Sex (A)	1	2865.120	1.29
Dependency (B)	1	19511.495	8.76*
A × B	1	.056	.00
Nurturance (C)	1	18944.888	8.51*
B × C	1	17931.349	8.05*
A × C	1	101.481	.05
A × B × C	1	1.817	.00
Error	16	2226.625	

*$p < .01$.

TABLE 2
Adjusted Cell Means, in Seconds, for the Test Puzzle

Group	High Dependent	Low Dependent	Nurturance Totals
Nurturance			
Boys	122.870	119.536	
Girls	141.266	136.649	
Total	264.136	256.185	520.321
Nurturance deprivation			
Boys	230.756	115.838	
Girls	256.863	142.888	
Total	487.619	258.726	746.345
Dependency totals	751.755	514.911	

NOTE. Equality of cell variances is assumed in the analysis. Since there are equal n's in each cell any inequality would be overcome by the robustness of the P test. Total variance for the test is the mean square error term in Table 1.

Hypothesis 1 is supported by the significant overall effect of nurturance. Further, a comparison between cell means of high-dependent children under nurturance and nurturance deprivation (Table 2) shows that this is a function of the interaction between nurturance deprivation and high dependency. A similar comparison for low-dependent children (Table 2) reveals a nonsignificant nurturance effect.

Evidence for Hypothesis 2 is provided by comparing the total mean for the high-dependent subjects with that of the low-dependent subjects under nurturance deprivation (Table 2). The significant difference between these groups again reveals a notable interaction between high dependency and nurturance deprivation but not between low dependency and nurturance deprivation. Moreover, a nonsignificant difference between high- and low-dependency groups within the nurturant condition (Table 2) points out the similarity of negligible interactive effects between the nurturance condition and high or low dependency.

No significant main effect of sex was evident from the main analysis. A look at Table 2, however, shows slightly better efficiency for the boys under each of the four dependency-nurturance situations.

DISCUSSION

The findings sustain the hypothesis that there is a close correspondence between adult nurturant behavior and child dependency, with children high in dependency keenly sensitive to changes in nurturance level. This awareness may be attributable to the highly dependent child's response to nurturance as a rewarding state of affairs, the removal of which results in a stressful, anxiety-producing situation. Thus, any setting in which dependency-gratifying behaviors are absent may be defined as stressful for a highly dependent child. Such stress may well interfere with efficient performance on a complex task. Further, the higher the child's dependency level, the more stressful the situation may seem and the more heightened his dependency behavior may become, with concomitant decreasing efficiency in performance. That such changes may be inferred from a performance measure is indicated by the results obtained from the dependency and performance analysis. This effect appears to be a general one, since no significant differences between sexes were found.

In the case of children low in dependency, adult nurturance may have only minimal reward effects and its deprivation may not be stressful. The behavior of such children may reflect either a quick adjustment merely to the event of a situational difference or, in fact, show no change at all.

The inefficient performance of highly dependent children under deprivation of nurturance and the lack of a significant effect for children low in dependency are consistent with the above notion of situational stress.

Although stress may enhance performance on a simple task, as seen in Hartup's (1958) study, it is reasonable to assume that it serves as an interference in the more complex task used in this study. Thus, both the present findings and those of Hartup provide explicit behavioral evidence for differential changes in dependency as shown by Beller's (1959) perceptual studies.

The finding of no sex differences is open to a number of interpretations. It was expected that the presence of a female experimenter might possibly bring about interactive effects. For example, it is reasonable to expect that under both nurturance and nurturance-deprivation conditions the performance of the females would be positively affected by the female experimenter. This result did not appear in the analysis. To further substantiate this, it is necessary that a similar study with a larger number of subjects be carried out using experimenters of both sexes.

On the other hand, the slight superiority in efficiency of the boys may also be a function of task relevance rather than sex differences. (The puzzle depicted a male television repairman at work.) Kagan and Moss (1962) have shown that dependency behavior in children between the ages 3–6 shows little resemblance to that of adult behavior or even to that of the later childhood years. (It is not until later childhood that a reliable relationship to adult dependency behavior is seen.) Such instability can account for the lack of a clear-cut difference in dependency ratings between sexes in this investigation.

Whatever reason is cited for failure to find sex differences in dependency, it appears that in studies of child dependency at the preschool level, no distinction on the basis of sex is necessary. Except for the possibility (not tested here) that a male experimenter might produce different effects on the two sexes, in contrast to the lack of such a difference for a female experimenter, boys and girls at the preschool level are similar in response to variations in adult nurturance.

Although a study such as this can give some explicit cues to the nature of the relationships of nurturance and dependency to performance, it is quite another matter to reach a full understanding of dependency changes under varied nurturant conditions. A short-term study, where it is possible to measure confidently only such discrete variables as performance, can, at best, serve as a basis for discussion of inferred dependency change and as a preliminary step in the longitudinal type of investigation needed for a truly sufficient study of dependency. Such an investigation might be carried out in a classroom situation over a period of a year using specific times within the normal routine for the manipulation of nurturance and securing definitive ratings of dependency. With extraneous factors, such as performance and sex (and perhaps others) partialed out by studies such as the present one, this long-term approach could finally bring to light the true relationship between the motives of nurturance and dependency.

References

Beller, E. K. Dependence and independence in young children. *Journal of Genetic Psychology*, 1955, **87**, 25–35.

———. Dependency and autonomous achievement striving related to orality and anality in early childhood. *Child Development*, 1957, **28**, 287–315.

———. Exploratory studies of dependency. *Transactions of the New York Academy of Sciences*, 1959, **21**, 414–425.

Guenther, W. C. *Analysis of variance*. Englewood Cliffs, N. J.: Prentice-Hall, 1964.

Hartup, W. W. Nurturance and nurturance withdrawal in relation to the dependency behavior of pre-school children. *Child Development*, 1958, **29**, 191–201.

Heathers, G. Emotional dependence and independence in nursery school play. *Journal of Genetic Psychology*, 1955, **87**, 37–57.

Kagan, J., & Moss, H. A. *Birth to maturity: A study in psychological development*. New York: Wiley, 1962.

Moustakos, C. E., Sigel, I., & Schalock, H. An objective method for the measurement and analysis of child-adult interaction. *Child Development*, 1956, **27**, 109–134.

Murray, H. *Explorations in personality*. New York: Oxford University Press, 1938.

Sears, R. R. Dependency motivation. *Nebraska Symposium on Motivation*, 1963, **11**, 25–64.

Chapter 5

Courtesy the Peace Corps by Ray Witlin

An Overview of Human Life and Growth

All of existence is continuous and related. A search for beginnings and causes of life reveals psychological, physiological, biological, biochemical, and physical structures built upon and of each other.

Every organism and its environment have dynamic, reciprocal relationships. Affecting each other and being affected by each other, neither can be understood without the other, nor can either be what it *is* without the other. The cool air under the tree does not exist without the tree, nor would the tree exist without air. An interesting interaction between plants and landscape can be seen in coastal areas where conservation projects are carried out. A beach which was washed away by a hurricane now stretches smoothly into the Atlantic, backed by sand dunes built by plants. The plants were dead Christmas trees stuck into the sand and then reinforced by living plants which, finding nutrients and moisture enough in the sand, sent down a network of tough roots, which held the sand in the dunes.

More remarkable even than the building of beaches is the interaction of the human baby with his environment, his family. A human baby grows into a human child as he lives in a human family, calling forth maternal and paternal responses from two adults whose behavior could not be parental if he were not there.

Varieties of Interaction Between the Individual and His World

The story of child development begins with the interactions of a small package of DNA and ends with an adult human being living in a complex social network. Everyone has some beliefs and hypotheses as to how these many changes take place. Nobody has explained it all in a comprehensive theory, but many theorists have described and explained parts of it. A theory depends first of all on the point of view from which the observer looks at the human scene and consequently on the phenomena which he observes. Theories of growth and development usually have a biological flavor. Learning experiments may suggest the influence of physics. Research in social relationships often involves sociology and perhaps anthropology. This chapter deals with six types of interactions which represent different ways of looking at human phenomena. They are: equilibration, growth and development, learning, maturation, evolutionary adaptation, and heredity.

Equilibration

The organism constantly regulates its life processes so as to maintain physical and mental states within certain limits.

Homeostasis

Homeostasis is a balance which the organism maintains within itself during the processes of living and as environmental influences affect its internal conditions. Since the balance is continually upset and re-created, through a complex of interactions, it can be called a dynamic equilibrium. Through activities that are mostly unconscious, the individual keeps his blood sugar at a definite level, his water content within a given range, his oxygen content just so. Breathing and heartbeat speed up or slow down from their average rates to restore disturbed balances. The mechanisms of homeostasis regulate sleeping and waking states, activity and rest. Pressures and depleted tissues may register consciously as felt needs, leading to such purposeful interactions with the environment as eating, drinking, and eliminating.

Looming large in the life of a newborn infant, the problems of homeostasis dwindle throughout infancy and childhood. By about 3 months of age basic physiological processes are well controlled. At any time throughout the life span, however, when the balance is seriously threatened, when biological demands become crucial or urgent, the individual drops his higher-order activities, such as giving a lecture or playing tennis, in order to restore the balance within his body.

Psychological Equilibrium

The search for balance occurs in the mental realm as well as in the physical. Equilibration is the process of achieving a state of balance. Sooner or later, the state of equilibrium is upset and a new one must be created. Equilibration includes selecting stimuli from the world, seeking this or that kind, more or less, paying attention to some of them and using some in more complex mental operations. When you consider all the sounds, sights, tastes, and other perceptions available, it follows that a person could not possibly attend to all of them at once. There must be ways of selecting stimuli and avoiding or reducing psychological conflict. In Walter's words: "... there are mechanisms within the brain which act like traffic cops for information and actually damp down and modify the action of the receptors themselves. It has been shown that the information which is allowed to reach the brain from the outside world is a function of its novelty and significance. The level of the receptor itself, the actual eye or ear, is cut down, as though the central nervous system were to say: 'I'm not interested in what you're sending me'" [48, p. 109]. What Walter is describing is very much akin to homeostasis of physiological functions, the maintenance of satisfactory internal conditions.

Equilibration is one of Piaget's principles of mental development [34, pp. 5–8]. Action can be provoked when equilibrium is upset by finding a new object, being asked a question, identifying a problem; in fact, by any new experience. Equilibrium is reestablished by reaching a goal, answering a question, solving a problem, imitating, establishing an effective tie or any other resolution of the difference between the new factor or situation and the mental organization already existing. Equilibration results in the successive stages of intelligence which Piaget describes.

Equilibration, in Piaget's theory, includes two complementary processes through which the person proceeds to more complex levels of organization—*assimilation*, which is the taking in from the environment what the organism can deal with and *accommodation*, the changing of the organism to fit external circumstances. Just as the body can assimilate foods and not other substances, so the mind can take in certain aspects and events in the external world and not others. Existing structures or *schemas* incorporate experiences which fit them or which almost fit them.

A schema is a pattern of action and/or thought. A baby develops some schemas before he is born and has them for starting life as a newborn. With simple schemas, he interacts with his environment, working toward equilibrium. He achieves equilibrium over and over again, by using the schemas available to him at the moment. For example, a baby has a furry toy kitten which he knows as *kitty*. When given a small furry puppy he calls it *kitty*, strokes it and pats it, assimilating the puppy to an existing schema. A new little horse on wheels requires accommodation, since it is too different to be assimilated into the schema for dealing with *kitty*. It looks different; it feels different; it is not good for stroking and patting, but something can be done with the wheels which cannot be done with *kitty*. A new pattern of action is required. The child accommodates by changing and organizing existing schemas to form a schema for dealing with *horsey*. Thus the child grows in his understanding of the world and his ability to deal with his experiences in meaningful ways. Assimilation conserves the structural systems that he has while accommodation effects changes through which he copes more adequately with his environment and behaves in increasingly complex ways.

When homeostasis presents no problems, such as hunger, thirst, or fatigue, a person looks for something to do, something interesting, a new experience. If equilibrium were completely satisfying in itself, then surely he would sit or lie quietly doing nothing. In looking for action, the child seems to be trying to upset his state of equilibrium, as though equilibration were fun! And so it is. Activity is intrinsic in living tissue, brain cells included. Curiosity, exploration, competence, and achievement motivation are all outgrowths of the human propensity for enjoying the process of equilibration. The first stage of the process, perception of a problem, an incongruity or discrepancy, involves tension and a feeling of incompleteness. Something is missing or something is wrong.

The baby pushes himself forward to grasp a toy that is out of reach. The 4-year-old makes a mailbox which is necessary for his game of postman. The first grader sounds out a new word. Each child reduces a feeling of tension as he creates a new equilibrium. The equilibration (achievement of new balance) makes him into a slightly different person from what he has been, a person who can move forward a bit, a person who has made his own mailbox and can therefore make other things, a person who can read another word. Thus equilibration is a way of describing behavior development. New and more complex behavior occurs as it is demanded by the person's relationship with his surroundings.

When a person's schemas are adequate to deal with the situation in which he finds himself, he reacts automatically. For example, the response of a hungry breast-fed baby of 3 months would be quite automatic when offered his mother's breast. A 10-year-old would automatically answer the question "What is two times two?" When the schemas are not quite adequate to the situation, the child uses what he has, changing them slightly into actions which do solve the problem. For instance, the baby would change his behavior sufficiently to cope with a bottle and the 10-year-old with "$2x = 4$. What does x equal?" The change which takes place at the same time within the child is the development of a new behavior pattern or schema. A pleasant feeling of curiosity and satisfaction accompanies successful adjustments to demands for new behavior.

A person feels uneasy when he encounters a situation in which his resources are very inadequate. In order to provoke uneasiness, the problem must be somewhat similar to those which a person can solve, but not similar enough for him to succeed with. Such a problem for the baby mentioned might be a cup of milk. For the 10-year-old it might be an equation such as $5x - 49/x = 20x/5$. If the situation is so far removed from a person's past experience that his schemas for dealing with it are extremely inadequate, then he will have no reaction to it. He will not notice it. He will not select from the environment the stimuli which would pose the problem. The baby will not try to drink out of a carton full of cans of milk. The child won't attempt to solve $xY - x5 - 144 = 1062 + 2300$.

Familiar objects in unfamiliar guise produce unpleasantness, uneasiness, or even fear. (Chimpanzees are afraid of the keeper in strange clothes, an anesthetized chimp, a plaster cast of a chimp's head. Human babies are afraid of strangers.) In order to be frightened or to get the unpleasant feeling, the subject must first have residues of past experience with which to contrast the present experience. Thus does incongruity arise, with its accompanying unpleasant feeling tone. If the individual can cope with the situation successfully, he achieves equilibration and its accompanying pleasant feeling tone. Stimuli preferred and chosen are those that are slightly more complex than the state of equilibrium that the individual has already reached. Thus he moves on to a new state of equilibrium [36].

Growth and Development

The child's body becomes larger and more complex while his behavior increases in scope and complexity. If any distinction is made between the two terms, growth refers to size, and development to complexity. However, the two are often used interchangeably and this is what we have done. The terms *growth* and *development* were borrowed from the physical field, but they are commonly understood in connection with mental and personality characteristics. One can say, "He has grown mentally," or "He has developed mentally." The statement means "He is now functioning on a more complex intellectual level." Or one can speak of growth of personality and development of attitudes. Listening in on second grade and fifth grade classrooms in the same school building will reveal differences in subject matter interests and in mode of thinking.

Growth or development can be shown to have taken place either by comparing younger and older individuals at the same moment of time or by comparing the same individuals at two different points of time. When the measures of some characteristic of a number of individuals are averaged by age groups, the averages of the successive age groups show what growth has taken place. If each individual is measured only once, that is, if there are different people at each age, the study is *cross-sectional*. If the same individuals are measured at each successive age, the study is *longitudinal*. If some individuals do not remain available for continued study and new ones are added, the study is called *mixed longitudinal*. In a cross-sectional study, growth status at each age is investigated, and inferences regarding growth are drawn from *differences* between any groups. *Change* in status from age to age can be inferred only if the individuals at the two ages can be assumed to be comparable in all relevant ways. In a longitudinal study both growth status at each age and change in status from age to age can be investigated more precisely, because the same individuals are involved and actual growth patterns are established for individuals.

Principles of Growth

There are a number of generalizations about growth which are more apparent with respect to physical growth but which, as far as research can show, are also true for psychological growth. We will elaborate on nine such statements about growth at this point, some of them with subheadings.

Variation of Rates. Rates of growth vary from one individual to another, and they vary within one individual. An organism grows at varying rates, from one time to another. The organs and systems grow at varying rates, at different times. There is a sex difference in rates and terminals. Various group differences can be shown. It is no wonder that comparisons of growth require facts obtained by highly controlled methods.

An organism and its parts grow at rates which are different at different times. The body as a whole, as measured by height and weight, shows a pattern of velocity that is fast in infancy, moderate in the preschool period, slow during the school

292 Preschool Children

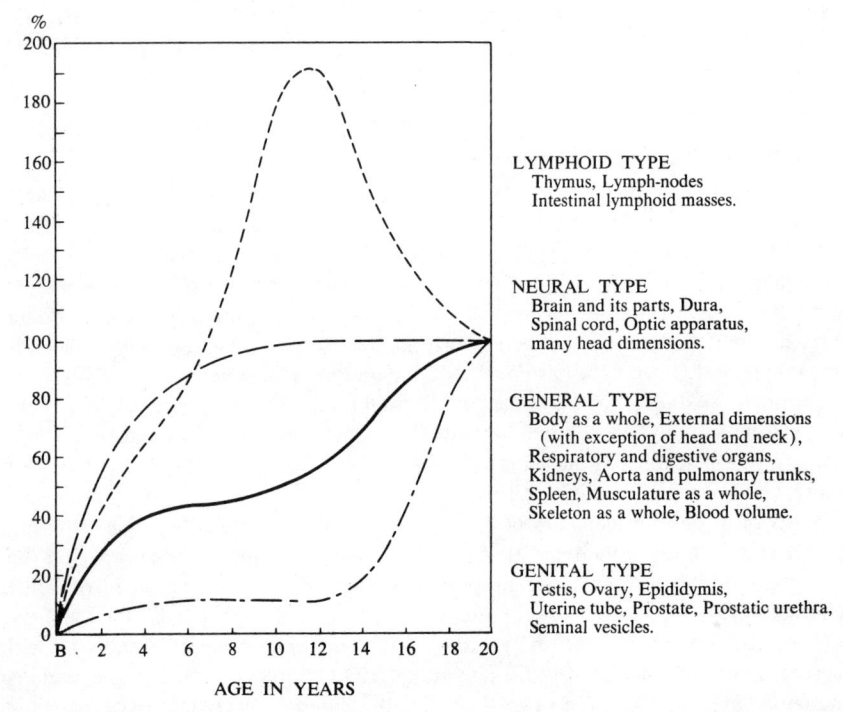

Figure 5-1. Growth curves of the body as a whole and of three types of tissue. Values at each age are computed as percentages of values for total growth.

SOURCE: Reproduced by permission from J. A. Harris, C. M. Jackson, D. G. Paterson, and R. E. Scammon, *The Measurement of Man*. Minneapolis: University of Minnesota Press, 1930.

LYMPHOID TYPE
Thymus, Lymph-nodes
Intestinal lymphoid masses.

NEURAL TYPE
Brain and its parts, Dura,
Spinal cord, Optic apparatus,
many head dimensions.

GENERAL TYPE
Body as a whole, External dimensions
(with exception of head and neck),
Respiratory and digestive organs,
Kidneys, Aorta and pulmonary trunks,
Spleen, Musculature as a whole,
Skeleton as a whole, Blood volume.

GENITAL TYPE
Testis, Ovary, Epididymis,
Uterine tube, Prostate, Prostatic urethra,
Seminal vesicles.

years, and fast in the beginning of adolescence. Figure 5-1 illustrates growth velocities of different types of tissue, expressed as percentages of maturity for each age. The general type of growth, which represents not only height and weight, but muscles, skeleton, and most of the internal organs, is illustrated by a sigmoid curve, an elongated S. The brain and related tissues grow in a different pattern of velocity, very fast during the first 2 years, moderately until about 6, and very little after that. The growth curve for genital tissue is almost the reverse of that of neural tissue. The genital system grows very little during infancy and childhood and very fast in adolescence. The fourth curve in Figure 5-1 represents the lymph system which grows rapidly throughout infancy and childhood, reaches a peak just before puberty, and then decreases in size throughout adolescence.

Rates of growth vary from one individual to another. Some children are fast growers, some moderate, and some slow in regard to the number of years taken to reach maturity. Periods of fast and slow growth vary as to when they occur and for how long. One child begins the pubescent growth spurt earlier or later than another, grows faster or slower during the spurt, and finishes sooner or later.

There are sex differences in rates. Early in fetal life, girls show evidence of maturing faster than boys, especially in skeletal development. At birth, girls are four weeks ahead of boys skeletally. Boys' skeletal development is about 80 percent of that of girls' from birth to maturity [44, p. 43]. Girls are ahead of boys in dentition, as measured by eruption of permanent teeth. Although sex differences in height and weight before the preadolescent growth spurt are very slight, favoring boys, sexual maturity and its antecedent growth spurt occur in girls about two years before they do in boys. Therefore, there is a period of about two years when girls are taller and heavier than boys. At all ages, girls are more mature physiologically.

Individual Differences in Terminals. It is obvious, yet it is essential in understanding growth, to recognize that for different people maturity comes at different points. You have only to walk down the street to observe that some people grow until they are over 6 feet tall, others stop at 5 feet, and most people stop in between. Measurable mental growth stops at different times for different individuals too. The average girl reaches height and weight terminals before the average boy. Little is known about mental growth terminals.

Dynamic Interrelations in Growth. It would be surprising if different measures of growth were not related to each other. A tremendous number of studies have probed into the question of interrelationships of growth-controlling and regulating mechanisms.

Correlations between measures of growth can be between measures in the same field (physical–physical, mental–mental, and so on), or in different fields (physical–mental, mental–emotional). Skeletal development, assessed by X rays of the wrist, is at present the best indicator of physiological maturity, although if body proportions could be quantified and scaled in some manageable way, this might prove even more useful. Fat thickness in childhood is also a measure of general physiological maturity [16]. Sexual maturity and eventual height can be predicted with good accuracy from measurements of skeletal maturity. A general factor of bodily maturity operating throughout the growth period influences the child's growth as a whole, including his skeleton, size, physiological reactions, and possibly intelligence. Influencing factors of more limited scope operate independently of the general factor and of each other. One of these limited factors controls baby teeth, another permanent teeth, another the ossification centers in the skeleton and probably several others regulate brain growth. This is why various measures of physical growth have low positive correlations with each other. If there were only one controlling factor, then the different measures would presumably all correlate highly or even perfectly with one another [44].

Studies of the relation between physical and mental growth show a small but consistent positive correlation, bearing out the hypothesis of a general factor which influences all growth processes. This relationship has been studied from age 6½ onward, comparing the mental ages or academic achievement, or both, of early maturing youngsters with those of late maturers [1, 24, 39, 40, 42]. A study of children at the extremes of distributions of mental traits showed gifted boys to be significantly ahead of retarded boys in measures of physical growth [24]. A small positive correlation between mental ability and size is also found in adults [45]. As an example of the relationships between growth and personality, there is good evidence that early maturers feel more adequate and more comfortable about themselves than do late maturers [23, 31].

Optimal Tendency. An organism behaves as though it were seeking to reach its maximum potential for development in both structure and function. Even though growth is interrupted, such as in periods of inadequate food supply, the child (or organism) makes up for the lean period as soon as more and better food is available, returning to his characteristic pattern of growth. Only if the deprivation is severe, or if it occurs throughout a critical period, will he show permanent effects from it.

During the deprivation period, the organism adapts by slowing growth and cutting down on the use of energy.

All sorts of adaptive arrangements are worked out when there are interferences with the normal course of development, as though the child is determined to reach his best potential by another route when one is blocked. The child with poor eyesight seeks extra information from his other senses. Babies with a tendency toward rickets drink cod liver oil freely if permitted to, selecting their own diets from a wide variety of simple foods [7]. For northern white children, the characteristics of the home were found to be most important in determining how well the child did at school, but for southern black children the characteristics of the school were more important than those of the home. "It is as if the child drew sustenance from wherever it was available. When the home had more to offer, it became more determining; but when the school could provide more stimulation than the home, then the school became the more influential factor." [5, p. 106].

"Every breach in the normal complex of growth is filled through regenerative, substantive, or compensatory growth of some kind.... Insurance reserves are drawn upon whenever the organism is threatened.... Herein lies the urgency, the almost irrepressible quality of growth" [18, p. 165]. This principle has been recognized as working in physical realms as well as organic, where there seems to be a self-stabilizing or target-seeking property of certain systems [49].

Differentiation and Integration. From large global patterns of behavior, smaller, more specific patterns emerge. Later the small, specific patterns can be combined into new, complicated, larger patterns. For example, a photographic study of human beginnings shows an 11½ weeks' fetus reacting to being stroked on the right cheek [18, p. 25]. The fetus contracted the muscles of his neck, trunk, and shoulder, causing his whole body to bend away from the stimulus and the arms and hands to move backward. When a newborn infant is stroked on the cheek he turns toward the stimulus, pursing his lips and opening his mouth when his lips touch something. Thus he shows a new, specialized response pattern which involves a small part of his body instead of the whole. As he grows older, the rooting response changes and becomes integrated with other behavior patterns. Instead of turning toward food when he is touched near the mouth, he turns toward the breast or bottle when he sees it. His hands come into play in guiding food toward his mouth. Later he uses a knife and fork. He is integrating behavior patterns of eyes and hands with the rooting pattern, forming a smoothly functioning whole.

Examples can also be taken from purely intellectual fields, such as mathematics. There is a stage of maturity at the end of infancy when a child knows *one, two* and *a-lot-of*. At 5, he has differentiated *three* and *four* out of *a-lot-of*. By 6, numbers up to ten have true meaning. Using these differentiated concepts, he next combines them in addition and subtraction to form new and more complicated concepts. Conceptual differentiation and integration are at work as the student moves up through algebra and geometry into higher mathematics. There remains an undifferentiated sphere where each person stops in his progress in mathematics.

Developmental Direction. Certain sequences of development take place in certain directions, in reference to the body. The motor sequence takes two such directions, cephalocaudal (head to tail) and proximodistal (midline to outer extremities). Like all animals, the child grows a relatively large, complex head region early in life, whereas the tail region or posterior is small and simple. As he becomes older, the region next to the head grows more, and finally, the end region grows. Coordination follows the same direction, the muscles of the eyes coming under control first, then the neck muscles, then arms, chest, and back, and finally the legs. The motor sequence illustrates the proximodistal direction by the fact that the earliest controlled arm movements, as in reaching, are large movements, controlled mostly by shoulder muscles. Later the elbow is brought into play in reaching, then the wrist, and then the fingers.

Normative Sequence. The sequence of motor development has long been noticed and understood as one of the ways of nature. "A child must creepe ere he walke."

As the structures of the body mature in their various sequences, they function in characteristic ways, provided that the environment permits appropriate interaction. The resulting behavior patterns appear in an orderly sequence. Sequences have been described for locomotion, use of hands, language, problem solving, social behavior, and other kinds of behavior [6, 19, 20]. During the decade of the thirties, the bulk of research in child development was normative, delineating sequences of development and designating average ages for the patterns observed. The classic viewpoint, exemplified by Gesell, stressed normative sequences as an unfolding. While some lip service was paid to the necessity of an environment, development was thought of largely as an inner process. Today interaction between organism and environment is recognized as basic to development. The change in viewpoint has come about to some extent because of the broadening of areas of child study to include a variety of cultures, at home and abroad. Although child development continues to take place in orderly sequences, exceptions can be found [8]. Hence normative sequences cannot be considered as universal, but must be understood as occurring in particular kinds of environments.

Epigenesis. Growth takes place upon the foundation which is already there. New parts arise out of and upon the old. Although the organism becomes something new as it grows, it still has continuity with the past and hence shows certain consistencies over time. Through interactions with the environment, the organism continues to restructure itself throughout life, being at each moment the product of the interaction which took place in the previous moment between organism and environment. A toddler's body results from interactions of a baby's body with food, water, and air. The motor pattern of walking is derived and elaborated from creeping and standing. Writing is built from scribbling.

Critical Periods. There are certain limited times during the growth period of any organism when it will interact with a particular environment in a specific way. The result of interactions during critical periods can be especially beneficial or harmful. The prenatal period includes specific critical periods for physical growth. The first three months are critical for the development of eyes, ears, and brain, as shown by defects in children whose mothers had German measles during the first three months of pregnancy. Apparently those organs are most vulnerable to the virus of German measles when they are in their periods of rapid growth.

Experiments on vision with human and animal infants reveal critical ages for the development of visual responses, times when the infant will either show the response without experience or will learn it readily [14]. If the visual stimulus is not given at the critical age (as when baby monkeys are reared in darkness), the animal later learns the response with difficulty, or not at all.

Psychological development also shows critical periods in the sense that certain behavior patterns are acquired most readily at certain times of life. Critical periods in personality development include the period of primary socialization, when the

296 Preschool Children

infant makes his first social attachments [38] and develops basic trust [11]. A warm relationship with a mother figure is thought to be essential among the experiences which contribute to a sense of trust [4]. This type of critical period is probably not so final and irreversible as is a critical period for the development of an organ in the embryo. If the term "critical period" is applied to the learning of skills such as swimming and reading, then it should be understood that it signifies the most *opportune* time for learning and not the only one [30].

Stage Theories of Development

The last three principles of growth are incorporated in theories of child development which present growth occurring in stages. Each stage is created through epigenesis, behavior patterns being organized and reorganized in an orderly sequence. Thus past, present, and future development are related and can be understood as an ongoing process. Small pieces of behavior can be interpreted in terms of the stage when they occur instead of being invested with one meaning. For example, crying at 1 month of age was seen to be an active attempt to overcome interference with sucking, whereas crying at 1 year of age was found to be a passive mode of response to environmental frustration [26]. Stage theories encourage research which establishes ways of predicting future development [22].

This book is organized in stages of development, leaning heavily on two stage theories: Erikson's theory of personality growth, and Piaget's theory of the growth of intelligence. The ages which correspond with the various stages are only approximations or rough landmarks. While it is useful to be able to anchor stage concepts to some sort of chronology, it is important to realize that stages are only age-related and not age-determined. The growth principle, *variation of rates*, applies here.

Erikson's Stages. Erikson's theory might be called epigenetic in a double sense. Not only does it portray epigenetic stages, but it was built upon Freud's theory and yet is a new organization and a unique creation. Freud proposed psychosexual stages of development, each of which used a certain zone of the body for gratification of the id (the unconscious source of motives, strivings, desires, and energy). The ego, which mediates between the demands of the id, the outside world, and the superego, "represents what may be called reason and common sense, in contrast to the id, which contains the passions" [15, p. 15]. The superego or ego ideal corresponds roughly to *conscience*. Freud's psychosexual stages are: *oral*, when the mouth is the main zone of satisfaction, about the first year; *anal*, when pleasure comes from anal and urethral sensations, the second and third years; *phallic*, the third and fourth years, a time of pleasure from genital stimulation; *oedipal*, also genital but now, at 4 and 5 years, the child regards the parent of the opposite sex as a love object and the same-sex parent as a rival; *latency*, from 6 to around 11, when sexual cravings are repressed (made unconscious) and the child identifies with the parent and peers of his own sex; *puberal* when mature genital sexuality begins.

Erikson uses Freud's concepts in his theory of psychosocial development, adding to the complexity of each stage and also adding three stages above the puberal, thus dealing with adulthood as a time for growth. Progress through the stages takes place in an orderly sequence. In making his stages psychosocial as well as psychosexual, Erikson recognizes the interaction between individual and culture as contributing to personal growth. While Freud's theory has a great deal to say about pathology, Erikson's offers a guide to both illness and health of personality. For each stage, there are problems to be solved within the cultural context. Thus each stage is a critical period for development of certain attitudes, convictions, and abilities. After the satisfactory solution of each crisis, the person emerges with an increased sense of unity, good judgment and capacity to "do well" [12, p. 92]. The conflicts are never completely resolved nor the problems disposed of forever. Each stage is described with a positive and negative outcome of the crisis involved. The stages are [11, pp. 247–274]:

1. *Basic trust versus basic mistrust.* Similar to Freud's oral stage, the development of a sense of trust dominates the first year. Success means coming to trust the world, other people, and himself. Since the mouth is the main zone of pleasure, trust grows on being fed when hungry, pleasant sensations when nursing, and the growing conviction that his own actions have something to do with pleasant events. Consistent, loving care is trust-promoting. Mistrust develops when trust-promoting experiences are inadequate, when the baby has to wait too long for comfort, when he is handled harshly or capriciously. Since life is never perfect, shreds of mistrust are woven into the fabric of personality. Problems of mistrust recur and have to be solved later, but when trust is dominant, healthy personality growth takes place.

2. *Autonomy versus shame and doubt.* The second stage, corresponding to Freud's anal period, predominates during the second and third year. Holding on and letting go with the sphincter muscles symbolizes the whole problem of autonomy. The child wants to do for himself with all of his powers: his new motor skills of walking, climbing, manipulating; his mental powers of choosing and deciding. If his parents give him plenty of suitable choices, times to decide when his judgment is adequate for successful outcomes, then he grows in autonomy. He gets the feeling that he can control his body, himself, and his environment. The negative feelings of doubt and shame arise when his choices are disastrous, when other people shame him or force him in areas where he could be in charge.

3. *Initiative versus guilt.* The Oedipal part of genital stage of Freudian theory, 4 and 5 years, is to Erikson the stage of development of a sense of initiative. Now the child explores the physical world with his senses and the social and physical worlds with his questions, reasoning, imaginative, and creative powers. Love relationships with parents are very important. Conscience develops. Guilt is the opposite pole of initiative.

4. *Industry versus inferiority.* Solutions of problems of initiative and guilt bring about entrance to the stage of developing a sense of industry, the latency period of Freud. The child is now ready to be a worker and producer. He wants to do jobs well instead of merely starting them and exploring them. He practices and learns the rules. Feelings of inferiority and inadequacy result when he feels he cannot measure up to the standards held for him by his family or society.

5. *Identity versus role diffusion.* The Freudian puberal stage, beginning at the start of adolescence, involves resurgence of sexual feelings. Erikson adds to this concept his deep insights into the adolescent's struggles to integrate all the roles he has played and hopes to play, his childish body concept with his present physical development, his concepts of his own society and the value of what he thinks he can contribute to it. Problems remaining from earlier stages are reworked.

6. *Intimacy versus isolation.* A sense of identity is the condition for ability to establish true intimacy, "the capacity to commit himself to concrete affiliations and partnerships and to develop the ethical strength to abide by such commitments" [11, p. 263]. Intimacy involves understanding and allowing oneself to be understood. It may be, but need not be, sexual. Without intimacy, a person feels isolated and alone.
7. *Generativity versus self-absorption.* Involvement in the well-being and development of the next generation is the essence of generativity. While it includes being a good parent, it is more. Concern with creativity is also part of it. Adults need to be needed by the young, and unless the adults can be concerned and contributing, they suffer from stagnation.
8. *Ego integrity versus despair.* The sense of integrity comes from satisfaction with one's own life cycle and its place in space and time. The individual feels that his actions, relationships, and values are all meaningful and acceptable. Despair arises from remorseful remembrance of mistakes and wrong decisions plus the conviction that it is too late to try again.

Figure 5-2 shows the normal timing of Erikson's stages of psychosocial development. The critical period for each stage is represented by a swelling of the rope which stretches throughout life. The ropes indicate that no crisis is ever solved completely and finally, but that strands of it are carried along, to be dealt with at different levels. As one rope swells at its critical period, the other ropes are affected and interact. Solutions to identity problems involve problems in all the other stages. The metaphor of the rope can also be extended by thinking of the personalities of a family's members as being intertwined ropes. When the parents' Generativity strands are becoming dominant, the infant's Trust strand is dominant. The two ropes fit smoothly together, indicating a complementary relationship between the personalities of infant and parents.

Piaget's Stages. Figure 5-2 shows Piaget's stages in the development of intelligence. Piaget is concerned with the nature of knowledge and how it is acquired. His studies of infants and children have revealed organizations of structures by which the child comes to know the world. The structural units are *schemas*, patterns of action and/or thought. As the child matures, he uses his existing schemas to interact, transforming them through the process of equilibration. Each stage of development is an advance from the last one, built upon it by reorganizing it and adapting more closely to reality. Reorganization and adaptation go on continuously, but from one time to another the results differ from each other. Piaget has broken this series of organizations of structures into units called periods and stages. There are three periods, each of which extends the previous one, reconstructs it, and surpasses it [35, pp. 152-159]. Periods are divided into stages which have a constant sequence, no matter whether the child achieves them at a slow or fast pace. Progress through the periods and stages is affected by organic growth, exercise and experience, social interaction or equilibration. The periods are:

1. *Sensorimotor.* Lasting from birth until about 2, sensorimotor intelligence exists without language and symbols. Practical and aimed at getting results, it works through action-schemas [35, p. 4]. Beginning with the reflex patterns present at birth, the baby builds more and more complex schemas through a succession of six stages. Figure 5-2 lists the names of the stages. During this period the baby constructs a schema of the permanence of objects. He comes to know

An Overview of Human Life and Growth   299

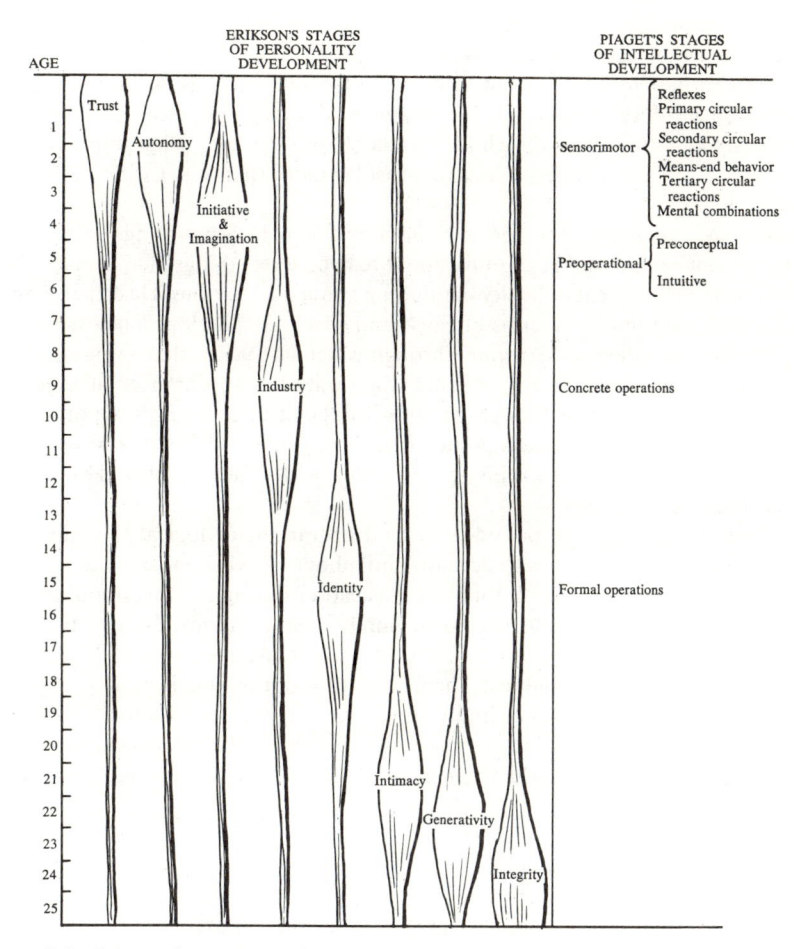

Figure 5-2. Schematic representation of Erikson's stages of psychosocial development, with names of Piaget's stages of the development of intelligence.

that things and people continue to exist even when he cannot see them and he realizes that they move when he is not looking. He learns control of his body in space. He begins to use language to imitate and to make internal representations of reality.

2. *Preoperational.* Sometimes this period, from about 2 to 7, is considered a subperiod of the whole time from 2 to 11. It is distinctly different, however, from the sensorimotor period and the period which comes around 7, the period of concrete operations. Two stages, preconceptual and intuitive thought, are included. The preoperational period is marked by the *semiotic* function and imitation. The semiotic function, often called symbolizing, is the use of an indicator or sign as distinct from the object or event to which it refers [35, pp. 52–91]. For example, the bell that announces dinner is perceived as distinct from the food but as indicating food. Achievements show much use of his new representational abilities, in deferred imitation (imitation starting after the

model has disappeared), symbolic play, drawing, mental images, and verbal representation. The child thinks that names are essential parts of the objects to which they refer. When he gives a reason, it is in terms of how he wants things to be. He sees no need to come to the same conclusions as anyone else because he does not realize the existence of viewpoints other than his own. Throughout this stage the child becomes more flexible in his thinking, more able to use past experience and to consider more than one aspect of an event at a time.

3. *Concrete operations.* The period from about 7 to 11 years of age is essentially the time when the child can think about real, concrete things in systematic ways, although he has great difficulty in thinking about abstractions. He orders, counts, classifies, and thinks in terms of cause and effect. He develops a new concept of permanence, called *conservation*, through which he realizes that amount, weight, volume, and number stay the same when outward appearances of objects or groups are changed. Although he finds it difficult to change his hypotheses, he learns to take other people's points of view and comes to feel that his reasoning and his solutions to problems should check with other people's. His thinking has become socialized.

4. *Formal operations.* The period of formal operations or logical thought begins at about 11 and continues to develop until about 15, when the individual has the mental operations for adult thinking. Instead of having to think about concrete objects, he can think and reason in purely abstract terms. He can think systematically, combining all factors in a situation so as to exhaust all possibilities. He makes hypotheses and tests them. This type of thinking is basic to logic and to the scientific method. The limitation of this stage is a confusion of what could and should be with what is practically possible. The adolescent resists the imperfections in the world when he can construct ideal arrangements in his mind.

Learning

Learning occurs when behavior changes as a result of experience. Experiments on newborn infants have demonstrated learning. As children grow older and their behavior more complex, the variables which influence behavior also increase in number and complexity. Thus different types of learning are described.

Conditioning

Conditioning, or learning by association, is the establishing of a connection between a stimulus and a response. In *classical conditioning*, the kind made famous by Pavlov, a neutral stimulus is presented with another stimulus which elicits an innate response. After several such presentations, the neutral stimulus is given without the other stimulus and the response occurs. Pavlov sounded a buzzer when he gave food to his dog. Eventually the dog salivated at the sound of the buzzer.

Operant, or instrumental, conditioning is done by rewarding the desired response whenever it occurs. Operant conditioning techniques have been developed for use in a wide variety of situations, with animal and human subjects. By rewarding small pieces of behavior, complex patterns can be built up, thus "shaping" or modifying the behavior of the subject. This technique has proved very useful in treating behavior disorders in infants, children, retardates, and the mentally ill.

Conditioning has been used to explore the abilities of infants and to show that newborn babies do learn [27]. Papoušek taught newborn babies to turn their heads to the sound of a buzzer by using a combination of classical and operant conditioning methods [32]. A bell was sounded and if the infant turned to the left, he was given milk. If he did not turn, head-turning was elicited by touching the corner of his mouth with a nipple. Then he was given milk. Newborns were slow to condition, taking an average of 18 days, whereas at 3 months, only 4 days were required and by 5 months, 3 days. Two-month-old infants learned to operate a mobile by means of head-pressing on their pillows [49]. Until recently, the problem for experimenters was to find a way of delivering rewards which would be contingent on a response that the infant was able to make. The ingenious arrangement of the mobile and an activating device in the pillow revealed not only that infants could learn instrumentally (by operant conditioning) but also that they showed enormous involvement and pleasure in the process of controlling stimulation.

Reinforcement

One of the laws of learning which Thorndike formulated in 1905 is the law of effect: "Any act which in a given situation produces satisfaction becomes associated with that situation, so that when the situation occurs, the act is more likely to recur also" [46, p. 203]. This principle is the basis of learning through reinforcement or rewards and punishment. Rewards and punishments, or positive and negative reinforcements, can be given to oneself or to others. It is not always possible to predict what will be rewarding and punishing, since previous experience and the state of the person at the time contribute to the meaning the particular reinforcement has. Havighurst has shown that rewards and punishments change with the age and maturity of the individual and that the development of the reward-punishment system varies from one culture to another [21]. These findings have important implications for educating children from minority subcultures.

Different schedules of reinforcement have different effects on learning by operant conditioning. Response strength is measured by the number of nonreinforced trials required to extinguish the behavior. Intermittent (random) reinforcement results in a much stronger response than does continuous reinforcement. This finding has practical implications for parents and teachers. For example, if the child finds that whining is never rewarded, he will soon stop whining, but if his parents give in occasionally and reward him with what he wants, then whining will be strengthened [41].

Punishment can be very effective in controlling children's behavior, but used without understanding of its complexity, punishment can have undesired effects. Important variables are timing, intensity, relationship between agent and recipient, cognitive structure (reasoning), and consistency [33].

Verbal Mediation

After the child acquires language, he grows in the ability to use words in solving problems and learning. By 5 or 6 years, the ability can be demonstrated by the child's solution of problems which are most easily done with the aid of a principle such as "Always choose the big one" or "It's the color that counts in finding the answer."

Observational Learning

Children learn many behavior patterns through watching and listening and then patterning their behavior according to what they have observed. Social learning, especially, is facilitated by modeling or imitating. Bandura and his associates have done many experiments to show the conditions under which children will learn through observation. One important finding is that children will imitate without any external reinforcement being given. That is, modeling is its own reward. Bronfenbrenner [5] has summarized information on factors affecting the modeling process, under three headings:

Characteristics of the Subject. The child must be able to perceive and to perform the actions and to be interested in observing and imitating.

Characteristics of the Stimulus Act. It is easier to imitate a complex action if it is broken into a series of components and labeled. The child then takes part in increasingly complex interactions.

Characteristics of the Model. The power of the model to induce imitation increases as:

1. The child sees the model as competent, high in status and controlling resources.
2. The child has already experienced the model as rewarding and nurturant.
3. The model is an important source of the child's comfort and support, such as parents, peers, and older children.
4. The child sees the model as similar to himself.
5. Several models show the same behavior.
6. The behavior demonstrated is typical of a group to which the child belongs or wants to belong.
7. The child sees the model rewarded for his behavior. (If he sees the model punished, he is likely not to imitate the behavior unless he gets into a situation where he does not anticipate punishment for performing the actions.)

Bronfenbrenner points out that the Soviets employ all of these principles of modeling in their educational system, where great use is made of the peer group for inducing adult-approved behavior in children. The teacher serves as a competent, high-status, resource-controlling model. The other characteristics of potent models are exemplified by peers.

Social Learning

When a child learns how to think, feel and behave as a member of a certain group, or in a particular role, the process is called social learning. *Socialization* refers to the teaching done by members of the groups or institution in order that social learning may occur in the child. Social learning occurs in people of all ages, but much of it takes place in childhood, as the individual learns appropriate values, attitudes and behavior patterns. Parents are the primary socializers. Siblings and other family members also teach. Teachers and peers are important socializing agents, and then other members of the community.

Socialization refers to both the present and the future. The child learns to behave appropriately as the child he now is, but he also learns attitudes, values and skills that he will use in the future. From interacting with his father, he learns the father role as well as the son role. Similarly, he observes his various socializers as worker, manager, host, citizen, teacher, and in all the many roles that they play in his society. His socializers make varying use of the different methods of teaching implied by the types of learning sketched above. The child learns some specific information and skills, as well as values and attitudes. Thus he is gradually socialized into his family, community and nation through a process which maintains the values and behavior patterns of that group.

Maturation

As the child's bodily structures grow, they change in size and complexity, becoming more and more the way they will be in the mature state. Bodily functions likewise change as the structures do. The whole process is called maturation. Although maturation is controlled by hereditary factors, the environment must be adequate to support it. The growth principle of normative sequence is reflected in maturation, since structures and functions mature in an orderly, irreversible sequence. Since maturation is little affected by experience, its effects are the same throughout a species. An impoverished environment slows the process of maturation more than it changes quality or sequence.

Certain behavior patterns are due to maturation more than to learning because they are relatively independent of experience. Many developmental processes involve both maturation and learning. Examples of processes which are largely maturational are the motor sequence and the emergence of language. In all but the most abnormal environments, infants go through regular sequences of raising the head, raising the chest, sitting, creeping, standing with support, and so on.

Some theories of development stress the role of maturation in determining behavior. Gesell is one of the best known of these theorists, since his writings had a great deal of influence on parents and child care authorities of his time. Gesell's descriptions of behavior stages led many parents to feel that they could do little to influence their children's behavior and that they must enjoy his good stages and wait patiently while he grew out of unattractive, annoying, or disturbing stages. While Piaget recognizes the importance of maturation, he also stresses the necessity for the child to interact, explore, and discover for himself in order to build his mental structures. Mental growth cannot be forced or hurried, however, since its counterpart is physical maturation. "Mental growth is inseparable from physical growth: the maturation of the nervous and endoctrine systems, in particular, continues until the age of sixteen" [35, p. vii].

Evolutionary Adaptation

The behavior patterns which develop through maturation can be traced back in the history of the species or the phylum. These fixed action patterns evolved as the animal adapted to a certain environment. *Ethology* is the study of the relation between animal behavior and environment. Ethology has influenced the study of human development, offering insight into certain kinds of behavior which cannot be explained as learning or fully understood as maturation. Lorenz pointed out the implications of ethology for understanding certain forms of human behavior [28]. Bowlby has integrated psychoanalytic theory with ethology [4]. Ainsworth [2] has done extensive research on attachment behavior, the main focus of the ethological approach to human development.

The adaptive behavior pattern becomes fixed in form, appearing as an innate skill in every member of a species, even though he has not had opportunities to learn [9]. A specific stimulus from the environment activates the particular behavior pattern, as though it were a key, unlocking the mechanism. Thus the behavior is sometimes called an *innate response mechanism*, or IRM. For example, a toad's catching response is released by a small, moving object, a 9-week-old gosling gives an intense fear reaction to his first sight of a hawk, and a stickleback fish will attack a red spot that resembles the red underbelly of another stickleback.

Bowlby points out that the environment to which a species is adapted is the environment in which it evolved into its present form [4, p. 59]. Most likely, when man first emerged as a distinct species, he lived by hunting and gathering in a savannah environment, much like today's most primitive societies and not unlike the ground-dwelling primates [2]. Mother–infant reciprocal behavior was adapted to protecting the infant so as to insure his survival. The baby's unlearned, spontaneous patterns of crying, clinging, and sucking brought him (and still bring him) into contact with the mother. Other aspects of attachment behavior, maturing a little later, serve to maintain and strengthen the contacts with the mother, who was (and still is) adapted or genetically programmed to respond with specific action patterns. In the urban environment of today, close physical contact of mother and baby is not necessary for protecting the baby from predators, but babies still behave as though it were and mothers still respond to their infants' behavior with innate action patterns. Closeness of mother and baby has other advantages, however, in terms of normal development.

Human behavior is largely labile, with relatively few fixed action patterns. The individual can make many adaptations, can learn a great deal. He is equipped with a few innate behavior mechanisms, such as attachment behavior and certain patterns of fear behavior, which have various kinds of value.

Heredity

While most students of child development will study the mechanisms of heredity in a biology course, we include a brief account here. After all, the mechanisms of heredity are what start the child developing and what control the course of development.

Biological Inheritance

The human being is composed of two main types of cells. By far the larger number of cells are the *body* cells. These are the cells which compose the skeleton, skin, kidneys, heart, and so on. A minority of cells are the *germ* cells. In the male, germ cells are called *spermatazoa* (the singular is spermatazoon), usually shortened to *sperm*: in the female, the germ cells are *ova* (the singular is *ovum*).

Each body cell is composed of several different parts, the most important of which for our present discussion are the *chromosomes*, of which there are 46, arranged in 23 pairs. The sizes and shapes of the chromosomes can be determined by viewing a prepared cell through an electron microscope. Twenty-two of the pairs of chromosomes are composed of two highly similar chromosomes, though each pair differs in certain respects from every other pair. These 22 pairs are similar

An Overview of Human Life and Growth   305

Chromosomal material attenuated
— Cell Membrane
— Cytoplasm
— Nuclear Membrane
— Nucleolus
— Spindle
— Centriole

Spindle enlarging chromosomes can be seen

Chromosomes arranged more regularly near center

Chromosomes separate

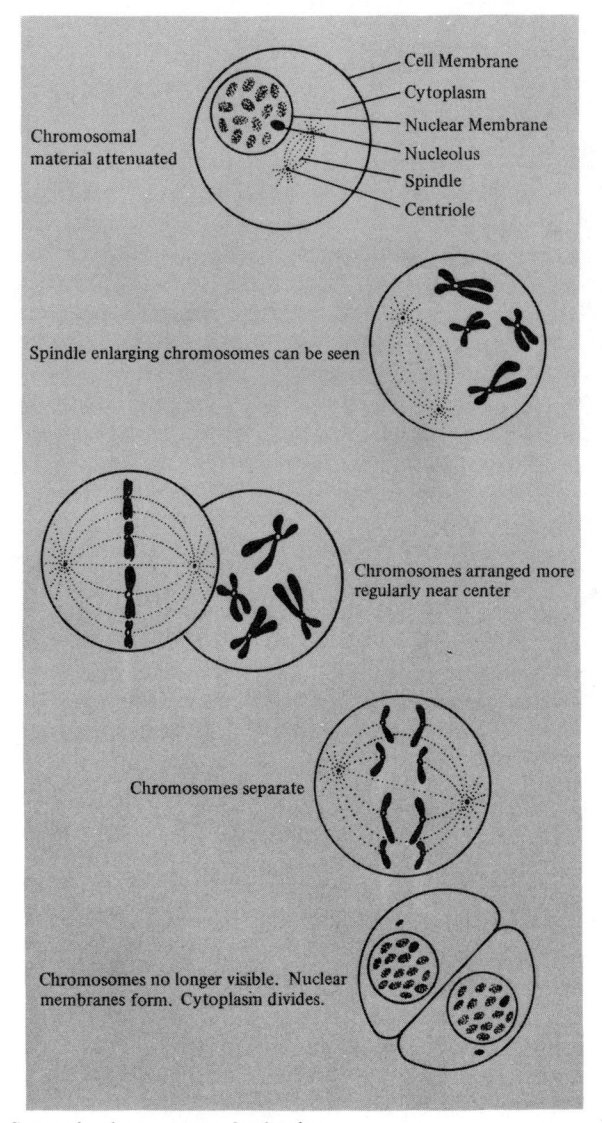

Chromosomes no longer visible. Nuclear membranes form. Cytoplasm divides.

Figure 5–3. Stages in the process of mitosis.
SOURCE: Adapted from P. A. Moody, *Genetics of Man*, Figure 3.2, p. 28. W. W. Norton, 1967.

in males and females. In males, the twenty-third pair is composed of two chromosomes which are unequal in size. The larger one is an *X chromosome*; the smaller is a *Y chromosome*. In females, the twenty-third pair is composed of two X chromosomes. When, in the course of growth, a body cell divides to form two new cells, it goes through the process of *mitosis*. The result of mitosis is that each of the new cells has exactly the same kind and number of chromosomes as the first cell had before it divided. Figure 5–3 shows the process of mitosis.

DNA, a substance in the chromosomes, is the carrier of the genetic code which transmits characteristics from one generation to the next. Figure 5–4 shows a

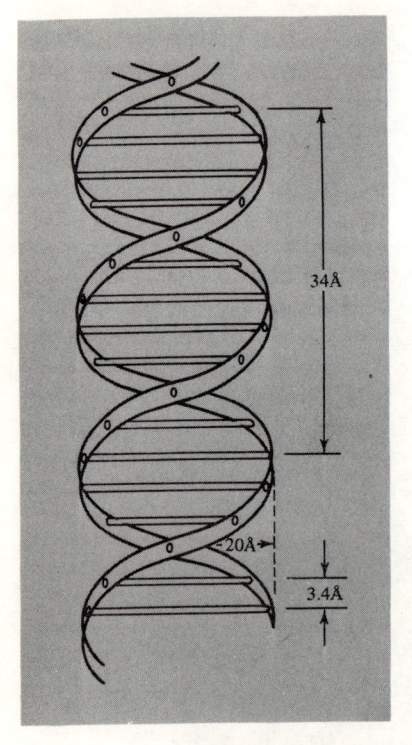

Figure 5-4. DNA takes the form of a double helix.

SOURCE: Adapted from G. W. Burns, *The Science of Genetics*. New York: The Macmillan Company, 1969, Figure 14-9, p. 258.

model of the DNA molecule, in the shape of a double helix or spiral ladder. The genes, carriers of specific instructions for growth, are arranged in linear order on the spirals. The two spirals can come apart like a zipper. Then each half produces another half.

Dominant and Recessive Genes. A recent story [43], which might be called *science prediction* rather than *science fiction*, went like this: a young couple had been quietly holding hands in a secluded corner of the campus. Then one of them said, "Let's match cards." Each pulled out a printed card containing a few holes. They put one on top of the other. None of the holes matched. They embraced happily. Like most human beings, each carried a few dangerous recessive genes out of the thousand or more which can cause birth defects. Since it takes a recessive gene from each parent to produce a characteristic which does not show in either parent, the young couple could safely plan to have children. Or if not with complete assurance, at least they would know that they were not endangering their future children as far as their own dangerous recessives were concerned. Suppose two of the holes had matched. Each of the couple was carrying a recessive gene for cystic fibrosis. For each conception, chances would be one in four for a child with two recessives and hence having cystic fibrosis, two in four for a child carrying one recessive, like the parents, and not showing the defect, and one in four for a normal child with two normal genes. And suppose they conceived a defective embryo. It could be diagnosed early in pregnancy and aborted, if they so chose.

Although at the moment when this is being written, the story is only prediction, the technology on which it is based is of the present. Many physical characteristics, including a large number of defects, are inherited according to simple Mendelian law, as illustrated in our story. Some other defects, such as color-blindness, are sex linked, which means that they are dominant in the male and recessive in the female. A male shows the defect when he carries only one gene for it, but the female does not suffer unless she has two such genes.

Heredity works in more complicated ways, also. Genes work in concert with one another and with the environment. The mechanisms of *crossing over* and *independent assortment* add enormously to the variety of genetic combinations possible. Genes "turn on" and off at various times during the life cycle. For example, the control of sexual maturation is considerably influenced by heredity.

Gene Blends. Many characteristics are the results of more than one pair of genes. Skin color in human beings is such a characteristic. It is not determined in all-or-none way, as is seed color in peas. Rather, in spite of popular belief to the contrary, a child's skin color is almost never darker than the skin of the darker parent, nor lighter than the skin of the lighter parent. If the child's skin is darker than either parent's, it is only a shade darker. At least two pairs of genes are considered to be active in determining skin color; there may be three or more.

Standing height is another human characteristic which is the result of many different genes working at least in part in a literally additive way, although blending of the kind which determines skin color may also be operating. A human being's height is the sum of the lengths of many different bones and many pieces of cartilage. Each bone's length is probably determined by one or more genes, and varies somewhat independently of the length of every other bone. Height is therefore a *polygenic* trait. (In addition, of course, the variation in heights of a group of individuals is affected by environmental factors such as diet and disease.)

Meiosis. Although each individual receives the chromosomes from germ cells of the parents, the offspring of the same parents do not receive identical chromosomes. The explanation of this difference between brothers and sisters lies in the process of *miosis*, the formation of germ cells, sperm, and ova.

Figure 5–5 shows the development of sperm which contain only 2 single chromosomes, since to show 23 would be unnecessarily complicated. In the diagram the primordial germ cell, the *spermatogonium*, is shown as containing two pairs of chromosomes. In the process of meiosis, the spermatogonium divides into two cells called *secondary spermatocytes*, each of which has one of the members of each pair of chromosomes. Each chromosome is composed of two *chromatids*. Each spermatocyte divides into two *spermatids*, each of which has one of the chromatids from the eight chromatids which are shown to have been in the original spermatogonium. From each spermatid develops a sperm. Therefore, from each male primordial germ cell result four sperm, each containing 23 single chromosomes.

The development of each ovum is similar to the development of each sperm, except that from each female primordial germ cell (called an *obgonium*) there result not four ova, but one. But it, like each sperm, contains 23 chromatids from among the 92 chromatids present in the obgonium. Since the obgonium begins meiosis with two X chromosomes, every ovum contains an X chromosome. The spermatogonium, which begins meiosis with one X and one Y chromosome, results in four sperms, two of which contain an X apiece and two a Y. If an X-bearing sperm fertilizes an ovum, the new individual will have two X chromosomes, and will be female. If a Y-bearing sperm fertilizes an ovum, the new individual will have one Y chromosome and one X chromosome, and will be a male.

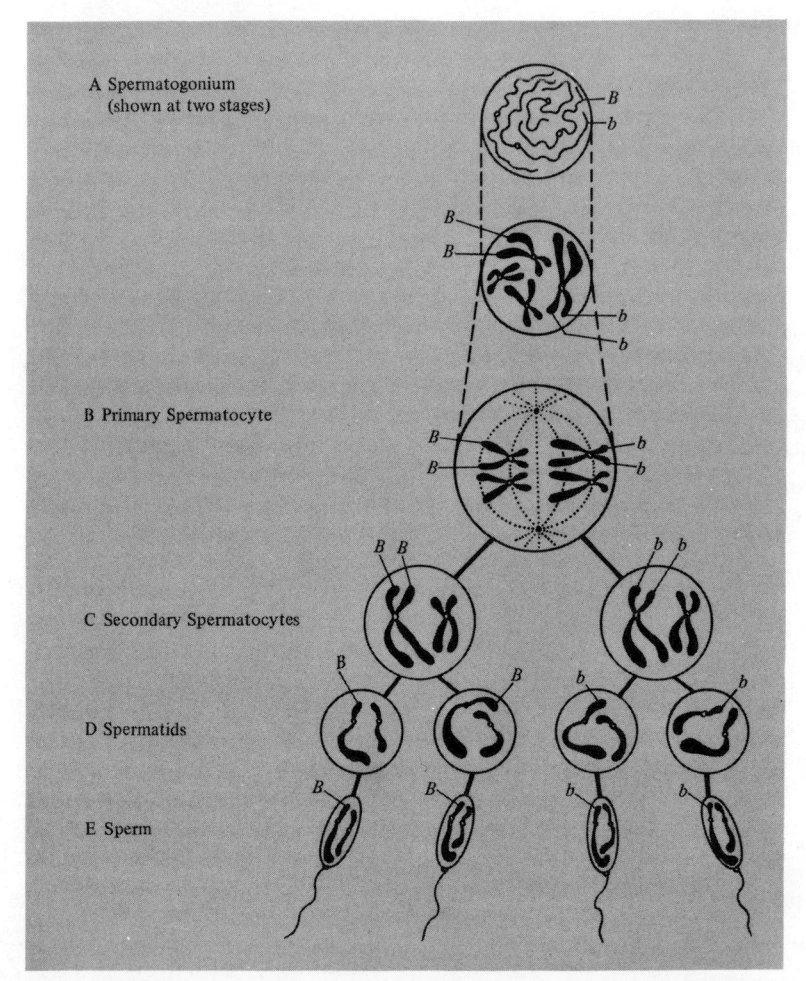

Figure 5-5. Meiosis provides the mechanism by which a heterozygous male produces sperm of two kinds: half of them containing the dominant gene, *B*, half of them containing its recessive allele, *b*.

Source: Adapted from P. A. Moody, *Genetics of Man*, Figure 3.7, p. 34. W. W. Norton, 1967.

In the same way, if one parent has two genes for any trait, each offspring will receive from that parent the same kind of genetic material as any other offspring. But if a parent has unlike genes for a trait, half of the offspring (other things being equal, which they often are not) will receive one kind of gene (e.g., the dominant gene) and half will receive the other. The process of meiosis explains part of the genetic difference between brothers and sisters, including the fact that a given father and mother are likely to have both sons and daughters.

Behavior Genetics

Not only are body form and coloration inherited from generation to generation, but different kinds of functioning are, also. The ability to roll the tongue is one of these functions. One of the authors of this book (MSS) can roll her tongue; RCS cannot. All three of their daughters can. Since this ability is known to be a dominant characteristic, we know that RCS is homozygous recessive. Some of our grandchildren may turn out to be like Grandpa. Our daughters are heterozygous for this characteristic. If their husbands are also heterozygous, we could predict that our grandchildren will be tongue-rollers in the ratio of 3:1.

(Incidentally, the genetic ratios hold only for large populations, not for small samples. Since we expect that the total number of our grandchildren will be six, they might all be tongue-rollers.)

The inheritance of certain defects in mental functioning can be described in terms of chromosomes [29]. Down's syndrome (Mongolism), a type of mental retardation accompanied by distinctive physical anomalies, occurs when an extra chromosome is attached to the chromosome numbered 21, making a total of 47 instead of the normal 46 chromosomes. Klinefelter's syndrome, incomplete sexual development along with lowered intelligence in males, involves two X chromosomes in addition to a Y. Turner's syndrome, in which females have only one X chromosome, includes defective spatial abilities. Males with an XXY condition are more likely than normals to be tall, aggressive, and mentally defective.

The transmission of all-or-none traits, such as tongue-rolling and Down's syndrome, can be explained by basic rules of genetics. When many genes are involved and when the characteristic is highly complex, such as intelligence or emotional stability, *heritability* is studied by *quantitative genetics*. Heritability of a characteristic can be estimated by comparing correlations between groups of known genetic similarity. Since the heredity of animals can be controlled, they can be used for experimental work in heredity. In working with humans, investigators have to use groups which vary in known degrees, from identical twins to unrelated persons. Results of many studies on inheritance of intelligence and personality indicate that there are indeed significant hereditary components in both [47].

Intelligence. Figure 5–6 shows median (average) sizes of correlations between measured intelligence of persons of different degrees of genetic similarity [13]. Unrelated persons living apart show no correlation (−.01). Identical twins reared together are very similar (.87). Identical twins reared apart are more closely correlated than those in any other relationship group (.75). Intelligence of parents and children correlates significantly (.50). Heredity components have been found in the following intellectual abilities, listed in order of weight of influence by heredity: word fluency, verbal ability (including spelling and grammar), spatial ability, clerical speed and accuracy, reasoning, number ability, and memory [47].

Personality. There is evidence for heritability of several dimensions of personality, the main ones of which are usual activity level; expression of emotions frankly in interpersonal relationships; degree of planning ahead rather than behaving impulsively [47]; extraversion–introversion [37].

Age Trends. Correlations between intelligence of children and parents are low negative in early infancy, zero at around a year, low positive at the end of the second year, and moderate (.5) in early childhood and thereafter [10]. This pattern is true of children and parents living apart, as well as of those living together. Correlations between stature of parents and children also increase throughout the early preschool years [16].

Sex Differences in Heritability. There is evidence that girls are controlled by heredity more than boys are, most likely because the X chromosome, of which girls have two and boys one, carries more hereditary material than does the Y

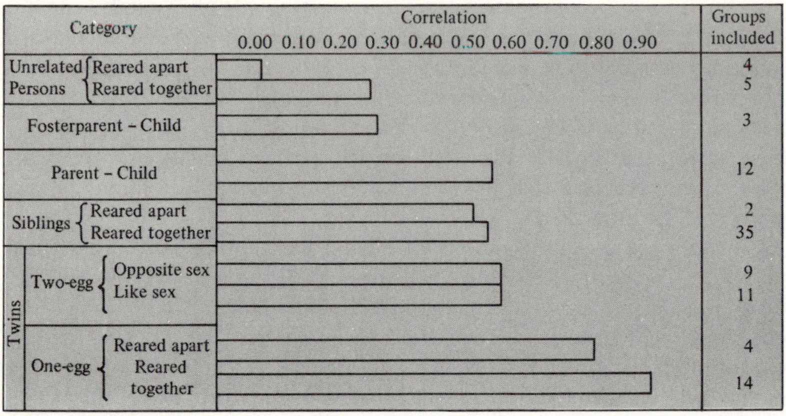

Category	Correlation 0.00–0.90	Groups included
Unrelated Persons — Reared apart		4
Unrelated Persons — Reared together		5
Fosterparent – Child		3
Parent – Child		12
Siblings — Reared apart		2
Siblings — Reared together		35
Twins, Two-egg — Opposite sex		9
Twins, Two-egg — Like sex		11
Twins, One-egg — Reared apart		4
Twins, One-egg — Reared together		14

Figure 5–6. Median correlation coefficients for intelligence test scores showing degree of similarity between performances of people of varying degrees of relatedness under different and similar environmental conditions.
SOURCE: Data from L. Erlenmeyer-Kimling and L. F. Jervik. *Science*, 1964, **142**, 1477–79.

chromosome. After age 13, measurements of stature correlate more highly for father–daughter than for father–son and for mother–daughter than for mother–son [17]. Data from the Berkeley Growth Study indicated that girls' intellectual functioning is more genetically determined than boys and that the impact of the environment is greater upon boys than upon girls [3]. High school boys and girls, studied by a twin control method, showed stronger heritability for girls than for boys on a battery of tests of achievements and aptitudes [25].

Summary

A baby, like all organisms, interacts continuously with his environment. He and his parents influence each other and change each other. Child development is described from different theoretical viewpoints, offering different ways of interpreting and understanding. Six types of interaction are described briefly in this chapter.

Equilibration is a process of regulation which the organism carries on in physical and intellectual modes. Homeostasis is the maintaining of the organism within certain physical limits such as those of chemical content and temperature. Psychological equilibrium involves regulating stimulation to an optimal level and also progressing toward more complex levels of mental organization. Piaget's notion of equilibration includes two complementary processes, accommodation and assimilation. Assimilation is the taking in and using of material from the environment; accommodation is changing the schemas to adjust to reality as it is experienced. Equilibration is enjoyable, as shown by children's curiosity and exploration, looking for problems and incongruities to be solved.

Growth and development, terms which can be used interchangeably, refer to increasing size and complexity of structure and function. The following principles or generalizations hold for many kinds of growth and development: variation in rates between individuals, between sexes, within the organism and of the organism in time; individuals differ in time of reaching maturity; measures of growth are interrelated; organisms behave as though they were seeking to achieve maximum

An Overview of Human Life and Growth 311

potential, searching for substitute sources of nurture when the usual ones are not available; specific patterns of behavior are differentiated out of larger, global patterns, and then specific patterns are integrated into larger, complex patterns; certain sequences of physical and motor development take place in directions (cephalo-caudal and proximo-distal) in relation to the body; certain behavior patterns mature in orderly sequences; growth is based on a foundation, the organism interacting with the environment to transform itself; critical periods are specific times when the organism will interact with the environment in specific ways which may be harmful or beneficial.

Stage theories, including Erikson's and Piaget's, explain development as proceeding epigenetically, being reorganized on more and more complex levels which occur in an orderly sequence. Erikson's psychosocial theory uses Freud's psychosexual stages as a base and develops a theory of the healthy personality. The eight stages of man's development involve the development of basic trust versus basic mistrust; autonomy versus doubt and shame; initiative versus guilt; industry versus inferiority; identity versus role diffusion; intimacy versus isolation; generativity versus self-absorption; ego integrity versus despair. Piaget shows how children develop intelligence in the process of dealing with the world and coming to know it. His sensorimotor period, spanning infancy, is subdivided into six stages. The preoperational period, from around 2 to 7, includes the stages of preconceptual and intuitive thought. The period of concrete operations comprises the school years, and the period of formal operations (logical thought), adolescence.

Learning is the change in behavior due to experience. Different methods of learning include classical conditioning, when a neutral stimulus becomes associated with a response due to pairing of the neutral stimulus with a stimulus which normally elicits the response; operant conditioning, when a response is established as a result of rewarding it, a method used widely for shaping behavior; verbal mediation, the use of words in problem solving or self-instruction; observational learning, a complex process of imitating some of the behavior of other people, according to the characteristics of the child himself, the stimulus, and the model. Reinforcement includes rewards and punishments, both of which operate in complex ways.

Maturation is the growth toward maturity of the body, its structures, and functions—growth which is relatively independent of experience. Most developmental processes involve both maturation and learning.

Evolutionary adaptation accounts for certain behavior patterns which mature quickly into a complex and relatively fixed form. The environment to which a species is adapted is the one in which it emerged in its present form. Attachment behavior in the human infant is most easily understood in terms of evolutionary adaptation.

Hereditary characteristics in human beings are sometimes the result of single pairs of genes, but often of numbers of genes working together. Most human beings carry several dangerous recessive genes, which will do no harm unless matched with the same dangerous genes from the partner in reproduction. Birth defects can be predicted on a chance basis, and some with certainty. An ovum contains an X chromosome, a sperm either an X or a Y. The source of sex differences is in the X and Y chromosomes, including differences in heritability, females being more influenced by heredity. These functions include intelligence and many of its components and also certain personality dimensions. Correlations

312 Preschool Children

between physical and mental measurements of parents and children increase during the preschool period.

References

1. Abernethy, E. M. Relationships between physical and mental growth. *Mono. Soc. Res. Child Devel.*, 1936, **1**:7.
2. Ainsworth, M. D. S. Object relations, dependency and attachment: A theoretical review of the infant–mother relationship. *Child Devel.*, 1969, **40**, 969–1025.
3. Bayley, N., & Schaefer, E. S. Correlations of maternal and child behaviors with the development of mental abilities: Data from the Berkeley growth study. *Mono. Soc. Res. Child Devel.*, 1964, **29**:6.
4. Bowlby, J. *Attachment and loss.* Vol. I: *Attachment.* London: Hogarth, 1969.
5. Bronfenbrenner, U. *Two worlds of childhood.* New York: Russell Sage Foundation, 1970.
6. Bühler, C. *The first year of life.* New York: Day, 1930.
7. Davis, C. M. Self-selection of diet by newly weaned infants. *Am. J. Dis. Child.*, 1928, **36**, 651–679.
8. Dennis, W. Causes of retardation among institutional children: Iran. *J. Genet. Psychol.*, 1960, **96**, 46–60.
9. Eibl-Eibesfeldt, I. Concepts of ethology and their significance in the study of human behavior. In H. W. Stevenson, E. H. Hess, & H. L. Rheingold (Eds.), *Early behavior.* New York: Wiley, 1967, pp. 127–146.
10. Eichorn, D. H. Developmental parallels in the growth of parents and their children. In *Newsletter of Division on Devel. Psychol.*, Washington, D. C.: American Psychological Association, Spring, 1970.
11. Erikson, E. H. *Childhood and society.* New York: Norton, 1963.
12. Erikson, E. H. *Identity, youth and crisis.* New York: Norton, 1968.
13. Erlenmeyer-Kiling, L. K., & Jarvik, L. F. Genetics and intelligence: A review. *Sci.*, 1964, **142**, 1477–1479.
14. Fantz, R. L. The origin of form perception. *Sci. Am.*, 1961, **204**, 66–72.
15. Freud, S. *The ego and the id.* New York: Norton, 1962.
16. Garn, S. M. Fat thickness and developmental status in childhood and adolescence. *J. Am. Medic. Assoc.*, 1960, **99**, 746–751.
17. Garn, S. M. Body size and its implications. In L. W. Hoffman & M. L. Hoffman (Eds.), *Review of child development research.* Vol. 2. New York: Russell Sage Foundation, 1966, pp. 529–561.
18. Gesell, A. *The embryology of behavior.* New York: Harper, 1945.
19. Gesell, A., & Thompson, H. *The psychology of early growth.* New York: Macmillan, 1938.
20. Halverson, H. M. An experimental study of prehension in infants by means of systematic cinema records. *Genet. Psychol. Mono.*, 1931, **10**, 107–286.
21. Havighurst, R. J. Minority subcultures and the law of effect. *Am. Psychol.*, 1970, **25**, 313–322.
22. Hunt, J. M., & Bayley, N. Explorations into patterns of mental development and prediction from the Bayley scales of infant development. Paper presented at the Fifth Minnesota Symposium on Child Psychology, Minneapolis, May 2, 1970.

23. Jones, M. C., & Mussen, P. H. Self-conceptions, motivations, and interpersonal attitudes of early- and late-maturing girls. *Child Devel.*, 1958, **29**, 492–501.
24. Ketcham, W. A. Relationship of physical and mental traits in intellectually gifted and mentally retarded boys. *Merrill-Palmer Quart.*, 1960, **6**, 171–177.
25. Klinger, R. Sex differences in heritability assessed by the Washington pre-college test battery of achievement/aptitude measures. Paper presented at the meeting of the Society for Research in Child Development, Santa Monica, Calif., March 27, 1969.
26. Lewis, M. The meaning of a response, or why researchers in infant behavior should be oriental metaphysicians. *Merrill-Palmer Quart.*, 1967, **13**, 7–18.
27. Lipsitt, L. P. Learning in the human infant. In H. W. Stevenson, E. H. Hess, & H. L. Rheingold (Eds.), *Early behavior.* New York: Wiley, 1967, pp. 225–247.
28. Lorenz, K. *King Solomon's ring.* New York: Crowell, 1952.
29. McClearn, G. E. Behavioral genetics: An overview. *Merrill-Palmer Quart.*, 1968, **14**, 9–24.
30. McGraw, M. B. Major challenges for students of infancy and early childhood. *Am. Psychol.*, 1970, **25**, 754–756.
31. Mussen, P. H., & Jones, M. C. The behavior-inferred motivations of late- and early-maturing boys. *Child Devel.*, 1958, **29**, 61–67.
32. Papoušek, H. Experimental studies of appetitional behavior in human newborns and infants. In H. W. Stevenson, E. H. Hess, & H. L. Rheingold (Eds.), *Early behavior.* New York: Wiley, 1967, pp. 249–277.
33. Parke, R. D. Effectiveness of punishment as an interaction of intensity, timing, age, nurturance and cognitive structuring. *Child Devel.*, 1969, **40**, 213–235.
34. Piaget, J. *Six psychological studies.* New York: Random House, 1967.
35. Piaget, J., & Inhelder, B. *The psychology of the child.* New York: Basic Books, 1969.
36. Sackett, G. P. Effects of rearing conditions upon the behavior of rhesus monkeys (Macca Mulatta). *Child Devel.*, 1965, **36**, 855–868.
37. Scarr, S. Social introversion-extraversion as a heritable response. *Child Devel.*, 1969, **40**, 823–832.
38. Scott, J. P. Early experience and the organization of behavior. Belmont, Calif.: Brooks/Cole. 1968.
39. Shuttleworth, F. K. The physical and mental growth of girls and boys age six to nineteen in relation to age at maximum growth. *Mono. Soc. Res. Child Devel.*, 1939, **4**:3.
40. Simon, M. D. Body configuration and school readiness. *Child Devel.*, 1959, **30**, 493–512.
41. Stevenson, H. W. Learning and reinforcement effects. In T. D. Spencer & N. Kass (Eds.), *Perspectives in child psychology.* New York: McGraw-Hill, 1970, pp. 325–355.
42. Stone, C. P., & Barker, R. G. Aspects of personality and intelligence in postmenarcheal and premenarcheal girls of the same chronological age. *J. Comp. Psychol.*, 1937, **23**, 439–455.
43. Sullivan, W. If we master the gene. *New York Times*, June 14, 1970.
44. Tanner, J. M. *Education and physical growth.* London: University of London Press, 1961.

45. Tanner, J. M. Relation of body size, intelligence test scores and social circumstances. In P. Mussen, J. Langer, & M. Covington (Eds.), *Trends and issues in developmental psychology.* New York: Holt, Rinehart and Winston, 1969.
46. Thorndike, E. L. *The elements of psychology.* New York: Seiler, 1905.
47. Vandenberg, S. G. Human behavior genetics: Present status and suggestions for future research. *Merrill-Palmer Quart.*, 1969, **15**, 121–154.
48. Walter, G. Comments in J. M. Tanner & B. Inhelder (Eds.), *Discussions on child development.* Vol. I. New York: International Universities, 1953.
49. Watson, J. S., & Ramey, C. T. Reactions to response-contingent stimulation in early infancy. Unpublished paper. University of California at Berkeley, 1970.

Readings in
An Overview of Human Life and Growth

In an earlier and possibly in some ways happier time, man was considered the final and triumphant item of creation, the master and user of other living things. Even the early evolutionary biologists considered that man stood at the apex of evolution; they did not seem aware of the possibility that the process of evolution might continue, resulting in the appearance of new species. They seemed even less aware of the possibility that the evolutionary process of man resulted in a creature who had within him the seeds of his own destruction, like the sabre-toothed tiger, whose overdeveloped canine teeth prevented him from ingesting his prey.

Ecology is the branch of biology which studies the relationship of living things to their environment, including other living things. Recently ecologists have included man as the subject of their study. In general the results of their investigations have been frightening. Especially in North America man is seen as a fouler of his environment—air, water, and soil—to such an extent that ecologists say that if present trends go unchecked, man may make his continued existence impossible.

In the first article in this chapter William W. Ballard, a biologist, describes some of the facts about man's evolutionary development and speculates about the future. He makes the important distinction between man as a species and men as individuals who together make up the species. Each individual has characteristics of the species which have arisen during the course of evolution, but each individual has his own personal history, during which he has learned some ways of behaving that may be, in the long run, maladaptive for the species.

Lawrence K. Frank, the author of the second article, gave form, direction, and impetus to the field of child development. Frank's genius provided a flow of ideas for research, education, and theory. He was responsible for establishing child development centers, the parent education movement, and interdisciplinary research. In the article presented here, Frank shows his characteristic warmth and wonder while analyzing the growth processes at work in infants. He shows how the child elaborates his individuality through interaction. In the terms used by Ballard in the first article, Frank shows how the "second computer" begins, based on the beginnings of the "first computer."

Erikson and Piaget, the authors of the third and fourth selections, are also primarily concerned with the development of the "second computer." But both are explicit in their statement that their theories are based on biology. Although both are dealing with psychological material, they start from biological characteristics of man.

The epigenetic theory of Erik H. Erikson is represented by the next essay, taken from his book Identity, Youth and Crisis. *An artist, teacher, and philosopher thoroughly* trained in Freudian psychoanalysis, Erikson has made enormous contributions to the field of child development. His theory is built upon Freudian theory, which he extends and develops into a way of understanding and describing the healthy personality throughout life. Erikson describes stages of personality growth, showing for each one a relation of personality to bodily development and to interaction with the culture. Each stage is derived from and built upon the one preceding it. The organization of this book is shaped by Erikson's stages in childhood and adolescence. The content is influenced by his thinking.

Jean Piaget, the world-famous Swiss psychologist, is the author of the fourth piece in this section. Piaget is primarily a genetic epistemologist, a scientist-philosopher who investigates the production of knowledge. He has developed a comprehensive theory of the mental structures through which human beings build their concept of reality and deal with it. Piaget has stimulated psychological research all over the world. Americans have produced hundreds of studies in response to his theories and findings. Like Erikson's theory of personality development, Piaget's account of the growth of intelligence is epigenetic and interactional. Piaget's theory is very compatible with a child development point of view, because the child's mind is seen as resulting from biologically given beginnings, actively engaged with the environment.

In the concluding selection in this chapter, Myrtle McGraw admonishes students of child development, particularly students of the development of very young children, that those who study growth need to be aware of the complexity and interrelatedness of their subject matter. To those who make applications of research knowledge about children she makes a plea for the careful consideration of terms, the continuous viewing of the child as a multifaceted organism, and the importance of adult guidance which changes synchronously with the child's development.

The Rise and Fall of Humanity

William W. Ballard

The reading which follows is the last part of a lecture titled "The Rise and Fall of Humanity." In the first part Ballard summarizes the development of living things during the course of 4 billion years of earth history, the accelerating growth of knowledge in the last few thousand years, and the serious threats to man's continued existence which have stemmed from this knowledge. Basically, Ballard says, the present crisis has arisen because there are too many people on the earth and they are demanding more than the earth can provide. These things have happened because man as a species of animal is composed of men as individuals.

To maximize the amount of life that can be supported in a given ecosystem, a large number of species of plants, animals and decomposers are brought into

Reprinted from *Dartmouth Alumni Magazine*, 1970, 62 (6), 60–64. By permission of the author, the Dartmouth Alumni College, and the *Dartmouth Alumni Magazine*.

balance, each occupying its own niche and following its own instructions to make the best of the things available to it while contributing to the flow of energy and the recycling of materials. If one species in the ecosystem gets out of balance the whole community develops an instability that may either result in an irreversible change in its character, or in the control or rejection of the destabilizing element.

The human species has been manipulating its environment since the invention of agriculture, favoring the plants and animals that serve it for food, repressing or even exterminating others. Where this was overdone—e.g., Mesopotamia, the Near East, Yucatan—ghost cities and records of dead cultures remain to show how powerfully nature can strike back. Quite recently we have begun to use the treasure trove of fossil fuels to grow the food to satisfy the multiplying demands of our own population, and we congratulate ourselves on having temporarily freed ourselves from the normal restrictions of the natural world. It is a dangerous game we are playing.

No good asking why the human *species* takes these risks. A species is an invention of the mind, a generalization. Only human *individuals* actually walk and breathe and make decisions and it is the collection of individuals who have been doing what I say the species has been doing. What went wrong with human individuals, that they have gotten their species and their environment into such a mess? The other face of this question is, what is an individual supposed to be doing, and within what limits is he supposed to be held?

The Primary Computer   To simplify, I shall restrict the latter question to animals rather than plants or decomposers. I shall pick animals that are not on a rampage, animals that have (so far as we can tell) no conscious reasoning ability, no thoughts, loyalties, hopes or faiths. Some kind of earthworm or some frog will do. I assume that whatever one of these animals does, any choice that it makes, is determined by its inherited computer system. It receives from its ancestors a scanning mechanism which reports what all the circumstances around and inside it are at the moment. This information is checked against an inherited memory encoded in its central nervous system. The computer then not only orders up the strategy and tactics that had met that sort of situation successfully before, but directs what every cell, what every organ, what the whole earthworm or frog must be doing to contribute to that response. (Directions for unsuccessful responses are not encoded in this primary computer, because they simply are not inherited.)

To see what this genetic computer requires the individual worm or frog to do, let us follow his life history, watching him obey and reconstructing from what he does the nature of the commands.

1. As a member of a bisexual species he (or she) starts as a fertilized egg, a single diploid individual with unique heterozygous genic individuality. First, *he develops*. Since the fertilized egg is insulated to a degree from the outside world, his computer works at first mostly on internal information. It refers to the inherited memory in the chromosomes and brings out instructions of various intricate sorts to the ultrastructures of the cell, programmed so that the cell divides into two, then four, then eight cells ... until the word gets back to the multiplied computers in the multiplied cells that it is time to activate their

inherited instructions for differentiation. Tissues and organs are formed, in such sorts and such patterns as have enabled the species to survive so far. The new individual acquires the sensory and neural apparatus for bringing in more and more information from the outside, and this is referred to the more and more specialized computer developing out of the inherited instructions, in a central nervous system (in the case of a frog, a brain and spinal cord). He begins to move about, respire, feed, excrete, defend himself, in directions and at rates calculated to be appropriate to the sensed state of affairs from moment to moment. This is quite a trick for a self-built computer to bring off, and as an embryologist I wish I understood more of how it is done.

2. The young earthworm or pollywog, having broken loose from its protective envelopes and used up its dowry of yolk, is next under orders to *reach adulthood*. He recognizes dangers and opportunities by continually referring the information flowing in from his sensory apparatus to his inherited memory. He certainly has not learned his behavioral responses from his parents, never having met them. It is the inherited computer which tells him what to do from one millisecond to the next. He survives or not, partly by luck but also partly according to whether his own inherited variant of the species-specific computer will deliver the right answers to the problems of his own day and place. (The *species* survives by offering up enough varieties so that some individuals will have what the new situations demand, the wastage of the other individuals being a necessary part of the cost. No other way has yet been discovered for meeting the demands of an unpredictable future, i.e. winning a game the rules for which have not yet been written.)

3. Our earthworm or frog, if lucky, finds himself a sexually mature individual, with his instructions to reproduce now turned on. These instructions, activated by seasonal or other environmental signals, operate upon particular genes, particular cells, particular organs, and particular behavioral mechanisms set off through the nervous system. Without knowing it, much less knowing why, the animal seeks out a mate, copulates, and shares in the production of fertilized eggs that bring us again to phase 1 of the cycle.

4. Having blindly and without thought followed his instructions to (1) develop, (2) make do, survive, gain strength, and (3) reproduce, our earthworm or frog subsequently (4) *dies*. It is the ancient law. So far as the interests of the individual are concerned, it is absurd.

But now how about man? How unique is he? Does he not learn by experience and education, manage his own life, consciously determine what jobs he shall tackle, what ends he shall serve? My argument that he too is run by an inherited computer program rests partly on the observed fact that (1) he develops, (2) he makes every effort to reach maturity, (3) if lucky enough he sets the cycle going again, and (4) he dies. There is nothing unique about that. Experience, learning, individual preferences serve only for minor embellishments.

I select one case to illustrate that an animal's program is mostly inherited. Four to six weeks after fertilization (depending on temperature) a salamander embryo will have used up its yolk and must by then have acquired an elaborate repertoire of locomotor, hunting-sensory, food-grabbing and swallowing behavior to keep itself fed and growing. Does the individual learn this behavior by trial and error? No. Starting a day before any of his muscles were mature enough to contract, you can rear him in a dilute anesthetic solution until he has reached the feeding stage. Put him back into pond water, and in twenty minutes the anesthetic will have worn off and he is swimming, hunting, grabbing and swallowing like a normal tadpole. One is seeing here the computer-controlled maturation of a computer-controlled behavior. No practice, no learning. The individual within which this remarkable apparatus matures is an expendable pawn, and the apparatus is not for his enjoyment of life, it is to keep the species going.

The Secondary Computer There is such an inherited program in the human individual, but there is much more. The baby does not so much learn to walk as to develop the inherited capacity to walk; but then he can learn a dance that no man has ever danced before, he can paint a picture with a brush clasped between his toes. During late fetal life and his first six or eight years he gradually matures a second computer system superimposed on, controlling and almost completely masking the ancient frog-type computer. The evolutionary history of this new device is traceable back to, and in some respects beyond, the time of origin of the modern mammals 70 million or more years ago. It has progressed farthest in particular mammalian orders—the carnivores, hoofed animals, bats, whales and primates, and least in the egg-laying mammals and marsupials.

The new trend has worked certain real advantages, and has been kept under reasonable control, in the higher mammals, but it is my strong suspicion that its over-development in man is the root of our trouble. Like the dinosaurs, we contain in our own structure the reason why we will have to go. Robinson Jeffers[1] said it: "We have minds like the fangs of those forgotten tigers, hypertrophied and terrible."

Up to a point, the development of brain and spinal cord follows the same course in frog and man. Sense organs, cranial and spinal nerves, principal subdivisions of the brain, basic fiber tract systems, all form in strictly comparable fashion in both. But the adult human brain is a far different thing from the adult frog brain. It continues the multiplication and interconnection of neurons during a far longer growth period, and adds to the elementary or frog-type apparatus two principal complicating tissues that far overshadow the earlier developments. One is often called reticular substance, the other is the cerebral cortex.

The reticular substance is so called because it is an interweaving of small centers of gray substance with short bundles and interspersed mats of axons (the white substance), quite different from the simple contrast between gray and white substance seen in primitive animals and in early embryos. The frog brain is not without this sort of tissue, but in the brains of advanced vertebrates like the teleost fishes, the reptiles and the birds, it becomes indescribably complex. The modern mammals push this development to still higher orders of magnitude.

Although neurological science is not yet ready with answers to most specific questions about what happens where in the central nervous system, the

[1] R. Jeffers, "Passenger Pigeons," in *The Beginning and the End.*

new techniques of exploration within the brain suggest that in and through the reticular substance the connections for integrating sensory information with the devices for evaluation and for making decisions and coordinated responses are multiplied exponentially.

Thus, an electrode planted within a single neuron in the reticular substance of the hindbrain can give startling evidence that this one cell is receiving and reacting to sensations reported from widely scattered parts of the body, and sending out coded pulses as a calculated response. Your own brain contains hundreds of millions, probably billions of such cells, every one individually a computer.

The neurologists can now stimulate chosen localized areas through implanted electrodes, either hooked up to wires dangling from the cage ceiling or activated through miniaturized transmitters healed in under the scalp and controlled by radio transmission. In such experiments, stimuli delivered to many parts of the reticular substance cause the animal to react as though he were flooded with agreeable sensation. If the cat or rat or monkey learns how to deliver the stimulus to himself by pressing a pedal, he will do so repeatedly and rapidly, until he falls asleep exhausted. As soon as he wakes up, he goes to pounding the pedal again.

There are other reticular areas which have the reverse effect. If the stimulus comes at rhythmical intervals and the animal discovers that he can forestall it by pressing the pedal, he quickly learns to regulate his life so as to be there and step on it just in time. What kind of sensation such a stimulus produces in him can only be guessed by the experimenter. One might suppose that these areas of reticular substance which have such opposite effects are there to add into the computer's analysis of the situation at the moment a go signal or a stop signal for particular alternative choices, or a sense of goodness or badness, satisfaction or distress, urgency or caution, danger or relaxation. A value judgment, in other words.

It is not difficult to see the survival value of such a device. No doubt the basic mechanism exists in the brains of fishes and frogs, though I am not aware that experiments have been done to locate it. In the reticular substance of mammals, however, we see it hugely developed. The result of overdoing this might produce an awareness of the good and bad features of so very many facets of a situation as to delay and perplex the individual in calculating his single coordinated response.

Mammals are also conspicuously good at remembering experiences from their own lives as individuals, and these memories are loaded with value judgments. There is still no clear answer as to where or in what coded form these new personal memories are stored. But an animal with all this added to the ancestral memory, enhanced with perhaps casually acquired and unwisely generalized connotations of goodness and badness, might predictably be endowed with excessive individuality, prone to unnecessarily variable behavior, chosen more often for self-satisfaction than in the interest of species survival.

The other evolutionary development, the formation of the cerebral cortex, is almost unknown in vertebrates other than mammals, and is feeble in some of these. Cerebral cortex is a tissue of awesome complexity, and our techniques for analyzing what happens in it are still highly inadequate. Stimulation of willing human subjects, in chosen spots exposed surgically, or radio stimulation of these areas through permanently installed electrodes operated by healed-in transistor devices, evoke feelings referred to a particular part of the body, or cause normal-appearing localized movements, e.g. the flexion of an arm or a finger, time and again, upon repetition of the signal. Other areas produce more generalized sensory or motor or emotional or physiologic effects. The patient, his brain exposed under local anesthesia, does not know when the stimulus is applied. When the electrode touches a particular spot of his cortex he may report that he is suddenly remembering a scene identifiable as to time and place, but the memory blacks out when the current is off. Stimulation of other areas may elicit emotions of sexual attraction or anxiety or rage graded according to the intensity of the signal.

More wide-ranging experiments with cats, monkeys or barnyard stock, singly or in groups, free to move in large caged areas, show the possibility of turning on and off a great range of complex emotions, behavior, and even personality traits, by local stimulation.[2] The effect produced through a permanently planted electrode is area specific. Though not predictable before the first stimulus is given, the response is repeated with each stimulus, many times a day or over periods of months or years.

In subjective comparison of mammals with greater or less personal individuality one gets the impression that the degrees of freedom of choice, of imaginative recognition of possible ways to react to situations, of storage capacity and retentiveness of memory, and the richness of association, are correlated with the intricacy and amount of the cerebral cortex and reticular substance. Animals highest on both scales include porpoises, elephants, cats and dogs, apes, and people.

One cannot underestimate the effects on the human species of other evolutionary trends that came to a climax in us, for instance the development of upright posture that frees the hands, the reshaping of the fingers for grasping and manipulating, the perfection of binocular vision that can bring into focus either the hands or the far distance at will. Far more significant than these was the development of speech, made possible by and controlled in a particular small area of the new cerebral cortex. This expanded the powers of the human secondary computer by orders of magnitude, even in comparison with that of close relatives like apes.

We no longer communicate with each other by baring teeth, raising hackles and flaunting rumps, but in symbolic language. We can make abstractions and generalizations and artificial associations. Through speech we can feed into the recording apparatus of each other's secondary computers not only the vast and rather accidental store of individually acquired and long-lasting memories of our own experience, but also the loads of approval or disapproval which we deliberately or unwittingly put upon them. We increasingly remove ourselves into created worlds of our own, calculating our choices by reference to a memory bank of second-hand ghosts of other people's experiences and feelings, prettied up or uglified with value judgments picked up who knows where, by whom, for what reason.

[2] J. M. R. Delgado, 1969, *Physical Control of the Mind*.

Language gave a fourth dimension to the powers of the secondary computer, and writing a fifth dimension. We can now convince each other that things are good or bad, acceptable or intolerable, merely by agreeing with each other, or by reciting catechisms. With writing we can color the judgments of people unborn, just as our judgments are tailored to the whim of influential teachers in the past.

Symbols have given us the means to attach a value judgment to some abstract noun, some shibboleth, and transfer this by association to any person or situation at will. We invent, we practice, we delight in tricks for saying things indirectly by poetry and figures of speech, that might sound false or trite or slanderous or nonsensical if we said them directly. A more normally constructed animal, a porpoise or an elephant, mercifully spared such subtleties, might well look at human beings and see that each one of us has become to some degree insane, out of touch with the actual world, pursuing a mad course of options in the imagined interest of self rather than of species.

The primary computer is still there, programmed in the interest of species survival. With his new powers, man should do better than any other animal at understanding the present crisis and generating an appropriate strategy and tactics. Instead, the effort is drowned out in the noise, the flicker-bicker, the chattering flood of directives from the personalized secondary computer. In pursuit of his own comfort and his own pleasure, man wars against his fellows and against the good earth.

The frame of each person is like a racing shell with two oarsmen in it, back to back, rowing in opposite directions. The one represents the ancient computer system, comparing the personal situation of the moment with an inherited value system and driving the person to perform in such a way that the species will survive, irrespective of how absurd his own expendable life may be. The other represents the secondary computer system, probably located in reticular substance and cerebral cortex, surveying chiefly the memories of childhood and adult life, and deciding how to act according to the value-loaded store of personal experience.

It is this runaway evolutionary development of our superimposed second computer that has produced our inventors, our artists, our saints and heroes, our poets, our thinkers. Our love and hate, ecstasy and despair. The infinite variety of human personalities. It has also atomized the species into a cloud of ungovernable individuals. We split our elections 48 to 52, make laws to break them, and either ignore community priorities or establish them by political blind-man's-buff in frivolous disregard of real emergencies. Six experts will come violently to six different decisions on how to meet a crisis because their personal histories lead them to weight the same data differently. Each of us can see bad logic and conflicts of interest affecting the judgment of most of our associates; it is more difficult to detect them in ourselves. Our individually acquired prejudices have been built into our secondary computers.

Yet it is a glorious thing to feel the uniqueness, the power of decision, the freedom of being human. Who would prefer to be even so wonderful a creature as a dog, an elephant, a horse, a porpoise? I believe nevertheless that just this ungovernable power of the human individual, the essence of our humanity, is the root of our trouble.

The California biologist Garrett Hardin, in a famous essay called "The Tragedy of the Commons," showed that this accounts for practically all the facets of our apocalyptic crisis, from the population explosion to runaway technology.[3] He is referring to the community pasture where anyone may feed his animals. Overgrazing will bring erosion and irreversible deterioration in it. Each herdsman, calculating the advantage and disadvantage to himself of putting out one more animal to graze, balancing his small share of the possible damage against his sole ownership of the extra income, adds another animal in his own interest, and another, and another. All do, and all lose together. The tragedy is the inescapable disaster when each herdsman pursues his own advantage without limit, in a limited commons. This is the tragedy that leaves us with too many human mouths to feed, soil impoverished and washed or blown away, forests skinned off, lakes ruined, plastic bottles and aluminum cans scattered over the countryside, rivers clogged with dead fish, bilge oil spreading on public waters, streets and highways made obscene with advertisements. It is what gives us choking smog, the stink and corruption below paper mills and slaughter houses, the draining of one well by another in a falling water table, the sneaking of radioactive wastes into the air and the oceans.

All these, Hardin makes clear, are problems with *no technological solution.* To be sure, the technology stands ready, but the trouble starts with some individual, you, me, whose response to a situation is to give highest priority to his personal chance of profit, or his family's, or his country's. He has a vivid sense of the value to himself of his own freedom, but the total effects of all such freedoms on the species and on the natural world which supports it is invisible or far out of focus. The technology might just as well not exist.

Some of these problems that will not be solved by technology alone can indeed be brought under control by compacts, treaties, and other agreements between willing groups, or by laws imposed by the majority upon a minority in the common interest. Hardin, however, puts the finger on the population problem as the worst example of the worst class of problems, in which all of us must restrict the freedom of all of us, when none of us want to. He is properly skeptical of conscience or altruism as forces for uniting the community when nearly all of us are still daring to gamble on the continued capacity of the commons to withstand collapse. What is needed, he says, is a fundamental extension of morality.

My way of agreeing with him is to say that human nature is our chief enemy because the species-preserving function of our primary computer has not yet been built into the secondary computer which generates our human nature. It is by now clear that our nature as individuals is not so much inherited as learned by babies as they grow into people, in and from their individual, accidental and culture-bound experiences. We need to incorporate into the decision-making apparatus that will really control them a new survival morality, a system of values the principal axiom of which is that anything which threatens the welfare of the species is bad, anything that serves to bring the species into harmony with its environment is good. We must, each of us, because of this inner drive, regulate our numbers and our selfish wants as rigorously as the

---

[3] G. Hardin, 1968, *Science* 162: 1243. The Tragedy of the Commons.

forces of natural selection would have done had we not learned how to set them aside.

Do we know how to create a human nature that can keep the species going without undue sacrifice of the privilege and joy of being human? How much freedom must we give up? Do we want to? Is there time?

Basic Processes in Organisms

Lawrence K. Frank

If we are to understand the infant as a persistent, but ever changing, organism, we need to think in terms that are dynamic, which calls for a recognition of the ongoing processes by which the infant grows, develops, matures and ages while continually functioning and behaving. As a young mammalian organism, the human infant lives by much the same basic physiological processes as other mammals.

The recognition of process has come with the acceptance of such recently formulated conceptions as that of self-organization, self-stabilization, self-repair and self-direction which are characteristic not only of organisms but of various man-made machines such as computers and systems designed to operate a planned sequence of activities with the use of positive and negative feedbacks. (Wiener 1961; Von Foerster and Zopf 1962). The organism may be said to be "programmed" by its heredity but capable of flexible functioning through the life cycle.

Moreover, it must be re-emphasized that each infant differs to a greater or lesser extent from all other infants, exhibiting not only individual variation but also displaying a considerable range of intra-individual variability, or continually changing functioning and physiological states, especially during the early months of life when the infant is not yet fully organized or capable of adequate self-stabilization.

Since most of our knowledge of infancy and childhood is derived from observations and measurements of selected variables, responses to stimuli, at a given time or a succession of times, we do not gain an adequate conception of the continuous, dynamic processes of living organisms, especially since we tend to focus upon the outcomes, without recognizing the processes which produce them. Accordingly, some account of these basic processes and how they operate may provide a conceptual model for understanding the multidimensional development of infants during the first year of life. Whatever is done to and for the infant, what privations, frustrations and deprivations he may suffer, what demands and coercions he must accept, what spontaneous activity and learning he displays, may be viewed as expressions of his basic functioning processes.

Every experience in the life of an infant evokes some alteration in these

From *The Importance of Infancy*, by Lawrence K. Frank. Copyright © 1966 by Random House, Inc. Reprinted by permission.

organic processes whereby he manages not only to survive but to grow and develop, to learn while carrying on his incessant intercourse with the surrounding world. Thus, by focusing on the organic processes we may discover what is taking place when we speak of adjustment, learning, adaptation, and the transitions encountered at critical stages in his development.

The concept of mechanism indicates or implies a deterministic relationship between antecedent and consequent, usually as a *linear* relationship in which the consequent is proportional to the antecedent. The concept of *process* involves a dynamic, *non-linear* operation, whereby the same process, depending upon where, when, how, and in what quantities or intensities it operates, may produce different products which may be all out of proportion to that which initiates or touches off the process. For example the process of fertilization and gestation operates in all mammals to produce the immense variety of mammalian young. But different processes may produce similar or equivalent products, an operation which has been called "equifinality" by Bertalanffy (1950).

A brief discussion of the six basic processes operating in organisms will indicate how the infant organism is able to persist and survive by continually changing and is thereby able to cope with the particular version of infant care and rearing to which he is subjected.

These six processes are: The Growth Process, The Organizing Process, The Communicating Process, The Stabilizing Process, The Directive or Purposive Process and The Creative Process. (Frank 1963.)

The Growth Process   The infant who has been growing since conception continues, with a brief interruption and often some loss of weight, to grow incrementally, adding gradually to his size and weight. His growth may be slowed down by inadequate or inappropriate feeding, by some difficulties in digesting and assimilating whatever foodstuff he be given, or by a variety of disturbances and dysfunctions. A continuing upward trend in weight is expected as an expression of normal development, although recent cautions have been expressed on the undesirability of too rapid increase in weight and the vulnerability of a fat, waterlogged infant.

This incremental growth in size and weight indicates that the infant is maintaining an excess of growth over the daily losses through elimination of urine and feces, through skin and lungs, and also in the replacement of many cells that are discarded. Thus, millions of blood corpuscles are destroyed and replaced each day, the iron of those destroyed being salvaged and reused. Likewise, cells of the skin and lining of the gastrointestinal tract, of the lungs, kidneys, liver, indeed of almost all organ systems, except the central nervous system and brain, are continually being replaced at different rates.

Probably more vitally significant but less clearly recognized is the continual replacement of the chemical constituents of cells, tissues and bony structures, like the skeleton and the teeth in which different chemicals are discarded and new materials are selected out of the blood stream to replace them. Here we see a dramatic illustration of the statement that an organism is a configuration which must continually change in order to survive, a conception which is wholly congruous with the recently formulated assumption of the world as an aggregate of highly organized complexes of energy transformations.

Growth, incremental and replacement, is a major functioning process, gradually producing an enlarging infant as the growing cells differentiate, specialize and organize to give rise to the varied tissues and organ systems in the developing embryo and fetus. In this prenatal development the creative process is also operating to produce the unique, unduplicated human infant along with the operation of the organizing process.

The Organizing Process   Only recently has the process of self-organization been recognized in scientific thinking as basic to all organisms which start with some kind of genetic inheritance and undergo multiplication and duplication of cells with differentiation and specialization of components that become organized into a living organism. (Von Foerster and Zopf 1962.) Thus the initial development of an infant takes place through the operation of the growth and the organizing processes which continue to operate throughout its life, maintaining the organism as it undergoes various transitions and transformations and copes with the many discontinuities encountered in its life cycle.

Since the normal infant arrives fully equipped with all the essential bodily components and organ systems, the growth process and the organizing process operate to incorporate the intakes of food, water and air into its ever changing structure-functioning. Most of the highly organized foodstuffs, proteins, fats and carbohydrates, are progressively broken down, disorganized and randomized, and the products of these digestive operations are then circulated through the blood stream from which the constituent cells, tissues and fluids select out what they need for metabolism and organize these into their specialized structure-functioning components. The recent dramatic findings in molecular biology show how this organizing process operates within the cell as the DNA (the carrier of the genetic information) of the genes directs the production of the various proteins and the utilization of the minerals and vitamins for the growth and multiplication of cells and the maintenance of their functioning.

Also of large significance for the understanding of organic processes are the sequential steps in the utilization of food stuffs for metabolism involving many steps and numerous specialized enzymes and catalysts. Unfortunately some infants suffer from so-called metabolic errors when one or more of these steps in the metabolic sequence is missing or inadequate and therefore his growth and development and healthy functioning are jeopardized.

In the self-organizing organism we encounter circular and reciprocal operations in which every component of the organism by its specialized functioning, gives rise to, and maintains, the total organism of which it is a participant; concurrently, the total organism reciprocally governs when, what and how each of these components must function and operate to maintain the organized whole. This capacity for self-organizing arises from the autonomy of each component of an organism which over millions of years of evolution has developed its own highly individualized and specialized functioning within the total organic complex but functions according to the requirements of the organism in which it operates.

Communication Process   Obviously, these autonomous components which give rise to growth and organization must continually communicate, internally and with the external "surround." The infant has an inherited communication network in his nervous system, his circulatory system, and his lymphatic system. Through these several channels every constituent of an organism continually communicates with all others, directly or indirectly, and with different degrees of speed in communication. Each component continually sends and receives messages whereby its functioning operations are regulated, synchronized, articulated and related to all others, with greater or less immediacy. The infant is born with most of these internal communications already functioning, having been in operation for varying periods of its prenatal development but with the central nervous system still immature. The infant also has the sensory apparatus for various inputs, of light, of sound, touch, taste and smell, also for pain, heat and cold, and for gravity and for atmospheric pressure changes. But the infant is also initially prepared for dealing with the varying intensities and durations of these intakes and impacts, gradually increasing his capacity for filtering, buffering, mingling and transducing these inputs whereby he may monitor these sensory communications according to his ever changing internal, physiological states and the kinesthetic and proprioceptive messages by which he continually orients himself and gradually achieves an equilibrium in space.

The infant must carry on this incessant intercourse with the world more or less protected by adults from too severe or hazardous impacts and provided with the food and care required by his helpless dependency. But the infant often must try to defend himself from what his caretakers try to impose on him or compel him to accept, as in feeding, toilet training, etc. Under this treatment much of the infant's energies may be expended in these efforts to maintain his stability and integrity against unwelcomed and uncongenial treatment which may interfere with his normal functioning and compromise his growth and development and learning as a unique organism. Thus we may say that the growth and organizing processes contribute to and are dependent upon the communication process, which operates through the inherited receptors of the infant which may become progressively altered, refined, and increasingly sensitized through learning. Quite early the infant may become receptive to nonverbal communications such as tones of voice, smiling, tactile comforting, or painful treatment.

Stabilizing Process   Since the world presents so many different and continually varying messages and impacts, organisms must be able to cope with the ever changing flux of experience and maintain their integrity and functional capacities by monitoring all their organic functions. While all other organisms have evolved with their species-specific range of sensory awareness and capacity for perception and for living in their ancestral life zones, the human infant, and a few other mammals are able to live in a wide variety of climates and habitations and maintain their internal world within fairly close limitations upon intra-organic variability. This becomes possible through the operation of the stabilizing process.

The stabilizing process operates through a network of physiological feedbacks, both negative and positive, to maintain a dynamic equilibrium and is not limited to the concept of homeostasis which Cannon used to describe the maintenance of the fluid internal environment. The stabilizing process maintains continually changing physiological states. At birth it is not fully developed or operationally effective and hence the infant needs continual care, protection, and appropriate nutrition. But as he grows and develops he increasingly regulates his internal functioning by responding appropriately to the various inputs and outputs, intakes, and outlets. Obviously an infant who must grow, both incrementally and by replacement, cannot tolerate too stable an internal environment which might prevent or limit such growth and adaptive functioning. With his increasing exposure to the world the infant learns to calibrate all his sensory inputs and increasingly to "equalize his thresholds," as Kurt Goldstein (1939) has pointed out.

Not the least significant and often stressful experience under which an infant must maintain his internal stability are the varying practices of child care and feeding, the efforts of parents to regularize his functioning and compel him to conform to whatever regimen of living they wish to establish. Clearly the stabilizing process is essential to the infant's survival and to his continuing growth and development and the variety of learning which he must master. Happily, most infants achieve a progressive enlargement of their capacity for living and for self-regulation and self-stabilization to assume an autonomy expressing their integrity in the face of often uncongenial treatment and surroundings.

The Directive or Purposive Process With the achievement of motor coordination and locomotion, by creeping and crawling, and then assuming an erect posture and learning to walk, the infant enlarges the purposive or goal seeking process which involves continual scanning, probing and exploring the world and developing his selective awareness and patterned perception, and especially the ability to ignore or to reject what may interfere or distract him in his endeavor to attain remote or deferred goals. Obviously, the purposive process cannot operate effectively until the infant has achieved a considerable degree of internal stabilization and of neuro-muscular coordination, and the ability to cope with a three dimensional, spatial world.

Since the child initially is attracted or impelled by whatever he may become aware of or has an impulse to seek, to handle, to put into his mouth, or otherwise to manipulate, the purposive process is frequently blocked and the child may be severely punished in his attempts to develop his autonomous mastery of his small world. Thus the purposive process operates differentially in each infant who is likely to be attracted by and responsive to different dimensions of his environment at different times; these early explorations provide an endless sequence of learning experiences which involve, not only the actual world of nature, but the wide range of artifacts and of highly individuated personalities with whom he is in contact. With language the infant learns to deal with people and verbal symbols of language for goal seeking.

The Creative Process As noted earlier, the creative process begins to operate early in gestation to produce a unique infant as a human organism with the same basic organic functions and similar or equivalent components which, however, are different in each infant. From birth on, therefore, each infant is engaged in creating a highly selective environment or a "life space" that is as congenial and appropriate for his individualized organism, with its peculiar needs and capacities, as is possible under the constraints and coercions imposed by others upon his growth, development, functioning, and learning. In infancy and childhood the individual is more creative than in any other period in his life cycle, but this creativity may be either ignored or discouraged by those who are intent upon making the child conform as nearly as possible to their image or ideal of attainment.

Within recent years the purposive and creative processes have become major foci in the studies of early child growth, development and education, but it must be remembered that the purposive and creative processes cannot operate independently because they are inextricably related to and dependent upon the other four basic processes which reciprocally contribute to the operation of these two processes.

Most of the training and education of the infant and young child involves curbing, regulating, focusing, and patterning, and also evoking the communicating and stabilizing and directive processes which are more amenable to intervention and control by others. Through supervision and regulation of these processes the child is largely molded, patterned, and oriented into the kind of organism-personality favored by his parents and appropriately prepared for living in his cultural and social order. As he grows older the infant is expected to learn the required conduct for group living and to master the various symbol systems by which he can relate cognitively to the world and negotiate with other people. It appears that learning as an expression of the purposive and the creative processes may be compromised and sometimes severely distorted or blocked when the child is expected or compelled to alter the organizing, communicating, and stabilizing processes, as required by his parents and other more experienced persons.

In the discussion of humanization we will see how the young mammalian organism is transformed into a personality for living in a symbolic cultural world and for participating in a social order, through the various practices of infant care and rearing that are focused upon, and directly intervene in, the operation of these six basic organic processes. But each infant is a highly individualized organism who develops his own idiosyncratic personality through the development and utilization of his basic organic processes.

Bibliography

BERTALANFFY, L. VON, "Theory of Open Systems in Physics and Biology," *Science*, CXI, 1950, pp. 27–29. See also Yearbooks of Society for General Systems Research.

FRANK, L. K., "Human Development—An Emerging Discipline," in *Modern Perspectives in Child Development*, In honor of Milton J. E. Senn, Eds. Albert J. Solnit and Sally Provence, New York: International Universities Press, 1963.

―――. "Potentiality: Its Definition and Development," in *Insights and the Curriculum*, Yearbook, Association for Supervision and Curriculum Development, Washington, D.C.: National Education Association, 1963.

GOLDSTEIN, KURT, *The Organism*, New York: American Book Company, 1939.

VON FOERSTER, HEINZ, and ZOPF, JR., GEORGE W., Eds., *Principles of Self Organizing Systems*, London: Pergamon Press, 1962.

WIENER, NORBERT, *Cybernetics*, Cambridge and New York: M.I.T. Press and John Wiley and Sons, Inc., 1961.

The Life Cycle: Epigenesis of Identity

Erik H. Erikson
HARVARD UNIVERSITY

Whenever we try to understand growth, it is well to remember the *epigenetic principle* which is derived from the growth of organisms *in utero*. Somewhat generalized, this principle states that anything that grows has a ground plan, and that out of this ground plan the parts arise, each part having its time of special ascendancy, until all parts have arisen to form a functioning whole. This, obviously, is true for fetal development where each part of the organism has its critical time of ascendance or danger of defect. At birth the baby leaves the chemical exchange of the womb for the social exchange system of his society, where his gradually increasing capacities meet the opportunities and limitations of his culture. How the maturing organism continues to unfold, not by developing new organs but by means of a prescribed sequence of locomotor, sensory, and social capacities, is described in the child-development literature. As pointed out, psychoanalysis has given us an understanding of the more idiosyncratic experiences, and especially the inner conflicts, which constitute the manner in which an individual becomes a distinct personality. But here, too, it is important to realize that in the sequence of his most personal experiences the healthy child, given a reasonable amount of proper guidance, can be trusted to obey inner laws of development, laws which create a succession of potentialities for significant interaction with those persons who tend and respond to him and those institutions which are ready for him. While such interaction varies from culture to culture, it must remain within "the proper rate and the proper sequence" which governs all epigenesis. Personality, therefore, can be said to develop according to steps predetermined in the human organism's readiness to be driven toward, to be aware of, and to interact with a widening radius of significant individuals and institutions.

It is for this reason that, in the presentation of stages in the development of the personality, we employ an epigenetic diagram analogous to the one employed in *Childhood and Society* for an analysis of Freud's psychosexual stages.[1] It is, in fact, an implicit purpose of this presentation to bridge the theory of infantile sexuality (without repeating it here in detail) and our knowledge of the child's physical and social growth.

In Diagram 1 the double-lined squares signify both a sequence of stages and a gradual development of component parts. In other words, the diagram formalizes a progression through time of a differentiation of parts. This indicates (1) that each item of the vital personality to be discussed is systematically related to all others, and that they all depend on the proper development in the proper sequence of each item; and (2) that each item exists in some form before "its" decisive and critical time normally arrives.

Reprinted from *Identity, Youth and Crisis*, Copyright © 1968 by W. W. Norton & Company, Inc., pp. 92–96. By permission.

[1] See Erik H. Erikson, *Childhood and Society*, 2nd ed., New York: W. W. Norton, 1963, Part I.

DIAGRAM 1

	1	2	3	4	5	6	7	8
VIII								Integrity vs. Despair
VII							Generativity vs. Stagnation	
VI						Intimacy vs. Isolation		
V	Temporal Perspective vs. Time Confusion	Self-Certainty vs. Self-Consciousness	Role Experimentation vs. Role Fixation	Apprenticeship vs. Work Paralysis	Identity vs. Identity Confusion	Sexual Polarization vs. Bisexual Confusion	Leader- and Followership vs. Authority Confusion	Ideological Commitment vs. Confusion of Values
IV				Industry vs. Inferiority	Task Identification vs. Sense of Futility			
III			Initiative vs. Guilt		Anticipation of Roles vs. Role Inhibition			
II		Autonomy vs. Shame, Doubt			Will to Be Oneself vs. Self-Doubt			
I	Trust vs. Mistrust				Mutual Recognition vs. Autistic Isolation			

331

If I say, for example, that a sense of basic trust is the first component of mental vitality to develop in life, a sense of autonomous will the second, and a sense of initiative the third, the diagram expresses a number of fundamental relations that exist among the three components, as well as a few fundamental facts for each.

Each comes to its ascendance, meets its crisis, and finds its lasting solution in ways to be described here, toward the end of the stages mentioned. All of them exist in the beginning in some form, although we do not make a point of this fact, and we shall not confuse things by calling these components different names at earlier or later stages. A baby may show something like "autonomy" from the beginning, for example, in the particular way in which he angrily tries to wriggle his hand free when tightly held. However, under normal conditions, it is not until the second year that he begins to experience the whole critical alternative between being an autonomous creature and being a dependent one, and it is not until then that he is ready for a specifically new encounter with his environment. The environment, in turn, now feels called upon to convey to him its particular ideas and concepts of autonomy in ways decisively contributing to his personal character, his relative efficiency, and the strength of his vitality.

It is this encounter, together with the resulting crisis, which is to be described for each stage. Each stage becomes a crisis because incipient growth and awareness in a new part function go together with a shift in instinctual energy and yet also cause a specific vulnerability in that part. One of the most difficult questions to decide, therefore, is whether or not a child at a given stage is weak or strong. Perhaps it would be best to say that he is always vulnerable in some respects and completely oblivious and insensitive in others, but that at the same time he is unbelievably persistent in the same respects in which he is vulnerable. It must be added that the baby's weakness gives him power; out of his very dependence and weakness he makes signs to which his environment, if it is guided well by a responsiveness combining "instinctive" and traditional patterns, is peculiarly sensitive. A baby's presence exerts a consistent and persistent domination over the outer and inner lives of every member of a household. Because these members must reorient themselves to accommodate his presence, they must also grow as individuals and as a group. It is as true to say that babies control and bring up their families as it is to say the converse. A family can bring up a baby only by being brought up by him. His growth consists of a series of challenges to them to serve his newly developing potentialities for social interaction.

Each successive step, then, is a potential crisis because of a radical change in perspective. Crisis is used here in a developmental sense to connote not a threat of catastrophe, but a turning point, a crucial period of increased vulnerability and heightened potential, and therefore, the ontogenetic source of generational strength and maladjustment. The most radical change of all, from intrauterine to extrauterine life, comes at the very beginning of life. But in postnatal existence, too, such radical adjustments of perspective as lying relaxed, sitting firmly, and running fast must all be accomplished in their own good time. With them, the interpersonal perspective also changes rapidly and often radically, as is testified by the proximity in time of such opposites as "not letting mother out of sight" and "wanting to be independent." Thus, different capacities use different opportunities to become full-grown components of the ever-new configuration that is the growing personality.

Equilibrium

Jean Piaget
UNIVERSITY OF GENEVA

The psychological development that starts at birth and terminates in adulthood is comparable to organic growth. Like the latter, it consists essentially of activity directed toward equilibrium. Just as the body evolves toward a relatively stable level characterized by the completion of the growth process and by organ maturity, so mental life can be conceived as evolving toward a final form of equilibrium represented by the adult mind. In a sense, development is a progressive equilibration from a lesser to a higher state of equilibrium. From the point of view of intelligence, it is easy to contrast the relative instability and incoherence of childhood ideas with the systematization of adult reason. With respect to the affective life, it has frequently been noted how extensively emotional equilibrium increases with age. Social relations also obey the same law of gradual stabilization.

An essential difference between the life of the body and that of the mind must nonetheless be stressed if the dynamism inherent in the reality of the mind is to be respected. The final form of equilibrium reached through organic growth is more static and, above all, more unstable than the equilibrium toward which mental development strives, so that no sooner has ascending evolution terminated than a regressive evolution automatically starts, leading to old age. Certain psychological functions that depend closely on the physical condition of the body follow an analogous curve. Visual acuity, for example, is at a maximum toward the end of childhood, only to diminish subsequently; and many other perceptual processes are regulated by the same law. By contrast, the higher functions of intelligence and affectivity tend toward a "mobile equilibrium." The more mobile it is, the more stable it is, so that the termination of growth, in healthy minds, by no means marks the beginning of decline but rather permits progress that in no sense contradicts inner equilibrium.

It is thus in terms of equilibrium that we shall try to describe the evolution of the child and the adolescent. From this point of view, mental development is a continuous construction comparable to the erection of a vast building that becomes more solid with each addition. Alternatively, and perhaps more appropriately, it may be likened to the assembly of a subtle mechanism that goes through gradual phases of adjustment in which the individual pieces become more supple and mobile as the equilibrium of the mechanism as a whole

From *Six Psychological Studies*, by Jean Piaget. Copyright © 1967 by Random House, Inc. Reprinted by permission.

becomes more stable. We must, however, introduce an important distinction between two complementary aspects of the process of equilibration. This is the distinction between the variable structures that define the successive states of equilibrium and a certain constant functioning that assures the transition from any one state to the following one.

There is sometimes a striking similarity between the reactions of the child and the adult, as, for example, when the child is sure of what he wants and acts as adults do with respect to their own special interests. At other times there is a world of difference—in games, for example, or in the manner of reasoning. From a functional point of view, i.e., if we take into consideration the general motives of behavior and thought, there are constant functions common to all ages. At all levels of development, action presupposes a precipitating factor: a physiological, affective, or intellectual need. (In the latter case, the need appears in the guise of a question or a problem.) At all levels, intelligence seeks to understand or explain, etc. However, while the functions of interest, explanation, etc., are common to all developmental stages, that is to say, are "invariable" as far as the functions themselves are concerned, it is nonetheless true that "interests" (as opposed to "interest") vary considerably from one mental level to another, and that the particular explanations (as opposed to the function of explaining) are of a very different nature, depending on the degree of intellectual development. In addition to the constant functions, there are the variable structures. An analysis of these progressive forms of successive equilibrium highlights the differences from one behavioral level to another, all the way from the elementary behavior of the neonate through adolescence.

The variable structures—motor or intellectual on the one hand and affective on the other—are the organizational forms of mental activity. They are organized along two dimensions—intrapersonal and social (interpersonal). For greater clarity we shall distinguish six stages or periods of development which mark the appearance of these successively constructed structures:

1. The reflex or hereditary stage, at which the first instinctual nutritional drives and the first emotions appear.

2. The stage of the first motor habits and of the first organized percepts, as well as of the first differentiated emotions.

3. The stage of sensorimotor or practical intelligence (prior to language), of elementary affective organization, and of the first external affective fixations. These first three stages constitute the infancy period—from birth till the age of one and a half to two years—i.e., the period prior to the development of language and thought as such.

4. The stage of intuitive intelligence, of spontaneous interpersonal feelings, and of social relationships in which the child is subordinate to the adult (ages two to seven years, or "early childhood").

5. The stage of concrete intellectual operations (the beginning of logic) and of moral and social feelings of cooperation (ages seven to eleven or twelve, or "middle childhood").

6. The stage of abstract intellectual operations, of the formation of the personality, and of affective and intellectual entry into the society of adults (adolescence).

Each of these stages is characterized by the appearance of original structures whose construction distinguishes it from previous stages. The essentials of these successive constructions exist at subsequent stages in the form of substructures onto which new characteristics have been built. It follows that in the adult each stage through which he has passed corresponds to a given level in the total hierarchy of behavior. But at each stage there are also temporary and secondary characteristics that are modified by subsequent development as a function of the need for better organization. Each stage thus constitutes a particular form of equilibrium as a function of its characteristic structures, and mental evolution is effectuated in the direction of an ever-increasing equilibrium.

We know which functional mechanisms are common to all stages. In an absolutely general way (not only in comparing one stage with the following but also in comparing each item of behavior that is part of that stage with ensuing behavior), one can say that all action—that is to say, all movement, all thought, or all emotion—responds to a need. Neither the child nor the adult executes any external or even entirely internal act unless impelled by a motive; this motive can always be translated into a need (an elementary need, an interest, a question, etc.).

As Claparède (1951) has shown, a need is always a manifestation of disequilibrium: there is need when something either outside ourselves or within us (physically or mentally) is changed and behavior has to be adjusted as a function of this change. For example, hunger or fatigue will provoke a search for nourishment or rest; encountering an external object will lead to a need to play, which in turn has practical ends, or it leads to a question or a theoretical problem. A casual word will excite the need to imitate, to sympathize, or will engender reserve or opposition if it conflicts with some interest of our own. Conversely, action terminates when a need is satisfied, that is to say, when equilibrium is re-established between the new factor that has provoked the need and the mental organization that existed prior to the introduction of this factor. Eating or sleeping, playing or reaching a goal, replying to a question or resolving a problem, imitating successfully, establishing an affective tie, or maintaining one's point of view are all satisfactions that, in the preceding examples, will put an end to the particular behavior aroused by the need. At any given moment, one can thus say, action is disequilibrated by the transformations that arise in the external or internal world, and each new behavior consists not only in re-establishing equilibrium but also in moving toward a more stable equilibrium than that which preceded the disturbance.

Human action consists of a continuous and perpetual mechanism of readjustment or equilibration. For this reason, in these initial phases of construction, the successive mental structures that engender development can be considered as so many progressive forms of equilibrium, each of which is an advance upon its predecessor. It must be understood, however, that this functional mechanism, general though it may be, does not explain the content or the structure of the various needs, since each of them is related to the organization of the particular stage that is being considered. For example, the sight of the same object will occasion very different questions in the small child who is still incapable of classification from those of the older child whose ideas are more extensive and systematic. The interests of a child at any given moment depend on the system of ideas he has acquired plus his affective inclinations, and he tends to fulfill his interests in the direction of greater equilibrium.

Before examining the details of development we must try to find that which is common to the needs and interests present at all ages. One can say, in regard to this, that all needs tend first of all to incorporate things and people into the subject's own activity, i.e., to "assimilate" the external world into the structures that have already been constructed, and secondly to readjust these structures as a function of subtle transformations, i.e., to "accommodate" them to external objects. From this point of view, all mental life, as indeed all organic life, tends progressively to assimilate the surrounding environment. This incorporation is effected thanks to the structures or psychic organs whose scope of action becomes more and more extended. Initially, perception and elementary movement (prehension, etc.) are concerned with objects that are close and viewed statically; then later, memory and practical intelligence permit the representation of earlier states of the object as well as the anticipation of their future states resulting from as yet unrealized transformations. Still later intuitive thought reinforces these two abilities. Logical intelligence in the guise of concrete operations and ultimately of abstract deduction terminates this evolution by making the subject master of events that are far distant in space and time. At each of these levels the mind fulfills the same function, which is to incorporate the universe to itself, but the nature of assimilation varies, i.e., the successive modes of incorporation evolve from those of perception and movement to those of the higher mental operations.

In assimilating objects, action and thought must accommodate to these objects; they must adjust to external variation. The balancing of the processes of assimilation and accommodation may be called "adaptation." Such is the general form of psychological equilibrium, and the progressive organization of mental development appears to be simply an ever more precise adaptation to reality.

Reference

CLAPARÈDE, E. *Le développement mental*. Neuchâtel: Delachaux et Niestlé, 1951.

Major Challenges for Students of Infancy and Early Childhood

Myrtle B. McGraw
BRIARCLIFF COLLEGE

It is not possible to pinpoint any particular ideologies or theories that have given rise to the present interest in early childhood development. The forces were many; they were complex and intertwined. Sputnik shocked the nation out of a state of educational complacency. The disparity of educational opportunities and achievements of children from differing socioeconomic and ethnic groups was brought to light. Then it was determined that children from less favorable environments entered school with their educational handicaps already established. To alleviate this situation, the federal government set up Head Start programs. The outcome of the Head Start programs has led to the claim that even the pre-kindergarten period is too late—education begins in the cradle. Furthermore, since the body of knowledge doubles every 10 years, the amount of knowledge one must master favors an early beginning.

Clearly, the goal of this current wave of concern is to develop the optimum potentials of all children. The pressure is on learning, early learning. It seems clear that the infant and toddler are capable of learning a great deal, *if* the opportunities for learning are properly presented. It also seems evident that the principles of learning derived from laboratory studies of animals or college students are inadequate when it comes to dealing with rapid behavior development of the human infant. The prevailing notion is that these goals can be achieved by manipulation of the environments in which the child lives. To some extent these ideas are reinforced by experiments of the effects of "sensory deprivation," "prolonged isolation," and the comparative effects of "enriched and impoverished" environments. Such studies have been conducted on animals, children, and adults. Once again, the emphasis seems to be shifting to the environmental side of the scale, but it is not locked in with the old heredity-environment dichotomy. It is generally recognized now that nature-nurture are interdependent forces, and to try to separate them clouds inquiry. A few studies (Fowler, 1962; McGraw, 1935; Moore, 1960) have demonstrated that the performances of the young *in particular activities* can be advanced beyond normal expectancy. But we have not as yet learned how to develop to the maximum *all potentials of the growing child*. To do this we shall need new theories or concepts of development that transcend the established principles of learning.

1. *Challenge for the Researchers of Growth* The present corps of growth scientists are the legatees of a vast body of concepts, theories, and research strategies inherited from the "psychological establishment." Of course, the growth scientists will be drawn from many disciplines and from diverse areas of psychology, other than developmental. Already it is apparent that some

Reprinted from *American Psychologist*, August 1970, 25, 754–756 by permission of the American Psychological Association.

dyed-in-the-wool experimentalists are selecting the human infant in preference to animals for special investigations. The challenge for all the students of growth —regardless of their scientific expertise and theoretical orientation—is to scan their legacy of knowledge and skills and to have the courage to rule out those theories and techniques that are not applicable to the study of a complex, ever-changing phenomenon, such as growth. Many experimentalists fail to take into account that their own preconceptions may operate as uncontrolled variables within a particular situation. Will the experimentalist, skillful in the manipulation of the variables and instruments of measurement, become able to recognize that the way the infant is held or positioned may also be a factor in the results obtained? Will the examiner be so focused on the toddler's response to the items set before him that he fails to detect that the child's wiggling and climbing off the chair and running toward the door is his way of saying that there is pressure on his bladder? Will researchers trained to use the IQ or just chronological age be able to devise strategies to evaluate a multiplicity of systems constantly in flux, each system influencing another and in different degrees? All growth and development is not in the form of accretion. The growth scientists will need to design methods that reveal the rises and falls, the pulsations and rhythms manifest in the growth of a given function. An understanding of these pulsations and rhythms may become promising guidelines for the development of optimum potentials of the growing child. Strategies developed in other disciplines (e.g., communication theories) may provide suggestive models for evaluating constantly changing phenomena, such as rapid growth during the early years. There is evidence that many of the current investigators (Endler, Boulter, & Osser, 1968) are alert to the problem, and that is the first step to improving methodologies.

2. *The Challenge of Cultural Acceptance of Scientific Theories* In the past, it has been traditional for scientists, especially those dealing with basic sciences, to be removed from the applied aspects of their findings. They were searching for fundamental truths, and whatever society did with it was none of their concern. On the other hand, many atomic physicists have begun to voice a sense of responsibility for the way society makes use of their knowledge. During this century we have been able to see how many psychological theories have been applied and misapplied to the matter of child rearing and education. If the periods of infancy and the early years are as important for total development as generally contended, then it is reasonable to expect the behavioral scientists to take some responsibility for the way in which their thoughts and theories are adopted into the cultural patterns of child management. Just how this can be done is not clear because it has never been systematically undertaken by any scientific discipline. The general public has faith in science and mass media and is quick to announce, "Science proves thus and so." Sometimes the misapplication of a theory may be ascribed to the use of a particular word, perhaps a word that was originally drawn from another discipline.

Let us consider for a moment some current thoughts that have the potential for creating parental anxiety. Take the question of "critical periods" as applied to learning. The concept was first used by embryologists. It was reinforced by Lorenz's (1935) study of imprinting. Recently, it has been emphasized in connection with studies of the effects of an impoverished environment. It has been asserted that if the impoverishment occurs at critical periods in development, then the damage done may be irreversible. Back in 1935, the writer applied the term "critical periods" to the acquisition of motor skills during infancy. If the agreed meaning of "critical periods" carries the idea that whatever is attained in development or learning must be achieved during a specified period, then the term should not be applied to normal behavioral growth. In the aforementioned instance, it was intended to signify that there are *opportune* times when specific activities can most economically be learned. If one misses that opportune time, then the methods of instruction should be altered for later learning of the same function. It is the irreversibility of damage done that adds emotion and fear to the "critical period" concept.

Just the amount of emphasis attached to certain concepts can also distort their meaning when adopted into the culture. Take, for example, the current emphasis on cognition. No investigator would contend that cognition operates independently of other aspects of learning. Yet, merely because it is the focus of investigative activity, cognition, like personality adjustment of old, is a kind of umbrella for all other goals: expose the child to the right knowledge, in the right way, and at the right time—then the job would be well done.

Perhaps most urgently of all, the growth scientists need to review the accepted principles of learning as they have been articulated and generally accepted. These principles of learning were determined largely by studies of animal subjects in laboratory situations and studies of children in the classroom. As stated above, there is every reason to suspect that they are not applicable to the process of growth taking place during infancy and during the early years. There is a pressing need for totally new guidelines for the benefit of those persons responsible for the management and socialization of the child from birth to three years of age. Obviously the most dominant force is change, change in the organism and change in behavior from day to day. Consistency in parental management does not mean setting up a pattern or rule and sticking to it. It means, rather, dealing with a child in a manner consistent with his developmental changes. To do this effectively requires knowledge, sensitivity, intuition, and flexibility. So the challenge is to orient mothers and teachers toward the concept of change, not toward stability in the ordinary sense. Parents should be taught to observe, to scan, and to detect the nonverbal as well as verbal signals of growth within the child and to design methods of instruction accordingly.

The United States may well be at the threshold of institutional reorganization for the care and education of the young. To develop maximum potentials of children of this age will require special preparation on the part of those responsible for this age group. They need to be not only knowledgeable but intuitive and observant. We have long adhered to the tradition that the biological parents are the ones best qualified to bring up young children. Whether we continue to follow that tradition or turn the education of the young over to specialists—kibbutz fashion—the personnel will require special preparation quite unlike that offered to elementary school teachers or even mothers of today.

The growth scientists are challenged to provide a theoretical frame of reference for the education of this crucial age group. And they are advised also to take account of the way in which their theories and pronouncements are adopted into the culture so that the growing child of today can confidently meet the social changes of the twenty-first century.

References

ENDLER, N. S., BOULTER, L. R., & OSSER, H. *Contemporary issues in developmental psychology*, New York: Holt, Rinehart and Winston, 1968.

FOWLER, W. Teaching a two-year-old to read: An experiment in early childhood reading. *Genetic Psychology Monographs*, 1962, 66, 181–283.

LORENZ, K. J. Der Kumpan in der Umwelt des Vogels. Der Artgenosse als auslösendes Moment sozialer Verhaltungsweisen. *Journal of Ornithology* (*Leipzig*), 1935, 83, 137–213.

MCGRAW, M. B. *Growth, a study of Johnny and Jimmy*. New York: Appleton-Century, 1935.

MOORE, O. K. *Automated responsive environments*. Hamden, Conn.: Basic Education, Inc., 1960. (Film)

author index

NOTE: Pages referring to bibliographic references are in *italics*. Pages have been given for authors who are mentioned on the text page only by reference number. In those cases, the following italic page must be consulted for the reference number. Pages in **boldface** refer to selections by the authors themselves.

A

Abernethy, E. M., 293, *312*
Achs, R., 63, *71*
Adamson, J. M., 227, *246*
Ainsworth, M. D. S., 215, 216, *242*, 303, 304, *312*
Albert, J., 133, 139, *140*
Allen, L., 67, *71*, 92, *112*
Almy, M., 125, *132*, 152, *177*
Altman, L. K., 23, *36*
Amatruda, C. S., 89, *112*
Ames, L. B., 81, 82, *111*, 234, *242*
Anisfeld, M., 101, *111*, 157, *177*
Applefeld, S. W., 165, *179*
Aronfreed, J., 228, *242*, 250, 254, *261*
Aronoff, F. W., 164, *177*

B

Bacon, M. K., 236, *243*
Baker, C. T., 92, *114*
Baldwin, A. L., 223, *242*
Balfour, G., 85, *111*
Ballard, W. W., **316-324**

Bandura, A., 221, 239, *242*, *243*, 255, *261*
Barclay, A., 267, *268*
Barker, R. G., 293, *313*
Barry, H., 236, *243*
Baruch, D. W., 214, *243*
Baumrind, D., 6, *36*, 217, *243*
Bayer, L. M., 56, 57, *61*
Bayley, N., 56, *61*, 95, *111*, 117, *124*, 134, *140*, 296, 310, *312*
Beach, D. R., 139, *139*
Becenti, M., **149-150**
Bee, H. L., 96, 108, *111*
Béhar, M., 14, 16, *36*
Bell, R. Q., 26, *39*, 63, *72*, 217, *246*
Beller, E. K., *246*, 280, 281, 282, 284, *285*
Bellugi-Klima, U., 105, 106, 107, *111*
Belmont, L., 33, *36*
Benda, C. E., 63, *71*
Bereiter, C., 173, *177*, 181, 185, *188*
Berko, J., 106, *111*, 143, *148*
Berkowitz, L., 252, *261*
Berland, T., 21, *36*
Berlyne, D. E., 136, *139*, 181, *188*
Bernbach, H. A., 99, *111*

Author Index

Bernstein, B., 141, *148*
Bertalanffy, L. von, 325, *329*
Biller, H. B., 239, 240, *243*, **263-269**, 273, *278*
Birch, H. G., 33, *36*, 95, 96, *112*
Birns, B., 95, *112*
Black, A. E., 6, *36*
Blank, M., 173, *177*, 181, *188*
Blau, B., 155, *177*
Bloom, B. S., 117, *123*, 184, *188*
Boehm, L., 232, *243*
Borstelmann, L. J., 239, *243*, 263, 264, *268*
Bostian, K. E., 63, *72*
Botstein, A., 63*n*, *71*
Boulter, L. R., 338, *340*
Bowlby, J., 24, *36*, 214, 215, *243*, 296, 303, 304, *312*
Boyd, E., 51, *62*
Brain, D. J., 25, *36*
Breckenridge, M. E., 7, 8, 10, 19, 20, 29, *36*
Breznitz, S., *243*
Bricker, W., 189, *197*
Bridger, W., 95, *112*
Bronfenbrenner, U., 230*n*, *243*, 294, 302, *312*
Bronson, G. W., 225, *243*
Brown, D. G., 239, *243*, 265, *268*, 269, 270, 271, 272, *278*
Brown, R., 104, 107, *111*
Brozek, J., 57, *61*
Bruner, J. S., 108, *111*, 172, *177*, 181, *188*
Bruning, J. L., 266, *268*
Bryan, J. H., 251, 256, 258, 259, *261*, *262*
Bryden, M. P., 84, *112*
Bühler, C., 295, *312*
Bullis, G. E., 10, *37*
Burn, M. H., 87, *111*
Burrowes, A., 257, *262*
Burton, R. V., 156, *179*
Butterfield, E. C., 185, *188*

C

Calder, R., 17, *36*
Callender, W. M., 184, *188*
Cambroune, B., 232, *244*

Cardinaux-Hilfiker, V., 25, *36*
Carlson, P., 101, *111*, 157, *177*
Carrothers, G. E., 33, *37*
Cazden, C. B., 105, 107, *111*
Chan, M. M. C., 58, *62*
Chang, K. S. F., 58, *62*
Charlesworth, R., 154, 163, 177, *178*, **189-197**
Chaudhuri, N. C., 102, *111*
Child, I. L., 217, 236, *243*, 246
Chinsky, J. M., 139, *139*
Chittenden, E. A., **124-132**
Church, J., 100, *114*
Claparède, E., 335, *336*
Clapp, W. F., 217, *243*
Clements, E. M. B., 58, *61*
Cleveland, S. E., 235, *244*
Coates, B., *197*, 256, 259, *261*
Cohen, M. B., 104, *111*
Connor, W. H., 252, *261*
Corah, N. L., 79, *111*
Cornoni, J., 15, *38*
Cramer, P., 79, *111*
Crandall, V. C., 5, *37*
Crandall, V. J., 6, *37*, 155, *177*
Culhane, J., 175, *177*
Cusumano, D. R., 267, *268*

D

Dale, P. S., 99, *111*
Dales, R. J., 164, *178*
Darcy, N., 140, *148*
Davis, C. M., 294, *312*
Davis, W. A., 223, *243*
Davy, A. J., 235, *244*
Day, D., 133, 139, *140*
Delgado, J. M. R., 321*n*
Dement, W. C., 19, *39*
Dennis, W., 117, *123*, 295, *312*
Descoeudres, A., 79, *111*
Deutsch, M., 172, *177*
DeVries, R., 120, 122, *123*
Diaz-Guerrero, R., *112*
DiBartolo, R., 215, *243*, **279-285**
Dickie, J. P., 173, *177*
Dierks, E. C., 16, 19, *37*
Distler, L., 239, 245, 252, *262*
Dixon, C. M., 165, *177*

Donaldson, M., 85, *111*
Dorman, L., 4, *37*
Dorn, M. S., 240, *246*
Dowley, E. M., 27, *38*, 171, *179*
Dressler, M., 51, *62*
Duckworth, L. H., 163, *177*
Dudley, D. T., 18, *37*
Dunn, L. M., 90, *111*, 264, *268*
Dupertuis, C. W., 56, *61*
Durrett, M. E., 235, *244*

E

Edwards, C. D., 235, *246*
Eibl-Eibesfeldt, I., 304, *312*
Eichorn, D. H., 10, *37*, 309, *312*
Eininger, M. A., 195, *197*
Elkind, D., 76, *111*, **180-188**
Ellis, R. W. B., 60, *61*
Emmerich, W., 217, 221, *244*
Endler, N. S., 338, *340*
Endsley, R. C., 225, *245*, 270, *278*
Englemann, S., 173, *177*, 181, 185, *188*
Erikson, E. H., 3, *37*, **41-46**, 157, *177*, 214, *244*, 296, 297, *312*, **330-333**
Erlenmeyer-Kiling, L. K., 309, *312*
Ervin, S., 106, *113*
Ervin-Tripp, S., 109, *112*
Escalona, S. K., 5, *37*

F

Fagot, B. I., 237, *244*
Fantz, R. L., 295, *312*
Feagans, L., 260, *262*
Feldman, C., 110, *112*, **140-148**
Ferguson, L. R., 236, *244*
Fisher, S., 235, *244*
Fishman, J. A., 141, *148*
Flavell, J. H., 139, *139*, 259, *261*
Flick, G. L., 34, *37*
Floyd, J., 189, *197*
Fohrman, M. H., 46, *62*
Forrester, N. J., 200, *211*
Fowler, W., 119, *123*, 181, 185, *188*, 337, *340*
Frank, L. K., **324-329**
Fraser, C., 104, *111*
Frederick, F., 257, *262*

Freud, S., 296, *312*
Friedlander, B., 235, *246*

G

Gaer, E. P., 103, *112*
Garai, J. E., 29, *37*
Garn, S. M., 293, 309, 310, *312*
Gellermann, L. W., 136, *139*
Gesell, A., 10, *37*, 89, *112*, 294, 295, *312*
Gever, B. E., 101, *112*
Gewirtz, J. L., 189, *197*
Gibson, E. J., 168, *177*
Gilbert, D. C., 214, *244*
Glazer, J. A., 154, 163, *178*, *197*
Goldberg, M. B., 48, *61*
Golden, M., 95, *112*
Goldfarb, W., 63n, *71*
Goldstein, K., 328, *329*
Goldstein, L. S., 172, *178*
Goldwasser, A., 230, *245*
Goldwasser, M., 230, *245*
Gollerkeri, S. B., 31, *37*
Goodenough, E. G., 161, *178*
Goodman, J., *38*
Goodnow, J. J., 170, *178*
Gordon, I., 234, *244*
Gospondinoff, E. J., 79, *111*
Gottesman, I. I., 185, *188*
Gottschalk, J., 84, *112*
Gray, S. W., 174, 175, *178*, **198-211**
Green, M., 189, *197*
Greenberg, J. H., 105, *112*
Greulich, W. W., 15, 16, *37*
Griffiths, R., 158-161, *178*
Groseclose, E., 175, *178*
Gross, J. B., 79, *111*
Gross, P., 259, *261*
Grusec, J., 252, 256, *261*
Guenther, W. C., 283, *285*
Guilford, J. P., 89, *112*
Gustavson, K., 63, *71*
Gutteridge, M. V., 27, 29, *37*
Gwinn, J. L., 25, *37*

H

Hagen, J. W., 27, *38*
Hagman, R. R., 225, *244*

Hall, M., 271, *278*
Halverson, C. F., Jr., 26, *39*, **63-72**
Halverson, H. M., 295, *312*
Handlon, B. J., 259, *261*
Hansman, C., 51, *62*
Hardin, G., 323*n*
Harper, R., 63, *71*
Harris, F. R., 32, *38*
Harris, M., 256, *261*
Hartshorne, H., 258, 260, *261*
Hartup, W. W., 154, 163, *177*, *178*, **189-197**, 217, *244*, 256, 259, *261*, 270, 271, 272, 277, *279*, 280, 284, *285*
Harwitz, M., 79, *113*
Hatfield, E. M., 10, *37*
Hathaway, M. L., 58, *61*
Havighurst, R. J., 172, *178*, 223, 228, 229, *243*, *245*, 301, *312*
Hazlitt, V., 79, 80, 98, *112*
Heathers, G., 280, *285*
Hebb, D. O., 248, *261*
Heider, G. M., 134, *139*
Heinicke, C. M., 227, *244*
Hertzig, M. E., 95, 96, *112*
Hess, E. H., 181, *188*
Hess, R. D., 107, *112*, 232, 234, *244*
Hetherington, E. M., 240, *244*, 267, *268*
Hicks, S. E., 6, *37*
Hildreth, G., 32, 33, 34, *37*
Hitchcock, E. A., 227, *246*
Hjertholm, E., 100, 101, *113*
Hodges, W. L., 95, *112*
Hoffman, M. L., 155, *178*, 229, *244*
Holmes, F. B., 226, *244*
Holt, B. G., 6, *39*
Holtzman, W. H., *112*
Honzik, M. P., 67, *71*, 92, *112*
Hooper, F., 122, *124*
Hulsebus, R. C., 76, *114*
Hunt, J. McV., 118*n*, 120, *123*, *124*, 181, *188*, 296, *312*
Huston, A. C., 239, *243*
Huttenlocher, J., 85, *112*
Hyde, D. M., 87, *112*

I

Ilg, F., 10, *37*

Inhelder, B., 74, 80, 84, 100, *114*, 298, 299, 303, *313*
Isen, A. M., 252, *262*
Ito, P. K., 60, *61*

J

Jackson, R. L., 8, *37*
Jarvik, L. F., 309, *312*
Jeffers, R., *319*
Jensen, A. R., 99, *112*, 185, *188*
Jersild, A. T., 163, *178*, 226, *244*
Jessor, R., 234, *244*
John, E., 225, *244*
John, V. P., 172, *178*
Johnson, O. C., 16, *39*
Johnston, M. K., 32, *38*
Jones, H., 118, *123*
Jones, M. C., 293, *313*
Jones, R., 74, *113*
Jones, T. D., 27, *38*
Jordan, J., 134*n*
Joynt, D., 232, *244*

K

Kagan, J., 5, *38*, 67, *71*, 132, 133, *139*, *139*, *140*, 217, *244*, 284, *285*
Kahana, B., 219, *244*
Kahana, E., 219, 220, *244*
Kami, C., 181, *188*
Kaplan, S. A., 48, *61*
Karnes, M. B., 173, *178*
Katz, D., 78, *113*
Katz, I., 235, *244*
Katz, R., 78, *113*
Keith, R. A., 271, *278*
Keliher, A. V., 175, *178*
Keller, E. D., 195, *197*
Kellogg, R., 168, *178*
Kelly, C. S., 32, *38*
Kendler, T. S., 99, *113*
Ketcham, W. A., 293, *313*
Kiil, V., 60, *61*
Kintz, B. L., 266, *268*
Klaus, R. A., 174, *178*, **198-211**
Klinger, R., 310, *313*
Koch, H. L., 218, 223, 224, *244*
Koch, M. B., 214, *245*

Kofsky, E., 79, *113*
Kogut, M. D., 48, *61*
Kohlberg, L., 100, 101, *113*, **116-124**, 130, *132*, 236, *245*, 257, 260, *262*
Kohn, N., 122, *124*
Korslund, M. K., 18, *38*
Kreitler, H., 238, *245*
Kreitler, S., 238, *245*
Kugelmass, S., *243*
Kurokawa, M., 6, *38*

L

Lambert, W. E., 141, *148*
Lansky, L. M., 270, 271, 272, 277, *279*
Laurendeau, M., 121, *124*
Learned, J., 82, *111*
Lee, L. C., 79, *113*
Lee, M. M. C., 58, *62*
Leeper, S. H., 164, *178*
Lenneberg, E. H., 103, 107, *113*
Lenrow, P. B., 254, *262*
Lesser, G. S., 175, *178*
Lev, J., 195, *197*
Levin, H., 20, *39*, 217, 238, *246*
Levine, V. E., 60, *62*
Lewin, K. W., 25, *37*
Lewis, M., 79, *113*, 296, *313*
Liddle, E. A., 240, *246*
Liebert, R. M., 258, *262*
Lindquist, E. R., 201, 204, *211*
Lipsitt, L. P., 301, *313*
Long, L., 85, *113*
Lorenz, K., 303, *313*
Lorenz, K. J., 338, *340*
Lovell, K., 87, 104, *113*
Lowrey, G. H., 7, 9, 10, *39*
Lubchenco, L. O., 51, *62*
Lueck, E., 27, *38*
Luria, A. R., 232, *245*
Luria, Z., 230*n*, 232, *245*

M

McCall, R., 134*n*
McCandless, B. R., **269-279**
McCaskill, C. L., 27, 29, *38*
McClearn, G. E., 309, *313*

Maccoby, E. E., 20, 27, *38*, *39*, 155, *178*, 215, 216, 229, *245*
McDavid, J. W., 175, *178*
MacFarlane, J. W., 67, *71*, 92, *112*
McGraw, M. B., 296, *313*, **337-340**
Mackay, D. H., 58, *62*
McKay, G., 270, 272, 277, *279*
Maclay, I., 25, *36*
Maher, B. A., 133, *140*
Maller, J. B., 258, 260, *261*
Marcus, I. M., 23, *38*
Marks, I. M., 225, 232, *245*
Marshall, H., *245*
Matthews, C. A., 46, *62*
Maurer, A., 226, *245*
May, M. A., 258, 260, *261*
Maynard, O., 164, *178*
Mead, M., 31, *38*, 236, *245*
Meichenbaum, D., *38*
Mendel, G., 6, *38*
Mendez, O. A., 95, 96, *112*
Menyuk, P., 109, *113*
Meredith, H. V., 13, *38*, 51, 58, *62*
Merrill, M. A., 89, 91, 95, *115*
Meyers, C. B., 95, *114*
Michael, N. B., 56, *61*
Michelson, N., 60, *62*
Midlarsky, E., 251, 259, *262*
Milgram, N. A., 68, *72*
Miller, D. R., 232, *245*
Miller, G. A., 109, *114*
Miller, J. O., 95, *113*, 175, *178*, 200, 210, *211*
Miller, P., 125, *132*
Miller, W., 106, *113*
Mills, C. A., 58, 60, *62*
Minton, C., 134*n*
Minuchin, P., 4, *38*
Mischel, W., 258, *262*
Moore, O. K., 337, *340*
Moore, S. B., 155, *178*
Morrisett, L., 119, *124*
Morse, L. M., 16, 19, *37*
Moss, A., 95, *112*
Moss, H. A., 5, *38*, 67, *71*, 217, *244*, 284, *285*
Moustakos, C. E., 280, *285*
Mumbauer, C. C., 95, *113*

Murphy, G., 89, *113*
Murphy, L. B., 5, *38*
Murphy, M. N., 7, 8, 10, 19, 20, 29, *36*
Murray, H., 281, *285*
Mussen, P. H., 215, 229, 239, *245*, *246*, 252, 260, *262*, 293, *313*
Muzio, J. N., 19, *39*

N

Najarian, P., 117, *123*
Nakamura, C. Y., 2, *38*
Nelson, V. L., 92, *114*
Nesbitt, E. L., 23, *39*
Neugarten, B. L., 219, *245*
Newson, E., 20, *38*, 238, *245*
Newson, J., 20, *38*, 238, *245*
Newton, P., 220, 221, *246*

O

O'Dell, S., 168, *178*
Oetzel, R. M., 236, *245*
Ogilvie, D. M., 216, *245*
Olson, W. C., 29, *38*
Osborn, D. K., 225, *245*
Oskamp, S., 235, *246*
Osler, S. F., 79, *113*
Osser, H., 338, *340*
Ozer, M. N., 68, *72*

P

Palmer, C. E., 60, *62*
Palmer, F. H., 93, 95, *113*, *114*, 174, *178*
Papoušek, H., 301, *313*
Parke, R. D., 301, *313*
Parker, A. L., 229, *245*
Parten, M. B., 194, *197*
Paskal, V., 250, *261*
Patterson, G. E., 189, *197*
Patterson, G. R., 237, *244*
Peal, E., 141, *148*
Pearson, L., 133, *140*
Peck, R. F., 228, 229, *245*

Pederson, F. A., 3, 26, *38*, *39*, 63, *72*, *113*, 133, 138, *140*, 263, *268*
Penfield, W., 109, *113*
Peterson, H. G., Jr., 25, *37*
Phillips, W., 133, 139, *140*
Piaget, J., 74, 75, 76, 77, 84, 87, 88, 98, 100, 102, *113*, *114*, 121, *124*, 126, 131, *132*, 141, *148*, 158, *179*, 187, *188*, 231, 232, *245*, 259, *262*, 289, 298-300, 303, *313*, **333-336**
Pinard, A., 121, *124*
Poteat, B. W., 76, *114*
Prelinger, E., 161, *178*
Preston, A., 6, *37*
Proshansky, H., 220, 221, *246*
Pryor, H. B., 11, *38*
Pufall, P. B., 85, *114*
Pyle, S. I., 15, 16, *37*, *38*

R

Rabinovitch, M. S., 84, *112*
Rabson, A., 6, *37*
Radin, N., 181, *188*
Rafferty, J., 155, *177*
Rainwater, L., 277, *279*
Ramey, C. T., 301, *314*
Read, K. H., 169, *179*
Rebelsky, F., 4, *37*, 232, *245*
Reed, R. B., 15, *38*, 53, *62*
Rees, A. H., 93, *114*, 174, *178*
Repucci, N. D., **132-139**
Reynolds, E. L., 60, *62*
Rheingold, H., 117, *124*, 181, *188*
Ricciuti, H. N., 77, *114*
Richardson, S. A., 234, *244*
Rifkin, S. H., 97, *114*
Robertson, J., 24, *39*
Robinson, H., 117, 119, *124*
Roffwarg, H. P., 19, 20, *39*
Rogers, M. M., 2, *38*
Rosen, B. C., 217, *246*
Rosenberg, B. G., 238, *246*, 265, *269*
Rosenblatt, I. E., 220, *244*
Rosenhan, D., 215, *246*, **247-263**
Rosman, B., 133, 139, *140*
Ross, D., 239, *243*

Ross, S. A., 239, *243*
Rossi, S. I., 77, *114*
Rutherford, E., 215, *246*, 252, 260, *262*
Ryckman, D. B., 95, *114*

S

Sackett, G. P., 291, *313*
Sava, S. G., 181, 186, *188*
Scarr, S., 134, *140*, 161, 309, *313*
Schacter, S., 250, *262*
Schaefer, A. E., 16, *39*
Schaefer, C. E., *179*
Schaefer, E. S., 134, *140*, 310, *312*
Schaffer, H. R., 184, *188*
Schalock, H., 280, *285*
Scheinfeld, A., 29, *37*
Scheinfeld, D., 234, *244*
Schell, R. E., 236, 237, *246*
Schlesinger, E. R., 23, *39*
Schneider, D. J., 253, *262*
Schwarz, J. C., 225, *246*
Scott, J. P., 181, 184, *188*, 296, *313*
Scott, L., 76, *111*
Scott, P. M., 156, *179*
Scrimshaw, N. S., 10, *39*
Sears, P. S., 171, *179*
Sears, R. R., 20, *39*, 217, 238, *246*, 280, *285*
Seltzer, A. R., *246*
Seyler, A., 21, *36*
Shapiro, S., 23, *39*
Shaw, R. E., 85, *114*
Sheldon, W. H., 26, *39*, 53-56, *62*
Shen, M., 110, *112*, **140-148**
Sher, M. A., 270, 271, 277, *279*
Sherk, L., 260, *262*
Shimizu, S. N. S., 48, *61*
Shipman, V. C., 107, *112*, 232, *244*
Shuttleworth, F. K., 293, *313*
Siegel, A. E., 227, *246*
Siegel, M., 63, *71*
Sigel, I., 122, *124*, 280, *285*
Silber, J. W., 236, 237, *246*
Simon, M. D., 293, *313*
Singer, J. E., 250, *262*

Sitkei, E. G., 95, *114*
Skeels, H. M., 93, *114*
Skinner, B F., 189, 191, *197*
Skipper, D. S., 164, *178*
Skubiski, S. L., 252, 256, *261*
Sloan, W., 68, *72*
Slobin, D. L., 105, 106, *114*
Smart, M. S., 31, *39*
Smart, R. C., 31, *39*
Smedslund, J., 121, *124*
Smilansky, S., 162, 173, *178*
Smith, E. W., 63, *72*
Smith, F., 109, *114*
Smith, H. P., 165, *179*
Smith, M. B., 252n
Smith, M. E., 2, *39*, 98, *114*
Smock, C. D., 6, *39*
Snow, A. C., 165, *179*
Solomon, F., 173, *177*, 181, *188*
Sontag, L. W., 60, *62*, 92, *114*
Spearman, C., 120, *124*
Spicker, H. H., 95, *112*
Spitz, R. A., 24, *39*
Springer, D., 82, *114*
Staub, E., 253, 260, *262*
Stephens, J. M., 125, 130, *132*
Stevenson, H. W., 181, *188*, 195, *197*, 234, *246*, 301, *313*
Stingle, K. G., *278*
Stolz, L. M., 227, *246*, 263, *269*
Stone, C. P., 293, *313*
Stone, L. J., 100, *114*
Streissguth, A. P., 96, *114*
Strodtbeck, F. L., 181, *188*
Stuart, H. C., 15, *38*, 53, *62*, 64, *72*
Stutsman, R., 89, *114*
Suchman, R. G., 79, *114*
Sullivan, W., 306, *313*
Sutherland, I., 60, *62*
Sutton-Smith, B., 152, *179*, 238, *246*, 265, *269*
Swanson, G. E., 232, *245*
Swartz, J. D., *112*
Sweetser, D. A., 219, *246*
Swift, J., 189, *197*
Sylvia, K., 133, *140*
Syrdal, A. K., 85, *114*
Szalay, G. C., 48, *62*

T

Tanner, J. M., 10, *39*, 51, 58, *62*, 292, 293, *313*, *314*
Tapie, L. L., *112*
Terman, L. M., 89, 91, 95, *114*, *115*
Thomas, A., 95, 96, *112*
Thomas, P. J., 271, *279*
Thompson, H., 295, *312*
Thompson, K. S., 235, *246*
Thompson, N. L., Jr., **269-279**
Thompson, W. R., 248, *261*
Thorndike, E. L., 89, *115*, 301, *314*
Thurstone, L. L., 95, *115*
Thurstone, T. G., 95, *115*
Tighe, T. J., 100, *115*
Torrance, E. P., 153, *179*
Tough, J., 108, *115*
Trabasso, T., 79, *114*

U

Ugurel-Semin, R., 259, *262*
Unger, S. M., 229, 233, *246*
Uzgiris, I. C., 118*n*, *124*

V

Van de Castle, R. L., 226, *246*
Vandenberg, S. G., 309, *314*
Vickers, V. S., 64, *72*
Vinacke, W. E., 215, *243*, **279-285**
Von Foerster, H., 324, 326, *329*
Vygotsky, L. S., 100, *115*

W

Walbeck, N., 256, 258, *261*
Waldrop, M. F., 26, *39*, **63-72**, 217, *246*
Walker, H., 195, *197*
Walker, R. N., 26, *39*
Walter, W. G., 10, *39*, 289, 294, *314*
Walters, R. H., 221, *243*
Wann, K. D., 240, *246*
Ward, W. D., 239, *246*, 271, *279*

Watson, E. H., 7, 9, 10, 11, *39*
Watson, J. S., 301, *314*
Watts, A. F., 98, *115*
Wechsler, D., 90, *115*
Weidenfeller, E. W., 165, *179*
Weikart, D. P., 173, 174, 175, *179*
Weinstein, K. K., 219, *245*
Weir, R. H., 102, 104, 106, 107, *115*
Weisberg, R. W., 101, *112*
Weisstein, N., 133, *140*
Welch, L., 85, *113*, 133, *140*
Wellman, B. L., 27, 29, *38*
Wender, P. H., 3, *38*, *113*, 133, 138, *140*
Werner, H., 78, 86, 87, *115*
Wetzel, N. C., 12, *39*
Whipple, D. V., **46-62**
White, B. L., *39*
White, G. M., 252, 256, 257, *262*, *263*
White, S. H., 183, *188*
Whiting, J. W. M., 217, *246*
Wiener, N., 324, *329*
Wilcox, J. A., 214, *243*
Williams, C. D., 17, *39*
Williams, J. E., 235, *246*
Wilson, D. C., 60, *62*
Winterbottom, M. R., 6, 8, *40*
Witherspoon, R. L., 164, *178*
Wittrock, M. C., 77, *114*
Wohlwill, J. F., 87, *115*
Wolf, M. M., 32, *38*
Woodruff, C. W., 8, *40*
Wright, B., 258, 259, *263*

Y

Yarrow, L. J., 117, *124*
Yarrow, M. R., 156, *179*
Yeager, J., 100, 101, *113*
Youniss, J., 100, *115*

Z

Zigler, E., 185, *188*, 236, *245*
Zimny, G. H., 165, *179*
Zook, E. A., 270, 271, 272, 277, *279*
Zopf, G. W., Jr., 324, 326, *329*

subject index

A

Accidents, 21-26
Accommodation, 126-131, 289-291, 336
Achievement, 5-6
Acquisition of language, 102-110
Activity and passivity, 5
Aggression, 4, 220-222
Altruism in children, 247-263
Androgyny, 56-57
Anger, 220-222
Anomalies, physical, 26, 63-72
Assessing growth, methods of, 11-15
Assimilation, 126-131, 289-291, 336
Attachment, 215-216
Autonomy
   nursery education and, 169
   sense of, 2-3
   vs. shame and doubt, 41-44, 297

B

Battered children, 25
Behavior genetics, 308-310
Bilingualism, 109, 140-148, 149-150
Birth, size at, 51-52
Body build, 26, 53-57
Body image, 235-236

C

Care of ill and injured children, 24-25
Causality concepts, 88-89
Character development, 228-233
Child abuse, 25
Chromosomes, 304-307
Class concepts, 77-80
Class differences, intelligence tests, 95-97
Cognition, 231-232
Cognitive development, 124-132
   parental stimulation of, 107-108
Compensatory education, 172-176
Competence, 5-6
Compliance, 155-156
Concept training, 173-174
Concrete operations, 300
Conditioning, 300-301
Conscience, development of, 4
Coordination, motor, 26-29
Creative materials, 165-168
Creativity, 151-171
Critical periods, 337-340
   principle of, 295-296
Cultural influences on moral development, 231-233
Culture and language, 102

D

Dependency, 216-218, 279-285
Deprivation, educational, 171-172
Deprived children, self concept of, 234
Developmental direction, principle of, 8-9, 294-295
Developmental sequence, motor, 27-29
Differences in terminals, principle of, 293

354 Subject Index

Differentiation and integration, principle of, 152-153, 294
Disadvantaged children, 171-172
 education for, 172-176, 180-188, 198-211
Diseases, 21-24
Discovery, teaching, 174
Dramatic play, 162-163

E

Early Training Project, 198-211
Ecology, 316-324
Ectomorph, 53-57
Education, 124-132, 180-211, 337-340
Egocentrism, 100-102
Emotional development, 214-228
Endomorphy, 53-54, 57
Environmental influences, physical growth, 57-60
Epigenesis, 295, 330-333
Equilibration, 127, 288-291, 333-336
Erikson's stages, 296-298
Errors of measurement, intelligence, 92
Ethnic differences, intelligence tests, 95-97
Evolution, 316-324
Evolutionary adaptation, 303-304
Exploratory behavior, 4
Eye preference, 34-35

F

Family members, perceptions of roles of, 240
Fat, growth of, 8
Father, influence on child, 217, 239-240
Father absence, 239-240, 263-269, 275n
Fear, 225-228
Feeding, 16-19
Fitness, physical, 31-32
Formal operations, 300
Freud's psychosexual stages, 296-297
Friendly behavior, 154-156

G

Generativity, sense of, 298
Genes, 306-309

Genetic influences, physical growth, 51-57
Genetics, 304-310, 316-324
Grammar, acquisition of, 104-106
Grandparent love, 219-220
Growth, 46-62
 methods of assessing, 11-15
 nature of, 46-49
 principles of, 291-296
 processes of, 324-329
 standards of, 11-12
Guilt, sense of, 44-46

H

Hand preference, 32-35
Health, 19-22
Height tables, 11-12
Heredity, 304-310
 intelligence and, 116-119
Homeostasis, 288-289
Humor, 163-164
Hyperactivity, 63-72

I

Identification with parents, 239
Identity, sense of, 297
Identity vs. role diffusion, 330-333
Illnesses, 21-26
Imaginary playmates, 163
Imagination, 156-168
Imaginative play, 158-161
Impulsivity, 63-72, 132-140
Individual differences, motor, 27
Industry, sense of, 297
Information processing, 132-140
Inheritance, biological, 304-308
Initiative, sense of, 3-6, 156-157, 297
 nursery education and, 169-170
Initiative vs. guilt, 44-46
Integrity, sense of, 298
Intellectual development, 73-115, 116-150, 180-188
 imagination and, 157-158
 nursery education and, 170-171
Intelligence, 116-124
 Piagetian, 120-132, 333-336

Intelligence quotient, 89-91
Intelligence tests, 89-97
Interrelationships in growth, 293
Intimacy, sense of, 298

J

Jealousy, 222-224

L

Labelling, 140-148
Language
  creative, 160-161
  moral development and, 232-233
  uses of, 99-102
  See also Bilingualism
Language development, 97-110, 140-148
Laterality, 32-35
Learning, 300-303
Love, 214-220
  sibling, 218-219

M

Masculinity-femininity, 269-279
Maturation, 303
Measurement, intelligence, 89-97
Meiosis, 307-308
Mesomorphy, 53-57
Moral development, 228-233, 247-263
Motor development, 26-35
Music and dance, 164-165

N

Normative sequence, principle of, 295
Nursery education, 169-171
Nursery school, 180-188
Nurturance, 214-215, 279-285
Nutrition, 16-19
  physical growth and, 57

O

Object constancy, 140-148
Optimal tendency, principle of, 293-294
Organs (*see* Tissue and organ growth)

P

Parent-child relations, 214-218, 222-224, 228-231, 239-240, 263-269
Peer relations, 153-156, 189-197
Percentile tables
  height, 11-12
  weight, 12
Personality development, 2-6, 41-72, 213-246, 330-333
Physical anomalies, 26, 63-72
Physical care, 16-23
Physical development, 7-26
Physical growth, 46-62
Piaget's stages, 298-300
Piagetian intelligence, 120-132, 333-336
Play, 132-140, 151-211
Posture, 29-31
Prediction of IQ, 92-94
Preoperational stage, 299-300
Preoperational thinking, 74-89
Principles of development
  critical periods, 16, 295-296
  developmental direction, 8, 294-295
  differences in terminals, 293
  differentiation and integration, 152-153, 294
  dynamic interrelations in growth, 293
  optimal tendency, 293-294
  variation of rates, 291-293
Private speech, 100-102
Proportions, 8-11
Prosocial behavior, 247-263
Psychological equilibrium, 289-291
Psychometric intelligence, 116-119

Q

Quantity concepts, 85-88

R

Race differences, 269-279
Reflectivity, 132-140
Reinforcement, 301
  positive social, 189-197
Religion, 240-241
Reversal-shift problems, 99
Rivalry, 222-224

S

Schemas, 289
Secular trend, 58
Self concepts, 233-236
Sensorimotor play, 153
Sensorimotor stage, 298-299
Sensory aspects of eating, 18-19
Sex differences, 273-279
   dependency, 279-285
   expectations of behavior, 236-238
   initiative, 6
   motor, 29
   physical growth, 48-52
   teaching of, 238-239
Sex role development, 263-269
Sex role identification, 239-240, 269-279
Sex typing, 236-240
Shame and doubt, 41-44
Siblings, 218-219, 222-224
Skeletal age, 15-16
Sleep, 19-21
Social-class concepts, 77-80
Social-class differences, intelligence tests, 95-97
Social development, 153-156, 189-197, 213-246, 247-285
   school-age, 247-263
Social learning, 302-303
Social play (*see* Play)
Socialization, 213-246
Socialized speech, 101
Sociodramatic play, 162-163, 173
Space concepts, 82-85
Speech, development of, 97-110
Stage theories of development, 296-300
Symbolism, 161-162

T

Teaching language, 107-109
Thinking, 74-89
Thought, relationship with language, 98
Time concepts, 80-82
Tissue and organ growth, 8-11
Trust, sense of, 297

V

Variation of rates, principle of, 291-293
Verbal mediation, 99-100, 301-302
Vertical diffusion, 209
Vocabulary, 102-103
Volition and moral development, 232

W

Weight tables, 12